"Movement — Fifth Avenue" by John Marin

THE ANNALS
OF
AMERICA

THE ANNALS OF AMERICA

Volume 13

1905 - 1915

The Progressive Era

William Benton, *Publisher*

ENCYCLOPÆDIA BRITANNICA, INC.

Chicago London Toronto Geneva Sydney Tokyo Manila

The editors wish to express their gratitude for permission to reprint
material from the following sources:

Doubleday & Company, Inc., for Selection 58, from *Toboganning on Parnassus*, by Franklin P. Adams, Copyright 1911 by Doubleday & Company, Inc.

Hart Schaffner & Marx for Selection 59, from MS in their possession.

Harvard University Press for Selections 27, 28, from *This Was America*, ed. by Oscar Handlin, Cambridge, Mass.: Harvard University Press, Copyright 1949 by the President and Fellows of Harvard College.

Holt, Rinehart and Winston, Inc. for Selection 99, from *Chicago Poems*, by Carl Sandburg, Copyright 1916 by Holt, Rinehart and Winston, Inc., Copyright 1944 by Carl Sandburg.

Houghton Mifflin Company for Selection 66, from *The Promised Land*, Copyright 1912 by Houghton Mifflin Company.

William White Howells for Selection 64, from *Harper's Monthly Magazine*, September 1912, Copyright © 1912 by Harper's Magazine, Inc.

The Estate of Rufus M. Jones for Selection 112, from *The Survey*, April-September 1915.

The Macmillan Company for Selection 87, from *An Economic Interpretation of the Constitution of the United States*, by Charles A. Beard, Copyright 1913, 1935 by The Macmillan Company, renewed 1963 by William Beard and Miriam Vagts. Also for Selection 90, from *The Congo and Other Poems*, by Vachel Lindsay, Copyright 1914 by The Macmillan Company, renewed 1942 by Elizabeth C. Lindsay.

Ellen C. Masters for Selection 119, from *The Spoon River Anthology*, by Edgar Lee Masters, New York: The Macmillan Company, 1914, 1942.

Carl Rausenbush for Selection 21, from *Christianity and the Social Crisis*, by Walter Rauschenbusch.

The Estate of John D. Rockefeller for Selection 43, from *Random Reminiscences of Men and Events*, by John D. Rockefeller, Copyright 1909 by Doubleday & Company, Inc., renewed 1936 by John D. Rockefeller.

Roosevelt University, Labor Education Division for Selections 72, 101, from *Songs of Work and Freedom*, ed. by Edith Fowke and Joe Glazer.

Stanford University Press for Selection 42, from *Changing Conceptions of Education*, by Ellwood P. Cubberley.

CODED SOURCES IN THIS VOLUME

PRFA

[United States Department of State] *Papers Relating to Foreign Affairs.* Compiled annually since 1861 except for 1869 with supplements issued periodically. Title changed to *Papers Relating to Foreign Relations of the United States* in 1870 and to *Foreign Relations of the United States* in 1947. Washington, 1862 *et seq.*

Record

Congressional Record. A record of the proceedings of Congress from March 3, 1873, to date, arranged by number of Congress and by session. Washington, 1874 *et seq.*

Richardson

A Compilation of the Messages and Papers of the Presidents 1789-1897. Edited by James D. Richardson. In 10 vols. Washington, 1896-1899. New edition extended to 1908. Washington, 1909. Supplementary edition extended to 1917. In 20 vols. with pages renumbered and divisions into volumes altered. New York, 1920.

Statutes

The Public Statutes at Large of the United States of America from the Organization of the Government in 1789, etc., etc. In 79 vols. as of August 1966. 1845 *et seq.* Vol. 28, Washington, 1915.

TWA

This Was America. Edited by Oscar Handlin. Cambridge, 1949.

United States Reports [Supreme Court].

198 U.S. 45   Vol. 198, pp. 45ff.;
221 U.S. 1   Vol. 221, pp. 1ff.

Contents

1906

1907

1908

Index of Authors, 578

THE PROGRESSIVE ERA
In Pictures

Consumer Technology 53-62

Industry continued to expand in established centers and moved gradually
into new territory in the West and South. The mainspring
of sustained growth was technology, bringing both new products
and new processes to American industry and providing a great
impetus to the now-habitual American optimism.

The Progressive Era 187-200

Progressivism, a broad reform movement rooted primarily in the
middle class, was in many ways reminiscent of the wave of
reform sentiment in the 1840s and 1850s. It was, however, less
self-righteously crusading and more self-consciously defensive; in
many ways it was a barrier erected by the middle class against
both radicalism and monopoly capital.

Urban America 289-302

The continuing growth of the cities finally made America
literally an urban nation as the population balance shifted in favor
of the cities between 1910 and 1920. At the same time new
developments in transportation and communication were drawing
the whole country closer to a common cultural center.

Scenes of Diversity 383-396

A sense of optimism and even gaiety pervaded the decade before
World War I. America had moved into the front rank of nations
in both economic and political power, and the future seemed
to promise unlimited material and spiritual progress.

Art and the Future 439-448

The decade was an exciting one for American art. The Armory
Show brought the best of contemporary European art to the
U.S. and, indirectly, caused more appreciation of the work
of adventurous native artists. The film was rapidly developing as an
art form. And architecture, led by Frank Lloyd Wright, was
moving surely into the modern period.

Progressive Politics 475-486

Under the vigorous leadership of Theodore Roosevelt and the
idealism of Wilson, America found itself becoming more and more
embroiled in foreign affairs. The legacy of the Monroe Doctrine,
of the Open Door, and of the Spanish-American War was an
uncomfortable new responsibility for an inexperienced nation.

Introduction

If revolution means change that is sweeping and abrupt, then a good case could be made that the United States underwent a revolution during the first decades of the twentieth century. No shots were fired, no aristocrats were guillotined, no new form of government was instituted. But a new generation seized power and used it to implement new programs in new ways. The revolution goes by the name of Progressivism; and it would be hard to exaggerate its importance in the latter day development of our nation.

It was a paradoxical revolution, which is one reason why it fascinates historians. It was unique, compared to Populism or the New Deal, in arising not out of depression, but in a time of prosperity. It found its main adherents not among the poor, who had real reason to rebel, but among the middle class. It declared war on corporate privilege, and numbered among its staunchest supporters many who had grown wealthy by partaking of such privilege. Its leaders advocated reforms in the 1900s that they had bitterly condemned in the 1890s. And the Republican Party that pioneered them was within less than a generation the very symbol of reaction.

It is tempting to say that Progressivism grew out of Populism, but in many ways they were distinct movements. Populism was rural based and local in its appeal, Progressivism urban and nationwide. Populism reflected the needs and desires of the dispossessed at a time of economic trial, Progressivism the conscience of the well-to-do during a period of prosperity. Populism tried but failed to recruit middle-class support, Progressivism was led by the very men who had turned their backs on the earlier movement.

From these differences arose others, less tangible, but going to the heart of the style and philosophy of these two movements of reform. Progressive thought tended to be better informed and more moderate than that of the Populists and, because it was not burdened by the feelings of the exploited in society, tended to be less rancorous in tone. The two assigned the responsibility for America's problems in significantly different ways. Whereas the Populists blamed others — Wall Street, the railroads, the monopolists — the Progressivists blamed themselves. If the country had somehow lost its way, then they were responsible; the guilt attached to them. And where the Populists tended to be simplistic both in their accusations and in their suggested solutions, the Progressivists tended to be speculative in their approach, and were often of two minds on the great social, economic, and political issues that engaged them. Thus, in their view, corporations might be a menace, but they were also the product of social evolution and possessed of distinct advantages. Militant labor unions might pose a threat to the national security, but the conditions of modern life demanded that they exist. The "new immigrants" flowing into the country by the hundreds of thousands might pollute the nation's blood, but it made more sense to help them than to hate them.

All this does not mean, of course, that explanations cannot be assigned for the rise of the Progressive movement, or for its special character. Reform had been in the air for a generation, and if the Populists had been unable to exploit it politically, it remained a potent force. Economic developments also contributed to the unleashing of middle-class reform sentiments. In the fifteen-year interval between 1897 and 1912 consumer prices rose by about 62 percent, from a low (1926 = 100) of 46.6 to a high of 75.5. For men on salaries or fixed income, and lacking organization wherewith to demand higher pay, this development was as critical as declining prices had been for the farmers. Moreover, it occurred at a time when the great corporations were consolidating their hold on the American economy. (See, for example, Selections 2, 13, 15, 27-28, 51, 59-62, 70, 73, 80-81, 95-96, and 100.)

The trend to monopolization goes back at least to the 1870s, when John D. Rockefeller established his Standard Oil empire, but it gathered momentum with each decade. Of the 318 trusts in the United States in 1904, eighty-two with a capitalization of less than $2 billion were organized before 1898, and 236 with a capitalization of over $6 billion in the six years after that date. The trend did not stop there, despite the "trustbusting" of the Roosevelt and Taft administrations. The Pujo Commission discovered in 1913, for example (see Selection 80), that the Morgan-Rockefeller interests held directorships in 112 corporations valued at $22 billion, or more than 10 percent of the wealth of the country.

Although these factors help to explain why a middle-class reform movement occurred around the turn of the century, they do not adequately explain its fervor, the quality of the men enlisted in it, and its extraordinarily wide support. (For a while, it seemed as if everybody in the country was a reformer. In 1912 the three major candidates — Roosevelt, Taft, and Wilson — each offered formidable Progressive credentials.) Something else was going on as well — something that is not revealed by economic tables. One theory suggests that a social revolution — a status upheaval, as it is called — had been occurring for three decades, and that it reached its apex in the years before World War I.

What Henry Adams wrote of one section of the country applied to all. "Down to 1850," he declared, "and even later, New England society was still directed by the professions. Lawyers, physicians, professors, merchants were classes, and acted not as individuals, but as though they were clergymen and each profession was a church." Furthermore, whatever their calling, these men had much in common; Anglo-Saxon by background, Protestant in religion, British by cultural orientation, they were usually well educated and just wealthy enough to be able to reject the ethic they dismissed as "crass commercialism."

The triumph of industrialism downgraded their role, not so much by depriving them of income or opportunity as by putting new eminences above them. Compared to the captains of industry like Carnegie and the Rockefellers, they were simply less important. To make matters worse, the usurpers had no redeeming qualities of breeding or culture. Their fortunes came to them through the use of ungentlemanly tactics, and ungentlemanly they remained. "If our civilization is destroyed, as Maculay predicted," Henry Demarest Lloyd declared bitterly, "it will not be by his barbarians from below. Our barbarians come from above."

What has been called the trauma of the middle class can be illustrated by the experience of two professions. Clergymen spoke with increasingly less authority as America turned to worship at the shrine of profits. One indication of their decline is the rapidity with which bankers and businessmen replaced them on the boards of trustees of major universities. In the cities they became almost the paid lackeys of wealthy congregations, and the poor stopped going to church at all (to Protestant churches, at least). Andrew Carnegie wrote a book called *The Gospel of Wealth;* the title itself bespeaks the change. (For writings by and about Carnegie, see Volume 11, Selections 18, 49, and 50, and Volume 13, Selection 14.) And Russell Conwell, though nominally a clergyman, did not act like any clergyman of a century before. He wrote a lecture, "Acres of Diamonds," and delivered it some 6,000 times, with total earnings, including royalties from its sale in published form, of $8,000,000. Its theme, too, was wealth. "To secure wealth is an honorable ambition," Conwell cried, "and is one great test of a person's usefulness to others. . . . I say, get rich, get rich!" (See Volume 11, Selection 55.)

The experience of lawyers was similar, although as a class they did not suffer financially (just the opposite). But they surrendered the proud heritage and ethics of their profession. Tocqueville had commented fifty years before on the extraordinary influence and sense of responsibility of the legal profession in America, on its high standards of inquiry and criticism. He probably would not have said the same in 1900. It would be wrong to assert that the law became a captive, but it is true enough that success in the law usually meant hiring one's services to men who were richer, less well educated, and often less scrupulous than oneself. As J. P. Morgan once said to his associate, Judge Elbert Gary, "Well, I don't know as I want a lawyer to tell me what I cannot do. I hire him to tell me how to do what I want to do."

The theory argues that Progressivism aimed at restoring the former elite to positions of influence. It attempted to find a place in industrial America for abiding preindustrial virtues and values. It did not reject the present, but neither did it reject the great legacy of the past. It hoped to achieve its goals by eradicating corruption, ignorance, and want, and by imposing restraints on the captains of American industry that would be sufficient, not to deprive them of profits, but to bend them to an ethic higher than mere profit. (See, for writings bearing on the above remarks, Selections 10-11, 17, 21, 23, 32, 34, 43, 45, 50, 58, 67-68, 76, 83, 90, 105-106, 110, and 119.)

Many of the characteristics of the Progressives lend credence to the theory. Most important, perhaps, was the religiosity, the tone of moral fervor, that ran through the movement. It was a convention among Progressive spokesmen to use Biblical language in pursuit of secular ends. "We stand at Armageddon and we battle for the Lord!" cried Theodore Roosevelt to the Bull Moosers in 1912; whereupon the assembled thousands broke out in a rendition of "On-ward, Christian Soldiers." Woodrow Wilson injected morality into politics at every opportunity. And the literature of the period also makes the point. Charles Sheldon's *In His Steps: What Would Jesus Do?*, one of the great best sellers of history (more than 8,000,000 copies had been sold by 1945), was published in 1897. It tells of a minister and his congregation who decide to carry on their daily lives as Jesus would do were He to return. It turns out that Jesus would become a Progressive.

The Protestant religious influence went deeper than that. The Progressive was often burdened with a deep sense of personal guilt. Those who have not read Lincoln Steffens' *The Shame of the Cities* sometimes fail to know where he placed the blame. "We are responsible," he wrote, "not our leaders, since we follow them." The remark was typical of the muckrakers (as Roosevelt called them), who often unearthed corruption only to beat their breasts in self-castigation. (For examples of this attitude, see Volume 12, Selections 114-116 and 123, and in this volume, Selections 20-21, 32, 34, 43, 45, 52, 57, 68, and 90.)

Another revealing trait of the Progressives is their high respect for intellect and scholarship. Hardly any era in American history has been richer in works of the mind. It produced (among others) Herbert Croly and Walter Lippmann writing on politics (see Selections 45 and 95); Thorstein Veblen on economics (see Volume 12, Selection 119); Charles A. Beard on history (see Selection 87); Louis D. Brandeis and Oliver Wendell Holmes, Jr., on law (see Selections 3 and 6); William James, George Santayana, Abraham Flexner, and John Dewey on philosophy and education (see Volume 12, Selection 110, and in this volume, Selections 49, 52, and 57); Franz Boas on sociology (see Volume 14, Selections 42 and 85). And their thought became an important part of the Progressive crusade. In a sense, all these scholars were involved in the same pursuit: a war on formalism, on the shibboleths that for decades past had constrained their intellectual realms.

Above all, the Progressive shared a faith in democracy, and what goes with it, a conviction that laws could settle the most complex social problems. Our modern image of turn-of-the-century America — a place where gentlemen in straw hats passed their time courting ladies in bustles — is of course distorted. But this pleasant picture contains one element of truth: the country was still young, perhaps naïve, but certainly optimistic. These, perhaps, were the deepest qualities of the Progressives. Uncowed by the enormous difficulties confronting them, they set out to prove that not even smoking factories and filthy tene-

ments and corruption in all walks of life belied the dreams of American statesmen of an earlier day. They attempted nothing less than to unite the best of
two epochs. As Woodrow Wilson put it in 1912, "The New Freedom is only
the old revived and clothed in the unconquerable strength of modern America."

William Howard Taft was Theodore Roosevelt's handpicked successor when
he retired from the White House in 1908. Roosevelt discreetly departed for
Africa to get in some long delayed hunting and to allow Taft to have the
spotlight. However, Taft was an inept politician, and the memory of Teddy
shone all the brighter as Taft bungled time after time. Distress signals started
to fly across the Atlantic. The old *Life* magazine printed this one in 1910:

> Teddy, come home and blow your horn,
> The sheep's in the meadow, the cow's in the corn.
> The boy you left to 'tend the sheep
> Is under the haystack fast asleep.

Roosevelt returned in June and for a while made no public statements. But
personal differences grew into political ones, and by late 1911 Roosevelt was
ready to declare war on his protégé. (For statements by Taft, and for others'
views of the events and policies of his administration, see Selections 40, 51, 56,
62-63, 67, 74, and 76.)

He started too late. The rank and file loved him, but the Republican profes-
sionals had already decided on Taft in 1912, and he was renominated on the
first ballot. But T. R. was never a quitter. "If you wish me to make the fight,"
he told a rump convention of insurgents, "I will make it, even if only one state
should support me." He was nominated by the newly formed Progressive or
"Bull Moose" Party in August, on a platform that included demands for tariff
reduction, prohibition of child labor, minimum wages for women, stricter regulation of industry, direct election of Senators, a nationwide preferential primary
system, the initiative, referendum, and recall, and women's suffrage — a platform, in short, that translated the New Nationalism into a political program.
(For discussions by Roosevelt and by others of the Progressive program, see
Selections 51, 62, and 69.)

The nation got most of the program — although it had to wait for some of
its elements for twenty years — but not Roosevelt. With two strong Republicans running, it was obvious to the Democrats that the election was theirs, and
the only question was, who should receive the prize? For a while it seemed
that the choice would be Champ Clark of Missouri, but he just failed to win
on the early ballots, and then old William Jennings Bryan announced that he
was throwing his support to Woodrow Wilson, the governor of New Jersey.
Wilson was a neophyte in politics who had gained a reputation as a scholar
and as president of Princeton University. After one of the more interesting
campaigns in our history, he was elected, gaining a smashing victory in the
electoral college. But he received only a little more than six million votes —
fewer than Bryan in any of his three defeats — and was outpolled by the two
Republicans together by a million votes.

Eugene Debs, running on the Socialist ticket, polled nearly a million votes. Clearly, for a considerable body of Americans, not even the moderate reform impulse within the major parties was sufficient to the needs of the day. (For discussions of American socialism during this period, see Volume 12, Selections 94, 104, and 122, and in this volume, Selections 4, 6-7, 11, 31, 44, 68, and 71.)

Wilson had offered the New Freedom as an alternative to the New Nationalism of Roosevelt. There was not much difference. True, the two men emphasized different aspects of the problems that both faced. With regard to trusts, for example, Roosevelt felt that, though they indeed violated the canons of laissez faire, they were economically necessary and should be regulated rather than destroyed. Wilson did not want to destroy them either, but he saw the problem from the point of view of the individual, who, he thought, had to be protected from the monopolists. Thus their different approaches resulted in different rhetorics, but their programs were remarkably similar. (For early statements by Wilson, see Selections 55, 70, and 82.)

Wilson made an immediate start on realizing the New Freedom by summoning Congress into special session on April 7, 1913, to enact a new tariff law. He surprised the country by reviving a practice that had died out a century before, and appeared in person before a joint session of both houses. ("Why didn't I think of that?" Roosevelt is said to have remarked.) Wilson worked long and hard to get a good bill, and the Underwood-Simmons Tariff represented the first genuine tariff reform since the Civil War. (See Selections 34, 40, 79, and 84.) The law contained one revolutionary provision. In order to compensate for an anticipated decrease in customs revenue, the framers took advantage of the Sixteenth Amendment, which had been ratified just before Taft left office, and imposed the first modern federal income tax. This, of course, is still with us today.

While the work of revising the tariff proceeded, Congress busied itself with another important plank in Wilson's platform. The country had been plagued ever since the demise of the Second Bank of the United States by an inelastic system of credit and currency, a plethora of paper money, and a highly unstable banking establishment. A National Monetary Commission chaired by Senator Nelson Aldrich of Rhode Island had studied the problem from 1908 to 1912; it ended up by recommending the formation of a new national bank. True to the heritage of Andrew Jackson, the Democratic Congress turned the idea down and appointed its own panel under Representative Arsène Pujo of Louisiana. We got no national bank, but we did get the Federal Reserve Act of December 23, 1913, which established another institution that continues to this day. (See Selections 73 and 80-81.)

A third notable action of Wilson's first administration was the establishment of the Federal Trade Commission and the passage of the Clayton Antitrust Act, both in 1914. Together, they put teeth into government machinery for controlling trusts for the first time. Even so, trustbusting in the old sense was not the order of the day. Instead, Wilson inaugurated experiments from 1915 on with the type of government-business collaboration that would set the pattern of "normalcy" during the 1920s and would be the prescription for recovery in the early New Deal. A trust was no longer considered illegal merely because it was big, but only if its bigness did real economic harm. This too was an enduring concept. (For various views of the trusts during this period, see Selections 61-62, 70, 95-96, and 100; and in Volume 14, Selections 51, 61, and 71-72.)

The leading event of Wilson's two terms, however — he was reelected in 1916 by a whisker over Charles Evans Hughes — was not the passage of progressive domestic legislation, but the world war into which the country was slowly but inexorably drawn from 1915 on. Consideration of that must be left to the next volume.

One other notable figure deserves mention here. He is Mark Twain, who perforce is less than adequately represented in the pages of the *Annals,* but whose spirit broods over this volume (he died in 1910) and the two or three that precede it. An excerpt from his story "Captain Stormfield's Visit to Heaven" appears here, as Selection 22; other fugitive but fascinating pieces by the great humorist appear in Volume 10. Would that there were more — but how could one reasonably stop short of the whole?

Captain Stormfield might be described as a practical theist, a down-to-earth fellow who ends up in Heaven (instead of hell, where he expects to go) because his heart is in the right place. As such, he was not wholly unrepresentative of the times, although Mark Twain himself was rather timid about publishing the story, fearing that it would offend the orthodox. In fact, there was much talk during these years about the proper role of religion in an industrial society. Some held that the church must increasingly serve secular ends and proclaimed a social gospel marked more by good works than by faith. But the 1900s was also a period of revivalism in religion, when men like Dwight L. Moody and Billy Sunday demanded adherence to older creeds that, to them and their many followers, seemed as relevant as ever. Indeed, this is just one more of the innumerable paradoxes of Progressivism. (For writings dealing with these matters in this volume, see Selections 7, 21, 23, 32, 108-109, and 112.)

Chronology: 1905 - 1915

1905

April 17. In *Lochner v. New York,* the Supreme Court holds that New York State law regulating hours of bakery workers is unconstitutional; dissent by Justice Holmes protests that decision is based on an "economic theory which a large part of the country does not entertain."

May 31. After decisively defeating the Russian fleet, Japan asks President Roosevelt to mediate in Russo-Japanese War, which has continued since February 1904; conflict has endangered Open Door Policy in China when fighting involves Manchuria, a Chinese province. **June 8.** Roosevelt invites both powers to peace conference. **July 29.** Before conference convenes, Secretary of War Taft (with Roosevelt's sanction) makes agreement with Japanese foreign minister that the U.S. will not interfere with Japanese imperialist actions in Korea if Japan will cede all its claims in the Philippines. **Aug. 9-Sept. 5.** Peace conference held at Portsmouth, New Hampshire, gives Japan control of Korea and strengthens its position in Manchuria, but Japan receives no indemnity and only half (instead of all) of Sakhalin Island. In following year Roosevelt receives Nobel Peace Prize for his efforts as mediator.

June 27-July 8. Industrial Workers of the World is founded in Chicago by Eugene V. Debs, William D. ("Big Bill") Haywood, and others; organization seeks to unite all workers and establish control by unions over production. Its main success is among miners and migratory workers in Western states. By World War I, split over socialism and subjected to severe legal harassment, it suffers a sharp decline in membership.

June. Eighteen-hour train service begins between New York and Chicago with New York Central's "Twentieth Century Limited" and Pennsylvania Railroad's "fastest long-distance train in the world." Within a week both trains are wrecked, with a loss of 19 lives. **Nov. 8.** Chicago and North Western Railway runs first train equipped with electric lights, from Chicago to California.

Oct. 3. Theatrical producer David Belasco opens first of a series of Western plays, *The Girl of the Golden West,* in Pittsburgh, where it runs for three years. Play is later written as an opera by Giacomo Puccini and opens at New York's Metropolitan Opera House. It is first opera based on an American theme.

Dec. 30. Chairman Charles Evans Hughes, appointed by the governor of New

York, presides over last of 57 hearings of investigation into scandals in the life insurance business; hearings have involved many prominent financial figures and lead to wide reforms, as well as making Hughes nationally known.

In this and the following year, George Santayana, teacher of philosophy at Harvard University, publishes his five-volume *The Life of Reason,* which he calls a "biography of the human intellect." Work consists of *Reason in Common Sense, Reason in Society, Reason in Religion, Reason in Art,* and *Reason in Science.* Daniel de Leon publishes *Socialist Reconstruction of Society.*

Zane Grey, author of a series of often violent Western novels, publishes *The Spirit of the Border;* total sales of Grey's books is estimated at 15 million.

First Rotary Club is founded in Chicago, meeting at each member's office in rotation. Clubs, consisting of at least one member of each local business or profession, are spread widely in the U.S. by 1910 and later in foreign countries. In 1922 name becomes Rotary International.

Mount Wilson Observatory completed; it has been established by George Ellery Hale near Pasadena, California, as a department of the Carnegie Institution of Washington (D.C.).

1906

March 12. In *Hale* v. *Henkel,* the Supreme Court rules that witnesses in antitrust suits may be compelled to testify against their corporations and to produce corporation documents without a plea of immunity.

April 7. Act of Algeciras is signed by Italy, France, Spain, Germany, Great Britain, Austria-Hungary, and the U.S.; settlement of status of Morocco upholds independence and territorial integrity of the country. Germany has asked President Roosevelt to arrange international conference after France has sought to establish a protectorate; while Act appears to accede to Germany's viewpoint, it actually sets up French-Spanish police and an international bank to control Moroccan finances. Austria-Hungary has been the only country to back Germany in the conference.

April 18. Most severe earthquake in U.S. history, followed by fire, destroys most of San Francisco's central area; damage is estimated at about $400 million, and about 700 lives are lost. Rescue workers commandeer all available automobiles to transport injured and aged; this is first time automobiles (about one per 800 of population) have been thought of as anything but a useless toy.

June 30. Reports by muckrakers result in passage of Pure Food and Drug Act, which requires statement of contents of packages and prohibits manufacture and sale of adulterated foods and drugs. On the same day, Meat Inspection Act is passed, largely as a result of exposure of filthy conditions in Chicago meat-packing plants made in Upton Sinclair's *The Jungle,* published earlier in the year.

Nov. 9. President Roosevelt sails on a battleship to visit Panama Canal Zone in first trip ever made outside the U.S. by a President in office.

Dec. 4. Reverend Algernon S. Crapsey, former High Episcopal clergyman who has become a rationalist and denies the divinity of Christ, is convicted by an ecclesiastical court of heresy after a trial that has lasted since April and drawn the attention of the U.S. and England.

Dec. 24. Reginald A. Fessenden demonstrates for the first time broadcasting of voice and music by radio; operators aboard many ships at sea report hearing the broadcast.

"O. Henry" (William Sidney Porter) publishes his first collection of short stories of New York City, *The Four Million*. Most famous for his New York stories, O. Henry writes more than 250 stories between 1899 and his death in 1910; many of the best of these concern the South and the West.

"Typhoid Mary," who under a number of assumed names has worked as a cook in institutions and private homes, is finally found eight years after it has become known that, although well herself, she is a carrier of typhoid fever. Because it is impossible to alter her carrier state, she is confined by health authorities for 23 years until her death.

During New York theater season of this year, six plays by George Bernard Shaw are shown: *Caesar and Cleopatra, Arms and the Man, Man and Superman, John Bull's Other Island, Major Barbara,* and *Mrs. Warren's Profession;* the last is raided by police as obscene and is closed after one performance.

1906 - 1909

Aug. 23. First president of Cuba asks U.S. help in putting down revolt resulting from election disputes. **Sept. 29.** After holding off for more than a month, President Roosevelt appoints Secretary of War Taft as provisional governor and sends troops to the island. Insurrectionists are disbanded within two weeks, but U.S. administration does not cease until January 28, 1909.

1907

February. President Roosevelt confers with San Francisco school board, which, on reopening of schools after earthquake, has

ordered segregation of children of Oriental parentage in a separate school; Japan's protest against this discrimination has led to fear of an international crisis. San Francisco authorities agree to withdraw ruling on condition federal government act to exclude Japanese laborers. **Feb. 24.** Japan in "gentlemen's agreement" agrees to withhold passports of laborers who plan to travel to the U.S. and recognizes right of U.S. to refuse admission to those whose passports have originally been intended for travel to another country. **March 13.** School board rescinds segregation order. **March 14.** Authorized by Congress, Roosevelt excludes Japanese laborers from the continental U.S. **Dec. 16.** Most of U.S. Navy ("Great White Fleet") leaves on world cruise to exhibit U.S. naval strength. President Roosevelt has planned move partly to show Japan that U.S. concessions do not result from fear of Japanese power.

March 13. Financial Panic of 1907 begins with fall of stock market. **Oct. 21.** Run on Knickerbocker Trust Company of New York lasts until reserves are gone, and many other banks throughout the U.S. fail. Widespread unemployment and enormous increase in food prices lead to congressional inquiry into currency and banking systems, and finally to Federal Reserve Act of 1913.

March 21. U.S. Marines land in Honduras during revolution to protect American lives and large capital investments in banana plantations from dangers of war.

April 1. Panama Canal Commission is reorganized; Secretary of War Taft is to direct project, and Lieutenant Colonel George W. Goethals, of Army Corps of Engineers, is appointed to direct construction, which has been virtually at a standstill because of malaria and yellow fever in area and disagreement over whether canal shall be lock construction or sea level. When completed in 1914, canal runs 40 miles from Atlantic to Pacific oceans and costs about $365 million.

May 1907. First observance of Mother's Day is held in a church in Philadelphia; by 1911 every state celebrates Mother's Day on the second Sunday in May. Mother's Day is formalized by Congress on May 7, 1914, and two days later President Wilson asks for display of flag to express "our love and reverence for the mothers of our country."

June 15-Oct. 18. Second Hague Peace Conference meets; it has been called in 1904 but postponed because of Russo-Japanese War. The U.S. fails in attempt to establish a World Court, but Monroe Doctrine is reinforced when Conference agrees that armed force must not be used to collect debts owed by any American nation; agreement has been proposed by Argentina during Venezuelan crisis.

June 19. Western cattle grazing interests meet in Denver to protest President Roosevelt's land reservation policy. Repeal of the Forest Reserve Act of 1891, which allows closing of timber areas for creation of national parks, is effected by a rider to an appropriation bill. However, Roosevelt adds 21 reserves to bill before he signs it.

Nov. 14. Central American Peace Conference, arranged by U.S. Secretary of State Elihu Root with Mexico, meets in Washington as result of war in Central America. Five countries organize a Central American Court of Justice and sign treaty of peace.

Nov. 16. Oklahoma, formerly Oklahoma and Indian territories, is admitted to the U.S. as forty-sixth state. Citizens have voted to name the state Sequoya after Indian creator of Cherokee alphabet, but Congress has refused. Population is 1,414,000, more than five times that of 1890. Constitution includes prohibition of liquor.

Lee de Forest develops thermionic amplifier tube, an improvement of his Audion amplifier, which makes possible telephone transmission across the continent.

First Nobel Prize for Physics awarded to an American goes to Albert A. Michelson of the University of Chicago for his work in spectroscopy and metrology.

State prohibition laws are adopted in Georgia and Alabama.

Walter Rauschenbusch of Rochester (New York) Theological Seminary publishes *Christianity and the Social Crisis*, first of a series of books advocating application of principles of Christianity to social problems.

College of Agriculture and Mechanic Arts is established in Honolulu; first classes begin in following year. College becomes University of Hawaii in 1920.

Florenz Ziegfeld, former theatrical manager, presents his first revue, *The Follies of 1907*, in New York City; series of extravaganzas continues for 23 years.

First daily comic strip begins in the *San Francisco Chronicle*; drawn by H. C. ("Bud") Fisher, it is at first titled, "Mr. Mutt" and later "Mutt and Jeff."

1907 - 1915

Best sellers of the period, some of which continue to sell to the present day, are Harold Bell Wright's *The Shepherd of the Hills, The Calling of Dan Matthews, The Winning of Barbara Worth*, and *The Eyes of the World*; John Fox, Jr.'s *The Trail of the Lonesome Pine*; *The Circular Staircase* by Mary Roberts Rinehart; Gene Stratton Porter's *A Girl of the Limberlost, The Harvester, Laddie*, and *Michael O'Halloran*; *Mother* by Kathleen Norris; *Riders of the*

Purple Sage by Zane Grey; *Pollyanna* by Eleanor Hodgman Porter; *Tarzan of the Apes* by Edgar Rice Burroughs; and *Penrod* by Booth Tarkington.

1908

Feb. 3. In Danbury Hatters' case (*Loewe v. Lawlor*), the Supreme Court rules unanimously that boycott of industry by a labor union comes within the Sherman Antitrust Act as a conspiracy in restraint of trade and is, therefore, illegal. This is first time the Sherman Act has been applied to labor unions.

April 2. People's Party meets and nominates Thomas E. Watson of Georgia for President. **May 1.** United Christian Party nominates Daniel B. Turney of Illinois. **May 10.** Socialists meet and nominate Eugene V. Debs of Indiana. **June 16.** Republican Party at Chicago meets and nominates President Roosevelt's choice, William Howard Taft of Ohio, for President and James S. Sherman of New York for Vice-President; Roosevelt, having promised not to run again, feels that Taft will carry out his policies. Platform stresses need for stronger antitrust legislation, backs Roosevelt's conservation program, and promises tariff reduction. **July 2.** Socialist Labor Party meets and nominates August Gillhaus of New York. **July 10.** Democrats at Denver nominate William Jennings Bryan for President and John W. Kern as his running mate. Platform is antimonopoly, promises tariff reduction, and favors income tax. **July 15.** Prohibition Party meets and nominates Eugene W. Chafin of Illinois. **July 27.** Independence Party meets and nominates Thomas L. Hisgen of Massachusetts.

May 13. White House Conservation Conference, called by President Roosevelt, is attended by congressmen, Supreme Court justices, members of the Cabinet, and state governors; immediate reason for calling Conference has been report of the Inland Waterways Commission that problem of crowded water routes cannot be separated from other problems of natural resources. **June 8.** National Conservation Commission is formed, with Gifford Pinchot as head. Commission's report on water, timber, soil, and mineral resources, submitted to Roosevelt in the following year, is first attempt to list them systematically.

May 28. Congress passes legislation regulating child labor in Washington, D.C., in hope that the states will follow suit.

May 30. National Monetary Commission established by the Aldrich-Vreeland Currency Act. Representing both houses of Congress, Commission is authorized to study U.S. and foreign banking and currency systems. Report made in 1912 is the basis of the Federal Reserve Act of 1913.

Oct. 1. Henry Ford introduces his Model T car; cost, $850. By 1909 his company is producing 19,000 automobiles annually, more than any other manufacturer. By turning out only one model (customers may have "any color, as long as it is black"), Ford is able to attain such efficiency that price has dropped to $310 by 1926.

Nov. 3. William Howard Taft and James S. Sherman defeat Bryan and Kern by popular vote of 7,675,000 to 6,412,000; electoral vote is Taft, 321; Bryan, 162. Republicans still dominate both House and Senate.

Nov. 30. U.S. and Japan sign Root-Takahira Agreement, which extends concessions made to Japan in 1905; it provides that both will uphold the Open Door Policy in China, support Chinese independence, and maintain the "existing status quo" in the Pacific, which Japan assumes to be U.S. recognition of its imperialistic aims in Korea and Manchuria.

Dec. 2. Federal Council of the Churches of Christ in America is established in Philadelphia; it represents almost all Protestant churches.

In *Adair* v. *United States,* the Supreme Court invalidates a provision of the Erdman Act of 1898 that prohibits interstate railroads from requiring workers to agree not to join unions (yellow-dog contracts). Opinion is that union membership is not an interstate matter.

In *Muller* v. *Oregon,* the Supreme Court holds that an Oregon law limiting women's working hours is not unconstitutional.

The 47-story Singer Building in New York City is completed; but soon the Metropolitan Life Insurance Building (50 stories) is built, and in 1913 the Woolworth Building of 60 stories tops them both.

Gertrude Stein, expatriate American author, having settled in Paris in 1903 in a house that becomes a center for visiting artists and writers, publishes her first book, *Three Lives.*

"Ashcan School" of painting is established by a group of former newspaper illustrators when they begin painting unglamorous people and areas of New York City; group includes, among others, Robert Henri, John Sloan, and George Luks.

Movie houses called nickelodeons, first established in McKeesport, Pennsylvania, in 1905 by John P. Harris and Harry Davis, now number about 8,000 throughout the country. Usually set up in empty stores, they show continuous movies with piano accompaniment, and tickets cost five cents.

1909

Feb. 12. Sixty Negro and white leaders issue call for national conference on the Negro on the hundredth anniversary of Abraham Lincoln's birth. **May 30.** Conference convenes in New York; result is formation of the National Association for the Advancement of Colored People (N.A.A.C.P.) to fight for Negro rights by legal means.

April 6. Arctic explorer Robert Edwin Peary, his Negro aid, Matthew Henson, and four Eskimos finish final dash from advance base to latitude 90 degrees north, first time in recorded history that men have reached the North Pole. **Sept. 1.** Dr. Frederick Cook of New York claims to have reached North Pole in previous year, but claim is discredited because of insufficient proof.

July 12. Congress submits Sixteenth (income tax) Amendment to the Constitution to the states for ratification; it is not finally ratified until 1913.

Payne-Aldrich Tariff is enacted by a special session of Congress to fulfill Republican campaign pledges, which have led public to expect reduced rates. Rates are revised downward to an average of about 38 percent on the value of goods imported, but tariff is actually increased on several hundred competitive items. In public controversy, President Taft defends this tariff as the best ever enacted by the Republican Party, but public disappointment helps Democrats win control of Congress 1910.

Leo H. Baekeland patents his thermosetting plastic, Bakelite; later it is used in many ways industrially, especially as an electric insulator. Invention is a major advance in U.S. plastics industry.

Herbert D. Croly publishes his first book on U.S. social and political problems, *The Promise of American Life.* Croly later founds weekly magazine, the *New Republic;* cofounder and associate editor is Walter Lippmann.

Daniel H. Burnham, architect and city planner, proposes his "city beautiful" plan for Chicago, which is 30 years ahead of its time in awareness of need for transportation, parks, and living space on a metropolitan area basis. Robie House in Chicago, designed by Frank Lloyd Wright, is completed; it is the most famous example of his "prairie" style.

First substantial animated cartoon in the United States is shown; it is entitled *Gertie the Dinosaur* and consists of 10,000 drawings by newspaper cartoonist Winsor McCay.

1909 - 1911

July 15, 1909. In effort to maintain balance of foreign control in China and safeguard American investment, President Taft seeks permission from Chinese regent for participation of U.S. private banks in international development of China. **July 4, 1911.** As a result of this "dollar diplomacy," Japan and Russia, urged by European nations, confirm each other's special interests in Manchuria, openly defying U.S.-sponsored Open Door Policy.

1910

Feb. 8. Boy Scouts of America is chartered; the U.S. is the twelfth country of the world to set up organized scouting after movement has been started in England by publication in 1908 of *Scouting for Boys* by Lieutenant General R. S. S. Baden-Powell; Baden-Powell has originally intended that his ideas be used by already existing boys' organizations. **March 17.** Camp Fire Girls is organized by Mr. and Mrs. Luther Halsey Gulick, Mrs. Ernest Thompson Seton, and other prominent educators.

March 19. Progressives led by George W. Norris, Nebraska Republican, revolt successfully against dictatorial powers of House Speaker Joseph Cannon of Illinois ("Cannonism") when they pass amendment to House rules providing that Rules Committee be elected by House rather than appointed by the speaker, who, in addition, is made ineligible for membership on the Committee.

March 26. Immigration Act of 1907 is amended to exclude paupers, criminals, anarchists, and diseased persons from the U.S.

May. Halley's Comet passes the sun without the occurrence of disaster as predicted; many have believed that the earth will pass through the comet's tail and that everything on the earth will be destroyed.

June 18. Mann-Elkins Railroad Act is passed; law continues movement to strengthen powers of Interstate Commerce Commission over railroads and other carriers and communications systems provided for in Hepburn Act of 1906. Rulings of Commission are made binding pending appeals to courts, and corporations are to furnish proof of unreasonableness.

June 25. Congress establishes postal savings bank system recommended by President Taft; specific post offices are made depositories of funds on which 2 percent interest is paid; system continues until 1967.

June 25. In extension of corrupt practices acts passed by many states, Congress passes Publicity Act requiring U.S. representatives to file reports of campaign contributions received.

June 25. Congress passes Mann Act (White-Slave Traffic Act), which prohibits transportation of women across state lines for immoral purposes.

Aug. 31. Theodore Roosevelt, on return from Africa and Europe, makes New Nationalism speech in Kansas. He is increasingly estranged from Taft administration, convinced that Taft has been too cautious in continuing liberal Republican policies, and is angered by scandals in administration of conservation program. Actually, Taft administration begins more than twice as many antitrust actions as that of Roosevelt.

Sept. 7. Long dispute between Great Britain and the U.S. over Newfoundland fishing rights is settled by The Hague Court; commission is formed to settle disputes over fishing regulations, and the U.S. is allowed some concessions in Newfoundland waters. Award is confirmed by Great Britain and the U.S. in 1912.

Nov. 8. In fall elections, Democrats capture control of the House of Representatives; although Senate remains Republican, actually it is dominated by insurgents who have ties with Democrats. Victor Berger of Wisconsin is first Socialist ever elected to Congress. More than half the states elect Democratic governors, including Woodrow Wilson in New Jersey. Franklin Delano Roosevelt is elected to New York State Senate.

1910 census shows a population of 91,972,000, which includes 8,795,000 immigrants arrived since 1900; almost 46 percent of people live in places of 2,500 or more. Of people over 25 years old, less than half have completed grade-school education, and about 4 percent have graduated from college; but illiteracy has decreased since 1900 from 10.7 percent to 7.7 percent.

By this year prohibition laws have been enacted by Maine, Kansas, North Dakota, Georgia, Alabama, Oklahoma, Mississippi, North Carolina, Tennessee, and several hundred towns in Massachusetts.

Robert Millikan of the University of Chicago measures electric charge carried by an electron and later shows that the charge is constant. His work confirms much basic physical theory and inspires important advances in physics.

Educator Abraham Flexner publishes his report *Medical Education in the United States and Canada;* written for the Carnegie Foundation for the Advancement of Teaching, the report exposes inferior standards in the 155 U.S. medical schools and results in closing of many and reorganization of most others.

First U.S. air meet is held at Los Angeles, with audiences averaging 35,000 per day who watch all meet air speed records broken by Louis Paulhan of France and Glenn Curtiss of the U.S. Although many men want to fly, only five airplanes have been sold to individuals in the three years since first commercially made plane was produced.

1910 - 1911

First voluntary agreements for arbitration in labor disputes are set up in New York at instigation of Louis D. Brandeis and in Chicago after negotiation by Sidney Hillman of United Garment Workers. International Ladies' Garment Workers' Union achieves improvement in sweatshop system and garment industry in New York, especially after Triangle fire of 1911, which kills 146 workers and results in revision of New York building code and labor laws.

Andrew Carnegie, after giving funds to the Temple of Peace at The Hague, sets up the Carnegie Endowment for International Peace with a fund of $10 million; in 1911 he establishes the Carnegie Corporation of New York to support educational projects with an endowment of $125 million. By this date he has already donated more than $60 million in accordance with his belief that wealth should be distributed for the good of the world.

1911

Jan. 21. National Progressive Republican League is formed by Senator Robert M. La Follette of Wisconsin and others. League urges general adoption of direct primaries; direct election of senators; and state constitution reforms to permit initiative, referendum, and recall.

Jan. 26. President Taft proposes reciprocal reduction of tariffs between the U.S. and Canada. **July 22.** U.S. Congress approves. Advanced to conciliate Canadian reaction to Payne-Aldrich Tariff of 1909, the proposals result in talk in the U.S. of annexing Canada, which arouses hostility of Canadian nationalists. **Sept. 21.** Made an issue in Canada, proposed agreement is repudiated when antireciprocity Conservatives win Canadian elections.

February. New automobile era begins when electric self-starter is demonstrated by General Motors; invented by Clyde J. Coleman in 1899, it has been perfected in this year by Charles F. Kettering. Invention makes it possible for women to drive without a male companion to crank the engine should it stop.

March 7. Twenty thousand U.S. troops are sent to Mexican border to protect interests of U.S. citizens during revolution led by liberal Francisco Madero against dictatorship; fighting has been so close to the border that crowds of U.S. citizens gather to watch. **April 14.** President Taft demands that Mexico cease fighting along the border. **May 25.** Madero's forces are victorious when Mexican President Díaz retires into exile after 34 years of control.

May 15. In *Standard Oil Company of New Jersey et al.* v. *United States,* Supreme Court orders Standard Oil Company dissolved on ground that it engages in "unreasonable" restraint of trade; thus, Court accepts "rule of reason" as principle for regulation of large corporations under Sherman Antitrust Act.

May 29. In *United States* v. *American Tobacco Company,* Supreme Court finds the "tobacco trust" to be in violation of the Sherman Antitrust Act in attempting to restrain commerce and effect a monopoly in the tobacco business.

July 7. Threat of complete extermination of fur seals in the North Pacific results in treaty signed by the U.S., Great Britain (for Canada), Russia, and Japan that outlaws pelagic sealing for 15 years north of the 30th parallel; the U.S. is given control of the area. Increase of seal herds has been prevented because seals killed are usually migrating pregnant females.

Oct. 16. Progressive Republicans meet in Chicago and nominate Robert M. La Follette for the Presidency.

Dec. 18. The U.S. abrogates 1832 treaty with Russia because Russia refuses to honor passports of Jewish U.S. citizens and those of various clergymen.

Socialist mayors are elected in 18 cities after campaigns advocating municipal ownership of public utilities and local transportation. Since 1900, era of municipal reform has been due in large part to muckrakers' exposures of graft and corruption.

Elmer Sperry patents the gyrocompass;

he later perfects the gyroscope and invents the automatic pilot.

1911 - 1914

Naturalistic novelist Theodore Dreiser publishes first novel in 11 years, *Jennie Gerhardt,* and the next year publishes *The Financier,* first book of a trilogy based on the life of a millionaire streetcar manufacturer; second book, *The Titan,* is published in 1914, but the third, *The Stoic,* not until 1947, two years after Dreiser's death.

1911. The *Masses,* proletarian magazine, is founded in New York; it later becomes the *Liberator* and then the *New Masses.* **1912.** Harriet Monroe begins publishing *Poetry* magazine in Chicago. **1914.** The *New Republic* magazine begins publication; it is founded and edited by Herbert Croly along with other Progressives, most notably Walter Lippmann.

1911 - 1920

Novelist Edith Wharton publishes her best-known novel, *Ethan Frome,* New England tragedy; later she publishes *The Reef, The Custom of the Country, Summer,* and, in 1920, *The Age of Innocence,* which wins the Pulitzer Prize.

1912

Jan. 6. New Mexico becomes forty-seventh state of the U.S. after numerous efforts to attain statehood have failed until 1910, when Congress has passed enabling legislation.

Jan. 12. Lawrence, Massachusetts, textile workers begin strike to protest reduction of wages that follows enactment of minimum hours law; lasting for two months and characterized by violence, strike demonstrates the power of the Industrial Workers of the World, which for the first time becomes influential in the East.

Feb. 14. Arizona, formerly part of New Mexico Territory, becomes forty-eighth state of the U.S. In previous August, President Taft has vetoed congressional resolution admitting it to statehood because of clause in state constitution providing for recall of judges by popular vote, which Taft feels will limit judicial independence. Arizona is admitted after removing clause but immediately reinserts it on becoming a state.

Feb. 25. Theodore Roosevelt, now alienated from Conservative Republicans and closer to Progressives who have backed Senator La Follette, consents to run against Taft for presidential nomination if asked.

March 7. U.S. Senate passes general arbitration agreement signed with France and Great Britain that provides for referral of international disputes to the Hague Court; but passage is not achieved until amendments proposed by Senator Henry Cabot Lodge of Massachusetts weaken it by adding reservations in cases that involve the Monroe Doctrine and Oriental exclusion from the U.S. and by requiring consent of the U.S. Senate before arbitration can be submitted to the Court.

April 7. Socialist Labor Party meets and nominates Arthur E. Reimer of Massachusetts for President. **May 12.** Socialists meet and again nominate Eugene V. Debs. **June 18.** Republicans meeting at Chicago are controlled by conservative elements, who exclude most Theodore Roosevelt backers by not seating contested delegations; President Taft and Vice-President Sherman are renominated, but Sherman dies on October 30. Platform advocates conservation, a corrupt practices act, financial reform, strict regulation of trusts, and a lower protective tariff. **June 22.** Roosevelt followers meet, declare Taft nomination fraudulent, and call upon Roosevelt to head third party. **July 2.** At Democratic convention in Baltimore, Woodrow Wilson of New Jersey is nominated for President on the forty-sixth ballot, after William Jennings Bryan swings support to him from Champ Clark of Missouri; Thomas R. Marshall of Indiana is nominated for Vice-President. Platform is like Republicans' on conservation, a corrupt practices act, and financial reform but stresses outlawing of monopolies, and tariff for revenue only. **Aug. 7.** Progressive ("Bull Moose") Party, meeting at Chicago, nominates Roosevelt for President and Hiram W. Johnson of California for Vice-President. Platform stresses tariff revision, changes in state and federal election laws, stricter control of combinations in industry, women suffrage, and reforms in labor laws for women and children.

April 14-15. "Unsinkable" steamship *Titanic* collides with iceberg and sinks with loss of more than 1,500 persons. Investigation shows that ship carried too few lifeboats and had been ordered to proceed at high speed through dangerous waters. **May 1.** Federal authorities order all steamships to provide enough lifeboats for all passengers.

Aug. 2. U.S. Senate passes resolution proposed by Senator Lodge expressing concern over possession by a non-American corporation of any strategic area in the Western Hemisphere; question has arisen when Japan is found to be negotiating with an American syndicate for an area of Lower California (Mexico). Known as the Lodge Corollary, resolution broadens scope of Monroe Doctrine to cover foreign corporations.

Aug. 14. U.S. Marines land in Nicaragua to prevent foreign occupation of possible canal route across the isthmus; foreign intervention has been threatened when Nicaragua has delayed payments of loans from European countries and U.S. banks that have been guaranteed by Nicaraguan customs revenues. Action is taken by authority of President Taft, although the U.S. Senate has failed to ratify various proposed U.S.-Nicaraguan agreements authorizing U.S. intervention.

Aug. 24. Domestic parcel post system is authorized; service begins in following year.

Nov. 5. Woodrow Wilson is elected President with a popular vote of 6,297,000 to 4,119,000 for Roosevelt and 3,487,000 for Taft; Socialist Debs receives 901,000 votes, twice as many as in any previous election. According to popular vote, Wilson is a minority President, but his electoral majority is greatest in U.S. election history to this time: Wilson, 435 (40 states); Roosevelt, 88 (6 states); Taft, 8 (2 states).

Alaska becomes an organized territory of the U.S. after 16 months of argument in Congress, but Alaskan legislature is restricted far more as to taxing and licensing powers than those of earlier territories.

By this year many states have passed laws controlling wages and hours, factory working conditions, and labor of women and children. Massachusetts passes first minimum wage law (invalidated by the Supreme Court in 1923); New York passes 54-hour-week labor law; and Congress passes eight-hour-day law for all federal workers.

Government-sponsored illustrations of engineering work on the Panama Canal are published; executed by etcher-lithographer Joseph Pennell, they are the first popularly successful artistic treatment of industrial or engineering themes.

Columbia University founds School of Journalism with bequest from newspaper publisher Joseph Pulitzer, who has died in the previous year.

Alexis Carrel, whose important work has been done at the University of Chicago and later at the Rockefeller Institute, receives Nobel Prize in Physiology and Medicine; award is for his work in transplanting organs and blood vessels and in suturing blood vessels. Two years later, Carrel performs first successful heart surgery on an animal by cutting off blood circulation for several minutes.

William Randolph Hearst begins to acquire control of a chain of newspapers. By 1934, chain consists of 30 newspapers, as well as 6 magazines, a Sunday supplement, a features syndicate, a newsreel, and 2 wire services.

1912 - 1914

Aug. 24, 1912. Congress passes Panama Canal Act, which provides toll-free passage of Canal for American vessels engaged in coastwise trade, although Hay-Pauncefote Treaty has provided entire equality for all nations. **March 5, 1914.** After British protest that Act shows bad faith on part of the U.S., President Wilson asks repeal of exemption, which Congress passes on June 11.

1912 - 1915

Amy Lowell publishes *A Dome of Many-Coloured Glass,* her first poetry collection, in 1912, and in 1914, *Sword Blades and Poppy Seed,* which contains her first free verse. Robert Frost publishes (in London) his first book of poetry, *A Boy's Will,* in 1913, and in the following year *North of Boston;* by 1915 he is recognized as a major poet. Va-

chel Lindsay's poem "General William Booth Enters into Heaven" appears in *Poetry* magazine in 1913, his *Congo and Other Poems* appearing a year later. Carl Sandburg's poetry is first recognized when he receives *Poetry* award in 1914 for poems about Chicago.

Liberal historian Charles Austin Beard reaches a wide audience with his analyses of major factors in the development of the U.S. government, *The Supreme Court and the Constitution* in 1912, *An Economic Interpretation of the Constitution of the United States* in 1913, and *The Economic Origins of Jeffersonian Democracy* in 1915.

1913

January-April. Garment workers' strike begins in New York City when 150,000 workers leave their jobs in protest against long hours, low wages, and refusal of employers to recognize union. Strike spreads to Boston and ends when workers win concessions on all three points.

Feb. 17. Armory Show opens at 69th Regiment Armory in New York City; organized by Association of Painters and Sculptors, it is the first full-scale presentation in the U.S. of contemporary European work, abstract, Cubist, Impressionist, and Postimpressionist. Show has revolutionary effects on public taste in the U.S., both for European art and for new departures and experiments by American artists.

Feb. 22. Liberal Mexican President Madero is assassinated by reactionaries under General Victoriano Huerta; Huerta is recognized by European nations but not by the U.S., which has supported Madero and has resisted pressures by U.S. business interests to support Huerta. **March 11.** President Wilson, in speech disapproving Huerta regime, ends "dollar diplomacy," stating that the U.S. will no longer support special business interests in foreign countries.

Feb. 25. Sixteenth Amendment to the U.S. Constitution is declared ratified. It authorizes Congress to tax income from all sources without regard to a census and without apportionment among the states.

Feb. 28. Report by House committee headed by Representative Arsène Pujo that has inquired into a reported "money trust" states that concentration of money and financial power is increasing by means of business consolidations, interlocking directorates, questionable stock purchases, and other financial maneuvers; report lends impetus to moves for banking and currency reforms.

March 4. Congress separates U.S. Department of Commerce and Labor into two departments, both with Cabinet status, and sets up federal mediation board to settle labor disputes.

April 8. President Wilson appears before Congress to deliver his message on tariff revision; he is first President since John Adams to deliver a message to Congress in person; Thomas Jefferson has set precedent in 1801, when he has his address read by a clerk.

April 24. Secretary of State William Jennings Bryan achieves last of 21 ratifications of arbitration treaties with foreign countries; treaties provide that no signing country will resort to war until disputes have been submitted to arbitration by an international commission, which must be allowed one year to submit a report.

May 14. John D. Rockefeller, in greatest single philanthropic act in U.S. history up to this time, donates $100 million to establish the Rockefeller Foundation; it is chartered by the state of New York.

May 31. Seventeenth Amendment to the Constitution is declared ratified and in effect. It provides for election of U.S. senators directly by the people of each state, instead of by state legislatures.

Aug. 16. Mexican leader Huerta refuses President Wilson's proposal of an armistice when new revolution breaks out, leading to Wilson policy of "watchful waiting" and strict arms embargo. **Oct. 27.** In answer to demands of business that the U.S. intervene, Wilson declares that the U.S. never again will seek territory by conquest. **Nov. 7.** Wilson demands Huerta's resignation and upon Huerta's refusal announces U.S. policy of support of revolutionists. Early in following year, arms embargo is lifted to allow shipments to revolutionists, and Veracruz is blockaded by U.S. warships to prevent entry of arms sent to Huerta from Europe.

Oct. 3. Congress passes Underwood Tariff Act; average duties are reduced to 30 percent, and some important raw materials are admitted free. To compensate for anticipated losses of revenue, a tax of 1 percent is levied on corporate incomes of more than $4,000, under the new sixteenth constitutional amendment.

Dec. 23. President Wilson, after a long congressional debate and in defiance of banking interests, signs Federal Reserve Act, first basic overhaul of U.S. banking system since 1863. Act provides for division of U.S. into 8 to 12 reserve districts and for a Federal Reserve Board of 7 members authorized to regulate financial reserves, currency, and credit. National banks are required to become members of the system, but membership of state banks is made voluntary.

In Minnesota rate cases, the Supreme Court upholds Minnesota law that regulates railroad rates within the state, finding that such laws are valid if they do not conflict with U.S. interstate laws.

Béla Schick devises Schick test for susceptibility to diphtheria. Large-scale testing and immunization of susceptible children sharply cut incidence of disease, which has been a major cause of death, especially in children.

Thomas Hunt Morgan of Columbia University publishes *Heredity and Sex* following research on the fruit fly to test the Mendelian law of inheritance. In previous years, Morgan has discovered that characteristics of flies are sex linked and has described characteristics of linkages.

Willa Cather, having resigned as editor of *McClure's* magazine in the previous year to write, publishes her novel *O Pioneers!*

1913 - 1914

Ford Motor Company sets up first moving assembly line, based on meat-packers' system of conveyor belts. Ford pays workers unheard-of minimum wage of $5 per day and shocks industry by establishing a 40-hour workweek. Assembly-line system results in lowering of prices of Model T Fords; more than 15 million are produced by 1927.

1913 - 1915

Feb. 14, 1913. President Taft vetoes immigration bill that requires a literacy test; a similar bill has been vetoed by President Cleveland in 1896; in 1915 President Wilson vetoes another such bill on ground that

the people of the U.S. have not voted to reverse a policy that has been in effect since the beginning of U.S. history.

Hollywood becomes the center of the motion-picture industry, replacing New York City. Serial films are beginning to be popular. Music-hall performer Charles Spencer Chaplin begins (December 1913) his movie career in producer Mack Sennett's one-reel slapstick Keystone Comedies. *The Birth of a Nation,* 12-reel film masterpiece directed by David Wark Griffith, and based on *The Clansman* by Thomas Dixon, is first exhibited (February 1915) in Los Angeles under the title of the book; its public opening is at New York's Liberty Theater on March 3 with new title suggested by Dixon. A story of the Reconstruction era that establishes all essentials of film narrative technique, it becomes one of the greatest moneymakers in film history. Its apparent racist tone and sympathetic treatment of the Ku Klux Klan are strongly protested by Northern liberals and Negro leaders.

1914

Feb. 13. American Society of Composers, Authors and Publishers (ASCAP) is organized in New York City at a meeting of more than 100 persons involved in the music field; composer Victor Herbert is largely responsible for calling meeting.

April 9. Party of U.S. sailors is arrested in Tampico, Mexico, when they go ashore for supplies; they are released with apologies by authorities, but U.S. commander, Admiral Henry T. Mayo, on his own initiative demands hoisting of American flag on Mexican soil and special 21-gun salute by Mexicans. **April 14.** Feeling that he must support Mayo, President Wilson orders U.S. fleet to Tampico Bay, five days later requesting authorization from Congress to use force to uphold U.S. rights. **April 21.** Before authorization is granted on April 22, U.S. forces shell and occupy Veracruz to forestall delivery of arms by approaching German ship. Incident causes anti-U.S. feeling in Mexico that brings two countries close to war.

April 25. Argentina, Brazil, and Chile (the ABC powers) offer to arbitrate U.S.-Mexican dispute is quickly accepted by President Wilson and Huerta. **May 20-June 30.** Commission, meeting in Ontario, Canada, rejects indemnity claims of U.S. but proposes resignation of Huerta. **June 24.** Plan is rejected by Mexico but has effect of forcing Huerta's resignation on July 15. **Nov. 23.** U.S. occupation forces withdraw from Veracruz, and in next year new anti-Huerta government is recognized by the U.S.

May 8. Congress passes Smith-Lever Act; Department of Agriculture and land-grant colleges of the states are to work together to establish system of education for farmers. Funds for program are to be provided equally by federal and state governments.

Aug. 1. Germany declares war on Russia. **Aug. 3.** Germany declares war on France and a day later invades Belgium. **Aug. 4.** Great Britain declares war on Germany. President Wilson issues proclamation of U.S. neutrality in Russo-German conflict. **Aug. 5.** U.S. neutrality proclamation is broadened to include Anglo-German war, and President Wilson offers his good offices to belligerents to negotiate peace. **Aug. 19.** Wilson asks Americans to be neutral "in thought as well as in action." Controversy between U.S. and warring powers over rights of neutral shipping, seizure of contraband materials (as well as classification of contraband), and effective blockade continues into following year.

Aug. 15. Panama Canal is officially opened to traffic.

Sept. 26. Congress passes Federal Trade Commission Act as part of President Wilson's program; Act seeks to eliminate unfair business practices in interstate commerce. Federal Trade Commission, which replaces Bureau of Corporations, is authorized to investigate and control activities of persons and corporations. Banks, common carriers, and communications enterprises are excluded, since other federal laws apply to these.

Oct. 15. Congress passes Clayton Antitrust Act, which refines and extends powers of federal government under Sherman Antitrust Act of 1890. Labor and farm organizations are exempted from regulations applying to "combinations in restraint of trade," and the use of court injunctions in labor disputes is severely limited, though these provisions are later weakened by rulings of the courts.

This year marks end of high tide of European immigration to the U.S. in the decade 1905-1914. During these years nearly 10.5 million people enter the U.S. Three-fourths of immigrants come from Slavic and southern regions of Europe, and less than 15 percent from western and northern Europe.

Robert H. Goddard patents his liquid-fuel rocket, which uses liquid ether and oxygen, although he does not fire this type of rocket until 1926. Known as the father of U.S. rocketry, Goddard later develops theory of rockets fired in stages as method for reaching the moon. His 1919 report "A Method of Reaching Extreme Altitudes" is a classic to the present day.

Theodore W. Richards receives Nobel Prize for Chemistry for his work in discovering the exact atomic weights of a large number of elements; he is first American honored in chemistry.

1914 - 1915

German occupation of neutral (and unprepared) Belgium leads to movement advocating preparedness in the U.S. Such organizations as the National Security League, the League to Enforce Peace, the American Defense Society, and the American Rights Committee are formed, backed by such men as Theodore Roosevelt, Henry Cabot Lodge, and William Howard Taft.

1915

Jan. 25. Alexander Graham Bell in New York speaks to Dr. Thomas A. Watson in San Francisco in first transcontinental telephone call. They are the same two men who made first telephone call in 1876 from telephones in adjoining rooms; Bell's words are the same: "Mr. Watson, come here. I want you." **July 27.** First direct wireless service between the U.S. and Japan is established. **Oct. 21.** First transatlantic radiotelephone communication is made when message is completed between Arlington, Virginia, and the Eiffel Tower in Paris.

Jan. 28. Congress combines Revenue Cutter Service and Lifesaving Service to form U.S. Coast Guard.

Feb. 4. Germany announces that enemy merchant ships in British waters will be sunk on sight and that no effort will be made to rescue passengers and personnel; neutral vessels may enter war zone at their own risk. **Feb. 10.** U.S. reply states that loss of American vessels or lives will be considered a clear "violation of neutrality" for which Germany will be held strictly responsible. Germany attempts to persuade U.S. to warn citizens against travel on ships

of belligerent nations, but State Department does nothing.

February. Founding of Washington Square Players (later the Theater Guild) in New York advances modern drama. In following summer, Provincetown Players is organized in Massachusetts by group of New Yorkers who produce early plays of Eugene O'Neill.

May 1. Germany warns that Americans traveling on ships in British waters do so at their own risk. **May 7.** British steamer *Lusitania* is sunk by German submarine off Ireland. Almost 1,200 people are drowned, including 128 Americans. **May 13.** Secretary of State Bryan reluctantly signs note drafted by President Wilson protesting sinking and demanding reparations for lost U.S. lives and an end to unrestricted submarine warfare. **May 28.** Germany replies that sinking is justified, since *Lusitania* was armed; although it was not armed, *Lusitania* carried munitions cargo. **June 7.** Secretary Bryan refuses to sign second Wilson *Lusitania* note demanding German promises, because he fears it will lead to U.S. involvement in war, but President Wilson, after accepting Bryan's resignation (June 8), sends it on June 9. **July 21.** Third *Lusitania* note warns Germany that future acts that violate U.S. rights will be considered "deliberately unfriendly."

July 28. President Wilson sends U.S. Marines to Haiti when internal disorders and revolution endanger lives and interests of foreign residents. **Sept. 16.** Haitian-U.S. treaty is signed, making Haiti virtually a U.S. protectorate.

Aug. 10. First military training camp for civilians ("Plattsburgh idea," which later spreads) is opened at Plattsburgh, New York.

Aug. 15. *New York World* begins publication of papers acquired by U.S. Secret Service that expose plans for sabotage, espionage, and propaganda involving many German-Americans, Hamburg-American Steamship Line officials, and members of German Embassy staff, as well as consuls. German government officials are recalled.

Aug. 19. British steamer *Arabic* is sunk by Germans with loss of two American lives, although submarine commanders have been instructed not to sink liners without warning. **Sept. 1.** German ambassador to the U.S. promises that liners will not be sunk without warning and without safety for the lives of nonbelligerents, a policy that is continued throughout the year. **Oct. 5.** German apologies and assurances of an indemnity for loss of lives are considered a diplomatic triumph for the U.S.

September. President Wilson, against his judgment, consents to U.S. loans to warring nations; U.S. bankers immediately negotiate $500 million loan with Britain and France. During next year and a half, U.S. investors purchase about $2.3 billion in bonds of belligerent countries — about 100 times as many from the Allies as from Germany.

Dec. 4. Strongest effort of peace groups, which feel that U.S. interests are not affected by the war, is made by Henry Ford, when he sends peace ship *Oskar II* to Europe in unsuccessful attempt to achieve negotiated end to war.

Dec. 4. Georgia grants new charter to Ku Klux Klan, beginning revival that reaches height in early Twenties, not only in the South but in Northern and Midwestern states.

Dec. 7. President Wilson, his opposition to preparedness altered by *Lusitania* sinking, presents plan for defense measures to Congress; the next month he begins tour of country speaking in behalf of this program.

Eighty-acre tract in northwestern Colorado and northeastern Utah is set aside to establish Dinosaur National Monument; area has been found to be rich in fossils, including dinosaur remains. Monument is enlarged to about 200,000 acres in 1938.

Taxi industry begins when automobile owners discover that people will pay for a short automobile ride. Fare is a "jitney" (a nickel), and cars soon are called jitneys legally.

New York Society for the Suppression of Vice moves legally to suppress Margaret Sanger's *Family Limitation*, a work on birth control that court finds "contrary not only to the law of the state, but to the law of God."

Edgar Lee Masters publishes *Spoon River Anthology*, his collection of short poems that reveal dishonesty and brutality of lives of inhabitants of the small town. Van Wyck Brooks publishes *America's Coming-of-Age*.

Manifest Destiny

In many ways the United States was unique among the community of nations, and the various aspects of its uniqueness had a decisive influence on public attitudes and official policy. Separation from Europe by 3,000 miles of ocean, a vast continent available for settlement and exploitation, and the lack of any powerful neighbors all combined to shape 19th-century America. Geographical isolation from Europe prompted a desire to keep the Western Hemisphere free of European interests and conflicts. This attitude became public policy in the Monroe Doctrine of 1823. The open continent, a growing population, and the quest for new opportunities coalesced into the concept of Manifest Destiny. The lack of strong neighbors meant that the United States was pretty well able to have its own way in North America.

Goaded by Manifest Destiny and a limited imperialism, the United States was able, in the course of a century, to settle the continent. Large land cessions were acquired from Mexico by war, and the various boundary disputes with Canada were settled, though not without much irritation on both sides. Conflicting territorial claims with Mexico continued to exist well past the middle of the 20th century. There was also intermittent talk of adding Canada and Mexico to the national domain, but such proposals never materialized.

Under the auspices of the Monroe Doctrine, the United States became the policeman of the Western Hemisphere, on the whole keeping it safe from foreign inroads and secure for native economic development. Frequent intervention, from the Civil War on, in the political life of Latin-American countries and of the Caribbean islands was prompted by the desire to stabilize their governments and protect a variety of American interests. The active interventionism of the first three decades of the 20th century has more recently been renounced in favor of security alliances and economic cooperation under such titles as the Good Neighbor Policy or the Alliance for Progress.

Maps prepared by Uni-Map Inc., Palatine, Ill.
for Encyclopaedia Britannica, Inc.

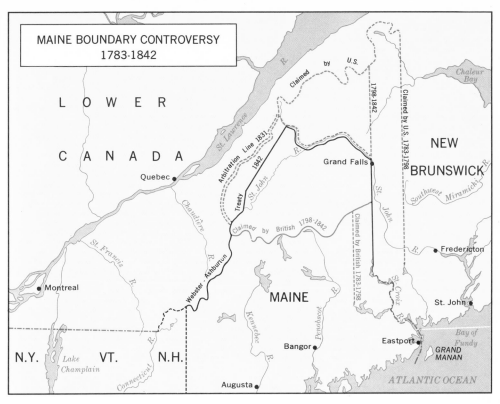

MAINE BOUNDARY CONTROVERSY
1783-1842

LOWER

CANADA

St. Lawrence R.

Claimed by U.S.

1798-1842

Claimed by U.S. 1783-1798

Chaleur
Bay

NEW

BRUNSWICK

Quebec

Arbitration Line 1831

1842

Treaty

St. John R.

Grand Falls

Southwest Miramichi R.

Chaudière R.

Claimed by British 1798-1842

St. John R.

Fredericton

St. Francis R.

Webster-Ashburton

St. John R.

Claimed by British 1783-1798

Montreal

MAINE

Kennebec R.

Penobscot R.

St. Croix R.

St. John

N.Y.

Lake
Champlain

VT.

R.

N.H.

Bangor

Eastport

Bay of
Fundy

GRAND
MANAN

Connecticut R.

Augusta

ATLANTIC OCEAN

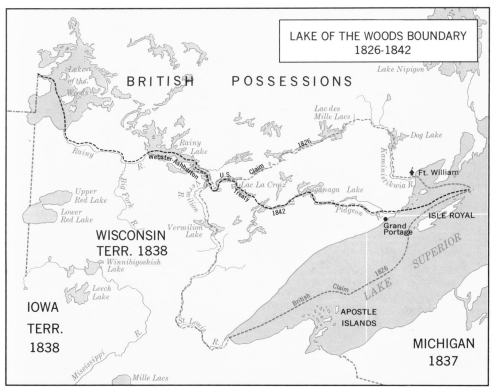

LAKE OF THE WOODS BOUNDARY
1826-1842

Lake of
the Woods

BRITISH   POSSESSIONS

Lake Nipigon

Lac des
Mille Lacs

Dog Lake

Rainy R.

Rainy
Lake

Webster-Ashburton

1826

Kaministikwia R.

Ft. William

Rainy R.

Big Fork R.

Vermilion R.

U.S.   Claim

Lac La Croix

Treaty

1842

Saganaga Lake

Pidgeon

ISLE ROYAL

Upper
Red Lake

Lower
Red Lake

Grand
Portage

WISCONSIN
TERR. 1838

Winnibigoshish
Lake

Vermilion
Lake

LAKE SUPERIOR

1826

IOWA

Leech
Lake

British   Claim

APOSTLE
ISLANDS

TERR.

St. Louis R.

1838

Mississippi R.

Mille Lacs

MICHIGAN

1837

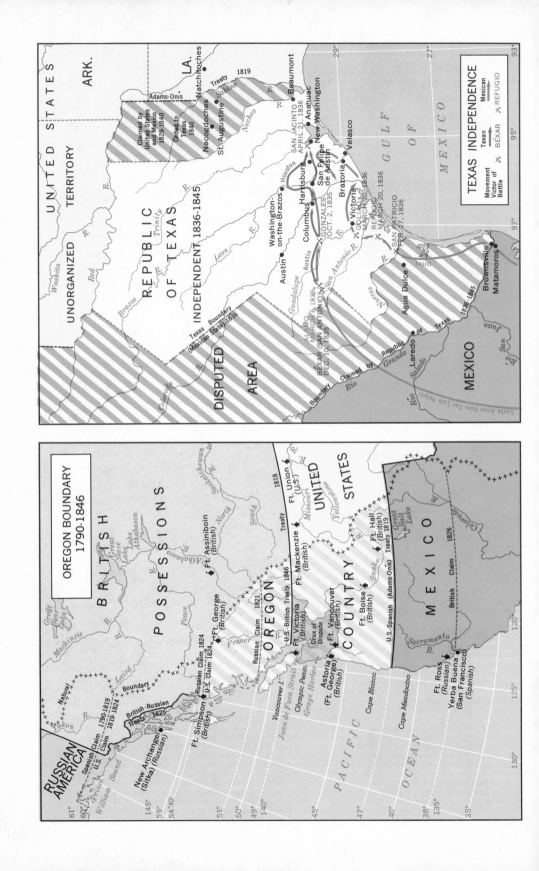

OREGON BOUNDARY 1790-1846

RUSSIAN AMERICA

BRITISH POSSESSIONS

UNITED STATES

OREGON COUNTRY

MEXICO

PACIFIC OCEAN

Spanish Claim 1790-1819
U.S. Claim 1819-1824
Russian Claim 1824
U.S. Claim 1824
British-Russian Treaty 1825
Natural Boundary
New Archangel (Sitka) (Russian)
Ft. Simpson (British)
Ft. George (British)
Vancouver I.
Ft. Victoria (British)
U.S.-British Treaty 1846
Russian Claim 1821
Crux of Dispute
Ft. Vancouver (British)
Ft. George (Astoria) (British)
Olympic Penin.
Juan de Fuca Strait
Grays Harbor
Cape Blanco
Cape Mendocino
Ft. Ross (Russian)
Yerba Buena (San Francisco) (Spanish)
Sacramento R.
British Claim 1826
U.S.-Spanish (Adams-Onis)
Ft. Hall (British) Treaty 1819
Snake R.
Ft. Boise (British)
Ft. Mackenzie (British)
Ft. Assinniboin (British)
Ft. Union (U.S.) 1818 Treaty
Missouri R.
Yellowstone R.
Great Salt Lake
Colorado R.
Lake Athabasca
Great Slave Lake
Credit Henry Lake
Mackinzie R.
Peace R.
Fraser R.
Laird R.
Yukon R.
Prince William Sound
Saskatchewan R.
North R.
South R.

TEXAS INDEPENDENCE

UNITED STATES

ARK.

LA.

UNORGANIZED

UNITED STATES TERRITORY

REPUBLIC OF TEXAS INDEPENDENT 1836-1845

DISPUTED AREA

MEXICO

GULF OF MEXICO

Adams-Onis Treaty 1819
Claimed by United States and Mexico 1829-1840
Ceded to Texas 1840
Natchitoches
Beaumont
Anahuac
SAN JACINTO APRIL 21, 1836
New Washington
San Felipe de Austin
Velasco
Harrisburg
Houston
Columbus
Brazoria
GONZALES OCT. 2, 1835
Victoria
GOLIAD MARCH 20, 1836
REFUGIO MARCH 14, 1836
SAN PATRICIO FEB. 27, 1836
ALAMO MARCH 6, 1836
BÉXAR (SAN ANTONIO) DEC. 10, 1835
Washington-on-the-Brazos
Austin
Agua Dulce
Texas Republic
Laredo
Brownsville
Matamoros
Texas Boundary (Mexican State) 1816
1836-1845
Boundary
Santa Anna from San Luis Potosí
Nacogdoches
St. Augustine
Sabine R.
Neches R.
Trinity R.
Brazos R.
Colorado R.
Guadalupe R.
San Antonio R.
Nueces R.
Rio Grande
Rio Salado
San Juan R.
Red R.
Washita R.
Leon R.

Movement of Battle
Victor of Battle: Texan, Mexican
BÉXAR ✗
REFUGIO ✗

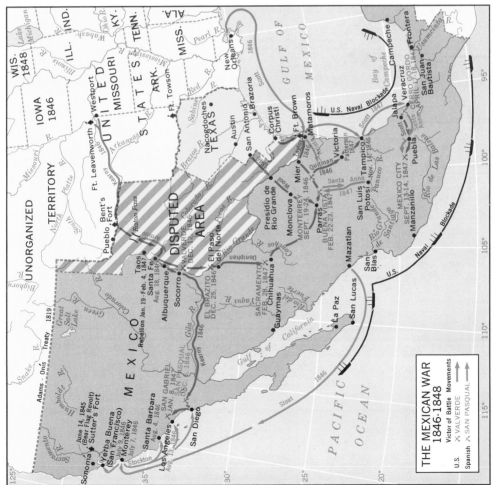

THE MEXICAN WAR
1846-1848

Victor of Battle Movements

U.S. ⤻⤻ ⤒ VALVERDE

Spanish ⤒ SAN PASQUAL

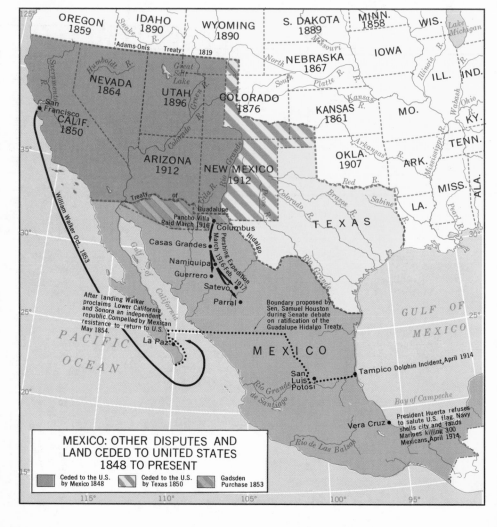

MEXICO: OTHER DISPUTES AND
LAND CEDED TO UNITED STATES
1848 TO PRESENT

Ceded to the U.S. by Mexico 1848

Ceded to the U.S. by Texas 1850

Gadsden Purchase 1853

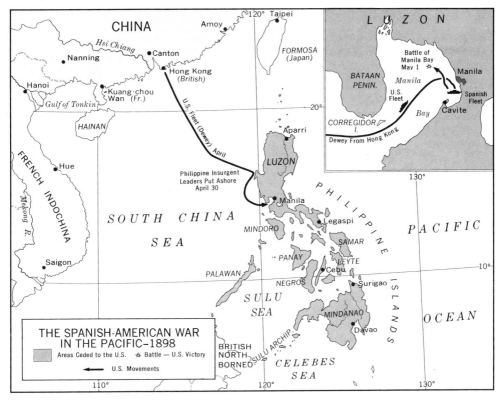

THE SPANISH-AMERICAN WAR IN THE PACIFIC–1898

Areas Ceded to the U.S. ☆ Battle — U.S. Victory

← U.S. Movements

Map labels (Pacific):

CHINA
Amoy
120° Taipei
Nanning
Hsi Chiang
Canton
FORMOSA (Japan)
Hanoi
Hong Kong (British)
Kuang-chou Wan (Fr.)
Gulf of Tonkin
20°
HAINAN
U.S. Fleet (Dewey) April
Aparri
FRENCH INDOCHINA
Hue
LUZON
Mekong R.
Philippine Insurgent Leaders Put Ashore April 30
Manila
PHILIPPINE
SOUTH CHINA SEA
Legaspi
PACIFIC
MINDORO
SAMAR
PANAY
LEYTE
Saigon
Cebu
10°
PALAWAN
NEGROS
Surigao
ISLANDS
SULU SEA
MINDANAO
OCEAN
Davao
BRITISH NORTH BORNEO
SULU ARCHIP.
CELEBES SEA
110°
120°
130°

Inset (Luzon):

LUZON
Battle of Manila Bay May 1 ☆
Manila
BATAAN PENIN.
Manila
U.S. Fleet
Spanish Fleet
CORREGIDOR I.
Bay
Cavite
Dewey From Hong Kong
130°

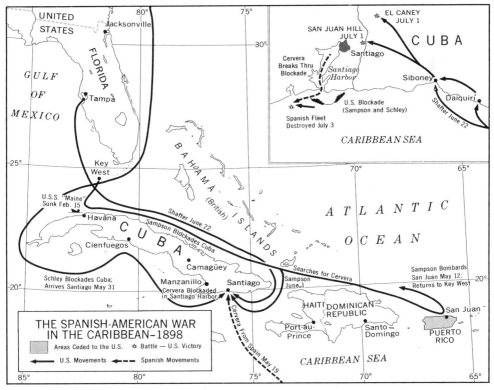

THE SPANISH-AMERICAN WAR IN THE CARIBBEAN–1898

Areas Ceded to the U.S. ☆ Battle — U.S. Victory

← U.S. Movements   ⇐--- Spanish Movements

Map labels (Caribbean):

UNITED STATES
80°
75°
Jacksonville
FLORIDA
GULF OF MEXICO
30°
Tampa
25°
Key West
U.S.S. "Maine" Sunk Feb. 15
Havana
Shafter June 22
Sampson Blockades Cuba
BAHAMA ISLANDS (British)
CUBA
Cienfuegos
ATLANTIC OCEAN
Camagüey
Searches for Cervera
Sampson Bombards San Juan May 12; Returns to Key West
20°
Schley Blockades Cuba; Arrives Santiago May 31
Manzanillo
Santiago
Sampson June 1
San Juan
Cervera Blockaded in Santiago Harbor
HAITI
DOMINICAN REPUBLIC
PUERTO RICO
Cervera From Spain May 19
Port-au-Prince
Santo Domingo
CARIBBEAN SEA
85°
80°
75°
70°
65°

Inset (Cuba):

EL CANEY JULY 1 ☆
SAN JUAN HILL JULY 1 ☆
CUBA
Santiago
Cervera Breaks Thru Blockade
Santiago Harbor
Siboney
Daiquirí
U.S. Blockade (Sampson and Schley)
Shafter June 22
Spanish Fleet Destroyed July 3
CARIBBEAN SEA
70°
65°

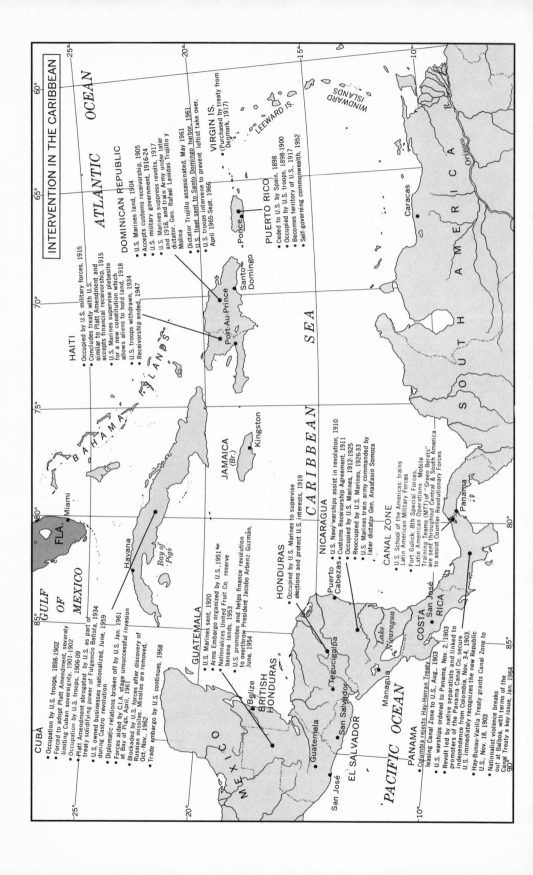

INTERVENTION IN THE CARIBBEAN

HAITI
- Occupied by U.S. military forces, 1915
- Concludes treaty with U.S. similar to Platt Amendment and accepts financial receivership, 1915
- U.S. Marines supervise plebiscite for a new constitution which allows aliens to hold land, 1918
- U.S. troops withdrawn, 1934
- Receivership ended, 1947

DOMINICAN REPUBLIC
- U.S. Marines land, 1904
- Accepts customs receivership, 1905
- U.S. military government, 1916-24
- U.S. Marines suppress revolts, 1917
- U.S. Marines intervene and train Army under later dictator, Gen. Rafael Lenidas Trujillo y Molina
- Dictator Trujillo assassinated, May 1961
- U.S. fleet sent to Santo Domingo harbor, 1961
- U.S. troops intervene to prevent leftist take over, April 1965-Sept. 1966

VIRGIN IS.
(Purchased by treaty from Denmark, 1917)

PUERTO RICO
- Ceded to U.S. by Spain, 1898
- Occupied by U.S. troops, 1898-1900
- Occupied by U.S. troops, 1917
- Becomes territory of U.S., 1917
- Self-governing commonwealth, 1952

CUBA
- Occupation by U.S. troops, 1898-1902
- Forced to adopt Platt Amendment, severely limiting Cuban sovereignty, 1901-1902
- Occupation by U.S. troops, 1906-09
- Platt Amendment abrogated by U.S. as part of treaty solidifying power of Fulgencio Batista, 1934
- U.S. owned businesses nationalized, June, 1959 during Castro revolution
- Diplomatic relations broken off by U.S. Jan. 1961
- Forces aided by C.I.A. stage unsuccessful invasion at Bay of Pigs, April, 1961
- Blockaded by U.S. forces after discovery of Russian missiles. Missiles are removed, Oct.-Nov. 1962
- Trade embargo by U.S. continues, 1968

GUATEMALA
- U.S. Marines sent, 1920
- Arms Embargo organized by U.S., 1951
- Nationalizes United Fruit Co. reserve banana lands, 1953
- U.S. promotes and helps finance revolution to overthrow President Jacobo Arbenz Guzmán, June 1954

HONDURAS
- Occupied by U.S. Marines to supervise elections and protect U.S. interests, 1919

NICARAGUA
- U.S. Navy warships assist in revolution, 1910
- Customs Receivership Agreement, 1911
- Occupied by U.S. Marines, 1912-1925
- Reoccupied by U.S. Marines, 1926-33
- U.S. Marines train army commanded by later dictator Gen. Anastasio Somoza

CANAL ZONE
- U.S. School of the Americas: trains Latin American Military Forces
- Fort Gulick: 8th Special Forces, Latin American Operations, Mobile Training Teams (MTT) of "Green Berets" are sent throughout Central & South America to assist Counter-Revolutionary Forces

PANAMA
- Columbia rejects Hay-Herran Treaty leasing Canal Zone to U.S. Aug. 1903
- U.S. warships ordered to Panama, Nov. 2, 1903
- Revolt led by native separatists and promoters of the Panama Canal Co., linked to independence from Colombia, Nov. 3-4, 1903
- U.S. immediately recognizes the new Republic U.S., Nov. 18, 1903
- Hay-Bunau-Varilla Treaty grants Canal Zone to U.S.
- Nationalist violence breaks out at Balboa, with terms of the Canal Treaty a key issue, Jan. 1964

ATLANTIC OCEAN

PACIFIC OCEAN

GULF OF MEXICO

CARIBBEAN SEA

SOUTH AMERICA

MEXICO

BAHAMA ISLANDS

WINDWARD ISLANDS

LEEWARD IS.

Miami
Havana
Bay of Pigs
Kingston
JAMAICA (Br.)
Port-Au-Prince
Santo Domingo
Ponce
Caracas
Orinoco
Panama
San José
COSTA RICA
Puerto Cabezas
Managua
Lake Nicaragua
Tegucigalpa
San Salvador
EL SALVADOR
Guatemala
GUATEMALA
Belize
BRITISH HONDURAS
San José
FLA.

1905

1.

THEODORE ROOSEVELT: Corollary to the Monroe Doctrine

*In 1902 Germany, Italy, and England blockaded the coast of Venezuela in an effort
to collect debts that it had refused to pay. President Roosevelt, concerned about
the presence of Europeans in the vicinity of the uncompleted Panama Canal, made
a show of naval force and urged U.S. mediation. Two years later, when European
powers threatened forcibly to collect debts owed them by the Dominican Republic,
the United States again intervened to make the collection. In his annual messages
to Congress in 1904 and 1905, Roosevelt formulated his "corollary" to the Monroe
Doctrine, urging a new role for the United States — that of international policeman
for the Western Hemisphere. In the message of 1905, which is reprinted here in
part, he spelled out in detail how the role was to be conceived.*

Source: Richardson, XI, pp. 1131-1181.

ONE OF THE MOST EFFECTIVE instruments for
peace is the Monroe Doctrine as it has been
and is being gradually developed by this nation and accepted by other nations. No other policy could have been as efficient in
promoting peace in the Western Hemisphere and in giving to each nation thereon
the chance to develop along its own lines. If
we had refused to apply the doctrine to
changing conditions, it would now be completely outworn, would not meet any of the
needs of the present day, and, indeed,
would probably by this time have sunk into
complete oblivion.

It is useful at home and is meeting with
recognition abroad because we have adapted
our application of it to meet the growing
and changing needs of the Hemisphere.
When we announce a policy such as the
Monroe Doctrine, we thereby commit ourselves to the consequences of the policy,
and those consequences from time to time
alter. It is out of the question to claim a
right and yet shirk the responsibility for its
exercise. Not only we but all American republics who are benefited by the existence
of the doctrine must recognize the obligations each nation is under as regards foreign
peoples, no less than its duty to insist upon
its own rights.

That our rights and interests are deeply
concerned in the maintenance of the doc-

Theodore Roosevelt; portrait by John Singer Sargent

trine is so clear as hardly to need argument. This is especially true in view of the construction of the Panama Canal. As a mere matter of self-defense we must exercise a close watch over the approaches to this canal; and this means that we must be thoroughly alive to our interests in the Caribbean Sea.

There are certain essential points which must never be forgotten as regards the Monroe Doctrine. In the first place, we must as a nation make it evident that we do not intend to treat it in any shape or way as an excuse for aggrandizement on our part at the expense of the republics to the south. We must recognize the fact that in some South American countries there has been much suspicion lest we should interpret the Monroe Doctrine as in some way inimical to their interests, and we must try to convince all the other nations of this continent once and for all that no just and orderly government has anything to fear from us.

There are certain republics to the south of us which have already reached such a point of stability, order, and prosperity that they themselves, though as yet hardly consciously, are among the guarantors of this doctrine. These republics we now meet, not only on a basis of entire equality but in a spirit of frank and respectful friendship, which we hope is mutual. If all of the republics to the south of us will only grow as those to which I allude have already grown, all need for us to be the especial champions of the doctrine will disappear, for no stable and growing American republic wishes to see some great non-American military power acquire territory in its neighborhood. All that this country desires is that the other republics on this continent shall be happy and prosperous; and they cannot be happy and prosperous unless they maintain order within their boundaries and behave with a just regard for their obligations toward outsiders.

It must be understood that under no circumstances will the United States use the Monroe Doctrine as a cloak for territorial aggression. We desire peace with all the world, but perhaps most of all with the other peoples of the American continent. There are, of course, limits to the wrongs which any self-respecting nation can endure. It is always possible that wrong actions toward this nation or toward citizens of this nation in some state unable to keep order among its own people, unable to secure justice from outsiders, and unwilling to do justice to those outsiders who treat it well, may result in our having to take action to protect our rights; but such action will not be taken with a view to territorial aggression, and it will be taken at all only with extreme reluctance and when it has become evident that every other resource has been exhausted.

Moreover, we must make it evident that we do not intend to permit the Monroe Doctrine to be used by any nation on this continent as a shield to protect it from the consequences of its own misdeeds against foreign nations. If a republic to the south of us commits a tort against a foreign nation, such as an outrage against a citizen of that nation, then the Monroe Doctrine does not force us to interfere to prevent punishment of the tort, save to see that the punishment does not assume the form of territorial occupation in any shape.

The case is more difficult when it refers to a contractual obligation. Our own government has always refused to enforce such contractual obligations on behalf of its citizens by an appeal to arms. It is much to be wished that all foreign governments would take the same view. But they do not; and in consequence we are liable at any time to be brought face to face with disagreeable alternatives. On the one hand, this country would certainly decline to go to war to prevent a foreign government from collecting a just debt; on the other hand, it is very inadvisable to permit any foreign power to take possession, even temporarily, of the customhouses of an American republic in order to enforce the payment of its obligations; for such temporary occupation might turn into a permanent occupation.

The only escape from these alternatives may at any time be that we must ourselves undertake to bring about some arrangement by which so much as possible of a just obligation shall be paid. It is far better that this country should put through such an arrangement, rather than allow any foreign country to undertake it. To do so insures the defaulting republic from having to pay debt of an improper character under duress, while it also insures honest creditors of the republic from being passed by in the interest of dishonest or grasping creditors. Moreover, for the United States to take such a position offers the only possible way of insuring us against a clash with some foreign power. The position is, therefore, in the interest of peace as well as in the interest of justice. It is of benefit to our people; it is of benefit to foreign peoples; and most of all it is really of benefit to the people of the country concerned.

This brings me to what should be one of the fundamental objects of the Monroe Doctrine. We must ourselves in good faith try to help upward toward peace and order those of our sister republics which need such help. Just as there has been a gradual growth of the ethical element in the relations of one individual to another, so we are, even though slowly, more and more coming to recognize the duty of bearing one another's burdens, not only as among individuals but also as among nations.

———◆———

When I say I believe in a square deal I do not mean, and nobody who speaks the truth can mean, that he believes it possible to give every man the best hand. If the cards do not come to any man, or if they do come, and he had not got the power to play them, that is his affair. All I mean is that there shall not be any crookedness in the dealing.

THEODORE ROOSEVELT, speech in Dallas, April 5, 1905

2.

David Wilcox: Government Control of Railroad Rates

*The establishment of the Interstate Commerce Commission (ICC) in 1887 was hailed
by reformers as an important first step toward federal regulation of big business.
Key provisions of the act creating the commission were that railroad rates be made
public and that they be "reasonable," but the term was vague, and for the most part
the railroads, aided by sympathetic court decisions, were able to avoid regulation.
Continued agitation by the Grangers, the Populists, and other groups prompted
Congress to investigate the question of railroad rates. President Theodore Roosevelt
favored the move and urged Congress in 1904 to strengthen the ICC. During the first
months of 1905, the House Committee on Interstate and Foreign Commerce held
hearings on various proposals to amend the Interstate Commerce Act. Portions of the
testimony of David Wilcox, president of the Delaware and Hudson Company, are
reprinted here. Wilcox testified on January 21, 1905.*

Source: 58 Congress, 3 Session, House Document No. 422, pp. 226-239.

Mr. Wilcox. When I applied to the chairman of this committee for a hearing, I did not apply on behalf of the Delaware and Hudson Company but on behalf of its employees and security holders and on behalf of those who are dependent upon them. My constituency, I may say, is perhaps 100,000; probably that.

What has been the cause of the prosperity of this property and upon what depend its 100,000 people? Upon nothing else in the world but the income of the property. Without the income the property is of no value. Without the income there would be no incentive to operate it; and, therefore, necessarily, any proposition which tends to place in the hands of the government, however ably administered, the question as to whether or not this substantial mass of property shall earn anything, which tends to qualify or limit its earning capacity, affects not the company; for these companies,

gentlemen, are of very little real importance. They are artificial persons. They are the means by which the property of the owners is held together and is made productive. That is all there is of it.

If the American people so wish, the corporations may die. But what is to become of the people who are interested in them? What is to become of this enormous mass of property, upon which rests the prosperity not merely of the class whom I have named but also of those who sell supplies to them, and of the communities through which they pass, and of the communities which will be built up by their extension? It seems to me that that is the serious question — What effect is what you may do here going to have upon the future welfare, productiveness, and value of the greatest single industrial interest of the country?

It is a great responsibility, gentlemen. I do not come here as an extremist. If you can devise anything which will be to the benefit of the country as a whole, who will welcome it more than those who are interested in the railroad property? Why should they not? As I said a moment ago, it is the greatest single interest there is in the country. It has $8-$10 billion worth of the country's accumulated wealth. As the Delaware and Hudson Company has grown to become a favorite object of investment with estates and institutions which have a more or less fiduciary character, so is it the case with the very large mass of this property generally.

Now, gentlemen, great as I feel my own responsibility with reference to the company with which I am connected, I realize that the responsibility of this committee is very, very much more serious. It may pass an act which shall put it in the power of those who, however well-intentioned they are — and I do not wish to join the superheated gentlemen who sometimes want to have the Interstate Commerce Commission abolished because they are not doing anything, and I will say that they are not railroad men, that I ever heard of — yet, having the power, may do great harm. I do not share in that feeling toward the commission. But, as I say, gentlemen, you may pass an act that will so compromise the value of the property and the prosperity of the communities of the country that it will bring widespread disaster. On the other hand, you may pass an act which will fail of operation.

Some people say that the present act has not accomplished what was hoped, although I do not agree with that exactly. But you may do the same thing, not intentionally but unintentionally, and the act which you may pass may become a gold brick in legislation. And there are those two great possibilities. You may pass an act which will so compromise the value of the greatest mass of accumulated resources of the country that its efficiency will in a measure cease, or

at any rate become less, or you may pass an act which will fail of accomplishing the desired results, and this agitation may go on, stimulated and kept on foot in the methods which you gentlemen know so well, apparently ad infinitum.

What I say, gentlemen, is that it is a very, very serious moment when an Anglo-Saxon government undertakes the charge of people's money and says how much they shall earn by the exercise of their constitutional rights of liberty and property. And it should be recognized that possibly we are at the parting of the ways, and that if this be done it will go on until those constitutional guarantees have but little value, and the only profession worth exercising in the country will be that of holding office in some administrative board.

I do not want to exaggerate, but the committee is certainly aware of the fact that Congress has no special power over carriers. What the Constitution provides is that Congress may regulate commerce among the states or with foreign nations. The shipper is engaged in interstate commerce just as much as the carrier. The manufacturer who ships is engaged in interstate commerce equally with the carrier, and if the plan is to be adopted that the earnings of those who are engaged in this interstate commerce are to be regulated by a governmental and administrative board, it applies just as much to the shippers as to the carriers. There is no substantial difference between them. It applies to everybody. So that it is, as I say, a question that affects the entire community.

The Chairman. You think there is no difference in the legal status of a common carrier and a shipper?

Mr. Wilcox. Of course, Mr. Chairman, I trust that I have practised law long enough to have some idea of what the difference is.

The Chairman. You said no substantial difference.

Mr. Wilcox. No, sir; there is no substantial difference in the power to regulate. The common carrier is bound to charge reasonable rates and not to discriminate. Now, when you have got beyond that I do not think there is a great deal of difference. The common carriers do not derive their franchises from the federal government after all; they derive them from the states, and I do not believe that there is any substantial reason for discriminating between a corporation which is engaged in interstate commerce and anybody else who is engaged in interstate commerce. In fact, I think the right to liberty and property, which is guaranteed by the Fifth Amendment, is a right of a corporation as much as an individual, and my impression is that it has been settled by the Supreme Court of the United States. . . .

I said that I was not one of those who believe in abolishing the Interstate Commerce Commission. Of course the great benefit of that commission has been the settlement of claims without controversy. In that manner it has settled over 90 percent of the claims which have come before it. That is the business way of carrying on business, for the parties to settle. I do not know of any business, gentlemen, which is carried on successfully by third parties who have no interest in the ultimate result and no business which is carried on by lawsuit.

Business by lawsuit would be a thing to be abhorred, a thing which would be impossible. That is where the Interstate Commerce Commission has been useful. The difficulty has arisen out of the other 10 percent. I do not think so because they quote what Judge Schoonmaker said as showing that the commission then realized that it had not power to fix rates. That was the construction given to the language of Commissioner Schoonmaker by Judge Brewer.

I suppose that the committee, by the discussions that have been had, has been fully advised of the fact that upon the record there is no question of the reasonableness of rates per se. Upon a brief which I shall have the pleasure of filing that matter is fully argued out. It admits of no question. Even as those advances from 1899 until 1903, regarding which the commission reported last year to the Senate — even as to them the commission itself says that it does not claim that they were unreasonable.

In an article in the *North American Review*, which was written by one of the most productive of the commissioners last June, the same statement was repeated, that he did not claim that they were unreasonable, but simply that the government ought to have the right to fix them. That is simply and baldly that the government should fix future rates. There is nobody complaining; there is no case and there has never been a case, as I have no doubt that the committee has been informed over and over again, of unreasonable rates which have been sustained; but the position of the commissioner who wrote this article was that, as a matter of right, the government should always intervene in these circumstances.

Now, that advance in rates amounted to what? Thirty-nine thousandths of a cent per ton per mile. And it is interesting to notice that in the report for 1902, in commenting upon the relation of rates between 1898 and 1902, the commission uses the expression that the rates were about the same. Now, the difference between those two years consisted of a difference of forty-one thousandths of a cent, and the commission said that the rates were about the same, and the commission said that the increase in gross earnings was due to the increased volume of traffic.

When they came to comparing the rates of 1899 and those of 1903, the difference was thirty-nine thousandths of a cent, two thousandths of a cent less than they had been between 1898 and 1902, when the commission said they were about the same. Nevertheless, this difference of thirty-nine thousandths of a cent was described as having made enormous additions to the expenses of railway transportation, although a difference of forty-one thousandths of a cent, taking the two previous corresponding years for purposes of comparison, was described as leaving the rates about the same. I suppose that the committee has also been fully advised of the fact that the Elkins Law covers the subject of rebates. The Interstate Commerce Commission has so said in its last two annual reports, that that subject is fully covered. So that I shall not stop to talk about that.

But the matter to which I wish to call the attention of the committee is the matter of discrimination between localities. As to that question of discrimination between localities, that is a matter, gentlemen, which you will always have with you. It is a question that arises naturally from the desire for commercial advancement. It is the natural result of commercial rivalry. I have no doubt you remember the language of the Supreme Court in which it points out, with a great deal of elaboration and vigor, that it is not all discriminations and all preferences which establish a cause of complaint, but that they must be undue or unjust, and that the existence of preferences can never be overcome.

Claims that preferences exist or are undue or unjust, as I have just said, arise from the feeling which everyone has that he desires equal treatment with his neighbor and that his place desires equal treatment. They are difficult questions. They give the railroad companies a great deal of concern. They are questions between the localities rather than with the railroads, and they are questions which affect the railroads only, as they almost invariably lead to a reduction of their revenue.

The efforts of the traffic officials of the road to meet the necessities of the shippers and to enable their manufacturers and shippers to ship to farther markets all the time are what have led, more, in my belief, than anything else, to the downward course of rates, which has been practically continuous. When you consider the increase in the cost of materials in the past few years, it is not too much to say that that has been a continuous course.

The traffic official is constantly endeavoring to enable his own patrons to reach farther markets. Now, there cannot be any question that that encourages competition, enables the consumer to have the benefit of constantly increasing sources of supply, and yet, naturally, when the dealers in the farther markets find that a new element of competition has entered they claim that they are prejudiced and that the first market is receiving an undue preference.

You can straighten a worm, but the crook is in him and only waiting.
Samuel L. Clemens ("Mark Twain")

3.

R. W. Peckham, J. M. Harlan, and O. W. Holmes, Jr.: *Lochner* v. *New York*

In a 5 to 4 decision handed down on April 17, 1905, the Supreme Court reversed the rulings of two New York courts in the important case of Lochner v. New York. *A New York state law of 1897 had set the hours of bakers at no more than ten a day or sixty a week.* Lochner, *the owner of a bakery, had been fined $50 for violating the law. The Supreme Court, in declaring the law unconstitutional, ruled that it interfered with the right of free contract under the Fourteenth Amendment, and, furthermore, that it was outside the legal police powers of the state. The following selection comprises portions of three opinions: the dissent of Justice Harlan, who was joined in it by two other justices; the dissent of Justice Holmes; and the opinion for the majority by Justice Peckham. The decision dealt a serious blow to social welfare legislation for a generation.*

Source: 198 U.S. 45.

Mr. Justice Peckham. The indictment, it will be seen, charges that the plaintiff in error violated the 110th Section of Article 8, Chapter 415, of the Laws of 1897, known as the Labor Law of the State of New York, in that he wrongfully and unlawfully required and permitted an employee working for him to work more than sixty hours in one week. There is nothing in any of the opinions delivered in this case, either in the Supreme Court or the Court of Appeals of the state, which construes the section, in using the word "required," as referring to any physical force being used to obtain the labor of an employee. It is assumed that the word means nothing more than the requirement arising from voluntary contract for such labor in excess of the number of hours specified in the statute.

There is no pretense in any of the opinions that the statute was intended to meet a case of involuntary labor in any form. All the opinions assume that there is no real distinction, so far as this question is concerned, between the words "required" and "permitted." The mandate of the statute that "no employee shall be required or permitted to work" is the substantial equivalent of an enactment that "no employee shall contract or agree to work" more than ten hours per day; and as there is no provision for special emergencies, the statute is mandatory in all cases.

It is not an act merely fixing the number of hours which shall constitute a legal day's work but an absolute prohibition upon the employer, permitting, under any circumstances, more than ten hours work to be done in his establishment. The employee may desire to earn the extra money which would arise from his working more than the prescribed time, but this statute forbids the employer from permitting the employee to earn it.

The statute necessarily interferes with the right of contract between the employer and employees concerning the number of hours in which the latter may labor in the bakery of the employer. The general right to make a contract in relation to his business is part of the liberty of the individual protected by the Fourteenth Amendment of the federal Constitution (*Allgeyer* v. *Louisiana*, 165 U.S. 578). Under that provision no state can deprive any person of life, liberty, or property without due process of law. The right to purchase or to sell labor is part of the liberty protected by this amendment, unless there are circumstances which exclude the right.

There are, however, certain powers existing in the sovereignty of each state in the Union somewhat vaguely termed "police powers," the exact description and limitation of which have not been attempted by the courts. Those powers, broadly stated and without, at present, any attempt at a more specific limitation, relate to the safety, health, morals, and general welfare of the public. Both property and liberty are held on such reasonable conditions as may be imposed by the governing power of the state in the exercise of those powers, and with such conditions the Fourteenth Amendment was not designed to interfere. . . .

The state, therefore, has power to prevent the individual from making certain kinds of contracts, and in regard to them the federal Constitution offers no protection. If the contract be one which the state, in the legitimate exercise of its police power, has the right to prohibit, it is not prevented from prohibiting it by the Fourteenth Amendment. Contracts in violation of a statute, either of the federal or state government, or a contract to let one's property for immoral purposes, or to do any other unlawful act could obtain no protection from the federal Constitution as coming under the liberty of person or of free contract.

Therefore, when the state, by its legislature, in the assumed exercise of its police powers, has passed an act which seriously limits the right to labor or the right of contract in regard to their means of livelihood between persons who are *sui juris* (both employer and employee), it becomes of great importance to determine which shall prevail — the right of the individual to labor for such time as he may choose, or the right of the state to prevent the individual from laboring or from entering into any contract to labor beyond a certain time prescribed by the state.

This Court has recognized the existence and upheld the exercise of the police powers of the states in many cases which might fairly be considered as border ones, and it has, in the course of its determination of questions regarding the asserted invalidity of such statutes, on the ground of their violation of the rights secured by the federal Constitution, been guided by rules of a very liberal nature, the application of which has resulted, in numerous instances, in upholding the validity of state statutes thus assailed. . . .

It must, of course, be conceded that there is a limit to the valid exercise of the police power by the state. There is no dispute concerning this general proposition. Otherwise the Fourteenth Amendment would have no efficacy and the legislatures of the states would have unbounded power, and it would be enough to say that any piece of legislation was enacted to conserve the morals, the health, or the safety of the people; such legislation would be valid, no matter how absolutely without foundation the claim might be. The claim of the police power would be a mere pretext — become another and delusive name for the supreme sovereignty of the state to be exercised free from constitutional restraint.

This is not contended for. In every case that comes before this Court, therefore, where legislation of this character is concerned and where the protection of the federal Constitution is sought, the question necessarily arises: Is this a fair, reasonable, and appropriate exercise of the police power of the state, or is it an unreasonable, unnecessary, and arbitrary interference with the right of the individual to his personal liberty or to enter into those contracts in relation to labor which may seem to him appropriate or necessary for the support of himself and his family? Of course the liberty of contract relating to labor includes both parties to it. The one has as much right to purchase as the other to sell labor.

This is not a question of substituting the judgment of the Court for that of the legislature. If the act be within the power of the state, it is valid, although the judgment of the Court might be totally opposed to the enactment of such a law. But the question would still remain — Is it within the police power of the state? — and that question must be answered by the Court.

The question whether this act is valid as a labor law, pure and simple, may be dismissed in a few words. There is no reasonable ground for interfering with the liberty of person or the right of free contract by determining the hours of labor in the occupation of a baker. There is no contention that bakers as a class are not equal in intelligence and capacity to men in other trades or manual occupations, or that they are not able to assert their rights and care for themselves without the protecting arm of the state, interfering with their independence of judgment and of action. They are in no sense wards of the state.

Viewed in the light of a purely labor law, with no reference whatever to the question of health, we think that a law like the one before us involves neither the safety, the morals, nor the welfare of the public, and that the interest of the public is not in the slightest degree affected by such an act. The law must be upheld, if at all, as a law pertaining to the health of the individual en-

gaged in the occupation of a baker. It does not affect any other portion of the public than those who are engaged in that occupation. Clean and wholesome bread does not depend upon whether the baker works but ten hours per day or only sixty hours a week. The limitation of the hours of labor does not come within the police power on that ground.

It is a question of which of two powers or rights shall prevail — the power of the state to legislate, or the right of the individual to liberty of person and freedom of contract. The mere assertion that the subject relates though but in a remote degree to the public health does not necessarily render the enactment valid. The act must have a more direct relation, as a means to an end, and the end itself must be appropriate and legitimate before an act can be held to be valid which interferes with the general right of an individual to be free in his person and in his power to contract in relation to his own labor. . . .

We think the limit of the police power has been reached and passed in this case. There is, in our judgment, no reasonable foundation for holding this to be necessary or appropriate as a health law to safeguard the public health or the health of the individuals who are following the trade of a baker. If this statute be valid, and if, therefore, a proper case is made out in which to deny the right of an individual, *sui juris,* as employer or employee, to make contracts for the labor of the latter under the protection of the provisions of the federal Constitution, there would seem to be no length to which legislation of this nature might not go. . . .

It is impossible for us to shut our eyes to the fact that many of the laws of this character, while passed under what is claimed to be the police power for the purpose of protecting the public health or welfare, are, in reality, passed from other motives. We are justified in saying so when, from the character of the law and the subject upon which it legislates, it is apparent that the public health or welfare bears but the most remote relation to the law. The purpose of a statute must be determined from the natural and legal effect of the language employed; and whether it is or is not repugnant to the Constitution of the United States must be determined from the natural effect of such statutes when put into operation and not from their proclaimed purpose. . . .

It is manifest to us that the limitation of the hours of labor as provided for in this section of the statute under which the indictment was found and the plaintiff in error convicted has no such direct relation to and no such substantial effect upon the health of the employee as to justify us in regarding the section as really a health law. It seems to us that the real object and purpose were simply to regulate the hours of labor between the master and his employees (all being men, *sui juris*) in a private business not dangerous in any degree to morals or in any real and substantial degree to the health of the employees. Under such circumstances the freedom of master and employee to contract with each other in relation to their employment, and in defining the same, cannot be prohibited or interfered with without violating the federal Constitution.

The judgment of the Court of Appeals of New York as well as that of the Supreme Court and of the County Court of Oneida County must be reversed and the case remanded to the County Court for further proceedings not inconsistent with this opinion.

Mr. Justice Harlan, with whom Mr. Justice White and Mr. Justice Day concurred, dissenting.

While this Court has not attempted to mark the precise boundaries of what is called the police power of the state, the existence of the power has been uniformly recognized, both by the federal and state courts. All the cases agree that this power extends at least to the protection of the lives, the health, and the safety of the public against the injurious exercise by any citizen of his own rights. . . .

Speaking generally, the state, in the exercise of its powers, may not unduly interfere with the right of the citizen to enter into contracts that may be necessary and essential in the enjoyment of the inherent rights belonging to everyone, among which rights is the right "to be free in the enjoyment of all his faculties; to be free to use them in all lawful ways; to live and work where he will; to earn his livelihood by any lawful calling; to pursue any livelihood or avocation." This was declared in *Allgeyer* v. *Louisiana*. . . . But in the same case it was conceded that the right to contract in relation to persons and property or to do business within a state may be "regulated and sometimes prohibited when the contracts or business conflict with the policy of the state as contained in its statutes." . . .

I take it to be firmly established that what is called the liberty of contract may, within certain limits, be subjected to regulations designed and calculated to promote the general welfare or to guard the public health, the public morals, or the public safety. "The liberty secured by the Constitution of the United States to every person within its jurisdiction does not impart," this Court has recently said, "an absolute right in each person to be, at all times and in all circumstances, wholly freed from restraint. There are manifold restraints to which every person is necessarily subject for the common good." *Jacobson* v. *Massachusetts*. . . .

Granting, then, that there is a liberty of contract which cannot be violated even under the sanction of direct legislative enactment, but assuming, as according to settled law we may assume, that such liberty of contract is subject to such regulations as the state may reasonably prescribe for the common good and the well-being of society, what are the conditions under which the judiciary may declare such regulations to be in excess of legislative authority and void? Upon this point there is no room for dispute; for the rule is universal that a legislative enactment, federal or state, is never to be disregarded or held invalid unless it be, beyond question, plainly and palpably in excess of legislative power. . . .

If there be doubt as to the validity of the statute, that doubt must therefore be resolved in favor of its validity, and the courts must keep their hands off, leaving the legislature to meet the responsibility for unwise legislation. If the end which the legislature seeks to accomplish be one to which its power extends and if the means employed to that end, although not the wisest or best, are yet not plainly and palpably unauthorized by law, then the court cannot interfere. In other words, when the validity of a statute is questioned, the burden of proof, so to speak, is upon those who assert it to be unconstitutional (*M'Culloch* v. *Maryland*). . . .

Let these principles be applied to the present case. By the statute in question it is provided that,

> No employee shall be required or permitted to work in a biscuit, bread, or cake bakery or confectionery establishment more than sixty hours in any one week, or more than ten hours in any one day, unless for the purpose of making a shorter work day on the last day of the week; nor more hours in any one week than will make an average of ten hours per day for the number of days during such week in which such employee shall work.

It is plain that this statute was enacted in order to protect the physical well-being of those who work in bakery and confectionery establishments. It may be that the statute had its origin, in part, in the belief that employers and employees in such establishments were not upon an equal footing, and that the necessities of the latter often com-

pelled them to submit to such exactions as unduly taxed their strength. Be this as it may, the statute must be taken as expressing the belief of the people of New York that, as a general rule, and in the case of the average man, labor in excess of sixty hours during a week in such establishments may endanger the health of those who thus labor.

Whether or not this be wise legislation it is not the province of the Court to inquire. Under our systems of government the courts are not concerned with the wisdom or policy of legislation. So that in determining the question of power to interfere with liberty of contract, the Court may inquire whether the means devised by the state are germane to an end which may be lawfully accomplished and have a real or substantial relation to the protection of health as involved in the daily work of the persons, male and female, engaged in bakery and confectionery establishments.

But when this inquiry is entered upon I find it impossible, in view of common experience, to say that there is here no real or substantial relation between the means employed by the state and the end sought to be accomplished by its legislation (*Mugler* v. *Kansas, supra*). Nor can I say that the statute has no appropriate or direct connection with that protection to health which each state owes to her citizens (*Patterson* v. *Kentucky, supra*); or that it is not promotive of the health of the employees in question (*Holden* v. *Hardy, Lawton* v. *Steele, supra*); or that the regulation prescribed by the state is utterly unreasonable and extravagant or wholly arbitrary (*Gundling* v. *Chicago, supra*). Still less can I say that the statute is, beyond question, a plain, palpable invasion of rights secured by the fundamental law (*Jacobson* v. *Massachusetts, supra*).

Therefore, I submit that this Court will transcend its functions if it assumes to annul the statute of New York. It must be remembered that this statute does not apply to all kinds of business. It applies only to work in bakery and confectionery establishments, in which, as all know, the air constantly breathed by workmen is not as pure and healthful as that to be found in some other establishments or out-of-doors.

Professor Hirt in his treatise on the "Diseases of the Workers" has said:

> The labor of the bakers is among the hardest and most laborious imaginable, because it has to be performed under conditions injurious to the health of those engaged in it. It is hard, very hard work, not only because it requires a great deal of physical exertion in an overheated workshop and during unreasonably long hours, but more so because of the erratic demands of the public, compelling the baker to perform the greater part of his work at night, thus depriving him of an opportunity to enjoy the necessary rest and sleep, a fact which is highly injurious to his health.

Another writer says:

> The constant inhaling of flour dust causes inflammation of the lungs and of the bronchial tubes. The eyes also suffer through this dust, which is responsible for the many cases of running eyes among the bakers. The long hours of toil to which all bakers are subjected produce rheumatism, cramps, and swollen legs. The intense heat in the workshops induces the workers to resort to cooling drinks, which together with their habit of exposing the greater part of their bodies to the change in the atmosphere is another source of a number of diseases of various organs. Nearly all bakers are pale-faced and of more delicate health than the workers of other crafts, which is chiefly due to their hard work and their irregular and unnatural mode of living, whereby the power of resistance against disease is greatly diminished. The average age of a baker is below that of other workmen; they seldom live over their fiftieth year, most of them dying between the ages of forty and fifty. . . .

We judicially know that the question of the number of hours during which a workman should continuously labor has been, for a long period, and is yet, a subject of serious consideration among civilized peoples and by those having special knowledge of the laws of health. Suppose the statute prohibited labor in bakery and confectionery establishments in excess of eighteen hours each day. No one, I take it, could dispute the power of the state to enact such a statute. But the statute before us does not embrace extreme or exceptional cases. It may be said to occupy a middle ground in respect of the hours of labor. What is the true ground for the state to take between legitimate protection, by legislation, of the public health and liberty of contract is not a question easily solved, nor one in respect of which there is or can be absolute certainty.

There are very few, if any, questions in political economy about which entire certainty may be predicated. One writer on relation of the state to labor has well said: "The manner, occasion, and degree in which the state may interfere with the industrial freedom of its citizens is one of the most debatable and difficult questions of social science." . . .

We also judicially know that the number of hours that should constitute a day's labor in particular occupations involving the physical strength and safety of workmen has been the subject of enactments by Congress and by nearly all of the states. Many, if not most, of those enactments fix eight hours as the proper basis of a day's labor.

I do not stop to consider whether any particular view of this economic question presents the sounder theory. What the precise facts are it may be difficult to say. It is enough for the determination of this case, and it is enough for this Court to know, that the question is one about which there is room for debate and for an honest difference of opinion. There are many reasons of a weighty, substantial character, based upon the experience of mankind, in support of the theory that, all things considered, more than ten hours' steady work each day, from week to week, in a bakery or confectionery establishment may endanger the health and shorten the lives of the workmen, thereby diminishing their physical and mental capacity to serve the state and to provide for those dependent upon them. If such reasons exist that ought to be the end of this case, for the state is not amenable to the judiciary, in respect of its legislative enactments, unless such enactments are plainly, palpably, beyond all question inconsistent with the Constitution of the United States.

We are not to presume that the state of New York has acted in bad faith. Nor can we assume that its legislature acted without due deliberation, or that it did not determine this question upon the fullest attainable information and for the common good. We cannot say that the state has acted without reason nor ought we to proceed upon the theory that its action is a mere sham. Our duty, I submit, is to sustain the statute as not being in conflict with the federal Constitution, for the reason — and such is an all-sufficient reason — it is not shown to be plainly and palpably inconsistent with that instrument. Let the state alone in the management of its purely domestic affairs, so long as it does not appear beyond all question that it has violated the federal Constitution. This view necessarily results from the principle that the health and safety of the people of a state are primarily for the state to guard and protect.

I take leave to say that the New York statute, in the particulars here involved, cannot be held to be in conflict with the Fourteenth Amendment without enlarging the scope of the amendment far beyond its original purpose and without bringing under the supervision of this Court matters which have been supposed to belong exclusively to the legislative departments of the several states when exerting their conceded power to guard the health and safety of their citizens by such regulations as they in their wisdom deem best. Health laws of every description constitute, said Chief Justice Marshall, a part of that mass of legislation which "embraces everything within the territory of a state, not surrendered to the general government; all which can be most advantageously exercised by the states themselves." (Gibbons v. Ogden). . . .

A decision that the New York statute is void under the Fourteenth Amendment will, in my opinion, involve consequences of a far-reaching and mischievous character; for such a decision would seriously cripple the inherent power of the states to care for the lives, health, and well-being of their citizens. Those are matters which can be best controlled by the states. The preservation of the just powers of the states is quite as vital as the preservation of the powers of the general government. . . .

The judgment in my opinion should be affirmed.

Mr. Justice Holmes. I regret sincerely that I am unable to agree with the judgment in this case and that I think it my duty to express my dissent.

This case is decided upon an economic theory which a large part of the country does not entertain. If it were a question whether I agreed with that theory, I should desire to study it further and long before making up my mind. But I do not conceive that to be my duty, because I strongly believe that my agreement or disagreement has nothing to do with the right of a majority to embody their opinions in law. It is settled by various decisions of this Court that state constitutions and state laws may regulate life in many ways which we as legislators might think as injudicious or if you like as tyrannical as this, and which equally with this interfere with the liberty to contract. Sunday laws and usury laws are ancient examples. A more modern one is the prohibition of lotteries.

The liberty of the citizen to do as he likes so long as he does not interfere with the liberty of others to do the same, which has been a shibboleth for some well-known writers, is interfered with by school laws, by the Post Office, by every state or municipal institution which takes his money for purposes thought desirable, whether he likes it or not. The Fourteenth Amendment does not enact Mr. Herbert Spencer's *Social Statics*.

The other day we sustained the Massachusetts vaccination law *(Jacobson v. Massachusetts)*. . . . United States and state statutes and decisions cutting down the liberty to contract by way of combination are familiar to this Court *(Northern Securities Co. v. United States)*. . . . Two years ago we upheld the prohibition of sales of stock on margins or for future delivery in the constitution of California *(Otis v. Parker)*. . . . The decision sustaining an eight-hour law for miners is still recent *(Holden v. Hardy)*. . . .

Some of these laws embody convictions or prejudices which judges are likely to share. Some may not. But a constitution is not intended to embody a particular economic theory, whether of paternalism and the organic relation of the citizen to the state or of laissez-faire. It is made for people of fundamentally differing views, and the accident of our finding certain opinions natural and familiar or novel and even shocking ought not to conclude our judgment upon the question whether statutes embodying them conflict with the Constitution of the United States.

General propositions do not decide concrete cases. The decision will depend on a judgment or intuition more subtle than any articulate major premise. But I think that the proposition just stated, if it is accepted, will carry us far toward the end. Every opinion tends to become a law. I think that the word "liberty" in the Fourteenth

The Bettmann Archive

Oliver Wendell Holmes, Jr.; photo dated 1910

Amendment is perverted when it is held to prevent the natural outcome of a dominant opinion, unless it can be said that a rational and fair man necessarily would admit that the statute proposed would infringe fundamental principles as they have been understood by the traditions of our people and our law.

It does not need research to show that no such sweeping condemnation can be passed upon the statute before us. A reasonable man might think it a proper measure on the score of health. Men whom I certainly could not pronounce unreasonable would uphold it as a first installment of a general regulation of the hours of work. Whether in the latter aspect it would be open to the charge of inequality I think it unnecessary to discuss.

4.

Manifesto of the Industrial Workers of the World

The Industrial Workers of the World, otherwise known as the "Wobblies," was organized in Chicago in 1905. The difference between this union and the rest of American organized labor was its revolutionary goal of organizing all the world's labor force against the capitalist system, which was to be replaced by a new social order. Founded largely as a protest against the American Federation of Labor, the "Wobblies" never gained popular support. Their willingness to promote labor strife and violence turned public opinion, as well as the constituted authorities, against them. Printed below is the IWW Manifesto, adopted at the first convention. Father Thomas Hagerty, a Roman Catholic priest, is credited with writing part of it; and it was signed by many socialists, including Eugene Debs, who eventually rejected the organization.

Source: *Proceedings of the First Convention of the Industrial Workers of the World,* New York, n.d., pp. 3-6.

SOCIAL RELATIONS AND GROUPINGS only reflect mechanical and industrial conditions. The *great facts* of present industry are the displacement of human skill by machines and the increase of capitalist power through concentration in the possession of the tools with which wealth is produced and distributed.

Because of these facts, trade divisions among laborers and competition among capitalists are alike disappearing. Class divisions grow ever more fixed and class antagonisms more sharp. Trade lines have been swallowed up in a common servitude of all workers to the machines which they tend. New machines, ever replacing less productive ones, wipe out whole trades and plunge new bodies of workers into the ever growing army of tradeless, hopeless unemployed. As human beings and human skill are displaced by mechanical progress, the capitalists need use the workers only during that brief period when muscles and nerves respond most intensely. The moment the laborer no longer yields the maximum of profits, he is thrown upon the scrap pile, to starve alongside the discarded machine. A *dead line* has been drawn, and an age limit established, to cross which, in this world of monopolized opportunities, means condemnation to industrial death.

The worker, wholly separated from the land and the tools, with his skill of craftsmanship rendered useless, is sunk in the uniform mass of wage slaves. He sees his power of resistance broken by craft divisions, perpetuated from outgrown industrial stages. His wages constantly grow less as his hours grow longer and monopolized prices grow higher. Shifted hither and thither by the demands of profit-takers, the laborer's home no longer exists. In this helpless condition he is forced to accept whatever humiliating conditions his master may impose. He is submitted to a physical and intellectual examination more searching than was the chattel slave when sold from the auction block.

Laborers are no longer classified by differences in trade skill, but the employer assigns them according to the machines to which they are attached. These divisions, far from representing differences in skill or interests among the laborers, are imposed by the employers that workers may be pitted against one another and spurred to greater exertion in the shop, and that all resistance to capitalist tyranny may be weakened by artificial distinctions.

While encouraging these outgrown divisions among the workers, the capitalists carefully adjust themselves to the new conditions. They wipe out all differences among themselves and present a united front in their war upon labor. Through employers' associations, they seek to crush, with brutal force, by the injunctions of the judiciary and the use of military power, all efforts at resistance. Or when the other policy seems more profitable, they conceal their daggers beneath the Civic Federation and hoodwink and betray those whom they would rule and exploit. Both methods depend for success upon the blindness and internal dissensions of the working class. The employers' line of battle and methods of warfare correspond to the solidarity of the mechanical and industrial concentration, while laborers still form their fighting organizations on lines of long-gone trade divisions.

The battles of the past emphasize this lesson. The *textile* workers of Lowell, Philadelphia, and Fall River; the *butchers* of Chicago, weakened by the disintegrating effects of trade divisions; the *machinists* on the Santa Fe, unsupported by their fellow workers subject to the same masters; the long-struggling *miners* of Colorado, hampered by lack of unity and solidarity upon the industrial battlefield, all bear witness to the helplessness and impotency of labor as at present organized.

This worn-out and corrupt system offers no promise of improvement and adaptation. There is no silver lining to the clouds of darkness and despair settling down upon the world of labor. This system offers only a perpetual struggle for slight relief within wage slavery. It is blind to the possibility of establishing an industrial democracy wherein there shall be no wage slavery, but where the workers will own the tools which they operate and the product of which they alone will enjoy.

It shatters the ranks of the workers into fragments, rendering them helpless and impotent on the industrial battlefield.

Separation of craft from craft renders industrial and financial solidarity impossible. Union men scab upon union men; hatred of worker for worker is engendered, and the workers are delivered helpless and disintegrated into the hands of the capitalists. Craft jealousy leads to the attempt to create trade monopolies.

Prohibitive initiation fees are established that force men to become scabs against their will. Men whom manliness or circumstances have driven from one trade are thereby fined when they seek to transfer membership to the union of a new craft.

Craft divisions foster political ignorance among the workers, thus dividing their class at the ballot box as well as in the shop, mine, and factory.

Craft unions may be and have been used to assist employers in the establishment of monopolies and the raising of prices. One set of workers are thus used to make harder the conditions of life of another body of laborers.

Craft divisions hinder the growth of class consciousness of the workers, foster the idea of harmony of interests between employing exploiter and employed slave. They permit the association of the misleaders of the workers with the capitalists in the civic fed-

Members of a committee governing the Industrial Workers of the World in New York

erations, where plans are made for the perpetuation of capitalism and the permanent enslavement of the workers through the wage system.

Previous efforts for the betterment of the working class have proven abortive because limited in scope and disconnected in action.

Universal economic evils afflicting the working class can be eradicated only by a universal working-class movement. Such a movement of the working class is impossible while separate craft and wage agreements are made favoring the employer against other crafts in the same industry and while energies are wasted in fruitless jurisdiction struggles which serve only to further the personal aggrandizement of union officials.

A movement to fulfill these conditions must consist of one great industrial union embracing all industries, providing for craft autonomy locally, industrial autonomy internationally, and working-class unity generally. It must be founded on the class struggle, and its general administration must be conducted in harmony with the recognition

of the irrepressible conflict between the capitalist class and the working class. It should be established as the economic organization of the working class, without affiliation with any political party.

All power should rest in a collective membership.

Local, national, and general administration, including union labels, buttons, badges, transfer cards, initiation fees, and per capita tax should be uniform throughout.

All members must hold membership in the local, national, or international union covering the industry in which they are employed, but transfers of membership between unions, local, national, or international, should be universal.

Workingmen bringing union cards from industrial unions in foreign countries should be freely admitted into the organization.

The general administration should issue a publication representing the entire union and its principles which should reach all members in every industry at regular intervals.

A *central defense fund,* to which all members contribute equally, should be established and maintained.

All workers, therefore, who agree with the principles herein set forth, will meet in convention at Chicago the 27th day of June, 1905, for the purpose of forming an economic organization of the working class along the lines marked out in this manifesto.

Representation in the convention shall be based upon the number of workers whom the delegate represents. No delegate, however, shall be given representation in the convention on the numerical basis of an organization unless he has credentials bearing the seal of his union, local, national or international, and the signatures of the officers thereof, authorizing him to install his union as a working part of the proposed economic organization in the industrial department in which it logically belongs in the general plan of organization. Lacking this authority, the delegate shall represent himself as an individual.

5.

Daniel De Leon: The Political Power of Labor

Daniel De Leon was the leader of the Socialist Labor Party and, according to his followers, the founder of industrial unionism. After the Chicago convention of the Industrial Workers of the World adjourned in July 1905, he went on a speaking tour and in Minneapolis gave one of his best-known addresses. Originally called "The Preamble of I.W.W.," the title was later changed to "Socialist Reconstruction of Society." In it he summarized his views of how labor could use its economic and political power to effect the change to a socialist system. Portions of De Leon's address, delivered on July 10, are reprinted below.

Source: *Socialist Landmarks,* New York, 1952, pp. 218-228.

THE PREAMBLE OF THE INDUSTRIAL WORKERS of the world poses well both the political and the economic movement of labor and places them in their proper relation toward each other.

Inestimable is the value, dignified the posture of the political movement. It affords the labor movement the opportunity to ventilate its purposes, its aspirations, and its methods, free, over and aboveboard, in the noonday light of the sun, whereas otherwise, its agitation would be consigned to the circumscribed sphere of the rat hole. The political movement renders the masses accessible to the propaganda of labor; it raises the labor movement above the category of a "conspiracy"; it places the movement in line with the spirit of the age, which, on the one hand, denies the power of "conspiracy" in matters that not only affect the masses but in which the masses must themselves be intelligent actors, and, on the other hand, demands the freest of utterance.

In short and in fine, the political movement bows to the methods of civilized discussion: *It gives a chance to the peaceful solution of the great question at issue.* By proclaiming the urgency of political as well as of industrial unity, the preamble amply and sufficiently proclaims the affinity of the economic with the political movement. At the same time, by expressly proclaiming that the "taking and holding" is an act that falls wholly within the province of the economic organization, the preamble has locked a dangerous switch, a switch running into which would bring grave danger, the danger of rendering the Socialist, which means the labor movement, illusory, and a roosting place for the "intellectual" riff-raff of bourgeois society.

The ballot is a weapon of civilization; the ballot is a weapon that no revolutionary movement of our times may ignore except at its own peril; the Socialist ballot is the emblem of *right*. For that very reason the Socialist ballot is

> weaker than a woman's tears,
> Tamer than sleep, fonder than
>   ignorance,
> Less valiant than the virgin in the
>   night,
> And skilless as unpractised infancy,

unless it is backed by the *might* to enforce it. That requisite might is summed up in the industrial organization of the working class.

Now, mind you, that *might* the labor movement needs, as much, I would almost say, against the political movements its own breath heats into being as against the capitalist tyrant himself. It needs that might against the capitalist tyrant to put the quietus upon him; it also needs that might to prevent the evil consequences to which, in this corrupt atmosphere of bourgeois society, the political movement is inevitably exposed. The two points are vital. Much, infinitely more than appears at first sight, hangs thereby.

Despite the sharply marked economic feature of the labor movement, the principle that it is bound to take on a political form also is founded on no fine-spun theory. Even discounting the force of the sociologic arguments . . . which point to the inevitableness of the political manifestation of the labor movement, there is a consideration . . . which, when properly weighed, places the matter beyond the peradventure of a doubt. That consideration is the existence of universal suffrage in the land.

The institution is so bred in the bones of the people that, although it has become a gravel in the shoe of the capitalist, he, powerful though he is, dares not abolish it outright. Among such a people, chimerical is the idea of expecting to conduct a great movement, whose palpable aim is a Socialist Revolution, to the slogan of "Abstinence from the ballot box!" The proposition cannot choose but brand its supporters as freaks. Whether the economic movement wills it or not, its political phase will assert itself on the political field. Men from its own ranks and men from outside its ranks will raise the standard of labor politics.

Nor will the capitalist be slow in endeavoring, while humoring the thing, to draw the sting from it. Watchfully though he guards his political burg, he will, from time to time, carefully select some "promising" candidate from the labor ticket, and allow him admission or, maybe, he is sometimes taken napping and some labor candidate slips through the fingers of his outposts at the ballot box. Subjected to the lures and wiles at the disposal of the capitalist, these successful labor candidates in the parliaments of capitalism, ten to one, succumb. They succumb either because of their own inherently corrupt souls or their muddleheadedness. In either case they betray the working class; the effect is harmfully felt by the economic movement.

Against this danger there is but one protection — the Industrial, that is, the class-conscious economic organization to keep that ballot straight. Nothing short of such an economic organization will prevent the evil, because nothing short of such an economic organization can keep sharp the edge of the special sword wielded by the political movement of labor. . . . It is purely *destructive.* The economic movement may take a little at a time. It may do so because its function is ultimately to "take and hold" the full plants of production and save them for the human race. The political movement, on the contrary, has an entirely different function: Its function is wholly to tear down the political burg of capitalist tyranny.

It follows herefrom that the political movement of labor may not even remotely partake even of the appearance of compromise. It exemplifies the revolutionary aim of the labor movement; it must be uncompromisingly revolutionary. This fact dictates the conduct of the successful political candidates of labor in the parliaments of capitalism. The principle found expression in the celebrated maxim uttered by William Liebknecht, when he was still in the full vigor of his Socialist aspirations — *"Parlamentiren ist paktiren,"* to parliamentarize is to compromise, to log-roll, to sell out. . . .

Without the *might* of the class-conscious economic movement back of the political, the political movements that the labor movement inevitably promotes in America will not only be divided but, as a further result, will promote that confusion of thought that runs into corruption and that, reacting back upon the economic movement itself, helps to scuttle its efficiency. It surely is no accident that, without exception, all the labor candidates so far allowed by the capitalist class to filter through their garrisons at their election defiles, whenever the office to which they were allowed to be returned elected was of any importance, have uniformly "parliamentarized," that is, "log-rolled," in short, sold out the revolution. We saw it happen during the heyday of the K. of L.; we saw it happen more recently in Haverhill, in Brockton, in the Massachusetts legislature, in Paterson, in Sheboygan; we see it happening now in Milwaukee.

It is a matter of self-protection with the economic organization to watch and control the political. Skilless as unpractised infancy, a danger to labor itself, is the sword of labor's ballot without the might of the class-conscious economic organization to whet its edge, to keep it sharp, and to insist upon its being plied over the skull of the foe, to insist upon that at the peril of the muddleheads, of the weakling, of the traitor.

There now remains only one point to consider, and I am through. It is the point with regard to the necessity of the industrial organization in order to supplement the right of the ballot with the might requisite to put the quietus upon the capitalist class itself. The point implies what is generally but wrongly meant by *"the general strike,"* a term that, through misuse by its own advocates, who have hitherto placed the cart before the horse, is greatly misunderstood and should be replaced by the more appropriate term of *"the general lockout of the capitalist class."*

Political power is reached through the ballot box. But the ballot box is not an open field; it is a veritable defile. That defile is held by the agents of the capitalist class. The election inspectors and returning boards are capitalist appointees; they are veritable garrisons with which the capitalist class holds the defile. To imagine that these capitalist garrisons of the election defiles will complacently allow the candidates of the revolution, whose program is the dismantling of the political burg of capitalism, peacefully to file through is to indulge in a mooncalf's vision. The revolutionary ballot of labor is counted out now; it has been counted out from the first day of its appearance; it will be counted out even more extensively in the future. . . .

The futility of the ballot alone, however triumphant, was strikingly illustrated nine years ago during the first Bryan campaign. The political temperature against the plutocratic rulers of the land had risen to a point where they, for a moment, considered the battle at the ballot box lost in advance. That, however, did not disconcert them. Through their national mouthpiece, Mark Hanna, they threatened to stop production. In other words, they threatened to go on strike.

The threat was no idle bombast. They could. It was known that they could. Craft unionism placed it in their power to do so. The threat had its effect. But let the capitalist attempt, under the pressure of the political temperature raised by the ballot of labor — let him attempt to strike. In possession of the might conferred and implied by the industrial organization of their class, the working class would forthwith *lock out the capitalist class.* Without political organization, the labor movement cannot triumph; without economic organization, the day of its political triumph would be the day of its defeat.

Industrialism means might. Craft unionism means impotence. All the plants of production, aye, even the vast wealth for consumption, is today in the keeping of the working class. It is workingmen who are in charge of the factories, the railroads, the mines, in short, all the land and machinery of production; and it is they, also, who sit as watchdogs before the pantries, the cellars, and the safe-deposit vaults of the capitalist class; aye, it is they who carry the guns in the armies.

But this place of vantage is of no avail to them under craft unionism. Under craft unionism, only one craft marches into the battlefield at a time. By idly looking on, the other crafts scab it upon the combatant. What with that and the likewise idle onlooking of those divisions of the workers who man the commissary department, so to speak, of the capitalist class, the class struggle presents, under craft unionism, the aspect of petty riots in which the empty stomachs and empty hands of the working class are pitted against the full ones of the employing class.

Was this ignorance? Was this treason? Whether it was treason or ignorance, the turning in the long lane has been reached. Both the present conduct of craft unionism and the future conduct of industrial unionism were well portrayed by one of the delegates at the Chicago Convention. Illustrating the point with the five fingers of his right hand far apart, he showed that to be the posture of the craft or autonomous unions — disconnected from one another for all practical work, and good only to act as a fan, a fan that had hitherto done nothing but scare the flies away from the face of the capitalist class — and proceeding thereupon to illustrate the further point by drawing his five fingers tightly into a compact fist, he showed that to be the posture of industrial unionism — a battering ram that would leave the face of the capitalist class looking materially different from the way it looked when it was merely fanned.

The impotence wherewith the right of the working class has hitherto been smitten is now to be transformed into a might without which that right is but mockery. The signal for that transformation was struck last week at the convention of the Industrial Workers of the World; and the word has gone out, as it could go out from no other country but America, in language that fits our full-grown capitalist development —

> Unite! Unite on the economic field upon the only basis on which economic unity is possible — the basis of the solidarity of the working class, the only solid fact from which political unity can be reflected! Unite! Unite upon the only economic principle capable of backing up the right of the labor ballot with the might to enforce it! Unite for the general strike at the ballot box, to overthrow the political robber burg of capitalism, backed by the general strike against, or, rather, the general lockout of, the capitalist class from the industrial fields that it has usurped. Unite for the emancipation of the working class, and to save civilization from a catastrophe!

6.

Louis D. Brandeis: The Law and the Laboring Classes

Louis D. Brandeis, called by one historian "the most socially conscious lawyer of his generation," was deeply concerned about the fact that the legal profession was almost always found on the side of big business in its disputes with labor. Asked to speak at Harvard University in May 1905 about opportunities in the law, Brandeis eloquently argued the view that lawyers — especially young lawyers — could and should become advocates of the poor and the dispossessed. The speech, which is reprinted here in part, was delivered at Phillips Brooks House on May 5.

Source: *Business — A Profession,* Boston, 1914, pp. 313-327.

IT IS TRUE THAT AT THE PRESENT time the lawyer does not hold as high a position with the people as he held seventy-five or indeed fifty years ago; but the reason is not lack of opportunity. It is this: Instead of holding a position of independence, between the wealthy and the people, prepared to curb the excesses of either, able lawyers have, to a large extent, allowed themselves to become adjuncts of great corporations and have neglected the obligation to use their powers for the protection of the people. We hear much of the "corporation lawyer" and far too little of the "people's lawyer." The great opportunity of the American Bar is and will be to stand again as it did in the past, ready to protect also the interests of the people.

Mr. Bryce, in discussing our Bar, said, in his *American Commonwealth:*

> But I am bound to add that some judicious American observers hold that the last thirty years have witnessed a certain decadence in the Bar of the great cities. They say that the growth of the enormously rich and powerful corporations willing to pay vast sums for questionable services has seduced the virtue of some

counsel whose eminence makes their example important.

The leading lawyers of the United States have been engaged mainly in supporting the claims of the corporations; often in endeavoring to evade or nullify the extremely crude laws by which legislators sought to regulate the power or curb the excesses of corporations.

Such questions as the regulation of trusts, the fixing of railway rates, the municipalization of public utilities, the relation between capital and labor call for the exercise of legal ability of the highest order. Up to the present time the legal ability of a high order which has been expended on those questions has been almost wholly in opposition to the contentions of the people. The leaders of the Bar, without any preconceived intent on their part, and rather as an incident to their professional standing, have, with rare exceptions, been ranged on the side of the corporations, and the people have been represented, in the main, by men of very meager legal ability.

If these problems are to be settled right, this condition cannot continue. Our country

Louis Brandeis

is, after all, not a country of dollars but of ballots. The immense corporate wealth will necessarily develop a hostility from which much trouble will come to us unless the excesses of capital are curbed through the respect for law as the excesses of democracy were curbed seventy-five years ago. There will come a revolt of the people against the capitalists unless the aspirations of the people are given some adequate legal expression; and to this end cooperation of the abler lawyers is essential.

For nearly a generation the leaders of the Bar have, with few exceptions, not only failed to take part in constructive legislation designed to solve in the public interest our great social, economic, and industrial problems, but they have failed likewise to oppose legislation prompted by selfish interests. They have often gone further in disregard of commonweal. They have often advocated, as lawyers, legislative measures which as citizens they could not approve, and have endeavored to justify themselves by a false analogy. They have erroneously assumed that the rule of ethics to be applied to a lawyer's advocacy is the same where he acts for private interests against the public as it is in litigation between private individuals.

The ethical question which laymen most frequently ask about the legal profession is this: How can a lawyer take a case which he does not believe in? The profession is regarded as necessarily somewhat immoral because its members are supposed to be habitually taking cases of that character. As a practical matter, the lawyer is not often harassed by this problem, partly because he is apt to believe, at the time, in most of the cases that he actually tries, and partly because he either abandons or settles a large number of those he does not believe in. But the lawyer recognizes that in trying a case his prime duty is to present his side to the tribunal fairly and as well as he can, relying upon his adversary to present the other side fairly and as well as he can. Since the lawyers on the two sides are usually reasonably well-matched, the judge or jury may ordinarily be trusted to make such a decision as justice demands.

But when lawyers act upon the same principle in supporting the attempts of their private clients to secure or to oppose legislation, a very different condition is presented. In the first place, the counsel selected to represent important private interests possesses usually ability of a high order, while the public is often inadequately represented or wholly unrepresented. Great unfairness to the public is apt to result from this fact. Many bills pass in our legislatures which would not have become law if the public interest had been fairly represented; and many good bills are defeated which, if supported by able lawyers, would have been enacted. Lawyers have, as a rule, failed to consider this distinction between practice in courts involving only private interests and practice before the legislature or city council involving public interests. Some men of high professional standing have even endeavored to justify their course in advocating professionally legislation which in their character as citizens they would have voted against.

Furthermore, lawyers of high standing have often failed to apply in connection with professional work before the legislature or city council a rule of ethics which they would deem imperative in practice before the court. Lawyers who would indignantly retire from a court case in the justice of which they believed, if they had reason to think that a juror had been bribed or a witness had been suborned by their client, are content to serve their client by honest arguments before a legislative committee, although they have as great reason to believe that their client has bribed members of the legislature or corrupted public opinion. This confusion of ethical ideas is an important reason why the Bar does not now hold the position which it formerly did as a brake upon democracy, and which I believe it must take again if the serious questions now before us are to be properly solved.

Here, consequently, is the great opportunity in the law. The next generation must witness a continuing and ever increasing contest between those who have and those who have not. The industrial world is in a state of ferment. The ferment is in the main peaceful, and, to a considerable extent, silent; but there is felt today very widely the inconsistency in this condition of political democracy and industrial absolutism. The people are beginning to doubt whether in the long run democracy and absolutism can coexist in the same community; beginning to doubt whether there is a justification for the great inequalities in the distribution of wealth, for the rapid creation of fortunes, more mysterious than the deeds of Aladdin's lamp. The people have begun to think; and they show evidences on all sides of a tendency to act.

Those of you who have not had an opportunity of talking much with laboring men can hardly form a conception of the amount of thinking that they are doing. With many these problems are all-absorbing. Many workingmen, otherwise uneducated, talk about the relation of employer and employee far more intelligently than most of the best-educated men in the community. The labor question involves for them the whole of life; and they must, in the course of a comparatively short time, realize the power which lies in them. Often their leaders are men of signal ability, men who can hold their own in discussion or in action with the ablest and best-educated men in the community.

The labor movement must necessarily progress. The people's thought will take shape in action; and it lies with us, with you to whom in part the future belongs, to say on what lines the action is to be expressed; whether it is to be expressed wisely and temperately, or wildly and intemperately; whether it is to be expressed on lines of evolution or on lines of revolution. Nothing can better fit you for taking part in the solution of these problems than the study and preeminently the practice of law. Those of you who feel drawn to that profession may rest assured that you will find in it an opportunity for usefulness which is probably unequaled. There is a call upon the legal profession to do a great work for this country.

Lawsuit, n. A machine which you go into as a pig and come out of as a sausage.
Ambrose Bierce, *The Devil's Dictionary*

7.

Songs of Parody and Protest

Many of the most popular labor songs of the period around the turn of the century were either evocations or direct parodies of the gospel songs of a generation or more earlier. The reason is not far to seek: gospel songs were known and sung by workingmen everywhere, so that the tunes, at least, were familiar; and the churches were regarded by the working class as fundamentally anti-labor and as supporters of the capitalist system. Joe Hill was a labor organizer and songwriter for the Industrial Workers of the World (IWW); the refrain of his best-known song, "The Preacher and the Slave," became almost the motto of the American labor movement in the years before World War I. "Hold the Fort" was originally an English version of a gospel song, but it was adopted by American workers and sung at many labor rallies.

❦ THE PREACHER AND THE SLAVE

Long-haired preachers come out every night,
Try to tell you what's wrong and what's right,
But when asked about something to eat,
They will answer with voices so sweet:

Chorus:
You will eat (you will eat), bye and bye (bye and bye),
In that glorious land in the sky (way up high).
Work and pray (work and pray), live on hay (live on hay),
You'll get pie in the sky when you die (that's a lie!).

And the starvation army they play,
And they sing and they clap and they pray,
Till they get all your coin on the drum —
Then they tell you when you're on the bum.

If you fight hard for children and wife —
Try to get something good in this life —
You're a sinner and bad man, they tell;
When you die you will sure go to Hell.

Working men of all countries, unite!
Side by side we for freedom will fight.
When the world and its wealth we have gained,
To the grafters we'll sing this refrain:

Last chorus:
You will eat (you will eat), bye and bye, (bye and bye),
When you've learned how to cook and to fry (way up high).
Chop some wood (chop some wood) — 'twill do you good (do you good)
And you'll eat in the sweet bye and bye (that's no lie!).

JOE HILL

✿ HOLD THE FORT

We meet today in freedom's cause
   And raise our voices high;
We'll join our hands in union strong
   To battle or to die.

Chorus:
Hold the fort, for we are coming,
   Union men be strong;
Side by side we battle onward,
   Victory will come.

Look my comrades, see the union
   Banners waving high;
Reinforcements now appearing,
   Victory is nigh.

See our numbers still increasing,
   Hear the bugles blow;
By our union we will triumph
   Over every foe.

8.

Principles of the Niagara Movement

Although Booker T. Washington was still the most respected and best-known Negro leader in the United States in 1905, a group of educated Northern Negroes was dissatisfied with his program. A minority of articulate Negroes urged greater economic opportunity, more and better education, and political equality for all Negroes. The Niagara Movement, so called because the group originally met in the proximity of Niagara Falls in July 1905, represented this impatient minority. The twenty-nine Negro ministers, lawyers, editors, teachers, and businessmen who attended the meeting, called by W. E. B. Du Bois, issued the following Declaration of Principles. The movement eventually merged into the National Association for the Advancement of Colored People.

Source: *Cleveland Gazette*, July 22, 1905.

THE MEMBERS OF THE CONFERENCE, known as the Niagara Movement, assembled in annual meeting at Buffalo, July 11, 12, and 13, 1905, congratulate the Negro Americans on certain undoubted evidences of progress in the last decade, particularly the increase of intelligence, the buying of property, the checking of crime, the uplift in homelife, the advance in literature and art, and the demonstration of constructive and executive ability in the conduct of great religious, economic, and educational institutions.

At the same time, we believe that this

class of American citizens should protest emphatically and continually against the curtailment of their political rights. We believe in manhood suffrage; we believe that no man is so good, intelligent, or wealthy as to be entrusted wholly with the welfare of his neighbor.

We believe also in protest against the curtailment of our civil rights. All American citizens have the right to equal treatment ·in places of public entertainment according to their behavior and deserts.

We especially complain against the denial of equal opportunities to us in economic life; in the rural districts of the South this amounts to peonage and virtual slavery; all over the South it tends to crush labor and small business enterprises; and everywhere American prejudice, helped often by iniquitous laws, is making it more difficult for Negro Americans to earn a decent living.

Common-school education should be free to all American children, and compulsory. High-school training should be adequately provided for all, and college training should be the monopoly of no class or race in any section of our common country. We believe that, in defense of its own institutions, the United States should aid common-school education, particularly in the South, and we especially recommend concerted agitation to this end. We urge an increase in public high-school facilities in the South, where the Negro Americans are almost wholly without such provisions. We favor well-equipped trade and technical schools for the training of artisans, and the need of adequate and liberal endowment for a few institutions of higher education must be patent to sincere well-wishers of the race.

We demand upright judges in courts, juries selected without discrimination on account of color, and the same measure of punishment and the same efforts at reformation for black as for white offenders. We need orphanages and farm schools for de-

pendent children, juvenile reformatories for delinquents, and the abolition of the dehumanizing convict-lease system.

We note with alarm the evident retrogression in this land of sound public opinion on the subject of manhood rights, republican government, and human brotherhood; and we pray God that this nation will not degenerate into a mob of boasters and oppressors, but rather will return to the faith of the fathers, that all men were created free and equal, with certain unalienable rights.

We plead for health — for an opportunity to live in decent houses and localities, for a chance to rear our children in physical and moral cleanliness.

We hold up for public execration the conduct of two opposite classes of men: the practice among employers of importing ignorant Negro American laborers in emergencies, and then affording them neither protection nor permanent employment; and the practice of labor unions of proscribing and boycotting and oppressing thousands of their fellow toilers simply because they are black. These methods have accentuated and will accentuate the war of labor and capital, and they are disgraceful to both sides.

We refuse to allow the impression to remain that the Negro American assents to inferiority, is submissive under oppression, and apologetic before insults. Through helplessness we may submit, but the voice of protest of 10 million Americans must never cease to assail the ears of their fellows so long as America is unjust.

Any discrimination based simply on race or color is barbarous, we care not how hallowed it be by custom, expediency, or prejudice. Differences made on account of ignorance, immorality, poverty, or disease may be legitimate methods of reform, and against them we have no word of protest; but discriminations based simply and solely on physical peculiarities, place of birth, color [of] skin, are relics of that unreasoning human savagery of which the world is and ought to be thoroughly ashamed.

We protest against the "Jim Crow" car, since its effect is and must be to make us pay first-class fare for third-class accommodations, render us open to insults and discomfort, and to crucify wantonly our manhood, womanhood, and self-respect.

We regret that this nation has never seen fit adequately to reward the black soldiers who, in its five wars, have defended their country with their blood and yet have been systematically denied the promotions which their abilities deserve. And we regard as unjust the exclusion of black boys from the military and Navy training schools.

We urge upon Congress the enactment of appropriate legislation for securing the proper enforcement of those articles of freedom, the Thirteenth, Fourteenth, and Fifteenth Amendments of the Constitution of the United States.

We repudiate the monstrous doctrine that the oppressor should be the sole authority as to the rights of the oppressed. The Negro race in America, stolen, ravished, and degraded, struggling up through difficulties and oppression, needs sympathy and receives criticism; needs help and is given hindrance; needs protection and is given mob violence; needs justice and is given charity; needs leadership and is given cowardice and apology; needs bread and is given a stone. This nation will never stand justified before God until these things are changed.

Especially are we surprised and astonished at the recent attitude of the Church of Christ — of an increase of a desire to bow to racial prejudice, to narrow the bounds of human brotherhood, and to segregate black men in some outer sanctuary. This is wrong, unchristian, and disgraceful to the 20th century civilization.

Of the above grievances we do not hesitate to complain, and to complain loudly and insistently. To ignore, overlook, or apologize for these wrongs is to prove ourselves unworthy of freedom. Persistent, manly agitation is the way to liberty, and toward this goal the Niagara Movement has started and asks the cooperation of all men of all races.

At the same time we want to acknowledge with deep thankfulness the help of our fellowmen from the Abolitionist down to those who today still stand for equal opportunity and who have given and still give of their wealth and of their poverty for our advancement.

And while we are demanding, and ought to demand, and will continue to demand the rights enumerated above, God forbid that we should ever forget to urge corresponding duties upon our people:

The duty to vote.

The duty to respect the rights of others.

The duty to work.

The duty to obey the laws.

The duty to be clean and orderly.

The duty to send our children to school.

The duty to respect ourselves, even as we respect others.

This statement, complaint, and prayer we submit to the American people and to Almighty God.

Inequality is as dear to the American heart as liberty itself.

WILLIAM DEAN HOWELLS

9.

Richard R. Wright, Jr.: The Negro in the Labor Movement

The growing Negro population in many Northern cities at the turn of the century occasioned there the first serious evidences of race prejudice and violence since the Civil War. Herded into the poorer sections of the city, the first generation of Southern Negroes in the North found their economic lot a most difficult one. Sometimes their only opportunity for work was at the expense of the white worker — for example, when Negroes were used as strikebreakers. R. R. Wright, Jr., pastor of Chicago's (Negro) Trinity Mission, was greatly concerned about the social and economic conditions of his parishioners. In the following article, published in October 1905, and reprinted here in part, he surveyed the Negro's role in the Chicago labor movement from 1900 to 1905.

Source: *Charities*, October 7, 1905: "The Negro in Times of Industrial Unrest."

THE SCOPE OF THIS PAPER is limited to the local situation in Chicago. The writer has for six years observed conditions among workingmen in this, the most rapidly growing Negro city population in the country, a population which in the last forty years has increased twice as rapidly as the total population of Chicago and sixteen times as rapidly as the total Negro population of the country.

The question of earning a living — how to get a job and how to hold a job — is the most serious and most difficult question now confronting the Chicago Negro. He must work where he can rather than where he will. Times of industrial unrest, of which there are many in this city, have often offered to him opportunities for work which were before closed. The three most significant instances of such unrest in which Negroes had conspicuous part were the building trades' strike of 1900, the stockyards' strike of 1904, and the teamsters'

strike of 1905. Prior to 1900, Negroes played but little part in the industrial situation on account of the smallness of the Negro population.

During 1899 and early 1900 one of the most powerful labor organizations in Chicago was that of the building trades, which controlled almost absolutely the building situation in the city. Over against them, however, was the growing organization of building contractors, slowly preparing to meet the labor men. The contractors were the aggressors in the struggle which began February 5, 1900, against what they called the "tyranny" of the Building Trades' Council, which had prohibited the use of machinery and apprentices, and "made possible the limitation of a man's work to one-half his capacity." The contractors held in brief that there should be no limitation of work, no restriction upon the use of machinery or tools, an eight-hour day at 50 cents per hour, one and one-half pay for overtime and double pay for Sundays, a committee on arbitration, and a three-years' agreement.

Up to this time Negroes had done but little work in the building trades. The unions, in order to limit competition, had not seen fit to invite them to join, and had in many instances refused, by blackballing, Negroes who presented themselves for membership. Most of the Negroes, therefore, who had come from the South with their trades found it easier and quite as lucrative to go into domestic and personal service. Some gave up their trades and others alternated between waiters' work and porters' work, and doing the odd jobs in their line which came to them as nonunion men.

The boycott of the building contractors was followed by a general strike of the building trades, and this was the opportunity of the nonunion laborer and, along with him, of the Negro. The strike lasted all the summer, and the number of Negroes increased until they were an important issue. There was, however, no wholesale importation from the South. [In] one of the largest buildings in the city, the Mandel Department Store, a large number of Negroes were employed, and their presence caused much violence, despite police protection. Violence, however, did not frighten the Negroes, and more peaceful means were used. The Chicago Federation of Labor, representing all the organized labor bodies of the city, issued an appeal to the Negroes, which because of its significance is given here:

The frequency with which unscrupulous employers of labor are of late supplanting white men by their colored brethren in times of industrial troubles is a question of most serious moment to the wage earners of this country. In calling attention to this question it is not our intention to arouse sentiment which might lead to race prejudice, or a race war, which would be deplorable in its results, but rather in a friendly spirit to lay before our colored brethren a statement of facts which we hope may convince them of their error. . . . We do not even condemn them, believing they are more justly entitled to our sympathy and support.

In the slavery days, now happily gone by, when the traffic in human flesh and blood remained a blot on our civilization, the Negro was unable to free himself from the bondage. His white brother rose in arms and declared that the slave should be free. Today the Negro is being used to keep the white man in industrial slavery. The colored man, more simple in his ways, with fewer wants and these more easily satisfied, is contented to work under conditions which are irksome to the white workman, and he is today, perhaps unconsciously, being used to try to drag the white man down to a level lower than was the Negro before he was freed from slavery. . . .

It is to remedy this that we appeal to him, to welcome him into our fold, to elevate him to our standard, and to better his condition as well as our own. The trades-union movement knows no race or color. Its aims are the bettering of the condition of the wage earner, whatever his color or creed. In this spirit we appeal to the colored workman to join us in our work. Come into our trades unions, give us your assistance, and, in return, receive our support so that race hatred may be forever buried, and the workers of the country united in a solid phalanx to demand what we are justly entitled to — a fair share of the fruits of our industry.

This appeal was taken seriously by many Negroes, who left the ranks of strikebreakers to join the unions. Some of these indeed became so zealous for the cause of unionism that they even tried the persuasion of violence upon other members of their race when words were not found strong enough to stop them from work.

The strike ended in the fall; the Building Trades' Council was disrupted and the unions left in a weak condition. But in the recuperation many more Negroes were among the membership of the unions than before. Of these the Negro membership of the hod carriers was especially strong, for in this kind of work the Negroes had been the strongest competitors.

The next great struggle in which Negroes were engaged was the stockyards' strike. On Tuesday, July 12, nearly 50,000 men, many of whom were Negroes, stopped work at the command of Michael Donnelly, president of the Amalgamated Meat Cutters and Butcher Workmen, who had organized the stockyards' unions and who conducted the strike. The grounds for the strike were the refusal of the packers to grant to the unskilled men a minimum wage of 18½ cents per hour and an equalization of the wages of skilled men. The strike was general in the West and involved all the large houses.

Ten days later, however, the packers and labor men came to a tentative agreement. On July 23, the men applied for their former positions. But in a few hours they were called out again, as it was charged that the packers discriminated in hiring the old men. Thus began a second strike, which was to continue nearly two months. The packers determined to break the strike after the efforts at peace failed. To do this they turned to the Negroes.

For more than twenty years there had been Negroes employed in the stockyards. Both Mr. Armour and Mr. Swift were friendly to them. There had been but little premeditated effort to break the strike, and in recruiting strikebreakers there was very little system. Employment agencies, private individuals, "runners," and others scoured the city. Thousands of Negroes were imported and in a few days more than 10,000 Negroes were in the various plants. Lodging houses, commissaries, and pleasure rooms were hastily provided; Negroes were eager to seize the situation. . . . Most of the Negroes employed were unskilled and were so indiscriminately gotten that it cannot be said that they were effective workers, or even the better type of strikebreakers. They

served a purpose, however, by the greatness of their numbers, of weakening the strikers.

Within one month, an industry which had used 95 percent white labor now threatened to use 85 percent Negro labor. It was more than unionism could bear. The more thoughtless strikers and their friends used violence and made it positively dangerous for a black face to appear in "Packingtown." But the thoughtful few saw another side of the subject and used persuasion and proffers of future friendliness to Negroes. Negro preachers, political leaders, and others were asked to urge the strikebreakers to quit work. On August 24, 1904, a telegram was sent to Booker T. Washington by prominent members of the Chicago Federation of Labor to this effect: "Organized labor of Chicago, representing 250,000 men and women of all races, respectfully requests you to address a mass meeting of colored people in this city on the subject, 'Should Negroes Become Strike-breakers?'" The telegram included also expressions concerning the efforts of the unions to overcome race prejudice.

On September 9, the strike ended, the unions surrendered unconditionally, and the men went back to work. The majority of the Negroes had not gained in proficiency and quit or were discharged. A fair proportion remained. Today no industry in Chicago employs more Negroes than the packing industries, where in nearly every branch they may find employment.

The teamsters' strike began April 6 in sympathy for the garment workers of the mail-order house of Montgomery Ward & Co., who had been upon a strike since November. On Friday, April 7, seventy-one teamsters employed by that firm quit work. The next day strikebreakers, among them many Negroes, took their places and delivered goods under police protection. There was a brief but futile effort at settlement; then a grim determination on the part of both employers and teamsters to win. The strike spread to the Railway Express drivers; department store drivers; coal drivers; parcel and baggage delivery drivers; furniture, lumber, and truck drivers; and other teamsters who refused to deliver goods to strikebound houses, in all about 5,000 men.

Among the first strikebreakers were a large number of Negroes. Negroes drove for such firms as Marshall Field, Carson, Pirie, Scott & Co., J. V. Farwell, Johnson Chair Co., and others who had not before employed Negro teamsters. The coal companies were freshly manned almost entirely with Negroes. This was, as usual, the signal for violence. For 105 days there was a fierce struggle; and for at least 40 days it seemed that there was war. Over 500 cases of violence were known to the police, and at least a score of deaths resulted. During the second month the teamsters weakened considerably, and the end came July 20 when the Teamsters' Joint Council declared the strike off, without condition. The coal teamsters, however, did not go back to work, but kept up the strike against the coal companies who were employing Negroes. August 23, however, the coal teamsters decided to call off; but at this writing, August 30, policemen are still guarding Negro drivers of coal wagons.

After the first three weeks of the strike, Negroes constituted an ever decreasing number of strikebreakers. Of the total number of men employed by the Employers' Association, there were 700 white men from Chicago to 200 Negroes; 4,300 white men were imported from St. Louis, Toledo, Buffalo, Cleveland, Minneapolis, Indianapolis, Omaha, Peoria, Rock Island, Moline, Davenport, and other cities, while about 450 Negroes were brought from St. Louis and 150 from Kansas City. At the end of the strike there were only about 2 percent Negro strikebreakers. The cause of this decrease was chiefly the violence which the strike incited.

Officers of the Employers' Association assure me that the Negroes were quite as competent as the whites, but that white strikebreakers objected to working with them; and that Negroes were often especially singled out for violent attacks by strikers and strike sympathizers. The race issue was raised by strikers, encouraged by exaggerated reports of some of the daily papers. The populace was in a fever, condemning Negro strikebreakers more than white strikebreakers, and deriding and committing violence upon them, even when they did not approve of the grounds of the strike. Many of the Negroes left their work voluntarily; but the majority remained until they were discharged. Now about 80 Negroes hold places gotten during the strike.

After this review, one comes to the question: Why do Negroes become strikebreakers? A prominent labor editor of this city writes me in answer to this question that the cause is "a certain prejudice which exists against them (Negroes) in the minds of white men, no matter how we might try to disguise the feeling, which operates against them in securing employment under normal conditions." Of course it must be borne in mind that Negroes seldom constitute the majority of strikebreakers. The public is in danger of being misled upon this point. In the teamsters' strike the impression was abroad that Negroes were the majority of strikebreakers. No less a personage than a Negro secretary of the Teamsters' Union wrote me that Negroes constituted 90 percent of the strikebreakers during the first weeks of the strike, and 40 percent at the time of this writing (July 1). The fact is Negroes never made up as high as 90 percent of the strikebreakers, and July 1 were only about 5 percent.

The bulk of Negro workmen never consisted of strikebreakers. Nor are Negroes opposed to unions. Many struck with the unions and remained loyal to them at the stockyards. In the teamsters' strike, while there were 800 Negro strikebreakers, the unions held a membership of nearly 2,000 Negro teamsters, and 1 of their number represented the coal drivers at the Philadelphia convention of the Brotherhood of Teamsters in August. There are a half-dozen Negro delegates to the Chicago Federation of Labor and several Negro local union officers. Yet it still remains that in times of industrial peace the more desirable places are closed against Negroes, either because the employers will not hire them or the men will not work with them.

Negroes become strikebreakers, also, because of the high wages paid during strikes. The union scale, and even higher, is paid. Teamsters receive $4 and $5 per day, which is paid every evening. Lodging was often furnished and sometimes board. This has great force with the unemployed and discontented classes.

The relation of Negroes to industrial unrest makes it clear that whatever the Negro is to have in the labor world must be won by him against odds and held by superior force. Only as the Negro develops into a strong competitor will he be recognized. Many examples of this occur each year. A case at the stockyards is typical. Several years ago a Negro "boner" came from Kansas City, where he had followed his trade as a union man. He was not admitted to the union in Chicago. Here "boning" was considered a "white man's" job, and members of the union, though outwardly friendly to the Negro, privately advised one another to "knock the Negro" if he aspired to anything except a "Negro's job." But during the strike Negroes got the opportunity to develop proficiency as "boners." Now it is no longer considered "a white man's job," and the Negroes who work at it are being urged to join the union.

The part which Negroes have played as strikebreakers has caused a higher value to be put upon their labor than before. Often an employer did not employ a Negro simply "because he had never had any," or "because he preferred whites," or because at some time in the past he had had some trouble with an individual Negro. Thus the door of opportunity is closed until this employer is forced to take Negro strikebreakers. This was the case in many instances during the last strike, and in most cases the efficiency and courage of the Negroes was surprising. . . .

On the other hand, the part of Negroes in strikes is bringing the unions to deal with less of insincerity than heretofore with the Negroes. They are beginning to realize in fact what they have asserted in theory, that the cause of labor cannot be limited by color, creed, or any other extraneous condition. They have shown the commendable spirit of welcoming the Negroes when they have been able to win their places. Today, as never before, unionism, which has often meant the crowding out of Negro laborers, is in an increasingly friendly attitude toward black men. This increase will be more and more as the Negroes increase in competency and intelligence.

A big man is a big man whether he's a president or a prizefighter.
JOHN L. SULLIVAN, greeting to Theodore Roosevelt in the White House.

10.

Félix Klein: The American Philanthropist

The Abbé Félix Klein, a professor at the Institut Catholique in Paris, was a liberal Catholic who considered the American branch of the Church to be more congenial than that of his native land. To test this belief, he made several visits to the United States, and the product of a tour in 1904 was the book Au Pays de "la vie intense," *published the following year. Klein visited several American cities and on the whole formed a favorable impression of the country. He was particularly struck by the behavior of rich Americans, and he wrote at length on the difference between the European wealthy class and its counterpart in the United States. Reprinted here is Klein's description of Andrew Carnegie, whom Klein considered a good example of the enlightened American philanthropist.*

Source: *In the Land of the Strenuous Life*, Chicago, 1905, pp. 202-205.

MERE MONEYMAKING is for Andrew Carnegie but half the task; it is necessary to employ it well. Hence his book *The Gospel of Wealth*. One may or may not share his opinions, but at least one must own that they are not wanting in a certain nobility. A man who, having risen from the ranks himself, thinks and speaks thus is a man in a thousand. As his ideas are not exclusively personal but are shared by many influential people, they are worth a moment's consideration.

Like that of most Americans, his philosophy is based on optimism. "The good old times" were not "good old times" according to him. The present state of things must be accepted and utilized just as it is. Communism is absurd; there is no alternative for the great employers of labor between ruin and an immense fortune. But they should consider themselves only as the trustees or administrators and use their wealth for the common good. When they have expended what is necessary for the comfortable maintenance and education of their family, the surplus ought to be applied by them to public interests.

There are but three modes of disposing of surplus wealth: it can be left to the family of the decedents, it can be bequeathed for public purposes, or it can be distributed by its possessors during their lives. Parents should of course educate their children and give them as far as possible the means of earning their own livelihood; and — an important consideration — it is also just to provide for them in moderation, if they accept the highly commendable mission of laboring for public ends without regard to pecuniary considerations. Beyond this, he considers it most injudicious for men to leave great fortunes to their children, as great sums bequeathed often work more for the injury than for the good of the recipients.

On the other hand, to bequeath one's fortune by will shows that a man is content to wait until he is dead before he becomes of much use in the world; and he is not to be extolled for doing what he cannot help. For what merit is there in such forced benevolence? From all this, Mr. Carnegie concludes that a graduated inheritance tax is a wise and salutary measure. According to him, the third mode of employing wealth is the only one worthy of a man, a Christian, and a good citizen. . . .

Like the Fathers of the Church, our American millionaire extols the happiness of laboring for the good of his fellows; and he seeks his ideal in the teaching of Christ. But he desires that one should recognize the changed conditions of this age and reproduce the spirit rather than the letter of the Gospel. Nine-tenths of the money spent in indiscriminate charity is wasted, and probably often does more harm than good. Everyone has, of course, met with individual cases where timely aid may be of real benefit; but it is society, and not the wealthy man, which has the mission of helping the really destitute. The individual administrator of his surplus wealth should aid those who are striving courageously, should assist those who desire to rise, but rarely or never should he do all. His role is to multiply, for those who wish to profit by them, the means of improvement, both physical and moral — everything, in fact, which tends to develop the education of the people, such as public institutions of various kinds, parks, baths, medical schools, picture galleries, universities.

But besides this, the wealthy man should devote himself, his time, and his experience to the wise administration of his gifts so that they should not have a degrading or pauperizing effect on the recipients. In the case of a library or a park, for instance, he should insist on the community being taxed to maintain them, as an endowed institution is liable to become the prey of a clique. Such is the solution which Mr. Carnegie offers to the mysterious difficulties which seem to bar the kingdom of Heaven to the rich.

11.

Jack London: How I Became a Socialist

At the peak of his popularity as a writer of fiction, Jack London began to lecture and to publish tracts on the American free-enterprise system. His negative attitude toward capitalism, and especially toward vast concentrations of unearned wealth, finally led him to socialism. The following selection, taken from his book War of the Classes, *published in 1905, tells of his conversion.*

Source: *War of the Classes*, New York, 1905, pp. 267-278.

It is quite fair to say that I became a Socialist in a fashion somewhat similar to the way in which the Teutonic pagans became Christians — it was hammered into me. Not only was I not looking for Socialism at the time of my conversion but I was fighting it. I was very young and callow, did not know much of anything, and though I had never even heard of a school called "Individualism," I sang the paean of the strong with all my heart.

This was because I was strong myself. By strong I mean that I had good health and hard muscles, both of which possessions are easily accounted for. I had lived my childhood on California ranches, my boyhood hustling newspapers on the streets of a healthy Western city, and my youth on the ozone-laden waters of San Francisco Bay and the Pacific Ocean. I loved life in the open, and I toiled in the open, at the hardest kinds of work. Learning no trade, but drifting along from job to job, I looked on the world and called it good, every bit of it. Let me repeat, this optimism was because I was healthy and strong, bothered with neither aches nor weaknesses, never turned down by the boss because I did not look fit, able always to get a job at shoveling coal, sailorizing, or manual labor of some sort.

And because of all this, exulting in my young life, able to hold my own at work or fight, I was a rampant individualist. It was very natural. I was a winner. Wherefore I called the game, as I saw it played, or thought I saw it played, a very proper game for MEN. To be a MAN was to write man in large capitals on my heart. To adventure like a man, and fight like a man, and do a man's work (even for a boy's pay) — these were things that reached right in and gripped hold of me as no other thing could. And I looked ahead into long vistas of a hazy and interminable future, into which, playing what I conceived to be MAN'S game, I should continue to travel with unfailing health, without accidents, and with muscles ever vigorous. As I say, this future was interminable. I could see myself only raging through life without end like one of Nietzsche's *blond beasts,* lustfully roving and conquering by sheer superiority and strength.

As for the unfortunates, the sick and ailing and old and maimed, I must confess I hardly thought of them at all, save that I vaguely felt that they, barring accidents, could be as good as I if they wanted to real hard, and could work just as well. Accidents? Well, they represented FATE, also spelled out in capitals, and there was no getting around FATE. Napoleon had had an accident at Waterloo, but that did not dampen my desire to be another and later Napoleon. Further, the optimism bred of a

The Bettmann Archive

Jack London, photographed about 1905

stomach which could digest scrap iron and a body which flourished on hardships did not permit me to consider accidents as even remotely related to my glorious personality.

I hope I have made it clear that I was proud to be one of nature's strong-armed noblemen. The dignity of labor was to me the most impressive thing in the world. Without having read Carlyle or Kipling, I formulated a gospel of work which put theirs in the shade. Work was everything. It was sanctification and salvation. The pride I took in a hard day's work well done would be inconceivable to you. It is almost inconceivable to me as I look back upon it. I was as faithful a wage slave as ever capitalist exploited. To shirk or malinger on the man who paid me my wages was a sin, first, against myself, and, second, against him. I considered it a crime second only to treason, and just about as bad.

In short, my joyous individualism was dominated by the orthodox bourgeois ethics. I read the bourgeois papers, listened to the bourgeois preachers, and shouted at the sonorous platitudes of the bourgeois politicians. And I doubt not, if other events had not changed my career, that I should have evolved into a professional strikebreaker (one of President Eliot's American heroes) and had my head and my earning power irrevocably smashed by a club in the hands of some militant trades unionist.

Just about this time, returning from a seven months' voyage before the mast, and just turned eighteen, I took it into my head to go tramping. On rods and blind baggages I fought my way from the open West, where men bulked big and the job hunted the man, to the congested labor centers of the East, where men were small potatoes and hunted the job for all they were worth. And on this new *blond-beast* adventure I found myself looking upon life from a new and totally different angle. I had dropped down from the proletariat into what sociologists love to call the "submerged tenth," and I was startled to discover the way in which that submerged tenth was recruited.

I found there all sorts of men, many of whom had once been as good as myself and just as *blond-beastly;* sailormen, soldiermen, labormen, all wrenched and distorted and twisted out of shape by toil and hardship and accident, and cast adrift by their masters like so many old horses. I battered on the drag and slammed backgates with them, or shivered with them in boxcars and city parks, listening the while to life histories which began under auspices as fair as mine, with digestions and bodies equal to and better than mine, and which ended there before my eyes in the shambles at the bottom of the Social Pit.

And as I listened my brain began to work. The woman of the streets and the man of the gutter drew very close to me. I saw the picture of the Social Pit as vividly as though it were a concrete thing, and at the bottom of the Pit I saw them, myself above them, not far, and hanging on to the slippery wall by main strength and sweat. And I confess a terror seized me. What

when my strength failed, when I should be unable to work shoulder to shoulder with the strong men who were as yet babes unborn?

And there and then I swore a great oath. It ran something like this: *All my days have worked hard with my body, and according to the number of days I have worked, by just that much am I nearer the bottom of the Pit. I shall climb out of the Pit, but not by the muscles of my body shall I climb out. I shall do no more hard work, and may God strike me dead if I do another day's hard work with my body more than I absolutely have to do.* And I have been busy ever since running away from hard work.

Incidentally, while tramping some 10,000 miles through the United States and Canada, I strayed into Niagara Falls, was nabbed by a fee-hunting constable, denied the right to plead guilty or not guilty, sentenced out of hand to thirty days' imprisonment for having no fixed abode and no visible means of support, handcuffed and chained to a bunch of men similarly circumstanced, carted down country to Buffalo, registered at the Erie County Penitentiary, had my head clipped and my budding mustache shaved, was dressed in convict stripes, compulsorily vaccinated by a medical student who practised on such as we, made to march the lockstep, and put to work under the eyes of guards armed with Winchester rifles — all for adventuring in *blond-beastly* fashion. Concerning further details deponent sayeth not, though he may hint that some of his plethoric national patriotism simmered down and leaked out of the bottom of his soul somewhere — at least, since that experience he finds that he cares more for men and women and little children than for imaginary geographical lines.

To return to my conversion. I think it is apparent that my rampant individualism was pretty effectively hammered out of me, and something else as effectively hammered in. But, just as I had been an individualist without knowing it, I was now a Socialist without knowing it, withal, an unscientific one. I had been reborn, but not renamed, and I was running around to find out what manner of thing I was. I ran back to California and opened the books. I do not remember which ones I opened first. It is an unimportant detail anyway. I was already It, whatever It was, and by aid of the books I discovered that It was a Socialist. Since that day I have opened many books, but no economic argument, no lucid demonstration of the logic and inevitableness of Socialism affects me as profoundly and convincingly as I was affected on the day when I first saw the walls of the Social Pit rise around me and felt myself slipping down, down, into the shambles at the bottom.

12.

VINCENT BRYAN: "In My Merry Oldsmobile"

Ransom E. Olds founded the Olds Motor Works in the 1890s, and it soon began production of the Oldsmobile. As a publicity stunt, Olds sent two of his cars across the country to the Lewis and Clark Exposition in Portland, Oregon, in 1905. The hazardous journey over muddy, pitted roads attracted the public's attention, and Vincent Bryan, one of Tin Pan Alley's leading lyricists, collaborated with the famous showman Gus Edwards to produce a song commemorating the feat. "In My Merry Oldsmobile" helped make the Oldsmobile famous in the country for years to come.

IN MY MERRY OLDSMOBILE

Young Johnnie Steel has an Oldsmobile;
  He loves a dear little girl;
She is the queen of his gas machine;
  She has his heart in a whirl.
Now when they go for a spin, you know,
  She tries to learn the auto, so
He lets her steer while he gets her ear
  And whispers soft and low:

They love to spark in the dark old park
  As they go flying along.
She says she knows why the motor goes —
  The sparker's awfully strong.
Each day they spoon to the engine's tune —
  Their honeymoon will happen soon.
He'll win Lucile with his Oldsmobile
  And then he'll fondly croon:

Chorus:
"Come away with me Lucile,
In my merry Oldsmobile.
Down the road of life we'll fly,
Automobubbling you and I.
To the church we'll swiftly steal,
Then our wedding bells will peal;
You can go as far as you like with me,
In my merry Oldsmobile."

1906

13.

WILLIAM P. HEPBURN: Regulation of Railroad Rates

Congress' attempt to regulate the railroads through the creation of the Interstate Commerce Commission in 1887 had proved largely ineffectual. In 1905 and 1906 a new interest in tighter governmental control led to the passage of the Hepburn Act. Named for its sponsor, Representative William Hepburn of Iowa, the act empowered the commission to regulate rates after complaints were registered by dissatisfied shippers. Hepburn stated his position in a speech to the House on February 7, 1906, a portion of which is reprinted here. He wanted neither to strip the railroads of all their rate-making powers nor to keep the commission the weak regulating body that it was.

Source: *Record,* 59 Cong., 1 Sess., p. 2253.

MR. CHAIRMAN, this is a great question. Any proposition of law that involves an interest so great as the railway interests of the United States ought to be regarded with solicitude by those who are charged with responsibility in that behalf.

One-twelfth of all the wealth in the United States is involved in greater or less degree in this bill. The earnings of the railways are so colossal that $2,100,000,000 mark the amount of this great interest in one year. Our whole wealth production is but ten times more than that. Think how colossal this is. But the aggregate of investments, the aggregate of annual earnings does not mark fairly the importance of this subject to the American people. Think how dependent we are for our prosperity, for the comforts of life even, upon the common carriers of the land. Think of the infinite

of the transactions between the carriers and those they serve — millions and millions of transactions.

And yet, Mr. Chairman, the gentleman from Massachusetts [Mr. McCall] announced the astonishing doctrine that with all these varied and varying interests, with all of these interests, the people cannot separate themselves from, they cannot separate their connection with, the railways — yet in all of these multiplied transactions there shall be no practical arbiter, no one to settle disputes except one of the parties in interest. . . .

The courts [have] proved inadequate because of these reasons: The subject of the controversy in all of the cases that I can conceive is an involved one to the plaintiff; the knowledge and information that would enable the plaintiff to maintain his action for an overcharge are not in his possession. He could not give that expert testimony as to all the elements that would enter into the composition of a just and reasonable charge or an overcharge while a knowledge of all these facts are in the hands of his adversary, and therefore he could not recover.

That is one of the difficulties, not with the courts but because of the peculiarities of the subject of controversy. The courts have not been adequate and therefore some other means had to be substituted. With what abhorrence would we look upon a proposition, if gentlemen should make it, with reference to controversies other than of this class that were certain to rise and be numerous in the community, providing that one of the parties alone should determine the rightfulness of the controversy; and yet that is what is involved in all of these multitudes of possible disputes between carrier and shipper.

It is the carrier that fixes the rate. He imposes upon the other party the necessity of accepting his rate. There is no escape from it. He may pay the charge and then the common law, says the gentleman from Maine [Mr. Littlefield], gives him a remedy and allows him to recover for the overcharge. Ah, how barren is that remedy, and while it is a known fact that the cases where such suits might be instituted are counted by millions, none is ever brought because of the expense, because of the delay, because of the inability to secure the proof whereby a judgment is within the limits of possibility. Therefore it is futile to talk about the courts as they are constituted furnishing that remedy that ought to be somewhere existent.

Now, what do we do by this bill? The gentlemen who oppose it have discussed it as though it conferred upon the Railway Commission the power to establish schedules and rates. They have, I think, sometimes purposely set up this bogie for the purpose of combating it. No one has proposed that. The jurisdiction of the commission is limited, as is its power limited, by this law. They cannot at pleasure establish a rate. Before their jurisdiction attaches it must be ascertained that a wrong has been

"Congress — Who's In It and Who Owns It"; cartoon by Jacob Burck reflecting the opinion that big money interests were able to maneuver the politicians

done, an overcharge has been made, a wrong in an extravagant, unreasonable rate, because the law today and the common law provide that the carriers' charge shall be just and reasonable. That is the limit to which he is permitted to go in fixing his tariff of schedules.

Now, under the operation of this bill, if it should become a law, it is necessary for someone to allege a violation of the statute — that a crime, in other words, has been done — because the overcharge is a crime, as well as being prohibited, and remedies furnished civilly by the courts. He has committed a crime. What then? Investigation follows, and if it is ascertained that the carrier is in violation of the law, then the jurisdiction of the commission attaches, and it is permitted to do what? Fix a rate? Oh, no;

oh, no. It is permitted to establish a just, reasonable, and fairly remunerative rate that shall be the maximum rate that the carrier shall charge. That is all.

Can you think of any legislative effort in the direction of control more conservative than this? First, the carrier must be in the wrong — the carrier must be a criminal. His criminality must be ascertained. When it is ascertained by a dispassionate commission, then a rate within limitations, fair and certain and well-defined, may be established as the maximum that the carrier may charge, leaving the feature of flexibility still remaining in the rate, and permitting the carrier to charge that lower sum that the exigencies of business or the activities of competition may make it prudent and wise for him to adopt.

14.

FINLEY PETER DUNNE: Lithrachoor and Andhrew Carnaygie

Between 1898 and 1910 Finley Peter Dunne was the leading satirist of American life and customs. His two colorful characters, Mr. Dooley, an Irish saloonkeeper, and Mr. Hennessy, the saloon's most faithful customer, discoursed in often biting terms on war, politics, religion, and the famous personalities of the time. In 1906 Dunne allowed Dooley and Hennessy to discuss Andrew Carnegie's widely admired philanthropic enterprise: the donation of libraries to cities and towns around the country. Mr. Dooley explained that a Carnegie library was "a large, brown-stone, impenethrible buildin' with th' name iv th' maker blown on th' dure" — but he also pointed out that the libraries were often empty because Carnegie had neglected to donate any books.

Source: *Dissertations by Mr. Dooley*, New York, 1906: "The Carnegie Libraries."

"HAS ANDHREW CARNAYGIE given ye a libry yet?" asked Mr. Dooley.

"Not that I know iv," said Mr. Hennessy.

"He will," said Mr. Dooley. "Ye'll not escape him. Befure he dies he hopes to crowd a libry on ivry man, woman, an'

child in th' counthry. He's given them to cities, towns, villages, an' whistlin' stations. They're tearin' down gas-houses an' poor-houses to put up libries. Befure another year, ivry house in Pittsburg that ain't a blast-furnace will be a Carnaygie libry. In some places all th' buildin's is libries. If ye

write him f'r an autygraft he sinds ye a libry. No beggar is iver turned impty-handed
fr'm th' dure. Th' pan-handler knocks an'
asts f'r a glass iv milk an' a roll. 'No, sir,'
says Andhrew Carnaygie. 'I will not pauperize this onworthy man. Nawthin' is
worse f'r a beggar-man thin to make a pauper iv him. Yet it shall not be said iv me
that I give nawthin' to th' poor. Saunders,
give him a libry, an' if he still insists on a
roll tell him to roll th' libry. F'r I'm humorous as well as wise,' he says.''

"Does he give th' books that go with
it?" asked Mr. Hennessy.

"Books?" said Mr. Dooley. "What ar-re
ye talkin' about? D'ye know what a libry
is? I suppose ye think it's a place where a
man can go, haul down wan iv his fav'rite
authors fr'm th' shelf, an' take a nap in it.
That's not a Carnaygie libry. A Carnaygie
libry is a large, brown-stone, impenethrible
buildin' with th' name iv th' maker blown
on th' dure. Libry, fr'm th' Greek wurruds,
libus, a book, an' ary, sildom, — sildom a
book. A Carnaygie libry is archytechoor,
not lithrachoor. Lithrachoor will be ripri-
sinted. Th' most cillybrated dead authors
will be honored be havin' their names
painted on th' wall in distinguished comp-
'ny, as thus: Andhrew Carnaygie, Shakespeare; Andhrew Carnaygie, Byron; Andhrew Carnaygie, Bobby Burns; Andhrew
Carnaygie, an' so on. Ivry author is guaranteed a place next to pure readin' matther
like a bakin'-powdher advertisemint, so that
whin a man comes along that niver heerd iv
Shakespeare he'll know he was somebody,
because there he is on th' wall. That's th'
dead authors. Th' live authors will stand
outside an' wish they were dead.

"He's havin' gr-reat spoort with it. I r-
read his speech th' other day, whin he laid
th' corner-stone iv th' libry at Pianola, Ioway. Th' entire popylation iv this lithry cin-
ter gathered to see an' hear him. There was
th' postmaster an' his wife, th' blacksmith
an' his fam'ly, the station agent, mine host
iv th' Farmers' Exchange, an' some sthray

live stock. 'Ladies an' gintlemen,' says he.
'Modesty compels me to say nawthin' on
this occasion, but I am not to be bulldoz-
ed,' he says. 'I can't tell ye how much pleasure I take in disthributin' monymints to th'
humble name around which has gathered so
manny hon'rable associations with mesilf. I
have been a very busy little man all me life,
but I like hard wurruk, an' givin' away me
money is th' hardest wurruk I iver did. It
fairly makes me teeth ache to part with it.
But there's wan consolation. I cheer mesilf
with th' thought that no matther how
much money I give it don't do anny particular person anny good. Th' worst thing ye
can do f'r anny man is to do him good. I
pass by th' organ-grinder on th' corner with
a savage glare. I bate th' monkey on th'
head whin he comes up smilin' to me window, an' hurl him down on his impecyoon-
yous owner. None iv me money goes into
th' little tin cup. I cud kick a hospital, an' I
lave Wall Sthreet to look afther th' widow
an' th' orphan. Th' submerged tenth, thim
that can't get hold iv a good chunk iv th'
goods, I wud cut off fr'm th' rest iv th'
wurruld an' prevint fr'm bearin' th' haughty
name iv papa or th' still lovelier name iv
ma. So far I've got on'y half me wish in
this matther.

" 'I don't want poverty an' crime to go
on. I intind to stop it. But how? It's been
holdin' its own f'r cinchries. Some iv th' gr-
reatest iv former minds has undertook to
prevint it an' has failed. They didn't know
how. Modesty wud prevint me agin fr'm
sayin' that I know how, but that's nayether
here nor there. I do. Th' way to abolish
poverty an' bust crime is to put up a
brown-stone buildin' in ivry town in th'
counthry with me name over it. That's th'
way. I suppose th' raison it wasn't thried
befure was that no man iver had such a
name. 'Tis thrue me efforts is not appre-
cyated ivrywhere. I offer a city a libry, an'
oftentimes it replies an' asts me f'r something to pay off th' school debt. I rayceive
degraded pettyshuns fr'm so-called proud

Finley Peter Dunne, American humorist who wrote under the name of Mr. Dooley; caricature by "Spy"

methropolises f'r a gas-house in place iv a libry. I pass thim by with scorn. All I ask iv a city in rayturn f'r a fifty-thousan'-dollar libry is that it shall raise wan millyon dollars to maintain th' buildin' an' keep me name shiny, an' if it won't do that much f'r lithrachoor, th' divvle take it, it's onworthy iv th' name iv an American city. What ivry community needs is taxes an' lithrachoor. I give thim both. Three cheers f'r a libry an' a bonded debt! Lithrachoor, taxation, an' Andhrew Carnaygie, wan an' insiprable, now an' foriver! They'se nawthin' so good as a good book. It's betther thin food; it's betther thin money. I have made money an' books, an' I like me books betther thin me money. Others don't, but I do. With these few wurruds I will con-clude. Modesty wud prevint me fr'm sayin' more, but I have to catch a thrain, an' cannot go on. I stake ye to this libry, which ye will have as soon as ye raise th' money to keep it goin'. Stock it with useful readin', an' some day ye're otherwise pauper an' criminal childher will come to know me name whin I am gone an' there's no wan left to tell it thim.'

"Whin th' historyan comes to write th' histhry iv th' West he'll say: 'Pianola, Ioway, was a prosperous town till th' failure iv th' corn crop in nineteen hundherd an' wan, an' th' Carnaygie libry in nineteen hundred an' two. Th' govermint ast f'r thirty dollars to pave Main Sthreet with wooden blocks, but th' gr-reat philanthropist was firm, an' the libry was sawed off on th' town. Th' public schools, th' wurruk-house, th' wather wurruks, an' th' other penal instichoochions was at wanst closed, an' th' people begun to wurruk to support th' libry. In five years th' popylation had deserted th' town to escape taxation, an' now, as Mr. Carnaygie promised, poverty an' crime has been abolished in th' place, th' janitor iv th' buildin' bein' honest an' well paid.'

"Isn't it good f'r lithrachoor, says ye? Sure, I think not, Hinnissy. Libries niver encouraged lithrachoor anny more thin tombstones encourage livin'. No wan iver wrote annythin' because he was tol' that a hundherd years fr'm now his books might be taken down fr'm a shelf in a granite sepulcher an' some wan wud write 'Good' or 'This man is crazy' in th' margin. What lithrachoor needs is fillin' food. If Andhrew wud put a kitchen in th' libries an' build some bunks or even swing a few hammocks where livin' authors cud crawl in at night an' sleep while waitin' f'r this enlightened nation to wake up an' discover th' Shakespeares now on th' turf, he wud be givin' a rale boost to lithrachoor. With th' smoke curlin' fr'm th' chimbley, an' hundherds iv potes settin' aroun' a table loaded down with pancakes an' talkin' pothry an' prize-fightin', with hundherds iv other potes stacked up nately in th' sleepin'-rooms an' snorin' in wan gran' chorus, with their wives holdin' down good-payin' jobs as libraryans or cooks, an' their happy little childher playin' through th' marble corrydors, Andhrew Carnaygie wud not have lived in vain. Maybe that's th' on'y way he knows how to live. I don't believe in libries. They pauperize lithrachoor. I'm f'r helpin' th' boys that's now on th' job. I know a pote in Halsted Sthreet that wanst wrote a pome beginnin', 'All th' wealth iv Ind,' that he sold to a magazine f'r two dollars, payable on publycation. Lithroachoor don't need advancin'. What it needs is advances f'r th' lithrachoors. Ye can't shake down posterity f'r th' price.

"All th' same, I like Andhrew Carnaygie. Him an' me ar-re agreed on that point. I like him because he ain't shamed to give publicly. Ye don't find him puttin' on false whiskers an' turnin' up his coat-collar whin he goes out to be benivolent. No, sir. Ivry time he dhrops a dollar it makes a noise like a waither fallin' down-stairs with a tray iv dishes. He's givin' th' way we'd all like to give. I niver put annything in th' poor-box, but I wud if Father Kelly wud rig up like wan iv them slot-machines, so that whin I stuck in a nickel me name wud appear over th' altar in red letthers. But whin I put a dollar in th' plate I get back about two yards an' hurl it so hard that th' good man turns around to see who done it. Do good be stealth, says I, but see that th' burglar-alarm is set. Anny benivolent money I hand out I want to talk about me. Him that giveth to th' poor, they say, lindeth to th' Lord; but in these days we look f'r quick returns on our invistmints. I like Andhrew Carnaygie, an', as he says, he puts his whole soul into th' wurruk."

"What's he mane be that?" asked Mr. Hennessy.

"He manes," said Mr. Dooley, "that he's gin'rous. Ivry time he gives a libry he gives himsilf away in a speech."

15.

David Graham Phillips: The Political Trust

David Phillips' "The Treason of the Senate," published in 1906, was a muckraking sensation. Going into dramatic and vivid detail, Phillips exposed the alliance between influential senators and big business interests. The following selection focuses upon the "treachery" (according to Phillips) of one important senator, Nelson W. Aldrich of Rhode Island. Aldrich, a veteran senator with twenty-five years' experience, was one of the group of Old Guard Republicans that dominated Congress from about 1880 to 1910. Phillips accused Aldrich of being the head of the Senate group that thwarted all social welfare legislation and kept the Congress of the United States a distinctly unrepresentative body. Phillips' exposé first appeared in Cosmopolitan *magazine from February through November 1906.*

Source: *Cosmopolitan,* April 1906.

For the organizer of this treason we must look at Nelson W. Aldrich, senior senator from Rhode Island.

Rhode Island is the smallest of our states in area and thirty-fourth in population — 1,250 square miles, less than 500,000 people, barely 70,000 voters with the rolls padded by the Aldrich machine. But size and numbers are nothing; it contains as many sturdy Americans proportionately as any other state. Its bad distinction of supplying the enemy with a bold leader is due to its ancient and aristocratic constitution, changed once, away back before the middle of the last century, but still an archaic document for class rule.

The apportionment of legislators is such that one-eleventh of the population, and they the most ignorant and most venal, elect a majority of the legislature — which means that they elect the two United States senators. Each city and township counts as a political unit; thus, the five cities that together have two-thirds of the population are in an overwhelming minority before twenty almost vacant rural townships — their total population is not 37,000 — where the ignorance is even illiterate, where the superstition is medieval, where tradition and custom have made the vote an article of legitimate merchandising.

The combination of bribery and party prejudice is potent everywhere; but there come crises when these fail "the interests" for the moment. No storm of popular rage, however, could unseat the senators from Rhode Island. The people of Rhode Island might, as a people and voting almost unanimously, elect a governor; but not a legislature. Bribery is a weapon forbidden those who stand for right and justice — who "fights the devil with fire" gives him choice of weapons, and must lose to him, though seeming to win. A few thousand dollars put in the experienced hands of the heelers and the senatorial general agent of "the interests" is secure for another six years.

The Aldrich machine controls the legislature, the election boards, the courts — the entire machinery of the "republican form of government." In 1904, when Aldrich needed a legislature to reelect him for his fifth consecutive term, it is estimated that carrying the state cost about $200,000 — a small sum easily to be got back by a few minutes of industrious pocket-picking in Wall Street; but a very large sum for Rhode Island politics, and a happy augury of a future day, remote, perhaps, but inevitable, when the people shall rule in Rhode Island. Despite the bribery, despite the swindling on registration lists and all the chicane which the statute book of the state makes easy for "the interests," Aldrich elected his governor by a scant 800 on the face of the returns. His legislature was, of course, got without the least difficulty — the majority for "the interests" is on joint ballot 75 out of a total of 117.

The only reason Aldrich disturbed himself about the governorship was that, through the anger of the people and the carelessness of the machine, a people's governor had been elected in 1903 and was up for reelection; this people's governor, while without any power whatever under the constitution, still could make disagreeable demands on the legislature, demands which did not sound well in the ears of the country and roused the people everywhere to just what was the source of the most respectable politician's security. So, Aldrich, contrary to his habit in recent years, took personal charge of the campaign and tried to show the people of Rhode Island that they were helpless and might as well quiet down, accept their destiny and spare his henchmen the expense and labor of wholesale bribery and fraud.

But, as a rule, Aldrich no longer concerns himself with Rhode Island's petty local affairs. "Not until about a year or so before it comes time for him to be elected again does he get active," says his chief henchman, Gen. Charles R. Brayton, the state's boss. "He doesn't pay much attention to details." Why should he? Politically, the state is securely "the interests" and his; financially, "the interests" and he have incorporated and assured to themselves in perpetuity about all the graft — the Rhode Island Securities Company, capitalized at and paying excellent dividends upon $39 million, representing an actual value of less than $9 million, owns, thanks to the munificence of the legislature, the state's street and trolley lines, gas and electric franchises, etc., etc.

It began in a street railway company of Providence in which Aldrich, president of the Providence Council and afterwards member of the legislature, acquired an interest. The sugar trust's Searles put in $1,500,000 shortly after the sugar trust got its license to loot through Aldrich at Washington; the legislature passed the necessary laws and gave the necessary franchises; Senator Steve Elkins and his crowd were invited in; more legislation; more franchises, more stocks and bonds, the right to loot the people of the state in perpetuity. Yes, Aldrich is rich, enormously rich, and his mind is wholly free for the schemes he plots and executes at Washington. And, like all the other senators who own large blocks of stocks and bonds in the great drainage companies fastened upon America's prosperity, his service is not the less diligent or adroit because he himself draws huge dividends from the people.

EARLY TRAINING OF ALDRICH

HE WAS BORN in 1841, is only sixty-four years old, good for another fifteen years, at least, in his present rugged health, before "the interests" will have to select another for his safe seat and treacherous task. He began as a grocery boy, got the beginning of one kind of education in the public schools and in an academy at East Greenwich, Rhode Island. He became clerk in a fish store in Providence, then clerk in a grocery, then bookkeeper, partner, and is still a wholesale grocer. He was elected to the legislature, applied himself so diligently to the work of getting his real education that he soon won the confidence of the boss, then Senator Anthony, and was sent to Congress, where he was Anthony's successor as boss and chief agent of the Rhode Island interests. He entered the United States Senate in 1881.

In 1901 his daughter married the only

"The Making of a Senator: When Will the People Stand from Under?"; cartoon from "Puck"

son and destined successor of John D. Rockefeller. Thus, the chief exploiter of the American people is closely allied by marriage with the chief schemer in the service of their exploiters. This fact no American should ever lose sight of. It is a political fact; it is an economic fact. It places the final and strongest seal upon the bonds uniting Aldrich and "the interests."

When Aldrich entered the Senate twenty-five years ago at the splendid full age of forty, the world was just beginning to feel the effects of the principles of concentration and combination, which were inexorably and permanently established with the discoveries in steam and electricity that make the whole human race more and more like one community of interdependent neighbors. It was a moment of opportunity, an unprecedented chance for Congress, especially its deliberate and supposedly sagacious senators, to "promote the general welfare" by giving those principles free and just play in securing the benefits of expanding prosperity to all, by seeing that the profits from the cooperation of all the people went *to* the people. Aldrich and the traitor Senate saw the opportunity. But they saw in it only a chance to enable a class to despoil the masses.

Before he reached the Senate, Aldrich had fifteen years of training in how to legislate the proceeds of the labor of the many into the pockets of the few. He entered it as the representative of local interests engaged in robbing by means of slyly worded tariff schedules that changed protection against the foreigner into plunder of the native. His demonstrated excellent talents for sly, slippery work in legislative chambers and committee rooms and his security in his seat against popular revulsions and outbursts together marked him for the position of chief agent of the predatory band which was rapidly forming to take care of the prosperity of the American people.

Various senators represent various divisions and subdivisions of this colossus. But Aldrich, rich through franchise grabbing, the intimate of Wall Street's great robber barons, the father-in-law of the only son of *the* Rockefeller — Aldrich represents the colossus. Your first impression of many and conflicting interests has disappeared. You now see a single interest, with a single agent-in-chief to execute its single purpose — getting rich at the expense of the labor and the independence of the American people. And the largest head among the many heads of this monster is that of Rockefeller, father of the only son-in-law of Aldrich and his intimate in all the relations of life!

There are many passages in the Constitution in which a Senate, true to its oath and mindful of the welfare of the people and of the nation, could find mandates to stop wholesale robbery and similar practices.

And yet, what has the Senate done — the Senate, with its high-flown pretenses of reverence for the Constitution? It has so legislated and so refrained from legislating that more than half of all the wealth created by the American people belongs to less than 1 percent of them; that the income of the average American family has sunk to less than $600 a year; that of our more than 27 million children of school age, less than 12 million go to school, and more than 2 million work in mines, shops, and factories.

And the leader, the boss of the Senate for the past twenty years has been — Aldrich!

In vain would "the interests" have stolen franchises, in vain would they have corrupted the public officials of states and cities if they had not got absolute and unshakable control of the Senate. But, with the Senate theirs, how secure, how easy, and how rich the loot!

SOURCE OF HIS POWER

THE SOLE SOURCE of Aldrich's power over the senators is "the interests" — the sole source, but quite sufficient to make him permanent and undisputed boss. Many of the senators, as we shall in due time and in detail note, are, like Depew and Platt, the direct agents of the various state or sectional subdivisions of "the interests," and these senators constitute about two-thirds of the entire Senate. Of the remainder, several know that if they should oppose "the interests" they would lose their seats; several others are silent because they feel that to speak out would be useless; a few do speak out, but are careful not to infringe upon the rigid rule of "senatorial courtesy," which thus effectually protects unblushing corruptionists like Aldrich, obsequious servants of corruption like Spooner, traitors to party as well as the people like Gorman, from having disagreeable truths dinged into their ears.

Tillman will "pitchfork" a president but not a senator, and not the Senate in any but the most useless, futile way — this, though none knows better than he how the rights and the property of the people are trafficked in by his colleagues of both parties, with a few exceptions. There are a few other honest men from the South and from the West, as many of the few honest Republicans as honest Democrats. Yet party allegiance and "senatorial courtesy" make them abettors of treason, allies of Aldrich and Gorman.

"Senatorial courtesy!" We shall have to return to it, as it is the hypocritical mask behind which the few senators who pose as real representatives of the people hide in silence and inaction.

The greatest single hold of "the interests" is the fact that they are the "campaign contributors" — the men who supply the money for "keeping the party together" and for "getting out the vote." Did you ever think where the millions for watchers, spellbinders, halls, processions, posters, pamphlets, that are spent in national, state, and local campaigns, come from? Who pays the big election expenses of your congressman, of the men you send to the legislature to elect senators? Do you imagine those who foot those huge bills are fools? Don't you know that they make sure of getting their money back, with interest, compound upon compound?

Your candidates get most of the money for their campaigns from the party committees; and the central party committee is the national committee with which congressional and state and local committees are affiliated. The bulk of the money for the "political trust" comes from "the interests." "The interests" will give only to the "political trust." And that means Aldrich and his Democratic (!) lieutenant, Gorman of Maryland, leader of the minority in the Senate. Aldrich, then, is the head of the "political trust" and Gorman is his right-hand man. When you speak of the Republican Party, of the Democratic Party, of the

"good of the party," of the "best interests of the party," of "wise party policy," you mean what Aldrich and Gorman, acting for their clients, deem wise and proper and "Republican" or "Democratic."

To relate the treason in detail would mean taking up bill after bill and going through it, line by line, word by word, and showing how this interpolation there or that excision yonder meant millions on millions more to this or that interest, millions on millions less for the people as merchants, wage or salary earners, consumers; how the killing of this measure meant immunity to looters all along the line; how the alteration of the wording of that other "trifling" resolution gave a quarter of a cent a pound on every one of hundreds of millions of pounds of some necessary of life to a certain small group of men; how this innocent-looking little measure safeguarded the railway barons in looting the whole American people by excessive charges and rebates. Few among the masses have the patience to listen to these dull matters — and, so, "the interests" and their agents have prosperity and honor instead of justice and jail.

No railway legislation that was not either helpful to or harmless against "the interests"; no legislation on the subject of corporations that would interfere with "the interests" which use the corporate form to simplify and systematize their stealing; no legislation on the tariff question unless it secured to "the interests" full and free license to loot; no investigations of wholesale robbery or of any of the evils resulting from it — there you have in a few words the whole story of the Senate's treason under Aldrich's leadership, and of why property is concentrating in the hands of the few and the little children of the masses are being sent to toil in the darkness of mines, in the dreariness and unhealthfulness of factories instead of being sent to school; and why the great middle class — the old-fashioned Americans, the people with the incomes of from $2,000 to $15,000 a year — is being swiftly crushed into dependence and the repulsive miseries of "genteel poverty." The heavy and ever heavier taxes of "the interests" are swelling rents, swelling the prices of food, clothing, fuel, all the necessities, and all the necessary comforts. And the Senate both forbids the lifting of those taxes and levies fresh taxes for its master.

A JUGGLER OF LEGISLATION

How DOES ALDRICH WORK? Obviously, not much steering is necessary when the time comes to vote. "The interests" have a majority and to spare. The only questions are such as permitting a senator to vote and at times to speak against "the interests" when the particular measure is mortally offensive to the people of his particular state or section. Those daily sham battles in the Senate! Those paradings of sham virtue! Is it not strange that the other senators, instead of merely busying themselves at writing letters or combing their whiskers, do not break into shouts of laughter?

Aldrich's real work — getting the wishes of his principals, directly or through their lawyers, and putting these wishes into proper form if they are orders for legislation or into the proper channels if they are orders to kill or emasculate legislation — this work is all done, of course, behind the scenes. When Aldrich is getting orders, there is of course never any witness. The second part of his task — execution — is in part a matter of whispering with his chief lieutenants, in part a matter of consultation in the secure secrecy of the Senate committee rooms.

Aldrich is in person chairman of the chief Senate committee — Finance. There he labors, assisted by Gorman, his right bower, who takes his place as chairman when the Democrats are in power; by Spooner, his

left bower and public mouthpiece; by Allison, that Nestor of craft; by the Pennsylvania Railroad's Penrose; by Tom Platt of New York, corruptionist and lifelong agent of corruptionists; by Joe Bailey of Texas, and several other sympathetic or silent spirits. Together they concoct and sugar-coat the bitter doses for the people — the loot measures and the suffocating of the measures in restraint of loot. In the unofficial but powerful steering committee — which receives from him the will of "the interests" and translates it into "party policy" — he works through Allison as chairman, but Allison's position is recognized as purely honorary.

Also, Aldrich sits in the powerful Interstate Commerce Committee; there, he has his "pal," the brazen Elkins of West Virginia, as chairman. He is not on the Committee on Appropriations; but Allison is — is its chairman — and Cullom of Illinois is there — and in due time we shall endeavor to get better acquainted with both of them. In the Commerce Committee, he has Frye of Maine to look after such matters as the projected, often postponed but never abandoned loot through ship subsidy; in the Pacific Railroad Committee he has the valiant soldier, the honest lumber and railway multimillionaire, the embalmed-beef hero, Alger, as chairman; in the Post-Office and Post-Roads Committee, which looks after the railways' postal graft, a clean steal from the Treasury of upward of 10 million a year — some put it as high as 30 million — he has Penrose as chairman. In that highly important committee, the one on rules, he himself sits; but mouthpiece Spooner is naturally chairman. Their associates are Elkins and Lodge — another pair that need to be better known to the American people. Bailey is the chief "Democratic" member. What a sardonic jest to speak of these men as Republicans and Democrats!

WHEN THE CURTAIN WAS LIFTED

THESE COMMITTEES carry on their colorless routine and also their real work — promoting thievish legislation, preventing decent legislation, devising ways and means of making rottenest dishonesty look like honesty and patriotism — these committees carry on their work in secrecy. *Public* business in profound privacy! Once Vest, angered by some misrepresentation made by Aldrich, had part of the minutes of a meeting of the Finance Committee read in open Senate — a gross breach of "senatorial courtesy!" Before the rudely lifted curtain was dropped, the country had a rare, illuminatory view of Aldrich. Here is this official minute:

> At a meeting of the Committee on Finance on March 17, 1894, on motion of Mr. Aldrich, the committee proceeded to a consideration of the provisions (of the Wilson bill) in regard to an income tax. Mr. Aldrich moved that the whole provision be stricken out of the bill.

He and Allison, that lifelong professional friend of the "plain people," had both voted aye. A pitiful sight he and Allison were, flustering and red, as this damning fact was read in open Senate, with the galleries full and all the reporters in their places! It is the only time the people have ever had a look at Aldrich in his shirt sleeves and hard at his repulsive but remunerative trade. But the people do not need to see the processes. They see, they feel, they suffer from the finished result — the bad law enacted, the good law killed.

When Bacon, in 1903, moved to call on the Department of Commerce and Labor for full facts about the selling of American goods at prices from ¼ to a full 100 percent cheaper abroad than at home, Aldrich at once moved to refer the resolution to his committee; and his motion was carried. A year later, Bacon reminded the Senate of his former resolution and of how it was sleeping in Aldrich's committee, and reintroduced it.

He backed it up with masses of facts — how "our" sewing machines sell abroad for $15 and here for $25; how "our" borax, a Rockefeller product, costs 7½ cents per pound here and only 2½ cents abroad; how "our" nails, a Rockefeller-Morgan product, sell here for $4.50 a keg and abroad for $3.10; how the foreigner gets for $1 as much of "our" window glass as we get for $2; how Schwab, in a letter to Frick on May 15, 1899, had said that, while steel rails sold here at $28 a ton, he could deliver them in England for $16 a ton and make $4 a ton profit; how the beef trust sold meat from 25 to 50 percent dearer in Buffalo than just across the Canadian line; how the harvester trust sold its reapers cheaper on the continent of Europe than to an Illinois farmer coming to its main factory at Chicago; how on every article in common use among the American people of city, town, and country, "the interests" were boldly robbing the people.

And Mr. Aldrich said, "Absurd!" And the Senate refused even to call upon the Department of Labor for the facts.

An illustration of another form of Aldrich's methods: When House and Senate disagree on a bill, each appoints a Conference Committee; and the two committees meet and try to find common ground. At one of these conferences — on the War-Tax Bill — Aldrich appeared, as usual in all matters which concern "the interests," at the head of the Senate conferees. He pressed more than a score of amendments to a single paragraph in the House measure. The House committee resisted him, and he slowly retreated, yielding point after point, until finally he had yielded all but one. He said: "Well, gentlemen of the House, we of the Senate have yielded practically everything to your body. We dare not go back absolutely empty-handed." And the House conferees gave him the one remaining point — the "mere trifle."

It afterward appeared that this was probably the only one of his more than a score of amendments that he really wanted; the others were mere blinds. For, that "mere trifle" subtly gave the tobacco "interests" (Rockefeller-Ryan) a license to use the war-revenue tax on tobacco to extort an additional 4 or 5 cents a pound from the consumer! There are half a dozen clauses, at least, in the present so-called Dingley tariff that protect the many-sided Standard Oil trust alone. But it takes an expert to find them, and doubtless many have escaped detection. But you may be sure that they work all right!

THE MAN WHO LAUGHS

Such is Aldrich, the senator. At the second session of the last Congress his main achievements, so far as the surface shows, were smothering all inquiry into the tariff and the freight-rate robberies, helping Elkins and the group of traitors in the service of the thieves who control the railway corporations to emasculate railway legislation, helping Allison and Bailey to smother the bill against the food poisoners for dividends. During the past winter he has been concentrating on the "defense of the railways" — which means not the railways, nor yet the railway corporations, but simply the Rockefeller-Morgan looting of the people by means of their control of the corporations that own the railways.

Has Aldrich intellect? Perhaps. But he does not show it. He has never in his twenty-five years of service in the Senate introduced or advocated a measure that shows any conception of life above what might be expected in a Hungry Joe. No, intellect is not the characteristic of Aldrich — or of any of these traitors or of the men they serve. A scurvy lot they are, are they not, with their smirking and cringing and voluble palaver about God and patriotism and their eager offerings of endowments for hospitals and colleges whenever the American people so much as looks hard in their direction!

There are at Washington three figures of prime importance: Root, the great Ryan-Morgan lawyer; Millionaire Joe Cannon, posing as a good fellow with little besides his income and — through the campaign contributors, that is, the interests, that is, the "party" — ruling the House to leave as little for Aldrich to do as is consistent with keeping the people deluded as to who and what really runs their national public administration. Aldrich is the third, and the most significant and powerful. He is hardly so contemptible as the other two — though, doubtless if it were necessary for him to adapt himself to the role of Pecksniff or Iago, he would take to it like a snake to squirming.

Aldrich is rich and powerful. Treachery has brought him wealth and rank, if not honor, of a certain sort. He must laugh at us, grown-up fools, permitting a handful to bind the might of our 80 million and to set us all to work for them.

———————◆———————

Reader, suppose you were an idiot. And suppose you were a member of Congress. But I repeat myself.

Samuel L. Clemens ("Mark Twain")

Now and then an innocent man is sent to the legislature.

Kin Hubbard

Broad Street, New York, with sidewalk stock brokers at work near the New York Exchange, 1905

CONSUMER TECHNOLOGY

The inventiveness of America was quickly applied to the consumer market. The practical inventor determined to advance knowledge, fill a need, and create a product, all at once; with a strong orientation toward the market, it is little wonder that potential backers and the public itself tended to class inventions as either saleable or toys. The development of mass production techniques such as the assembly line and the vertical corporation structure both depended upon and helped to create their counterpart, the mass market. In the classical theory of American capitalism, in which both "enlightened self-interest" and Henry Ford loom large, the creation of jobs by invention and mass production creates and spreads the wealth with which the product is bought. Wealth and prosperity are their own best promoters and guarantees. The system also creates the unexpected: advertising and public relations were sufficiently well developed by World War I to require both internal and external regulation.

(Top) Panorama of Pittsburgh, 1905; (left) interior of the Homestead Steel Works; (below) coal barges lining the banks of the Ohio River at Pittsburgh on the way to the mills; (right) the great steam hammer in mill at South Bethlehem, Pennsylvania; (bottom right) tipple-loading coal cars at a mine in Clarksburg, West Virginia

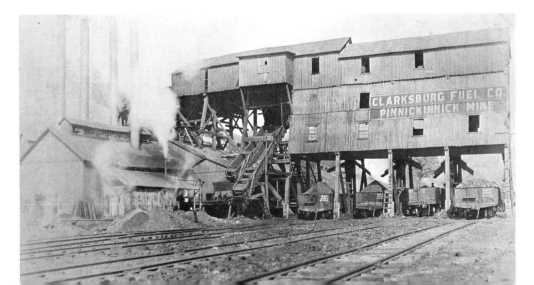

Furnaces of the Tennessee Coal, Iron, and Railroad Company, Ensley, Alabama, 1906

Southern industry, growing slowly, consisted largely of light industry such as textiles and various agriculture-based enterprises. But heavy industry was making gradual inroads; the Tennessee Coal and Iron Co. was in 1907 the second largest steel manufacturer in the United States. As elsewhere, the wealth of industry spread less rapidly and less evenly than the "enlightened self-interest" theory required. Outside ownership — Northerner J. P. Morgan acquired Tennessee Coal and Iron in the panic of 1907 — also drained away profits and other potential benefits.

Waterfront of Mobile, Alabama, about 1905, with Alabama Iron Works at left

(Above) Cotton mill at Tupelo, Mississippi, with workers' living quarters in the foreground; (below) cotton mills of the Roanoke Co., Virginia, with inferior housing for the workers

(Above) **Interior of the Niagara Falls Power Company generators, first on the American side, 1910; (below) Edison with a model for an electric power station; (below right) Marconi sending the first wireless message**

The automobile was the test case for the new mass methods of production and distribution, and by these means it was changed rapidly from a luxury toy to a popular middle-class recreation. The growth of allied industries and products, from gasoline to highways, led directly to the establishment of the automobile as both a personal necessity and the mainstay of the entire economy. The airplane was slower to develop commercially, mainly because of the greater amount of basic research required for the design and construction of practical aircraft.

Photograph of the instant of take-off on the first flight of the Wright brothers' plane on the beach at Kitty Hawk, North Carolina, December 17, 1903; (below left) glider experiment, 1908; (below right) flight of a Farnham Biplane in a public demonstration at Philadelphia

"Body drop" at the end of the assembly line at the Ford plant, 1914

Assembling magnetos at the Ford plant during the early evolution of the assembly line technique; (right) Henry Ford seated in his first car, 1896; (below) fitting the motor to the chassis, 1913

The country was not quite ready for cars: (Top) A carriage and harness dealer has taken on Fords as a sideline; Model T on a rural road; (below) steam equipment employed in roadbuilding

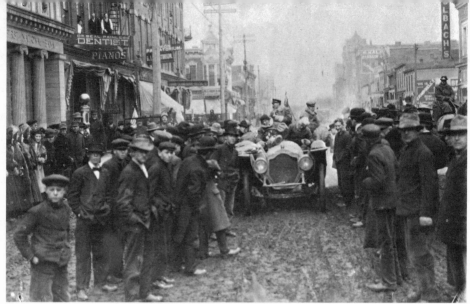

A crowd gathers in Grand Island, Nebraska, to inspect one of the contestants in the New York-to-Paris automobile race held in 1908

Family out on a Sunday drive in southern Vermont on a "Vermont superhighway," 1906; (below) Worden and Durea rounding a turn during the 1905 Vanderbilt Cup race

16.

John Vaughn: Thirty Years of the Telephone

The first telephone ever seen by the public was shown at the Centennial Exposition held at Philadelphia in 1876. Its inventor, Alexander Graham Bell, was remarkable not so much for his theoretical discoveries as for his ability to make use of materials and insights that had been available for a generation. The telephone, like many other technological advances, was the result of a laboratory accident. But it might have been wasted on someone less intent on transmitting vocal sounds electrically — a conception that grew out of the system of "visible speech" developed by Bell's distinguished father, Alexander Melville. Bell was the third generation of distinguished Scottish phoneticists. John Vaughn's article, first published in 1906, is reprinted here in part. In it he described how dependent business and life generally had become on the new device. A half century later that dependence had become almost total.

Source: *Scribner's*, September 1906: "The Thirtieth Anniversary of a Great Invention."

Considering how vital a factor is the telephone in today's business world, we find it hard to realize that but thirty years have passed since Bell obtained his first patent. It is only a quarter of a century since his great invention began to revolutionize commercial modes of communication. Thousands of visitors to the Centennial Exhibition saw what was then called the "talking toy." Few of them predicted its astonishing success.

But there are many capitalists that regret their failure to invest in the Bell Company's stock when it was first placed on the market. Still, it should be said that the telephone had not then proved itself indispensable in business, and it was unparalleled as a practical application of electricity; hence only unusually keen foresight could have gauged the instrument's possibilities. Bell himself says, "Even after our company was formed, not one of us fully realized the overwhelming importance of the invention."

Bell is still alive, very much alive, indeed, a vigorous, big-brained man, many-sided in his intellectual and social sympathies, a regent of the Smithsonian Institution and an ex-president of the National Geographic Society. . . .

Born in Edinburgh, Scotland, in 1847, Bell studied at Edinburgh and London Universities. His father's health failing, the family removed, in 1870, to Canada and settled on a farm. In 1873 the future inventor of the telephone became professor of vocal physiology in Boston University. At that time he was trying to perfect an apparatus intended to make language sounds visible to deaf and dumb persons. The Boston School Committee invited him to test the apparatus in the Horace Mann School for Deaf-Mutes. Success did not crown his efforts, but his failure was quickly forgotten in his newborn conviction that articulate speech could be conveyed electrically — a conviction forced on him by some unexpected results in his experiments.

His visible-speech apparatus comprised two electromagnets, connected by a wire, and two steel rods fastened to the poles of the magnets. These were the principal parts. It occurred to him that if membranes were drawn tightly across small-sized boxes, and the steel rods were arranged to beat against the membranes, in consonance with voice impulses, the result would be the reproduction at one membrane of the vocal sounds directed against the other membrane. But this theory could not be translated into steel and copper, and Bell turned his attention to multiplex telegraphy. The basement of his house in Boston was fitted up as a laboratory for experimental research.

One day a wire, snapping in two, sent a sound through another wire which had attached to each end a thin sheet-iron disk a few inches in circumference. Could that sound be repeated? Experiment gave an affirmative answer. Then arose the important query, "Could vocal sounds be transmitted thus?" A parchment diaphragm, with a sheet-iron button in the center, was stretched across the mouth of a thin metal cylinder about three inches in diameter. A glimpse inside that metal tube would have shown us features not unknown in today's perfected receiver — two magnets with poles wound with wire and, between the magnets, a small strip of soft iron.

A precisely similar instrument, with a wire running from its coils, was left in charge of Bell's assistant, while Bell, with the wire connected with his tubular iron-cased telephone, ascended to the attic of his house. The assistant, a bright young man, was directed to remain in the laboratory and to keep the receiver at his ear. Bell, holding the diaphragm a few inches from his lips, said in ordinary conversational tones, "Can you hear me?"

In a moment the assistant came bounding up the stairs. "Mr. Bell," he excitedly called out, "I heard your question plainly!"

The telephone was born!

It required a year's hard work, however, to mold the invention into patentable form. Meanwhile, the friends of the young inventor turned into Job's comforters and tried to discourage him. His talking toy would never bring him a dollar. Let him stick to his work in multiplex telegraphy. Therein

he would be sure to meet with success.

Fortunately for the world, Bell had inherited a goodly share of Scotch stubbornness and acumen, and he persevered in his endeavors to make electricity convey articulate speech. His reward reached him in the shape of his famous patent of March 7, 1876. Probably no other private document has ever caused so much litigation. The highest courts, however, sustained Bell's claims; and the owners of the patent were at last permitted to enjoy in peace the fruits of their property. . . .

In 1877 the telephone appeared as a public utility. At first its progress was slow. Experience soon demonstrated that, while the receiver operated by the magneto-transmitter reproduced words clearly, it was not efficient enough for business needs. But it had been proved that electric currents could be utilized to convey articulate speech, and, when the need of more powerful transmitters and receivers became apparent, the Bell Company turned to battery power.

Edison, the wizard of the electrical world, was first in the field, and his carbon transmitter was the only one used for some time. He utilized the discovery of the French physicist Count du Moncel, that, when two ends of a severed circuit are brought into contact, the resistance of the contact is variable with and proportionate to the pressure between them. This battery transmitter permitted the current to be varied by the resistance changes in the transmitter, these changes being caused by voice vibrations.

This invention was a long stride in advance in telephony. Edison and Berliner, practically at the same time, made a contribution of still greater value, however, when it occurred separately to them to combine the induction coil with the transmitter.

The true nature of the carbon transmitter's mode of operation was made known in 1878 by Professor Hughes of London. His "microphone" proved that, to obtain the best results with resistance changes due to changes in pressure, it is necessary to have a light contact. Since then all transmitters have been constructed on the light-contact plan.

In 1877 the first long-distance line was built. It connected Boston and Salem and was sixteen miles long. In these days, when lines run from Portland, Me., to Omaha, Neb. — cities 1,700 miles apart — it sounds like cheap sarcasm to style sixteen miles of wire a long-distance line. Yet the Boston-Salem telephone line was so denominated in sober earnest — in 1877. It is interesting to learn that it was the only line erected under Bell's personal superintendence. Two years passed away before a longer line was demanded by increasing use of the telephone, Boston and Lowell being brought into communication with each other then.

In the light of today's marvelous telephonic achievements, the following excerpt from the Bell Company's first prospectus reads like a jest:

> The proprietors [of the Bell patents] are now prepared to furnish telephones for the transmission of articulate speech between instruments not more than twenty miles apart.

Twenty miles? Verily, the days of small things have passed! The proprietors of the same patents are now prepared to furnish telephones for the transmission of articulate speech halfway across the continent. We should remember, however, that telephony was a new art when our republic was only 101 years old. The United States was a year older before the first telephone exchange was started. "Hello, Central!" was first heard in 1878. Today, the exchanges are numbered by the thousand, the telephones by the million.

Various industries, unknown thirty years ago, but now sources of employment to many thousands of workers, depend entirely on the telephone for support. Numerous factories making lead sheathing, dynamos,

motors, generators, batteries, office equipments, cables, and many other appliances would have to close down and thus throw their operatives into idleness and misery if the telephone bell should cease to ring. The Bell Companies employ over 87,000 persons and, it may be added, pay them well. Many of these employees have families to maintain; others support their parents or aid younger brothers and sisters. It is safe to say that 200,000 people look to the telephone for their daily bread.

These figures may be supplemented by the number of telephones in use (5,698,000), by the number of miles of wire (6,043,000) in the Bell lines, and by the number of conversations (4,479,500,000) electrically conveyed in 1905. The network of wire connects more than 33,000 cities, towns, villages, and hamlets.

Such tremendous growth as these statistics show would imply not only a steadily increasing appreciation of the telephone but would also suggest improved instruments, more skilled operators, and better service. There would be no flattery in such suggestion. Electrical science has undergone radical reformation since 1876. Telephony has raised the utilization of electricity to the height of a profession. Of course such advances have not been won without cost. Fortunes were spent in experiment and investigation before a dollar came back. Communication by the first telephone was limited to a few thousand feet. Now, conversation can be carried on by persons 1,600 miles apart. Tomorrow, long-distance lines will span the continent; and the day after, oceanic telephony will be a commonplace of mercantile routine. But science and money had to collaborate for years before they could work the miracle of enabling Boston and Omaha to talk together. . . .

American hurry and nervousness have influenced the telephone's line of advance. In the old days people would forget to ring off, and then "Central" had no means of determining when conversation was closed and the line was released, except by sending questions along the wires of the telephone users. Now, if, after you have put down your receiver, the other subscriber still holds his own wire, his little supervisory lamp tells that fact to "Central." Comparison of the complicated and expensive apparatus in use now with the apparatus of twenty years ago would prove that telephone engineers have spared no pains to minimize the work required of the subscriber. Today he does absolutely nothing, unless lifting the receiver to his ear is accounted something.

It is not assumed that machinery can take the place of human intelligence. Automatism has, however, been applied in all cases where it would save time and secure accuracy. For example, an operator receives a call for a certain number. Is the called line engaged? Into its jack is thrust lightly, by way of query, the metal plug, or tip, of the proper calling cord. *Click-click* is the response. The line wanted is busy. No words are needed. Other special signals are employed for various questions between different exchanges, and there are signals for operators in even the same exchange.

Some future philosophic historian of the nineteenth century may aver that the telephone appeared in response to mankind's demand for a quick-communication medium, usable by all persons. Bell was merely the unconscious agent of the Power which guides progress. . . .

The United States . . . is preeminently the land of the "'phone." In Berlin there is one telephone to every seventeen families; in Paris, one to every twenty-two families; in London, one to every fifty-eight families. American figures show a much higher ratio of intelligence and business enterprise. New York has one telephone to every twelve families; Boston, one to every six families; San Francisco had, on Jan. 1, 1906, one telephone to every four families. Since 1880 the Bell Companies alone have increased their mileage of wire about 50 percent. Yet the population of the country has, during

the same time, increased at only one-tenth of that rate. The rural districts should not be left unnoticed. They had 260,000 miles of single wire and 267,000 telephones in use during 1905. All Europe had last year only 2,044,200 miles of wire. Yet that grand division contains about five times as many inhabitants as the United States.

But Europe is unprogressive compared with us. Outside its cities, the telephone is little used. Here, its imperious call is heard everywhere — in the huge department store, thronged with city crowds; in lonely lumber camps, buried in the depths of primeval forests; in the rice swamps of our Gulf states; on the vast wheat ranches of the West; in the mines of Pennsylvania or Colorado — in short, wherever American energy is turning raw material into wealth. The most urgent need of trade or commerce — of wealth production or wealth distribution — is quick communication. Hence it is a truism nowadays that expansion of business means increased telephonage. But, if business aids the telephone, it is also true that the telephone aids business — creates it, indeed, under certain circumstances. Spread a network of telephone wires over a backward rural community and note the surprising improvement visible in a few years. The people have been awakened, stirred into activity, educated up to higher standards.

If public demand has made the Bell companies supreme in the field of telephony, be it remembered that the telephone has made itself indispensable in business. This benefit is a direct benefit. Incidentally the companies, by employing labor and paying good wages, help every city wherein they maintain an exchange. Telephony is a new art and has opened new avenues of employment, especially to women. The manager of the New York exchange, in 1878, found himself hurriedly compelled to augment his force of employees owing to rapid increase in the use of the telephone. It was impossible to obtain competent men enough. By accident he learned that a young woman had charge of the switchboard in the exchange in Bridgeport, Conn. Her success gave him a hint; and in a few days young women were installed in all his switchboard operator chairs. The Bridgeport young lady was the first telephone operator of her sex in the United States. Today the companies have more than 20,000 women operators in their employ. Telephony enables them all to earn larger wages than they would receive in any other occupation.

Thirty years ago every noted physicist in the world would have scoffed and scorned a proposition to convey speech by wire. Bell says of himself, "Had I known more about electricity and less about sound, I should never have invented the telephone." So simple was its mechanism that the first telephone was characterized as the very hardi-hood of invention. It bears no resemblance to the complicated apparatus to be seen in any central exchange in this year of grace, 1906.

Marvelous, indeed, is the progress which has been made since the war-stirring patent of 1876 was issued. Hundreds of keen minds have cooperated to produce the perfected telephone of today. Nevertheless, in science, as in reform, it is the first step that costs. The world cannot forget its obligation to the inventor of the original telephone. Two countries have the right to be especially proud of him — Scotland, the land of his birth, and the United States, the land of his adoption. Each country has a splendid beadroll of names illustrious in applied science. Yet it is safe to say that posterity will honor none of them more highly than the name of Alexander Graham Bell.

17.

UPTON SINCLAIR: The Meat-Packers of Chicago

The Chicago Union Stockyards were controlled by a few large companies that composed the "beef trust" and monopolized the processing and distribution of meat in the United States. Upton Sinclair, at the time a recent convert to socialism, worked in the stockyards to gather material for an exposé of the meat-packing industry. The Jungle, published in 1906, dealt with the poverty-stricken lives of the workers at the yards and the highly unsanitary conditions in the packing plants. The publicity attending the novel was instrumental in prompting the congressional investigations of 1906, out of which came the Pure Food and Drug Act and the Meat Inspection Act. Portions of three chapters of The Jungle *are reprinted below.*

Source: *The Jungle*, New York, 1906, pp. 39-47, 112-117, 160-162.

ENTERING ONE OF THE DURHAM BUILDINGS, they found a number of other visitors waiting; and before long there came a guide to escort them through the place. They make a great feature of showing strangers through the packing plants, for it is a good advertisement. But . . . Jokubas whispered maliciously that the visitors did not see any more than the packers wanted them to.

They climbed a long series of stairways outside of the building to the top of its five or six stories. Here were the chute, with its river of hogs, all patiently toiling upward; there was a place for them to rest to cool

Upton Sinclair with his son; photographed at Princeton Farm in 1906 at the time that "The Jungle" was published

off, and then through another passageway they went into a room from which there is no returning for hogs.

It was a long, narrow room, with a gallery along it for visitors. At the head there was a great iron wheel, about twenty feet in circumference, with rings here and there along its edge. Upon both sides of this wheel there was a narrow space, into which came the hogs at the end of their journey; in the midst of them stood a great burly Negro, bare-armed and bare-chested. He was resting for the moment, for the wheel had stopped while men were cleaning up. In a minute or two, however, it began slowly to revolve, and then the men upon each side of it sprang to work. They had chains which they fastened about the leg of the nearest hog, and the other end of the chain they hooked into one of the rings upon the wheel. So, as the wheel turned, a hog was suddenly jerked off his feet and borne aloft.

At the same instant the ear was assailed by a most terrifying shriek; the visitors started in alarm, the women turned pale and shrank back. The shriek was followed by another, louder and yet more agonizing — for once started upon that journey, the hog never came back; at the top of the wheel he was shunted off upon a trolley and went sailing down the room. And meantime another was swung up, and then another, and another, until there was a double line of them, each dangling by a foot and kicking in frenzy — and squealing. The uproar was appalling, perilous to the eardrums; one feared there was too much sound for the room to hold — that the walls must give way or the ceiling crack. There were high squeals and low squeals, grunts, and wails of agony; there would come a momentary lull, and then a fresh outburst, louder than ever, surging up to a deafening climax. It was too much for some of the visitors — the men would look at each other, laughing nervously, and the women would stand with hands clenched, and the blood rushing to their faces, and the tears starting in their eyes.

Meantime, heedless of all these things, the men upon the floor were going about their work. Neither squeals of hogs nor tears of visitors made any difference to them; one by one they hooked up the hogs, and one by one with a swift stroke they slit their throats. There was a long line of hogs, with squeals and lifeblood ebbing away together; until at last each started again and vanished with a splash into a huge vat of boiling water.

It was all so very businesslike that one watched it fascinated. It was pork-making by machinery, pork-making by applied mathematics. And yet somehow the most matter-of-fact person could not help thinking of the hogs; they were so innocent, they came so very trustingly; and they were so very human in their protests — and so perfectly within their rights! They had done nothing to deserve it; and it was adding insult to injury, as the thing was done here, swinging them up in this cold-blooded, impersonal way, without a pretense at apology, without the homage of a tear. Now and then a visitor wept, to be sure; but this slaughtering machine ran on, visitors or no visitors. It was like some horrible crime committed in a dungeon, all unseen and unheeded, buried out of sight and of memory.

One could not stand and watch very long without becoming philosophical, without beginning to deal in symbols and similes, and to hear the hog-squeal of the universe. Was it permitted to believe that there was nowhere upon the earth, or above the earth, a heaven for hogs, where they were requited for all this suffering? Each one of these hogs was a separate creature. Some were white hogs, some were black; some were brown, some were spotted; some were old, some were young; some were long and lean, some were monstrous. And each of them had an individuality of his own, a will of his own, a hope, and a heart's desire; each was full of self-confidence, of self-importance, and a sense of dignity. And trusting and strong in faith he had gone about his business, the while a black shadow hung over him and a horrid Fate waited in his pathway.

Now, suddenly, it had swooped upon him and had seized him by the leg. Relentless, remorseless, it was; all his protests, his screams, were nothing to it — it did its cruel will with him, as if his wishes, his feelings, had simply no existence at all; it cut his throat and watched him gasp out his life. And now was one to believe that there was nowhere a god of hogs, to whom this hog-personality was precious, to whom these hog-squeals and agonies had a meaning? Who would take this hog into his arms and comfort him, reward him for his work well done, and show him the meaning of his sacrifice? Perhaps some glimpse of all this was in the thoughts of our humble-minded Jurgis, as he turned to go on with the rest of the party, and muttered: "Dieve — but I'm glad I'm not a hog!"

The carcass hog was scooped out of the vat by machinery, and then it fell to the second floor, passing on the way through a wonderful machine with numerous scrapers, which adjusted themselves to the size and shape of the animal and sent it out at the other end with nearly all of its bristles removed. It was then again strung up by machinery and sent upon another trolley ride; this time passing between two lines of men, who sat upon a raised platform, each doing a certain single thing to the carcass as it came to him.

One scraped the outside of a leg; another scraped the inside of the same leg. One, with a swift stroke, cut the throat; another, with two swift strokes, severed the head, which fell to the floor and vanished through a hole. Another made a slit down the body; a second opened the body wider; a third, with a saw, cut the breastbone; a fourth loosened the entrails; a fifth pulled them out — and they also slid through a hole in the floor. There were men to scrape each side and men to scrape the back; there were men to clean the carcass inside, to trim it and wash it. Looking down this room, one saw, creeping slowly, a line of dangling hogs a hundred yards in length; and for every yard there was a man, working as if a demon were after him. At the end of this hog's progress every inch of the carcass had been gone over several times; and then it was rolled into the chilling room, where it stayed for twenty-four hours, and where a stranger might lose himself in a forest of freezing hogs.

Before the carcass was admitted here, however, it had to pass a government inspector, who sat in the doorway and felt of the glands in the neck for tuberculosis. This government inspector did not have the manner of a man who was worked to death; he was apparently not haunted by a fear that the hog might get by him before he had finished his testing. If you were a sociable person, he was quite willing to enter into conversation with you and to explain to you the deadly nature of the ptomaines which are found in tubercular pork;

and while he was talking with you you could hardly be so ungrateful as to notice that a dozen carcasses were passing him untouched. This inspector wore a blue uniform with brass buttons, and he gave an atmosphere of authority to the scene, and, as it were, put the stamp of official approval upon the things which were done in Durham's.

Jurgis went down the line with the rest of the visitors, staring open-mouthed, lost in wonder. He had dressed hogs himself in the forest of Lithuania; but he had never expected to live to see one hog dressed by several hundred men. It was like a wonderful poem to him, and he took it all in guilelessly — even to the conspicuous signs demanding immaculate cleanliness of the employees. Jurgis was vexed when the cynical Jokubas translated these signs with sarcastic comments, offering to take them to the secret rooms where the spoiled meats went to be doctored.

The party descended to the next floor, where the various waste materials were treated. Here came the entrails, to be scraped and washed clean for sausage casings; men and women worked here in the midst of a sickening stench, which caused the visitors to hasten by, gasping. To another room came all the scraps to be "tanked," which meant boiling and pumping off the grease to make soap and lard; below they took out the refuse, and this, too, was a region in which the visitors did not linger.

In still other places men were engaged in cutting up the carcasses that had been through the chilling rooms. First, there were the "splitters," the most expert workmen in the plant, who earned as high as fifty cents an hour, and did not a thing all day except chop hogs down the middle. Then there were "cleaver men," great giants with muscles of iron; each had two men to attend him — to slide the half carcass in front of him on the table and hold it while he chopped it, and then turn each piece so that he might chop it once more.

His cleaver had a blade about two feet long, and he never made but one cut; he made it so neatly, too, that his implement did not smite through and dull itself — there was just enough force for a perfect cut, and no more. So through various yawning holes there slipped to the floor below — to one room, hams; to another, forequarters; to another, sides of pork.

One might go down to this floor and see the pickling rooms, where the hams were put into vats, and the great smoke rooms, with their air-tight iron doors. In other rooms they prepared salt pork — there were whole cellars full of it, built up in great towers to the ceiling. In yet other rooms they were putting up meat in boxes and barrels, and wrapping hams and bacon in oiled paper, sealing and labeling and sewing them. From the doors of these rooms went men with loaded trucks, to the platform where freight cars were waiting to be filled; and one went out there and realized with a start that he had come at last to the ground floor of this enormous building.

Then the party went across the street to where they did the killing of beef — where every hour they turned four or five hundred cattle into meat. Unlike the place they had left, all this work was done on one floor; and instead of there being one line of carcasses which moved to the workmen, there were fifteen or twenty lines, and the men moved from one to another of these. This made a scene of intense activity, a picture of human power wonderful to watch. It was all in one great room, like a circus amphitheater, with a gallery for visitors running over the center.

Along one side of the room ran a narrow gallery, a few feet from the floor, into which gallery the cattle were driven by men with goads which gave them electric shocks. Once crowded in here, the creatures were prisoned, each in a separate pen, by gates that shut, leaving them no room to turn around; and while they stood bellowing and plunging, over the top of the pen there eaned one of the "knockers," armed with a sledge hammer and watching for a chance to deal a blow. The room echoed with the thuds in quick succession and the stamping and kicking of the steers. The instant the animal had fallen, the "knocker" passed on to another; while a second man raised a lever, and the side of the pen was raised and the animal, still kicking and struggling, slid out to the "killing bed."

Here, a man put shackles about one leg and pressed another lever, and the body was jerked up into the air. There were fifteen or twenty such pens, and it was a matter of only a couple of minutes to knock fifteen or twenty cattle and roll them out. Then once more the gates were opened and another lot rushed in; and so out of each pen there rolled a steady stream of carcasses, which the men upon the killing beds had to get out of the way.

The manner in which they did this was something to be seen and never forgotten. They worked with furious intensity, literally upon the run — at a pace with which there is nothing to be compared except a football game. It was all highly specialized labor, each man having his task to do; generally this would consist of only two or three specific cuts, and he would pass down the line of fifteen or twenty carcasses, making these cuts upon each. First, there came the "butcher," to bleed them; this meant one swift stroke, so swift that you could not see it — only the flash of the knife; and before you could realize it, the man had darted on to the next line, and a stream of bright red was pouring out upon the floor. This floor was half an inch deep with blood, in spite of the best efforts of men who kept shoveling it through holes; it must have made the floor slippery, but no one could have guessed this by watching the men at work.

The carcass hung for a few minutes to bleed; there was no time lost, however, for there were several hanging in each line, and one was always ready. It was let down to the ground, and there came the "heads-man," whose task it was to sever the head with two or three swift strokes. Then came the "floorsman" to make the first cut in the skin; and then another to finish ripping the skin down the center; and then half a dozen more in swift succession to finish the skinning. After they were through, the carcass was again swung up; and while a man with a stick examined the skin to make sure that it had not been cut, and another rolled it up and tumbled it through one of the inevitable holes in the floor, the beef proceeded on its journey. There were men to cut it, and men to split it, and men to gut it and scrape it clean inside. There were some with hose which threw jets of boiling water upon it, and others who removed the feet and added the final touches. In the end, as with the hogs, the finished beef was run into the chilling room, to hang its appointed time.

The visitors were taken there and shown them, all neatly hung in rows, labeled conspicuously with the tags of the government inspectors — and some, which had been killed by a special process, marked with the sign of the "Kosher" rabbi, certifying that it was fit for sale to the Orthodox. And then the visitors were taken to the other parts of the building to see what became of each particle of the waste material that had vanished through the floor; and to the pickling rooms, and the salting rooms, the canning rooms, and the packing rooms, where choice meat was prepared for shipping in refrigerator cars, destined to be eaten in all the four corners of civilization. Afterward they went outside, wandering about among the mazes of buildings in which was done the work auxiliary to this great industry.

There was scarcely a thing needed in the business that Durham and Company did not make for themselves. There was a great steam-power plant and an electricity plant. There was a barrel factory, and a boiler-repair shop. There was a building to which the grease was piped and made into soap and lard; and then there was a factory for making lard cans, and another for making soap boxes. There was a building in which the bristles were cleaned and dried for the making of hair cushions and such things; there was a building where the skins were dried and tanned; there was another where heads and feet were made into glue, and another where bones were made into fertilizer. No tiniest particle of organic matter was wasted in Durham's.

Out of the horns of the cattle they made combs, buttons, hairpins, and imitation ivory; out of the shinbones and other big bones they cut knife and toothbrush handles, and mouthpieces for pipes; out of the hoofs they cut hairpins and buttons before they made the rest into glue. From such things as feet, knuckles, hide clippings, and sinews came such strange and unlikely products as gelatin, isinglass, and phosphorus, bone-black, shoe-blacking, and bone-oil. They had curled-hair works for the cattle tails, and a "wool pullery" for the sheepskins; they made pepsin from the stomachs of the pigs, and albumen from the blood, and violin strings from the ill-smelling entrails. When there was nothing else to be done with a thing, they first put it into a tank and got out of it all the tallow and grease, and then they made it into fertilizer.

All these industries were gathered into buildings nearby, connected by galleries and railroads with the main establishment; and it was estimated that they had handled nearly a quarter of a billion of animals since the founding of the plant by the elder Durham a generation and more ago. If you counted with it the other big plants — and they were now really all one — it was, so Jokubas informed them, the greatest aggregation of labor and capital ever gathered in one place. It employed 30,000 men; it supported directly 250,000 people in its neighborhood, and indirectly it supported 500,000. It sent its products to every country in the civilized world, and it furnished the food for no less than 30 million people! . . .

"Bubbly Creek" is an arm of the Chicago River and forms the southern boundary of the yards; all the drainage of the square mile of packing houses empties into it, so that it is really a great open sewer a hundred or two feet wide. One long arm of it is blind, and the filth stays there forever and a day. The grease and chemicals that are poured into it undergo all sorts of strange transformations, which are the cause of its name; it is constantly in motion, as if huge fish were feeding in it, or great leviathans were disporting themselves in its depths. Bubbles of carbonic acid gas will rise to the surface and burst, and make rings two or three feet wide.

Here and there the grease and filth have caked solid, and the creek looks like a bed of lava; chickens walk about on it, feeding, and many times an unwary stranger has started to stroll across and vanished temporarily. The packers used to leave the creek that way, till every now and then the surface would catch on fire and burn furiously, and the Fire Department would have to come and put it out. Once, however, an ingenious stranger came and started to gather this filth in scows, to make lard out of; then the packers took the cue, and got out an injunction to stop him, and afterwards gathered it themselves. The banks of "Bubbly Creek" are plastered thick with hairs, and this also the packers gather and clean.

And there were things ever stranger than this, according to the gossip of the men. The packers had secret mains, through which they stole billions of gallons of the city's water. The newspapers had been full of this scandal — and once there had been an investigation and an actual uncovering of the pipes; but nobody had been punished, and the thing went right on.

And then there was the condemned-meat industry, with its endless horrors. The people of Chicago saw the government inspectors in Packingtown, and they all took that to mean that they were protected from diseased meat; they did not understand that these 163 inspectors had been appointed at the request of the packers, and that they were paid by the United States government to certify that all the diseased meat was kept in the state. They had no authority beyond that; for the inspection of meat to be sold in the city and state the whole force in Packingtown consisted of three henchmen of the local political machine!

And shortly afterward one of these, a physician, made the discovery that the carcasses of steers which had been condemned as tubercular by the government inspectors, and which therefore contained ptomaines, which are deadly poisons, were left upon an open platform and carted away to be sold in the city; and he insisted that these carcasses be treated with an injection of kerosene — and was ordered to resign the same week! So indignant were the packers that they went farther, and compelled the mayor to abolish the whole Bureau of Inspection; so that since then there has not been even a pretense of any interference with the graft. There was said to be $2000 a week hush-money from the tubercular steers alone; and as much again from the hogs which had died of cholera on the trains, and which you might see any day being loaded into boxcars and hauled away to a place called Globe, in Indiana, where they made a fancy grade of lard. . . .

There was another interesting set of statistics that a person might have gathered in Packingtown — those of the various afflictions of the workers. When Jurgis had first inspected the packing plants with Szedvilas, he had marveled while he listened to the tale of all the things that were made out of the carcasses of animals, and of all the lesser industries that were maintained there; now he found that each one of these lesser industries was a separate little inferno, in its way as horrible as the killingbeds, the source and fountain of them all. The workers in each of them had their own peculiar diseases. And the wandering visitor might be skeptical about all the swindles, but he could not be skeptical about these, for the worker bore the evidence of them about on his own person — generally he had only to hold out his hand.

There were the men in the picklerooms, for instance . . . scarce a one of these that had not some spot of horror on his person. Let a man so much as scrape his finger pushing a truck in the picklerooms and he might have a sore that would put him out of the world; all the joints in his fingers might be eaten by the acid, one by one. Of the butchers and floorsmen, the beef-boners and trimmers, and all those who used knives, you could scarcely find a person who had the use of his thumb; time and time again the base of it had been slashed, till it was a mere lump of flesh against which the man pressed the knife to hold it. The hands of these men would be criss-crossed with cuts, until you could no longer pretend to count them or to trace them. They would have no nails, — they had worn them off pulling hides; their knuckles were swollen so that their fingers spread out like a fan.

There were men who worked in the cooking rooms, in the midst of steam and sickening odors, by artificial light; in these rooms the germs of tuberculosis might live for two years, but the supply was renewed every hour. There were the beef luggers, who carried two-hundred-pound quarters into the refrigerator cars; a fearful kind of work, that began at four o'clock in the morning, and that wore out the most powerful men in a few years.

There were those who worked in the chilling rooms, and whose special disease was rheumatism; the time limit that a man could work in the chilling rooms was said to be five years. There were the wool pluckers, whose hands went to pieces even sooner than the hands of the pickle men; for the pelts of the sheep had to be painted with acid to loosen the wool, and then the pluckers had to pull out this wool with their bare hands, till the acid had eaten their fingers off. There were those who made the tins for the canned meat; and their hands, too, were a maze of cuts, and each cut represented a chance for blood poisoning.

Some worked at the stamping machines, and it was very seldom that one could work long there at the pace that was set and not give out and forget himself and have a part of his hand chopped off. There were the "hoisters," as they were called, whose task it was to press the lever which lifted the dead cattle off the floor. They ran along upon a rafter, peering down through the damp and the steam; and as old Durham's architects had not built the killing room for the convenience of the hoisters, at every few feet they would have to stoop under a beam, say four feet above the one they ran on; which got them into the habit of stooping, so that in a few years they would be walking like chimpanzees.

Worst of any, however, were the fertilizer men, and those who served in the cooking rooms. These people could not be shown to the visitor, for the odor of a fertilizer man would scare any ordinary visitor at a hundred yards; and, as for the other men who worked in tank rooms full of steam, and in some of which there were open vats near the level of the floor, their peculiar trouble was that they fell into the vats; and when they were fished out, there was never enough of them left to be worth exhibiting, — sometimes they would be overlooked for days till all but the bones of them had gone out to the world as Durham's Pure Leaf Lard!

With one member trimming beef in a cannery and another working in a sausage factory, the family had a first-hand knowledge of the great majority of Packingtown swindles. For it was the custom, as they found, whenever meat was so spoiled that it could not be used for anything else, either to can it or else to chop it up into sausage. With what had been told them by Jonas, who had worked in the pickle rooms, they could now study the whole of the spoiled-meat industry on the inside, and read a new and grim meaning into that old Packingtown jest — that they use everything of the pig except the squeal.

Jonas had told them how the meat that was taken out of pickle would often be found sour, and how they would rub it up with soda to take away the smell and sell it to be eaten on free-lunch counters; also of all the miracles of chemistry which they performed, giving to any sort of meat, fresh or salted, whole or chopped, any color and any flavor and any odor they chose.

In the pickling of hams they had an ingenious apparatus, by which they saved time and increased the capacity of the plant — a machine consisting of a hollow needle attached to a pump; by plunging this needle into the meat and working with his foot, a man could fill a ham with pickle in a few seconds. And yet, in spite of this, there would be hams found spoiled, some of them with an odor so bad that a man could hardly bear to be in the room with them. To pump into these the packers had a second and much stronger pickle which destroyed the odor — a process known to the workers as "giving them thirty percent."

Also, after the hams had been smoked, there would be found some that had gone to the bad. Formerly these had been sold as "Number Three Grade," but later on some ingenious person had hit upon a new device, and now they would extract the bone, about which the bad part generally lay, and insert in the hole a white-hot iron. After this invention there was no longer Number One, Two, and Three Grade — there was only Number One Grade. The packers were always originating such schemes — they had what they called "boneless hams," which were all the odds and ends of pork stuffed into casings; and "California hams," which were the shoulders, with big knuckle joints, and nearly all the meat cut out; and fancy "skinned hams," which were made of the oldest hogs, whose skins were so heavy and coarse that no one would buy them — that is, until they had been cooked and chopped fine and labeled "headcheese!"

It was only when the whole ham was spoiled that it came into the department of Elzbieta. Cut up by the two-thousand-revolutions-a-minute flyers, and mixed with half a ton of other meat, no odor that ever was in a ham could make any difference. There was never the least attention paid to what was cut up for sausage; there would come all the way back from Europe old sausage that had been rejected, and that was moldy and white — it would be dosed with borax and glycerine, and dumped into the hoppers, and made over again for home consumption. There would be meat that had tumbled out on the floor, in the dirt and sawdust, where the workers had tramped and spit uncounted billions of consumption germs. There would be meat stored in great piles in rooms; and the water from leaky roofs would drip over it, and thousands of rats would race about on it.

It was too dark in these storage places to see well, but a man could run his hand over these piles of meat and sweep off handfuls of the dried dung of rats. These rats were nuisances, and the packers would put poisoned bread out for them; they would die, and then rats, bread, and meat would go into the hoppers together. This is no fairy story and no joke; the meat would be shoveled into carts, and the man who did the shoveling would not trouble to lift out a rat even when he saw one — there were things that went into the sausage in comparison with which a poisoned rat was a tidbit.

There was no place for the men to wash their hands before they ate their dinner, and so they made a practice of washing them in the water that was to be ladled into the sausage. There were the butt ends of smoked meat, and the scraps of corned beef, and all the odds and ends of the waste of the plants that would be dumped into old barrels in the cellar and left there.

Under the system of rigid economy which the packers enforced, there were some jobs that it only paid to do once in a long time, and among these was the cleaning out of the waste barrels. Every spring they did it; and in the barrels would be dirt and rust and old nails and stale water — and cartload after cartload of it would be taken up and dumped into the hoppers with fresh meat and sent out to the public's breakfast. Some of it they would make into "smoked" sausage — but as the smoking took time, and was therefore expensive, they would call upon their chemistry department and preserve it with borax and color it with gelatine to make it brown. All of their sausage came out of the same bowl, but when they came to wrap it, they would stamp some of it "special," and for this they would charge two cents more a pound.

———◆———

Edible, adj. *Good to eat, and wholesome to digest, as a worm to a toad, a toad to a snake, a snake to a pig, a pig to a man, and a man to a worm.*
AMBROSE BIERCE, *The Devil's Dictionary*

18.

JOHN A. RYAN: The Right to a Living Wage

Inspired by Pope Leo XIII's 1891 encyclical Rerum novarum, *John Ryan wrote his doctor's dissertation on the rights of workers and published it in 1906. In arguing, as had the pope, that government had a responsiblity to workers, Ryan reflected the liberal Catholic position that the Church must play a meaningful social role. Ryan maintained that a living wage was a basic right of workers, and not, as many others believed, a benefit to be conferred by a benevolent and paternalistic state; and he also described what a "living wage" meant in modern society. The following selection is taken from his book.*

Source: *A Living Wage*, New York, 1906, Ch. 18: "The Obligation of the State."

THE OBLIGATION OF PROVIDING the laborer with a Living Wage has been fully outlined in its individual and class aspects. There remains only the question of the extent to which it rests upon the state. That baneful heritage of the 18th century, the doctrine that a minimum of state regulation of industry means a maximum of industrial freedom for the individual, no longer counts any considerable number of adherents. It is demonstrably false in theory, and it has been completely discredited in practice. Negatively, liberty is absence of restraint; positively, it is the power to act and to enjoy.

Now the restraints to action and enjoyment are not all political and legal; consequently the individual may possess the fullest immunity from governmental interference and yet be hindered by some other restraints, such as the strength, cunning, or selfishness of his fellows, from doing and enjoying those things that are essential to reasonable life. Whenever this happens, the absence of state intervention means the presence of insuperable obstacles to real and effective liberty. In a word, political and legal freedom are not an adequate safeguard to the welfare of the individual.

As the Comte de Mun told the French Chamber of Deputies:

Liberty does not consist in a theoretical right but in the possibility of exercising it. The power to be free, in a regime which puts the workingman's life at the mercy of supply and demand; which exposes himself, his wife, and his children to the hardships of a competition that knows no moderation; which sets no limit to his exploitation except the interests of those who employ him — the power to be free in such conditions, when the need of subsistence is so pressing as to permit of no waiting, no choice, no hesitation, does not exist and consequently the laborer is not free.

The economic history of the 19th century furnishes abundant proof of these statements and an overwhelming refutation of the nonintervention theory. Perhaps the clearest and most logical instance is to be found in the conditions prevailing in the mines and factories of England before the passage of the Factory Acts.

Some of the opponents of state intervention in industry may be conveniently classed with the juvenile bully who resents the "interference" of parent or teacher in his relations with younger and weaker boys, and with the burglar or highwayman who objects to the activity of the policeman. These are the possessors of superior bargaining power who realize that if government will only let them alone they will be able successfully to exploit their weaker fellows. Their opposition is natural in the same sense that selfishness is natural. Those who oppose state regulation of industry on higher grounds than self-interest usually misconceive its concrete effects.

From this point of view, laws may be divided into two classes: those which actually restrict the liberty of all or a majority of the citizens; and those which limit the freedom of all potentially, but of only a few actually. The first class regulates the simpler, more frequent, and more general activities of everyday life, and puts some practical restriction on the freedom of nearly every person. Yet they bring to him more freedom than they take away. For example, the ordinance forbidding a man to monopolize the street or the sidewalk curtails to that extent his liberty but secures him the larger liberty of immunity from the inconvenience that would be produced by similar unreasonable conduct on the part of his fellows. . . .

As an abstract proposition, the state has both the right and the duty to compel all employers to pay a Living Wage. The function of the state is to promote the social welfare. The social welfare means in practice the welfare of all individuals over whom the state has authority; and the welfare of the individual includes all those conditions that assist in the pursuit of his earthly end, namely, the reasonable development of his personality. The primary business of the state, then, is to protect men in the enjoyment of those opportunities that are essential to right and reasonable life. They may be summed up in the phrase "natural rights."

In addition to this, the state is charged with the obligation of promoting social prosperity. That is to say, its task is not merely to provide men with the opportunities that are absolutely essential to right living but also to furnish, as far as practicable, the conditions of wider and fuller life. Since man's capacity for progress is indefinite, the state will fail in its mission of furthering social welfare unless it does something toward securing to him the external conditions of something more than the minimum of reasonable personal development. State activity in the first sense is mainly protective and restrictive; in the second, auxiliary and cooperative.

Now, a law requiring employers to pay a Living Wage would evidently be an instance of state activity in the primary sense, for it would be an attempt to protect natural rights and to provide one of the essential conditions of reasonable human life. Even those who hold that the sole function of the state is to safeguard individuals against violence and injustice, in other words, to protect life and property, could logically admit that the enactment of such a law would not be an undue exercise of power. To compel a man to work for less than a Living Wage is as truly an act of injustice as to pick his pocket. In a wide sense it is also an attack upon his life. An ordinance prohibiting this species of oppression would, therefore, be a measure for the protection of life and property.

The question of the legal enforcement of a Living Wage is, consequently, one of expediency. It has two distinct phases. We may ask whether a universal Living Wage is economically feasible; and, supposing it to be workable, whether legal enactment could bring it about. The former inquiry does not concern itself with the productive resources of the country, since . . . these are ample to supply all the inhabitants with the requisites of a decent livelihood, but with the consequences that might be expected to follow the establishment of a universal Living Wage in our present industrial system. The difficulties that it suggests remain substantially the same whether this condition be attained through trade union action, the payment of sufficiently high prices by consumers, or legal enactment.

This question is frequently answered in the negative, on the ground that if all the laborers who are at present underpaid were to receive a Living Wage, there would be such a rise in the price of the goods and services that they produce as to cause a corresponding decline in demand. Instead of insufficient wages, we should have the evil of insufficient employment. President Hadley says that society, that is, the consuming public, regards the making of a certain amount of product as worth only so much, and if compelled to pay more will diminish the quantity that it consumes. Professor Smart maintains that the decreased demand would result in the laborers being put on short time, so that their Living Wage would prove a misnomer.

President Hadley's contention is true in a general way, but it is subject to two important qualifications. It implies, or at least will seem to many to imply, that the consumers look upon the low prices at which certain products sell as a full and precise equivalent of the fixed and necessary "worth" of these articles; and it easily leads to an exaggerated idea of the part taken by consumers in creating these prices. Why do consumers regard certain products of underpaid labor as worth no more than they now sell for? Because the low wages resulting from excessive competition among both employers and

workers have enabled these prices to become customary. As Professor Smart points out, the proposition that women's wages are low because the goods that they turn out are cheap, puts — so far as the question of primary causality is concerned — "the cart before the horse."

The initiative in reducing prices comes from the producers not from the public. Once prices are down, however, the public accepts them so eagerly that to raise them and the low wages underlying them constitutes a very difficult problem. This is the explanation of low prices and the real significance of the consumer's estimate of the "worth" of low priced goods. President Hadley would, indeed, be one of the first to subscribe to this view, but his language . . . can be construed in support of an exaggerated notion of the rigidity and significance of the evaluations made by the consumer. That society regards the prices that it pays for cheap goods as an "equivalent" of the labor expended in producing them, is true in the sense that it will not voluntarily offer to pay more; it is not necessarily true in the sense that society would not pay more for these goods rather than do without them.

And this brings us to the second qualification to be made concerning President Hadley's statement, and likewise with regard to that of Professor Smart. A rise in the price of an article will always be followed by a falling off in the demand for it, *other conditions remaining unchanged*. If, however, it is accompanied by a corresponding increase in the purchasing power of consumers, actual and potential, there need be no diminution in the amount sold. The prices of most of the necessities of life have risen greatly in the last seven years, yet the effective demand for them has not decreased. The contrary has, in fact, occurred, thus exemplifying the general rule that high prices mean greater industrial activity and a smaller volume of unemployment. Whether the establishment of a Living Wage in all the industries in which it does not now exist would bring with it sufficient demand to continue or increase the number at present employed, cannot be mathematically determined beforehand.

This much, however, may be confidently affirmed: of the actual and potential consumers affected, the richest section would probably buy as much as they did before prices rose; another section would certainly reduce its consumption; some of the laborers formerly underpaid would increase their consumption; and some of them would become consumers of these particular goods for the first time. Hence the effect of a rise in prices consequent upon the universal application of the Living Wage principle would be less simple as well as less serious than the statements of the above-mentioned writers seem to imply.

A second objection is drawn from the assumption that even though the higher range of prices should cause no decrease in demand or in employment, it would swallow up completely the rise in remuneration. What the laborer gained in wages he would lose in the highest cost of living. To put it technically, there would be a rise in nominal but not in real wages. . . .

The workers whose remuneration was raised to the Living Wage level would not be in the same condition of economic advantage or disadvantage relatively to other economic classes as they were before the rise. There is no more reason for expecting this outcome than there was for the prediction, formerly made, that all the gains effected by trade union action would be neutralized by the higher prices that the unionists would be obliged to pay as consumers. As a matter of fact, group after group have through organization obtained increases in wages without suffering anything like an equivalent loss in the purchasing power of their individual dollars. Experience has

shown that whenever one economic class has gained in money income at the apparent expense of other classes, a part of the gain has been not merely nominal, and a part of it has been not only in appearance, but in fact at the expense of the other classes.

Thus far the discussion of both of the objections that we have been considering has proceeded on the assumption that the rise in prices would be *fully equivalent* to the rise in wages. The assumption concedes too much. Part of the increased labor cost would come out of interest; part out of profits; part out of the saving effected through the elimination of incompetent employers; and part out of the increased efficiency of both labor and capital. Some of the employers who found it impossible to pay a Living Wage and at the same time obtain the usual rate of interest on their own capital invested in the business would content themselves with a somewhat lower rate. They would do this rather than go out of business.

Some of those who were unable to pay the old rate on borrowed capital would offer a lower rate, thereby lessening the demand for capital and exerting a downward pressure on the rate of interest. And this downward pressure would be reinforced by the action of those capitalist-employers who withdrew from business and threw their capital on the market rather than accept a smaller return from their investment. Moreover, since competition is never perfect, and since some businessmen do get money more cheaply than others in similar circumstances, some of the borrowers whom we are considering would succeed in renewing their loans at a lower rate than that which generally prevailed. Some lenders would submit to this condition in preference to the risk of faring worse elsewhere. Finally, there are some employers who would be able and willing to take a part of the added labor cost out of their personal profits. That is, they would be willing to do so rather than cease to be employers or attempt to saddle all the increased expense on the selling price of the product.

To deny these general statements concerning the capitalist-employer, the loan-capitalist, and the employer in his capacity of profit receiver is to contend that all the individuals of these three classes would absolutely refuse to accept a lower return for their money or their activity than they now obtain. It is to maintain that of all the agents of production only the laborer will ever submit to a reduction in his share of the product. Needless to say, this theory is contradicted by experience. Both interest and profits *have* fallen, and there is no good reason to think that they have already reached an irreducible minimum. On the contrary, it is practically certain that the general rate of interest must, independently of the Living Wage question, suffer a further decline.

Perhaps a majority of the small employers would not, or could not, continue their present functions if their personal returns were diminished; but this is by no means the case with all. The situation in which employers who were compelled to raise the compensation of their underpaid employees to the plane of a Living Wage would find themselves, is this: The sources from which the additional wage payments can be drawn are only three; namely, the selling price of the product, interest, and profits. Now the difficulty of raising prices to a level sufficiently high — and of maintaining them there — to provide for all the increased labor cost is so great that many employers will find it easier and more satisfactory to secure a portion of the necessary funds from one or both of the other two sources. In the third place, some of the more competent or better situated employers at present pay substantially a Living Wage in circumstances and industries in which their competitors generally fail to do so, and could under other conditions take care of a large proportion of the business now carried on by the latter.

When the Living Wage became universal, they would not find it necessary to raise prices to any appreciable extent, while many of their less-competent competitors would be forced to the wall. This "survival of the fittest" might proceed so far that prices would ultimately reach the old level, owing to the satisfactory profits obtained by the "survivors" through the increased volume of sales. At any rate, it is certain that a large number of incompetent employers are now able to continue their functions, not because their services are needed by the community but because they pay a smaller wage than their competitors; and that the elimination of these from any cause whatever would reduce the total cost of production and enable their labor force to find employment at better wages with the more competent employers.

In the fourth place, a part of the increase in wages would be derived from the increased productivity of the industries in which the rise occurred. The higher wage enjoyed by the laborers would give them a higher physical and mental efficiency, and consequently a greater productive power, while the increased labor cost of production would compel businessmen to introduce better machinery and a better organization of industry. Most of the improvements of the last century in methods of production seem to have originated in the pressure exerted upon employers and by the demands of labor. As long as they could secure the advantages of cheap production through cheap labor, employers generally declined to undertake the exertion, risk, and expense of discovering or introducing new processes. A similar condition obtains today in many of the industries in which labor is underpaid, and a similar course would be adopted by many employers if they found it no longer possible to hire workers for less than a Living Wage.

In general, it may be said that the arguments against the economic feasibility of a universal Living Wage are reducible to two. The first is that the national product of food and other articles of necessity and comfort would not be adequate; the second, that the machinery of distribution could not be so modified as to achieve the desired result. It is difficult to see how any American economist can take the former contention seriously. . . . Our natural resources and productive capacity are more than sufficient to furnish the entire population with the requisites of a decent livelihood. . . .

The objections based on the difficulty of obtaining the required modification of the distributive process are far from being conclusive. They can all be, and have been, urged against every effort that has ever been made, by trade union action or otherwise, to better the condition of any group of workers; for they all turn on the supposed evil consequences of a higher cost of production and higher prices to the consumer. If there is any difference between the economic and social effects of the gains that labor has already struggled for and secured, and those that would result from the universal application of the Living Wage principle, it is a difference only of degree. Yet experience has shown that gains in wages invariably mean a real improvement in the condition of those obtaining them and rarely involve any hardship worth considering to other classes or to the community at large.

The discussion of this point may be fitly closed with a citation from two investigators [Sidney and Beatrice Webb] of the very highest authority.

We desire to emphasize the point that whatever political objections there may be to the fixing by law of a national minimum wage, and whatever practical difficulties there may be in the way of carrying it out, the proposal, *from the point of view of abstract economics,* is open to no more objection than the fixing by law of a national minimum of sanitation, or a national minimum of leisure, both of which are, in principle, embodied in our factory legislation. Indeed, a minimum wage, since it would in no way interfere with the fullest use of machinery and plant, or otherwise check productivity, would seem to be even less open to economic criticism than a limitation of the hours of labor.

The obstacles to the legal enactment and enforcement of a Living Wage in America are great but not necessarily insuperable. There is, in the first place, that perverse individualism which prefers irrational liberty and industrial anarchy to a legal regime of order and justice. This spirit is still sufficiently potent to render exceedingly difficult those changes in the federal Constitution and in the constitutions of the several states which would be a preliminary requisite to any such legislation. After the law had been enacted, the willingness of the unemployed, always numerous in the class affected by the new statute, to sell their labor below the legal rate through fear of not obtaining employment otherwise would constitute a serious menace to its successful enforcement. In the case of illegal agreements entered into from this motive, both of the contracting parties would be interested in violating the law. Nevertheless, there are good grounds for believing that an honest and sustained attempt to secure a Living Wage by legal enactment would meet with a fair measure of success.

Public opinion is changing very rapidly in its attitude toward government regulation of industry, and especially with regard to the question of legislative repression of abuses. It is coming to see that unregulated competition has proved itself inadequate to protect the consumer against monopoly and extortionate prices, and the producer against exploitation and starvation wages. Very probably a large majority of the voters of the country agree with President Roosevelt that, if the federal government does not now possess the power to regulate corporations adequately, the national Constitution ought to be changed accordingly. Once an amendment of this character has been effected, constitutional modifications empowering Congress and the state legislatures to pass a minimum wage law could readily be obtained. Thus the greatest of the obstacles to a universal Living Wage by legal enactment would have disappeared.

After the law had been placed on the statute books, organized labor and a large section of the underpaid workers who were not organized would be vitally and actively interested in its enforcement. The penalties attached to its violation could be made sufficiently heavy to deter all but the boldest employers and the most reckless workingmen. Even if it were observed in the case of, say, only one-fifth of the workers previously underpaid, there would be so much gained, and according as the public came to realize the reasonableness and necessity of the new legislation, the proportion of instances in which it was violated would rapidly decrease.

Owing to differences in the cost of living and other conditions, the greater part of such legislation would have to come from the several states rather than from the national Congress. Its terms in detail and its enforcement could best be determined and secured through a commission, empowered to adjust it to different industries and different centers of population. Precisely the same principle is embodied in the legislation which at present authorizes state railway commissions to fix reasonable rates for the transportation of passengers and freight. Their power to lay down maximum rates on the basis of a reasonable return from investments is at bottom the power to limit, indirectly, of course, the incomes of the stockholders. The wage commissions would attack the opposite extreme of industrial in-

justice by fixing a minimum rate of remuneration for the workingmen. . . .

Until such time as a general Living Wage law becomes a reality, the state could apply the principle partially. The various legislative authorities, national, state, and municipal, should enact legislation providing that all adult employees in the public services or employed by private firms on work done by contract for the public receive a wage adequate to the decent maintenance of themselves and their families. While the number of laborers affected by the law would be comparatively small, the moral effect on public opinion and on purely private wage contracts would be very considerable.

Similar legislation could without difficulty be enacted and successfully applied to all quasi-public industries of a monopolistic character, such as, railroads, street railways, and telegraph, telephone, and express companies. Professor T. S. Adams maintains that a compulsory arbitration law — which would necessarily include the power to determine rates of wages — covering these industries is immediately feasible. When it is recalled that in the highly prosperous year of 1903 more than three-fourths of a million adult males in steam-railway occupations received less than a Living Wage, the direct benefits to be derived from this partial extension of the Living Wage principle are readily perceived.

Several indirect methods may be mentioned through which the state could extend the field in which a Living Wage would prevail. The first is legislation limiting the working day to eight hours and fixing the minimum age at which children would be permitted to become wage earners at sixteen years. The immediate effect of these measures would be a diminution in product and an increase in the demand for labor. An increase in the price of labor — a rise in wages — would follow necessarily. In general, the objections offered to this argument are identical with those urged against a universal Living Wage, namely, an increased cost of production and a rise in the price of the finished product. . . .

Two other methods of state action to which attention will be called are housing and old-age pensions. "No problem," says a recent writer, "presents so many startling aspects as the problem of the housing of the working people." The overcrowded condition in which so many of them are forced to exist involves the "destruction of home-life, weakening of parental influence, falling off of religious faith, changed relation of the sexes, absence of privacy, intrusion of strangers upon the family life, the use in common of facilities of living where propriety and decency demand the restriction to a single family, the constant sight and sound of debasing influences from which escape is impossible."

The state could build dwellings and sell them to the worst-off of the underpaid workers for less than cost, on condition that they be paid for in small installments without interest. The direct gain in comfort to the beneficiaries of this action is obvious; the indirect gain in the form of self-respect, self-confidence, hopefulness, and courage, ambition and ability to contend for better wages and a higher economic position, would be of even greater importance.

Finally, the state ought to give every laborer who has become permanently incapacitated for work through old age, and whose wages have not been sufficient to make provision for his declining years, an annual pension. The man that has toiled faithfully during all the vigorous portion of his life has a valid claim against society for this amount. It is, in fact, a part of the Living Wage that is due him for his lifework. A system of old-age pensions would, moreover, afford considerable relief to many underpaid and moderately paid workers who are now burdened with the support of relatives that are no longer able to earn their own living. Freed from this charge, many of the former would enjoy a Living Wage in the full sense of the phrase, while others would approach it much more closely than they do at present. State relief of the incapacitated has become an especially urgent problem in this machine age, when the laborer's working life comes to a close so much earlier than formerly.

These forms of state assistance would, of course, entail a heavy financial burden and increased taxation. One method of providing the required funds may be briefly touched upon because of its general bearing on the problem of distribution. A progressive tax on incomes and inheritances could be so framed as to furnish the means of carrying out the projects of housing and old-age pensions on a very large scale. The rate on inheritance would naturally be higher than that on incomes.

Speaking of the former method of taxation, Andrew Carnegie has written:

> Of all forms of taxation, this seems to be the wisest. Men who continue hoarding great sums all their lives, the proper use of which for public ends would work good to the community, should be made to feel that the community in the form of the state, cannot be deprived of its proper share. By taxing estates heavily at death, the state marks its condemnation of the selfish millionaire's unworthy life.
>
> It is desirable that nations should go much further in this direction. Indeed, it is difficult to set bounds to the share of a rich man's estate which should go at his death to the public through the agency of the state, and by all means such taxes should be graduated, beginning at nothing upon moderate sums to dependents and increasing rapidly as the amounts swell, until of the millionaire's hoard, as of Shylock's, at least
> —— The other half
> Comes to the privy coffer of the state.

The argument for a graduated tax, increasing in rate with the size of the estate, is as valid in the case of incomes as in that of inheritance. In both, the rich man is compelled to give up to the community a larger percentage of his wealth than the man of moderate means because, the richer a man is, the less hardship does he suffer when his possessions are diminished by a given fraction. If it be objected that to apply the proceeds of these forms of taxation to the purposes here advocated is to take from the rich and give to the poor, the charge may be passed over as correct in substance. It implies, however, a false notion of the morality of the proposal.

The state is bound not only to protect its citizens in the enjoyment of their natural rights to the effective opportunity of gaining a decent livelihood by their labor but to compensate, as far as practicable, those persons for whom it has failed to provide such opportunity. For this purpose, taxes must be levied, and they should be apportioned in accordance with the resources of the citizens.

19.

George M. Cohan: "You're a Grand Old Flag"

George M. Cohan wrote the words and music for "You're a Grand Old Flag" for the musical show George Washington, Jr., *which opened on Broadway, with Cohan in the leading role, in 1906. The original title was "You're a Grand Old Rag," a phrase used by a Civil War veteran who had referred affectionately to the flag in that manner in a conversation with Cohan. The audience did not seem to be pleased by this bit of jocular familiarity, and so Cohan changed "Rag" to "Flag." The song was an immediate hit and sold over a million copies of sheet music, and it enjoyed a revival during both world wars.*

Source: "You're A Grand Old Flag," New York, 1906.

❦ YOU'RE A GRAND OLD FLAG

There's a feeling comes a-stealing and it sets my brain a-reeling,
When I'm listening to the music of a military band.
Any tune like "Yankee Doodle" simply sets me off my noodle —
It's that patriotic something that no one can understand.
"Way down South in the land of cotton,"
    Melody untiring —
    Ain't that inspiring!
Hurrah! Hurrah! We'll join the jubilee,
    And that's going some
    For the Yankees, by gum.
Red, white, and blue, I am for you —
Honest, you're a grand old rag.

    Chorus:
    You're a grand old flag, though you're torn to a rag,
    And forever in peace may you wave.
    You're the emblem of the land I love,
    The home of the free and the brave.

Every heart beats true under red, white, and blue,
Where there's never a boast or brag;
"But should auld acquaintance be forgot,"
Keep your eye on the grand old flag.

I'm no cranky hanky-panky, I'm a dead square honest Yankee,
And I'm mighty proud of that old flag that flies for Uncle Sam.
Though I don't believe in raving every time I see it waving,
There's a chill runs up my back that makes me glad I'm what I am.
Here's a land with a million soldiers —
  That's if we should need 'em,
  We'll fight for freedom!
Hurrah! Hurrah! For every Yankee tar
  And old G.A.R.,
   Every stripe, every star,
Red, white, and blue, hats off to you —
  Honest, you're a grand old rag.

20.

Florence Kelley: Obstacles to Enforcing Child Labor Laws

The National Child Labor Committee, led by prominent liberals, such as Professor Felix Adler and Jane Addams, publicized the distressing conditions under which children worked and the unhealthy effects long working hours had on the young. At the third annual meeting of the committee, December 13-15, 1906, in Cincinnati, the status of child labor in this country was reviewed. Mrs. Florence Kelley, one of Jane Addams' associates at Hull House and a leading worker for the National Child Labor Committee, reported on the implementation of child labor laws in various states. She suggested some reasons why the laws were ineffectual and proposed ways to improve them. A portion of her report appears here.

Source: *Annals* of the American Academy of Political and Social Science, January 1907: "Obstacles to the Enforcement of Child Labor Legislation."

SIXTY YEARS AGO IN ENGLAND the great obstacle to the enforcement of child labor legislation, and even to the enactment of such legislation, was the attitude of the cotton manufacturers of that Kingdom, who went in delegations to Parliament and said, "Yes, there is child labor, and it is a good thing that the children should learn to work. We are carrying on schools to teach them to work. Moreover, it is good for the Kingdom that there should be child labor, for on that rests the commercial supremacy of the nation." And the only answer possible at that time was a purely theoretical statement that nothing can be so important as the life, the health, and welfare of the children of the nation.

We have not that obstacle in this country. No great delegations of manufacturers go to Congress, or to any legislature, and say, "Yes, there is child labor, and it is a good thing for the children, and for the republic." They do not go to Congress at all on this subject, or to any legislature — not at all. Through their trade organs the great manufacturers say: "There is no child labor in this country. If there were, it would be a bad thing. We do not employ young children. This is all exaggeration."

But they do employ children, and the children are working tonight. I know that children six, seven, and eight years old work this week in New York City tenements for reputable manufacturers. I have seen children in a cotton mill in Georgia whose employer told me they were ten years old, who were wretched dwarfs if they were really eight years old. That one man frankly showed children at work in his mill.

On the whole, however, the entire attitude of the manufacturing class has been revolutionized in sixty years. No one now says that it is a good thing for little children to work. The haggling now is as to whether a child shall legally begin at twelve, or at fourteen, or at sixteen years to work.

It is ultimately the attitude of mind of the nation that decides whether child labor laws shall be enforced after they are enacted. And the attitude of mind has changed (as it exhibits itself in speech and in print) from the bold claim that the commercial supremacy of England was more important than the welfare of the English race, to the hypocritical attitude of this country that we have not the evil and, therefore, need do nothing about it. I do not know which obstacle to the enforcement of law is more effective. The obstacle is there, and our legislation, taking the country over, is not effectively enforced.

There are three objective tests of the enforcement of our laws. One is the presence of children in school. This is now being shown in an interesting exhibit of industrial conditions in Philadelphia. There is a chart showing the attendance of the children of Chicago at school in the year 1902. A small block symbolizes the attendance in that year. For the following year the same block repeated symbolizes the attendance; but the next year, 1904, when the present drastic child labor law of Illinois had taken effect, the enrollment in the Chicago schools of the children of compulsory school age trebled. It required three times the original block to indicate the school attendance in the year after that new law took effect and was enforced. That statute carried 1,000 children out of the stockyards in a single week; and later it carried 2,200 children out of the mines of Illinois in another week, following the decision of the enlightened judge of the Peoria district. And the increased school enrollment showed whither the children went.

The second objective test of the enforcement of child labor laws is prosecution. The child labor law is enforced in Illinois by persistent prosecution. Hundreds of employers have paid thousands of dollars in fines, and the visible result of the success of those prosecutions is the presence of the children of compulsory school age in school. That is an infallible test of the effectiveness of the enforcement of the law which prohibits children working throughout the period of compulsory school attendance.

South of Baltimore — south of Louisville — there are no prosecutions; there is no compulsory school attendance. In any Southern state today, school attendance does not serve as a test of the efficiency of the protection of the children because there are not schools enough to enroll the children if they were all dismissed from the mills.

We enroll our children in New York

Overseer supervising a girl about 13 years old operating a bobbin-winding machine in the Yazoo City Yarn Mills, Mississippi, 1911; photo by Lewis Hine

City. I wish I might say that we kept them in school. We enroll them, at least, and the enrollment has increased under the recent efficient enforcement of the law in the factories by Commissioner Sherman. Even where there are not schools enough to admit the children, we can at least enroll them so that we may know where they are, and the opportunity to enroll them depends largely upon the efficiency of the prosecutions carried out by the factory inspectors.

The enforcement of the law depends not only on the quality of the men to whom the work of enforcing it is entrusted; it depends far more largely on the quality of the community in which those men hold office. There are few blacker chapters in the history of this republic than the ever recurring story of removal of efficient officers because they have attempted to enforce child labor laws in communities which were willing to have those laws on the statute books so long as they were not enforced, but either repealed the statutes or removed the officers as soon as there was any effective prosecution.

There is a brilliant example of this in the history of the city of New York. The Mercantile Employees' Law, when first drafted, provided that the same officer who enforced the law in factories should enforce it in the stores. But the Retail Dealers' Association of New York City objected and prevented the enactment of the statute until a compromise was achieved. That was in the days when we had a very efficient inspector in office, the only efficient one we ever had before Mr. Sherman. A compromise was achieved, and the enforcement of the law in stores was left to local boards of health.

The Retail Dealers' Association highly approved the appointment of a leading philanthropic merchant of New York to the position of commissioner of health. This gentleman said quite frankly when he took office that he did not mean to hold it long, that he had only two aims which he wished to achieve. One aim was to get free sterilized and pasteurized milk for the children of the tenements; the other aim was to cut out of the municipal budget the appropriation for local inspectors to enforce the child labor laws in stores. He achieved both these ends; he cut the municipal appropriation for the enforcement of the law in stores, and he established pasteurized milk for children in tenements. Then he resigned.

His successor cut out the pasteurized milk; and then we had neither mercantile inspection nor pasteurized milk. And to this day the child labor law has never been enforced in stores. Notice is served upon the incoming commissioner of health by the secretary of the Retail Dealers' Association that they do not consider it desirable that the law should be enforced in stores with the same rigor with which it is enforced in factories.

Two years ago I saw 150 children working illegally at 20 minutes past 10 o'clock at night in a perfectly reputable dry goods store in the city of New York on the Saturday night before Christmas. If one of those children had stolen any small article, a doll or a penknife, the heavy hand of the law would have carried that child promptly into the Juvenile Court. But 150 children were robbed of sleep in violation of the law; and the merchant, their employer who robbed them, has never been prosecuted to this day, and will never be prosecuted. The community does not insist that the great in New York City shall obey the law for the protection of the children; and no commissioner of health has had the moral courage to do that which his community does not wish done.

While the community in New York does sustain the commissioner of labor in his prosecutions of manufacturers who employ children illegally, no commissioner of health has instituted proceedings under a similar law against any merchant in the city except in the case of one or two obscure men down in the Lower East Side.

It is difficult to induce men of high ability to give up their chosen occupations to take a position which involves them in an oath that they will enforce a law when there is always a sword hanging over their heads if they do enforce that law. If there is a great clamor in the community by a few people that the law shall be enforced, the temptation is terribly strong to enforce it against obscure offenders violating it in a small way so as to make a record of something done without incurring powerful opposition for the official or for the law.

The third test of the enforcement of the child labor laws is the published records of the officials appointed to enforce them. The friends of the children are growing in numbers, but they often lack technical acquaintance with the subject. It may be said of many of us that our intentions are good, but we have never been working children; we have never been employers; we have, perhaps, never been teachers of working children, and we do not speak with authority. . . .

In the same industrial exhibition in Philadelphia of which I spoke, the most conspicuous objects are two huge signs which tell the story taken from the official records of Pennsylvania concerning enforcement of the child labor laws in manufacture and mercantile pursuits in that state. The latest available report is dated 1904, and this is the end of 1906.

One of those signs says, in large letters:

Pennsylvania — Children Employed, 40,140.
Children Illegally Employed, 3,243.
Prosecutions, 22.

The other sign says:

Pennsylvania — Children Employed, 40,140.
Children Illegally Employed, 3,243.
Fines Imposed, $750.
Average Cost of Violation of the
Child Labor Law in
Pennsylvania, 23 Cents.

Now, that is the sort of information for want of which we are not, on the whole, very intelligent about our working children in this country. The National Consumers' League, a volunteer philanthropic body, publishes every year a *Handbook of Child Labor Legislation.* Why is this book left to be published by a volunteer body? Why does not the United States Department of Commerce and Labor publish it? And why has the predecessor of that department not done so for the past twenty years? Why has the handbook been left to grow from a little leaflet of four pages, five years ago, to a little pamphlet of sixty-four pages now, published as a supplement to *The Annals* of the American Academy this year?

Why are the American people content to have thousands of undecipherable official pages of unmeaning figures published year after year? Why have we endured being left with no official means of ready comparison of the statutes of the different states and the prosecutions of violations of the child labor law in the different states? Whether in Ohio it costs 23 cents for every violation of the child labor law, or 23 dollars, or $230, or $2,300, we do not know. We do not know this for any state unless we sit down and carefully and laboriously make computations for ourselves, which may then perhaps be in error.

These, I believe, are the gravest obstacles at the present time to the enforcement of the child labor law: first, the general hypocrisy of the American people, believing that child labor is an evil, and that, therefore, we do not tolerate it — when there are working children on the streets before our eyes, every working day in the year, in every manufacturing city; second, the failure to make the work of enforcing the law a desirable and recognized profession into which the ablest men will willingly go.

Leonard Horner, the first of the English factory inspectors, held office thirty-four years. He laid the foundation for factory inspection throughout the world. His name goes down in history coupled with the name of Lord Shaftesbury — and honorably coupled with it. And from his day to the present the position of local factory inspector and shop inspector is an honorable one for which thoroughly efficient men eagerly compete in the English civil service. In America, we leave an inspector at the mercy of the most influential man whom it may be his duty to prosecute, and at the mercy of every turn of the political wheel; and then we wonder that we have not a race of noble martyrs who protect working children at cost of their own professional careers. And we fall to thinking that there is something hopeless in the effort to put better laws upon the statute book if then they are to sleep upon its pages.

The trouble is with ourselves. We get exactly the sort of care for the children through the officials that the community determines they shall have; and we register our indifference in accepting such printed records as we have now, obscuring the actual conditions of the working children in nearly all the states.

Where the employment of children is arrested, as is the case effectually in Illinois, partially in New York, partially in Massachusetts, the records are so clear that any schoolchild can understand them. The ability which makes it possible to arrest the growth of child labor makes it possible also to print records which we can all read and understand and use.

The next step which we need to take is to insist that this is a national evil, and we must have a national law abolishing it. We must also insist that this is a matter of great import to the people of this country, that the government must give us information not only through a bureau for the children in the federal government but through all the existing departments — the Census Bureau, the Department of Commerce and Labor, the Department of Education. We must demand trustworthy records in our state publications so that we shall not blush when a request comes to send a complete collection of our records for the use, for instance, of the Austrian government.

1907

21.

Walter Rauschenbusch: A Christian Alliance with Labor

The Social Gospel had existed as a movement for at least two decades before Walter Rauschenbusch wrote Christianity and the Social Crisis *in 1907, but it was he who gave it the vital intellectual foundation that it needed and spread its fame beyond the nation's boundaries. Rauschenbusch never forgot the circumstances of his pastorate in New York City's slum area, "Hell's Kitchen," where he saw before him a continuous "procession of men out of work, out of clothes, out of shoes, and out of hope." As a Christian Socialist he argued that labor's attempt to organize into unions was only a first step toward the formation of a socialist society that would see the dissolution of both the capitalist and the working class. The following selection is from the closing chapter of the book.*

Source: *Christianity and the Social Crisis,* New York, 1913: "What To Do."

THE MASSING OF LABOR in the factories since the introduction of power machinery has brought [the working class] into close contact with one another. Hard experience has taught them how helpless they are when they stand alone. They have begun to realize their solidarity and the divergence of their interests from those of the employers. They have begun to organize and are slowly learning to act together. The spread of education and cheap literature, the ease of communication, and the freedom of public meeting have rapidly created a common body of ideas and points of view among them.

The modern "labor movement" is the upward movement of this class. It began with local and concrete issues that pressed upon a given body of workingmen some demand for shorter hours or better wages, some grievance about fines or docking. . . .

But the labor movement means more than better wages and shorter hours for individual workingmen. It involves the struggle for a different status for their entire class. Other classes have long ago won a recognized standing in law and custom and public opinion — so long ago that they have forgotten that they ever had to win it. . . .

On the other hand, the working class has no adequate standing as yet. It did have in the guilds of former times, but modern industry and modern law under the laissez-faire principle dissolved the old privileges and reduced the working class to a mass of unrelated human atoms. Common action on their part was treated in law as conspiracy. In our country they have not yet won from their employers nor from public opinion the acknowledged right to be organized, to bargain collectively, and to assist in controlling the discipline of the shops in which they have to work. The law seems to afford them very little backing as yet. It provides penalties for the kind of injuries which workingmen are likely to inflict on their employers, but not for the subtler injuries which employers are likely to inflict on their workingmen. Few will care to assert that in the bitter conflicts waged between labor and capital the wrong has always been on one side. Yet when the law bares its sword, it is somehow always against one side. The militia does not seem to be ordered out against capital.

The labor movement must go on until public opinion and the law have conceded a recognized position to the labor unions and until the workingmen interested in a given question stand collectively on a footing of equality with the capitalists interested in it. This means a curtailment of power for the employers, and it would be contrary to human nature for them to like it. But for the working class it would be suicidal to forgo the attempt to get it. They have suffered fearfully by not having it. All the sacrifices they may bring in the chronic industrial warfare of the present will be cheap if they ultimately win through to an assured social and legal status for their class.

As long as the working class simply attempts to better its condition somewhat and to secure a recognized standing for its class organization, it stands on the basis of the present capitalistic organization of industry. Capitalism necessarily divides industrial society into two classes — those who own the instruments and materials of production, and those who furnish the labor for it. This sharp division is the peculiar characteristic of modern capitalism which distinguishes it from other forms of social organization in the past. These two classes have to cooperate in modern production.

The labor movement seeks to win better terms for the working class in striking its bargains. Yet whatever terms organized labor succeeds in winning are always temporary and insecure, like the hold which a wrestler gets on the body of his antagonist. The persistent tendency with capital necessarily is to get labor as cheaply as possible and to force as much work from it as possible. Moreover, labor is always in an inferior position in the struggle. It is handicapped by its own hunger and lack of resources. It has to wrestle on its knees with a foeman who is on his feet. Is this unequal struggle between two conflicting interests to go on forever? Is this insecurity the best that the working class can ever hope to attain?

Here enters socialism. It proposes to abolish the division of industrial society into two classes and to close the fatal chasm which has separated the employing class from the working class since the introduction of power machinery. It proposes to restore the independence of the workingman by making him once more the owner of his tools and to give him the full proceeds of his production instead of a wage determined by his poverty. It has no idea of reverting to the simple methods of the old handicrafts, but heartily accepts the power machinery, the great factory, the division of labor, the organization of the men in great regiments of workers as established facts in modern life and as the most efficient method of producing wealth.

But it proposes to give to the whole body of workers the ownership of these vast instruments of production and to distribute among them all the entire proceeds of their common labor. There would then be no capitalistic class opposed to the working class; there would be a single class which would unite the qualities of both. Every workman would be both owner and worker, just as a farmer is who tills his own farm or a housewife who works in her own kitchen. This would be a permanent solution of the labor question. It would end the present insecurity, the constant antagonism, the social inferiority, the physical exploitation, the intellectual poverty to which the working class is now exposed even when its condition is most favorable.

If such a solution is even approximately feasible, it should be hailed with joy by every patriot and Christian, for it would put a stop to our industrial war, drain off the miasmatic swamp of undeserved poverty, save our political democracy, and lift the great working class to an altogether different footing of comfort, intelligence, security, and moral strength. And it would embody the principle of solidarity and fraternity in the fundamental institutions of our industrial life. All the elements of cooperation and interaction which are now at work in our great establishments would be conserved, and, in addition, the hearty interest of all workers in their common factory or store would be immensely intensified by the diffused sense of ownership. Such a social order would develop the altruistic and social instincts just as the competitive order brings out the selfish instincts.

Socialism is the ultimate and logical outcome of the labor movement. When the entire working class throughout the industrial nations is viewed in a large way, the progress of socialism gives an impression of resistless and elemental power. It is inconceivable from the point of view of that class that it should stop short of complete independence and equality as long as it has the power to move on, and independence and equality for the working class must mean the collective ownership of the means of production and the abolition of the present two-class arrangement of industrial society. If the labor movement in our country is only slightly tinged with socialism as yet, it is merely because it is still in its embryonic stages. Nothing will bring the working class to a thorough comprehension of the actual status of their class and its ultimate aim

more quickly than continued failure to secure their smaller demands and reactionary efforts to suppress their unions. . . .

The cooperation of professional men outside the working class would contribute scientific information and trained intelligence. They would mediate between the two classes, interpreting each to the other, and thereby lessening the strain of hostility. Their presence and sympathy would cheer the working people and diminish the sense of class isolation. By their contract with the possessing classes they could help to persuade them of the inherent justice of the labor movement and so create a leaning toward concessions. No other influence could do so much to prevent a revolutionary explosion of pent-up forces. It is to the interest of all sides that the readjustment of the social classes should come as a steady evolutionary process rather than as a social catastrophe.

If the laboring class should attempt to seize political power suddenly, the attempt might be beaten back with terrible loss in efficiency to the movement. If the attempt should be successful, a raw governing class would be compelled to handle a situation so vast and complicated that no past revolution presents a parallel. There would be widespread disorder and acute distress, and a reactionary relapse to old conditions would, by all historical precedents, be almost certain to occur. It is devoutly to be desired that the shifting of power should come through a continuous series of practicable demands on one side and concessions on the other.

Such an historical process will be immensely facilitated if there are a large number of men in the professional and business class with whom religious and ethical motives overcome their selfish interests so that they will throw their influence on the side of the class which is now claiming its full rights in the family circle of humanity. On the other hand, the Christian idealists must not make the mistake of trying to hold the working class down to the use of moral suasion only, or be repelled when they hear the brute note of selfishness and anger.

The class struggle is bound to be transferred to the field of politics in our country in some form. It would be folly if the working class failed to use the leverage which their political power gives them. The business class has certainly never failed to use political means to further its interests. This is a war of conflicting interests which is not likely to be fought out in love and tenderness. . . .

It is fruitless to attempt to turn modern society back to conditions prevailing before power machinery and trusts had revolutionized it; or to copy biblical institutions adapted to wholly different social conditions; or to postpone the Christianizing of society to the millennium; or to found Christian communistic colonies within the competitive world; or to make the organized church the center and manager of an improved social machinery. The force of religion can best be applied to social renewal by sending its spiritual power along the existing and natural relations of men to direct them to truer ends and govern them by higher motives. . . .

We must repent of the sins of existing society, cast off the spell of the lies protecting our social wrongs, have faith in a higher social order, and realize in ourselves a new type of Christian manhood which seeks to overcome the evil in the present world, not by withdrawing from the world but by revolutionizing it. . . .

The force of the religious spirit should be bent toward asserting the supremacy of life over property. Property exists to maintain and develop life. It is unchristian to regard human life as a mere instrument for the production of wealth.

The religious sentiment can protect good customs and institutions against the inroads of ruthless greed and extend their scope. It can create humane customs which the law is impotent to create. It can create the con-

victions and customs which are later embodied in good legislation.

Our complex society rests largely on the stewardship of delegated powers. The opportunities to profit by the betrayal of trust increase with the wealth and complexity of civilization. The most fundamental evils in past history and present conditions were due to converting stewardship into ownership. The keener moral insight created by Christianity should lend its help in scrutinizing all claims to property and power in order to detect latent public rights and to recall the recreant stewards to their duty.

Primitive society was communistic. The most valuable institutions in modern life — the family, the school, and church — are communistic. The state, too, is essentially communistic and is becoming increasingly so. During the larger part of its history, the Christian Church regarded communism as the only ideal life. Christianity certainly has more affinity for cooperative and fraternal institutions than for competitive disunion. It should therefore strengthen the existing communistic institutions and aid the evolution of society from the present temporary stage of individualism to a higher form of communism.

The splendid ideal of a fraternal organization of society cannot be realized by idealists only. It must be supported by the self-interest of a powerful class. The working class, which is now engaged in its upward movement, is struggling to secure better conditions of life, an assured status for its class organizations, and, ultimately, the ownership of the means of production. Its success in the last great aim would mean the closing of the gap which now divides industrial society and the establishment of industry on the principle of solidarity and the method of cooperation. Christianity should enter into a working alliance with this rising class, and by its mediation secure the victory of these principles by a gradual equalization of social opportunity and power.

1908

22.

Samuel L. Clemens ("Mark Twain"): A Visit to Heaven

*Mark Twain's story "Extract from Captain Stormfield's Visit to Heaven" was
written or at least drafted in 1868 but not published for forty years. It was only one
of the many works of this master humorist that he was reluctant to reveal to the world,
lest it learn the bitterness in his heart. One may wonder why Clemens was afraid to
allow the story to appear, for, although it is opposed to organized religion, it is
deeply religious in another sense. The decision to publish at long last may have been
prompted by the author's belief that he would die in 1910 — when Halley's Comet,
under which he had been born, was to reappear. Incidentally, this belief was
confirmed; the perihelion of Halley's Comet was April 20, 1910, and Mark Twain died
the next day. In the following episode from his story, Captain Stormfield is given
a comprehensive briefing in the rules and customs of heaven by one McWilliams, an
older inhabitant. Cap and Sandy conduct their conversation while awaiting the
arrival of a recently deceased barkeep from Jersey City who expects to enjoy a
triumphant reception.*

Source: *Harper's Monthly*, January 1908.

I HAD BEEN HAVING CONSIDERABLE TROUBLE with my wings. The day after I helped the choir I made a dash or two with them, but was not lucky. First off, I flew thirty yards, and then fouled an Irishman and brought him down — brought us both down, in fact. Next, I had a collision with a Bishop — and bowled him down, of course. We had some sharp words, and I felt pretty cheap, to come banging into a grave old person like that, with a million strangers looking on and smiling to themselves.

I saw I hadn't got the hang of the steering, and so couldn't rightly tell where I was going to bring up when I started. I went afoot the rest of the day, and let my wings hang. Early next morning I went to a private place to have some practice. I got up on a pretty high rock, and got a good start, and went swooping down, aiming for a bush a little over three hundred yards off; but I couldn't seem to calculate for the wind, which was about two points abaft my beam. I could see I was going considerable to looard of the bush, so I worked my starboard wing slow and went ahead strong on the port one, but it wouldn't answer; I could see I was going to broach to, so I slowed down on both, and lit.

I went back to the rock and took another chance at it. I aimed two or three points to starboard of the bush — yes, more than that — enough so as to make it nearly a head wind. I done well enough, but made pretty poor time. I could see, plain enough, that on a head wind, wings was a mistake. I could see that a body could sail pretty close to the wind, but he couldn't go in the wind's eye. I could see that if I wanted to go a-visiting any distance from home, and the wind was ahead, I might have to wait days, maybe, for a change; and I could see, too, that these things could not be any use at all in a gale; if you tried to run before the wind, you would make a mess of it, for there isn't any way to shorten sail — like reefing, you know — you have to take it *all* in — shut your feathers down flat to your sides. That would *land* you, of course. You could lay to, with your head to the wind — that is the best you could do, and right hard work you'd find it, too. If you tried any other game, you would founder, sure.

I judge it was about a couple of weeks or so after this that I dropped old Sandy McWilliams a note one day — it was a Tuesday — and asked him to come over and take his manna and quails with me next day; and the first thing he did when he stepped in was to twinkle his eye in a sly way, and say —

"Well, Cap, what you done with your wings?"

I saw in a minute that there was some sarcasm done up in that rag somewheres, but I never let on. I only says —

"Gone to the wash."

"Yes," he says, in a dry sort of way,

"they mostly go to the wash — about this time — I've often noticed it. Fresh angels are powerful neat. When do you look for 'em back?"

"Day after tomorrow," says I.

He winked at me, and smiled.

Says I,

"Sandy, out with it. Come — no secrets among friends. I notice you don't ever wear wings — and plenty others don't. I've been making an ass of myself — is that it?"

"That is about the size of it. But it is no harm. We all do it at first. It's perfectly natural. You see, on earth we jump to such foolish conclusions as to things up here. In the pictures we always saw the angels with wings on — and that was all right; but we jumped to the conclusion that that was their way of getting around — and that was all wrong. The wings ain't anything but a uniform, that's all. When they are in the field — so to speak — they always wear them; you never see an angel going with a message anywhere without his wings, anymore than you would see a military officer presiding at a court-martial without his uniform, or a postman delivering letters, or a policeman walking his beat in plain clothes. But they ain't to *fly* with! The wings are for show, not for use.

"Old experienced angels are like officers of the regular army — they dress plain when they are off duty. New angels are like the militia — never shed the uniform — always fluttering and floundering around in their wings, butting people down, flapping here, and there, and everywhere, always imagining they are attracting the admiring eye — well, they just think they are the very most important people in heaven. And when you see one of them come sailing around with one wing tipped up and t'other down, you can make up your mind he is saying to himself: 'I wish Mary Ann in Arkansaw could see me now. I reckon she'd wish she hadn't shook me.' No, they're just for show, that's all — only just for show."

"I judge you've got it about right, Sandy," says I.

"Why, look at it yourself," says he.

"*You* ain't built for wings — no man is. You know what a grist of years it took you to come here from the earth — and yet you were booming along faster than any cannonball could go. Suppose you had to fly that distance with your wings — wouldn't eternity have been over before you got here? Certainly. Well, angels have to go to the earth every day — millions of them — to appear in visions to dying children and good people, you know — it's the heft of their business. They appear with their wings, of course, because they are on official service, and because the dying persons wouldn't know they were angels if they hadn't wings — but do you reckon they fly with them? It stands to reason they don't. The wings would wear out before they got half-way; even the pin feathers would be gone; the wing frames would be as bare as kite sticks before the paper is pasted on.

"The distances in heaven are billions of times greater; angels have to go all over heaven every day; could they do it with their wings alone? No, indeed; they wear the wings for style, but they travel any distance in an instant by *wishing*. The wishing carpet of the Arabian Nights was a sensible idea — but our earthly idea of angels flying these awful distances with their clumsy wings was foolish.

"Our young saints, of both sexes, wear wings all the time — blazing red ones, and blue and green, and gold, and variegated, and rainbowed, and ring-streaked-and-striped ones — and nobody finds fault. It is suitable to their time of life. The things are beautiful, and they set the young people off. They are the most striking and lovely part of their outfit — a halo don't *begin*."

"Well," says I, "I've tucked mine away in the cupboard, and I allow to let them lay there till there's mud."

"Yes — or a reception."

"What's that?"

"Well, you can see one tonight if you want to. There's a barkeeper from Jersey City going to be received."

"Go on — tell me about it."

"This barkeeper got converted at a Moody and Sankey meeting, in New York, and started home on the ferryboat, and there was a collision and he got drowned. He is of a class that think all heaven goes wild with joy when a particularly hard lot like him is saved; they think all heaven turns out hosannahing to welcome them; they think there isn't anything talked about in the realms of the blest but their case, for that day. This barkeeper thinks there hasn't been such another stir here in years as his coming is going to raise. And I've always noticed this peculiarity about a dead barkeeper — he not only expects all hands to turn out when he arrives but he expects to be received with a torchlight procession."

"I reckon he is disappointed, then."

"No, he isn't. No man is allowed to be disappointed here. Whatever he wants, when he comes — that is, any reasonable and unsacrilegious thing — he can have. There's always a few millions or billions of young folks around who don't want any better entertainment than to fill up their lungs and swarm out with their torches and have a high time over a barkeeper. It tickles the barkeeper till he can't rest, it makes a charming lark for the young folks, it don't do anybody any harm, it don't cost a rap, and it keeps up the place's reputation for making all comers happy and content."

"Very good. I'll be on hand and see them land the barkeeper."

"It is manners to go in full dress. You want to wear your wings, you know, and your other things."

"Which ones?"

"Halo, and harp, and palm branch, and all that."

"Well," says I, "I reckon I ought to be ashamed of myself, but the fact is I left them laying around that day I resigned from the choir. I haven't got a rag to wear but this robe and the wings."

"That's all right. You'll find they've been raked up and saved for you. Send for them."

"I'll do it, Sandy. But what was it you was saying about unsacrilegious things, which people expect to get, and will be disappointed about?"

"Oh, there are a lot of such things that people expect and don't get. For instance, there's a Brooklyn preacher by the name of Talmage, who is laying up a considerable disappointment for himself. He says, every now and then in his sermons, that the first thing he does when he gets to heaven will be to fling his arms around Abraham, Isaac, and Jacob, and kiss them and weep on them. There's millions of people down there on earth that are promising themselves the same thing. As many as sixty thousand people arrive here every single day that want to run straight to Abraham, Isaac, and Jacob, and hug them and weep on them. Now mind you, sixty thousand a day is a pretty heavy contract for those old people. If they were a mind to allow it, they wouldn't ever have anything to do, year in and year out but stand up and be hugged and wept on thirty-two hours in the twenty-four. They would be tired out and as wet as muskrats all the time.

"What would heaven be, to *them?* It would be a mighty good place to get out of — you know that, yourself. Those are kind and gentle old Jews, but they ain't any fonder of kissing the emotional highlights of Brooklyn than you be. You mark my words, Mr. T.'s endearments are going to be declined, with thanks. There are limits to the privileges of the elect, even in heaven. Why, if Adam was to show himself to every newcomer that wants to call and gaze at him and strike him for his autograph, he would never have time to do anything else but just that. Talmage has said he is going to give Adam some of his attentions, as

well as A., I., and J. But he will have to change his mind about that."

"Do you think Talmage will really come here?"

"Why, certainly, he will; but don't you be alarmed; he will run with his own kind, and there's plenty of them. That is the main charm of heaven — there's all kinds here — which wouldn't be the case if you let the preachers tell it. Anybody can find the sort he prefers, here, and he just lets the others alone, and they let him alone. When the Deity builds a heaven, it is built right, and on a liberal plan."

Sandy sent home for his things, and I sent for mine, and about nine in the evening we begun to dress. Sandy says —

"This is going to be a grand time for you, Stormy. Like as not some of the patriarchs will turn out."

"No, but will they?"

"Like as not. Of course they are pretty exclusive. They hardly ever show themselves to the common public. I believe they never turn out except for an eleventh-hour convert. They wouldn't do it then, only earthly tradition makes a grand show pretty necessary on that kind of an occasion."

"Do they all turn out, Sandy?"

"Who? — all the patriarchs? Oh, no — hardly ever more than a couple. You will be here fifty thousand years — maybe more — before you get a glimpse of all the patriarchs and prophets. Since I have been here, Job has been to the front once, and once Ham and Jeremiah both at the same time. But the finest thing that has happened in my day was a year or so ago; that was Charles Peace's reception — him they called 'the Bannercross Murderer' — an Englishman. There were four patriarchs and two prophets on the Grand Stand that time — there hasn't been anything like it since Captain Kidd came. Abel was there — the first time in twelve hundred years. A report got around that Adam was coming; well, of course Abel was enough to bring a crowd, all by himself, but there is nobody that can draw like Adam. It was a false report, but it got around, anyway, as I say, and it will be a long day before I see the like of it again.

"The reception was in the English department, of course, which is eight hundred and eleven million miles from the New Jersey line. I went, along with a good many of my neighbors, and it was a sight to see, I can tell you. Flocks came from all the departments. I saw Esquimaux there, and Tartars, Negroes, Chinamen — people from everywhere. You see a mixture like that in the Grand Choir, the first day you land here, but you hardly ever see it again. There were billions of people; when they were singing or hosannahing, the noise was wonderful; and even when their tongues were still, the drumming of the wings was nearly enough to burst your head, for all the sky was as thick as if it was snowing angels. Although Adam was not there, it was a great time anyway, because we had three archangels on the Grand Stand — it is a seldom thing that even one comes out."

"What did they look like, Sandy?"

"Well, they had shining faces, and shining robes, and wonderful rainbow wings, and they stood eighteen feet high, and wore swords, and held their heads up in a noble way, and looked like soldiers."

"Did they have halos?"

"No — anyway, not the hoop kind. The archangels and the upper-class patriarchs wear a finer thing than that. It is a round, solid, splendid glory of gold that is blinding to look at. You have often seen a patriarch in a picture, on earth, with that thing on — you remember it? — he looks as if he had his head in a brass platter. That don't give you the right idea of it at all — it is much more shining and beautiful."

"Did you talk with those archangels and patriarchs, Sandy?"

"Who — *I*? Why, what can you be thinking about, Stormy? I ain't worthy to speak to such as they."

"Is Talmage?"

"Of course not. You have got the same mixed-up idea about these things that everybody has down there. I had it once, but I got over it. Down there they talk of the heavenly King — and that is right — but then they go right on speaking as if this was a republic and everybody was on a dead level with everybody else, and privileged to fling his arms around anybody he comes across, and be hail-fellow-well-met with all the elect, from the highest down. How tangled up and absurd that is! How are you going to have a republic under a king? How are you going to have a republic at all, where the head of the government is absolute, holds his place forever, and has no parliament, no council to meddle or make in his affairs, nobody voted for, nobody elected, nobody in the whole universe with a voice in the government, nobody asked to take a hand in its matters, and nobody *allowed* to do it? Fine republic, ain't it?"

"Well, yes — it *is* a little different from the idea I had — but I thought I might go around and get acquainted with the grandees, anyway — not exactly splice the main brace with them, you know, but shake hands and pass the time of day."

"Could Tom, Dick, and Harry call on the Cabinet of Russia and do that? — on Prince Gortschakoff, for instance?"

"I reckon not, Sandy."

"Well, this is Russia — only more so. There's not the shadow of a republic about it anywhere. There are ranks, here. There are viceroys, princes, governors, sub-governors, sub-sub-governors, and a hundred orders of nobility, grading along down from grand-ducal archangels, stage by stage, til the general level is struck, where there ain't any titles. Do you know what a prince of the blood is, on earth?"

"No."

"Well, a prince of the blood don't belong to the royal family exactly, and he don't belong to the mere nobility of the kingdom; he is lower than the one, and higher than ʼother. That's about the position of the patriarchs and prophets here. There's some mighty high nobility here — people that you and I ain't worthy to polish sandals for — and *they* ain't worthy to polish sandals for the patriarchs and prophets. That gives you a kind of an idea of their rank, don't it? You begin to see how high up they are, don't you? Just to get a two-minute glimpse of one of them is a thing for a body to remember and tell about for a thousand years.

"Why, Captain, just think of this: if Abraham was to set his foot down here by this door, there would be a railing set up around that foot-track right away, and a shelter put over it, and people would flock here from all over heaven, for hundreds and hundreds of years, to look at it. Abraham is one of the parties that Mr. Talmage, of Brooklyn, is going to embrace, and kiss, and weep on, when he comes. He wants to lay in a good stock of tears, you know, or five to one he will go dry before he gets a chance to do it."

"Sandy," says I, "I had an idea that *I* was going to be equals with everybody here, too, but I will let that drop. It don't matter, and I am plenty happy enough anyway."

"Captain, you are happier than you would be the other way. These old patriarchs and prophets have got ages the start of you; they know more in two minutes than you know in a year. Did you ever try to have a sociable improving time discussing winds, and currents and variations of compass with an undertaker?"

"I get your idea, Sandy. He couldn't interest me. He would be an ignoramus in such things — he would bore me, and I would bore him."

"You have got it. You would bore the patriarchs when you talked, and when they talked they would shoot over your head. By

and by you would say, 'Good morning, your Eminence, I will call again' — but you wouldn't. Did you ever ask the slush boy to come up in the cabin and take dinner with you?"

"I get your drift again, Sandy. I wouldn't be used to such grand people as the patriarchs and prophets, and I would be sheepish and tongue-tied in their company, and mighty glad to get out of it. Sandy, which is the highest rank, patriarch or prophet?"

"Oh, the prophets hold over the patriarchs. The newest prophet, even, is of a sight more consequence than the oldest patriarch. Yes, sir, Adam himself has to walk behind Shakespeare."

"Was Shakespeare a prophet?"

"Of course he was; and so was Homer, and heaps more. But Shakespeare and the rest have to walk behind a common tailor from Tennessee by the name of Billings; and behind a horse doctor named Sakka, from Afghanistan. Jeremiah and Billings and Buddha walk together, side by side, right behind a crowd from planets not in our astronomy; next come a dozen or two from Jupiter and other worlds; next come Daniel and Sakka and Confucius; next a lot from systems outside of ours; next come Ezekiel and Mohamet Zoroaster, and a knife grinder from ancient Egypt; then there is a long string, and after them, away down toward the bottom, come Shakespeare and Homer, and a shoemaker named Marais, from the back settlements of France."

"Have they really rung in Mohamet and all those other heathens?"

"Yes — they all had their message, and they all get their reward. The man who don't get his reward on earth needn't bother — he will get it here, sure."

"But why did they throw off on Shakespeare that way, and put him away down there below those shoemakers and horse doctors and knife grinders — a lot of people nobody ever heard of?"

"That is the heavenly justice of it — they

warn't rewarded according to their deserts on earth, but here they get their rightful rank. That tailor Billings, from Tennessee, wrote poetry that Homer and Shakespeare couldn't begin to come up to; but nobody would print it, nobody read it but his neighbors, an ignorant lot, and they laughed at it. Whenever the village had a drunken frolic and a dance, they would drag him in and crown him with cabbage leaves, and pretend to bow down to him; and one night when he was sick and nearly starved to death, they had him out and crowned him, and then they rode him on a rail about the village, and everybody followed along, beating tin pans and yelling. Well, he died before morning. He wasn't ever expecting to go to heaven, much less that there was going to be any fuss made over him, so I reckon he was a good deal surprised when the reception broke on him."

"Was you there, Sandy?"

"Bless you, no!"

"Why? Didn't you know it was going to come off?"

"Well, I judge I did. It was the talk of these realms — not for a day, like this barkeeper business, but for twenty years before the man died."

"Why the mischief didn't you go, then?"

"Now, how you talk! The like of me go meddling around at the reception of a prophet? A mudsill like me trying to push in and help receive an awful grandee like Edward J. Billings? Why, I should have been laughed at for a billion miles around. I shouldn't ever heard the last of it."

"Well, who did go, then?"

"Mighty few people that you and I will ever get a chance to see, Captain. Not a solitary commoner ever has the luck to see a reception of a prophet, I can tell you. All the nobility, and all the patriarchs and prophets — every last one of them — and all the archangels, and all the princes and governors and viceroys, were there — and no small fry — not a single one. And mind you, I'm not talking about only the grandees from our world but the princes and patriarchs and so on from all the worlds that shine in our sky, and from billions more that belong in systems upon systems away outside of the one our sun is in. There were some prophets and patriarchs there that ours ain't a circumstance to, for rank and illustriousness and all that.

"Some were from Jupiter and other worlds in our own system, but the most celebrated were three poets, Saa, Bo, and Soof, from great planets in three different and very remote systems. These three names are common and familiar in every nook and corner of heaven, clear from one end of it to the other — fully as well known as the eighty Supreme Archangels, in fact — whereas our Moses, and Adam and the rest have not been heard of outside of our world's little corner of heaven, except by a few very learned men scattered here and there — and they always spell their names wrong, and get the performances of one mixed up with the doings of another, and they almost always locate them simply in our solar system, and think that is enough without going into little details such as naming the particular world they are from. It is like a learned Hindoo showing off how much he knows by saying Longfellow lives in the United States — as if he lived all over the United States, and as if the country was so small you couldn't throw a brick there without hitting him.

"Between you and me, it does gravel me, the cool way people from those monster worlds outside our system snub our little world, and even our system. Of course we think a good deal of Jupiter, because our world is only a potato to it, for size; but then there are worlds in other systems that Jupiter isn't even a mustard-seed to — like the planet Goobra, for instance, which you couldn't squeeze inside the orbit of Halley's comet without straining the rivets. Tourists from Goobra (I mean parties that lived and died there — natives) come here, now and then, and inquire about our world, and when they find out it is so little that a streak of lightning can flash clear around it in the eighth of a second, they have to lean up against something to laugh. Then they screw a glass into their eye and go to examining *us,* as if we were a curious kind of foreign bug, or something of that sort.

"One of them asked me how long our day was; and when I told him it was twelve hours long, as a general thing, he asked me if people where I was from considered it worthwhile to get up and wash for such a day as that. That is the way with those Goobra people — they can't seem to let a chance go by to throw it in your face that their day is three hundred and twenty-two of our years long. This young snob was just of age — he was six or seven thousand of his days old — say two million of our years — and he had all the puppy airs that belong to that time of life — that turning point when a person has got over being a boy and yet ain't quite a man exactly. If it had been anywhere else but in heaven, I would have given him a piece of my mind.

"Well, anyway, Billings had the grandest reception that has been seen in thousands of centuries, and I think it will have a good effect. His name will be carried pretty far, and it will make our system talked about, and maybe our world, too, and raise us in the respect of the general public of heaven. Why, look here — Shakespeare walked backwards before that tailor from Tennessee, and scattered flowers for him to walk on, and Homer stood behind his chair and waited on him at the banquet. Of course that didn't go for much *there,* amongst all those big foreigners from other systems, as they hadn't heard of Shakespeare or Homer either, but it would amount to considerable down there on our little earth if they could know about it. I wish there was something *in* that miserable spiritualism, so we could

send them word. That Tennessee village would set up a monument to Billings, then, and his autograph would outsell Satan's. Well, they had grand times at that reception — a small-fry noble from Hoboken told me all about it — Sir Richard Duffer, Baronet."

"What, Sandy, a nobleman from Hoboken? How is that?"

"Easy enough. Duffer kept a sausage shop and never saved a cent in his life because he used to give all his spare meat to the poor, in a quiet way. Not tramps — no, the other sort — the sort that will starve before they will beg — honest, square people out of work. Dick used to watch hungry-looking men and women and children, and track them home, and find out all about them from the neighbors, and then feed them and find them work. As nobody ever *saw* him give anything to anybody, he had the reputation of being mean; he died with it, too, and everybody said it was a good riddance; but the minute he landed here they made him a baronet, and the very first words Dick the sausage-maker of Hoboken heard when he stepped upon the heavenly shore were, 'Welcome, Sir Richard Duffer!' It surprised him some, because he thought he had reasons to believe he was pointed for a warmer climate than this one."

All of a sudden the whole region fairly rocked under the crash of eleven hundred and one thunder blasts, all let off at once, and Sandy says —

"There, that's for the barkeep."

I jumped up and says —

"Then let's be moving along, Sandy; we don't want to miss any of this thing, you know."

"Keep your seat," he says; "he is only just telegraphed, that is all."

"How?"

"That blast only means that he has been sighted from the signal station. He is off

Sandy Hook. The committees will go down to meet him, now, and escort him in. There will be ceremonies and delays; they won't be coming up the Bay for a considerable time yet. It is several billion miles away, anyway."

"*I* could have been a barkeeper and a hard lot just as well as not," says I, remembering the lonesome way I arrived, and how there wasn't any committee nor anything.

"I notice some regret in your voice," says Sandy, "and it is natural enough; but let bygones be bygones; you went according to your lights, and it is too late now to mend the thing."

"No, let it slide, Sandy, I don't mind. But you've got a Sandy Hook *here*, too, have you?"

"We've got everything here, just as it is below. All the States and Territories of the Union, and all the kingdoms of the earth and the islands of the sea are laid out here just as they are on the globe — all the same shape they are down there, and all graded to the relative size, only each State and realm and island is a good many billion times bigger here than it is below. There goes another blast."

"What is that one for?"

"That is only another fort answering the first one. They each fire eleven hundred and one thunder blasts at a single dash — it is the usual salute for an eleventh-hour guest; a hundred for each hour and an extra one for the guest's sex; if it was a woman we would know it by their leaving off the extra gun."

"How do we know there's eleven hundred and one, Sandy, when they all go off at once? — and yet we certainly do know."

"Our intellects are a good deal sharpened up, here, in some ways, and that is one of them. Numbers and sizes and distances are so great, here, that we have to be made so we can *feel* them — our old ways of counting and measuring and ciphering wouldn't

ever give us an idea of them, but would only confuse us and oppress us and make our heads ache."

After some more talk about this, I says: "Sandy, I notice that I hardly ever see a white angel; where I run across one white angel, I strike as many as a hundred million copper-colored ones — people that can't speak English. How is that?"

"Well, you will find it the same in any State or Territory of the American corner of heaven you choose to go to. I have shot along, a whole week on a stretch, and gone millions and millions of miles, through perfect swarms of angels, without ever seeing a single white one, or hearing a word I could understand. You see, America was occupied a billion years and more by Injuns and Aztecs, and that sort of folks, before a white man ever set his foot in it. During the first three hundred years after Columbus' discovery, there wasn't ever more than one good lecture audience of white people, all put together in America — I mean the whole thing, British Possessions and all; in the beginning of our century there were only 6,000,000 or 7,000,000 — say seven; 12,000,000 or 14,000,000 in 1825; say 23,000,000 in 1850; 40,000,000 in 1875.

"Our death rate has always been 20 in 1,000 per annum. Well, 140,000 died the first year of the century; 280,000 the twenty-fifth year; 500,000 the fiftieth year; about a million the seventy-fifth year. Now I am going to be liberal about this thing and consider that fifty million whites have died in America from the beginning up to today — make it sixty, if you want to; make it a hundred million — it's no difference about a few millions one way or t'other. Well, now, you can see, yourself, that when you come to spread a little dab of people like that over these hundreds of billions of miles of American territory here in heaven, it is like scattering a ten-cent box of homoeopathic pills over the Great Sahara and expecting to find them again. You can't expect us to amount to anything in heaven, and we *don't* — now that is the simple fact, and we have got to do the best we can with it.

"The learned men from other planets and other systems come here and hang around a while, when they are touring around the kingdom, and then go back to their own section of heaven and write a book of travels, and they give America about five lines in it. And what do they say about us? They say this wilderness is populated with a scattering few hundred thousand billions of red angels, with now and then a curiously complected *diseased* one. You see, they think we whites and the occasional nigger are Injuns that have been bleached out or blackened by some leprous disease or other — for some peculiarly rascally *sin,* mind you. It is a mighty sour pill for us all, my friend — even the modestest of us, let alone the other kind, that think they are going to be received like a long-lost government bond, and hug Abraham into the bargain. I haven't asked you any of the particulars, Captain, but I judge it goes without saying — if my experience is worth anything — that there wasn't much of a hooraw made over you when you arrived — now was there?"

"Don't mention it, Sandy," says I, coloring up a little; "I wouldn't have had the family see it for any amount you are a mind to name. Change the subject, Sandy, change the subject."

"Well, do you think of settling in the California department of bliss?"

"I don't know. I wasn't calculating on doing anything really definite in that direction till the family come. I thought I would just look around, meantime, in a quiet way, and make up my mind. Besides, I know a good many dead people, and I was calculating to hunt them up and swap a little gossip with them about friends, and old times, and one thing or another, and ask them how they like it here, as far as they have got. I reckon my wife will want to camp in the California range, though, because most all her departed will be there, and she likes to be with folks she knows."

"Don't you let her. You see what the Jersey district of heaven is, for whites; well, the Californian district is a thousand times worse. It swarms with a mean kind of leather-headed, mud-colored angels — and your nearest white neighbor is likely to be a million miles away. *What a man mostly misses, in heaven, is company* — company of his own sort and color and language. I have come near settling in the European part of heaven once or twice on that account."

"Well, why didn't you, Sandy?"

"Oh, various reasons. For one thing, although you *see* plenty of whites there, you can't understand any of them, hardly, and so you go about as hungry for talk as you do here. I like to look at a Russian or a German or an Italian — I even like to look at a Frenchman if I ever have the luck to catch him engaged in anything that ain't indelicate — but *looking* don't cure the hunger — what you want is talk."

"Well, there's England, Sandy — the English district of heaven."

"Yes, but it is not so very much better than this end of the heavenly domain. As long as you run across Englishmen born this side of three hundred years ago, you are all right; but the minute you get back of Elizabeth's time the language begins to fog up, and the further back you go the foggier it gets. I had some talk with a Mr. Spenser and a man by the name of Chaucer — old-time poets — but it was no use, I couldn't quite understand them, and they couldn't quite understand me. I have had letters from them since, but it is such broken English I can't make it out. Back of those men's time the English are just simply foreigners, nothing more, nothing less; they talk Danish, German, Norman French, and sometimes a mixture of all three; back of *them,* they talk Latin, and ancient British,

Irish, and Gaelic; and then back of these come billions and billions of pure savages that talk a gibberish that Satan himself couldn't understand. The fact is, where you strike one man in the English settlements that you can understand, you wade through awful swarms that talk something you can't make head nor tail of. You see, every country on earth has been overlaid so often, in the course of a billion years, with different kinds of people and different sorts of languages, that this sort of mongrel business was bound to be the result in heaven."

"Sandy," says I, "did you see a good many of the great people history tells about?"

"Yes — plenty. I saw kings and all sorts of distinguished people."

"Do the kings rank just as they did below?"

"No; a body can't bring his rank up here with him. Divine right is a good-enough earthly romance, but it don't go here. Kings drop down to the general level as soon as they reach the realms of grace. I knew Charles the Second very well — one of the most popular comedians in the English section — draws first rate. There are better, of course — people that were never heard of on earth — but Charles is making a very good reputation indeed, and is considered a rising man. Richard the Lion-hearted is in the prize-ring, and coming into considerable favor. Henry the Eighth is a tragedian, and the scenes where he kills people are done to the very life. Henry the Sixth keeps a religious-book stand."

"Did you ever see Napoleon, Sandy?"

"Often — sometimes in the Corsican range, sometimes in the French. He always hunts up a conspicuous place, and goes frowning around with his arms folded and his field glass under his arm, looking as grand, gloomy, and peculiar as his reputation calls for, and very much bothered because he don't stand as high, here, for a soldier as he expected to."

"Why, who stands higher?"

"Oh, a *lot* of people *we* never heard of before — the shoemaker and horse doctor and knife grinder kind, you know — clodhoppers from goodness knows where, that never handled a sword or fired a shot in their lives — but the soldiership was in them, though they never had a chance to show it. But here they take their right place, and Caesar and Napoleon and Alexander have to take a back seat. The greatest military genius our world ever produced was a bricklayer from somewhere back of Boston — died during the Revolution — by the name of Absalom Jones. Wherever he goes, crowds flock to see him. You see, everybody knows that if he had had a chance he would have shown the world some generalship that would have made all generalship before look like child's play and 'prentice work. But he never got a chance; he tried heaps of times to enlist as a private, but he had lost both thumbs and a couple of front teeth, and the recruiting surgeon wouldn't pass him. However, as I say, everybody knows, now, what he *would* have been, and so they flock by the million to get a glimpse of him whenever they hear he is going to be anywhere. Caesar, and Hannibal, and Alexander, and Napoleon are all on his staff, and ever so many more great generals; but the public hardly care to look at *them* when *he* is around. Boom! There goes another salute. The barkeeper's off quarantine now."

Sandy and I put on our things. Then we made a wish, and in a second we were at the reception place. We stood on the edge of the ocean of space and looked out over the dimness, but couldn't make out anything. Close by us was the Grand Stand — tier on tier of dim thrones rising up toward the zenith. From each side of it spread away the tiers of seats for the general public. They spread away for leagues and leagues — you couldn't see the ends. They were empty and still, and hadn't a cheerful look, but looked dreary, like a theater before anybody comes — gas turned down. Sandy says —

"We'll sit down here and wait. We'll see the head of the procession come in sight away off yonder pretty soon, now."

Says I —

"It's pretty lonesome, Sandy; I reckon there's a hitch somewheres. Nobody but just you and me — it ain't much of a display for the barkeeper."

"Don't you fret, it's all right. There'll be one more gunfire — then you'll see."

In a little while we noticed a sort of a lightish flush, away off on the horizon.

"Head of the torchlight procession," says Sandy.

It spread, and got lighter and brighter; soon it had a strong glare like a locomotive headlight; it kept on getting brighter and brighter till it was like the sun peeping above the horizon line at sea — the big red rays shot high up into the sky.

"Keep your eyes on the Grand Stand and the miles of seats — sharp!" says Sandy, "and listen for the gunfire."

Just then it burst out, "Boom-boom-boom!" like a million thunderstorms in one, and made the whole heavens rock. Then there was a sudden and awful glare of light all about us, and in that very instant every one of the millions of seats was occupied, and as far as you could see, in both directions, was just a solid pack of people, and the place was all splendidly lit up! It was enough to take a body's breath away. Sandy says —

"That is the way we do it here. No time fooled away; nobody straggling in after the curtain's up. Wishing is quicker work than traveling. A quarter of a second ago these folks were millions of miles from here. When they heard the last signal, all they had to do was to wish, and here they are."

The prodigious choir struck up —

> We long to hear thy voice,
> To see thee face to face.

It was noble music, but the uneducated

chipped in and spoilt it, just as the congregations used to do on earth.

The head of the procession began to pass, now, and it was a wonderful sight. It swept along, thick and solid, five hundred thousand angels abreast, and every angel carrying a torch and singing — the whirring thunder of the wings made a body's head ache. You could follow the line of the procession back, and slanting upward into the sky, far away in a glittering snaky rope, till it was only a faint streak in the distance. The rush went on and on, for a long time, and at last, sure enough, along comes the barkeeper, and then everybody rose, and a cheer went up that made the heavens shake, I tell you! He was all smiles and had his halo tilted over one ear in a cocky way, and was the most satisfied-looking saint I ever saw. While he marched up the steps of the Grand Stand, the choir struck up —

> The whole wide heaven groans,
> And waits to hear that voice.

There were four gorgeous tents standing side by side in the place of honor, on a broad-railed platform in the center of the Grand Stand, with a shining guard of honor round about them. The tents had been shut up all this time. As the barkeeper climbed along up, bowing and smiling to everybody, and at last got to the platform, these tents were jerked up aloft all of a sudden, and we saw four noble thrones of gold, all caked with jewels, and in the two middle ones sat old white-whiskered men, and in the two others a couple of the most glorious and gaudy giants, with platter halos and beautiful armor. All the millions went down on their knees, and stared, and looked glad, and burst out into a joyful kind of murmurs. They said —

"Two archangels! — that is splendid. Who can the others be?"

The archangels gave the barkeeper a stiff little military bow; the two old men rose; one of them said, "Moses and Esau welcome thee!" and then all the four vanished, and the thrones were empty.

The barkeeper looked a little disappointed, for he was calculating to hug those old people, I judge; but it was the gladdest and proudest multitude you ever saw — because they had seen Moses and Esau. Everybody was saying, "Did you see them? — I did — Esau's side face was to me, but I saw Moses full in the face, just as plain as I see you this minute!"

The procession took up the barkeeper and moved on with him again, and the crowd broke up and scattered. As we went along home, Sandy said it was a great success, and the barkeeper would have a right to be proud of it forever. And he said *we* were in luck, too; said we might attend receptions for forty thousand years to come and not have a chance to see a brace of such grand moguls as Moses and Esau. We found afterwards that we had come near seeing another patriarch, and likewise a genuine prophet besides, but at the last moment they sent regrets. Sandy said there would be a monument put up there, where Moses and Esau had stood, with the date and circumstances, and all about the whole business, and travelers would come for thousands of years and gawk at it, and climb over it, and scribble their names on it.

23.

CHARLES SPRAGUE SMITH: A Creedless Church for a Creedless People

The estrangement from religion of city dwellers at the beginning of the twentieth century deeply troubled many clergymen and was a challenge to such men as Charles Sprague Smith, managing director of the People's Institute in New York City. This organization scheduled many lectures on religious subjects, most of which stressed the universal morality underlying Western religions. Discussion periods followed the lectures, in the course of which members of the audience could express their views and reveal their doubts. In the following article Smith described the order of events during a typical evening at the Institute.

Source: *Independent,* January 2, 1908.

EVERY LARGER COMMUNITY is facing today the problem of what to do for those whom the church no longer attracts. For it is recognized by churchmen and nonchurchmen alike that the old Sabbath service which all attended at weekend and week beginning gave something man needs. Purely educational or diversional opportunities are not substitutes, while the appeal of the (so-called) ethical movement is thus far limited chiefly to the more intellectual.

The larger the community, the more heterogeneous its population, the graver and more complex this problem. In New York City an attempt has been made to solve it. The gathering place, Cooper Union Hall, is one dear to the people's heart. For there men who speak its speech, are inspired by its ideals, have addressed and still address great audiences. More than any other hall in America, more even than Faneuil Hall in Boston, Cooper Union has been and is a forum of democracy.

In 1898 a new organization, the People's Institute, began its work there. For the first year its field embraced, solely, evening addresses and discussions upon problems of the day. The proclaimed purpose was preparation for the intelligent discharge of civic duties. The frank way in which the work was done won in an unusual degree the confidence of the masses, distrustful ordinarily of any social-educational movement directed by men who do not themselves belong to the working class. For, from the platform, social reorganization on the basis of the recognition of solidarity, brotherhood was frankly declared to be the goal set. Of the speakers only knowledge and sincerity was demanded, none being excluded, save the preacher of revolution. Similarly, entire freedom of speech, within the bounds of courtesy, was the sole rule prescribed in the discussion following upon every address.

In the second year of its life, the Institute, relying upon the vantage of confidence won, began a church experiment. Similar methods were employed to those that had proved successful in the purely secular work. The sole limitations imposed were that there should be no attack of creed upon creed and no attempt to proselyte. The success, great at the start, vast audiences of all creeds and no creed gathering, has increased year by year. The seating capacity of the hall — 1,600 — is, during the larger part of the season, inadequate, from 50 to 200 persons usually standing. The speakers, almost always clergymen, represent all creeds, save the Catholic.

The themes are ethical and commonly religious. The element of worship is largely absent. Experience has suggested but one method of introducing this without giving offense to some element of the audience

and none should be offended. Music, that of a grand organ, would provide this medium, but there seems to be no place in the hall for such an organ, and there are no funds wherewith to provide one could place be found.

It can hardly be doubted that with a hall of much larger dimensions, properly equipped, the audience would speedily more than double in size. For the close air and the crowding of the present quarters, with the inadequacy of the music (piano and soloist) due to limited funds, keep many, especially of the well-to-do, away who, under different conditions, would gladly become regular attendants. Thus, one purpose sought by these gatherings, namely, the breaking down of the separating walls between class and class, is still in large degree defeated. But the problem of assembling regularly nonchurchgoers (with churchgoers) of all creeds and no creed and bringing to them, thru the teachings of the leaders in the pulpit, ethical and broadly religious instruction and inspiration can fairly be regarded as solved. Two-thirds, at least, of every Sunday audience are regular attendants.

Sit on the Cooper Union platform on a Sunday night and look out upon the mass gathered in that historic hall. It is not the usual church assembly. Ordinarily, women predominate where religious or ethical addresses are given. Here, among the 1,600 to 1,800 that fill the seats and line the walls, the brighter colors of woman's dress and headgear are as infrequent as bright-colored flowers, purple asters, for example, in a well-ordered grainfield. Fully 90 percent are men, and they have gathered from all over Manhattan Island. Not a few have come from towns lying along the Hudson. Some are Jerseyites who make this weekly pilgrimage to the city to be present at the unique assembly. There is no listlessness. Perhaps a weary Willie or two may be nodding (Cooper Union is very convenient to the Bowery, and the stream of flotsam and jetsam that moves up and down it), but the nodders are few. To look for the first time into that multitude of tense faces is an impressive experience.

The speaker of the evening, usually a clergyman, and one of the most eminent in the metropolitan pulpit, is discoursing about some religious or ethical theme. It may be an ethical treatment of a question of the day. As he develops his thought, if he shows not only a good grasp of his subject but also a sympathetic understanding of the people's way of thinking and feeling, there is a manifest deepening and quickening of life in the audience. You are sensible of waves of emotion sweeping thru the hall. The speaker pauses for a moment, and a burst of applause punctuates the interruption. Then he resumes. Perhaps a little later he seems to glide over the surface of things instead of penetrating to the depths, and you are conscious that minds are registering the fact and preparing to dispute the conclusions presented when the proper time comes.

The three-quarters of an hour or hour allotted for the address is coming to a close; the speaker, inspired by his audience, is drawing together in a masterly fashion the threads of his discourse and leading up to a stirring peroration. The interest becomes every moment more tense. As the last word is spoken, the applause reverberates from the low roof of the old hall. The audience will not let the speaker remain in his seat; he must advance to the edge of the platform and receive their enthusiastic greeting. They call him again and again forward. Gradually the intensity gives place to calm, and music intervenes to lull the minds back to restfulness.

Then follows the half or three-quarters of an hour devoted to discussion. The weak points, if any such there have been, in the argument have been noted and are ruthlessly uncovered by those who in succession take the floor. In general, the discussion shows a sincere desire to get at the whole truth, to relate what has been said to practical life. But the crank is also in evidence, the man, too, who is convinced that his scheme of social service is the cure-all. A ripple of excitement occasioned by the substance and method of their remarks not infrequently runs thru the hall, but the presiding officer, with the assistance of the audience, always succeeds in repressing all undue manifestations.

It is a revelation to one who has not before come close to the people. This revelation is a manifold one. You discern what the people are thinking about and how they are thinking about it, what their deepest desires and needs are, and how they think they ought to be satisfied. You seem to see — you do see, if you have been there frequently — how the stream of folk life is moving in this city and country of ours. And in your mind the movement here associates itself with the world movement outside and with the folk current across all the ages since social development began. The fundamental, straightforward striving for the right on the part of the people becomes also clear to you. There is splendid citizenship here, in the making, in this unschooled multitude, an immense force of righteousness, for all kinds of uplift, if rightly instructed and directed.

Gradually, on the old dial above the platform, the hands approach the hour of ten; the chairman stops the discussion, which usually has become somewhat languid, and the speaker of the evening, in a few brief sentences, sums up the lesson, the result of his own address and of the new thought developed by the discussion. The audience is thereby brought back again from its mental wandering to the heart of the theme and uplifted to the heights of vision and purpose to which the evening's work has sought to lead them.

Then comes the closing hymn, sung by

the audience rising. The hymnology of this People's Church has also its special interest. Part of the songs have been composed by those connected with the work, part selected from other hymnologies. All breathe the spirit of democracy, faith in humanity, in an intelligent ordering of the universe, progress toward a higher social ideal.

To multitudes (some 12,000 individuals yearly) this is the only church they know or care to frequent. To its services they look forward as to a haven of refuge, a fountain of refreshing from weekend to weekend. Every creed is represented, and every non-creed, religious and social. But at the door all that separates falls away and all elements merge in a true congregation, a brotherhood seeking for instruction, light, inspiration.

If you would hear the leading clergymen of New York at their best, do not seek them in their own pulpits, but go to Cooper Union. If you would understand what the thinkers of the past meant when they used the term *"Vox populi, vox Dei,"* go there also. If you would see democracy in the making, there is no place where you can get nearer to its fundamental processes than in that hall where Abraham Lincoln delivered the address that made him President, the hall that a workingman of New York, Peter Cooper, dedicated to the training of workingmen in the principles and practice of democracy.

If formulated, the creed of this creedless church would run, "Faith in the brotherhood of man and loyal service to the Power not ourselves that makes for righteousness."

24.

George E. Walsh: Entertainment for the Millions

The motion picture revolutionized popular entertainment in the United States in the first decade of the twentieth century. Where before most people had relied on entertaining themselves at home, now they flocked by the millions to the nickelodeons that grew up seemingly overnight in a hundred cities and a thousand towns. George E. Walsh wrote about the early years of the movie industry in an article for the Independent *that is reprinted here.*

Source: *Independent,* February 6, 1908: "Moving Picture Drama for the Multitude."

THE MOVING PICTURE DRAMA furnishes entertainment for the millions, literally reproducing comic, tragic, and great events to some 16 million people a week at a nominal cost of a nickel or a dime. The effect of this new form of pictorial drama on the public is without parallel in modern history, for it more graphically illustrates the panorama of life than the photographs and texts of the daily newspaper and intrudes upon the le-

gitimate theater through the actual dramatization of plays that have had a good run. The moving picture drama is for the multitude, attracting thousands who never go to the theater, and particularly appealing to the children. In the poorer sections of the cities where innumerable foreigners congregate, the so-called "nickelodeon" has held preeminent sway for the last year.

All of this has been developed within half

a dozen years, and the remarkable growth of the industry is due to the perfection of the biograph, vitagraph, kinetoscope or cinematograph — whichever name the moving picture machine goes by — within the last year or two. Edison first invented the moving picture machine, but he did not perfect it; and others rushed in to secure patents on its improvements which gave them certain protective rights. There have been upward of 200 patents taken out in the last five years on moving picture machines, and there are something like three-score names applied to the different machines in use. They are all essentially the same in at least one respect — they reproduce enlarged photographs on a screen at such a rapid rate that lifelike action of the actors is obtained thereby. The question of clearness and sharpness of outline, the speed of reproduction, and cost of operation concerns only the different owners of the patents and not the public.

The improvement of the biograph so that strips of photographs could be enlarged and reproduced was costly at first, and the exhibitions were made chiefly for advertising purposes. Large photographs had to be taken, and the cost of a strip of films was very great. Then, by improving the magnifying lens, it was found that pictures one-eighth the old size could be made equally serviceable. These magnifying lenses cost all the way from $25 to $100. The old biograph driven by a motor had to take and reproduce pictures at the rate of thirty a second, but the modern instrument can reproduce equally good results at fifteen per second. A complete outfit for a small exhibition hall can be obtained today for $125, but from this the cost runs up to almost any price desired.

In the last two years "nickelodeons" or moving picture theaters or exhibition halls have opened in nearly every town and village in the country, and every city from the Klondike to Florida and from Maine to California supports from two or three to several hundred. Millions of dollars have been invested in the shows, and it is estimated that on an average 2 million or 3 million people in this country attend the shows every day in the week.

The large companies engaged in renting the films for these biograph shows are chiefly responsible for the great changes in our cheap entertainment halls. These companies have invaded nearly every department of life to secure interesting photographs. The films used today are five-eighths by one and one-eighth of an inch in size, but they can be enlarged 200 times by the magnifying lens when thrown on the screen. They are projected on the screen and each separate picture is held there one-twentieth of a second. The continuous motion deceives the eye and produces perfect lifelike action. Where greater speed is desired, such as a reproduction of an automobile race or a fast mail train in motion, the speed of the machine is increased, until the eye is fairly deceived by the performance.

The most difficult and interesting feature of the industry is getting the photographs. In this work, intense rivalry exists between the different film-renting companies. A first-class set of films becomes a valuable asset, and it is in demand all over the country. The expense to the companies is frequently enormous. For instance, in photographing the Jeffries-Sharkey fight at Coney Island in 1899, the film company which secured the contract took 198,000 pictures and had over seven miles of film to exhibit. Besides paying the chief exhibitors in the fight a large sum, the film company had to go to great expense in lighting up and focusing the cameras for the work. Yet in spite of the thousands of dollars thus spent, the investment proved a financial success.

Most remarkable tricks can be played by the camera, as every photographer knows, but for reproduction in the biograph these tricks are intensified a thousandfold. For instance, the building of a skyscraper within a few minutes is a feat easily accomplished on the screen. In order to do this a camera is placed in position when the foundations begin, and, by means of slow time exposure extending over months, an exact reproduction of the building can be projected on the screen occupying less than ten minutes. When the old Star Theater in New York was demolished a number of years ago, a camera took time exposure pictures of the operation, and when finished it was possible to throw on the screen a perfect reproduction of the work. The theater could be demolished within five minutes, and by reversing the films rebuilt within the same period. The Passion Play has been reproduced by the machines, and when first presented in Paris it proved a huge success. In this country it has met with equal approval.

The biograph man is everywhere, and almost any day a pedestrian in our crowded streets may be made a part of a moving throng that flits across the screen to entertain immense multitudes. The story is told of an American who, while watching moving pictures in a hall in Paris, saw a reproduction of a Broadway throng at the noon hour. His interest in the old familiar scenes was intensified when he saw his own face and figure in the crowd. When he was close to the camera, he was still more surprised to see a valuable watch charm, which he had always worn attached to his fob, drop and disappear from sight. He had mourned the loss of this jewel for several months, but had no idea where it was lost. Then, out of the moving throng, appeared a young lady who suddenly stooped and picked up the charm from the pavement. The man gasped and dropped back in his seat when he recognized the features of the woman as she approached closer to the camera. A few weeks later he recovered his watch charm after he had cabled to the woman to ascertain if there was any truth in the strange coincidence or whether it was all fiction.

To secure lifelike exhibitions of strange and difficult scenes, the film renting concerns keep a corps of experts engaged all the time. One part of their work is to arrange theatrical groups in an outdoor theater constructed for this special purpose. The favorite place for the enactment of these outdoor scenes in New York is on the roof of some tall building where there is little danger of outside interruption. The roof theater is provided with glass screens and canvas roof to regulate the light. Up there on the roofs, plays are being enacted every clear day, with no audience. Elaborate scenery is provided, and the costumes of the actors are in many cases as accurate in detail as any used in our high-priced plays. Historical scenes are here enacted, and many popular and classic plays are attempted. The actors and actresses in these plays must be perfect in pantomime, but their ability in declamation does not count. The comic plays produced are the most popular. The average audience of the "nickelodeon" cares more for the comedy and *opera bouffe* than anything else. In some of the higher class plays, actors of high standing are employed during the day.

The demand for legitimate picture drama is growing, and within a short time most of our popular plays will be reproduced in the "nickelodeon" shortly after they have had a run on the road. More than this, the film companies are developing their own plays, paying experts in pantomime to invent plots and scenes which will show up well in moving pictures. In Paris this work has reached a higher development than in this country. A considerable class of expert pantomime actors depend entirely upon the film companies for their living. They receive all the way from $15 to $40 a week for their services.

Then, too, the storywriter comes in for a share of the profits of the new profession. A good story, suitable for moving picture reproduction, may sell from $5 to $30, or even more. The story is not written out in magazine form but is a brief description of scenes and acts which have a well-defined plot. Some of the companies are experimenting with the phonograph in connection with the moving pictures, by means of which the actors in the scenes will actually speak and declaim as the various pantomime scenes are thrown on the screen. This may be the next development in this method of furnishing cheap plays for the multitudes.

Outdoor scenes are also in demand, and these must be obtained by the photographer, who goes forth and risks life and limb. The man who stands in front of a fast-moving train to secure films invites certain risks that now and then result disastrously. The man who is run over by a train is not after all a real man. By means of a little trickery with the camera he appears to step directly in front of the engine, but it is a well-made-up dummy who is really run over. Moving pictures of bear fights and of animals ranging the wild woods are obtained with great difficulty, and when good films are thus procured, they are frequently used for exhibition before scientific societies. A swimming moose or a fight between two wild animals is of invaluable aid, sometimes, to students.

A storm at sea, with the inevitable shipwreck, may be imitated in the studio of the professional, but frequently the photographer faces great danger to secure films from actual life. The photographing of important events of the day is another startling feature of this new amusement method. If a steamship is wrecked on the rocks or a railroad train is demolished in a great accident, the filmmakers try to get good photographs of some important part of it. The first visit of the *Lusitania* to this port was photographed in a series of pictures that, when reproduced on the screen, will give a perfect lifelike birdseye view of the notable event. The building of great bridges and the construction of towerlike skyscrapers are made the subject of moving pictures. One cannot question the value of such pictures in preserving for all time views of important engineering and structural works.

In France they have succeeded in a way in coloring the films so that, when projected upon the screen, the lifelike movements are greatly improved. These colored films are now used in many of the higher priced places of amusement, but they cost something like 50 percent more than the ordinary black-and-white ones.

Courtroom scenes of noted trials are reproduced today in moving pictures so that the public can get perfect views of the actors in these great events. Photographs of great singers and artists in grand opera are made at considerable expense, so that it is only a matter of a few cents for the poorest to view Caruso, Eames, Nordica, or other prima donnas in their great roles on the stage. It brings grand opera, in a way, down to the level of the poorest, and when we consider the perfect reproduction of the voices in the modern phonograph and graphophone, there seems to be little left to be desired.

The employment of the moving picture exhibition for instructive purposes is also quite extensive. Travel pictures are popular methods of lecturers. Views of a country from the observation car of a moving train carry one through Europe and America. One can, for a few cents, view panoramic pictures of the famous canals of Venice with all their throngs of moving boats and people, or take a trip through the canals of Holland, or see the marketplaces of the great European centers. From the deck of steamers one gets moving pictures of the coast of Greenland, Iceland, or the islands of the South Pacific.

Even the growth of plants and flowers is observed. By time exposures extending over months, it is possible to reproduce exactly within a few minutes the budding and flowering of plants. Oranges spring from the flower and turn into golden fruit while you wait, or apples come into existence like magic on the trees which a few moments before were bare and leafless. There is, in fact, hardly a field which has not been exploited, and the use of the moving pictures increases every year as the experts study new methods and ways of securing films.

The average expense of running one of these halls for exhibiting moving pictures is placed from $150 to $250 a week, the greatest single item being for rent of hall and the next for wages of manager and assistants. The rent of the films runs as low as $50 a week for two changes of reels a week, and the cost of the projecting machine is as low as $10 and $15 a week. The actual cost of reproducing costly drama and important scenes of the day is thus more dependent upon the rent of buildings and wages of employees than upon the films and machines which are responsible for their exhibition. The field thus offers golden opportunities for those who can induce the multitudes to pay their nickels and dimes to witness up-to-date entertainments.

25.

FREDERICK DWIGHT: A Dim View of the Automobile

Frederick Dwight did not share the enthusiasm of many of his contemporaries for the automobile. He viewed it, in 1908, as an instrument designed to please the reckless few and to harm the cautious many. Dwight shuddered when he read the advertisements of auto manufacturers who proudly stated that their new models would travel at sixty miles an hour! Dwight lamented the fact that car owners were already ignoring the twenty-five-mile limits imposed in many cities. His article, originally titled "Automobiles: The Other Side of the Shield," is reprinted here in part.

Source: *Independent*, December 3, 1908.

EVERY NEW AND POPULAR DEVICE exercises more or less tyranny. The mob spirit is generated and people hasten to chant the praises of the idol for fear of being called "reactionaries," a curious class who are supposed to be capable of all sorts of contemptible acts. Yet merchants have to pause occasionally to "take stock" in order to find out just what their condition at the moment is, and there is nothing really eccentric in whispering a few doubts in the midst of a general chorus of adulation.

At the moment I am thinking of automobiles. The advertising columns of the papers contain daily hymns to them. The proceedings of motor clubs are set forth at length. Our magazines teem with "motor flights" and astonishing tours and articles upon the romance of motoring. All is harmony and enthusiasm. Only at rare intervals does some miserable "Pro Bono Publico" or "Indignant Citizen" raise an anonymous howl in the correspondence column of his favorite paper, cursing automobiles and wishing they had never been invented. A rather more comprehensive protest seems to have been made by citizens of Brussels, who are reported to have petitioned the authorities to assemble all the cars in the city and destroy them in one picturesque conflagration. But that was an isolated case.

Now it may be that a motor age, like a species of new Augustan Age, is about to dawn if aviation or some other novelty does not strangle it in its birth, and that it will be filled with blessings. But of course it does not follow that the period between the introduction and the complete development of automobiles is improved by them. At any rate, a reasonable counterblast to motor eulogies may not be out of place, and I propose to set down here some of the peculiar problems of the present time that have been produced by automobiles.

To begin with, although they are performing work in fields of usefulness, they have not as yet proved their necessity. That is, commercially, they are still in the experimental stage — too costly and unreliable to supplant horse-drawn vehicles widely. They are regarded doubtfully by emergency services, such as the fire and ambulance; and as an adjunct to armies have yet to demonstrate their value. The point I wish to make is obvious enough — that at the present time their conspicuous success has been achieved almost wholly as pleasure vehicles, so that their mention suggests to the average person only a new way of enjoying oneself.

The swiftness of their development to the present time has been astounding and may be illustrated by a contrast or two which could be duplicated in the experience of almost everyone. About six or seven years ago, an acquaintance of mine, a young man of large means, informed me that he had imported a French car and that it had cost him, duty paid, $4,000. He intended, I believe, to impress me by the amount of the investment, and succeeded in doing so. Four thousand dollars appeared a very great sum to expend for a rather uncertain machine. A

few days ago a friend of limited resources said that as soon as he "could afford it" he intended to buy a certain "racing runabout." They were not very expensive, he added, "only $4,000." The figure then seemed moderate, or at least not at all unusual.

The French car I have mentioned was, I think, of fifteen horsepower, and its owner declared it would maintain easily a speed of twenty-five miles an hour. Today the advertising columns of papers and magazines are strewn with notices of "roadsters" and "road racers" guaranteed by their makers to develop sixty horsepower or even higher, and to maintain a speed greater than a mile a minute.

In other words, an infancy of spindly, fragile "horseless carriages" has grown to a youth of mighty road engines continually increasing in size, in power, in cost of purchase and maintenance, and, naturally, in excellence of construction. One might think, too, that the rules of economics had been set at defiance, for the advance in outlay has been accompanied by a constantly broadening demand.

The reason, or at least one very conspicuous reason, for this excessive popularity is evident enough. It is the stimulation produced by motoring. Every rider knows the exultation arising from feeling the strength of the animal under him, and this sensation is reproduced and intensified in the easy and constant power of an automobile. But from the same circumstance arises its greatest menace. There is always a temptation to urge a fiery Thoroughbred to the limit of his speed. A rider, however, must take into account the endurance of the horse and finds a compensation for a moderate pace in the sense of companionship with a fine animal. Indeed, whether riding or driving a horse, the fact that the motive power is a living thing has an interest of its own. There is an atmosphere about horses. But there is none surrounding an automobile. The occupant has a powerful mechanism which can be driven, like a horse, at top speed, and the motives for refraining do not exist. So, naturally, excessive speeding has become a matter of common occurrence.

This, of course, is the most conspicuous evil. Motorists have exhibited the one worse attitude than defiance of law — indifference to it. The usual answer to such a charge is that only a small minority disregard the law, and the majority should not be held responsible for their conduct. In the first place, however, there are probably far more offenders than devotees of the "sport" are willing to admit. At any rate, one railway company after investigation reported that over one-half of the machines that crossed their road at a certain point within the period of observation were maintaining a speed not only in excess of the legal limit but so great that they could not have been stopped if a train had been passing. In the second place, there is practically no evidence that those who do keep within the law know or care what the provisions are. It is a matter of individual choice. They do not enjoy going at a reckless speed, that is all. Let them change their views, and is there the least assurance that the statutes would deter them? There are the familiar roadside signs: "Town limit. Motor vehicles limited to twelve miles an hour." Has any motor party ever taken such a warning seriously? The maximum placed by the inexperienced authorities is low, and no pretense of obeying is made.

And what if violators are arrested? Some inconvenience, a few dollars' fine — and that is all, as a rule. It is part of the game. Courts have not been able so far to persuade themselves that "overspeeding" is an offense serious enough to warrant imprisonment and confine themselves to fines and "reprimands." The prisoner looks contrite at the court's words, "peels off" the amount of the fine from a large roll of bills, and

sallies forth to try for another record, laughingly telling the officer who made the arrest, as he passes, that next time he won't be caught so easily.

In this there may be some exaggeration — but not very much. Only recently six men were arrested in New York after pursuit by a motorcycle policeman over the greater part of the island of Manhattan. The time was late night, a speed of forty miles an hour through the city streets was attained (according to the papers), the offenders united in urging the pursuing officer to "come on," and they were stopped at last only by the runaway gates on an East River bridge. The court, when they were arraigned, allowed all but the man who had been driving to go with fines of $2 each!

This suggests an interesting reflection. It is the apparently singular inability of our legislatures and courts to respond to new requirements. Assume, for example, that a dozen different devices, all as dangerous and alluring as automobiles, were introduced at the same time. Unless our solons grasped the situation far more quickly than has been the case with motor vehicles, years would pass, each one leaving a bloody trail of fatalities and mutilations, before an adequate policy were adopted.

The trouble seems to be that the legislators cling fondly to the idea that motor cars are still nothing but carriages without horses, to be dealt with in the same manner as the older vehicles. For instance, the authorities in general agree that upon public highways a speed greater than say twenty to twenty-five miles an hour is dangerous and should not be permitted. In order to achieve this result they resort to the time-honored methods of licensing cars and drivers, of requiring numbers, and finally of ordering the owners not to exceed the statutory limit. The inadequacy of such a policy appears to have been demonstrated. In spite of all the statutes, in Massachusetts within twelve months 62 persons were killed and

640 seriously injured in automobile accidents, while an insurance company has noted the killing, in a period of four weeks of the past summer, of 26 people and the injuring of 74 others in a similar manner. Indeed, punitive laws of the character are impossible of enforcement, except within limited areas, because of the vast expense for police involved and the great difficulty of catching offenders or taking the numbers accurately.

High-powered cars might with greater logic be regarded as morphine and cocaine are. Possessions and ability to use, when combined with an inborn passion, create a temptation that many are unable to resist. People are not permitted to procure or possess deadly drugs unless competent physicians have certified that they require them. A parallel provision would seem to be that cars capable of a harmful speed should not be allowed except under special conditions — as, for example, upon highways devoted to them exclusively as are railway tracks to trains.

It is certainly an absurd thing for the lawmakers to consume their gray matter in constructing statutes designed to prevent automobiles from going more than twenty miles an hour on the public roads, while at the same time and in the same jurisdiction manufacturers are permitted openly to urge everyone to buy their cars, warranted to maintain a speed of sixty miles an hour on those very roads! A preventive is needed, and if public opinion be at last shocked into an aggressive attitude, it seems probable that gearing or automatic governors will be insisted upon, so that the power to transgress will be removed.

There are at least two other evils which have arisen and more or less closely connected with overspeeding. Coachmen constitute a well-defined class, with rules of behavior and action resulting from long experience. Locomotive engineers are men of training and reliability. But the chauffeur is a new type. He has not been "standard-ized." He is of no particular race or years, and there are no traditions of his calling. Very probably he has not been in the personal service of another before, has an insufficient conception of discipline, and has introduced a new and serious form of offense for which at the present time there is no adequate remedy. It would be very unusual to see a coachman in his shirt sleeves driving his employer's horses and carriage at full speed around the neighborhood and so entertaining a wagonload of personal friends — also in shirt sleeves. But this seems to be an ordinary diversion of chauffeurs. They take the powerful cars which are in their custody, and, without the owner's permission, fill them with acquaintances as irresponsible as themselves and race over the country, occasionally killing or maiming innocent passersby, and then, too frequently, speeding away before they can be caught or their numbers taken. An Appellate Court in New York has decided that the owner of the machine is not responsible for the damage caused under such circumstances, and so his solicitude to see that the car is not taken out except upon his order is reduced to a minimum.

Then there is the destruction of roads. The macadam construction has done very well for horse-drawn vehicles. In fact, it is the best that is known, and the motor demands for smooth, hard surfaces have led communities at great expense to enlarge the macadamized areas. What are the results? First, the broad pad of the automobile tire destroys the surface rapidly and hurls clouds of dust over the houses and crops by the roadside, causing annoyance and at times seriously impairing rental values. Then, to meet these difficulties, the appearance of the highway is ruined by the application of a mixture of crude oil and tar, which is greasy and dingy and evil smelling. And it is also merely experimental. No one knows how much the dressing will really add to the highway's life under the strains of rushing cars.

These drawbacks and others that might be mentioned are those which communities as a whole sustain from the presence of automobiles. But there are some which are due to their demoralizing fascination. Thus a question that is frequently asked is — How can so many afford them? It is an ordinary thing to see a huge and expensive machine running smoothly along and crowded with men and women who look far from affluent. And many who never felt that they were in a position to purchase a horse and carriage at perhaps $1,000, maintainable for $800 a year, now indulge in automobiles costing several thousand dollars originally and $800 to operate for only two or three months.

A few sidelights of which I have been told may be cited here. They illumine in an interesting manner this apparently wonderful expansion of resources. A young clerk, dependent upon a presumably small salary, inherited $8,000. He spent $2,500 of it in the purchase of a car. A large employer of labor in one of our great cities had a clerk, a young married man, whose salary was less than $1,000 a year. One morning he appeared at the office in a handsome new automobile. My informant called him in, and in reply to questions, he explained that the car was his; that he himself had no money outside of his salary, but his wife possessed a dot of about $12,000 and "they thought they would put $2,500 of it into an automobile!" A resident of Boston said a year or two ago that one would be astonished to know the number of second mortgages that had been placed upon houses in the vicinity of his city to enable the owners to procure cars; and a lawyer of New York is responsible for the statement that in his office during the past winter there have been over 200 foreclosures of New York mortgages which had been created with the same end in view. Such cases are probably not very

exceptional and require no comment beyond the remark that they indicate a reckless extravagance which few, if any other, inventions have ever called forth.

In conclusion, it is not unfair to refer to the appearance of the occupants. Commentators have declared that the tendency of our development is toward a colorless and uninteresting civilization, devoid of highlights or any element of the picturesque. The average motorist of today is an argument for the contention. During the reign of horse-drawn vehicles, no costumes were too carefully designed. Under the new regime, nothing is too ugly. Hatless and coatless or wrapped in linen dusters and huge veils, men and women are reduced to one uninspiring, begoggled level. In place of the trim coachman erect on his box, one sees a creature clad in dingy cap and cotton duster, sitting on the small of his back, and so sunken that the crown of his head is almost on a level with the shoulder of the person by his side.

All this may seem dyspeptic, but it is not so intended. The point simply is that, in spite of the assertions of enthusiasts, I think the time when motor vehicles are desirable assets to society at large is yet to come, and that at present a certain excess must be charged to them in the debit column. They have engendered a reckless personal extravagance that must bring remorse and suffering to many some day. They have produced a new contempt for authority and an unusually lawless and irresponsible class. Finally, with little or no compensating advantage to the communities through which they hurry, they have caused the taxpayers heavy expense for roads, have almost driven the more leisurely from them, and have then proceeded to destroy the highways themselves. All of these things are doubtless curable and will be remedied in time. At present, however, they exist.

26.

Octave Chanute: The Wright Brothers' Flights

The flying machine was more an object of curiosity than anything else at the beginning of the twentieth century. Of the early experimenters in this mode of transportation, the Wright brothers, Orville and Wilbur, were the most successful. Their work shrouded in secrecy, they built and for the first time flew a heavier-than-air machine, with a twelve-horsepower engine, at Kitty Hawk, North Carolina, on December 17, 1903. When the Signal Corps of the U.S. Army invited proposals in 1907 for a flying machine, the Wright brothers won the bid and set to work. Octave Chanute, an engineer and aeronaut who had pioneered in gliding experiments, wrote a brief survey of their achievements for the Independent. *At the time of writing, the Wright brothers had not yet completed the flying machine for the Army.*

Source: *Independent*, June 4, 1908.

It will be remembered that last December the Signal Corps of the United States Army issued an advertisement inviting proposals for furnishing a "heavier-than-air flying machine" according to specifications attached. These specifications have been criticized by both foreign and American technical journals as being amazingly severe, but the officials answer, fairly enough, that they have only specified what some of the inventors in private interviews have stated that they could perform; that the government must be protected from being trifled with, and that the tests will be conducted with justice and liberality.

Notwithstanding the strictness of the specifications, no less than forty-one bids were received. Thirty-eight did not comply with the stipulations and three were accepted; these being those of J. F. Scott of Chicago (since withdrawn); of A. M. Herring of New York, who bid $20,000, and of Wright Brothers of Dayton, O., who proposed to deliver a flying machine in 200 days from the award (February 8, 1908) for a sum of $25,000, a very moderate price for such a unique apparatus.

It is now generally conceded that Wright Brothers have accomplished the extraordinary performances claimed by them in their letter to the *Aerophile* in 1905 and to the Aero Club of America in 1906. That, beginning with a first flight with a motor-driven flying machine, December 17, 1903, spending the season of 1904 in learning how to fly in circular courses, they succeeded in 1905 in perfecting modes of control with which they made at last continuous flights of eleven, twelve, fifteen, twenty, twenty-one, and twenty-four miles at speeds of about thirty-eight miles per hour, alighting in every case safely, ready to start again upon the replenishing of the fuel supply.

These experiments had been privately conducted on secluded grounds eight miles from Dayton, upon understandings with adjoining farmers and the press not to notice them in any way, but the last flight attracted so much attention that many came out with cameras to the practice grounds; and Wright Brothers, becoming alarmed lest their secrets should be discovered, stopped experimenting at once, dismantled the machine, and have not flown since. It would have been perhaps preferable to have first made one public demonstration, provided the crowd was not allowed to approach close to the machine, for the secrets of its construction are not easily discoverable when it is high in air, and then it would have been easy to organize a company to exploit and defend it.

Instead of that, Wright Brothers stated publicly what they had accomplished, and these statements were received with general incredulity by those who were not aware of what had previously been done, or those who did not know the Wrights. They inaugurated negotiations for the sale of their invention to various governments for war purposes, asking, it must be confessed, very high prices. Being somewhat opinionated as well as straightforward, they made two mistakes: the first, that the principal market for flying machines would be for war purposes (where cost is no object) instead of for sporting purposes, as more correctly judged by the French; and the second, that contracts could be obtained for a secret machine contingent upon making a flight of thirty or forty miles within one hour. Two years were therefore spent in fruitless negotiations. Wright Brothers seem now to have changed their point of view, but meanwhile large numbers of French aviators have begun experimenting, operating in public, and teaching each other, so that they have obtained promising results, although not yet equal to the American performances.

Under their contract with the United States government, Wright Brothers seem to have begun the preliminary tests of their machine in the beginning of May, but not to have been discovered by the press until the 8th. Instead of operating near their shop at Dayton, as in 1904 and 1905, they went to their former experimenting ground at Kill Devil Hills, south of Kitty Hawk, North Carolina. It is a forlorn spot on that long tongue of sand which stretches along the coast south of Norfolk, between the At-

lantic and Albemarle and Pamlico sounds. It is about as desolate a region as exists near civilization, only inhabited by a few fishermen and the lifesaving crews of the government. Its access is roundabout and tedious. This sandspit is two or three miles wide in the vicinity of the Kill Devil Hills.

Here the Wrights established their camp, assembled their machine, and began tuning it up. The reporters seem to have detected them from Manteo, a little town ten miles away on Roanoke Island, the seat of the first settlement by Sir Walter Raleigh in 1585, this being now doubly historic ground. There followed an amusing contest: the reporters naturally eager for information, and the Wrights so strongly resisting all attempts at description of their machine, that they stopped experimenting when the reporters came around. The latter have said that new and possibly improved methods of steering having been introduced, these are being tested with extreme caution — that caution which has contributed so much to the success of the Wright brothers.

On the 8th of May, ten ascensions were reported, all of them perfect, the longest being one and a half miles. This disclosed that the adjustment required a slight alteration. On the 10th, three flights were reported, one of them two miles at a speed of forty-six miles per hour. In landing, the gasoline engine gathered in some sand, and as a few grains of this are sufficient to produce cutting, it had to be carefully removed before other ascents were attempted. On the 13th, two very successful flights are reported, the longest being three miles, with the machine under perfect control.

On the 14th, three remarkable flights are reported as made by Orville Wright, in one of which he had another man on the machine. Then Wilbur Wright alone made a flight of eight miles at a speed of about forty-five miles an hour, at the close of which the machine was wrecked behind a sand dune. The operator had only a few scratches, and he explained that he had made a mistake by grasping the wrong lever of the steering gear recently installed, this being the one which directed the course downward, while the other lever directed it upward — a mistake very likely to occur with a nervous man operating a new arrangement.

The machine was sent back to Dayton (nearly 800 miles) for rebuilding. This ought not to occupy more than two weeks, when the adjusting tests will be resumed, the scene of which has not been disclosed.

The tests already made substantiate the absolute truth of what the Wrights have hitherto claimed as to their past achievements, and hold out good hopes that if no disastrous accident intervenes the Wright Brothers will be enabled to fulfill all the government requirements. They have until August 28 to make delivery, and thirty days after that for the tests, so that there seems to be sufficient time to rebuild the machine and to obtain thorough control over so novel and complicated an invention.

27.

Giuseppe Giacosa: Impressions of America

The Impressioni d'America *of Giuseppe Giacosa, an Italian dramatist who visited the United States in 1898, was published posthumously in 1908. The lack of tradition in American life, often said to be a sign of America's cultural inferiority to Europe, was not so regarded by Giacosa. His impressions were similar to those of many foreign observers, who were often struck by the restlessness, the constant changes, and the quick pace of life in America. To an Italian, accustomed to a more leisurely, ordered life, America offered an interesting contrast.*

Source: TWA, pp. 396-400.

ON THE LAST THURSDAY in November the United States celebrates Thanksgiving Day, a holiday proclaimed annually by the President to give thanks to God for the favors of the year. On this day New York was full of students from Yale and Princeton, the two most celebrated universities in America assembled for a football match which divided the whole city into two factions.

Today, New York did not show the sad brightness which is the mark of a holiday in all American cities. Early in the morning the midtown district, instead of being deserted of inhabitants, was more than usually full of uproarious people. All the faces were marked with a pleasant aspect and with that disposition to familiar communication

which children carry as of right and which shines even on adults. The immense metropolis seemed transformed into a little college town altogether wrapped up in the life of its students. . . .

Before the houses, the hotels, and the clubs, immense open carriages, their four horses bedecked with garlands, waited to take the spectators directly to the playing field. Troops of students marched like conquerors through the crowds, which burst into cheers to wish them success. This was a pleasant occasion, dedicated to the flower of American youth.

The game follows — a stupendous and elaborate exercise of strength and skill. In the evening, the streets and the theaters are jammed with students, but the flower of American youth has begun to fade and gives forth the odor of alcohol. The young men break into the theaters by force and are thrown out by violence. They do not indulge in those exhibitions of salacious gaiety by which our students on a spree compensate for distracting the peaceful spectators. Instead, the American boys emit an annoying, deafening yell on a single continuous note that expresses the immobility of their sluggish minds. No smiling, no laughing! Their supreme power, unmitigated by any grace, seems like that of a conquering soldiery.

They stagger tipsily through the streets, sunk in a dark drunkenness, without a ray of merriment. The less funereal beat time out loud, trying to march in step, but voices and step are independent of each other and agree only in wandering off on their own accounts. Their voices give off noises like the sound of drums muffled for a funeral, sounds so strained that they seem to express the delirium of the paralytic. What a difference from our lively and sparkling drinking songs and from the subtle exaltation that mounts to the brain from our wines! And their walk! A three-year-old could fell the most vigorous of these athletes like a log. Late at night many lie down like corpses in the gutter.

This brutal viciousness is equally characteristic of the rich and poor, even making allowance for differences in the quality of their drinking and of its inebriating capacity, for the latter rises in inverse proportion to the former. It is well known that in the very exclusive clubs the most fastidious members come in on foot, but go out in the small hours on the backs of their servants who bundle them into carriages, take them home, and put them to bed before they recover consciousness.

I judge that the American is more interested in getting drunk than in drinking. That statement may seem paradoxical, but is not. I have rarely seen an American, accustomed to drinking, sip a glass of liquor and show signs of savoring the aroma. They all act as if the bitter alcohol is unpleasant to the palate, and hurry the act of imbibing as if eager to get rid of the disagreeable substance. They do not drink, they guzzle. When they bring the glass to their lips and empty it at a gulp, it is clear that the column of liquor must sink like lead through the throat without affecting the taste.

The act of imbibing generally is not accompanied by any sign of pleasure. Deep and habitual drinkers reach the state of drunkenness without passing through the process of getting drunk. For them inebriety is not a height to be climbed, but a well into which to sink, and that not little by little, gradually, but purposely and deliberately. True, this process involves a conservation of energy; it imposes a rest and suspends the intellectual activity of minds, so heavily taxed and so thoroughly fatigued by business.

Americans feel a violent need to paralyze cerebral activity with external aids. Or perhaps the source of the invincible seductiveness of alcohol that steadily leads them to the ultimate stupor lies in their impatience for extreme sensations; they love to save time, to get there all at once. That is the same gross sensuality that reveals itself in a thousand ways, disdainful of delicacy, loving enormities, giganticism, excess.

The first product of the prodigies of mechanization that impressed me in the United States was the appearance of universal prosperity, and consequently the visible equality of social conditions. There was equality of dress, of fashions, of habits, of manners, and, above all, a kind of physiological equality; I don't venture to say equality of health, but the kind of healthy well-being that comes from sufficient, nutritious food.

In New York, toward evening, when the working day ends, miles of carriages scatter the innumerable crowds, which all day long conduct their affairs downtown, to all parts of the upper city. The six parallel elevated railway lines each run trains of five or six enormous coaches every five minutes, all jammed to overflowing with people. There the millionaire sits beside the porter and may well be asked by the conductor to get up and give his place to an old serving woman. Some elegant Wall Street bankers are marked by special clothes of English cut. But with that exception, no European would be able to pick out by eye who there represents the infinite variety of professions, trades, states, fortune, culture, education that may be encountered among the whole people.

The gentleman who sits at your side and can scarcely edge himself into the tiny space available while he nonchalantly reads his immense newspaper might with equal likelihood be the attorney of the richest railroad in the world, a shoe clerk, or a cab driver from City Hall Park just finishing his tour of duty. At most, some hands might betray the exercise of the more menial trades, and some odors, peculiar industries. But the shape and texture of the clothing in all shows the same care, the same cut, and almost the same easy circumstances; and in manners and speech all display the same vigorous sentiments of an egalitarian society and of personal dignity.

The stranger who wishes summarily to learn the home manners of the Americans will spend a Sunday in New York riding the length of an elevated line. For that purpose, the Ninth Avenue Line is best. It reaches from the edge of the harbor to the Harlem River, a distance of some twenty kilometers, and the entire journey costs five American cents. The structure of the railroad, following the gradual rises of the ground, generally runs at a height parallel to the first story of the houses, except when it comes to certain dips that furrow the city. There the line runs along the second, third, or fourth floors, and now and then even above the ridges of the roofs.

Leaving the Battery, at the edge of the harbor, the train passes first through the oldest part of New York, the *city* of business, of very old buildings given over in their ground floors to stores, to offices, banks, and establishments of all kinds. Every evening, as I have already said, this city of wealth, which finances the agricultural and industrial activity of the United States, entirely empties itself. No one sleeps there. The press of business forestalls the introduction of improvements; the streets remain narrow and tortuous, the houses, dark and inconvenient; the pavement is broken and buried under a layer of thick black mud, the air stagnant and fetid.

So the dollars are accumulated in ugliness, only to be spent in elegance. That accounts for the deathly silence that falls upon this deserted quarter of the town on holidays. The train moves up the avenue, cutting across the numbered streets which open in places on gardens and plazas or offer glimpses in the distance of the great North River, the Hudson, which is dotted with masts and sails and animated by the aerial seesaw of the ferryboats. Higher up, above Central Park, are the working-class quarters, monotonous, but spacious, convenient, well-furnished.

On Sunday, whoever watches these homes from an elevated train and knows something of the social condition of their inhabitants will believe himself witness of an Anglo-Saxon form of the dream that earned Faust his easy pardon. Every family passes the entire day in serene rest before the spacious windows. The father sits in his rocking chair, pipe in mouth; he reads and reads, from first to last line, the thirty-two large pages of his Sunday paper. Another illustrated paper of equal length busies the mother, seated in another rocking chair near another window. If there is a son in the family, and the house has a third window, there will without fail be a third paper and the same sight without variation, as in a figured tapestry.

Only the girls modify the monotony of

this silent and instructive felicity. Rich-blooded, blooming in blond or rosy beauty, they do not sit still but lean against the sills, looking curiously into the street, smiling at the passengers who fly by in the elevated, chatting with neighbors, making eyes at whoever notices them, nibbling almonds, and laughing continually with sincere freshness. It may be said, parenthetically, that nothing is more graceful than the bold, saucy, gay nimbleness of all these American girls; nothing is more refreshing than the open pleasure with which they encourage and receive the admiration, express or tacit, of passersby.

When the train runs at its highest along the level of the top floors, where more light enters, the whole interior equipment and furniture of the house becomes visible. There are pleasant draperies, cloths on the tables, nice curtains, copious and commodious furniture, in general an air of solidity and comfort which in Italy we do not see in our provincial cities, except perhaps for such exceptions as the homes of lawyers, doctors, judges, merchants. These people, be it understood, live by their own day's labor, with salaries of four or even three dollars a day, the ordinary pay of a worker. These are settled people; they neither owe nor are owed; they are not in danger of ruin; and their needs are not limited to that which barely keeps them from dying but also include what is desirable for living.

28.

Count Vay de Vaya und zu Luskod: The Land of Mammon and Moloch

The reputed quest of Americans for money and riches has led many foreign visitors to describe the United States as the land of Mammon. Count Vay de Vaya und zu Luskod, a Hungarian churchman who made frequent visits to America, was convinced that the country between 1903 and 1906 was devoted solely to work and to the accumulation of material possessions. The sacrifice and self-denial often made in the struggle for riches convinced him that Americans also worshiped Moloch, the god of human sacrifice. However, his observations were not entirely negative. He complimented the American on his ingenuity and pragmatic sense. A selection from his Inner Life of the United States *(1908) is reprinted below.*

Source: TWA, pp. 410-417.

IN THIS REALM of Mammon and Moloch everything has a value — except human life. Scientific brains cogitate how to turn the filthiest dross to account, but no one concerns himself about the sanguinary destruction in the ranks of mankind. Why? Because human life is a commodity the supply of which exceeds the demand. There are always fresh recruits to supply the place of those who fall in the battle; and steamships are constantly arriving at the neighboring ports, discharging their living human cargo still further to swell the phalanx of the instruments of cupidity.

It is true that the factory laborers of Pittsburgh get more money than farm-hands; but they have also to sacrifice much more. Day after day, week after week, year in, year out, their tired eyes rest upon nothing but glowing iron and molten steel. But, yet, there is some change — a constant recurrence of disasters, the bloody tax exacted by the Moloch of the furnaces, who claims his victim every day. If one could compute the fatal accidents that take place in a year at the Pittsburgh plants, the number would be incredibly large. And if one ascertained the extent to which preventive measures are taken to minimize this waste of life, one would find practically nothing done. Accidents are steadily on the increase.

How can the inhuman callousness with which the owners of the works regard the annihilation of their employees be accounted for? The only plausible answer is: the indifference of the employers is confirmed and rendered chronic by the ghastly calculation that there are more men outside the works than are required inside. Obsolete machinery and appliances are very often used instead of the expensive improvements for the simple reason that alterations would cost much more than the "death money" which the firms have to pay to the families of their victims.

The new Compensation Act, recently passed, actually protects the employer instead of the employee, for it not only lowers the rate but also provides that the injured workman who has no family in America is not entitled to compensation at all. Half the workmen leave their wives and families in their native land and arrive alone to commence their new existence; when such men happen to be injured or killed, their wives and children become paupers. This act is one of the most unjust, pernicious, and heartless ever passed by any nation, and is doubly unjust, pernicious, and heartless in view of the superabundance of capital, which is being further piled up hour by hour.

The most astonishing feature of this land of dollars is the absolute indifference and contempt of the rich toward the poor. One might well suppose that, in a democratic country, such as have risen from the lowest strata of society would entertain more liberal and humane sentiments toward the less fortunate. But in the struggle for gold there is no room for sentiment. One might perhaps suppose that a sense of duty at least would prompt them to kindly actions. Sad experience, however, teaches otherwise. Strange as it may seem, often the most unsympathetic and the most callous are those who have themselves graduated from the hard school of adversity.

In this eternal turmoil the worker's lot is hard in a special degree. But most difficult is that of the Hungarian and the Slav, who, while getting the least pay, do the most degrading and dangerous work. Usually these people are appointed as enginemen or as stokers in the foundries and blast furnaces, always where the heat is most intense and the danger most imminent. And the daily remuneration for such strenuous labor and appalling risk is only about $1.75.

It is hardly credible that men risk their lives for such a paltry pittance, yet so it is. When we consider that in Pittsburgh, lodgings, clothing, and all the necessities of life are very dear, the sum mentioned brings only half or a third of its value elsewhere in the country. How a man can live upon it, and even save from it, seems past comprehension. Yet while the immigrant cannot be said to live, he exists, and actually manages to put a little aside.

Most of the alien workmen have no families, and, having no homes, their wants are few and simple. They are not regular members of the social order; they are, as it were, outlaws. As many of them are herded together in rooms as can well be packed therein without regard to the requirements of decency or hygiene; others do not occupy rooms at all but find shelter from the elements in outhouses. There is no proper furniture in these hovels, simply rude wooden benches on which the occupants may lie down and sleep, closely crowded together. No comfort, no cleanliness, no light — the atmosphere is sickening.

To sustain life under such conditions is hardly conceivable. Is it surprising that various diseases decimate the denizens of these foul quarters? Often the most terrible epidemics rage The food is even worse than the lodging. The people, it is true, eat meat three times a day, but the meat is in nine cases out of ten unwholesome, as the recent meat trust scandals have sufficiently proved. The noxious effects of this tainted diet are aggravated by the fact that the workmen take very little farinaceous and vegetable food with it.

Their employment is dangerous; they have no homes; their workdays are gloomy and cheerless — what can their Sundays, their holidays be like? The program of their recreations is very brief. Ignorant of the language, they can enjoy no society; they are debarred from all pleasures except the questionable ones of drinking and gambling. And so the most sober-minded of them are induced to indulge in these vices.

Is there no one to rescue, to ameliorate, to help? Are there no millionaire employers with the enthusiasm to build cottages, plant gardens, and establish decent homes for their employees? Not seeing anything of these, I timidly asked various people to show me some of their benevolent schemes, and, at once, with an air of pride, they pointed to certain marble halls, lofty edifices, and gilded cupolas, "In memory of Mr. X.," "To the honor of Mr. Y.," and "For the glory of Mr. Z." I failed to understand, and said so; and then they explained that one of these palaces contained a famous collection of antediluvian skeletons, another some marvelous ancient parchments, while a third sheltered thousands of volumes.

Yet I could not quite see the connection between these magnificent specimens of architectural art and the practical well-being of the toilers. It seemed to me that they served much less for the benefit of the poor than for the glorification of the rich. And I thought how laudable it would be if Messrs. X., Y., and Z., instead of advertising their own wealth and greatness in this fashion, would erect humble yet clean and comfortable dwellings for their laborers.

Is it to be wondered at if these poor, neglected, good-natured creatures — having no wholesome counterattractions, no friends, no benevolent patrons — cannot resist the temptations lying in their path? Their environment and lusterless existence drive them into the abyss.

Alas! that men should be driven to earn their daily bread by such inhuman labor, such bloody sweat! How heart-rendering that man should sacrifice all his noblest aspirations and every lofty ideal, and, blindfolded by primitive instincts, should see nothing but the alluring, chimerical gold! In the effort and struggle to obtain it, he sacrifices peace, happiness, even God's precious gift of life, and risks what is more precious still — his immortal soul.

Yet materialism is an evil which, alas, is permeating the whole world, and it would be highly erroneous to endeavor to make any one nation responsible for this dangerous scourge, for it is universal. If it finds a more congenial soil in America, and there develops more formidable proportions, we must remember that in the New World everything is on a larger scale, everything is exaggerated. Each process is more intense and magnified. Life is something infinitely larger.

These rudimentary conditions in the United States are perfectly natural and the outcome of the general situation. Although one cannot help noticing these conditions, and though Americans themselves are the first to deplore them, it would not be just to look entirely on the black side and to criticize in a pessimistic spirit.

Labor, as such, in the New World is what strikes each new arrival most forcibly — labor which provides daily bread and occupation to rich and poor, labor which has become identical with the thought of terrestrial life, labor which is the chief object of existence and its highest ideal.

Work in the United States is everything, and everything has become work. Toil and relaxation, hours passed at the office or at home, only give pleasure when there is something to do. The old idea of *dolce far niente* is incomprehensible; fatigue, whether as a means of providing subsistence, or whether for distraction, or as a habit, becomes a necessity of life.

One must keep moving; rest is not understood and is avoided whenever possible unless rendered compulsory by a general breakdown. The impulses toward motion govern everyone; so much so that if they sit down their chairs must have rockers so that they may continue an action of some sort even when resting.

The day begins very early, about two hours earlier than in England, with a hurried toilet, a hasty breakfast, and the rush to the factories and offices. Time is far too valuable to permit a midday meal at home. There is not even time for proper food; the restaurants would find their efforts wasted if they advertised a good cuisine and well-appointed table. Instead, to attract the passersby, they put up notices with such inscriptions as "Quick lunch," "Hasty meals," "Chops in a minute." And on office doors at about midday we often see a card with the words, "Away for lunch; back in five minutes." The rest of the day, of the week, and of the year passes in the same way. This encumbered existence, as intense for the capitalist as for the laborer, gives American life its high pressure.

However disconcerted the stranger may be on arrival by this incoherent and whirling bustle, it will carry him away mechanically; he will become, in spite of himself, an atom in the general turmoil. One gets accustomed to it; then it becomes a necessity, and one adapts oneself to the novel life.

People come from many parts of the world — astute and stubborn Teutons, lazy and casual Latins, Orientals of vague dispositions — all amalgamating in a seething caldron, everything boiling and effervescing, everything glowing.

Work here is divided up, distributed, and multiplied among many elements, great or small. It is, in fact, a huge, unseen machine in which each individual, high or low, plays the part of one of the wheels. Each revolves, each whirls, each is in ceaseless activity.

Everything is done with great facility. Enterprises, manual or spiritual, simple or complicated, small or great, of little or much importance, are all initiated with the same simplicity. From the modest clerk whose only apparatus is a fountain pen, to officials who carry portfolios under their arms, equipment is reduced to a minimum. Everything that is superfluous or an encumbrance is dispensed with. There is no room for the useless.

The same tendency shows itself in all fields of labor, in every kind of negotiation. Simplicity reigns supreme. The formality and ceremonies of the Old World are dispensed with. In the largest companies, two or three directors meet in a casual way to decide in a few minutes on the disposition of millions. And if there is no time to lose when it comes to investing millions, that is even more the case among those who handle tools. The main feature of American work is the absence of waste, either of time or labor. The way in which the workman uits his work to the time and space at his command gives American labor its character. He spends less time at work than in other countries, yet has more to show. It is of course, to his interest to produce as much as possible, since he is generally on piecework. When he works by time, he is under a strict supervision and under high pressure; if he is not up to the standard, he will be dismissed immediately.

Thus the workman does his utmost, in his own interest, to keep up to the mark. The simplest laborer, even the newly arrived immigrant, does not have the long hours he was accustomed to; but he must adapt himself to the tension expected here. This relationship of toil to time is one of the main factors of the marvelous rate of production in this country.

Another is the division of labor. Where wages are high, hours short, and competition extreme, only a precise division of labor can assure the success of a factory. Only thus have Americans been able to secure their own markets against foreign competition and, in certain branches, to dominate European commerce as well.

The apparent confusion of machinery and humanity in the factory at work is at first sight quite bewildering. Everything is moving, revolving, hammering, or whirring. Looking more closely, one begins to perceive that the chaotic movement, the cacophony of sound, follows hard and fast rules. As each revolution of a wheel is ordered and each hammer only strikes to command, so each human limb moves only in coordination. As each wheel or lever of the vast machinery accomplishes only a certain action and produces only a part of an article, so each human hand is engaged only in one detail, performing and reperforming the same action, doing the same work to perpetuity. Whether or not it is desirable for the individual to become a piece of machinery is another question. But the division

of labor is simply wonderful, and so complex as to be almost incomprehensible to the uninitiated.

Like everything else in this country, this is the result of organic and natural development. The history of one of the great commercial enterprises sounds as incredible as a fairy tale, although in a novel edition appropriate to an age of smoke and invention. We hear descriptions that can hardly be believed of the time when formidable towns were wildernesses with only a few wooden huts, visited from time to time by peddlers who eventually erected booths, out of which grew many of the commercial undertakings that we admire at the present day.

This natural development explains the growth of these establishments and their complicated system of organization. The personnel adapted itself to conditions in the same way and increased until it attained its present size. Walking around the workshops and departments of Marshall Field and Company, the pride of Chicago, founded when the sixth city in the world had only just been begun, we are surprised to hear that the present owners themselves laid its foundation as a small shop.

If the relation of toil to time and the minute division of labor are the most prominent traits of the factories, in the shops it is the organization that impresses us most. These huge buildings, where dozens of elevators constantly shoot up and down, swarm with hundreds of employees and thousands of customers, elbowing their way hither and thither. The ability to organize and manage such a place is amazing.

It would, of course, be impossible to start such an establishment all at once; it could only develop and grow naturally to its present proportions. By this organic growth the largest commercial enterprises preserve the unity and intensity that they had when first established. Thus the manager, who is often the proprietor himself or the largest shareholder, continues to hold the threads of each department in his own hands, paying attention to the pettiest details and giving his employees the widest opportunities to show their worth.

Men, therefore, have a chance to improve themselves and to rise. Sometimes they are their own masters from the very beginning and sell matches in the street; sometimes they are hired by others as errand boys and the like. Their sphere of activity increases with their age, according to their gifts. The whole procedure maintains an organic relation between the development of the individual and his business. The magnate and his enterprise grow together by a continuity of work; at the same time, the business acquires its manifold character and the proprietor increases his business capacity. Only thus can we explain the great American businessman, who has every branch of his undertaking under his own control, just as in the old days when his whole stock in trade could be held in a box.

Everybody works in this country out of respect for work, and each individual tries to make his work as lucrative as possible. Labor that is not well paid is not understood. Rich and poor must be equally well remunerated. The richer and more comfortable a man is, the higher will be his prices or his fees. The idea in old countries, that people of independent means should not earn money, that the rich who work should do so gratuitously, or at least preserve the appearance of doing so, is inconceivable here.

The false shame of work, which is one of the drawbacks of our social life and national activity, is unknown in America. In fact, there, no one starts working without first fixing his price. There is no mystery or embarrassment. People talk as openly about it as about stocks and bonds, and the higher his price the more candidly will a man advertise the fact. Individual worth has its rise and fall as shares do, and clients take pride in making it known that they can afford the services of such and such a lawyer, doctor, speaker, and so on.

This is why America is the paradise of all artists, lecturers, and writers; in a word, of all mental work. For intellectual effort is not less respected and certainly is not less lavishly paid than any other kind of work. The fabulous salaries of celebrated singers and actors are proverbial, and every rising star regards an American tour as an El Dorado.

An El Dorado it is indeed, for while they sweep in the dollars, they also enjoy every social advantage, are received everywhere cordially, are feted in the most exclusive circles, and become leaders of society. For America is not only a state based on democratic principles, its inhabitants are out-and-out democrats, and its conceptions of work and the workman are essentially democratic.

The moral flabbiness born of the exclusive worship of the bitch-goddess SUCCESS. *That — with the squalid cash interpretation put on the word success — is our national disease.*

WILLIAM JAMES

There is not a single human characteristic which can be safely labeled as "American."

SAMUEL L. CLEMENS ("MARK TWAIN")

29.

CHARLES V. TEVIS: Tobacco War in Kentucky

The tobacco growers of Kentucky were at the mercy of many forces, not least among them the American Tobacco Company monopoly. In 1904, according to a Kentucky calculation, a man was lucky to raise tobacco for 30 cents a day. In an effort to get a better price, tobacco growers formed associations that gathered together all the tobacco grown in a particular region, set what seemed a fair price, and demanded it from the giant corporation's buyer. However, some independent growers were unwilling to join the associations. In order to persuade them — for their cooperation was essential to success — "Night Riders" terrorized them until they yielded. Charles Tevis described the activities of these "Night Riders" in an article for Harper's Weekly, *part of which appears here.*

Source: *Harper's Weekly*, February 8, 1908: "A Ku-Klux Klan of To-day: The Red Record of Kentucky's 'Night Riders.' "

THERE IS WAR IN KENTUCKY. In a score of towns what is virtually a state of martial law exists. In the farming districts, cellars have been fortified and loaded arms stacked within easy reach. The "Night Riders" are abroad.

Rivaling the notorious Ku Klux Klan in daring and in romantic interest, this internecine foe of the commonwealth of the Blue Grass state has burned a path to a disquieting dominance. By day the planters of tobacco, riding in companies, are doggedly proselytizing in protest against what they characterize as the oppressive methods of the American Tobacco Company. Their greeting is characteristic of whole-hearted Kentucky; generally their word of farewell is a warning, perhaps veiled, but menacing. By night, bands of masked men are roving the state with flaming torches and ready revolvers, leaving behind them a trail of devastation and bloodshed. . . .

That the bread and butter of 75 percent of the farmers of the state is endangered,

anarchy takes as an excuse for its sway. The so-called tobacco trust, the American Tobacco Company, has been defied by the planters. They are withholding their 1906, 1907, and, in some cases, their 1905 crops from the company's markets. This means that their product is not being marketed; that their pocketbooks for the year just past are minus approximately $35 million; that the banks are refusing them credit; that the insurance companies are declining to write "property risks" and even canceling policies; that the chance for a 1908 crop is remote; that a staggering blow is likely to be dealt at the life of Kentucky's greatest industry. . . .

In the course of months, 75,000 members were enrolled in the two big societies, the Burley Tobacco Association and the Dark Tobacco Association. This membership represented a tobacco pool of 350 million pounds, or more than 70 percent of the state's output. How formidable this farmer trust became can readily be seen. But the leaders of the movement appreciated the fact that for it to be successful there must be no nonunionists, and a greater crusade was instituted. As has been said, persuasions failed to bring all of the independent growers into the fold. Then came the Night Riders.

This was the beginning of a crusade of destruction which has up to this time caused the loss of $50 million worth of property and the sacrifice of several lives. As yet, nothing has served to check it. Not one, but a half-dozen companies, of from 200 to 500 men each (a strange commentary on Kentucky's percentage of ruffian citizenship, if the contentions of some are to be believed), are parading nightly, blackened ruins marking their progress.

On the night of the 2nd of March, 1906, they appeared suddenly in the streets of Princeton. They were on horseback, masked, armed, determined. With a preliminary scattering of shots, they applied the torch to several freight cars containing tobacco, some of which had been bought by the American Tobacco Company, and the rest owned by independents. Not until these fires had completely destroyed the tobacco did they leave the city and disappear into the darkness as mysteriously as they had come.

"A band of ruffians! They will not dare to repeat the outrage!" was the verdict, when the news of the raid was flashed over the state.

Close upon the heels of this event came a report that a band of mounted men, masked and armed, had burned the barns of a farmer near Hopkinsville. Simultaneously, other planters — all independents — communicated the intelligence that their crops had been "salted," or ruined by "dragging," or that their barns had been burned. These arrived from different parts of the state, and each stated that a band of mounted men . . . had committed the depredation.

"The trouble is confined to the few western counties that raise the greatest Burley crops. The hirelings who are doing the work will soon be apprehended and punished," said the wiseacres.

Then appeared the ominous skull and cross-bones on the front doors, fences, and barns of independents who were refusing to join in the fight against the tobacco trust. Letters threatening destruction of property and a whipping were sent out broadcast. A campaign of intimidation was waged, and the American Society of Equity's ranks were augmented. But the American Tobacco Company and its allied concerns pursued the even tenor of their way, strong in the support of those who laughed at threats and remained independent.

This was not well-advised. On the night of December 7 began a reign of terror that has no like in the history of Kentucky. Hopkinsville was the point of first attack. The citizens of this city, on that memorable evening, little suspected what the next few hours held for them. A raid by the mysterious band of "Night Riders" was far from their thoughts. Not until their slumbers were broken by the clatter of flying hoofs and the rattle of shots, and their sleep-burdened eyes blinded by the glare of burning buildings, did they realize the full meaning of a descent by the dreaded band.

In the face of a determined fire from the several detachments of the invaders, the men of the city, armed with all kinds of weapons, ventured from the protection of their homes to meet in alleys and in the shadows of buildings. Preachers, physicians, lawyers, merchants — men of all classes and characters — made up these squads, which, by daring dashes and sly maneuvers, at length joined for a concerted attack upon the marauders, who were holding the public square. There a pitched battle ensued.

The spectacle of fellow Kentuckians, perhaps neighbors, perhaps relatives, shooting at each other with deadly intent was painted red by the flames of the blazing warehouses. Shrieks of terror-stricken women were heard above the rattle of shots; and the cries of the wounded answered the shouts of new recruits to the ranks of the defenders. Slowly, fighting each step of retreat, the "Night Riders" were forced from street to street and alley to alley, and finally to the outskirts of the city. There, two of the raiders were seen to fall from their horses as the bullets flew among them. The army of citizens had by this time assumed formidable size, but in the face of its terrific fire the invaders made a last stand, while their fallen comrades were being placed upon their horses. Then, with a threat to repeat the outrage, the band galloped away. . . .

All sorts of strange stories sprang into life. It was said that the "Night Riders" had an organization modeled after that of the historic Ku Klux Klan; that there was one man at the head — one of the biggest growers in the state — and, under him, a high council of war, acting through captains, lieutenants, and different bands of privates; that this organization was statewide, its companies ready for their sinister work in every tobacco-producing section within the boundary lines of the state. Some declared that the bands made their headquarters in caves, that there lots were cast, and the fate of different independents decided. A few of the more imaginative even pictured wives and mothers making masks and hoods for their husbands and sons.

The contagion of fear quickly spread north and east from Hopkinsville, and both warnings from authentic sources and ill-timed appearances of strange groups of masked horsemen caused more than one body of citizens to prepare for defense. A cordon of guards was thrown about all the warehouses in Lexington. This example was followed in Maysville, Owingsville, Russell-ville, and a number of other towns. By day every stranger was an object of suspicion; by night sentries patrolled the streets. . . .

Then a band of "Peaceful Riders By Day" made its appearance. Gen. George W. Jett, one of the most influential planters in the state, was in command. It commenced its march in Bracken County, from East Augusta, where the 500 "soldiers" foregathered. From one farm to another went the company, soliciting signatures to a contract not to raise any tobacco in 1908 unless the tobacco trust "lays down," and advising, to use a mild term, those who refused to sign not to attempt to market any of their product. . . .

For two weeks this army paraded in Mason, Bracken, Boone, Kenton, and Campbell counties, preaching peace and prosperity through organization, and generously distributing "advice." During this period the "Night Riders" were not asleep. As if by concerted irregularity, they appeared at the most unexpected places, and their hand was heavy. Then came the second conference of the Society of Equity men and the representatives of the trust. The following statement was given out at the conclusion of the meeting by the District Board of the planters:

> In accordance with the understanding reached at Frankfort, a meeting was held in this city (Winchester) today (January 3), with Messrs. Smith and Walker of the American Tobacco Company. They offered to buy 10,000 hogsheads of tobacco pooled at 12 cents a pound, taking an equal percentage of all grades of tobacco. After a discussion it was determined that this amount was less than they were paying for 1906 tobacco, and even less than they are paying for the 1907 crop in winter order. A counter-proposition was submitted to them, to wit: that our Burley Association should offer 10,000 hogsheads at scheduled prices, which would average 15 cents a pound.
>
> We consider it a great concession on

our part to be willing to sell so small an amount of tobacco. But our proposition was rejected, and we were notified by the American Tobacco's representatives that they would not change one iota from the original proposition, and when asked if they would consider any further proposition in the nature of a compromise, they answered in the negative. . . .

We have come to the conclusion that the American Tobacco Company is using every endeavor to break down our organization and, if it can, disrupt it forever. Without appealing to the prejudice or passion of our people, we can state with truth that our disruption means bankruptcy and ruin for many of our farmers, and want and misery among a large part of Kentucky's citizenship. To obviate such a state of affairs, we will call upon the lawmaking and law-enforcing power of our state to join us in a movement that will forever put an end to such a trust. . . .

Just before this message reached the people came news of the third big raid of the "Night Riders," this time at Russellville, where several citizens were seriously wounded and $100,000 worth of property was destroyed.

The band entered the city shortly after midnight without a moment's warning. A detachment overpowered the police officials, binding them hand and foot. Another detachment went to the Louisville and Nashville railroad yards, where they took possession of every locomotive, fearing that whistles would be sounded and the alarm given to the countryside. The electric-light plant was also seized and its whistles spiked. Others of the band tied telegraph operators to doors and, at the point of revolvers, held up the telephone operators, many of them women, at the same time wrecking the apparatus. . . .

The following night the masked host rode in Campbell County, across the Ohio River from Cincinnati. On Monday, January 6, the "Riders" appeared almost simultaneously at the towns of Bethel, Sherburne, and Jackstown. The first, a village, was practically wiped off the map; all the American Tobacco Company's property at Sherburne was burned to the ground; and only a timely warning and a quick removal of the independent's tobacco at Jackstown saved that community. . . .

The destruction, up to the present time amounting to $50 million worth of property in the state, not to mention the killing and wounding of a score of people, has apparently but whetted the determination of the masked raiders to accomplish by dreadful might what peaceful conferences failed in doing.

Remember, my son, that any man who is a bear on the future of this country will go broke.

J. P. MORGAN, as reported by his son, Dec. 10, 1908. Often quoted as: "Don't sell this country short."

30.

Arthur Twining Hadley: The Constitution and Private Property

A number of historians writing around the turn of the century showed special interest in the character and role of private property in the United States, and especially in the relationship between property and democratic processes. One of these was Arthur Twining Hadley, whose contention that the Supreme Court was the crucial factor in the conflict between political democracy and industrial absolutism gains credence when the Court's many decisions opposing social welfare legislation between 1895 and 1908 are recalled. However, his assurance that Americans would always stop short of socialism must have been comforting to defenders of the status quo — both on and off the Court. The following comprises part of an article by Hadley published in 1908. The article was a revision of a lecture he had delivered at Berlin University.

Source: *Independent*, April 16, 1908: "The Constitutional Position of Property in America."

EUROPEAN OBSERVERS who study either the specific industrial questions which have come before the American people for their solution or the general relation between the industrial activity of the government and that of private individuals are surprised at a certain weakness of public action in all these matters. Our legislatures are often ready to pass drastic measures of regulation; they are rarely willing to pursue a consistent and carefully developed policy for the attainment of an industrial end. The people often declaim against the extent of the powers of private capital; they are seldom willing to put that capital under the direct management of the government itself. . . .

The fact is that private property in the United States, in spite of all the dangers of unintelligent legislation, is constitutionally in a stronger position, as against the government and the government authority, than is the case in any country of Europe. However much public feeling may at times move in the direction of socialistic measures, there is no nation which by its constitution is so far removed from socialism or from a socialistic order. This is partly because the governmental means provided for the control or limitation of private property are weaker in America than elsewhere, but chiefly because the rights of private property are more formally established in the Constitution itself.

This may seem a startling proposition; but I think a very brief glance at the known facts of history will be sufficient to support and sustain it. For property in the modern sense was a comparatively recent development in the public law of European communities. In the United States, on the contrary, property in the modern sense represents the basis on which the whole social order was established and built up. . . .

In the American colonies . . . where the public law of the United States first took its rise, conditions were wholly different [from those of Europe]. People wanted no military chieftain to protect them, no overlord to rule them. Each man was familiar with the use of a gun — how familiar the overwhelming losses of the British troops in the Revolutionary War, when brought face to face with untrained farmers, testify very clearly — and was ready to take his share in protecting the community against the attacks of the Indians or their French leaders. There was plenty of land for all — plenty of opportunity for the exercise of labor and the use of capital. That man did the most for society who worked hardest and saved most. Under such circumstances the laws were so framed and interpreted as to give the maximum stimulus to labor and the maximum rights to capital.

There was no military aristocracy which stood in the way. Governors were at times sent over from England who tried their best to assert Crown rights for themselves and their subordinates. But the net effect of the activity of these governors was probably to weaken rather than to strengthen the claims of feudal authority. . . .

At the time, therefore, when the United States separated from England, respect for industrial property right was a fundamental principle in the law and public opinion of the land. It was natural enough that this should be so at a period when every man either held property or hoped to do so. The strange thing is that this principle should have survived with so little change down to the present day. But there were certain circumstances connected with the adoption of the Constitution of the United States which provided for the perpetuation of this state of things — which made it difficult for public opinion in another and later age, when property holding was less widely distributed, to alter the legal conditions of the earlier period.

During the War of the Revolution, from 1775 to 1782, and in the years immediately thereafter, the American Union had been a league of independent states, and a very loose one. They had formed an organization for mutual protection in carrying on the war. But this organization, even while the war lasted, was very weak indeed. The im-

minence of a common danger, which threatened to involve all, and the personality of a few leaders, of whom George Washington was the most conspicuous, were the only things that enabled the different colonies to act together. When independence was conceded by England in 1782, and the restraints of common danger were removed, the hopeless weakness of the central government became obvious.

From 1783 to 1789 the United States had no means of securing concert of action at home or respect and consideration abroad. Clearheaded men felt the absolute necessity of centralization. The Constitution of 1788 was the result of a set of contracts, agreements, and compromises between two pretty evenly balanced parties — a states' rights party, which wished to limit the powers of the federal government, and a national party, which was anxious to set some practical control on the autonomy of the state government.

The delegates to the Convention of 1787 were concerned with questions of constitutional law in the narrower sense. They were not thinking of the legal position of private property. But it so happened that in making mutual limitations upon the powers of the federal and the state government, they unwittingly incorporated into the Constitution itself certain very extraordinary immunities to the property holders as a body.

It was in the first place provided that there should be no taking of private property without due process of law. The states' rights men feared that the federal government might, under the stress of military necessity, pursue an arbitrary policy of confiscation. The Federalists, or national party, feared that, under the influence of sectional jealousy, one or more of the states might pursue the same policy. This constitutional provision prevented the legislature or executive, either of the nation or of the individual states, from taking property without judicial inquiry as to the necessity, and without making full compensation even in case the esult of such inquiry was favorable to the overnment. No man foresaw the subse-uent effect of this provision in preventing majority of voters, acting in the legislature r through the executive, from disturbing xisting arrangements with regard to rail-oad building or factory operation until the ailroad stockholders or factory owners had ad the opportunity to have their case tried n the courts.

There was another equally important lause in the Constitution providing that no tate should pass a law impairing the obli-ation of contracts. In this case also a provi-ion which was at first intended to prevent ectional strife and to protect the people of ne locality against arbitrary legislation in nother became a means of strengthening ested rights as a whole against the possibil-ty of legislative or executive interference. Nor was the direct effect of these two lauses in preventing specific acts on the art of the legislature the most important esult of their existence. They were a pow-rful means of establishing the American ourts in that position of supremacy which hey enjoy under the Constitution; for vhenever an act of the legislature or the ex-cutive violated, or even seemed to violate, ne of these clauses, it came before the ourts for review. If the federal courts said hat the act of a legislature violated one of hese provisions it was blocked — rendered owerless by a dictum of the judges.

I do not mean that these two clauses in he Constitution were the chief source of udicial power. That power has been due rimarily to the traditional respect for the udicial office existing in the United States, vhich has rendered it almost impossible for any but men of learning and character to spire to it; and, secondarily, to the very great ability that certain of the early Ameri-can judges — notably Marshall, Story, and Kent — showed in expounding the law in such manner as to command universal ap-roval. But if these provisions did not lie at he foundation of the positive authority of the judges, they were unquestionably a most powerful instrument in practically lim-iting the authority of legislatures, and to that extent in strengthening the rights of the property holders.

The rights of individual owners against legislative interference were thus most fully protected. But how was it when property was in the hands of corporations?

Here also the power of control by the government was weakened and the rights and immunities of the property holders cor-respondingly strengthened by two events, whose effect upon the modern industrial sit-uation may be fairly characterized as fortu-itous. One of these was the decision in the celebrated Dartmouth College case in 1819; the other was the passage of the Fourteenth Amendment to the Constitution of the United States in 1868. I call their effect fortuitous, because neither the judges who decided the Dartmouth College case nor the legislators who passed the Fourteenth Amendment had any idea how these things would affect the modern industrial situation.

The Dartmouth College case dealt with an educational institution, not with an in-dustrial enterprise. The Fourteenth Amend-ment was framed to protect the Negroes from oppression by the whites, not to pro-tect corporations from oppression by the legislature. It is doubtful whether a single one of the members of Congress who voted for it had any idea that it would touch the question of corporate regulation at all. Yet the two together have had the effect of placing the modern industrial corporation in an almost impregnable constitutional posi-tion.

In 1816 the New Hampshire legislature attempted to take away the charter rights of Dartmouth College. Daniel Webster was employed by the college in its defense, and his reasoning so impressed the court that they committed themselves to the position that a charter was a contract; that a state, having induced people to invest money by certain privileges and immunities, could not at will modify those privileges and immunities thus granted. Whether the court would have taken so broad a position if the matter had come before it thirty or forty years later, when the abuses of ill-judged industrial charters had become more fully manifest, is not sure; but, having once taken this position and maintained it in a series of decisions, the court could not well recede from it. Inasmuch as many of the corporate charters granted by state legislation had an unlimited period to run, the theory that these instruments were contracts binding the state for all time had a very important bearing in limiting the field within which a legislature could regulate the activity of such a body, or an executive interfere with it.

Again, by the Fourteenth Amendment to the Constitution of the United States, every state was forbidden to interfere with the civil rights of any person or to treat different persons in an unequal way. This amendment to the Constitution, passed just after the close of the Civil War, was intended to prevent the Southern states readmitted, or on the point of being readmitted, to the Union from abridging the rights of the Negro members of the commonwealth. A number of years elapsed before the effect of this amendment upon the constitutional position of railroad and industrial corporations seems to have been fully realized.

But, in 1882, the Southern Pacific Railroad Company, having been, as it conceived, unfairly taxed by the assessors of a certain county in California, took the position that a law of the state of California taxing the property of a corporation at a different rate from that under which similar property of an individual would be taxed was in effect a violation of the Fourteenth Amendment to the Constitution, because a corporation was a person and therefore entitled to equal treatment. This view, after careful consideration, was upheld by the federal courts. A corporation, therefore, under the law of the United States, is entitled to the same immunities as any other person; and, since the charter creating it is a contract whose obligation cannot be impaired by the one-sided act of the legislature, its constitutional position as a property holder is much stronger than anywhere in Europe.

Under these circumstances, it is evident that large powers and privileges have been constitutionally delegated to private property in general and to corporate property in particular. I do not mean that property owners, and specifically the owners of corporate property, have more *practical* freedom from interference in the United States than they do in some other countries, notably in England. Probably they do not have as much. But their theoretical position — the sum of the conditions which affect their standing for the long future and not for the immediate present — is far stronger in the United States. The general status of the property owner under the law cannot be changed by the action of the legislature or the executive, or the people of a state voting at the polls, or all three put together. It cannot be changed without either a consensus of opinion among the judges, which should lead them to retrace their old views, or an amendment of the Constitution of the United States by the slow and cumbersome machinery provided for that purpose, or, last — and I hope most improbable — a revolution.

When it is said, as it commonly is, that the fundamental division of powers in the modern state is into legislative, executive, and judicial, the student of American institutions may fairly note an exception. The fundamental division of powers in the Constitution of the United States is between voters on the one hand and property owners on the other. The forces of democracy on one side, divided between the executive and the legislature, are set over against the forces of property on the other side, with the judiciary as arbiter between them, the Constitution itself not only forbidding the legislature and executive to trench upon the rights of property but compelling the judiciary to define and uphold those rights in a manner provided by the Constitution itself.

This theory of American politics has not often been stated. But it has been universally acted upon. One reason why it has not been more frequently stated is that it has been acted upon so universally that no American of earlier generations ever thought it necessary to state it. It has had the most fundamental and far-reaching effects upon the policy of the country. To mention but one thing among many, it has allowed the experiment of universal suffrage to be tried under conditions essentially different from those which led to its ruin in Athens or in Rome.

The voter was omnipotent — within a limited area. He could make what laws he pleased, as long as those laws did not trench upon property right. He could elect what officers he pleased, as long as those officers did not try to do certain duties confided by the Constitution to the property holders. Democracy was complete as far as it went, but constitutionally it was bound to stop short of *social* democracy. I will not go so far as to say that this set of limitations on the political power of the majority in favor of the political power of the property owner has been a necessary element in the success of universal suffrage in the United States. I will say unhesitatingly that it has been a decisive factor in determining the political character of the nation and the actual development of its industries and institutions.

31.

EUGENE V. DEBS: Capitalism and Socialism

In 1908 Eugene V. Debs was nominated for the presidency by the Socialist Party for the third time. He had become a national figure during the great Pullman Strike in 1894, during which he led the American Railway Union and was jailed for refusing to obey a federal injunction. Debs served six months in prison, from which he emerged a convert to socialism. He was a moderate, stressing the possibility of cooperation and harmony between labor and capital, and was thus able to attract increasing numbers of voters in his successive campaigns. Debs was living in Girard, Kansas, when news of his third nomination was received. People gathered in the plaza of the town to hear the famous Socialist speak. Debs's impromptu speech, a portion of which is reprinted here, was delivered on May 23, 1908, and summarized his aims for the Socialist Party.

Source: *Debs: His Life, Writings and Speeches,* Chicago, 1908: "The Issue."

Comrades, Ladies, and Gentlemen:

When I made inquiry a few moments ago as to the cause of this assembling I was told that it was the beginning of another street fair. I am quite surprised, and agreeably so, to find myself the central attraction. . . .

I did what little I could to prevent myself from being nominated by the convention now in session at Chicago, but the nomination sought me out, and, in spite of myself, I stand in your presence this afternoon the nominee of the Socialist Party for the presidency of the United States.

Long, long ago I made up my mind never again to be a candidate for any political office within the gift of the people. I was constrained to violate that vow because, when I joined the Socialist Party, I was taught that the desire of the individual was subordinate to the party will, and that when the party commanded, it was my duty to obey. . . .

Now, my friends, I am opposed to the system of society in which we live today, not because I lack the natural equipment to do for myself but because I am not satisfied to make myself comfortable knowing that there are thousands upon thousands of my fellowmen who suffer for the barest necessities of life. We were taught under the old ethic that man's business upon this earth was to look out for himself. That was the ethic of the jungle; the ethic of the wild beast. Take care of yourself, no matter what may become of your fellowman. Thousands of years ago the question was asked: "Am I my brother's keeper?" That question has never yet been answered in a way that is satisfactory to civilized society.

Yes, I am my brother's keeper. I am under a moral obligation to him that is inspired, not by any maudlin sentimentality but by the higher duty I owe to myself. What would you think of me if I were capable of seating myself at a table and gorging myself with food and saw about me the children of my fellow beings starving to death? . . .

I am in revolt against capitalism (and that doesn't mean to say, my friends, that I am hating you — not the slightest). I am opposed to capitalism because I love my fellowmen; and if I am opposing you I am opposing you for what I believe to be your good; and though you spat upon me with contempt, I should still oppose you to the extent of my power.

I don't hate the workingman because he has turned against me. I know the poor fellow is too ignorant to understand his self-interest, and I know that as a rule the workingman is the friend of his enemy and the enemy of his friend. He votes for men who represent a system in which labor is simply merchandise; in which the man who works the hardest and longest has the least to show for it.

If there is a man on this earth who is entitled to all the comforts and luxuries of this life in abundance, it is the man whose labor produces them. If he is not, who is? Does he get them in the present system? . . .

I am opposing the system under which we live today because I believe it is subversive of the best interests of the people. I am not satisfied with things as they are, and I know that no matter what administration is in power, even were it a Socialist administration, there will be no material change in the condition of the people until we have a new social system based upon the mutual economic interests of the whole people; until you and I and all of us collectively own those things that we collectively need and use.

That is a basic economic proposition. As long as a relatively few men own the railroads, the telegraph, the telephone, own the oilfields and the gasfields and the steel mills and the sugar refineries and the leather tanneries — own, in short, the sources and means of life — they will corrupt our politics, they will enslave the working class, they will impoverish and debase society, they will do all things that are needful to perpetuate their power as the economic masters and the political rulers of the people. Not until these great agencies are owned and operated by the people can the people hope for any material improvement in their social condition.

Is the condition fair today, and satisfactory to the thinking man?

According to the most reliable reports at

our command, as I speak here this afternoon, there are at least 4 million workingmen vainly searching for employment. Have you ever found yourself in that unspeakably sad predicament? Have you ever had to go up the street, begging for work, in a great city thronged with humanity — and, by the way, my friends, people are never quite so strange to each other as when they are forced into artificial, crowded, and stifled relationship. . . .

Nothing is more humiliating than to have to beg for work, and a system in which any man has to beg for work stands condemned. No man can defend it. Now the rights of one are as sacred as the rights of a million. Suppose you happen to be the one who has no work. This republic is a failure so far as you are concerned.

Every man has the inalienable right to work. . . .

Nature's storehouse is full to the surface of the earth. All of the raw materials are deposited here in abundance. We have the most marvelous machinery the world has ever known. Man has long since become master of the natural forces and made them work for him. Now he has but to touch a button and the wheels begin to spin and the machinery to whir, and wealth is produced on every hand in increasing abundance.

Why should any man, woman, or child suffer for food, clothing, or shelter? Why? The question cannot be answered. Don't tell me that some men are too lazy to work. Suppose they are too lazy to work, what do you think of a social system that produces men too lazy to work? If a man is too lazy to work, don't treat him with contempt. Don't look down upon him with scorn as if you were a superior being. If there is a man who is too lazy to work, there is something the matter with him. He wasn't born right or he was perverted in this system. You could not, if you tried, keep a normal man inactive, and if you did he would go stark mad. Go to any penitentiary and you will find the men there begging for the privilege of doing work.

I know by close study of the question exactly how men become idle. I don't repel them when I meet them. I have never yet seen the tramp I was not able to receive with open arms. He is a little less fortunate than I am. He is made the same as I am made. He is a child of the same Father. Had I been born in his environment, had I been subjected to the same things to which he was, I would have been where he is. . . .

Your material interest and mine in the society of the future will be the same. Instead of having to fight each other like animals, as we do today, and seeking to glorify the brute struggle for existence — of which every civilized human being ought to be ashamed — instead of this, our material interests are going to be mutual. We are going to jointly own these mammoth machines, and we are going to operate them as joint partners, and we are going to divide all the products among ourselves.

We are not going to send our surplus to the Goulds and Vanderbilts of New York. We are not going to pile up a billion of dollars in John D. Rockefeller's hands — a vast pyramid from the height of which he can look down with scorn and contempt upon the "common herd." John D. Rockefeller's great fortune is built upon your ignorance. When you know enough to know what your interest is, you will support the great party that is organized upon the principle of collective ownership of the means of life. This party will sweep into power upon the issue of emancipation just as republicanism swept into power upon the Abolition question half a century ago. . . .

What do I propose to do for [the] farmer? Nothing. I only want him to know that he is robbed every day in the week; and, if I can awaken him to the fact that he is robbed under the capitalist system, he will fall into line with the Socialist movement, and will march to the polls on election day, and instead of casting his vote to fasten the shackles upon his limbs more firmly, he will vote for his emancipation. All I have to do is to show that farmer, that day laborer, that tramp that they are victims of this system, that their interests are identical, that they constitute the millions, and that the millions have the votes. The Rockefellers have the dollars, but we have the votes; and when we have sense enough to know how to use the votes, we will have not only the votes but the dollars for all the children of men.

This seems quite visionary to some of you and especially to those of you who know nothing about economics. I could not begin to tell you the story of social evolution this afternoon; of how these things are doing day by day, of how the world is being pushed into socialism, and how it is bound to arrive, no matter whether you are for it or against it. It is the next inevitable phase of civilization. It isn't a scheme, it isn't a contrivance. It isn't anything that is made to order. The day is coming when you will be pushed into it by unseen hands whether you will or not. Nothing can be introduced until the people want it, and when the majority want it they will know how to get it.

I venture the prophecy that within the next five years you will be completely dispossessed. You are howling against the trusts, and the trusts are laughing at you. You keep on voting in the same old way, and the trusts keep on getting what you produce. You say Congress will give you some relief. Good heavens! Who will save us from Congress? Don't you know that Congress is made up almost wholly of trust lawyers and corporation attorneys? I don't happen to have the roll of this one, but with few exceptions they are all lawyers. Now, in the competitive system, the lawyer sells himself to the highest bidder the same as the workingman does. Who is the highest bidder? The trust and corporation, of course. So the trust buys the best lawyer

and the common herd gets the shyster. . . .

The world is just beginning to awaken and is soon to sing its first anthem of freedom. All the signs of the times are cheering. Twenty-five years ago there was but a handful of socialists; today there are a half million. When the polls are closed next fall you will be astounded. The Socialist movement is in alliance with the forces of progress. We are today where the Abolitionists were in 1858. They had a million and a quarter of votes. There was dissension in the Whig, Republican, and Free-Soil parties; but the time had come for a great change, and the Republican Party was formed in spite of the bickerings and contentions of men. Lincoln made the great speech in that year that gave him the nomination and afterward made him President of the United States.

If you had said to the people in 1858, "In two years from now the Republican Party is going to sweep the country and seat the President," you would have been laughed to scorn. The Socialist Party stands today where the Republican Party stood fifty years ago. It is in alliance with the forces of evolution, the one party that has a clear-cut, overmastering, overshadowing issue; the party that stands for the people, and the only party that stands for all the people. In this system we have one set who are called capitalists and another set who are called workers; and they are at war with each other.

Now, we Socialists propose that society in its collective capacity shall produce, not for profit but in abundance to satisfy human wants; that every man shall have the inalienable right to work and receive the full equivalent of all he produces; that every man may stand fearlessly erect in the pride and majesty of his own manhood.

Every man and every woman will then be economically free. They can, without let or hindrance, apply their labor, with the best machinery that can be devised, to all the natural resources, do the work of society and produce for all ; and then receive in exchange a certificate of value equivalent to that of their production. Then society will improve its institutions in proportion to the progress of invention. Whether in the city or on the farm, all things productive will be carried forward on a gigantic scale. All industry will be completely organized. Society for the first time will have a scientific foundation. Every man, by being economically free, will have some time for himself. He can then take a full and perfect breath. He can enjoy life with his wife and children because then he will have a home.

We are not going to destroy private property. We are going to establish private property — all the private property necessary to house man, keep him in comfort, and satisfy his wants. Eighty percent of the people of the United States have no property today. A few have got it all. They have dispossessed the people, and when we get into power we will dispossess them. We will reduce the workday and give every man a chance. We will go to the parks, and we will have music, because we will have time to play music and desire to hear it.

Is it not sad to think that not one in a thousand knows what music is? Is it not pitiable to see the poor, ignorant, dumb human utterly impervious to the divine influences of music? If humanity could only respond to the higher influences! And it would if it had time.

Release the animal, throw off his burden; give him a chance and he rises as if by magic to the plane of a man. Man has all of the divine attributes. They are in a latent state. They are not yet developed. It does not pay now to love music. Keep your eye on the almighty dollar and your fellowman. Get the dollar and keep him down. Make him produce for you. You are not your brother's keeper. Suppose he is poor! Suppose his wife is forced into prostitution! Suppose his child is deformed! And suppose he shuffles off by destroying himself! What is that to you?

But you ought to be ashamed. Take the standard home and look it in the face. If you know what that standard means, and you are a success, God help the failure!

Our conduct is determined by our economic relations. If you and I must fight each other to exist, we will not love each other very hard. We can go to the same church and hear the same minister tell us in good conscience that we ought to love each other, and the next day we approach some business transaction. Do we remember what the minister told us? No; it is gone until next Sunday. Six days in the week we are following the Golden Rule reversed. Now, when we approach a business transaction in competition, what is more natural than that we should try to get the better of it? — get the better of our fellowman? — cheat him if we can?

And, if you succeed, that fixes you as a businessman. You have all the necessary qualifications. Don't let your conscience disturb you — that would interfere with business.

Competition was natural enough at one time, but do you think you are competing today? Many of you think you are competing. Against whom? Against Rockefeller? About as I would if I had a wheelbarrow and competed with the Santa Fe from here to Kansas City. That is about the way you are competing; but your boys will not have even that chance — if capitalism lives that long. You hear of the "late" panic. It is very late. It is going to be very late. This panic will be with us five years from now, and will continue till then.

I am not a prophet. I can no more penetrate the future than you can. I do study the forces that underlie society and the trend of evolution. I can tell by what we have passed through about what we will have in the future; and I know that capitalism can be abolished and the people put in possession. Now, when we have taken possession and we jointly own the means of production, we will no longer have to fight each other to live; our interests, instead of being competitive, will be cooperative. We will work side by side. Your interest will be mine and mine will be yours. That is the economic condition from which will spring the humane social relation of the future.

When we are in partnership and have stopped clutching each other's throats, when we have stopped enslaving each other, we will stand together, hands clasped, and be friends. We will be comrades, we will be brothers, and we will begin the march to the grandest civilization the human race has ever known.

I did not mean to keep you so long this afternoon. I am sure I appreciate the patience with which you have listened to me. From the very depths of my heart I thank you, each of you — every man, woman, and child — for this splendid testimonial, this beautiful tribute, which I shall remember with gratitude and love until memory empties its urn into forgetfulness.

32.

The Social Gospel of the Protestant Churches

Instead of being in the vanguard of social change, the churches in the United States at the turn of the century had for the most part undertaken the defense of the status quo and adopted the values of middle- and upper-class Americans. Many denominational leaders came to realize that such a narrow mission would eventually alienate the great mass of society. Preachers of the new Social Gospel like Washington Gladden and Walter Rauschenbusch urged the churches to confront the economic and social problems of the workingman. By 1908 denominational groups were giving expression to a new sense of responsibility in such statements as the two "social creeds" reprinted here. The first was adopted by the General Conference of the Methodist Episcopal Church in May 1908; the second, a statement on "The Church and Modern Industry," was adopted by the first convention of the Federal Council of Churches in December 1908.

Source: *A Year Book of the Church and Social Service in the United States,* Harry F. Ward, ed., New York, 1916, pp. 197-198.
Federal Council of the Churches of Christ in America, Report of the First Meeting of the Federal Council, Philadelphia, 1908, Elias B. Sanford, ed., New York, 1909.

I.

Social Creed of the Methodist Episcopal Church

THE METHODIST EPISCOPAL CHURCH STANDS:

For equal rights and complete justice for all men in all stations of life.

For the principle of conciliation and arbitration in industrial dissensions.

For the protection of the worker from dangerous machinery, occupational disease, injuries, and mortality.

For the abolition of child labor.

For such regulation of the conditions of labor for women as shall safeguard the physical and moral health of the community.

For the suppression of the "sweating system."

For the gradual and reasonable reduction of the hours of labor to the lowest practical point, with work for all; and for that degree of leisure for all which is the condition of the highest human life.

For a release from employment one day in seven.

For a living wage in every industry.

For the highest wage that each industry can afford and for the most equitable division of the products of industry that can ultimately be devised.

For the recognition of the Golden Rule and the mind of Christ as the supreme law of society and the sure remedy for all social ills.

II.

The Church and Industry

1. This Federal Council places upon record its profound belief that the complex problems of modern industry can be interpreted and solved only by the teachings of the New Testament, and that Jesus Christ is final authority in the social as in the individual life. Under this authority and by application of this teaching, the contribution to human welfare by the church, whatever its lapses and its delays, has been incalculable. Out of the sacrifice and fervor of the centuries has come a fund of altruism which enriches today a thousand purposes for human betterment, some of which do not know the origin of their impulse. The interest of the church in men is neither recent nor artificial. No challenge of newly posted sentries can exclude it from the ground where are struggle and privation and need. It has its credentials and knows the watchword.

2. Christian practice has not always harmonized with Christian principle. By the force of economic law and of social custom individual life has been, at times, swerved from the straight course, and the organized church has not always spoken when it

should have borne witness, and its plea for righteousness has not always been uttered with boldness. Christianity has created both the opportunity and the principles of life. In the mighty task of putting conscience and justice and love into a "Christian" civilization, the church, with all its splendid achievements, has sometimes faltered. But it has gone farther and suffered more, a thousandfold, to accomplish this end than any other organized force the world has ever known.

3. The church now confronts the most significant crisis and the greatest opportunity of its long career. In part its ideals and principles have become the working basis of organizations for social and industrial betterment which do not accept its spiritual leadership and which have been estranged from its fellowship. We believe, not for its own sake but in the interest of the kingdom of God, the church must not merely acquiesce in the movements outside of it which make for human welfare but must demonstrate, not by proclamation but by deeds, its primacy among all the forces which seek to lift the plane and better the conditions of human life.

This Council, therefore, welcomes this first opportunity on behalf of the Churches of Christ in the United States officially represented to emphasize convictions which have been in fragmentary ways already expressed.

4. We recognize the complex nature of industrial obligations affecting employer and employee, society and government, rich and poor, and most earnestly counsel tolerance, patience, and mutual confidence; we do not defend or excuse wrongdoing in high places or in low, nor purpose to adapt the ethical standards of the Gospel to the exigencies of commerce or the codes of a confused industrial system.

5. While we assert the natural right of men — capitalists and workingmen alike — to organize for common ends, we hold that the organization of capital or the organiza-

tion of labor cannot make wrong right or right wrong; that essential righteousness is not determined by numbers either of dollars or of men; that the church must meet social bewilderment by ethical lucidity and by gentle and resolute testimony to the truth must assert for the whole Gospel its prerogative as the test of the rightness of both individual and collective conduct everywhere.

6. We regard with the greatest satisfaction the effort of those employers, individual and corporate, who have shown in the conduct of their business a fraternal spirit and a disposition to deal justly and humanely with their employees as to wages, profit sharing, welfare work, protection against accidents, sanitary conditions of toil, and readiness to submit differences to arbitration. We record our admiration for such labor organizations as have under wise leadership throughout many years, by patient cultivation of just feelings and temperate views among their members, raised the efficiency of service, set the example of calmness and self-restraint in conference with employers, and promoted the welfare not only of the men of their own craft but of the entire body of workingmen.

7. In such organizations is the proof that the fundamental purposes of the labor movement are ethical. In them great numbers of men of all nationalities and origins are being compacted in fellowship, trained in mutual respect, and disciplined in virtues which belong to right character and are at the basis of good citizenship. By them society at large is benefited in the securing of better conditions of work, in the Americanization of our immigrant population, and in the educational influence of the multitudes who in the labor unions find their chief, sometimes their only, intellectual stimulus.

8. We note as omens of industrial peace and goodwill the growth of a spirit of conciliation, and of the practice of conference and arbitration in settling trade disputes.

We trust profoundly that these methods may supplant those of the strike and the lockout, the boycott, and the blacklist. Lawlessness and violence on either side of labor controversies are an invasion of the rights of the people and must be condemned and resisted. We believe no better opportunity could be afforded to Christian men, employers and wage earners alike, to rebuke the superciliousness of power and the obstinacy of opinion than by asserting and illustrating before their fellows in labor contests the Gospel which deals with men as men and has for its basis of fraternity the Golden Rule.

We commend most heartily the societies and leagues in which employers and workingmen come together upon a common platform to consider the problems of each in the interest of both, and we urge Christian men more freely to participate in such movements of conciliation. We express our gratitude for the evidences that in ever widening circles the influence of the agencies established by some of the churches is distinctly modifying the attitude of the workingmen and the church toward each other.

9. We deem it the duty of all Christian people to concern themselves directly with certain practical industrial problems. To us it seems that the churches must stand —

For equal rights and complete justice for all men in all stations of life.

For the right of all men to the opportunity for self-maintenance, a right ever to be wisely and strongly safeguarded against encroachments of every kind.

For the right of workers to some protection against the hardships often resulting from the swift crises of industrial change.

For the principle of conciliation and arbitration in industrial dissensions.

For the protection of the worker from dangerous machinery, occupational disease, injuries, and mortality.

For the abolition of child labor.

For such regulation of the conditions of toil for women as shall safeguard the physical and moral health of the community.

For the suppression of the "sweating system."

For the gradual and reasonable reduction of the hours of labor to the lowest practicable point, and for that degree of leisure for all which is a condition of the highest human life.

For a release from employment one day in seven.

For a living wage as a minimum in every industry and for the highest wage that each industry can afford.

For the most equitable division of the products of industry that can ultimately be devised.

For suitable provision for the old age of the workers and for those incapacitated by injury.

For the abatement of poverty.

10. To the toilers of America and to those who by organized effort are seeking to lift the crushing burdens of the poor and to reduce the hardships and uphold the dignity of labor, this Council sends the greeting of human brotherhood and the pledge of sympathy and of help in a cause which belongs to all who follow Christ.

33.

Gentlemen's Agreement About Japanese Immigration

Japanese immigration to the West Coast increased markedly during the first years of the twentieth century. The hostility of native labor to Oriental competition led to discriminatory school laws in San Francisco in 1906, and other local legislation of the same kind seemed in the offing. In order to avoid further insults to the Japanese government, President Roosevelt negotiated a gentlemen's agreement with Japan in 1907. The exact terms of this executive agreement never have been revealed, but its gist is indicated in the following 1908 Department of Commerce and Labor report. The Japanese population continued to increase, owing to the proviso that wives be permitted to immigrate, and the agreement was therefore superseded by the much more stringent Immigration Act of 1924.

Source: *Reports of the Department of Commerce and Labor, 1908,* Washington, 1909, pp. 221-222.

To SECTION 1 OF THE IMMIGRATION ACT approved February 20, 1907, a proviso was attached reading as follows:

That whenever the President shall be satisfied that passports issued by any foreign government to its citizens to go to any other country than the United States or to any insular possession of the United States or to the Canal Zone are being used for the purpose of enabling the holders to come to the continental territory of the United States to the detriment of labor conditions therein, the President may refuse to permit such citizens of the country issuing such passports to enter the continental territory of the United States from such other country or from such insular possessions or from the Canal Zone.

This legislation was the result of a growing alarm, particularly on the Pacific Coast and in states adjacent to Canada and Mexico, that labor conditions would be seriously affected by a continuation of the then existing rate of increase in admissions to this country of Japanese of the laboring classes. The Japanese government had always maintained a policy opposed to the emigration to continental United States of its subjects belonging to such classes; but it had been found that passports granted by said government to such subjects entitling them to proceed to Hawaii or to Canada or Mexico were being used to evade the said policy and gain entry to continental United States.

On the basis of the above-quoted provision, the President, on March 14, 1907, issued a proclamation excluding from continental United States "Japanese or Korean laborers, skilled or unskilled, who have received passports to go to Mexico, Canada, or Hawaii, and come therefrom." Department Circular No. 147, dated March 26, 1907, which has been continued in force as Rule 21 of the Immigration Regulations of July 1, 1907, outlined the policy and procedure to be followed by the immigration officials in giving effect to the law and proclamation.

In order that the best results might follow from an enforcement of the regulations, an understanding was reached with Japan that the existing policy of discouraging the emigration of its subjects of the laboring classes to continental United States should be continued and should, by cooperation of the governments, be made as effective as possible. This understanding contemplates that the Japanese government shall issue passports to continental United States only to such of its subjects as are nonlaborers or are laborers who, in coming to the continent, seek to resume a formerly acquired domicile; to join a parent, wife, or children residing there; or to assume active control of an already possessed interest in a farming enterprise in this country; so that the three classes of laborers entitled to receive passports have come to be designated "former residents," "parents, wives, or children of residents," and "settled agriculturists."

With respect to Hawaii, the Japanese government of its own volition stated that, experimentally at least, the issuance of passports to members of the laboring classes proceeding thence would be limited to "former residents" and "parents, wives, or children of residents." The said government has also been exercising a careful supervision over the subject of the emigration of its laboring class to foreign contiguous territory.

It will be seen, therefore, that the report for the past fiscal year covers a novel phase of the immigration question, viz., the exclusion from the continental portion of this country of certain classes of aliens, such exclusion being based in part upon the provision of law mentioned, but principally upon the mutual understanding of the two countries affected, and to be brought about largely by said two countries uniting upon a policy, agreed by both to be necessary and desirable, one of the countries exercising control over the departure and the other over the admission of the persons whose emigration and immigration it is desired mutually to control.

Three generations from shirt sleeves to shirt sleeves.
Attributed to ANDREW CARNEGIE, 1908

34.

David Starr Jordan: The Moral Aspect of the Protective Tariff

Because protective tariffs favored big business, they were criticized by Progressive reformers who viewed them as a tool in the hands of the wealthy. From 1861 until 1909 tariffs continued to climb. But agitation for a downward revision also increased, until both major political parties promised to lower tariffs in 1908. The following selection, a speech by David Starr Jordan to the Economic Congress in London in August 1908, presents a moral argument for lowering tariffs. Jordan was president of Indiana University and, later, Stanford University.

Source: *Independent*, November 26, 1908.

EVERY ARGUMENT FOR AND AGAINST the protective tariff has been stated a thousand times. There is nothing new to be said. But at the bottom of every argument remains the necessary recognition of its primal iniquity. The fundamental idea in American polity is that of a square deal to all men, each standing on his own feet, with exclusive privileges or governmental aid to no man and to no class of men.

Inequality before the law, entail, primogeniture, church control of state, state control of church, class-consciousness and class legislation were evils in English polity which our fathers would not tolerate. On account of these they left England. They chose the hardships of Plymouth Rock and later the hazards of war rather than to put up with any of them. If there is one American idea or ideal to be segregated from the rest it is this of equality before the law. And it is this ideal which is violated absolutely and continuously in the theory and in the practice of the protective tariff.

The protective tariff is a device for enhancing the home price of the articles it covers by a tax on commerce, by forcing the body of citizens to pay tribute to producers at home. To these the state in futile fashion tries to guarantee "a reasonable profit." These producers may be capitalists or directors of industry, or they may be the laborers who contribute effort only, without responsibility for the way in which effort may be applied. It matters not whether capitalists or laborers, either or both, actually profit at your expense or mine or that of foreign producers. The protective tariff intends that they should thus profit, at least to a reasonable degree.

But in the theory of our republic it is no part of the state to guarantee to anyone "a reasonable profit," nor to protect anyone from a reasonable loss. Its function is to see fair play and freedom of operation. It is a breach of the principle of equality before the law that the state should do anything more. To guarantee anyone a reasonable profit is to do so at the expense of the rest. The theory is one of injustice, whatever its result in practice. In practice, whatever is gained on the one hand is lost on the other. Even if we could force foreigners to pay the tariff taxes, which is sometimes possible, their capacity as buyers is correspondingly decreased. International trade is barter, and

David Starr Jordan; photo by Arthur Dudley

every burden it carries works a corresponding loss to both parties in the transaction.

Moreover, as a matter of fact, the protective tariff yields little gain to the laborer, because continued immigration brings him new competitors and because he is in his turn one of the general public who suffer from the commerce tax. If wages are raised by the tariff, so is the cost of living, and the cost of living comes first. For the director or employer of labor, the case is, on the whole, not much better, because the cost of his product is enhanced by the tariff taxes on everything which enters into his process of manufacture. Insofar as a tariff is successful in gaining profit, it is so because it is virtually prohibitory. That the evils of prohibitory tariffs are so little felt by us is due to the fact that our country is a world in itself, with untaxed trade throughout a district comprising nearly a third of the specialized production area of the globe. Yet within this favored area, with all its vast range in competition, it is possible sometimes to monopolize production in some particular direction.

Such a monopoly we now call a trust. To the development of such monopolies the tariff naturally lends itself, though it would be unfair to declare it to be the parent of all trusts. It is enough to recognize that its general purpose is the same — the development through legal means of industrial and economic monopoly, of the enrichment of a class or of a group of classes at the expense of the citizens at large. This is theoretically contrary to American polity. If the principles of our republic in regard to "equal justice to all, exclusive privileges to none" are right, then the theory and the practice of the protective tariff are wrong. That it works through the method of indirect taxation disguises but does not justify its injustice.

The prohibitory tax on importable products is said to have brought its justification in the ultimate lowering of price of the articles concerned. The same claim is made in behalf of the trusts, and much evidence is brought forward in both cases to justify this claim. But the real cause of the reduction in price is seldom traceable to the trust or the tariff. Doubtless, for example, iron is cheaper in this country under a high tariff than it once was without the tariff. But the cheapening of all metals, protected and unprotected, is held to depend on the advance of the science and the arts of metallurgy. The cheapening of gold, a metal out of the range of tariff, is due to improved processes of contraction, and the change threatens to subvert the monetary basis of the world's credit and trade. Metals which have been cheapened in the United States have been similarly affected in England. It is not clear that the tariff in this matter holds any important relation of cause to effect. Nor would the general policy of taxing one group of men, or even one generation for the benefit of the next, be justified if it were so.

The tariff is defended on the ground of the value to the growing nation of the advancement of infant industries — of the development of diversified economies. We may not deny the importance of such development. We may admit that at many places and for definite periods there has been a financial gain to the community at large, through taxing the farmer to build up the manufacturer. We may admit that nation building has been hastened by it. But for all that it is not politically right nor just to do this, for the gain to one has gone with loss to others. The policy in practice assumes the form of a vested right which becomes in time a vested wrong. But even if we admit the past value of protection, the greater evil comes when we cannot let go. Around these vested rights other conditions grow up, and a change of any sort works havoc with related or associated interests. Justice to the new interests becomes possible only by the perpetuation of varied forms of injustice.

To touch the tariff in any way now sends a shock through the financial world, throughout the body politic. Tariff revision in our day is therefore an operation which can be based on no principles. It is a blind rush among various choices of evils. To put revision in the hands of friends of the tariff means still suppression of reform, the further extension of the evil itself. To put revision into other hands means a commercial crisis. And sooner or later commercial crisis must come. The only permanence lies in making tariff taxation like other taxation, a nonrespecter of persons, its sole function that of raising revenue. Justice is always blind, knowing nothing of indirect or ulterior advantages.

Historically, the theory of the infant industry has proved fallacious. There are in America today no infant industries. These infants have grown more rapidly than the nation has. Our huge industrial combinations overshadow the world. Just as in their alliance they dominate us, in similar degree they have the whip hand over other nations.

If anything American can take care of itself, it is our infant industries. Yet these organizations demand the tariff as a necessity of existence as insistently as ever they did. They exact tribute from all of us because they can get it. The lull in the self-assertion just at present is due to the handwriting on the wall, not to any lessening desire to be fed at the public expense.

The actual injury to American prosperity traceable to the tariff may not be enormously great. It has doubtless been exaggerated. It lends itself to exaggeration. It makes us angry when we think of it, and wrath carries always a magnifying glass. Its greatest evil is moral, not economic. It lies in the perversion of our theories of government, the introduction of the idea of class enrichment through legislation.

Doubtless much of the prosperity of the United States is due to the protective tariff — the prosperity of some of us. But in like degree the nonprosperity of some of us, some of the very same persons, for that matter, is due to the same national meddling with individual rights. The apparent prosperity of any community could be greatly enhanced by taking property away from half the people to put it into the hands of the others who know better how to use it. Some of this sort has lain at the foundation of British polity. It is the theory by which nobility and aristocracy justify themselves. It is not the theory of democracy. It is not the principle on which our nation was founded. Thus, behind all discussion of sources and means of prosperity, the fact remains that democratic justice, that fundamental equity between man and man, can never be realized in America so long as any trace of the protective tariff remains on our statute books. It is another illustration of the truth that "they enslave their children's children who make compromise with sin." This law applies to economic lapses, to timeserving legislation, as well as to moral sins.

35.

Hervey White: Our Rural Slums

The agitation of Progressive reformers in the first decade of the twentieth century had kept the needs of the urban poor before the public. The rural poor, on the other hand, had been all but forgotten. There were no settlement houses or private organizations available to help the "slum dwellers" in Upper New York State or in the Kentucky hill country. Hervey White's teaching experiences among the poor people in rural areas prompted him to write about them. The following selection is from an article published in 1908.

Source: *Independent,* October 8, 1908.

As POVERTY, IN ITS VARIOUS ASPECTS, has for many years been the chief subject of my observation, it was with deep interest and concern that I inquired into life and conditions during a short sojourn in the mountains of the Carolinas and a hasty tour through Tennessee and the much-benoveled Smokies. I was told, after I had decided to establish myself in our nearby and tiny group of the Catskills, that I would find back in the mountains much the same type of mountaineer as the Southern "cracker," only, of course, confined to smaller districts; and my finger was placed on the black blotch of illiteracy of the educational map of New York state, and I was supposed to experience the characteristic American shudder that determines us a republican and a free people when we behold that man who cannot read or write. . . .

As it had been my previous fortune to spend some years of work among the people of the poor districts of Chicago, it was but natural, with this life in the mountains, that comparisons would keep coming to me, and it was not long before I found myself saying that, if those were slums, why these are slums also. That it is not crowded tenements and bad air that create the slum type. It is not ignorance, which is, I think, a result rather than a cause. Indeed, I might go so far as to guess that poverty itself is not a cause, but an accompaniment. Why is it that some elements of society are on the downward trend? Why is it that others are on the upward? Why do peoples migrate West, South, East? Is it possible for us to get at fundamental reasons?

It is, however, our modern socialistic mode to say that poverty causes the slums; and, for the present, let us be anything rather than be out of fashion. Poverty is the cause. It is accepted. A working hypothesis under one is such a comfort. Now we can sit down, rent a desk, and begin our magazine reform-writing well established.

Poverty being the cause of the slum condition, it is easy to find its results back in the mountains. The soil is sterile, yielding but a precarious livelihood. Houses must be small. Families must be large. Ventilation in winter is of the worst. Drainage, even in a mountain country, is but questionable. Food is scanty and ill-prepared. Indigestion and bad teeth are the consequent. The orchards yield hard cider for those men who must take to alcoholism as a relief. Overworked and overburdened wives take to scolding and hysteria. Parents scream to each other and to their children. The children can but answer with screaming. Slums — oh, yes, we have them in our mountains. We have them on the wide breadth of our prairies. The "renters," the day laborers in agriculture, may be slum-bred as well as urban neighbors.

That curious little mechanism, the phonograph, has made the likeness of the two classes almost identical. The country songs and jokes are all turned slummy. It is grotesque, to put it but mildly, to hear that nasal metallic outrage from Fourteenth Street accepted under the name of comic song — it is grotesque, it is uncanny with democracy to hear it issuing from these mountainside dwellings; the slang, the jangle of the banjos, the blatant brawling of the latest "star" along the Bowery. The very babies catch up the refrain and sing in weazened, phonographic voices. The children bring them to school with imagined dances. Or some child has been to the city on a visit and the cakewalk takes the place of folklore games.

But the children in the schools — there is my subject; the hopes I had of them in the beginning; the same sickening sense of failure in the end that I experienced in my years of city teaching. It is true, I did in time accomplish the law of obedience; enforced, be it said, with the ever-threatening though sometimes hidden rod. It is true, also, that as months wore on I was rewarded with the spirit of enthusiasm and work — something unknown, I think, to every one of my pupils when I first entered. But it was at this point that my every effort failed when all should have been marching on to victory. For I was forced to admit in

the end that the pupils were not capable of continued effort or the fervor that comes from healthy self-advancement.

Like their city slummy cousins, they had to have constant change, a new stimulus in some dramatic presentation. In other words, they had to be amused. It was the old cry here in the remoteness of the mountains, "bread and circuses." There were slums, then, too, in Rome, you will remember. It is but the name and not the fact that changes.

My picture is lugubrious, pessimistic? The fault lies in my method of presentation, perhaps, rather than in the sum of my observation. Let us turn for a moment from the shadow and look at the same picture in the full sunshine, at noonday when all shadows minimize. It is well known, again, by those who are familiar with the poor districts, that there is no charity like that the poor show to the poor. All can tell of cases of a widow lending half of her last pail of coal to a suffering neighbor, where sharing what one has of necessities is the rule, instead of doling out from an undiminished superfluity. So we find the same law in our rural slums. The poorer people are, the more ready they are to share with others who are in need. It is not the well-to-do farmers from the valleys who give from their bank accounts to the needy. Their accepted excuse is, indeed, that their money is banked as soon as earned and they cannot break into the interest. As if, with these valley churchgoing Christians, interest were treasure laid in heaven; commanded by their Teacher instead of forbidden, so we twist and turn to argue for our greed.

An instance of this universal sharing was noticeable in the way my mountain children regarded their textbooks. It had only to be known that some boy had no book, that it was lost or torn, or that his father would not buy him one, when every book in the school was freely proffered. "He can use mine," or "He can sit with me," came from every quarter, no matter, even if he soiled the book or tore it. "It was made to use," was the careless, good-natured rejoinder. So it was with the paper, slates, and pencils. And it was the daily incident to see some pupil sharing pencils with two little boys who were known to be common thieves of pencils. "He stole all my pencils last week. Now he has traded them off or lost them. He has none to write with. Well, I have bought a new one. Let him take it. He does not know any better than to steal pencils. But, Sammy, mind you give me this one back."

Other faults and other failings were condoned. For example, there was one girl who had never known a father, but who was never slighted by the others in work or play. Not but that the distinction was known and felt keenly by them all, for slums as much as any have their social caste. But, "it is not her fault," was the universal dictum. And, if, in a quarrel, the matter did sometimes burst forth, it was invariably made up afterward with tears and embraces and there was genuine humility for the hardness, and meek repentance and loyal pledges for the future.

With the poor, too, both of city and of country, we often meet with that perfect hospitality so rarely, if ever, found in bourgeois homes. It is: "Come in. Sit down. Draw up to the fire. John, move back so that our guest can sit closer. We are about to sup. Won't you take a place at the table? Mary, get a plate from the cupboard." A jug of cider is brought up from the cellar. It is all with a smile and a hospitable wave of the hand. "Stay overnight with us. The storm outside is much too rough." This is treatment one still may meet with in the mountains.

As we sit, too, listening to the flood of talk and kindly interrogation, we may notice that the room is furnished in better taste than is met with in the favored farmhouses of the valley. It may partly be because the furniture is of the old fashion, which was in simpler, better lines than our modern factory vulgarities. But we will also see that the things that are of necessity modern, the wallpaper, the paint upon the wainscot, the print curtain that hangs to screen the cupboard, these are all in better taste than their rich neighbors. There is a harmony, a sense of relationship among them. They serve as an appropriate background for the household. An artist could not choose them better for a picture.

Why is it that to read a little, and to write, to go to church, to own a little property one does not use, almost always implies to be a little vulgar? Is it a necessary step in social evolution? The stage of the new rich? Of the second generation of peasant immigrants? Should we still be hopeful and look to the height of the development? Alas! We are in the toils again of speculation. Let us leave this sunshine picture of the poor and resuming our working hypothesis of poverty begetting slummery, climb into our chair once more before our desk and forge on with our magazine reform article.

I taught fifteen months in the rural schools of the Catskills. Nine of those months were spent in the school of which I have spoken. But the other six were in a school out toward the valley, comprising more the children of the well-to-do farmers, though sprinkled as well with renters and day laborers.

Now, without exception, I found that the children of these civilized, churchgoing, economizing "usurers" were far in advance of the poorer denizens of the mountains. Their intellects were better, their methods were more organized, they could understand and appreciate the benefit of a year's task, working at it a little every day. They could love work for its own sake as well as for the promotion that it gave them. They were not constantly harrowed and drawn aside from their duties by petty quarrels about their games upon the playground. Their very games were superior from a standpoint of organization, though they may not have been so picturesque, going in for baseball rather than for simpler old-time folk games. The curse of the Fourteenth Street phonograph was not upon them. They had bright, cheery, well-washed faces. They were neatly dressed, in sweatshop clothes it is true, but sweatshop products still have sense of order.

In the city their comparison would be found among the children of the well-to-do mechanics who live in some dreary, endless suburb, though where each one owns his little house and garden, or is trying to own it, or hoping so to do; where the boys still have ambition for distinction and the girls pound hammer and tongs music from cheap pianos, and everything is properly prosaic and we sense the foundation walls of our republic; yes, of our society, of our civilization, forgetting in our superficial, artistic, petulant rating that foundations are necessarily less delicate than spires, turrets, and the traceries of rose windows; than arch or column, capital or pediment.

It is difficult, is it not, to draw conclusions?

Even if one has a working hypothesis and a desk and a chair? It is difficult to remain seated in a chair.

I rise from mine in a hopeless conflict of rebellion.

36.

James J. Hill: The Natural Wealth of the Land and Its Conservation

President Roosevelt, whose experiences as a rancher had made him an enthusiastic conservationist, called a White House conference on conservation that was held May 13-15, 1908. It was attended by 44 governors and 500 other experts and public figures. The conservationists, who had pleaded for such a meeting, were alarmed by the waste of the nation's basic resources and were convinced that unless effective measures were taken, the country's natural wealth would be depleted within a century. James J. Hill, the head of the Great Northern Railway, surprised many people by his impassioned speech, a portion of which is reprinted here, supporting the creation of a national conservation program.

Source: *Conference on the Conservation of Natural Resources*, n.p., n.d.

THE TWOFOLD SIGNIFICANCE of this meeting is found in the comparative novelty of its subject matter and of the method by which it has been approached. The subject is the conservation of our national wealth and a careful study of our national economic resources. . . . It is this policy — the conservation of national resources, the best means of putting an end to the waste of the sources of wealth — which largely forms the subject matter of this conference. For the first time there is a formal national protest, under seal of the highest authority, against economic waste. . . .

"Of all the sinful wasters of man's inheritance on earth," said the late Professor Sha-

James J. Hill addressing the Richland County Fair in Wahpeton, N.D., 1909

ler, "and all are in this regard sinners, the very worst are the people of America." This is not a popular phrase but a scientific judgment. It is borne out by facts. In the movement of modern times, which has made the world commercially a small place and has produced a solidarity of the race such as never before existed, we have come to the point where we must to a certain extent regard the natural resources of this planet as a common asset, compare them with demands now made and likely to be made upon them, and study their judicious use. Commerce, wherever untrammeled, is wiping out boundaries and substituting the world relation of demand and supply for smaller systems of local economy.

The changes of a single generation have brought the nations of the earth closer together than were the states of this Union at the close of the Civil War. If we fail to consider what we possess of wealth available for the uses of mankind and to what extent we are wasting a national patrimony that can never be restored, we might be likened to the directors of a company who never examine a balance sheet.

The sum of resources is simple and fixed. From the sea, the mine, the forest, and the soil must be gathered everything that can sustain the life of man. Upon the wealth that these supply must be conditioned forever, as far as we can see, not only his progress but his continued existence on earth.

How stands the inventory of property for our own people? The resources of the sea furnish less than 5 percent of the food supply, and that is all. The forests of this country, the product of centuries of growth, are fast disappearing. The best estimates reckon our standing merchantable timber at less than 2 trillion feet. Our annual cut is about 40 billion feet. The lumber cut rose from 18 billion feet in 1880 to 34 billion feet in 1905; that is, it nearly doubled in twenty-five years. We are now using annually 500 feet board measure of timber per capita, as against an average of 60 feet for all Europe. The New England supply is gone. The Northwest furnishes small growths that would have been rejected by the lumberman thirty years ago. The South has reached its maximum production and begins to decline. On the Pacific Coast only is there now any considerable body of merchantable standing timber.

We are consuming yearly three or four times as much timber as forest growth restores. Our supply of some varieties will be practically exhausted in ten or twelve years; in the case of others, without reforesting, the present century will see the end. When will we take up in a practical and intelligent way the restoration of our forests?

Turning now to one of the only two remaining sources of wealth, the mine, we find it different from the others in an important essential. It is incapable of restoration or recuperation. The mineral wealth stored in the earth can be used only once. When iron and coal are taken from the mine, they cannot be restored; and upon iron and coal our industrial civilization is built. When fuel and iron become scarce and high-priced, civilization, so far as we can now foresee, will suffer as man would suffer by the gradual withdrawal of the air he breathes.

The exhaustion of our coal supply is not in the indefinite future. The startling feature of our coal production is not so much the magnitude of the annual output as its rate of growth. For the decade ending in 1905 the total product was 2,832,402,746 tons, which is almost exactly one-half the total product previously mined in this country. For the year 1906 the output was 414 million tons, an increase of 46 percent on the average annual yield of the ten years preceding. In 1907 our production reached 470 million tons. Fifty years ago the annual per capita production was a little more than one-quarter of a ton; it is now about 5 tons.

It is but eight years since we took the place of Great Britain as the leading coal-producing nation of the world, and already our product exceeds hers by over 43 percent, and is 37 percent of the known production of the world. Estimates of coal deposits still remaining must necessarily be somewhat vague, but they are approximately near the mark.

The iron industry tells a similar story. The total of iron ore mined in the United States doubles about once in seven years. It was less than 12 million tons in 1893, over 24 million tons in 1899, 47,740,000 tons in 1906, and over 52 million tons in 1907. The rising place of iron in the world's life is the most impressive phenomenon of the last century. In 1850 the pig-iron production of the United States amounted to 563,757 tons, or about 50 pounds per capita. Our production now is over 600 pounds per capita.

We do not work a mine, build a house, weave a fabric, prepare a meal, or cultivate an acre of ground under modern methods without the aid of iron. We turn out over 25 million tons of pig iron every year, and the production for the first half of 1907 was at the rate of 27 million tons. This is two and one-half times the product of Great Britain. It is nearly half the product of the whole world. And the supply of this most precious of all the metals is so far from inexhaustible that it seems as if iron and coal might be united in their disappearance from common life.

The large deposits of iron ore in this country are now located. For cheap iron we depend on the Lake Superior district, because of its high grade, the ease of extracting the ore from the mines, and its nearness to cheap transportation. At the rate of over 50 million tons per year, our present consumption, it would require over 2 billion tons to supply the demand for the next forty years, supposing it to remain stationary. This would approach the end of all the higher-grade ore in large deposits now in sight in this country. The product of other workings would be of inferior quality and higher cost, and remote from market. But production is certain to increase even more rapidly than in the past.

A few years ago a Swedish geologist prepared for his government a report which stated that the entire supply of the iron ore in the United States would be exhausted within the present century. The United States Geological Survey declared this an overestimate; but here is the conclusion of its own report, after a careful examination of the question in the light of the best authorities. I quote the official published document:

> Assuming the demand for iron ore during the present century may range from 50 million to 100 million tons per year, the Lake Superior district would last for from twenty-five to fifty years if it supplied the entire United States. But counting on the known supply elsewhere in the United States, the ore will last for a much longer period, though, of course, it must necessarily show a gradual but steady increase in value and in cost of mining, along with an equally steady decrease in grade.

The most favorable view of the situation forces the conclusion that iron and coal will not be available for common use on anything like present terms before the end of this century; and our industrial, social, and political life must be readjusted to meet the strains imposed by new conditions. Yet we forbid to our consumers access to the stores of other countries, while we boast of our increased exports, of that material for want of which one day the nation must be reduced to the last extremity.

We now turn to the only remaining resource of man upon this earth, which is the soil itself. How are we caring for that, and what possibilities does it hold out to the people of future support? We are only beginning to feel the pressure upon the land. The whole interior of this continent, aggregating more than 1.5 billion acres, has been occupied by settlers within the last fifty years. What is there left for the next fifty years? Excluding arid and irrigable areas, the latter limited by nature, and barely enough of which could be made habitable in each year to furnish a farm for each immigrant family, the case stands as follows: In 1906 the total unappropriated public lands in the United States consisted of 792 million acres. Of this area the divisions of Alaska, Arizona, California, Colorado, Idaho, Montana, Nevada, New Mexico, and Wyoming contained 195.7 million acres of surveyed and 509 million acres of unsurveyed land. Little of Alaska is fitted for general agriculture, while practically all of the rest is semiarid land, available only for grazing or irrigation. We have, subtracting these totals, 50 million acres of surveyed and 36.5 million acres of unsurveyed land as our actual remaining stock. And 21 million acres were disposed of in 1907. How long will the remainder last? No longer can we say that "Uncle Sam has land enough to give us all a farm."

Equally threatening is the change in quality. There are two ways in which the productive power of the earth is lessened; first by erosion and the sweeping away of the fertile surface into streams and thence to the sea, and second by exhaustion through wrong methods of cultivation. The former process has gone far. Thousands of acres in the East and South have been made unfit for tillage. . . .

Far more ruinous, because universal and continuing in its effects, is the process of soil exhaustion. It is creeping over the land from east to west. The abandoned farms that are now the playthings of the city's rich or the game preserves of patrons of sport bear witness to the melancholy change. . . . The soil of the West is being reduced in agricultural potency by exactly he same processes which have driven the farmer of the East, with all his advantage of nearness to markets, practically from the field.

Within the last forty years a great part of the richest land in the country has been brought under cultivation. We should, therefore, in the same time, have raised proportionately the yield of our principal crops per acre; because the yield of old lands, if properly treated, tends to increase rather than to diminish. . . .

But the fact of soil waste becomes startlingly evident when we examine the record of some states where single cropping and other agricultural abuses have been prevalent. Take the case of wheat, the mainstay of single-crop abuse. Many of us can remember when New York was the great wheat-producing state of the Union. The average yield of wheat per acre in New York for the last ten years was about 18 bushels. For the first five years of that ten-year period it was 18.4 bushels, and for the last five years, 17.4 bushels. Farther west, Kansas takes high rank as a wheat producer. Its average yield per acre for the last ten years was 14.16 bushels. For the first five of those years, it was 15.14 and for the last five years 13.18. Up in the Northwest, Minnesota wheat has made a name all over the world. Her average yield per acre for the same ten years was 12.96 bushels. For the first five years, it was 13.12, and for the last five, 12.8.

We perceive here the working of a uniform law, independent of location, of soil, or of climate. It is the law of diminishing return due to soil destruction. Apply this to the country at large and it reduces agriculture to the condition of a bank whose depositors are steadily drawing out more money than they put in.

What is true in this instance is true of our agriculture as a whole. In no other important country in the world, with the exception of Russia, is the industry that must be the foundation of every state at so low an ebb as in our own. According to the last census the average annual product per acre of the farms of the whole United States was worth $11.38. It is little more than a respectable rental in communities where the soil is properly cared for and made to give a reasonable return for cultivation. There were but two states in the Union whose total value of farm products was over $30 per acre of improved land. The great state of Illinois gave but $12.48, and Minnesota showed only $8.74. No discrimination attaches to these figures, where all are so much at fault.

Nature has given to us the most valuable possession ever committed to man. It can never be duplicated, because there is none like it upon the face of the earth. And we are racking and impoverishing it exactly as we are felling the forests and rifling the mines. Our soil, once the envy of every other country, the attraction which draws millions of immigrants across the seas, gave an average yield for the whole United States during the ten years beginning with 1896 of 13.5 bushels of wheat per acre. . . .

When the most fertile land in the world produces so much less than that of poorer quality elsewhere, and this low yield shows a tendency toward steady decline, the situation becomes clear. We are robbing the soil in an effort to get the largest cash returns from each acre of ground in the shortest possible time and with the least possible labor. This soil is not mere dead matter, subject to any sort of treatment with impunity. Chemically, it contains elements which must be present in certain proportions for the support of vegetation. Physically, it is made up of matter which supplies the principal plant food. This food, with its chemical constituents in proper admixture, is furnished by the decomposition of organic matter and the disintegration of mineral matter that proceed together. Whatever disturbs either factor of the process, whatever takes out of the soil an excessive amount of one or more of the chemical elements upon which plant growth depends, ends in sterility. Any agricultural methods that move in this direction mean soil impoverishment; present returns at the cost of future loss; the exhaustion of the land — exactly as the animal system is enfeebled by lack of proper nourishment.

Our agricultural lands have been abused in two principal ways: first, by single cropping, and, second, by neglecting fertilization. It is fortunate for us that nature is slow to anger and that we may arrest the consequence of this ruinous policy before it is too late. In all parts of the United States, with only isolated exceptions, the system of tillage has been to select the crop which would bring in most money at the current market rate, to plant that year after year, and to move on to virgin fields as soon as the old farm rebelled by lowering the quality and quantity of its return. It is still the practice; although diversification of industry and the rotation of crops have been urged for nearly a century and are today taught in every agricultural college in this country. The demonstration of the evils of single cropping is mathematical in its completeness. . . .

We frequently hear it said that the reduction in yield is due to the wearing out of the soil as if it was a garment to be destroyed by the wearing. The fact is that soils either increase or maintain their productivity indefinitely under proper cultivation. If the earth, the great mother of human and animal life, is to "wear out," what is to become of the race?

The two remedies are as well ascertained as is the evil. Rotation of crops and the use of fertilizers act as tonics upon the soil. We might expand our resources and add billions of dollars to our national wealth by conserving soil resources instead of exhausting them as we have the forests and the contents of our mines. For there is good au-

thority for the assertion that the farmer could take from the same area of ground in four years' grain crops as much as seven years now give him, leaving the products of the other three years when the land rested from grain as a clear profit due to better methods.

He can do far more than that by joining livestock raising with grain raising. Nature has provided the cattle to go with the land. There is as much money in livestock as there is in grain. Looked at in any way there is money in livestock: money for dairy products, money for beef, money for the annual increase, and most money of all for the next year's crop when every particle of manure is saved and applied to the land.

We need not consider at present really intensive farming, such as is done by market gardeners with high profit, or such culture as in France, in Holland, in Belgium, and in the island of Jersey produces financial returns per acre that seem almost beyond belief. The average in money per acre of the island of Jersey for each acre of cultivated land is over $250. What our people have to do is to cover less ground, cultivate smaller farms so as to make the most of them instead of getting a scant and uncertain yield from several hundred acres, and raise productivity by intelligent treatment to twice or three times its present level.

There is more money in this system. The net profit from an acre of wheat on run-down soils is very small; consequently decreasing the acreage of wheat under certain conditions will not materially decrease profits. . . .

I have dwelt upon the conservation of farm resources because of the commanding importance of this industry and because of its relation to our future. Nearly 36 percent of our people are engaged directly in agriculture. But all the rest depend on it. In the last analysis, commerce, manufactures, our home market, every form of activity runs back to the bounty of the earth by which every worker, skilled and unskilled, must be fed and by which his wages are ultimately paid. The farm products of the U.S. in 1906 were valued at $6,794,000,000 and in 1907 at $7,412,000,000. All of our vast domestic commerce, equal in value to the foreign trade of all the nations combined, is supported and paid for by the land. Of our farm areas only one-half is improved. It does not produce one-half of what it could be made to yield; not by some complex system of intensive culture, but merely by ordinary care and industry intelligently applied. It is the capital upon which alone we can draw through all the future, but the amount of the draft that will be honored depends on the care and intelligence given to its cultivation.

Were any statesman to show us how to add $7 billion annually to our foreign trade, it would be the sensation of the hour. The way to do this in agriculture is open. Our share in the increase would not be the percentage of profit allowed by successful trading but the entire capital sum. On the other side stands the fact that the unappropriated area suitable to farm purposes is almost gone and that we have been for the last century reducing the producing power of the country. Nowhere in the range of national purposes is the reward for conservation of a national resource so ample. Nowhere is the penalty of neglect so threatening.

By the fixed rate of increase in the past, we must count upon a population of over 200 million in the United States in the year 1950. . . . We shall have less and less of this agricultural wealth to part with as population increases. And as to enlarging greatly our sale of manufactured products in the world's markets, it is mostly a dream. We cannot finally compete there, except in a few selected lines, without a material lowering of the wage scale at home and a change in the national standard of living which our people are not ready to accept without a

struggle. When capital cannot find a profit, there will be no money for the payrolls of an unprofitable business. Doubtless as we grow we shall buy more and sell more, but our main dependence half a century ahead must be on ourselves. The nation can no more escape the operation of that law than can the man. It is time to set our house in order.

Not only the economic but the political future is involved. No people ever felt the want of work or the pinch of poverty for a long time without reaching out violent hands against their political institutions, believing that they might find in a change some relief from their distress. Although there have been moments of such restlessness in our country, the trial has never been so severe or so prolonged as to put us to the test. . . .

Every nation finds its hour of peril when there is no longer free access to the land or when the land will no longer support the people. Disturbances within are more to be feared than attacks from without. Our government is built upon the assumption of a fairly contented, happy, and prosperous people, ruling their passions, with power to change their institutions when such change is generally desired. It would not be strange if they should in their desire for change attempt to pull down the pillars of their national temple. Far may this day be from us! But since the unnecessary destruction of our land will bring new conditions of danger, its conservation, its improvement to the highest point of productivity promised by scientific intelligence and practical experiment appears to be a first command of any political economy worthy of the name.

I have endeavored to outline some of the principal issues at stake in the better conservation of our national resources, and especially that one about which all the others revolve and by whose fortunes we shall eventually stand or fall — the land itself. They are for us quite literally the issues of national existence. The era of unlimited expansion on every side, of having but to reach out and seize any desired good, ready provided for us by the hand that laid the foundations of the earth, is drawing to a close. The first task, it seems to me, must be to force home the facts of the situation into the public consciousness; to make men realize their duty toward coming generations exactly as the father feels it a duty to see that his children do not suffer want. In a democracy this is a first essential. In other forms of government one or two great men may have power to correct mistakes and to put in motion wise policies that centuries do not unsettle.

A part of the price of self-government is the acceptance of that high office and imperative duty as a whole by the people themselves. They must know, they must weigh, they must act. Only as they form and give effect to wise decisions can the nation go forward. And we should not be here today were it not that the principle of a conservation of national resources as the foremost and controlling policy of the United States henceforth is coming to be seen by many, and must be heartily accepted by all, as the first condition not only of continued material prosperity but also of the perpetuation of free institutions and a government by the people.

The work now being done by the Department of Agriculture and the agricultural colleges of the various states furnishes a broad and intelligent foundation upon which to build up a new era of national progress and prosperity. It calls for a wise, generous, and continuing policy on the part of both federal and state governments.

If this patriotic gospel is to make headway, it must be by just such organized missionary work as is here begun. It cannot go on and conquer if imposed from without. It must come to represent the fixed idea of the people's mind, their determination and their hope. It cannot be incorporated in our practical life by the dictum of any individual or any officer of nation or state in his official capacity. It needs the cooperation of all the influences, the help of every voice, the commendation of nation and state that has been the strength and inspiration of every worthy work on American soil for 120 years.

We return, for our gathering in council and for our plan of action for the future, to the model given us by the Fathers. State and nation are represented here, without jealousy or any ambition of superiority on either side, to apply to the consideration of our future such cooperation as that out of which this nation was born and by which it has won to worthy manhood. Reviving the spirit of the days that created our Constitution, the days that carried us through civil conflict, the spirit by which all our enduring work in the world has been wrought, taking thought as Washington and Lincoln took thought, only for the highest good of all the people, we may, as a result of the deliberations held and the conclusions reached here today, give new meaning to our future, new luster to the ideal of a republic of living federated states, may shape anew the fortunes of this country, and enlarge the borders of hope for all mankind.

The forests of America, however slighted by man, must have been a great delight to God; for they were the best He ever planted.

John Muir, *The American Forests*

1909

37.

THEODORE ROOSEVELT: The Conservation of Public Lands

President Roosevelt was a conservationist by nature. An enthusiastic outdoorsman, he also recognized that the industrial transformation of the United States since the Civil War had made coal, timber, and other natural resources vital to the welfare of the country. Thus, he supported the work of federally employed civil engineers and foresters. In a special message to Congress on January 22, 1909 (reprinted here in part), he urged the formation of nationally supervised agencies to conserve natural resources. His proposals included the creation of a Bureau of Mines, as well as the strengthening of the Inland Waterways Commission.

Source: Richardson, XI, pp. 1416-1426.

To the Senate and House of Representatives:

I transmit herewith a report of the National Conservation Commission, together with the accompanying papers. This report, which is the outgrowth of the Conference of Governors last May, was unanimously approved by the recent joint conference held in this city between the National Conservation Commission and governors of states, state conservation commissions, and conservation committees of great organizations of citizens. It is, therefore, in a peculiar sense, representative of the whole nation and all its parts.

With the statements and conclusions of this report I heartily concur, and I commend it to the thoughtful consideration both of the Congress and of our people generally. It is one of the most fundamentally important documents ever laid before the American people. It contains the first inventory of its natural resources ever made by any nation. In condensed form it presents a statement of our available capital in material resources, which are the means of progress, and calls attention to the essential conditions upon which the perpetuity, safety, and welfare of this nation now rest and must always continue to rest. It deserves, and should have, the widest possible distribution among the people. . . .

The National Conservation Commission wisely confined its report to the statement of facts and principles, leaving the Executive to recommend the specific steps to which these facts and principles inevitably lead. Accordingly, I call your attention to some of the larger features of the situation dis-

Theodore Roosevelt photographed in Colorado in 1905

closed by the report and to the action thereby clearly demanded for the general good.

WATERS

The report says:

Within recent months it has been recognized and demanded by the people, through many thousand delegates from all states assembled in convention in different sections of the country, that the waterways should and must be improved promptly and effectively as a means of maintaining national prosperity.

The first requisite for waterway improvement is the control of the waters in such manner as to reduce floods and regulate the regimen of the navigable rivers. The second requisite is development of terminals and connection in such manner as to regulate commerce.

Accordingly, I urge that the broad plan for the development of our waterways recommended by the Inland Waterways Commission be put in effect without delay. It provides for a comprehensive system of waterway improvement extending to all the uses of the waters and benefits to be derived from their control, including navigation, the development of power, the extension of irrigation, the drainage of swamp and overflow lands, the prevention of soil wash, and the purification of streams for water supply. It proposes to carry out the work by coordinating agencies in the federal departments through the medium of an administrative commission or board acting in cooperation with the states and other organizations and individual citizens.

The work of waterway development should be undertaken without delay. Meritorious projects in known conformity with the general outlines of any comprehensive plan should proceed at once. The cost of the whole work should be met by direct appropriation, if possible, but, if necessary, by the issue of bonds in small denominations.

It is especially important that the development of waterpower should be guarded with the utmost care both by the national government and by the states in order to protect the people against the upgrowth of monopoly and to insure to them a fair share in the benefits which will follow the development of this great asset which belongs to the people and should be controlled by them.

FORESTS

I urge that provision be made for both protection and more rapid development of the national forests. Otherwise, either the increasing use of these forests by the people must be checked or their protection against fire must be dangerously weakened. If we compare the actual fire damage on similar areas on private and national forest lands during the past year, the government fire patrol saved commercial timber worth as much as the total cost of caring for all national forests at the present rate for about ten years.

I especially commend to the Congress the facts presented by the commission as to the relation between forests and stream flow in its bearing upon the importance of the forest lands in national ownership. Without an understanding of this intimate relation the conservation of both these natural resources must largely fail.

The time has fully arrived for recognizing in the law the responsibility to the community, the state, and the nation which rests upon the private owners of private lands. The ownership of forest land is a public trust. The man who would so handle his forest as to cause erosion and to injure stream flow must be not only educated but he must be controlled.

The report of the National Conservation Commission says:

> Forests in private ownership cannot be conserved unless they are protected from fire. We need good fire laws, well-enforced. Fire control is impossible without an adequate force of men whose sole duty is fire patrol during the dangerous season.

I hold as first among the tasks before the states and the nation in their respective shares in forest conservation the organization of efficient fire patrols and the enactment of good fire laws on the part of the states.

The report says further:

> Present tax laws prevent reforestation of cut-over land and the perpetuation of existing forests by use. An annual tax upon the land itself, exclusive of the timber, and a tax upon the timber when cut is well-adapted to actual conditions of forest investment and is practicable and certain. It is far better that forest land should pay a moderate tax permanently than that it should pay an excessive revenue temporarily and then cease to yield at all.

Second only in importance to good fire laws, well-enforced, is the enactment of tax laws which will permit the perpetuation of existing forests by use.

LANDS

With our increasing population the time is not far distant when the problem of supplying our people with food will become pressing. The possible additions to our arable area are not great, and it will become necessary to obtain much larger crops from the land, as is now done in more densely settled countries. To do this, we need better farm practice and better strains of wheat, corn, and other crop plants, with a reduction in losses from soil erosion and from insects, animals, and other enemies of agriculture. The United States Department of Agriculture is doing excellent work in these directions and it should be liberally supported.

The remaining public lands should be classified and the arable lands disposed of to homemakers. In their interest the Timber and Stone Act and the commutation clause of the Homestead Act should be repealed, and the Desert-Land Law should be modified in accordance with the recommendations of the Public Lands Commission.

The use of the public grazing lands should be regulated in such ways as to improve and conserve their value.

Rights to the surface of the public land should be separated from rights to forests upon it and to minerals beneath it, and these should be subject to separate disposal.

The coal, oil, gas, and phosphate rights still remaining with the government should be withdrawn from entry and leased under conditions favorable for economic development.

MINERALS

The consumption of nearly all of our mineral products is increasing more rapidly than our population. Our mineral waste is about one-sixth of our product, or nearly $1 million for each working day in the year. The loss of structural materials through fire is about another million a day. The loss of life in the mines is appalling. The larger part of these losses of life and property can be avoided.

Our mineral resources are limited in quantity and cannot be increased or reproduced. With the rapidly increasing rate of consumption, the supply will be exhausted while yet the nation is in its infancy unless better methods are devised or substitutes are found. Further investigation is urgently needed in order to improve methods and to develop and apply substitutes.

It is of the utmost importance that a Bureau of Mines be established in accordance with the pending bill to reduce the loss of life in mines and the waste of mineral resources, and to investigate the methods and substitutes for prolonging the duration of our mineral supplies. Both the need and the public demand for such a bureau are rapidly becoming more urgent. It should cooperate with the states in supplying data to serve as a basis for state mine regulations. The establishment of this bureau will mean merely the transfer from other bureaus of work which it is agreed should be transferred and slightly enlarged and reorganized for these purposes.

CONCLUSIONS

The joint conference already mentioned adopted two resolutions to which I call your special attention. The first was intended to promote cooperation between the states and the nation upon all of the great questions here discussed. It is as follows:

> *Resolved,* that a joint committee be appointed by the chairman to consist of six members of state conservation commis-

sions and three members of the National Conservation Commission, whose duty shall be to prepare and present to the state and national commissions, and through them to the governors and the President, a plan for united action by all organizations concerned with the conservation of natural resources. . . .

The second resolution of the joint conference to which I refer calls upon the Congress to provide the means for such cooperation. The principle of the community of interest among all our people in the great natural resources runs through the report of the National Conservation Commission and the proceedings of the joint conference. These resources, which form the common basis of our welfare, can be wisely developed, rightly used, and prudently conserved only by the common action of all the people acting through their representatives in state and nation. Hence the fundamental necessity for cooperation. Without it we shall accomplish but little, and that little badly. The resolution follows:

> We also especially urge on the Congress of the United States the high desirability of maintaining a national commission on the conservation of the resources of the country, empowered to cooperate with state commissions to the end that every sovereign commonwealth and every section of the country may attain the high degree of prosperity and the sureness of perpetuity naturally arising in the abundant resources and the vigor, intelligence, and patriotism of our people.

In this recommendation I most heartily concur, and I urge that an appropriation of at least $50,000 be made to cover the expenses of the National Conservation Commission for necessary rent, assistance, and traveling expenses. This is a very small sum. I know of no other way in which the appropriation of so small a sum would result in so large a benefit to the whole nation.

38.

Report of the President's Commission on Country Life

The population of American cities in the early 1900s was increasing three times as fast as that of rural areas. Although the United States was clearly becoming a nation of cities, millions still lived in the country, and many Americans continued to retain, or at least to pay lip service to, the old Jeffersonian ideal of the yeoman farmer, rather than the merchant or worker, as the backbone of the nation. In order to preserve and strengthen country life, President Roosevelt established a commission to study living conditions in rural areas. The Country Life Commission's report, which was delivered to the Senate on February 9, 1909, stressed the importance of preserving a communal spirit in the open country, but it conceded that the chief cause of rural discontent was the increasing unprofitableness of farming. A portion of the concluding section of the report, "The General Corrective Forces That Should Be Set in Motion," is reprinted here.

Source: 60 Congress, 2 Session, Senate Document No. 705, pp. 48-65.

EVEN WHEN PERMANENTLY SETTLED, the farmer does not easily combine with others for financial or social betterment. The training of generations has made him a strong individualist, and he has been obliged to rely mainly on himself. Self-reliance being the essence of his nature, he does not at once feel the need of cooperation for business purposes or of close association for social objects. In the main, he has been prosperous and has not felt the need of cooperation. If he is a strong man, he prefers to depend on his own ability. If he is ambitious for social recognition, he usually prefers the society of the town to that of the country. If he wishes to educate his children, he avails himself of the schools of the city. He does not as a rule dream of rural organization that can supply as completely as the city the four great requirements of man — health, education, occupation, society. While his brother in the city is striving by moving out of the business section into the suburbs to get as much as possible of the country in the city, he does not dream that it is possible to have most that is best of the city in the country.

The time has come when we must give as much attention to the constructive development of the open country as we have given to other affairs. This is necessary, not only in the interest of the open country itself but for the safety and progress of the nation. . . .

The correctives for the social sterility of the open country are already in existence or under way, but these agencies all need to be strengthened and especially to be coordinated and federated; and the problem needs to be recognized by all the people. The regular agricultural departments and institutions are aiding in making farming profitable and attractive, and they are also giving attention to the social and community questions. There is a widespread awakening, as a result of this work. This awakening is greatly aided by the rural free delivery of mails, telephones, the gradual improvement of highways, farmers' institutes, cooperative creameries and similar organizations, and other agencies.

The good institutions of cities may often be applied or extended to the open country. It appears that the social evils are in many cases no greater in cities in proportion to the number of people than in country districts; and the very concentration of numbers draws attention to the evils in cities and leads to earlier application of remedies. Recently, much attention has been directed, for example, to the subject of juvenile crime, and the probation system in place of jail sentences for young offenders is being put into operation in many places. Petty crime and immorality are certainly not lacking in rural districts, and it would seem that there is a place for the extension of the probation system to towns and villages. . . .

The proper correctives of the underlying structural deficiencies of the open country are knowledge, education, cooperative organizations, and personal leadership. These we may now discuss in more detail. . . .

The subject of paramount importance in our correspondence and in the hearings is education. In every part of the United States there seems to be one mind, on the part of those capable of judging, on the necessity of redirecting the rural schools. There is no such unanimity on any other subject. It is remarkable with what similarity of phrase the subject has been discussed in all parts of the country before the commission. Everywhere there is a demand that education have relation to living, that the schools should express the daily life, and that in the rural districts they should educate by means of agriculture and country-life subjects. It is recognized that all difficulties resolve themselves in the end into a question of education.

The schools are held to be largely responsible for ineffective farming, lack of ideals, and the drift to town. This is not because the rural schools, as a whole, are declining, but because they are in a state of arrested development and have not yet put themselves in consonance with all the recently changed conditions of life. The very forces that have built up the city and town school have caused the neglect of the country school. It is probable that the farming population will willingly support better schools as soon as it becomes convinced that the schools will really be changed in such a way as to teach persons how to live. . . .

The most necessary thing now to be done for public-school education in terms of country life is to rouse all the people to the necessity of such education, to coordinate the forces that are beginning to operate, and to project the work beyond the schools for youth into continuation schools for adults. The schools must represent and express the community in which they stand, although, of course, they should not be confined to the community. They should teach health and sanitation, even if it is necessary to modify the customary teaching of physiology. The teaching should be visual, direct, and applicable. Of course, the whole tendency of the schools will be ethical if they teach the vital subjects truthfully; but particular care should be taken that they stand for the morals of the pupils and of the communities.

We find a general demand for federal encouragement in educational propaganda to be in some way cooperative with the states. The people realize that the incubus of ignorance and inertia is so heavy and so widespread as to constitute a national danger, and that it should be removed as rapidly as possible. It will be increasingly necessary for the national and state governments to cooperate to bring about the results that are needed in agricultural and other industrial education.

The consideration of the educational problem raises the greatest single question that has come before the commission and which the commission has to place before the American people. Education has now come to have vastly more significance than the mere establishing and maintaining of schools. The education motive has been taken into all kinds of work with the people, directly in their homes and on their farms, and it reaches mature persons as well as youths. Beyond and behind all educational work there must be an aroused, intelligent, public sentiment; to make this sentiment is the most important work immediately before us. The whole country is alive with educational activity. While this activity may all be good, it nevertheless needs to be directed and correlated, and all the agencies should be more or less federated.

The arousing of the people must be accomplished in terms of their daily lives or of their welfare. For the country people this means that it must be largely in terms of agriculture. Some of the colleges of agriculture are now doing this kind of work effectively, although on a pitiably small scale as compared with the needs. This is extension work, by which is meant all kinds of educational effort directly with the people, both old and young, at their homes and on their farms; it comprises all educational work that is conducted away from the institution and for those who cannot go to schools and colleges. The best extension work now proceeding in this country — if measured by the effort to reach the people in their homes and on their own ground — is that coming from some of the colleges of agriculture and the United States Department of Agriculture.

Within the last five or ten years, the colleges of agriculture have been able to attack the problem of rural life in a new way. This extension work includes such efforts as local agricultural surveys; demonstrations on farms; nature study and other work in schools; boys' and girls' clubs of many kinds; crop organizations; redirection of rural societies; reading clubs; library extension; lectures; traveling schools; farmers' institutes; inspections of herds, barns, crops, orchards, and farms; publications of many kinds; and similar educational effort directly in the field.

To accomplish these ends, we suggest the establishment of a nationwide extension work. The first or original work of the agricultural branches of the land-grant colleges was academic in the old sense; later there was added the great field of experiment and research; there now should be added the third coordinate branch, comprising extension work, without which no college of agriculture can adequately serve its state. It is to the extension department of these colleges, if properly conducted, that we must now look for the most effective rousing of the people on the land.

In order that all public educational work in the United States may be adequately studied and guided, we also recommend that the United States Bureau of Education be enlarged and supported in such a way that it will really represent the educational activities of the nation, becoming a clearinghouse and a collecting, distributing, and investigating organization. It is now wholly inadequate to accomplish these ends. In a country in which education is said to be the national religion, this condition of our one expressly federal educational agency is pathetic. The good use already made of the small appropriations provided for the Bureau shows clearly that it can render a most important service if sufficient funds are made available for its use.

It is of the greatest consequence that the people of the open country should learn to work together, not only for the purpose of forwarding their economic interests and of competing with other men who are organized but also to develop themselves and to establish an effective community spirit. This effort should be a genuinely cooperative or common effort in which all the associated persons have a voice in the management of the organization and share proportionately in its benefits. Many of the so-called cooperative organizations are really not such, for they are likely to be controlled in the interest of a few persons rather than for all and with no thought of the good of the community at large. Some of the societies that are cooperative in name are really strong, centralized corporations or stock companies that have no greater interest in the welfare of the patrons than other corporations have. . . .

While there are very many excellent agricultural cooperative organizations of many kinds, the farmers nearly everywhere complain that there is still a great dearth of association that really helps them in buying and selling and developing their communities. Naturally, the effective cooperative groups are in the most highly developed communities; the general farmer is yet insufficiently helped by the societies. The need is not so much for a greater number of societies as for a more complete organization within them and for a more continuous active work.

Farmers seem to be increasingly feeling the pressure of the organized interests that sell to them and buy from them. They complain of business understandings or agreements between all dealers from the wholesaler and jobber to the remote country merchants that prevent farmers and their organizations from doing an independent business.

The greatest pressure on the farmer is felt in regions of undiversified, one-crop farming. Under such conditions, he is subject to great risk of crop failure; his land is soon reduced in productiveness; he usually does not raise his home supplies and is therefore dependent on the store for his living; and his crop, being a staple and produced in enormous quantities, is subject to world prices and to speculation, so that he has no personal market. In the exclusive cotton and wheat regions, the hardships of the farmer and the monotony of rural life are usually very marked. Similar conditions are likely to obtain in large-area stock ranging, hay raising, tobacco growing, and the like. In such regions, great discontent is likely to prevail and economic heresies to breed. The remedy is diversification in farming, on the one hand, and organization, on the other.

The commission has found many organizations that seem to be satisfactorily handling the transporting, distributing, and marketing of farm products. They are often incorporated stock companies in which the cooperators have the spur of money investment to hold them to their mutual obligations. In nearly all cases, the most successful organizations are in regions that are strongly dominated by similar products, as fruit, dairy, grain, or livestock.

Two principles may be applied in these business societies: in one class, the organization is in the nature of a combination and attempts to establish prices and perhaps to control the production; in the other class, the organization seeks its results by studying and understanding the natural laws of trade and taking advantage of conditions and regulating such evils as may arise, in the same spirit as a merchant studies them, or as a good farmer understands the natural laws of fertility.

With some crops, notably cotton and the grains, it is advantageous to provide cooperative warehouses in which the grower may hold his products till prices rise; and also in which scientific systems of grading of the products may be introduced. In certain fruit regions, community packinghouses have proved to be of the greatest benefit. In the meantime, the cotton or grain in the warehouse becomes, for business purposes, practically as good as cash (subject to charge for insurance) in the form of negotiable warehouse receipts. This form of handling products is now coming to be well-understood, and, combined with good systems of farming, it is capable of producing most satisfactory results.

Organized effort must come as the voluntary expression of the people; but it is essential that every state should enact laws that will stimulate and facilitate the organization of such cooperative associations, care being taken that the working of the laws be not cumbersome. These laws should provide the association with every legal facility for the transaction of the business in which they are to engage. They are as important to the state as other organizations of capital and should be fostered with as much care, and their members and patrons be adequately safeguarded. It is especially important that these organizations be granted all the powers and advantages given to corporations or other aggregations of capital, to the end that they may meet these corporations on equal legal ground when it is necessary to compete with them. Such laws should not only protect the cooperative societies but should provide means that will allow the societies to regulate themselves, so that they may be safeguarded from becoming merely commercial organizations through the purchase or control of the stock by dealers in the products that they handle. It is not unlikely that federal laws may also be needed to encourage cooperation.

Organized associative effort may take on special forms. It is probable, for example, that cooperation to secure and to employ farm labor would be helpful. It may have for its object the securing of telephone service (which is already contributing much to country life and is capable of contributing much more), the extension of electric lines, the improvement of highways, and other forms of betterment. Particular temporary needs of the neighborhood may be met by combined effort, and this may be made the beginning of a broader permanent organization.

A method of cooperative credit would undoubtedly prove of great service. In other countries credit associations loan money to their members on easy terms and for long enough time to cover the making of a crop, demanding security not on the property of the borrower but on the moral warranty of his character and industry. The American farmer has needed money less, perhaps, than landworkers in some other countries, but he could be greatly benefited by a different system of credit, particularly where the lien system is still in operation. It would be the purpose of such systems, aside from providing loans on the best terms and with the utmost freedom consistent with safety, to keep as much as possible of the money in circulation in the open country where the values originate. The present banking systems tend to take the money out of the open country and to loan it in town or to town-centered interests. We suggest that the national bank examiners be instructed to determine, for a series of years, what proportion of the loanable funds of rural banks is loaned to the farmers in their localities in order that data may be secured on this question. All unnecessary drain from the open country should be checked in order that the country may be allowed and encouraged to develop itself.

It is essential that all rural organizations, both social and economic, should develop into something like a system, or at least that all the efforts be known and studied by central authorities. There should be, in other words, a voluntary union of associative effort, from the localities to the counties, states, and the nation. Manifestly, government in the United States cannot manage the work of voluntary rural organization. Personal initiative and a cultivated cooperative spirit are the very core of this kind of work; yet both state and national government, as suggested, might exert a powerful influence toward the complete organization of rural affairs.

Steps should be taken whereby the United States Department of Agriculture, the state departments of agriculture, the land-grant colleges and experiment stations, the United States Bureau of Education, the normal and other schools shall cooperate in a broad program for aiding country life in such a way that each institution may do its appropriate work at the same time that it aids all the others and contributes to the general effort to develop a new rural social life.

This commission has no desire to give advice to the institutions of religion nor to attempt to dictate their policies. Yet any consideration of the problem of rural life that leaves out of account the function and the possibilities of the church and of related institutions would be grossly inadequate. This is not only because in the last analysis the country-life problem is a moral problem, or that in the best development of the individual, the great motives and results are religious and spiritual, but because from the pure sociological point of view the church is fundamentally a necessary institution in country life. In a peculiar way the church is intimately related to the agricultural industry. The work and the life of the farm are closely bound together, and the institutions of the country react on that life and on one another more intimately than they do in the city. This gives the rural church a position of peculiar difficulty and one of unequaled opportunity. The time has arrived when the church must take a larger leadership, both as an institution and through its pastors, in the social reorganization of rural life.

The great spiritual needs of the country community just at present are higher personal and community ideals. Rural people need to have an aspiration for the highest possible development of the community. There must be an ambition on the part of the people themselves constantly to progress in all of those things that make the community life wholesome, satisfying, educative,

and complete. There must be a desire to develop a permanent environment for the country boy and girl of which they will become passionately fond. As a pure matter of education, the countryman must learn to love the country and to have an intellectual appreciation of it. More than this, the spiritual nature of the individual must be kept thoroughly alive. His personal ideals of conduct and ambition must be cultivated.

Of course the church has an indispensable function as a conservator of morals. But from the social point of view, it is to hold aloft the torch of personal and community idealism. It must be a leader in the attempt to idealize country life.

The country church doubtless faces special difficulties. As a rule it is a small field. The country people are conservative. Ordinarily the financial support is inadequate. Often there are too many churches in a given community. Sectarian ideas divide unduly and unfortunately. While there are many rural churches that are effective agents in the social evolution of their communities, it is true that as a whole the country church needs new direction and to assume new responsibilities. Few of the churches in the open country are provided with resident pastors. They are supplied mostly from the neighboring towns and by a representative of some single denomination. Sometimes the pulpit is supplied by pastors of different denominations in turn. Without a resident minister the churchwork is likely to be confined chiefly to services once a week. In many regions there is little personal visitation except in cases of sickness, death, marriage, christening, or other special circumstance.

The Sunday school is sometimes continued only during the months of settled weather. There are young people's organizations to some extent, but they are often inactive or irregular. The social activity of the real country church is likely to be limited to the short, informal meetings before and after services and to suppers that are held for the purpose of raising funds. Most of the gatherings are designed for the church people themselves rather than for the community. The range of social influence is therefore generally restricted to the families particularly related to the special church organization, and there is likely to be no sense of social responsibility for the entire community.

In the rural villages there are generally several or a number of churches of different denominations, one or more of which are likely to be weak. The salaries range from $400 to $1,000. Among Protestants there is considerable denominational competition and consequent jealousy or even conflict. United effort for cooperative activity is likely to be perfunctory rather than sympathetic and vital. The pastor is often overloaded with station work in neighboring communities.

It is not the purpose of the commission to discuss the difficulties of the rural church at this time nor to present a solution for them, but, in the interests of rural betterment, it seems proper to indicate a few considerations that seem to be fundamental.

In New England and in some other parts of the North, the tremendous drawback of denominational rivalry is fairly well recognized and active measures for church federation are well under way. This does not mean organic union. It means cooperation for the purpose of trying to reach and influence every individual in the community. It means that "some church is to be responsible for every square mile." When a community is over-churched, it means giving up the superfluous church or churches. When a church is needed, it means a friendly agreement on the particular church to be placed there. This movement for federation is one of the most promising in the whole religious field, because it does not attempt to break down denominational influence or standards of thought. It puts emphasis, not

on the church itself but on the work to be done by the church for all men, churched and unchurched.

It is possible that all parts of the country are not quite ready for federation, although a national church federation movement is under way. But it hardly seems necessary to urge that the spirit of cooperation among churches, the diminution of sectarian strife, the attempt to reach the entire community must become the guiding principles everywhere if the rural church is long to retain its hold.

The rural church must be more completely than now a social center. This means not so much a place for holding social gatherings, although this is legitimate and desirable, but a place whence constantly emanate influences that go to build up the moral and spiritual tone of the whole community. The country church of the future is to be held responsible for the great ideals of community life as well as of personal character.

There should be a large extension of the work of the Young Men's Christian Association into the rural communities. There is apparently no other way to grip the hearts and lives of the boys and young men of the average country neighborhood. This association must regard itself as an ally of the church, with a special function and a special field.

We must have a complete conception of the country pastorate. The country pastor must be a community leader. He must know the rural problems. He must have sympathy with rural ideals and aspirations. He must love the country. He must know country life, the difficulties that the farmer has to face in his business, some of the great scientific revelations made in behalf of agriculture, the great industrial forces at work for the making or the unmaking of the farmer, the fundamental social problems of the life of the open country.

Consequently, the rural pastor must have special training for his work. Ministerial colleges and theological seminaries should unite with agricultural colleges in this preparation of the country clergyman. There should be better financial support for the clergyman; in many country districts it is pitiably small. There is little incentive for a man to stay in a country parish, and yet this residence is just what must come about. Perhaps it will require an appeal to the heroic young men, but we must have more men going into the country pastorates, not as a means of getting a foothold but as a permanent work. The clergyman has an excellent chance for leadership in the country. In some sections he is still the dominating personality. But everywhere he may become one of the great community leaders. He is the key to the country church problem. . . .

While it is of course necessary that the farmer receive good remuneration for his efforts, it is nevertheless true that the money consideration is frequently too exclusively emphasized in farm homes. This consideration often obscures every other interest, allowing little opportunity for the development of the intellectual, social, and moral qualities. The open country abounds in men and women of the finest ideals; yet it is necessary to say that other ends in life than the making of more money and the getting of more goods are much needed in country districts; and that this, more than anything else, will correct the unsatisfying nature of rural life.

Teachers of agriculture have placed too much relative emphasis on the remuneration and production sides of country life. Money-hunger is as strong in the open country as elsewhere, and as there are fewer opportunities and demands for the expenditure of this money for others and for society, there often develops a hoarding and a lack of public spirit that is disastrous to the general good. So completely does the money-purpose often control the motive that other purposes in farming remain dormant. The complacent contentment in many rural neighborhoods is itself the very evidence of social incapacity or decay.

It must not be assumed that these deficiencies are to be charged as a fault against the farmer as a group. They are rather to be looked on as evidence of an uncorrelated and unadjusted society. Society is itself largely to blame. The social structure has been unequally developed. The townsman is likely to assume superiority and to develop the town in disregard of the real interests of the open country or even in opposition to them. The city exploits the country; the country does not exploit the city. The press still delights in archaic cartoons of the farmer. There is as much need of a new attitude on the part of the townsman as on the part of the farmer.

This leads us to say that the country ideals, while derived largely from the country itself, should not be exclusive; and the same applies to city and village ideals. There should be more frequent social intercourse on equal terms between the people of the country and those of the city or village. This community of interests is being accomplished to a degree at present, but there is hardly yet the knowledge and sympathy and actual social life that there should be between those who live on the land and those who do not. The businessmen's organizations of cities could well take the lead in some of this work. The country town in particular has similar interests with the open country about it; but beyond this, all people are bettered and broadened by association with those of far different environment.

Reform must come from within, not from without. You cannot legislate for virtue.

James Cardinal Gibbons, address, Baltimore, Sept. 13, 1909

39.

Theodore Roosevelt: The Threat of Japan

Theodore Roosevelt left the White House in 1909, with the confident expectation that President Taft, his handpicked successor, would continue his policies, especially in the realm of foreign affairs. In order to make clear his views, Roosevelt wrote a number of memorandums and letters during his last months in office, one of which is reprinted here. The letter, written on February 8, 1909, to Philander Knox, the newly appointed secretary of state, expressed Roosevelt's conviction that the next and most important threat to America's national interests and security would come, not from Germany, as many thought, but from Japan.

Source: Papers of Theodore Roosevelt, Manuscript Division, Library of Congress, pp. 120-126.

My Dear Senator Knox:

You are soon to become secretary of state under Mr. Taft. At the outset both he and you will be overwhelmed with every kind of work; but there is one matter of foreign policy of such great and permanent importance that I wish to lay it before the President-to-be and yourself. I speak of the relations of the United States and Japan.

It is utterly impossible to foretell as regards either foreign or domestic policy what particular questions may appear as at the moment of most engrossing interest. It may be that there will be no ripple of trouble between Japan and the United States during your term of service. It may very well be that you will have acute trouble about Cuba, or with Venezuela or in Central America, or with some European power; but it is not likely that grave international complications — that is, complications which can possibly lead to serious war — can come from any such troubles. If we have to interfere again in Cuba, or take possession of the island, it will be exasperating, and we may in consequence have to repeat our Philippine experiences by putting down an annoying but unimportant guerrilla outbreak. But this would represent mere-

ly annoyance. The same would be true of anything in Central America or Venezuela.

I do not believe that Germany has any designs that would bring her in conflict with the Monroe Doctrine. The last seven years have tended steadily toward a better understanding of Germany on our part, and a more thorough understanding on the part of Germany that she must not expect colonial expansion in South America. As for England, I cannot imagine serious trouble with her. The settlement of the Alaskan boundary removed the one grave danger. The treaties now before the Senate are excellent, and all we have to fear is some annoying, but hardly grave, friction in the event of the failure of the Senate to ratify them.

But with Japan the case is different. She is a most formidable military power. Her people have peculiar fighting capacity. They are very proud, very warlike, very sensitive, and are influenced by two contradictory feelings; namely, a great self-confidence, both ferocious and conceited, due to their victory over the mighty empire of Russia; and a great touchiness because they would like to be considered as on a full equality with, as one of the brotherhood of, Occidental nations, and have been bitterly humiliated to find that even their allies, the English, and their friends, the Americans, won't admit them to association and citizenship, as they admit the least advanced or most decadent European peoples. Moreover, Japan's population is increasing rapidly and demands an outlet; and the Japanese laborers, small farmers, and petty traders would, if permitted, flock by the hundred thousand into the United States, Canada, and Australia.

Now for our side. The events of the last three years have forced me to the clear understanding that our people will not permit the Japanese to come in large numbers among them; will not accept them as citizens; will not tolerate their presence as large bodies of permanent settlers. This is just as true in Australia and Colombia as in our Rocky Mountain and Pacific states; but at present the problem is more acute with us because the desire of the Japanese to come here has grown. The opposition to the presence of the Japanese, I have reluctantly come to feel, is entirely warranted, and not only must be, but ought to be, heeded by the national government in the interest of our people and our civilization; and this in spite of the fact that many of the manifestations of the opposition are unwise and improper to the highest degree.

To permit the Japanese to come in large numbers into this country would be to cause a race problem and invite and insure a race contest. It is necessary to keep them out. But it is almost equally necessary that we should both show all possible courtesy and consideration in carrying out this necessarily disagreeable policy of exclusion, and that we should be thoroughly armed, so as to prevent the Japanese from feeling safe in attacking us. Unfortunately, great masses of our people show a foolish indifference to arming, and at the same time a foolish willingness to be offensive to the Japanese.

Labor unions pass violent resolutions against the Japanese and almost at the same moment protest against strengthening our military resources on land or sea. Big corporations seek to introduce Japanese coolies so as to get cheap labor, and thereby invite agitation which they are powerless to quell. The peace societies, and senators and congressmen like Burton of Ohio, Perkins of California, Perkins of New York, Tawney of Minnesota, McCall of Massachusetts, and Bartholdt of Missouri blatantly or furtively oppose the Navy and hamper its upbuilding, while doing nothing whatever to prevent insult to Japan. The California legislature is threatening to pass the most offensive kind of legislation aimed at the Japanese, and yet it reelects a wretched creature like Perkins to the Senate although he has opposed, with his usual feeble timidity and so far as he dared, the upbuilding of the Navy, following Hale's lead.

We are therefore faced by the fact that our people will not tolerate, and ought not to tolerate, the presence among them of large bodies of Japanese; and that so long as they are here in large bodies there is always chance either of violence on the part of mobs or of indiscreet and improper action by the legislative bodies of the Western states under demagogic influence. Furthermore, in Hawaii the Japanese already many times outnumber the whites, and have shown on more than one recent occasion a spirit both truculent and insolent.

In Hawaii the trouble is primarily due to the shortsighted greed of the sugar planters and of the great employers generally, who showed themselves incapable of thinking of the future of their children and anxious only to make fortunes from estates tilled by coolie labor. Accordingly, they imported, first, masses of Chinese laborers and, then, masses of Japanese laborers. Throughout my term as President, I have so far as possible conducted our policy against this desire of the sugar planters, against the theory of turning Hawaii into an island of coolie-tilled plantations, and in favor of making it so far as possible the abode of small settlers.

With this purpose, I have done everything I could to encourage the immigration of southern Europeans to the islands, and have endeavored so far as I could in the absence of legislation to restrict the entrance of Asiatic coolies. So far as possible our aim should be to diminish the number of Japanese in the islands without any regard to the fortunes of the sugar planters, and to bring in Europeans, no matter of what ancestry, in order that the islands may be filled with a white population of our general civilization and culture.

As regards the mainland, our policy should have three sides and should be shaped, not to meet the exigencies of this year or next but to meet what may occur for the next few decades. Japan is poor and is therefore reluctant to go to war. Moreover, Japan is vitally interested in China and on the Asiatic mainland and her wiser statesmen will, if possible, prevent her getting entangled in a war with us, because whatever its result it would hamper and possibly ruin Japan when she came to deal again with affairs in China. But with so proud and sensitive a people neither lack of money nor possible future complications will prevent a war if once they get sufficiently hurt and angry; and there is always danger of a mob outbreak there just as there is danger of a mob outbreak here.

Our task therefore is on the one hand to meet the demands which our own people make and which cannot permanently be resisted, and on the other to treat Japan so courteously that she will not be offended more than is necessary; and at the same time to prepare our fleet in such shape that she will feel very cautious about attacking us. Disturbances like those going on at present are certain to occur unless the Japanese immigration, so far as it is an immigration for settlement, stops. For the last six months under our agreement with Japan it has been stopped to the extent that more Japanese have left the country than have come into it. But the Japanese should be

made clearly to understand that this process must continue and if there is relaxation it will be impossible to prevent our people from enacting drastic exclusion laws; and that in such case all of us would favor such drastic legislation.

Hand in hand with insistence on the stopping of Japanese immigration should go insistence as regards our own people that they be courteous and considerate, that they treat the Japanese who are here well; and above all that they go on with the building of the Navy, keep it at the highest point of efficiency, securing not merely battleships but an ample supply of colliers and other auxiliary vessels of every kind. Much of the necessary expense would be met by closing the useless Navy yards. By the way, the fighting Navy should not be divided; it should be kept either in the Pacific or in the Atlantic, merely a squadron being left in the other ocean, and this in such shape that, in the event of war, it could avoid attack and at once join the main body of fighting ships.

All this is so obvious that it ought not to be necessary to dwell upon it. But our people are shortsighted and have short memories — I suppose all peoples are shortsighted and have short memories. The minute we arrange matters so that for the moment everything is smooth and pleasant, the more foolish peace societies, led by men like ex-Secretary of State Foster and ex-Secretary of the Navy Long, clamor for a stoppage in the building up of the Navy. On the other hand, at the very moment when we are actually keeping out the Japanese and reducing the number of Japanese here, demagogues and agitators like those who have recently appeared in the California and Nevada legislatures work for the passage of laws which are humiliating and irritating to the Japanese and yet of no avail so far as keeping out immigrants is concerned; for this can be done effectively only by the national government.

The defenselessness of the coast, the fact

that we have no army to hold or reconquer the Philippines and Hawaii, the fact that we have not enough battleships nor enough auxiliaries in the Navy — all these facts are ignored and forgotten. On the other hand, the Japanese, if we do not keep pressure upon them, will let up in their effort to control the emigration from Japan to this country; and they must be continually reminded that unless they themselves stop it, in the end this country is certain to stop it, and ought to stop it, no matter what the consequences may be.

There is no more important continuing feature of our foreign policy than this in reference to our dealing with Japan; the whole question of our dealings with the Orient is certain to grow in importance. I do not believe that there will be war, but there is always the chance that war will come; and if it did come, the calamity would be very great. And while I believe we would win, there is at least a chance of disaster. We should therefore do everything in our power to guard against the possibility of war by preventing the occurrence of conditions which would invite war and by keeping our Navy so strong that war may not come or that we may be successful if it does come.

Sincerely yours,
THEODORE ROOSEVELT

[*Handwritten*] P.S. I enclose a copy of my telegram to the speaker of the California Lower House; this was really meant almost as much for Japan as for California, and sets forth, seemingly as incidental, what our future policy must be.

[*Handwritten*] If possible, the Japanese should be shown, what is the truth, that our keeping them out means not that they are inferior to us — in some ways they are superior — but that they are *different;* so different that, whatever the future may hold, at present the two races ought not to come together in masses.

40.

WILLIAM HOWARD TAFT: Defense of a High Tariff

Taft and the Republicans promised a lowering of tariffs during the 1908 campaign. When Taft took office he called a special session of Congress for this purpose. The House reported a bill that did lower most duties, but the Senate added over 800 amendments, and the final rates were little lower than in previous years. In spite of strong Midwestern opposition, the Payne-Aldrich Tariff was passed and signed by the President. In a speech at Winona, Minnesota, on September 17, 1909, a portion of which is reprinted here, Taft defended it as "the best tariff bill" ever passed.

Source: 61 Congress, 2 Session, Senate Document No. 164.

As LONG AGO AS AUGUST 1906, in the congressional campaign in Maine, I ventured to announce that I was a tariff revisionist and thought that the time had come for a readjustment of the schedules. I pointed out that it had been ten years prior to that time that the Dingley Bill had been passed; that great changes had taken place in the conditions surrounding the productions of the farm, the factory, and the mine, and that under the theory of protection in that time the rates imposed in the Dingley Bill in many instances might have become excessive; that is, might have been greater than the difference between the cost of production abroad and the cost of production at home, with a sufficient allowance for a reasonable rate of profit to the American producer.

I said that the party was divided on the issue, but that in my judgment the opinion of the party was crystallizing and would probably result in the near future in an effort to make such revision. I pointed out the difficulty that there always was in a revision of the tariff, due to the threatened disturbance of industries to be affected and the suspension of business, in a way which made it unwise to have too many revisions.

In the summer of 1907 my position on the tariff was challenged, and I then entered into a somewhat fuller discussion of the matter. It was contended by the so-called standpatters that rates beyond the necessary measure of protection were not objectionable because behind the tariff wall competition always reduced the prices and thus saved the consumer. But I pointed out in that speech what seems to me as true today as it then was, that the danger of excessive rates was in the temptation they created to form monopolies in the protected articles, and thus to take advantage of the excessive rates by increasing the prices, and therefore, and in order to avoid such a danger, it was wise at regular intervals to examine the question of what the effect of the rates had been upon the industries in this country, and whether the conditions with respect to the cost of production here had so changed as to warrant a reduction in the tariff, and to make a lower rate truly protective of the industry.

It will be observed that the object of the revision under such a statement was not to destroy protected industries in this country but it was to continue to protect them where lower rates offered a sufficient protection to prevent injury by foreign competition. That was the object of the revision as

advocated by me, and it was certainly the object of the revision as promised in the Republican platform.

I want to make as clear as I can this proposition, because, in order to determine whether a bill is a compliance with the terms of that platform, it must be understood what the platform means. A free trader is opposed to any protective rate because he thinks that our manufacturers, our farmers, and our miners ought to withstand the competition of foreign manufacturers and miners and farmers, or else go out of business and find something else more profitable to do. Now, certainly the promises of the platform did not contemplate the downward revision of the tariff rates to such a point that any industry theretofore protected should be injured. Hence, those who contend that the promise of the platform was to reduce prices by letting in foreign competition are contending for a free trade and not for anything that they had the right to infer from the Republican platform.

The Ways and Means Committee of the House, with Mr. Payne at its head, spent a full year in an investigation, assembling evidence in reference to the rates under the tariff, and devoted an immense amount of work in the study of the question where the tariff rates could be reduced and where they ought to be raised with a view to maintaining a reasonably protective rate, under the principles of the platform, for every industry that deserved protection. They found that the determination of the question, what was the actual cost of production and whether an industry in this country could live under a certain rate and withstand threatened competition from abroad, was most difficult. The manufacturers were prone to exaggerate the injury which a reduction in the duty would give and to magnify the amount of duty that was needed; while the importers, on the other hand, who were interested in developing the importation from foreign shores, were quite likely to be equally biased on the other side.

"Saved"; cartoon by W. A. Rogers for the New York "Herald," 1909

Mr. Payne reported a bill — the Payne Tariff Bill — which went to the Senate and was amended in the Senate by increasing the duty on some things and decreasing it on others. The difference between the House bill and the Senate bill was very much less than the newspapers represented. It turns out upon examination that the reductions in the Senate were about equal to those in the House, though they differed in character.

Now, there is nothing quite so difficult as the discussion of a tariff bill, for the reason that it covers so many different items, and the meaning of the terms and the percentages are very hard to understand. The passage of a new bill, especially where a change in the method of assessing the duties has been followed, presents an opportunity for various modes and calculations of the percentages of increases and decreases that are most misleading and really throw no light at all upon the changes made.

One way of stating what was done is to say what the facts show — that under the

Dingley law there were 2,024 items. This included dutiable items only. The Payne law leaves 1,150 of these items unchanged. There are decreases in 654 of the items and increases in 220 of the items. Now, of course, that does not give a full picture, but it does show the proportion of decreases to have been three times those of the increases. . . .

Now, the promise of the Republican platform was not to revise everything downward, and in the speeches which have been taken as interpreting that platform which I made in the campaign, I did not promise that everything should go downward. What I promised was that there should be many decreases, and that in some few things increases would be found to be necessary; but that on the whole I conceived that the change of conditions would make the revision necessarily downward — and that, I contend, under the showing which I have made, has been the result of the Payne Bill. I did not agree, nor did the Republican Party agree, that we would reduce rates to such a point as to reduce prices by the introduction of foreign competition. That is what the free traders desire. That is what the revenue tariff reformers desire; but that is not what the Republican platform promised, and it is not what the Republican Party wished to bring about.

To repeat the statement with which I opened this speech, the proposition of the Republican Party was to reduce rates so as to maintain a difference between the cost of production abroad and the cost of production here, insuring a reasonable profit to the manufacturer on all articles produced in this country; and the proposition to reduce rates and prevent their being excessive was to avoid the opportunity for monopoly and the suppression of competition, so that the excessive rates could be taken advantage of to force prices up.

Now, it is said that there was not a reduction in a number of the schedules where there should have been. It is said that there was no reduction in the cotton schedule. There was not. The House and the Senate took evidence and found from cotton manufacturers and from other sources that the rates upon the lower class of cottons were such as to enable them to make a decent profit — but only a decent profit — and they were contented with it; but that the rates on the higher grades of cotton cloth, by reason of court decisions, had been reduced so that they were considerably below those of the cheaper grades of cotton cloth, and that by undervaluations and otherwise the whole cotton schedule had been made unjust and the various items were disproportionate in respect to the varying cloths.

Hence, in the Senate, a new system was introduced attempting to make the duties more specific rather than ad valorem in order to prevent by judicial decision or otherwise a disproportionate and unequal operation of the schedule. Under this schedule it was contended that there had been a general rise of all the duties on cotton. This was vigorously denied by the experts of the Treasury Department. At last, the Senate, in conference, consented to a reduction amounting to about 10 percent on all the lower grades of cotton, and this reduced the lower grades of cotton substantially to the same rates as before and increased the higher grades to what they ought to be under the Dingley law and what they were intended to be.

Now, I am not going into the question of evidence as to whether the cotton duties were too high and whether the difference between the cost of production abroad and at home, allowing for a reasonable profit to the manufacturer here, is less than the duties which are imposed under the Payne Bill. It was a question of evidence which Congress passed upon, after they heard the statements of cotton manufacturers and such other evidence as they could avail themselves of. I agree that the method of taking evidence and the determination was made in a general way and that there ought to be other methods of obtaining evidence and reaching a conclusion more satisfactory. . . .

On the whole, however, I am bound to say that I think the Payne Tariff Bill is the best tariff bill that the Republican Party ever passed; that in it the party has conceded the necessity for following the changed conditions and reducing tariff rates accordingly. This is a substantial achievement in the direction of lower tariffs and downward revision, and it ought to be accepted as such. Critics of the bill utterly ignore the very tremendous cuts that have been made in the iron schedule which heretofore has been subject to criticism in all tariff bills. . . .

The high cost of living, of which 50 percent is consumed in food, 25 percent in clothing, and 25 percent in rent and fuel, has not been produced by the tariff, because the tariff has remained the same while the increases have gone on. It is due to the change of conditions the world over. Living has increased everywhere in cost — in countries where there is free trade and in countries where there is protection — and that increase has been chiefly seen in the cost of food products. In other words, we have had to pay more for the products of the farmer — for meat, for grain, for everything that enters into food. Now, certainly no one will contend that protection has increased the cost of food in this country, when the fact is that we have been the greatest exporters of food products in the world. It is only that the demand has increased beyond the supply, that farmlands have not been opened as rapidly as the population, and the demand has increased.

I am not saying that the tariff does not increase prices in clothing and in building and in other items that enter into the necessities of life, but what I wish to emphasize is that the recent increases in the cost of living in this country have not been due to the tariff. We have a much higher standard of living in this country than they have abroad, and this has been made possible by higher income for the workingman, the farmer, and all classes. Higher wages have been made possible by the encouragement of diversified industries, built up and fostered by the tariff.

Now, the revision downward of the tariff that I have favored will not, I hope, destroy the industries of the country. Certainly it is not intended to. All that it is intended to do, and that is what I wish to repeat, is to put the tariff where it will protect industries here from foreign competition but will not enable those who will wish to monopolize to raise prices by taking advantage of excessive rates beyond the normal difference in the cost of production.

If the country desires free trade, and the country desires a revenue tariff and wishes the manufacturers all over the country to go out of business, and to have cheaper prices at the expense of the sacrifice of many of our manufacturing interests, then it ought to say so and ought to put the Democratic Party in power if it thinks that party can be trusted to carry out any affirmative policy in favor of a revenue tariff. Certainly in the discussions in the Senate there was no great manifestation on the part of our Democratic friends in favor of reducing rates on necessities. They voted to maintain the tariff rates on everything that came from their particular sections. If we are to have free trade, certainly it cannot be had through the maintenance of Republican majorities in the Senate and House and a Republican administration.

———◆———

Taft is an amiable island, entirely surrounded by men who know exactly what they want. .

JONATHAN PRENTISS DOLLIVER, of President Taft, 1909

41.

Daniel H. Burnham and Edward H. Bennett: Plan of Chicago

At the turn of the century, Chicago was the railroad center of the country and the meat-packer for the world. After the catastrophic fire in 1871, the city had been rebuilt of more durable structures and was quickly spreading beyond the central Loop area. The innovations of the Chicago School, led by Louis Sullivan and Frank Lloyd Wright, had established an international reputation for the city as the home of modern urban architecture. Daniel Burnham, the chief architect of the World's Columbian Exposition in 1893 and already established as a city planner, devoted himself to devising a master plan for Chicago's growth. Trading on his experience at the fair, he and Edward Bennett developed, from 1906 to 1909, a program of planned growth that incorporated transportation facilities, park systems, and preservation of the miles of lakefront. The plan was presented to the public in 1909 and adopted by the city. Carried out under Burnham's leadership, the plan is still evident in the city's present layout. The following selection is the summary chapter from the plan.

Source: *Plan of Chicago*, Charles Moore, ed., Chicago, 1909, Ch. 8.

THE PLAN OF CHICAGO . . . is the result of a systematic and comprehensive study, carried on during a period of thirty months, with the sole purpose of mapping out an ideal project for the physical development of this city. Perfection of detail is not claimed, but the design as a whole is placed before the public in the confident belief that it points the way to realize civic conditions of unusual economy, convenience, and beauty.

It is fully realized that a plan calling for improvements on a scale larger and more inclusive than any heretofore proposed seems, on first consideration, beyond the financial ability of the community. If, however, the plan meets public approval, it can be executed without seriously increasing present burdens. The very growth of the city, creating as it does wealth greater than mines can produce, gives a basis of bond issues in excess of the utmost cost involved in carrying out this plan. The increase in the assessed value of real estate in the city of Chicago for the past ten years exceeds the expense required to put the plan into execution; and at the same time the very character of the proposed changes is such as to stimulate the increase in wealth. The public, therefore, has the power to put the plan into effect if it shall determine to do so.

It is quite possible that some revision of existing laws may be necessary in order to enable the people to carry out this project; but this is clearly within the power of the people themselves. The realization of the plan, therefore, depends entirely on the strength of the public sentiment in its favor. And what hope is there that the people will desire to make Chicago an ideal city? A brief survey of the past will help to form an opinion on this subject.

Sixty years ago, when Chicago was scarcely more than a village, it became apparent that in order to secure proper drainage the street levels must be raised to a considerable extent throughout what we know as the old city, from the main river to Twelfth Street, and also for a distance on the West and North Sides. This project, albeit a very formidable one for that time, was promptly entered upon and duly carried out, although it involved raising all the streets and most of the buildings throughout that large territory. For that day and generation the undertaking was much more serious than the reconstruction of the city thoroughfares now proposed.

Again, some fifty years ago, when the idea of creating great metropolitan park areas was new, Chicago undertook to acquire and improve a chain of parks surrounding the city on three sides. This scheme, which has well supplied the needs of Chicago until recent times, was carried out in such a manner that it never was burdensome. The creation of a park system for Chicago was not undertaken from motives of utility but purely because of a desire to make the city attractive; and the success was magnificent.

Later, in the '80s, the purification of the water of Lake Michigan by the diversion of the sewage became a public issue. Once again the people of Chicago rose to the occasion; and, after years of hard work, the Drainage Canal, built at a cost of $60 million, has been completed.

Next came the World's Fair, in the early '90s, and here also a result was accomplished which has never been surpassed either in scope or in architectural beauty. The cost of the Fair (over $20 million for grounds and buildings alone) was very large for that day. The fact that the Fair came into being here indicated that this people, generally regarded as a commercial community, were deeply appreciative of the higher forms of good order and municipal beauty.

The Chicago World's Fair, like the raising of the grades of the city, the creation of a complete system of parks and boulevards, and the building of the Drainage Canal, went far beyond anything of the same kind ever before undertaken by a city. These four works are the greatest ones which have been achieved by Chicago. They have proved the readiness of the people to take up large schemes of public improvement which at the time of their inception required great foresight and great faith in the future. Two of them were demanded by considerations exclusively practical, while the other two were not so regarded, but on the other hand were the expression of the deeper sense in man of the value of delightful surroundings. If an accurate statement of the costs of the four improvements could be made, it would probably show that about equal sums have been spent on the practical and on the aesthetic side.

Besides the public enterprises mentioned, the people of Chicago, either collectively or as individuals, have established many agencies for the improvement of the intellectual, social, moral, and aesthetic conditions. The Chicago Orchestra occupies land and buildings on Michigan Avenue which have a present value of over $1,250,000; and during the past twenty years private subscriptions have amounted to at least another $1 million, all expended for an organization purely artistic. The Art Institute building in Grant Park cost $700,000, and, since its completion in 1893, it has never been closed for a day. Besides its large and excellent art school, there is a good collection of the works of old and modern masters, which is constantly receiving additions. The Crerar Library has an endowment fund of $3,500,000, besides a substantial building fund; and the Newberry Library and the Armour Institute of Technology are other worthy public benefactions.

Especially notable are the educational foundations which contribute so largely to the intellectual life of the city and exert an influence throughout the Middle West — Lake Forest University, Northwestern University, and the University of Chicago. The last-named institution, established in 1892, has already taken its place among the foremost universities in this country, not only by reason of its endowment and property (representing more than $23 million) but also because of wise administration along a well-considered plan.

Quite in accord with the plan of Chicago is the Benjamin Franklin Ferguson Monument Fund of $1 million, the income of which is available for defraying the cost of statuary commemorating worthy men and women of America or important events in American history, to be erected in the parks and boulevards of the city under the direction of the trustees of the Art Institute. The Field Museum, representing gifts aggregating $9 million, is a further instance of loyalty to the city and a desire for its improvement.

Such enterprises and such gifts as those enumerated show what may be expected from individual benefactions as wealth increases and the idea of public service is encouraged. When opportunities for enriching the city are provided, individual citizens rise to the occasion and find true satisfaction in leaving memorials useful or agreeable to the people.

Mere increase in numbers does not warrant the belief that public sentiment in favor of extensive public works will grow in proportion to the population; but the history of the past does prove that the people of Chicago are always ready and anxious to follow when the way to great benefits is plainly open. We believe that the tendency which the community has shown by its acts points hopefully to the adoption of a great scheme of public improvement. In other words, Chicago, having already carried out large projects strictly on the lines of this report, may we not, therefore, confidently expect this people to go on doing as they have done?

There is a still stronger reason for the belief that the public will favor such a plan as is herein presented. It lies in the growing love of good order, due to the advance in education. Everyone knows that the civic conditions which prevailed fifty years ago would not now be tolerated anywhere; and everyone believes that conditions of today will not be tolerated by the men who shall follow us. This must be so, unless progress has ceased.

The education of a community inevitably brings about a higher appreciation of the value of systematic improvement and results in a strong desire on the part of the people to be surrounded by conditions in harmony with the growth of good taste; and as fast as the people can be brought to see the advantage to them of more orderly arrangement of the streets, transportation lines, and parks, it is well-nigh certain that they will bring about such desirable ends. Thus do the dreams of today become the commonplaces of tomorrow; and what we now deem fanciful will become mere matter-of-fact to the man of the future.

If the plan as a whole be approved by the majority of our citizens because it is found to be both practical and beautiful, the next question is as to what it commits us. In answering this query a general review of the principal elements composing the plan will be of value. The following list comprises the main items:

First, the improvement of the lakefront.

Second, the creation of a system of highways outside the city.

Third, the improvement of railway terminals and the development of a complete traction system for both freight and passengers.

Fourth, the acquisition of an outer park system and of parkway circuits.

Fifth, the systematic arrangement of the streets and avenues within the city in order to facilitate the movement to and from the business district.

Sixth, the development of centers of intellectual life and of civic administration, so related as to give coherence and unity to the city.

The improvement of the lakefront from Winnetka to the Indiana line is an economic necessity. As has been stated, the aggregate of the waste material seeking dumping ground on the lakeshore, because that is the cheapest place to deposit it, is not less than 1 million cubic yards per annum. This material is sufficient to produce annually from twenty-seven to thirty acres of land if used to build the lake parkways and park strips herein recommended. The park authorities would only have to furnish breakwaters and bridges and to finish the grounds. The utilization of this material in thirty years would produce all the lakefront land recommended in the report for the region between Grant and Jackson parks.

But long before the expiration of the thirty years, the amount of filling urgently seeking the lakefront dump will be enormously increased. This dirt should be utilized for the public benefit instead of being wasted as at present in the open lake, where it becomes detrimental to health and an interference to navigation. The dirt to be disposed of in building new traction tunnels under the principal streets of the city will go far toward the completion of the new lakeshore parks.

It is evident, therefore, that this improvement, involving the redemption of the entire lakefront, from Winnetka to the Indiana state line, and the creation of an extremely beautiful and useful public recreation ground, will involve very little public expense. There can be no doubt that this part of the plan of Chicago will be carried through; and in fact much is already being accomplished along these lines.

The interurban highway system can be realized very cheaply. Ninety-five percent of the necessary roads now exist as public highways, and the cost of acquiring the other 5 percent will be merely nominal. The diagram . . . is laid out with a radius of approximately sixty miles from the City Hall. The cost of widening that comparatively small portion of the roadways which require to be widened; the straightening of the few which need such treatment; the planting of trees along the highways; and the macadamizing of the roads are improvements that may be hastened by concerted intelligent action. The expense involved is comparatively small, but the economy and convenience to the public are very large. Is it not evident that this portion of the plan can be realized at no distant day provided a strong organization of active men shall be formed for the purpose of carrying it into effect?

The suggestions in regard to trunk lines, their rights-of-way, stations, and general conditions, are many and serious. The suggestions have been made for the purpose of bringing about the greatest economy of money and time, both in freight and passenger handling. If the recommendations herein contained will produce conditions really beneficial to the individual shipper and passenger, undoubtedly they will be found best for the railroads themselves.

The direct object in view is to free a large portion of the South Side from tracks and stations and restore it to business use; to double the capacity of the streets of the whole city by opening circulation to the north, west, and south, and by connecting the outlying parts in the best possible manner with the heart of the city. Over and above all these considerations, highly important as they all are, is economy in the freight handling of Chicago as a shipping center. The object here has been to find that general principle which, if applied, will give to the merchants, manufacturers, and jobbers of this city all the advantages that should naturally be theirs throughout the great territory dominated by Chicago.

If the general scheme herein proposed shall not be adopted by the public and the railroads, some other inevitably must be, because the very life of the community is involved in the solution of this problem. The commercial prosperity of the community is represented by the cost per ton of handling freight into and out of this territory as a shipping center. General changes in railroad conditions take years to accomplish. That will be the case if such a scheme as we recommend is carried out; but the public should remember that they will not be taxed to pay for it. When these improvements come they will be railroad enterprises, undertaken by the railroads and carried out by the railroads.

The traction recommendations contained in this report are already in progress, and no question need be raised as to whether or not this portion of work will be carried out. It has practically been decided upon and no doubt will be accomplished. The cost will be borne in part by the traction lines themselves and partly by the public.

The additional parks and parkways recommended are extensive, as should be the case. Although it is true that the men of forty years ago did devise a scheme which has been sufficient almost up to the present moment, it is also true that the number, location, and arrangement of the parks and parkways of Chicago today are entirely inadequate for its future development; and nothing is suggested in this report except what has seemed to be absolutely required. Fifty years ago before population had become dense in certain portions of the city, people could live without parks; but we of today cannot. We now regard the promotion of robust health of body and mind as necessary public duties, in order that the individual may be benefited and that the community at large may possess a higher average degree of good citizenship. And, after all has been said, good citizenship is the prime object of good city planning.

In some locations, parks and parkways are sufficient to accommodate the people in the immediate neighborhoods; other sections of this city, and suburbs which will soon become parts of this city, should be equally well-provided. "Nature," says President Charles W. Eliot, "is the greatest factor in the continuous education of man and woman." The extensive woodlands proposed are an addition not usually designed for American cities, although almost invariably used in Europe. The cost of these added parks and woodlands will be considerable, and it must be borne by the public; but it is a sane proposition that the people of Chicago and its suburbs should have the 60,000 acres of wooded territory as well as the great Bow . . . which will occupy from 600 to 800 additional acres.

The acquisition and completion of an outer park system may easily be carried through in ten years; and if the cost shall be distributed over that period of time, it will not prove burdensome. The returns will come in the shape of increase of health and joy of living for all the people; and incidentally the value of every real-estate holding in the city will be enhanced.

The land necessary for the Civic Center should be secured at once, while values at the point proposed are reasonable. For the time being, this land may be treated as park space; but the sites and the general scheme of grouping for the buildings should be approved, so that as the city, the county, and the general government outgrow their present structures, the new ones may take their appointed places, each one contributing its part to an orderly and convenient scheme. The adoption of such a scheme would save a very large amount of money in the purchase of public building sites and would create stability in real-estate values.

To the West Side, especially, the development of a Civic Center along the lines indicated is a matter of prime importance; for it will give to that portion of the city the needed impetus toward higher standards than now prevail there. At the same time it will benefit all other parts of the city, since it is for the advantage of Chicago as a whole that each portion shall be developed equally with every other portion. The cost of the Civic Center should be paid by the whole community.

The street plan as laid out involves a very considerable amount of money; but it will be found that in Chicago as in other cities the opening of new thoroughfares, although involving large initial expense, creates an increase in values due to increase in convenience and the provision for adequate sites for the increasing retail traffic of the city. The cost will amount to many millions of dollars, but the result will be continuous prosperity for all who dwell here; and such prosperity the city cannot have unless it becomes a convenient and pleasant place in which to live.

Finally, it seems probable that the schemes of outer highways and of all the lakefront improvements may come about quite naturally and with very little expense to the city; that the railways will pay most of the expense of their changes and improvements, thus leaving a portion of the cost of the traction system and all of the cost of the Civic Center, of the parks and parkways, and of the street development for the general public to meet. The community has ample financial ability to do its part without placing undue burdens upon the people.

Paris had not much more than half a million people, and her commercial prospects were far less than are ours today, when that municipality adopted a street improvement scheme involving over $260 million, and carried it to completion in thirty-five years. The motive of the French people in undertaking this enterprise was to create a great attraction for all men: a city so delightful as to insure continuous prosperity to the inhabitants. The success of the undertaking has amply justified the pains and the expense. People from all over the world visit and linger in Paris. No matter where they make their money, they go there to spend it; and every proprietor and workman in Paris benefits by reason of that fact.

Conditions in Chicago are such as to repel outsiders and drive away those who are free to go. The cream of our own earnings should be spent here, while the city should become a magnet, drawing to us those who wish to enjoy life. The change would mean prosperity, effective, certain, and forever continuous.

If, therefore, the plan is a good one, its adoption and realization will produce for us conditions in which business enterprises can be carried on with the utmost economy, and with the certainty of successful issue, while we and our children can enjoy and improve life as we cannot now do. Then our own people will become homekeepers, and the stranger will seek our gates.

You wrote me a lovely letter on my nintieth birthday. . . . What I have done looks small to me, but I have tried a good deal for the best I have known. . . . Don't you think that the best things are already in view? The opportunities for women, the growing toleration and sympathy in religion, the sacred cause of peace? I have lived like Moses, to see the entrance into the Promised Land. How much is this to be thankful for! My crabbed hand shows how time abridges my working powers, but I march to the brave music still.

JULIA WARD HOWE, letter to Mrs. Spofford, 1909

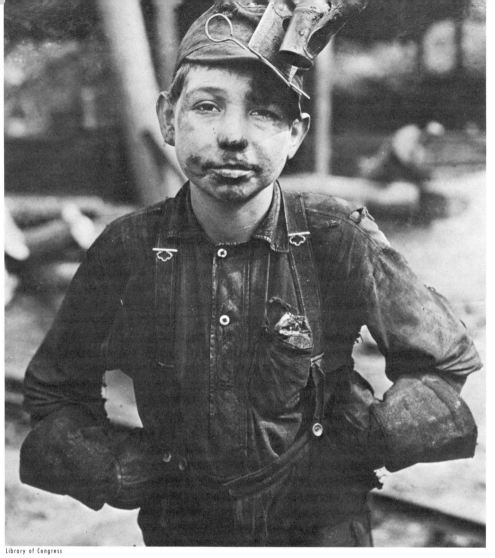

"Tipple Boy" at the Turkey Knob Mine, MacDonald, West Virginia; photographed by Lewis Hine, 1908

THE PROGRESSIVE ERA

The Progressive Era, from about 1895 to World War I, was a period of unrest, of agitation and reform. Progressivism was both a moral and a political movement and it found expression in ways as diverse as the Anti-Saloon League, the Clayton Anti-trust Act, and Roosevelt's Bull Moose Party. It was largely a movement of the middle class, a class threatened by monopoly capital on one side and labor unionism on the other; it was largely a movement of self defense, organizing the unprotected middle, and demanding, with varying success, reforms and reorganizations designed to forestall radical action by the dispossessed.

Much Progressive activity was sincere in motivation, but the element of fear was necessary for anything like a mass movement. The advance fronts of Progressive action, particularly its legislation, ran head on into the established conservatism of the courts, still grounded in 18th-century legal and economic theory and determined to defend the absolute sovereignty of property ownership against Socialist and Progressive alike. Progressivism held out against World War I as long as possible, but was finally absorbed in the new crusade. After the war its small chance of revival was ended by the wave of postwar disillusionment.

A brief moment away from the spinner. "Said she was 10. Been working over a year."

Laws limiting the hours of child employment had been common in New England in the 1850s where they supplemented compulsory-education laws. In the 1870s the Knights of Labor had conducted a campaign to prohibit child labor, but real results required the organization of the National Child Labor Committee in 1904; by 1910 there were 22 state committees and by 1914 all but one state had set a minimum working age, usually 14. Efforts to pass uniform federal legislation were, however, fruitless. Long delayed laws passed in 1916 and 1919 were promptly declared unconstitutional.

(Left) Girls at a mill in Georgia during lunch; (below) noon hour at mill in Meridian, Mississippi. Pictures on these and succeeding pages by Hine

(Top) At work in the Vivian Cotton Mill, Cherryville, N.C.; (left) John Tidwell. "Many of these youngsters smoke"; (below) girl going to work at a shoe factory in Kirksville, Mo.

Glass factory, Alexandria, Virginia. "Works day shift one week and night shift the next"

Bootblack at Third Avenue and 9th Street in New York. "Not an after school job." 1910

Boys working at canning machinery in the J. S. Farrand Packing Co., Baltimore, 1909. Hine was outraged at the danger of injury; (right) young boys at work in a West Virginia coal mine, 1908; (below) two generations of miners at the same mine, Turkey Knob, West Virginia. The older boys have already spent years in the mine and the future promises more of the same.

Freddie Reed, 14, of Springfield, Mass. "Left school as soon as he reached the legal age. Been working a few months"; (left) Judge Benjamin Barr Lindsey of the Denver Juvenile Court meeting boys under the court's jurisdiction during the Saturday morning "report day" session. Judge Lindsey was a pioneer in the handling of juvenile offenders produced in growing numbers by the pressures of industrial economy and urban life; (below) boys in uniform playing baseball on the playground of the New York Juvenile Asylum

Elizabeth Street, New York. Inside tenement a "great deal of clothes finishing is done," 1912; (right) "Municipal Playground" from "The Masses"

In 1915, the Commission on Industrial Relations observed that a "large part of our industrial population are . . . living in a condition of actual poverty," with one-third to one-half the wage earners living below a decent level. As a result, children of the poor died at three times the rate of middle-class children. In large cities up to 20% of the children were undernourished; only one-third of all children enrolled finished elementary school; less than 10% of children in public high schools graduated.

"Survival of the Unfittest." Construction work reveals a "backyard tenement" squeezed in between two larger buildings; New York City

Eugene Debs, highly successful labor organizer and perennial Socialist presidential choice

Elisabeth Gourley Flynn at Patterson, N.J., silk workers' strike, 1913; Samuel Gompers; (below) memorial parade for 146 victims, mostly girls, of the Triangle Shirtwaist Co. fire, 1911

Labor organizations proceeded in two quite different directions. The American Federation of Labor, under the strong conservative leadership of Samuel Gompers, strove constantly for orderly organization and bargaining. The operative theory was that labor was, as in classical economics, a commodity to be bartered at the best possible price, and that market power for labor was gained through labor unity. The insistence on respectability and political orthodoxy forced the AF of L to follow public opinion and even public hysteria, often to its own disadvantage. The Industrial Workers of the World differed in two major points: the organization of labor on industry rather than craft lines, thus including the hitherto unrepresented unskilled labor groups, and a gradually increasing radicalism which soon ran to violent anarchosyndicalism.

Burning miner's camp, Forbes, Colorado, 1914; (right) Big Bill Haywood, IWW leader; (below) ruins of the "Ludlow Colony" in Colorado, 1914

Campaign poster of the Socialist Party in the presidential election; (above left) ad for a lecture program in Philadelphia sponsored by Polish Socialists to raise money to aid the revolutionaries in Russia, 1905; (above right) cartoon from "The Masses": "To those who bend to power and lap its milk, Editors, Educators, Lawyers, Ministers." (Right) Another "Masses" view

J. P. Morgan, Jr. giving testimony at a hearing on industrial activities, c. 1915

The Sherman Antitrust Act of 1890 proved to be of minor value in regulating monopolistic tendencies in business. Always hampered by the courts, trust-busting under the Act dealt generally with companies already liable for prosecution for other, more explicitly illegal actions. After the Roosevelt-Taft period, sentiment shifted from the prosecution of trusts in themselves to trusts formed by or engaged in illegal or harmful practices.

Responses to the widespread social criticism were attacked as marginal: "Puck" cartoon calling for stronger antitrust action and another faulting Carnegie on the direction of his philanthropy

Graduates at Tuskegee parade past their white benefactors, among them Carnegie and President Eliot of Harvard, 1906; Tuskegee students plowing some of the more than 1,000 acres cultivated at the Institute in keeping with Booker T. Washington's ideas; (below) between classes

Negro school near Henderson, Kentucky; over half the students are absent doing farm work

The status of the Negro in the United States worsened progressively. Still concentrated in the South, most Negroes had been forced into the losing business of sharecropping. Effectively barred from real education — Alabama, for example, spent 514 percent more per white child on education in 1909 — Negroes found little opportunity for betterment. As the 20th-century northern migration began, practices in the North began slowly to emulate those of the South. Legal segregation was rendered unnecessary by the discovery that de facto segregation followed habitual and extralegal discrimination in housing, employment, and education.

(Left) Stocks still in use in Dover, Delaware, 1910; Jeff Shields, "Stonewall" Jackson's cook, at a Confederate rally

Executive Committee of the National Negro Business League; (below) W. E. B. Du Bois and Washington

Skilled Negro workers, few as they were, were barred from the AF of L or organized separately and pitted against white unions. By 1910 the disenfranchisement of Southern Negroes was virtually complete. It was becoming clear that the policies of Booker T. Washington were popular with whites in direct proportion to their ineffectiveness. In spite of Washington's compromises and accommodations, he could still be called "as bestial as a gorilla" by Thomas Watson, congressman, senator, and Populist presidential candidate. To repudiate Washington and to work for tangible results, the Niagara Movement was founded in 1905 under the leadership of W. E. B. Du Bois, distinguished scholar and educator. The movement evolved into the NAACP and Du Bois edited the group's organ "Crisis" until 1932.

42.

Ellwood P. Cubberley: Education and the Changing National Life

In the first decade of the twentieth century, the extraordinary industrial and manufacturing progress of the nation was evident to all, but there were some who were concerned whether other facets of American life were keeping pace. Ellwood Cubberley, a professor of education at Stanford University, was especially concerned about the ability of American education to meet the needs of the country's changed situation. A portion of his Changing Conceptions of Education *is reprinted here.*

Source: *Changing Conceptions of Education,* Boston, 1909, pp. 50-68.

From 1897 to 1907, our country experienced an unprecedented period of industrial development and national prosperity. It was a period marked by the concentration of capital and business enterprises in all fields; undertakings on a scale heretofore unattempted were begun; capital changed from a national to an international basis; "trusts," combinations, and associations were formed in all lines of business; the specialization of labor and the introduction of laborsaving machinery took place to an extent before unknown; new inventions destroyed old trades and threw hundreds out of employment; the immigration of people racially further removed from our own stock reached a maximum; city conditions everywhere became even more complex and potentially more dangerous; villages became more urban and a more cosmopolitan attitude began to pervade our whole life; the frontier practically disappeared; the national feeling was deepened and intensified, and the national government was called upon to do many things for the benefit of the people which it had become clearly evident that the states could not do.

Such periods of rapid development subject educational systems to increased strain. National progress outruns the possibility of education to keep pace with it. Many readjustments are called for, and readjustments are not easy to make, and cannot be made at once. The need of broad, general, and diversified training, adapted to the needs of the future rather than to the needs of the present or the past, becomes even more evident. The educational system is subjected to new and increased criticism. We hear this on all sides today. The practical man would make the school over; the conservative schoolmaster clings tenaciously to the past. Criticism and skepticism alike prevail. At last the tension becomes so great that something has to give way, and progress, often rapid progress, ensues. A new viewpoint is attained, a new inspiration directs our work, new means and methods are introduced, and often a new philosophy actuates the work of the school.

There are many reasons for thinking that our school system has entered on another such period of change and development now and that we are standing on the threshold of a new era in educational progress. The period since 1900 has certainly been a remarkable one. The number of new educational societies and associations which have been formed, and the number of congresses which have been held to promote some one phase or another of educational work, is so large that one can scarcely remember their names. The great educational awakening which has taken place in the Southern states is only paralleled by that started by Horace Mann in Massachusetts seventy years ago.

The large endowments for higher education and the deep interest taken in popular education by many laymen are certainly significant. The many state educational commissions which have been created within the past five years indicate a general dissatisfaction with existing conditions and a desire for change and improvement. The new interest in school hygiene and the physical welfare of the child indicates a new and a commendable desire to care for the bodies as well as the heads of our children. The great educational lessons to be learned from a study of the educational, political, and industrial progress of the German Empire during the past forty years are at last beginning to take root with us. Above all, the new and extensive interest in industrial and vocational training is especially significant of the changing conception of the function of the school and the classes in society which the school is in future expected to serve.

A right-about-face movement, too, is taking place in our educational theory. When the school first became conscious and critical of itself, it turned to methods and classroom procedure for lines of improvement, and psychology became its fundamental science. Its gaze was turned inward upon itself. Many reforms and improvements in methods and in the teaching process were made, but the advances in organization and in the enrichment of the curriculum have nearly all been forced upon the school by practical men from without. The school now shows signs of becoming conscious of itself in a new and truer direction; its gaze is now outward instead of inward, and the relation of the school to the world outside has now become a question of the first importance in educational procedure.

The school is essentially a time- and laborsaving device, created — with us — by democracy to serve democracy's needs. To convey to the next generation the knowledge and the accumulated experience of the past is not its only function. It must equally prepare the future citizen for the tomorrow of our complex life. The school must grasp the significance of its social connections and relations, and must come to realize that its real worth and its hope of adequate reward lies in its social efficiency. There are many reasons for believing that this change is taking place rapidly at present, and that an educational sociology, needed as much by teachers today as an educational psychology, is now in the process of being formulated for our use.

Child life is everywhere experiencing today a new lengthening of the period of dependence and training. In proportion as our social life becomes broader and more complex, a longer period of guidance becomes necessary to prepare the individual for active participation in it. As our industrial life becomes narrower and its processes more concealed, new and more extended training is called for to prepare the future worker for his task; to reveal to him something of the intricacy and interdependence of our modern social and industrial life, and to point out to him the necessity of each man's part. With the ever increasing subdivision and specialization of labor, the danger from class subdivision is constantly increasing, and the task is thrown more and more upon the school of instilling into all a social and a political consciousness that will lead to unity amid diversity and to united action for the preservation and betterment of our democratic institutions. The great numbers of aliens who yearly come to our shores and at once become a part of our industrial classes, many of whom are illiterate and few of whom have any real conception of the meaning of democratic life, add new emphasis to this point of view.

Five or six months of common school education each year for a few years are no longer enough; and on all sides the school year is being lengthened and the educational requirements increased. So marked has been the change in this direction within recent years that sixteen years of age bids fair to be the earliest time at which we will, ultimately, permit children to entirely cease attendance at some form of the public school.

Our school curriculum bids fair, too, to experience many modifications during the next one or two decades, and chiefly along a line that will lead toward preparation for increased social efficiency. Much antiquated material, adapted largely to the needs of a society that has preceded us, will doubtless be eliminated. New subjects and new points of emphasis in old subjects, better adapting the school to our changed and changing social and industrial life, will probably be added.

Our city schools will soon be forced to give up the exceedingly democratic idea that all are equal, and that our society is devoid of classes, as a few cities have already in large part done, and to begin a specialization of educational effort along many new lines in an attempt better to adapt the school to the needs of these many classes in the city life. City, town, and country schools alike have, in the past, directed most of their training to satisfying the needs of the children of the well-to-do classes and those headed for business life or the profes-

sions. More recently, most of the larger cities have provided some form of work leading to preparation for the executive positions in technical pursuits. The common wage earners, those who enter the industries as workmen, and the country boy and girl have been forced to take what was provided for the others, or to do without.

The situation has been somewhat analogous to that of the old colleges, with their Latin, Greek, and mathematics curriculum and their small student body and limited support. With the introduction of many new lines of work and the democratization of all instruction, the colleges have experienced a great increase in students and in popular favor and support. Our public schools are at present experiencing some such change, and it is one that is likely to increase rather than to diminish with time. Vocational schools and special-type schools of many kinds are likely soon to find a place in our more important school systems. There is some reason to hope, too, that the aim and direction of the country school and the small-town school will also change, and that in the future these will seriously turn their attention to the needs of rural life. Ever since the establishment of rural schools they have been giving instruction of a kind which has led to the city rather than to the farm. The introduction of manual training, domestic science, and agriculture would do much toward making the country school and the small-town school a more useful social institution.

A very significant change has also taken place since 1900 in the attitude assumed toward the study of education by our higher institutions of learning. The study of education, rather than the old "pedagogy," has recently become an important part of the work of most of our colleges and universities. Instead of a study of school methods and management only, the work has changed into a phase of political science, that of a study of means of improving the state and of advancing the public welfare. Nearly all of our universities and colleges now have such chairs or departments, and the state universities and our more democratic private institutions are now organizing professional schools for the training of teachers and educational leaders for the state. Active, capable, and mature young men are studying the subject, and many are preparing themselves for leadership in the work which will soon have to be done. The work begins at last to offer a good career, and the opportunities for useful service are almost unparalleled.

The instruction offered in a number of our normal schools has been revised recently to make it conform better to the new conception, and many indications point to education as a future high school subject of study, with ultimately a unit of credit for college entrance. Surely a study of the history, aims, purposes, and functions of public education in a democratic society such as our own ought to be as useful, either as a preparation for participation in active life or for the thinking required of a college freshman, as is the study of the history of medieval Europe or the reading of four books of Caesar.

The administration of education each year becomes a more important and a more dignified piece of work. If we could only cast off the antiquated and unsatisfactory method of awarding the selection of state and county superintendents to the Republican and Democratic parties, and open up these places to the competition of the brains of the whole country, as we have done with the high school principalship and the city superintendency, these positions would become among the most important within the gift of the state. The office of superintendent of city schools has in many places become one of much dignity and importance, and the office is being completely divorced from partisan or personal politics by all progressive communities. State superintendents

of public instruction and state boards of education are being entrusted with new functions, and a marked tendency toward a centralization of power and responsibility is manifest in many states. There is even good reason to believe that at last Congress has been touched by the new spirit in education and that it will, before long, perform the long-delayed task of raising the national Bureau of Education from a position inferior to that of the lifesaving service, the Bureau of Fish and Fisheries, or the meat-inspection service, to a position commensurate with the importance of education to us as a nation.

A people who express themselves as completely as we do in free political institutions, and whose whole life is experiencing such rapid changes and advances as our own, is increasingly dependent on education for guidance and progress. As a nation we have been slow to realize this. We have cared for higher or university education relatively well, and our secondary schools are in many places well provided for, but our elementary, supplementary, continuation, and vocational schools have been as yet but imperfectly developed. The recent German commission sent to this country to investigate our educational conditions mentioned this as one of our most vulnerable points.

The new period of advance which we now seem to be entering also bids fair to be very paternalistic, perhaps even socialistic, in the matter of education. The old principle, fought for so vigorously fifty or sixty years ago, that the wealth of the state must educate the children of the state, bids fair to be even further extended with a view to a greater equalization of both the burdens and the advantages of education. Poor and overburdened towns and districts will be supplied with sufficient means to enable them to provide a good school for their children, and the present great difference in tax rates, to provide practically the same educational advantages, will be in large part equalized by the state. There is, as yet, a small but a very significant tendency for the school to free itself from the financial control of the town board or city council and to erect itself as an independent and a coordinate branch of the town or city government, responsible only to the people for its work and its expense. There are many signs of an increasing centralization of management which will ultimately lead to greater efficiency. Many options which communities have today will in time be changed into obligations. The state oversight of private and parochial education is likely to increase slowly, especially along the lines of uniformity in statistics and records, sanitary inspection, common standards of work, and the enforcement of the attendance laws.

In particular, the attitude toward the control of the child is likely to change. Each year the child is coming to belong more and more to the state and less and less to the parent. In all that relates to proper care, kindness, education, and advantages, the child belongs to the parent; but when neglect, abuse, and the deprivation of the child of any natural right takes place, the child belongs to the state. The right to reasonably good treatment, proper care, an education, protection from vice, and protection from labor beyond his strength and years, the state will soon guarantee. The plea in defense that "the child is my child" will not be accepted much longer by society. Our future welfare is too thoroughly in the keeping of the child to permit of such a policy.

The movement for general education for all of the people has been essentially a democratic movement. Everywhere west of the Allegheny Mountains the girl has shared equally with the boy in all of the advantages provided. The masses, who have been the voting strength of the movement, have seen in it a chance for their children to rise, and educators and statesmen have seen in it the safety of the republic. School systems

with us are thoroughly democratic. An educational ladder for all who can afford it and have the mental capacity to use it extends from the kindergarten or primary school to and through the state university. Only in the states of the North Atlantic group, Maine alone excepted, has there been a failure to carry the system to its logical conclusion at the top.

The evils and shortcomings of democracy are many and call loudly for remedies and improvement. Whether we shall have remedies and improvement or not depends very largely on how the next generation is trained. The ideas taught in the school today become the actuating principles of democracy tomorrow. Because the school is so thoroughly a democratic institution and responds so quickly to democratic sentiment, the school has for long hesitated to touch, except in a very cautious manner, many of the evils and shortcomings of democracy. The greatest obstacle to intelligent educational and social progress is the lack of intelligence and grasp of democracy itself. It takes time and patience to educate and move the mass, yet in some way the school must touch these sores.

Our state governments are weak and inefficient, we say; the school must then teach, and teach in some effective manner, the principles of strong and effective government. Our city governments are corrupt, we hear; fundamental moral and economic principles must then be taught to the masses so that they may realize the importance of civic righteousness and understand as well who ultimately pays the bills for all mismanagement. Our people waste their money and their leisure in idle and profligate ways, we say; a knowledge of values and of how to utilize leisure time must then be taught. The list might be prolonged over pages, with similar conclusions.

Through all the complicated machinery of the school, some way must be found to awaken a social consciousness as opposed to class consciousness, to bring out the important social and civic lessons, to point out our social and civic needs, and to teach our young people how to live better and to make better use of their leisure time. Reading, writing, arithmetic, grammar, geography, and history, the staples of the elementary curriculum, are really of little value except as they are closely related with the needs and problems of our social, civic, and industrial life.

This new conception shifts the emphasis in education from methods to men, and this new conception has underlain many of the better courses of study issued for our schools during recent years. It also underlies much of the discussion of the present time. Teachers as a body, though, are not thoroughly conscious of such a purpose or need, and courses of study alone cannot produce results. If our schools are to become more effective social institutions, our teachers must become more effective social workers. What teachers need, as much as anything else, is a knowledge of democracy's needs and problems, and of conditions to be met. Our teaching force is composed largely of women, and women are seldom interested by nature in this point of view. Their training for generations has been along different lines. Those teachers who enter the work wholly by examination have little opportunity ever to acquire this point of view, and the examination door should be closed as soon as financial conditions will permit.

The time to impart ideals is during the training period, and an introduction to the social point of view and the social and industrial problems before us as a nation ought to be an essential part of the training of every normal school. A normal school which is essentially an apprentice school will inevitably turn out teachers with limited vision and little power of growth, while the call today for farsighted teachers of large adaptability is greater than ever before in our history.

The work of public education is destined in the near future to be one of the most important lines of work which our republic has to do. Its importance in a government such as ours can scarcely be overestimated. Each man with us is the captain of his own fate and the carver of his own destiny. It is within his power to do great good or to do great harm. To decide righteously and to act wisely he must know. Knowledge and training, if of the right type, can hardly be provided too extensively. The overeducated man is scarcely possible if an education adapted to his needs and station in life is given him.

The work of public education is with us, too, to a large degree, a piece of religious work. To engage in it is to enlist in the nation's service. Its call is for those who would dedicate themselves in a noble way. Those who would serve must be of the world, with red blood in their veins; they must know the world, its needs, and its problems; they must have largeness of vision and the courage to do and to dare; and they must train the youth with whom they come in contact for useful and efficient action.

This will never be a civilized country until we expend more money for books than we do for chewing gum.

ELBERT HUBBARD, *The Philistine*

43.

John D. Rockefeller: The Difficult Art of Giving

After 1885 John D. Rockefeller devoted himself to philanthropy. In the course of more than twenty years he had many opportunities to reflect upon the difficulties involved in giving away money. A moralist, Rockefeller was interested in seeing his money rehabilitate individuals and improve society. His Rockefeller Foundation, which distributed, and continues to distribute, millions of dollars a year, was organized in 1913 to develop systematic methods of philanthropy. The following selection is taken from a 1909 publication that discussed some of the problems of distributing large sums of money.

Source: *Random Reminiscences of Men and Events*, New York, 1909, pp. 139-160.

It is, no doubt, easy to write platitudes and generalities about the joys of giving and the duty that one owes to one's fellowmen, and to put together again all the familiar phrases that have served for generations whenever the subject has been taken up.

I can hardly hope to succeed in starting any new interest in this great subject when gifted writers have so often failed. Yet I confess I find much more interest in it at this time than in rambling on . . . about the affairs of business and trade. It is most difficult, however, to dwell upon a very practical and businesslike side of benefactions generally without seeming to ignore, or at least to fail to appreciate fully, the spirit of giving, which has its source in the heart, and which, of course, makes it all worthwhile.

In this country we have come to the period when we can well afford to ask the ablest men to devote more of their time, thought, and money to the public wellbeing. I am not so presumptuous as to attempt to define exactly what this betterment work should consist of. Every man will do that for himself, and his own conclusion will be final for himself. It is well, I think, that no narrow or preconceived plan should be set down as the best.

I am sure it is a mistake to assume that the possession of money in great abundance necessarily brings happiness. The very rich are just like all the rest of us; and if they get pleasure from the possession of money, it comes from their ability to do things which give satisfaction to someone besides themselves. . . .

THE BEST PHILANTHROPY

The best philanthropy, the help that does the most good and the least harm, the help that nourishes civilization at its very root, that most widely disseminates health, righteousness, and happiness, is not what is usually called charity. It is, in my judgment, the investment of effort or time or money, carefully considered with relation to the power of employing people at a remunerative wage, to expand and develop the resources at hand, and to give opportunity for progress and healthful labor where it did not exist before. No mere money giving is comparable to this in its lasting and beneficial results.

If, as I am accustomed to think, this statement is a correct one, how vast indeed is the philanthropic field! It may be urged that the daily vocation of life is one thing and the work of philanthropy quite another. I have no sympathy with this notion. The man who plans to do all his giving on Sunday is a poor prop for the institutions of the country.

The excuse for referring so often to the busy man of affairs is that his help is most needed. I know of men who have followed out this large plan of developing work, not as a temporary matter but as a permanent principle. These men have taken up doubtful enterprises and carried them through to success often at great risk and in the face of great skepticism, not as a matter only of personal profit but in the larger spirit of general uplift. . . .

THE GENEROSITY OF SERVICE

PROBABLY THE MOST GENEROUS people in the world are the very poor, who assume each other's burdens in the crises which come so often to the hard pressed. The mother in the tenement falls ill and the neighbor in the next room assumes her burdens. The father loses his work, and neighbors supply food to his children from their own scanty store. How often one hears of cases where the orphans are taken over and brought up by the poor friend whose benefaction means great additional hardship! This sort of genuine service makes the most princely gift from superabundance look insignificant indeed.

The Jews have had for centuries a precept that one-tenth of a man's possessions must be devoted to good works, but even this measure of giving is but a rough yardstick to go by. To give a tenth of one's income is well-nigh an impossibility to some, while to others it means a miserable pittance. If the spirit is there, the matter of proportion is soon lost sight of. It is only the spirit of giving that counts, and the very poor give without any self-consciousness. But I fear that I am dealing with generalities again.

The education of children in my early days may have been straightlaced, yet I have always been thankful that the custom was quite general to teach young people to give systematically of money that they themselves had earned. It is a good thing to lead children to realize early the importance of their obligations to others but, I confess, it is increasingly difficult; for what were luxuries then have become commonplaces now. It should be a greater pleasure and satisfaction to give money for a good cause than to earn it, and I have always indulged the hope that during my life I should be able to help establish efficiency in giving so that wealth may be of greater use to the present and future generations.

Perhaps just here lies the difference between the gifts of money and of service. The poor meet promptly the misfortunes which confront the home circle and household of the neighbor. The giver of money, if his contribution is to be valuable, must add service in the way of study, and he must help to attack and improve underlying conditions. Not being so pressed by the racking necessities, it is he that should be better able to attack the subject from a more scientific standpoint; but the final analysis is the same: his money is a feeble offering without the study behind it which will make its expenditure effective.

Great hospitals conducted by noble and unselfish men and women are doing wonderful work; but no less important are the achievements in research that reveal hitherto unknown facts about diseases and provide the remedies by which many of them can be relieved or even stamped out.

To help the sick and distressed appeals to

the kind-hearted always, but to help the investigator who is striving successfully to attack the causes which bring about sickness and distress does not so strongly attract the giver of money. The first appeals to the sentiments overpoweringly, but the second has the head to deal with. Yet I am sure we are making wonderful advances in this field of scientific giving. All over the world the need of dealing with the questions of philanthropy with something beyond the impulses of emotion is evident, and everywhere help is being given to those heroic men and women who are devoting themselves to the practical and essentially scientific tasks. It is a good and inspiring thing to recall occasionally the heroism, for example, of the men who risked and sacrificed their lives to discover the facts about yellow fever, a sacrifice for which untold generations will bless them; and this same spirit has animated the professions of medicine and surgery. . . .

THE FUNDAMENTAL THING IN ALL HELP

IF THE PEOPLE can be educated to help themselves, we strike at the root of many of the evils of the world. This is the fundamental thing, and it is worth saying even if it has been said so often that its truth is lost sight of in its constant repetition.

The only thing which is of lasting benefit to a man is that which he does for himself. Money which comes to him without effort on his part is seldom a benefit and often a curse. That is the principal objection to speculation — it is not because more lose than gain, though that is true — but it is because those who gain are apt to receive more injury from their success than they would have received from failure. And so with regard to money or other things which are given by one person to another. It is only in the exceptional case that the receiver is really benefited. But, if we can help

people to help themselves, then there is a permanent blessing conferred.

Men who are studying the problem of disease tell us that it is becoming more and more evident that the forces which conquer sickness are within the body itself, and that it is only when these are reduced below the normal that disease can get a foothold. The way to ward off disease, therefore, is to tone up the body generally; and, when disease has secured a foothold, the way to combat it is to help these natural resisting agencies which are in the body already. In the same way the failures which a man makes in his life are due almost always to some defect in his personality, some weakness of body, or mind, or character, will, or temperament. The only way to overcome these failings is to build up his personality from within, so that he, by virtue of what is within him, may overcome the weakness which was the cause of the failure. It is only those efforts the man himself puts forth that can really help him.

We all desire to see the widest possible distribution of the blessings of life. Many crude plans have been suggested, some of which utterly ignore the essential facts of human nature, and if carried out would perhaps drag our whole civilization down into hopeless misery. It is my belief that the principal cause for the economic differences between people is their difference in personality, and that it is only as we can assist in the wider distribution of those qualities which go to make up a strong personality that we can assist in the wider distribution of wealth. Under normal conditions the man who is strong in body, in mind, in character, and in will need never suffer want. But these qualities can never be developed in a man unless by his own efforts, and the most that any other can do for him is, as I have said, to help him to help himself.

We must always remember that there is not enough money for the work of human uplift and that there never can be. How vitally important it is, therefore, that the expenditure should go as far as possible and be used with the greatest intelligence!

I have been frank to say that I believe in the spirit of combination and cooperation when properly and fairly conducted in the world of commercial affairs on the principle that it helps to reduce waste; and waste is a dissipation of power. I sincerely hope and thoroughly believe that this same principle will eventually prevail in the art of giving as it does in business. It is not merely the tendency of the times developed by more exacting conditions in industry, but it should make its most effective appeal to the hearts of the people who are striving to do the most good to the largest number.

SOME UNDERLYING PRINCIPLES

AT THE RISK of making this chapter very dull, and I am told that this is a fault which inexperienced authors should avoid at all hazards, I may perhaps be pardoned if I set down here some of the fundamental principles which have been at the bottom of all my own plans. I have undertaken no work of any importance for many years which, in a general way, has not followed out these broad lines, and I believe no really constructive effort can be made in philanthropic work without such a well-defined and consecutive purpose.

My own conversion to the feeling that an organized plan was an absolute necessity came about in this way.

About the year 1890 I was still following the haphazard fashion of giving here and there as appeals presented themselves. I investigated as I could, and worked myself almost to a nervous breakdown in groping my way, without sufficient guide or chart, through this ever widening field of philanthropic endeavor. There was then forced upon me the necessity to organize and plan this department of our daily tasks on as distinct lines of progress as we did our business affairs; and I will try to describe the underlying principles we arrived at, and have since followed out, and hope still greatly to extend.

It may be beyond the pale of good taste to speak at all of such a personal subject — I am not unmindful of this — but I can make these observations with at least a little better grace because so much of the hard work and hard thinking are done by my family and associates, who devote their lives to it.

Every right-minded man has a philosophy of life, whether he knows it or not. Hidden away in his mind are certain governing principles, whether he formulates them in words or not, which govern his life. Surely his ideal ought to be to contribute all that he can, however little it may be, whether of money or service, to human progress.

Certainly one's ideal should be to use one's means, both in one's investments and in benefactions, for the advancement of civilization. But the question as to what civilization is and what are the great laws which govern its advance has been seriously studied. Our investments not less than gifts have been directed to such ends as we have thought would tend to produce these results. If you were to go into our office and ask our committee on benevolence or our committee on investment of what they consider civilization to consist, they would say that they have found in their study that the most convenient analysis of the elements which go to make up civilization runs about as follows:

1. Progress in the means of subsistence, that is to say, progress in abundance and variety of food supply, clothing, shelter, sanitation, public health, commerce, manufacture, the growth of the public wealth, etc.

2. Progress in government and law, that is to say, in the enactment of laws securing

justice and equity to every man, consistent with the largest individual liberty, and the due and orderly enforcement of the same upon all.

3. Progress in literature and language.

4. Progress in science and philosophy.

5. Progress in art and refinement.

6. Progress in morality and religion.

If you were to ask them, as indeed they are very often asked, which of these they regard as fundamental, they would reply that they would not attempt to answer; that the question is purely an academic one; that all these go hand in hand, but that historically the first of them — namely, progress in means of subsistence — had generally preceded progress in government, in literature, in knowledge, in refinement, and in religion. Though not itself of the highest importance, it is the foundation upon which the whole superstructure of civilization is built and without which it could not exist.

Accordingly, we have sought, so far as we could, to make investments in such a way as will tend to multiply, to cheapen, and to diffuse as universally as possible the comforts of life. We claim no credit for preferring these lines of investment. We make no sacrifices. These are the lines of largest and surest return. In this particular, namely, in cheapness, ease of acquirement, and universality of means of subsistence, our country easily surpasses that of any other in the world, though we are behind other countries, perhaps, in most of the others.

It may be asked: How is it consistent with the universal diffusion of these blessings that vast sums of money should be in single hands? The reply is, as I see it, that while men of wealth control great sums of money, they do not and cannot use them for themselves. They have, indeed, the legal title to large properties, and they do control the investment of them, but that is as far as their own relation to them extends or can

extend. The money is universally diffused in the sense that it is kept invested, and it passes into the pay envelope week by week.

Up to the present time no scheme has yet presented itself which seems to afford a better method of handling capital than that of individual ownership. We might put our money into the Treasury of the nation and of the various states, but we do not find any promise in the national or state legislatures, viewed from the experiences of the past, that the funds would be extended for the general weal more effectively than under the present methods, nor do we find in any of the schemes of socialism a promise that wealth would be more wisely administered for the general good. It is the duty of men of means to maintain the title to their property and to administer their funds until some man, or body of men, shall rise up capable of administering for the general good the capital of the country better than they can.

The next four elements of progress mentioned in the enumeration above, namely, progress in government and law, in language and literature, in science and philosophy, in art and refinement, we for ourselves have thought to be best promoted by means of the higher education. And accordingly we have had the great satisfaction of putting such sums as we could into various forms of education in our own and in foreign lands; and education not merely along the lines of disseminating more generally the known but quite as much, and perhaps even more, in promoting original investigation. An individual institution of learning can have only a narrow sphere. It can reach only a limited number of people. But every new fact discovered, every widening of the boundaries of human knowledge by research becomes universally known to all institutions of learning and becomes a benefaction at once to the whole race.

44.

Morris Hillquit: Socialism and Individualism in Industrial Life

Morris Hillquit, one of the leading theorists of the Socialist Party, also became the leader of the group of New Yorkers who controlled the party machinery. "Socialism," he once wrote, "is above all a philosophy of life and civilization," and in the early years of the century he was full of enthusiasm for an America that could assure mankind the decent life for which it yearned. In the following selection, taken from his Socialism in Theory and Practice, *Hillquit described what he felt to be the relationship of individualism to socialism. In dispassionate language, he traced the changes that industrialism had wrought in society and their effect on the average worker.*

Source: *Socialism in Theory and Practice,* New York, 1909, pp. 12-35.

WITH THE DEVELOPMENT of the simple tool into a variety of huge, steam-propelled machines specialized for the mass production of minute parts of commodities, the little workshop grew into the enormous modern factory in which hundreds and thousands of men are brought together from all parts of the country, organized into a complex hierarchy of labor; each one doing one small thing, each working into the hands of the other, all of them collectively producing one article which may have to go through numerous similar operations in other immense and complex factories before it turns into a commodity for direct consumption. The modern machine is a social tool, the modern factory is a social workshop, the modern workingman is a social servant, and the modern goods are social products.

Let us take the most simple articles of use: the coat we wear, the chair we sit on, the bed we sleep in, and ask ourselves: Who produced these articles? To answer that question we shall have to consider the unknown thousands who contributed to the work of their immediate design and manufacture, to the production and transportation of the material contained in them, to the work of constructing the wonderful machinery employed at the countless steps of the process, and to the work of operating the machinery of transportation, etc. In modern production the individual laborer is practically obliterated; what is before us is a worldwide community of socially organized labor of all gradations, from the highest and most skillful to the lowest and most common, working together collectively for the needs of our race.

And it is this collective labor of our times that sustains modern comforts and modern civilization. Were it possible for us to return to the regime of absolute individualism in production, to prepare our own food, make our own clothing, build our own dwellings, without taking advantage of the material prepared by others, without accepting the cooperation of our fellowmen, we should relapse into a state of savagery in less than a generation.

While the feature of individualism has been almost eliminated from the field of production by the last century, it has, during that period, shown much greater vitality in the sphere of management of our industries.

The management of our industries by individual capitalists for their own private benefit and in rivalry with each other — *industrial competition* — has for decades been the favorite topic of controversy between the adherents of the individualist philosophy and the partisans of the socialist school of political economy. To the sturdy individualist the competitive system of industry is the source of all blessings of civilization; he never tires of extolling the merits of that system as an incentive to industrial enterprise, inventiveness, and efficiency, as a character builder and lever of all social and individual progress. The socialist, on the other hand, points a warning finger to the evils of competition: the anarchy in management and waste in production which the system entails, and the tremendous social, economic, and ethical losses which it imposes on the producers, the consumers, and the community at large.

But while the discussion on the merits and demerits of competition is assuming ever more intense forms, the mute forces of economic evolution, unconcerned by theories and abstractions, are rapidly working toward a practical solution of the problem. The individual capitalist steadily yields his place in the industrial world to the corporation and the trust; and the latter combine and consolidate the independent managements of numerous individual concerns under one corporate direction and reorganize the management of industries, frequently on a national and even international scale. The irresistible growth of trusts and monopolies is the central fact of all recent economic development, and it sounds the death knell of individual competition.

The only sphere of our industrial life in which the principle of individualism has survived in all its pristine vigor is that of the appropriation or distribution of the products.

Although the instruments of production have become social in their character and use and indispensable to the entire working community, they are still owned and controlled by the individual capitalists. Although the production of goods is a collective process, and its management and direction are fast becoming so, it is still conducted principally for the benefit of the individual captains of industry. Although all useful members of the community collectively contribute to the so-called national wealth, only a comparatively small number of individuals share in it. In short, although the production of wealth is practically socialistic, its distribution is entirely individualistic.

And this contradiction between the modern methods of production and distribution is the only real issue between the individualist and the socialist in the domain of economic discussion.

The beneficiaries of the present system of wealth distribution have a very obvious material interest in maintaining it, and there never was a ruling class that did not have the abundant support of scientific and ethical theories to justify it in the continued enjoyment of its privileges. In the present case this function is being performed by the school of "individualistic" philosophers and moralizers.

The socialists, on the other hand, consider the present system of individual appropriation of social wealth as an anachronism, a survival of a past economic order, and a disturbing factor in the process of social, economic, and ethical progress. The main object of socialism is to adjust the principles of wealth distribution to those of production — to make the one as social and general in function and effect as the other already is.

45.

Herbert Croly: The Land of Promise

Herbert Croly, who founded the New Republic in 1914, was one of the leading Progressive spokesmen for government regulation of monopolies, rather than their destruction. His book The Promise of American Life (1909), a portion of which is reprinted here, influenced Theodore Roosevelt in formulating his New Nationalism, a phrase that was adopted from Croly's writings. The work also reflected Croly's deep and abiding faith in America's future.

Source: *The Promise of American Life,* New York, 1909, Chs. 1, 13.

THE FAITH OF AMERICANS in their own country is religious, if not in its intensity, at any rate in its almost absolute and universal authority. It pervades the air we breathe. As children we hear it asserted or implied in the conversation of our elders. Every new stage of our educational training provides some additional testimony on its behalf. Newspapers and novelists, orators and playwrights, even if they are little else, are at least loyal preachers of the truth. The skeptic is not controverted; he is overlooked. It constitutes the kind of faith which is the implication rather than the object of thought, and consciously or unconsciously it enters largely into our personal lives as a formative influence. We may distrust and dislike much that is done in the name of our country by our fellow countrymen; but our country itself, its democratic system, and its prosperous future are above suspicion. . . .

The higher American patriotism, on the other hand, combines loyalty to historical tradition and precedent with the imaginative projection of an ideal national promise. The land of democracy has always appealed to its more enthusiastic children chiefly as a land of wonderful and more than national possibilities. "Neither race nor tradition," says Professor Hugo Münsterberg in his volume on *The Americans,* "nor the actual past, binds the American to his countrymen, but rather the future which together they are building."

This vision of a better future is not, perhaps, as unclouded for the present generation of Americans as it was for certain former generations; but in spite of a more friendly acquaintance with all sorts of obstacles and pitfalls, our country is still figured in the imagination of its citizens as the land of promise. They still believe that somehow and sometime something better will happen to good Americans than has happened to men in any other country; and this belief, vague, innocent, and uninformed though it be, is the expression of an essential constituent in our national ideal.

The past should mean less to a European than it does to an American, and the future should mean more. To be sure, American life cannot with impunity be wrenched violently from its moorings any more than the life of a European country can; but our American past compared to that of any European country has a character all its own. Its peculiarity consists, not merely in its brevity but in the fact that from the beginning it has been informed by an idea. From the beginning Americans have been anticipating and projecting a better future. From the beginning the land of democracy has been figured as the land of promise. Thus the American's loyalty to the national tradition rather affirms than denies the imaginative projection of a better future.

An America which was not the land of promise, which was not informed by a prophetic outlook and a more or less constructive ideal, would not be the America bequeathed to us by our forefathers. In cherishing the promise of a better national future, the American is fulfilling rather than imperiling the substance of the national tradition. . . .

The better future, whatever else it may bring, must bring at any rate a continuation of the good things of the past. The drama of its fulfillment must find an appropriate setting in the familiar American social and economic scenery. No matter how remote the end may be, no matter what unfamiliar sacrifices may eventually be required on its behalf, the substance of the existing achievement must constitute a veritable beginning, because on no other condition can the attribution of a peculiar promise to American life find a specific warrant. On no other condition would our national promise constitute more than an admirable but irrelevant moral and social aspiration.

The moral and social aspiration proper to American life is, of course, the aspiration vaguely described by the word "democratic"; and the actual achievement of the American nation points toward an adequate and fruitful definition of the democratic ideal. Americans are usually satisfied by a most inadequate verbal description of democracy, but their national achievement implies one which is much more comprehensive and formative. In order to be true to their past, the increasing comfort and economic independence of an ever increasing proportion of the population must be secured, and it must be secured by a combination of individual effort and proper political organization.

Above all, however, this economic and political system must be made to secure results of moral and social value. It is the seeking of such results which converts democracy from a political system into a constructive social ideal; and the more the ideal significance of the American national promise is asserted and emphasized, the greater will become the importance of securing these moral and social benefits.

The fault in the vision of our national future possessed by the ordinary American does not consist in the expectation of some continuity of achievement. It consists rather in the expectation that the familiar benefits will continue to accumulate automatically. In his mind the ideal promise is identified with the processes and conditions which hitherto have very much simplified its fulfillment, and he fails sufficiently to realize that the conditions and processes are one thing and the ideal promise quite another. Moreover, these underlying social and economic conditions are themselves changing, in such wise that hereafter the ideal promise, instead of being automatically fulfilled, may well be automatically stifled.

For two generations and more the American people were, from the economic point of view, most happily situated. They were able, in a sense, to slide downhill into the valley of fulfillment. Economic conditions were such that, given a fair start, they could scarcely avoid reaching a desirable goal. But such is no longer the case. Economic conditions have been profoundly modified, and American political and social problems have been modified with them. The promise of American life must depend less than it did upon the virgin wilderness and the Atlantic Ocean, for the virgin wilderness had disappeared and the Atlantic Ocean has become merely a big channel.

The same results can no longer be achieved by the same easy methods. Ugly obstacles have jumped into view, and ugly obstacles are peculiarly dangerous to a person who is sliding downhill. The man who is clambering uphill is in a much better position to evade or overcome them. Americans will possess a safer as well as a worthier vision of their national promise as soon as they give it a house on a hilltop rather than in a valley. . . .

The conscious recognition of grave national abuses casts a deep shadow across the traditional American patriotic vision. The sincere and candid reformer can no longer consider the national promise as destined to automatic fulfillment. The reformers themselves are, no doubt, far from believing that whatever peril there is cannot be successfully averted. They make a point of being as patriotically prophetic as the most "old-fashioned democrat." They proclaim even more loudly their conviction of an indubitable and a beneficent national future. But they do not and cannot believe that this future will take care of itself.

As reformers they are bound to assert that the national body requires for the time being a good deal of medical attendance, and many of them anticipate that even after the doctors have discontinued their daily visits the patient will still need the supervision of a sanitary specialist. He must be persuaded to behave so that he will not easily fall ill again, and so that his health will be permanently improved. Consequently, just insofar as reformers are reformers, they are obliged to abandon the traditional American patriotic fatalism. The national promise has been transformed into a closer equivalent of a national purpose, the fulfillment of which is a matter of conscious work.

The transformation of the old sense of a glorious national destiny into the sense of a serious national purpose will inevitably tend to make the popular realization of the promise of American life both more explicit and more serious. As long as Americans be-

lieved they were able to fulfill a noble national promise merely by virtue of maintaining intact a set of political institutions and by the vigorous individual pursuit of private ends, their allegiance to their national fulfillment remained more a matter of words than of deeds; but now that they are being aroused from their patriotic slumber, the effect is inevitably to disentangle the national idea and to give it more dignity.

The redemption of the national promise has become a cause for which the good American must fight, and the cause for which a man fights is a cause which he more than ever values. The American idea is no longer to be propagated merely by multiplying the children of the West and by granting ignorant aliens permission to vote. Like all sacred causes, it must be propagated by the word and by that right arm of the word, which is the sword.

The more enlightened reformers are conscious of the additional dignity and value which the popularity of reform has bestowed upon the American idea, but they still fail to realize the deeper implications of their own program. In abandoning the older conception of an automatic fulfillment of our national destiny, they have abandoned more of the traditional American point of view than they are aware.

The traditional American optimistic fatalism was not of accidental origin, and it cannot be abandoned without involving in its fall some other important ingredients in the accepted American tradition. Not only was it dependent on economic conditions which prevailed until comparatively recent times, but it has been associated with certain erroneous but highly cherished political theories. It has been wrought into the fabric of our popular economic and political ideas to such an extent that its overthrow necessitates a partial revision of some of the most important articles in the traditional American creed.

The extent and the character of this revision may be inferred from a brief consideration of the effect upon the substance of our national promise of an alteration in its proposed method of fulfillment. The substance of our national promise has consisted, as we have seen, of an improving popular economic condition, guaranteed by democratic political institutions, and resulting in moral and social amelioration. These manifold benefits were to be obtained merely by liberating the enlightened self-interest of the American people. The beneficent result followed inevitably from the action of wholly selfish motives — provided, of course, the democratic political system of equal rights was maintained in its integrity. The fulfillment of the American promise was considered inevitable because it was based upon a combination of self-interest and the natural goodness of human nature.

On the other hand, if the fulfillment of our national promise can no longer be considered inevitable, if it must be considered as equivalent to a conscious national purpose instead of an inexorable national destiny, the implication necessarily is that the trust reposed in individual self-interest has been in some measure betrayed. No preestablished harmony can then exist between the free and abundant satisfaction of private needs and the accomplishment of a morally and socially desirable result.

The promise of American life is to be fulfilled not merely by a maximum amount of economic freedom but by a certain measure of discipline; not merely by the abundant satisfaction of individual desires but by a large measure of individual subordination and self-denial. And this necessity of subordinating the satisfaction of individual desires to the fulfillment of a national purpose is attached particularly to the absorbing occupation of the American people — the occupation, viz.: of accumulating wealth. The automatic fulfillment of the American national promise is to be abandoned, if at all, precisely because the traditional American confidence in individual freedom has resulted in a morally and socially undesirable distribution of wealth.

In making the concluding statement of the last paragraph I am venturing, of course, upon very debatable ground. Neither can I attempt in this immediate connection to offer any justification for the statement which might or should be sufficient to satisfy a stubborn skeptic. I must be content for the present with the bare assertion that the prevailing abuses and sins, which have made reform necessary, are all of them associated with the prodigious concentration of wealth and of the power exercised by wealth in the hands of a few men. I am far from believing that this concentration of economic power is wholly an undesirable thing, and I am also far from believing that the men in whose hands this power is concentrated deserve, on the whole, any exceptional moral reprobation for the manner in which it has been used. In certain respects they have served their country well, and in almost every respect their moral or immoral standards are those of the great majority of their fellow countrymen.

But it is none the less true that the political corruption, the unwise economic organization, and the legal support afforded to certain economic privileges are all under existing conditions due to the malevolent social influence of individual and incorporated American wealth; and it is equally true that these abuses and the excessive "money power" with which they are associated have originated in the peculiar freedom which the American tradition and organization have granted to the individual. Up to a certain point that freedom has been and still is beneficial. Beyond that point it is not merely harmful; it is by way of being fatal.

Efficient regulation there must be; and it must be regulation which will strike, not at the symptoms of the evil but at its roots. The existing concentration of wealth and financial power in the hands of a few irresponsible men is the inevitable outcome of the chaotic individualism of our political and economic organization, while at the same time it is inimical to democracy because it tends to erect political abuses and social inequalities into a system. The inference which follows may be disagreeable but it is not to be escaped. In becoming responsible for the subordination of the individual to the demand of a dominant and constructive national purpose, the American state will in effect be making itself responsible for a morally and socially desirable distribution of wealth.

The consequences, then, of converting our American national destiny into a national purpose are beginning to be revolutionary. When the promise of American life is conceived as a national ideal whose fulfillment is a matter of artful and laborious work, the effect thereof is substantially to identify the national purpose with the social problem. What the American people of the present and the future have really been promised by our patriotic prophecies is an attempt to solve that problem. They have been promised on American soil comfort, prosperity, and the opportunity for self-improvement; and the lesson of the existing crisis is that such a promise can never be redeemed by an indiscriminate individual scramble for wealth.

The individual competition, even when it starts under fair conditions and rules, results, not only, as it should, in the triumph of the strongest but in the attempt to perpetuate the victory; and it is this attempt which must be recognized and forestalled in the interest of the American national purpose. The way to realize a purpose is not to leave it to chance but to keep it loyally in mind and adopt means proper to the importance and the difficulty of the task. No voluntary association of individuals, resourceful and disinterested though they be, is competent to assume the responsibility. The problem belongs to the American na-

tional democracy, and its solution must be attempted chiefly by means of official national action.

Neither can its attempted solution be escaped. When they are confronted by the individual sacrifices which the fulfillment of their national promise demands, American political leaders will find many excuses for ignoring the responsibility thereby implied; but the difficulty of such an attempted evasion will consist in the reenforcement of the historical tradition by a logical and a practical necessity. The American problem is the social problem partly because the social problem is the democratic problem. American political and social leaders will find that in a democracy the problem cannot be evaded.

The American people have no irremediable political grievances. No good American denies the desirability of popular sovereignty and of a government which should somehow represent the popular will. While our national institutions may not be a perfect embodiment of these doctrines a decisive and a resolute popular majority has the power to alter American institutions and give them a more immediately representative character. Existing political evils and abuses are serious enough; but inasmuch as they have come into being, not against the will but with the connivance of the American people, the latter are responsible for their persistence. In the long run, consequently, the ordinary American will have nothing irremediable to complain about except economic and social inequalities.

In Europe such will not be the case. The several European peoples have, and will continue to have, political grievances because such grievances are the inevitable consequence of their national history and their international situation; and as long as these grievances remain, the more difficult social problem will be subordinated to an agitation for political emancipation. But the American people, having achieved democratic institutions, have nothing to do but to turn them to good account. Insofar as the social problem is a real problem and the economic grievance a real grievance, they are bound under the American political system to come eventually to the surface and to demand express and intelligent consideration. A democratic ideal makes the social problem inevitable and its attempted solution indispensable. . . .

Democracy must stand or fall on a platform of possible human perfectibility. If human nature cannot be improved by institutions, democracy is at best a more than usually safe form of political organization; and the only interesting inquiry about its future would be: How long will it continue to work? But if it is to work better as well as merely longer, it must have some leavening effect on human nature; and the sincere democrat is obliged to assume the power of the leaven. For him the practical questions are: How can the improvement best be brought about? and How much may it amount to? . . .

The real vehicle of improvement is education. It is by education that the American is trained for such democracy as he possesses; and it is by better education that he proposes to better his democracy. Men are uplifted by education much more surely than they are by any tinkering with laws and institutions, because the work of education leavens the actual social substance. It helps to give the individual himself those qualities without which no institutions, however excellent, are of any use, and with which even bad institutions and laws can be made vehicles of grace.

The American faith in education has been characterized as a superstition; and superstitious in some respects it unquestionably is. But its superstitious tendency is not exhibited so much in respect to the ordinary process of primary, secondary, and higher education. Not even an American can overemphasize the importance of proper teaching

during youth; and the only wonder is that the money so freely lavished on it does not produce better results.

Americans are superstitious in respect to education, rather because of the social "uplift" which they expect to achieve by socalled educational means. The credulity of the socialist in expecting to alter human nature by merely institutional and legal changes is at least equaled by the credulity of the good American in proposing to evangelize the individual by the reading of books and by the expenditure of money and words. Back of it all is the underlying assumption that the American nation by taking thought can add a cubit to its stature — an absolute confidence in the power of the idea to create its own object and in the efficacy of good intentions.

Do we lack culture? We will "make it hum" by founding a new university in Chicago. Is American art neglected and impoverished? We will enrich it by organizing art departments in our colleges and popularize it by lectures with lantern slides and associations for the study of its history. Is New York City ugly? Perhaps, but if we could only get the authorities to appropriate a few hundred millions for its beautification, we could make it look like a combination of Athens, Florence, and Paris. Is it desirable for the American citizen to be something of a hero? I will encourage heroes by establishing a fund whereby they shall be rewarded in cash.

War is hell, is it? I will work for the abolition of hell by calling a convention and passing a resolution denouncing its iniquities. I will build at The Hague a Palace of Peace which shall be a standing rebuke to the war lords of Europe. Here, in America, some of us have more money than we need and more goodwill. We will spend the money in order to establish the reign of the good, the beautiful, and the true.

This faith in a combination of good intentions, organization, words, and money is not confined to women's clubs or to societies of amiable enthusiasts. In the state of mind which it expresses can be detected the powerful influence which American women exert over American men; but its guiding faith and illusion are shared by the most hard-headed and practical of Americans. The very men who have made their personal successes by a rigorous application of the rule that business is business — the very men who in their own careers have exhibited a shrewd and vivid sense of the realities of politics and trade — it is these men who have most faith in the practical, moral, and social power of the subsidized word. The most real thing which they carry over from the region of business into the region of moral and intellectual ideals is apparently their bank accounts. The fruits of their hard work and their business ability are to be applied to the purpose of "uplifting" their fellow countrymen. A certain number of figures written on a check and signed by a familiar name, what may it not accomplish? . . .

The tradition of seeking to cross the gulf between American practice and the American ideal by means of education or the subsidized word is not to be dismissed with a sneer. The gulf cannot be crossed without the assistance of some sort of educational discipline; and that discipline depends partly on a new exercise of the "money power" now safely reposing in the strongboxes of professional millionaires. There need be no fundamental objection taken to the national faith in the power of good intentions and redistributed wealth. That faith is the immediate and necessary issue of the logic of our national moral situation. It should be, as it is, innocent and absolute; and if it does not remain innocent and absolute, the promise of American life can scarcely be fulfilled.

A faith may, however, be innocent and absolute without being inexperienced and credulous. The American faith in education is by way of being credulous and superstitious, not because it seeks individual and social amelioration by what may be called an educational process but because the proposed means of education are too conscious, too direct, and too superficial. Let it be admitted that in any one decade the amount which can be accomplished toward individual and social amelioration by means of economic and political reorganization is comparatively small; but it is certainly as large as that which can be accomplished by subsidizing individual good intentions. Heroism is not to be encouraged by cash prizes any more than is genius; and a man's friends should not be obliged to prove that he is a hero in order that he may reap every appropriate reward.

A hero officially conscious of his heroism is a mutilated hero.

In the same way art cannot become a power in a community unless many of its members are possessed of a native and innocent love of beautiful things; and the extent to which such a possession can be acquired by any one or two generations of traditionally inartistic people is extremely small. Its acquisition depends not so much upon direct conscious effort as upon the growing ability to discriminate between what is good and what is bad in their own native art. It is a matter of the training and appreciation of American artists rather than the cultivation of art. Illustrations to the same effect might be multiplied.

The popular interest in the higher education has not served to make Americans attach much importance to the advice of the highly educated man. He is less of a practical power in the United States than he is in any European country; and this fact is in itself a sufficient commentary on the reality of the American faith in education. The fact is, of course, that the American tendency to disbelieve in the fulfillment of their national promise by means of politically, economically, and socially reconstructive work has forced them into the alternative of attaching excessive importance to subsidized good intentions. They want to be "uplifted" and they want to "uplift" other people; but they will not use their social and political institutions for the purpose, because those institutions are assumed to be essentially satisfactory. The "uplifting" must be a matter of individual or of unofficial associated effort; and the only available means are words and subsidies.

There is, however, a sense in which it is really true that the American national promise can be fulfilled only by education; and this aspect of our desirable national education can, perhaps, best be understood by seeking its analogue in the training of the individual. An individual's education consists primarily in the discipline which he undergoes to fit him both for fruitful association with his fellows and for his own special work. Important as both the liberal and the technical aspect of this preliminary training is, it constitutes merely the beginning of a man's education. Its object is or should be to prepare him both in his will and in his intelligence to make a thoroughly illuminating use of his experience in life. . . .

Back of the problem of educating the individual lies the problem of collective education. On the one hand, if the nation is rendered incapable of understanding its own experience by the habit of dealing insincerely with its national purpose, the individual, just insofar as he himself has become highly educated, tends to be divided from his country and his fellow countrymen. On the other hand, just insofar as a people is sincerely seeking the fulfillment of its national promise, individuals of all kinds will find their most edifying individual opportunities in serving their country. In aiding the accomplishment of the collective purpose by means of increasingly constructive experiments, they will be increasing the scope and power of their own individual action.

The opportunities, which during the past few years the reformers have enjoyed to make their personal lives more interesting, would be nothing compared to the opportunities for all sorts of stirring and responsible work which would be demanded of individuals under the proposed plan of political and economic reorganization. The American nation would be more disinterestedly and sincerely fulfilling its collective purpose, partly because its more distinguished individuals had been called upon to place at the service of their country a higher degree of energy, ability, and unselfish devotion. If a nation, that is, is recreant to its deeper purpose, individuals so far as they are well educated are educated away from the prevailing national habits and traditions; whereas when a nation is sincerely attempting to meet its collective responsibility, the better individuals are inevitably educated into active participation in the collective task.

The reader may now be prepared to understand why the American faith in education has the appearance of being credulous and superstitious. The good average American usually wishes to accomplish exclusively by individual education a result which must be partly accomplished by national education. The nation, like the individual, must go to school; and the national school is not a lecture hall or a library. Its schooling consists chiefly in experimental collective action aimed at the realization of the collective purpose. If the action is not aimed at the collective purpose, a nation will learn little even from its successes. If its action is aimed at the collective purpose, it may learn much even from its mistakes.

No process of merely individual education can accomplish the work of collective education because the nation is so much more than a group of individuals. Individuals can be "uplifted" without "uplifting" the nation, because the nation has an individuality of its own which cannot be increased without the consciousness of collective responsibilities and the collective official attempt to redeem them. The processes of national and individual education should, of course, parallel and supplement each other. The individual can do much to aid national education by the single-minded and intelligent realization of his own specific purposes; but all individual successes will have little more than an individual interest unless they frequently contribute to the work of national construction. The nation can do much to aid individual education; but the best aid within its power is to offer to the individual a really formative and inspiring opportunity for public service. The whole round of superficial educational machinery — books, subsidies, resolutions, lectures, congresses — may be of the highest value, provided they are used to digest and popularize the results of a genuine individual and national educational experience; but when they are used, as so often at present, merely as a substitute for well-purposed individual and national action, they are precisely equivalent to an attempt to fly in a vacuum.

That the direct practical value of a reform movement may be equaled or surpassed by its indirect educational value is a sufficiently familiar idea — an idea admirably expressed ten years ago by Mr. John Jay Chapman in the chapter on "Education" in his *Causes and Consequences*. But the idea in its familiar form is vitiated, because the educational effect of reform is usually conceived as exclusively individual. Its effect *must,* indeed, be considered wholly as an individual matter just so long as reform is interpreted merely as a process of purification. From that point of view the collective purpose has already been fulfilled as far as it can be fulfilled by collective organization, and the *only* remaining method of social amelioration is that of the self-improvement of its constituent members. As President Nicholas Murray Butler of Columbia says, in his *True and False Democracy:*

We must not lose sight of the fact that the corporate or collective responsibility which it [socialism] would substitute for individual initiative is only such corporate or collective responsibility as a group of these very same individuals could exercise. Therefore, socialism is primarily an attempt to overcome man's individual imperfections by adding them together in the hope that they will cancel each other.

But what is all organization but an attempt, not to overcome man's individual imperfections by adding them together, so much as to make use of many men's varying individual abilities by giving each a sufficient sphere of exercise?

While all men are imperfect, they are not all imperfect to the same extent. Some have more courage, more ability, more insight, and more training than others; and an efficient organization can accomplish more than can a mere collection of individuals precisely because it may represent a standard of performance far above that of the average individual. Its merit is simply that of putting the collective power of the group at the service of its ablest members; and the ablest members of the group will never attain to an individual responsibility commensurate with their powers until they are enabled to work efficiently toward the redemption of the collective responsibility.

The nation gives individuality an increased scope and meaning by offering individuals a chance for effective service such as they could never attain under a system of collective irresponsibility. Thus under a system of collective responsibility the process of social improvement is absolutely identified with that of individual improvement. The antithesis is not between nationalism and individualism but between an individualism which is indiscriminate and an individualism which is selective. . . .

There is only one way in which popular standards and preferences can be improved. The men whose standards are higher must learn to express their better message in a popularly interesting manner. The people will never be converted to the appreciation of excellent special performances by argumentation, reproaches, lectures, associations, or persuasion. They will rally to the good thing only because the good thing has been made to look good to them; and so far as individual Americans are not capable of making their good things look good to a sufficient number of their fellow countrymen, they will on the whole deserve any neglect from which they may suffer. They themselves constitute the only efficient source of really formative education. Insofar as a public is lacking, a public must be created. They must mold their followers after their own likeness — as all aspirants after the higher individual eminence have always been obliged to do. . . .

It tends . . . to be socially as well as individually formative. The peculiarly competent individual is obliged to accept the responsibilities of leadership with its privileges and fruits. There is no escape from the circle by which he finds himself surrounded. He cannot obtain the opportunities, the authority, and the independence which he needs for his own individual fulfillment unless he builds up a following; and he cannot build up a secure personal following without making his peculiar performances appeal to some general human interest. The larger and more general the interest he can arouse, the more secure and the more remunerative his personal independence becomes. It by no means necessarily follows that he will increase his following by increasing the excellence of his work, or that he will not frequently find it difficult to keep his following without allowing his work to deteriorate. No formula reconciling the individual and the popular interest can be devised which will work automatically. The reconciliation must always remain a matter of victorious individual or national contrivance.

But it is nonetheless true that the chance of fruitful reconciliation always exists, and in a democracy it should exist under peculiarly wholesome conditions. The essential nature of a democracy compels it to insist that individual power of all kinds, political, economic, or intellectual shall not be perversely and irresponsibly exercised. The individual democrat is obliged no less to insist in his own interest that the responsible exercise of power shall not be considered equivalent to individual mediocrity and dependence. These two demands will often conflict; but the vitality of a democracy hangs upon its ability to keep both of them vigorous and assertive. Just insofar as individual democrats find ways of asserting their independence in the very act of redeeming their responsibility, the social body of which they form a part is marching toward the goal of human betterment.

It cannot be claimed, however, that the foregoing account of the relation between the individual and a nationalized democracy is even yet entirely satisfactory. No relation can be satisfactory which implies such a vast amount of individual suffering and defeat and such a huge waste of social and individual effort. The relation is only as satisfactory as it can be made under the circumstances. The individual cannot be immediately transformed by individual purpose and action into a consummate social type, any more than society can be immediately transformed by purposive national action into a consummate residence for the individual. In both cases amelioration is a matter of intelligent experimental contrivance based upon the nature of immediate conditions and equipped with every available resource and weapon.

In both cases these experiments must be indefinitely continued, their lessons candidly learned, and the succeeding experiments based upon past failures and achievements. Throughout the whole task of experimental educational advance the different processes of individual and social amelioration will be partly opposed, partly supplementary, and partly parallel; but insofar as any genuine advance is made, the opposition should be less costly and cooperation, if not easier, at least more remunerative.

The peculiar kind of individual self-assertion . . . has been adapted, not to perfect but to actual moral, social, and intellectual conditions. For the present Americans must cultivate competent individual independence somewhat unscrupulously, because their peculiar democratic tradition has hitherto discouraged and undervalued a genuinely individualistic practice and ideal. In order to restore the balance, the individual must emancipate himself at a considerable sacrifice and by somewhat forcible means; and to a certain extent he must continue those sacrifices throughout the whole of his career. He must proclaim and, if able, he must assert his own leadership, but he must be always somewhat on his guard against his followers. He must always keep in mind that the very leadership which is the fruit of his mastery and the condition of his independence is also, considering the nature and disposition of his average follower, a dangerous temptation; and while he must not for that reason scorn popular success, he must always conscientiously reckon its actual cost. And just because a leader cannot wholly trust himself to his following, so the followers must always keep a sharp lookout lest their leaders be leading them astray. For the kind of leadership which we have postulated above is by its very definition and nature liable to become perverse and distracting.

But just insofar as the work of social and individual amelioration advances, the condition will be gradually created necessary to completer mutual confidence between the few exceptional leaders and the many "plain people." At present the burden of establishing any genuine means of communication rests very heavily upon the exceptionally able individual. But after a number of exceptionally able individuals have imposed their own purposes and standards and created a following, they will have made the task of their successors easier.

Higher technical standards and more adequate forms of expression will have become better established. The "public" will have learned to expect and to appreciate more simple and appropriate architectural forms, more sincere and better formed translations of life in books and on the stage, and more independent and better equipped political leadership. The "public," that is, instead of being as much satisfied as it is at present with cheap forms and standards, will be prepared to assume part of the expense of establishing better forms and methods of social intercourse.

In this way a future generation of leaders may be enabled to conquer a following with a smaller individual expenditure of painful sacrifices and wasted effort. They can take for granted a generally higher technical and formal tradition, and they themselves will be freed from an overconscious preoccupation with the methods and the mechanism of their work. Their attention will naturally be more than ever concentrated on the proper discrimination of their subject matter; and just insofar as they are competent to create an impression or a following, that impression should be more profound and the following more loyal and more worthy of loyalty.

Above all, a substantial improvement in the purposes and standards of individual self-expression should create a more bracing intellectual atmosphere. Better standards will serve not only as guides but as weapons. Insofar as they are embodied in competent performances, they are bound also to be applied in the critical condemnation of inferior work; and the critic himself will assume a much more important practical job than he now has. Criticism is a comparatively neglected art among Americans because a sufficient number of people do not care whether and when the current practices are really good or bad.

The practice of better standards and their appreciation will give the critic both a more substantial material for his work and a larger public. It will be his duty to make the American public conscious of the extent of the individual successes or failures and the reasons therefor; and in case his practice improves with that of the other arts, he should become a more important performer, not only because of his better opportunities and public but because of his increase of individual prowess. He should not only be better equipped for the performance of his work and the creation of a public following but he should have a more definite and resolute conviction of the importance of his own job.

It is the business of the competent individual as a type to force society to recognize the meaning and the power of his own special purposes. It is the special business of the critic to make an ever larger portion of the public conscious of these expressions of individual purpose, of their relations one to another, of their limitations, and of their promises. He not only popularizes and explains for the benefit of a larger public the substance and significance of admirable special performance but he should in a sense become the standard-bearer of the whole movement.

The function of the critic hereafter will consist in part of carrying on an incessant and relentless warfare on the prevailing American intellectual insincerity. He can make little headway unless he is sustained by a large volume of less expressly controversial, individual, intellectual self-expression; but, on the other hand, there are many serious obstructions to any advancing intellectual movement, which he should and must overthrow. In so doing he has every reason to be more scrupulous and aggressive even than his brethren-in-arms. He must stab away at the gelatinous mass of popular indifference, sentimentality, and complacency, even though he seems quite unable to penetrate to the quick and draw blood.

For the time, the possibility of immediate constructive achievement in his own special field is comparatively small, and he is the less responsible for the production of any substantial effect, or the building up of any following except a handful of free lances like himself. He need only assure himself of his own competence with his own peculiar tools, his own good-humored sincerity, and his disinterestedness in the pursuit of his legitimate purposes in order to feel fully justified in pushing his strokes home.

In all serious warfare, people have to be really wounded for some good purpose; and in this particular fight there may be some chance that not only a good cause but the very victim of the blow may possibly be benefited by its delivery. The stabbing of a mass of public opinion into some consciousness of its active torpor, particularly when many particles of the mass are actively torpid because of admirable patriotic intentions — that is a job which needs sharp weapons, intense personal devotion, and a positive indifference to consequences.

Yet if the American national promise is ever to be fulfilled, a more congenial and a more interesting task will also await the critic — meaning by the word "critic" the voice of the specific intellectual interest, the lover of wisdom, the seeker of the truth.

Every important human enterprise has its meaning, even though the conduct of the affair demands more than anything else a hard and inextinguishable faith. Such a faith will imply a creed; and its realizations will go astray unless the faithful are made conscious of the meaning of their performances or failures. The most essential and edifying business of the critic will always consist in building up "a pile of better thoughts," based for the most part upon the truth resident in the lives of their predecessors and contemporaries, but not without its outlook toward an immediate and even remote future. There can be nothing final about the creed unless there be something final about the action and purposes of which it is the expression. It must be constantly modified in order to define new experiences and renewed in order to meet unforeseen emergencies. But it should grow, just insofar as the enterprise itself makes new conquests and unfolds new aspects of truth.

Democracy is an enterprise of this kind. It may prove to be the most important moral and social enterprise as yet undertaken by mankind; but it is still a very young enterprise, whose meaning and promise is by no means clearly understood. It is continually meeting unforeseen emergencies and gathering an increasing experience. The fundamental duty of a critic in a democracy is to see that the results of these experiences are not misinterpreted and that the best interpretation is embodied in popular doctrinal form. The critic consequently is not so much the guide as the lantern which illuminates the path. He may not pretend to know the only way or all the ways; but he should know as much as can be known about the traveled road.

Men endowed with high moral gifts and capable of exceptional moral achievements have also their special part to play in the building of an enduring democratic structure. In the account which has been given of the means and conditions of democratic fulfillment, the importance of this part has been underestimated; but the underestimate has been deliberate. It is very easy and in a sense perfectly true to declare that democracy needs for its fulfillment a peculiarly high standard of moral behavior; and it is even more true to declare that a democratic scheme of moral values reaches its consummate expression in the religion of human brotherhood. Such a religion can be realized only through the loving kindness which individuals feel toward their fellowmen and particularly toward their fellow countrymen; and it is through such feelings that the network of mutual loyalties and responsibilities woven in a democratic nation become radiant and expansive.

Whenever an individual democrat, like Abraham Lincoln, emerges, who succeeds in offering an example of specific efficiency united with supreme kindliness of feeling, he qualifies as a national hero of consummate value. But, at present, a profound sense of human brotherhood is no substitute for specific efficiency. The men most possessed by intense brotherly feelings usually fall into an error, as Tolstoi has done, as to the way in which those feelings can be realized. Consummate faith itself is no substitute for good work. Back of any work of moral conversion must come a long and slow process of social reorganization and individual emancipation; and not until the reorganization has been partly accomplished and the individual released, disciplined, and purified will the soil be prepared for the crowning work of some democratic Saint Francis.

Hence, in the foregoing account of a possible democratic fulfillment, attention has been concentrated on that indispensable phase of the work which can be attained by conscious means. Until this work is measurably accomplished, no evangelist can do more than convert a few men for a few years. But it has been admitted throughout that the task of individual and social regeneration must remain incomplete and impoverished until the conviction and the feeling of human brotherhood enters into possession of the human spirit. The laborious work of individual and social fulfillment may eventually be transfigured by an outburst of enthusiasm — one which is not the expression of a mood but which is substantially the finer flower of an achieved experience and a living tradition. If such a moment ever arrives, it will be partly the creation of some democratic evangelist — some imitator of Jesus who will reveal to men the path whereby they may enter into spiritual possession of their individual and social achievements, and immeasurably increase them by virtue of personal regeneration.

Be it understood, however, that no prophecy of any such consummate moment has been made. Something of the kind may happen in case the American or any other democracy seeks patiently and intelligently to make good a complete and a coherent democratic ideal. For better or worse, democracy cannot be disentangled from an aspiration toward human perfectibility, and hence from the adoption of measures looking in the direction of realizing such an aspiration. It may be that the attempt will not be seriously made, or that, if it is, nothing will come of it.

Mr. George Santayana concludes a chapter on "Democracy" in his *Reason in Society* with the following words:

> For such excellence to grow general mankind must be notably transformed. If a noble and civilized democracy is to subsist, the common citizen must be

something of a saint and something of a hero. We see, therefore, how justly flattering and profound, and at the same time how ominous, was Montesquieu's saying that the principle of democracy is virtue.

The principle of democracy *is* virtue, and when we consider the condition of contemporary democracies, the saying may seem to be more ominous than flattering. But if a few hundred years from now it seems less ominous, the threat will be removed in only one way. The common citizen can become something of a saint and something of a hero, not by growing to heroic proportions in his own person but by the sincere and enthusiastic imitation of heroes and saints; and whether or not he will ever come to such imitation will depend upon the ability of his exceptional fellow countrymen to offer him acceptable examples of heroism and saintliness.

46.

BEN B. LINDSEY: The Origin of the Juvenile Court

At the turn of the century, some professional social workers, lawyers, and judges, arguing that criminals were not born but made, sought to put into practice the theory that poor environmental conditions often contributed to crime. Judge Ben Lindsey of Colorado became a leading advocate of this view. He was especially concerned with changing the harsh treatment of juveniles who had run afoul of the law. The following selection is taken from a magazine article in which Judge Lindsey describes the beginnings of his Juvenile Court and the methods he used to deal with young criminals.

Source: *Everybody's Magazine*, December 1909: "The Beast and the Jungle."

THROUGH . . . TWO YEARS of quarreling and crusading, our court work for the children was going on very happily. It was a recreation for us all, and it kept me full of hope — for it was successful. We were getting

the most unexpected results. We were learning something new every day. We were deducing, from what we learned, theories to be tested in daily practice, and then devising court methods by which to apply

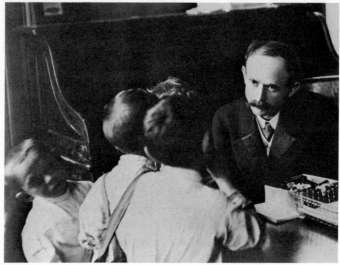

Benjamin Barr Lindsey talking to boys in his chamber during the early days of Juvenile Court

the theories that proved correct. It had all the fascination of scientific research, of practical invention, and of a work of charity combined. It was a succession of surprises and a continual joy.

I had begun merely with a sympathy for children and a conviction that our laws against crime were as inapplicable to children as they would be to idiots. I soon realized that not only our laws but our whole system of criminal procedure was wrong. It was based upon fear; and fear, with children, as with their elders, is the father of lies. I found that when a boy was brought before me, I could do nothing with him until I had taken the fear out of his heart; but, once I had gotten rid of that fear, I found — to my own amazement — that I could do anything with him.

I could do things that seemed miraculous, especially to the police, who seldom tried anything but abuse and curses, and the more or less refined brutalities of the "sweatbox" and the "third degree." I learned that instead of fear we must use sympathy, but without cant, without hypocrisy, and without sentimentalism. We must first convince the boy that we were his friends but the determined enemies of his misdeeds; that we wished to help him to do

right, but could do nothing for him if he persisted in doing wrong. We had to encourage him to confess his wrongdoing, teach him wherein it had been wrongdoing, and strengthen him to do right thereafter.

I found — what so many others have found — that children are neither good nor bad, but either strong or weak. They are naturally neither moral nor immoral — but merely unmoral. They are little savages, living in a civilized society that has not yet civilized them, often at war with it, frequently punished by it, and always secretly in rebellion against it, until the influences of the home, the school, and the church gradually overcome their natural savagery and make them moral and responsible members of society.

The mistake of the criminal law had been to punish these little savages as if they had been civilized, and by so doing, in nine cases out of ten, make them criminal savages. Our work, we found, was to aid the civilizing forces — the home, the school, and the church — and to protect society by making the children good members of society instead of punishing them for being irresponsible ones. If we failed, and the child proved incorrigible, the criminal law could then be invoked. But the infrequency with which we failed was one of the surprises of the work.

Take, for example, the case of Lee Martin and his "River Front Gang." He was a boy burglar, a sneak thief, a pickpocket, a jail breaker, and a tramp; and his "gang" was known to the newspapers as the most desperate band of young criminals in Denver. Lee Martin and another member of the gang named Jack Heimel were one night caught in a drugstore into which they had broken. And when I went to see them in jail, I found them strapped to the benches in their cells, bruised and battered from an interview with the police, in which they had been punished for refusing to "snitch" (tell) on their fellow members of the gang. This was before the passage of our Juvenile Court laws, and I wished to have an opportunity to try what I could do with these two boys. The police did not wish me to have them.

I told the boys that I intended to try to help them, and they sneered at me. I told them that I thought they had not been given "a square deal" — which was true — but they did not respond. I used what tact and sympathy I could to draw them out and get their side of the story of their war with society, but it took me something like a month of frequent visits to get them to trust me and to believe that I wished to help them. In the end I was successful. I got their story — a story too long to repeat here — but it proved to me that the boys had been as much sinned against as sinning. They had begun as irresponsible little savages, and they had been made desperate young criminals. Their parents had failed to civilize them, and the school and the church had never had an opportunity to try. I resolved to see if it was too late to begin.

The police captain assured me that it was. "You can't 'baby' Lee Martin," he said. "He's been in jail thirteen times, and it hasn't done him any good."

"Well, I'd like to see what we can do," I replied. "If we fail, we'll still have twelve times the best of the jail. It has cost this city, in officers' fees alone, over a thousand dollars to make a criminal of him. Let us see how much it will cost to turn him into an honest boy."

The officer reeled off a long list of Martin's offenses, and I retorted by showing a typewritten record of them, twice as long. "How in the world did you get 'em, Judge?" he said. "We couldn't *sweat* 'em out of him."

After a week of such argument, we got the case referred to our court. The boys were tried; and, of course, their guilt was clear. I sent them back to the jail under suspended sentence, and thought the matter over.

One night I had them brought to my chambers under guard, and, after a talk with Heimel, I sent him and the guard away, and concentrated on Martin. I decided to put my influence over him to the test. I told him of the fight I was making for him, showed him how I had been spending all my spare time "trying to straighten things out" for him and Heimel, and warned him that the police did not believe I could succeed. "Now, Lee," I said, "you can run away if you want to, and prove me a liar to the cops. But I want to help you, and I want you to stand by me. I want you to trust me, and I want you to go back to the jail there, and let me do the best I can."

He went. And he went alone — unguarded.

Then I put him and Heimel on probation, and in a few days they came to see me and brought "Red" Mike and Tommie Green, of the "River Front Gang." I talked to them about their offenses against the law, and told them I wanted to help them do what was right and live honest lives, unpersecuted by the police; and I praised Martin for his moral strength in going back to the jail alone. Before they left me, "Red" and Tommie had "snitched" on themselves, and I had two new probationers. One by one the others followed, until I had all seven members of the gang on my list, all confessed wrongdoers pledged to give up crime and make an honest effort to be "straight." Six of the seven are today honest young workmen; Lee Martin failed, after a long and plucky fight, and is now in the penitentiary. "The River Front Gang," to my knowledge, has been responsible for the reformation of thirty boys in Denver; and Lee Martin, in his time, did more to discourage crime than any policeman in the city. . . .

During the first two years of our work, 554 children were put on probation; only 31 were ever returned to the court again, and of these 31, a number were returned and sent to Golden because of the hopelessness of reforming them in their squalid homes.

One evening, a probationer brought four boys to my chambers with the announcement that they wished to "snitch" on themselves. They had been stealing bicycles — making a regular practice of it — and they had five such thefts to their discredit. I investigated their story and found it to be true. The police had a complete record of the thefts, and I tried — and got the boys to try — to recover the wheels, but we could not; they had been sold and resold and quite lost track of. A police officer, with whom I consulted, insisted that the boys should be arrested and sentenced to jail; and while I listened to him it dawned upon me what the difference was between the criminal procedure and the methods of our court.

"Officer," I said, "you are trying to save bicycles. I am trying to save boys. The boys are more important than the bicycles. And, if we can save the boys, we can save bicycles in the future that we could not save in the past." I put the boys on probation, with the understanding that, if they did not live up to their new resolve to be honest, I should be allowed to use their confessions against them. Not one of them failed me. The court helped them to get work and

they are honest and useful members of society today.

In one year, 201 boys came in this way to our court, voluntarily, and confessed their wrongdoing, and promised to "cut it out." . . . This achievement of our Juvenile Court has attracted more attention than anything else we have done; and yet it is not an isolated act; it is merely one of the results of the method.

The criminal law is founded on vengeance. It treats all criminals as born criminals, incorrigible and unforgivable. It is designed to save property, not to save men and it does neither: it makes more criminal than it crushes. I believe that the methods of our Juvenile Court could be applied to half the criminal cases on our calendars. The majority of our criminals are not born but made — and ill made. They can be remade as easily as the "River Front Gang" was remade if we would use the methods of Christianity on them and not those of a sort of fiendish paganism that exacts "an eye for an eye," and exacts it in a spirit of vengeance.

Does this read as if I were "crazy"? Do not think so. It is a conclusion based upon years of thoughtful experience. I have obtained a law in Colorado — the first of its kind in the history of jurisprudence, if that be anything against it! — by which an adult accused of crime can be tried as our children are tried and aided and corrected by the state as *parens patriae,* just as our children are aided and corrected. And I am willing to stake my faith on it that, if our courts and our prisons ever learn how to work under such a law, you will see not only children but grown men and women going from the courtrooms with their commitment papers in their hands and knocking on the gates of the prisons to be admitted.

Crazy? When I first told one of our deputy sheriffs that in future I should send boys to Golden without him, he said to my clerk: "Well, I've always heard Lindsey was crazy, but I never believed it till today!" And when a hardened young criminal went, from my court, 250 miles to the Buena Vista reformatory alone, and presented himself at the gates of the prison, "the sentry" (as I was afterward told) "almost fell off the walls." Crazy? Do you know that over half the inmates of reformatories, jails and prisons in this country are under twenty-five years of age? (Some authorities say under twenty-three.) . . .

I may be very crazy and yet not be as crazy as the people who in the face of these facts believe that the criminal methods of our civilization are anything but a gigantic crime and a stupendous folly. Some day our descendants will read of our methods of handling criminals as we now read of how our ancestors imprisoned the insane in chains and used the methods of a Siberian jailer on the inmates of the madhouse!

Never doubt it. Under our civil laws today, Masters of Discipline could be appointed — as Masters in Chancery are appointed — to aid and correct delinquents, especially young delinquents, in our cities; to allow them to repent and make reparation — as they cannot under our criminal procedure; to help them rise from immorality and clean their hands of crime — as no judge can help them now, without being guilty of "compounding a felony." That will come, some day. If not in *our* day, then so much the worse for us!

47.

Anonymous: The Achievement of Thomas A. Edison

Born at Milan, Ohio, in 1847, Thomas Alva Edison's formal education was limited to three months of public school at Port Huron, Michigan. At twelve he became a railroad newsboy and later worked as a telegraph operator. In 1868 he took out his first patent, for an electrical vote recorder. Numerous other inventions followed, including a "phonograph or speaking machine," and, most famous of all, the incandescent lamp, success with which came after the expenditure of $40,000 in fruitless experiments. On October 21, 1879, he succeeded in making a loop of carbonized cotton thread glow in a vacuum for forty hours. In his combined workshop and laboratory at Menlo Park, New Jersey, and later at West Orange, New Jersey, Edison was incessantly engaged in various forms of invention for more than fifty years and took out 1,033 patents up to April 1928. The article reprinted here in part, which summarized the economic effects of Edison's work (to 1909), first appeared in Scientific American.

Source: *Scientific American*, February 27, 1909.

As an inventor, Edison's chief characteristic is his pertinacity. "Genius is 2 percent inspiration and 98 percent perspiration," is an epigram of his, which has been worn threadbare by much newspaper use, but which contains the whole story of his intensely active career.

Edison is a utilitarian to his fingertips. He never yet invented a machine that could not be employed in everyday life. Long ago he made a brief excursion into the field of aerial navigation, and although his experiments were full of promise, he abandoned the investigation, largely because there was no immediate prospect of applying the flying machine to the needs of this world. Even his conversation is that of a man whose interests are essentially practical. He would never ramble off, for example, into a metaphysical discussion on man's place in the universe. He is a glorified Yankee inventor, a mechanic of real genius who, by dint of rare patience and indomitable energy, has raised himself to an enviable position among the most distinguished scientists of his time.

Despite the exceedingly practical bent of his faculties, he is a man of large ideas with a wonderful gift of what may be termed scientific penetration. Few engineers and physicists can grasp with anything like his swiftness of perception the meaning of simple phenomena, often accidental in their origin. The phonograph, for example, which, although not his greatest invention is probably the most marvelous in the eyes of the public, was suggested by experiments made with the telephone and automatic recording telegraph.

He was working on a machine provided with a disk of paper, similar to the present disk talking machine. On the traveling arm was a magnet which had an embossing point which embossed or indented dots and dashes on the paper, the platen having a grooved volute spiral on its surface. After recording Morse signals, a contact point swept over the record, and the indentations gave movement to the make and break and reproduced the signals on another line. When run at high speed, it would give a humming sound. He knew from the telephone about the movements of the diaphragm, and had caused his voice to work a ratchet wheel and toy figure. Then he conceived the idea of indenting by the voice and reproducing the sound by means of the indentations. The machine was made, but in cylinder form.

Then he decided to make a talking machine — with what success everyone knows. When the first operative machine was produced, he packed up the instrument and came to the office of the *Scientific American*. Without ceremony he placed the machine on the editor's desk and turned the crank. The machine literally spoke for itself. "Good morning," it said. "How do you do? How do you like the phonograph?" And thus the editors of the *Scientific American* constituted the first public audience that ever listened to the phonograph.

If ever an Edison invention was the product of unflagging pertinacity, it was the electric incandescent lamp. Strange to narrate, he began with the metallic filaments, which now threaten to supplant the carbon filament that he finally adopted. He abandoned the metallic filament, not because he failed to see its immense possibilities but because the proper metals could not be obtained cheaply enough until a few years ago. Indeed, some of them were mere laboratory rarities when he commenced his epoch-making researches. Before he began, he studied everything that had been done before him so that he could take up the work where his predecessors had ceased. When he finally decided that the filament must be made of carbon, he began a search for the proper raw material which may well be considered a quest for a scientific Holy Grail.

Men were dispatched to all quarters of the globe to search for fibers having the requisite properties. One of these scientific crusaders ransacked the Amazon jungles and tasted no meat for 116 days. The 80 varieties of bamboo and 3,000 specimens of fibers brought back by these emissaries were tested in Edison's laboratory, and all but 3 or 4 rejected. Night after night he and his assistants slept in the laboratory with resistance boxes for pillows and work benches and tables for beds. Food was passed in to them through the windows. Doggedness such as this was bound to bring success.

The same story could be told of every one of the hundreds of inventions that Edison has patented. The method of procedure (an object lesson to every inventor) is always the same. He invariably begins his investigations by a thorough course of reading, fully conscious that he is not the first in the field and that he must know where others failed. After a thorough review of the subject, he begins actual work — an expert who carefully avoids covering ground which has already been explored and who begins where others abandoned investigation. Experiments are made by the hundred and thousand. Model after model is built. Failure succeeds failure, until further efforts seem hopeless. For all that, more experiments are made and more models built. At last an experiment is conducted or a model constructed that seems faintly encouraging. A less-experienced inventor would be elated. Edison, however, regards the favorable result with suspicion. Not until the partial success has been confirmed by many repetitions of the experiment is he convinced that something has been achieved.

The activities of Mr. Edison have been of such great range, and his conquests in the domains of practical arts so extensive and varied, that it is somewhat difficult to estimate with any satisfactory degree of accuracy the money value of his inventions to the world.

First of all, let us mention the incandescent electric light and systems of distribution of electric light, heat, and power, which may justly be considered as the crowning inventions of Mr. Edison's life. Today, there are in the United States more than 41 million of these lamps connected to existing central station circuits in active operation. At the present time there are over 5,000 central stations in this country for the distribution of electric current for light,

heat, and power, with capital obligations amounting to not less than $1 billion. Besides the above-named 41 million incandescent lamps connected to their mains, there are about 500,000 arc lamps and 150,000 motors, using 750,000 horsepower, besides countless fan motors and heating and cooking appliances. The gross earnings of these central stations approximate the sum of $225 million yearly.

In addition to central stations, there are upward of 100,000 isolated or private plants in mills, factories, steamships, hotels, theaters, etc., owned by the persons or concerns who operate them. These plants represent an approximate investment of $500 million, and the connection of not less than 25 million incandescent lamps, or their equivalent.

Then there are the factories where these incandescent lamps are made, about forty in number, representing a total investment that may be approximated at $25 million.

The reader will naturally be disposed to ask whether it is intended to claim that Mr. Edison has brought about all this magnificent and wonderful growth of the electric lighting art. The answer to this is decidedly in the negative, for the fact is that he laid the foundation and erected a building thereon; and, in the natural progressive order of things, other inventors of more or less fame have added a wing here and a story there, until the resultant great structure has attained such magnificent proportions as to evoke the wonder and amazement of the beholder — but the old foundation and the fundamental building still remain to support the other parts.

Edison was the first man to devise, construct, and operate from a central station a practicable, life-size electric railroad which was capable of transporting, and did transport, passengers and freight at variable speeds over varying grades, and under complete control of the operator. While Mr. Edison's original broad ideas are embodied in present practice, the perfection of the modern electric railway is also greatly due to the labors and inventions of a large number of other well-known inventors.

The statistics of 1908 for American street and elevated railways show that within twenty-five years the electric railway industry has grown to embrace 38,812 miles of track on streets and for elevated railways, operated under the ownership of 1,238 separate companies, whose total capitalization amounts to the enormous sum of $4,123,834,598 in 1908. In the equipments owned by such companies, there are included 68,636 electric cars and 17,568 trailers and others, making a total of 86,204 of such vehicles. These cars and equipments earned over $425 million in 1907, in giving the public transportation, at a cost including transfers, of a little over 3 cents per passenger, for whom a 15-mile ride would be possible. No cheaper transportation is given in the world.

Some mention should also be made of the great electrical works of the country, in which the dynamos, motors, and other varied paraphernalia are made for electric lighting, electric railway, and other purposes. The productions of the General Electric Company alone, as shown by average annual sales of over $50 million, are of themselves a colossal item, but they do not comprise the total of the country's manufactures in these lines, which amount to five times as much again.

To Alexander Graham Bell is due the broad idea of transmission of speech by means of an electrical circuit. Mr. Edison invented and brought out the carbon transmitter, which is universally acknowledged to have been the needed device that made the telephone a commercial possibility, and has since led to its phenomenally rapid adoption and worldwide use. His inventions may be found in every one of the 7 million telephones employed in the country at the present day.

On a conservative estimate, at this writing, the investment has been not less than $800 million in now existing telephone systems, and no fewer than 10.5 billion talks over the lines during the year 1908. These figures relate only to telephone systems and do not include any details regarding the great manufacturing establishments engaged in the construction of telephone apparatus, of which there is an annual production amounting to at least $15 million per annum.

There is no way in which any definite computation can be made of the value of Mr. Edison's contributions in the art of telegraphy except, perhaps, in the case of his quadruplex telegraph, through which alone it is estimated that there has been saved from $15 million to $20 million in the cost of line construction in this country.

At Orange, N.J., may be found the National Phonograph Company, the Edison Business Phonograph Company, the Edison Phonograph Works, the Edison Manufacturing Company, the Edison Storage Battery Company, and the Bates Manufacturing Company. The importance of these industries will be apparent when it is stated that there are upward of 3,600 people employed, and an annual payroll of about $2,250,000.

There have been upward of 1,310,000 phonographs sold during the last twenty years, with and for which there have been made and sold no less than 97,845,000 records of a musical or other character. Phonographic records are now being manufactured at Orange at the rate of 75,000 a day, the annual sale of phonographs and records being approximately $7 million, including business phonographs. The figures given represent only about one-half of the entire business of the country in phonographs, records, cylinders, and supplies.

Taking next his inventions that pertain to "moving pictures," we find that from the inception of the moving-picture business to the present time, Edison has made upward of 13,100 projecting machines and many million feet of film carrying small photographs of moving objects. Although the moving-picture business is still in its youth, it calls for the annual production of thousands of machines and many million feet of films in Mr. Edison's shops, having a sale value of not less than $750,000. The annual product of the Edison Manufacturing Company in this line is only a fractional part of the total that is absorbed by the 10,000 or so moving-picture theaters and exhibitions which are in operation in the United States at the present time, and which represent an investment of some $40 million. Licensees under Edison patents in this country alone produce upward of 60 million feet of films, containing more than 1.5 billion separate photographs.

In making a somewhat radical change of subject, from moving pictures to cement, we find ourselves in a field in which Mr. Edison has made a most decided impression. His corporation in five years has grown to be the fourth largest producer in the United States, with a still increasing capacity. His plant, which occupies forty acres, represents an approximate investment of $4 million in quarries, railroads, and machinery. The production reaches a grand total of over 5 million barrels of cement up to the present date, having a value of about $4.5 million, exclusive of package. At the time of this writing, the rate of production is over 8,000 barrels of cement per day, or say 2.5 million barrels per year, having an approximate selling value of a little less than $2 million, with prospects of increasing in the near future to a daily output of 10,000 barrels.

48.

Harry McClintock: "Big Rock Candy Mountain"

Harry McClintock was one of the most colorful of the group of self-imposed exiles who flocked to the banner of the Industrial Workers of the World in the years after 1905. A tramp by choice, as well as by necessity, McClintock in a number of songs caught the flavor of the life of the free spirits who rode the boxcars and camped alongside the railroad tracks of the country. "Big Rock Candy Mountain" tells of the hobo's utopia; it is popular among children, who may have similar dreams.

BIG ROCK CANDY MOUNTAIN

One evening as the sun went down and the jungle fires were burning,
Down the track came a hobo hiking; he said "Boys, I'm not turning;
I'm heading for a land that's far away beside that crystal fountain.
I'll see you all this coming fall in the Big Rock Candy Mountain."

In the Big Rock Candy Mountain, it's a land that's fair and bright,
The handouts grow on bushes and you sleep out every night;
The boxcars all are empty and the sun shines every day.
I'm bound to go where there ain't no snow,
Where the sleet don't fall and the wind don't blow,
In the Big Rock Candy Mountain.

Chorus:
Oh, the buzzing of the bees in the cigarette trees,
By the soda water fountain,
By the lemonade springs where the bluebird sings,
In the Big Rock Candy Mountain.

In the Big Rock Candy Mountain you never change your socks,
Little streams of alkyhol comes trickling down the rocks.
Oh, the shacks all have to tip their hats, and the railroad bulls are blind.
There's a lake of stew and ginger ale too,
And you can paddle all around it in a big canoe,
In the Big Rock Candy Mountain.

In the Big Rock Candy Mountain all the cops have wooden legs,
The bulldogs all have rubber teeth and the hens lay soft-boiled eggs.
The boxcars all are empty and the sun shines every day.
I'm bound to go where there ain't no snow,
Where the sleet don't fall and the wind don't blow,
In the Big Rock Candy Mountain.

In the Big Rock Candy Mountain the jails are made of tin,
You can slip right out again as soon as they put you in.
There ain't no short-handled shovels, no axes, saws, nor picks.
I'm bound to stay where you sleep all day,
Where they hung the jerk that invented work,
In the Big Rock Candy Mountain.

1910

49.

Abraham Flexner: Medical Education in the United States

In 1908 the Carnegie Foundation for the Advancement of Teaching commissioned Abraham Flexner to survey the condition of medical education in the United States and Canada. Flexner spent a year visiting all of the institutions that represented themselves as medical schools and decided that almost all of them were "essentially private ventures, moneymaking in spirit and object." His report received front-page coverage and proved highly embarrassing to the medical profession. Many schools were forced to close (in Louisville they dwindled from seven to one, in Chicago, from fifteen to three), educational qualifications were raised and standardized, and the number of students allowed to study was limited. The change was a revolutionary one; and from it modern medical education was born. The following selection is from the third chapter of the report, "The Actual Basis of Medical Education."

Source: *Medical Education in the United States and Canada*, Bulletin No. 4, New York, 1910, pp. 28-51.

Taking a two-year college course, largely constituted of the sciences, as the normal point of departure, let us survey the existing status. The 155 medical schools of the United States and Canada fall readily into three divisions: the first includes those that require two or more years of college work for entrance; the second, those that demand actual graduation from a four-year high school or oscillate about its supposed "equivalent"; the third, those that ask little or nothing more than the rudiments or the recollection of a common school education.

To the first division, sixteen institutions already belong; six more, now demanding one year of college work, will fully enter the division in the fall of 1910 by requiring a second; and several more, at this date still in the second division, will shortly take the step from the high school to the two-year college requirement. The Johns Hopkins requires for entrance a college degree which, whatever else it represents, must include the three fundamental sciences, French, and German. No exception has ever been made to this degree requirement; but, recently, admission to the second-year class has been granted to students holding an A.B. degree earned by four years' study, the last of them devoted to medical subjects in institutions where those subjects were excellently taught.

At Harvard the degree requirement has been somewhat unsettled by a recent decision to admit students without degree provided they have had two years of college science; they are to be grouped as "special" students and are required to maintain higher standing in order to qualify for the M.D. degree. But as these students enter on a general rule and as a matter of course, and are, under a slight handicap, eligible to the M.D. degree, they are not accurately described as special. A special student is properly one whom no rule fits; one whose admission presents certain individual features requiring consideration on their merits. Such is not the case with the students under discussion; they enter just as regularly as the degree men, and without that limitation as to number which makes of the "special student" device something of a privilege. Harvard can thus admit any student who is eligible to the schools with the two-year college requirement.

The other institutions under discussion telescope the college and medical courses; the preliminary medical sciences constitute the bulk of two college years; the next two years are reckoned twice. They count simultaneously as third and fourth years of the college and as first and second years of the medical course. At their close the student gets the A.B. degree, but his medical education is already half over. Without exception, the schools belonging to this group are high-grade institutions. They differ considerably, however, in the degree of rigor with which their elevated entrance requirements have been enforced from the start.

At the University of Pennsylvania, for example, in a class of 114, admitted this year (1909-1910) on a one-year college basis, 75 (66 percent) are conditioned; at Ann Arbor, of 36 entering on the two-year college basis, only 8 are conditioned at all, and those mainly in organic chemistry; at Yale, which advanced in 1909-1910 from the high school to the two-year college basis, in a class of 23, there was only one partial condition in biology, and, best of all, failed members of last year's class on the old basis were refused readmission.

Experience elsewhere indicates that the percentage of conditions declines rapidly as students learn by forethought to adjust their work to their ultimate purpose and as the colleges facilitate adjustment by providing the requisite opportunities; both of which processes will be accelerated if the medical schools have the courage — and the financial strength — to close their doors to students who labor under anything more than a slight handicap. Here as elsewhere development follows hard upon actual responsibility.

Our second division constitutes the real problem; out of it additional high-grade medical schools to the number actually required must be developed. About fifty institutions, whose entrance standard approximates high school graduation, belong here. Great diversity exists in the quality of the student body of these institutions: the regents' certificates in New York, state board supervision in Michigan, the control of admission to their medical departments by the academic authorities of McGill and Toronto, insure as capable and homogeneous an enrollment as is obtainable at or about the high school level. A few others, not so well protected, are within measurable distance of the same category — the medical department of Tulane University and Jefferson Medical College (Philadelphia), for example. In general, however, the schools of this division are difficult to classify; for they freely admit students on bases that are not only hopelessly unequal to each other but are even incapable of reduction to a common denominator.

On their actual standards the catalog statements throw little light; there the requirements are cast in the form of a descending scale, running from the top, down. Equally acceptable in their sight are a bachelor's degree from a college or a university, a diploma from an "accredited" high school, an examination in a few speci-fied and several of a wide range of optional studies, and a certificate from the principal of a high school, normal school, or acade-my, from a "reputable instructor," from a state or city superintendent of education, or from a state board of medical examiners, that stamps the applicant as possessing the "equivalent" of a high school education.

Now it is clear that the alternatives at the top are mainly decorative. The real standard is perilously close to the "equivalent" that creeps in modestly at the bottom. There is, of course, no active prejudice anywhere against Ph.D.'s and A.M.'s and A.B.'s and B.Sc.'s; they are apt to be rather conspicu-ously exploited, when they drift in. But they do not set the pace; they do not deter-mine or even vitally affect the character of the school. In these instances the medical curriculum either contains the premedical subjects in an elementary form, or, what may be worse, tries to go ahead entirely without them.

The real standard is not influenced by the presence of degree men, and the wonder is that any of them sacrifice the advantage of a superior education by resorting to these institutions. The minimum is, then, the real standard; all else is permissive; for to the needs of those admitted at the bottom the quantity and quality of the instruction must in fairness conform.

To get at the real admission standard, then, of these medical schools, one must make straight for the "equivalent." On the methods of ascertaining and enforcing that, the issue hangs. Now the "equivalent" may be defined as a device that concedes the ne-cessity of a standard which it forthwith pro-ceeds to evade. The professed high school basis is variously sacrificed to this so-called equivalent. The medical schools under dis-cussion agree to accept at face value only graduation diplomas from "approved" or "accredited" high schools. These terms have a definite meaning: they indicate schools which, upon proper investigation, have been

recognized by the state universities of their respective states or by some other compe-tent educational organization — in New England, by the College Entrance Certifi-cate Board; in the Middle West, by the North Central Association. High schools and academies not acceptable at full value to state universities or to the bodies just named do not belong to the "approved" or "accredited" class; their diplomas and certif-icates are not, therefore, entitled to be re-ceived in satisfaction of the announced stan-dard. They are nevertheless freely accept-ed. . . .

If the standard were enforced, the candi-dates in question, not offering a graduation diploma from an accredited high school, would be compelled to enter by written ex-amination. But the examination is, as things stand, only another method of evasion. Nei-ther in extent nor in difficulty do the writ-ten examinations, in the relatively rare cases in which they are given, even approximate the high school standard. Nor are they meant to do so. Colleges with medical de-partments of the kind under discussion do not expect academic and medical students to pass the same or the same kind of exami-nation. A special set of questions is pre-pared for the medical candidates, including perhaps half the subjects, and each of these traversing about half the ground covered by the academic papers. . . .

There remains still a third method of cut-ting below an actual high school standard — the method indeed that provides much the most capacious loophole for the admis-sion of unqualified students under the cloak of nominal compliance with the high school standard. The agent in the transactions about to be described is the medical exam-iner, appointed in some places by voluntary agreement between the schools, elsewhere delegated by the state board or by the su-perintendent of public instruction acting in its behalf, for the purpose of dealing with students who present written evidence other than the diploma of an accredited high school. It is intended and expected that this official shall enforce a high school standard. In few states is this standard achieved. The Education Department in New York, the state boards in Minnesota and Michigan, maintain what may be fairly called a scholastically honest high school requirement; for they require a diploma representing an organically complete secondary school education, properly guaranteed, or, in default thereof, a written examination covering about the same ground; there is no other recourse.

Elsewhere the state board is legally powerless, as in Maryland, or unwilling to antagonize the schools, as in Illinois and Kentucky. The outside examiners, agreed on by the schools in the former case, designated by law in the latter, fall far short of enforcing a high school standard. The examiner, even where distinctly well intentioned, as in Kentucky, never gets sufficient control. The schools do not want the rule enforced, and the boards are either not strong enough or not conscientious enough to withstand them.

Besides, the examiners lack time, machinery, and encouragement for the proper performance of their ostensible office. They are busy men: here, a county official; there, a school principal; elsewhere, a high school professor. A single individual, after his regular day's work is over, without assistance of any kind, is thus expected to perform a task much more complicated than that for which Harvard, Columbia, and the University of Michigan maintain costly establishments.

There is no set time when candidates must appear. They drop in as they please, separately — now, before the medical school opens; again, long after; sometimes with their credentials; sometimes without them. There is no definite procedure. At times, the examiner concludes from the face of the papers; at times, from the face of the candidate. The whole business is transacted in a free and easy way. In Illinois, for example, the law speaks of "preliminary" edu-

cational requirements; the state board graciously permits them to become subsequents.

Students enter the medical schools, embark on the study of medicine, and, at their convenience, "square up" with one of the examiners. An evening call is arranged; there is an informal talk, aiming to elicit what "subjects" the candidate "has had." He may, after an interview lasting from thirty minutes to two hours, and rarely including any writing, be "passed" with or without "conditions"; if with conditions, the rule requires him to reappear for a second "examination" before the beginning of the sophomore year; but nothing happens if he postpones his reappearance until a short time before graduation. Besides, a condition in one subject may be removed by "passing" in another! "No technical questions are asked; the presumption is that the applicant won't remember details."

Formerly, written examinations were used in part; but they were given up "because almost everybody failed." And it may at any moment happen that an applicant actually turned down by one examiner will be passed by another. The most flagrantly commercial of the Chicago schools operate "premedical" classes where a hasty cram, usually at night, suffices to meet the academic requirements of the Illinois state board: "The examiner's no prude, he'll give a man a chance," said the dean of one of them. . . .

To all the disorder that prevails in schools of this grade in the United States, the Canadian schools at the same level present, with two exceptions, a forcible contrast. There, too, "equivalents" are accepted; but they are equivalents in fact as in name, for they are probed by a series of written examinations, each three hours in length, held at a stated time and place, only and actually in advance of the opening of the medical school, entrance to which is absolutely dependent on their outcome.

The quality of the student body thus accumulated in the schools under discussion bears out the above description. "The facilities are better than the students"; "The boys are imbued with the idea of being doctors; they want to cut and prescribe; all else is theoretical"; students accepted in chemistry or physics "don't know a barometer when they see it"; "It is difficult to get a student to *want* to repeat an experiment (in physiology). They have neither curiosity nor capacity." "The machinery doesn't stop the unfit." "Men get in, not because the country needs the doctors but because the schools need the money." "What is your honest opinion of your own enrollment?" a professor in a Philadelphia school was asked. "Well, the most I would claim," he answered, "is that nobody who is absolutely worthless gets in!"

We have still to deal with schools of our third division. They are most numerous in the South, but they exist in almost all medical "centers" — San Francisco, Chicago, — there plainly on the sufferance of the state board, for the law, if enforced, would stamp them out — St. Louis and Baltimore. Outside the South they usually make some pretense of requiring the "equivalent" of a high school education; but no examiner of any kind is employed, and the deans are extremely reluctant to be pinned down. Southern schools of this division, after specifying an impressive series of acceptable credentials ranging once more from university degrees downward, announce their satisfaction with a "grammar school followed by two years of a high school," or in default thereof a general assurance of adequate "scholastic attainments" by a state, city, or county superintendent, or some other person connected with education or purporting to be such; but the lack of such credentials is not very serious, for the student is admitted without them, with leave to procure them later.

Many of the schools accept students from the grammar schools. Credentials, if presented, are casually regarded and then usu-ally returned; a few may be found, rolled up in a rubber band in a dusty pigeonhole. There is no protection against fraud or forgery. At the College of Medicine and Surgery, Chicago, a thorough search for credentials or some record of them was made by the secretary and several members of the faculty, through desk drawers, safe, etc., but without avail. The school is nevertheless in "good standing" with the Illinois state board, and is "accredited" by the New York Education Department to the extent of three years' work.

At the Medical Department of the University of Georgia I was told: "We go a long way on faith." In visits to medical colleges certificates were found from nonexistent schools as well as from nonexistent places. Of course a few fairly competent students may be found sprinkled in these institutions. But for the most part, the student body gets in on the "equivalent." . . .

Statistical proof of inadequacy of preparation is furnished by what one may fairly call the abnormal mortality within schools operating on the basis of "equivalents." The standards of promotion in these schools watch narrowly the action of the state boards, which are usually lenient. The schools are too weak financially to do otherwise; doubtful points are resolved in the boy's favor. Hence the school examinations play less havoc than would follow tests strictly constructed in the public interest. Yet the mortality from one cause or another by the close of the first year runs from 20 to 50 percent.

At the Medico-Chirurgical College of Philadelphia, an initial first-year enrollment of 152 in October fell to 100 by the following January 1; of these, 60 passed without conditions, much less than one-half the original class enrollment; at Tufts, the entering class, 1908-1909, shows in the catalog an enrollment of 141 — 75 were promoted, with or without conditions, into the sophomore class; at Cornell, on its former high school basis, the failures at the close of the first year in a period of ten years averaged 28 percent; at Buffalo, the failed and conditioned of three successive first-year classes amounted to 40 percent of the total enrollment; at Vanderbilt, out of a class of 70, the dropped, conditioned, and failed amounted to 44 percent; at the College of Physicians and Surgeons, Atlanta, 70 percent, out of a class of 99.

In schools on the higher basis, *i.e.*, two years of college work or better, the instruction is more elaborate, the work more difficult, and the examinations harder; for scientific ideals rather than chances with the state board dominate. Yet the mortality drops decisively. At the Johns Hopkins, the mortality during three successive years averages less than 5 percent, only half of which is due to failure; at Ann Arbor, on the one-year college basis, the mortality is below 10 percent.

The exhibit made by institutions that have tried both standards is especially instructive. At the University of Missouri, during the last three years of the high school or equivalent basis, there was a mortality due to actual failure of 35 percent; during the following three years, when one year of college work was required, the mortality fell to 12½ percent. At the Medical Department of the University of Minnesota, during the last three years of the high school requirement, the mortality was 18 percent; in the three years following, on the basis of one year of college work, the mortality was about 10 percent. At the University of Virginia, in the last two years on the old basis, 38 percent of the students failed in one or more subjects; an increase in entrance requirements by one college year reduces the fatalities to 14 percent, despite the augmented difficulty of the work.

The Medical Department of the University of Texas has gradually advanced from a two-year high school basis to a four-year high school basis; on the lower standard there were 34 percent of hopeless failures in

1903 as against 13 percent of hopeless failures in 1908 on the higher. The requirement of a college year assists doubly — first, in eliminating the sham equivalents; next, in strengthening the equipment of those who actually persist. Canada accomplishes the former by means of the examinations already noticed, with the result that the mortality there is distinctly less than ours, at something like the same ostensible level.

The breaches made by the fatalities above described are repaired by immigration, which on investigation proves to be in most instances only another way of evading standards — entrance and other. To some extent, good students who find themselves in a poor school endeavor to retrieve their error by transferring themselves to a better; again, there is a certain amount of enforced emigration annually from schools that, like the University of Wisconsin, offer medical instruction in the first two years only. In the main, however, the "lame ducks" move, and, strangely enough, into schools that are at the moment engaged in rejecting a number equally lame. The interchange is veiled by pretended examinations; but the character of the examination can be guessed from the quality of the students that pass it.

Two standards are thus often broken at once: An ill-equipped student registers in a low-grade Chicago school. At the close of a year or two, he transfers to the College of Physicians and Surgeons, which might have declined him originally. He has thus circumvented its admission requirements. If, now, he has previously failed in the medical courses so far pursued, and succeeds "on examination" in passing, he has simultaneously circumvented the professional requirements as well. Instances of both kinds abound in schools at and below the high school basis. . . .

Is this the best that can be done? Will the actual enforcement of a real and adequate standard starve any section of the country in the matter of physicians? The question can be answered without guesswork or speculation.

The South requires something like 400 doctors annually. How high a standard can it enforce and still get them? In the year 1908-1909 there were 15,791 male students in four-year high schools in six Southern states — Alabama, Georgia, Louisiana, South Carolina, Virginia, and Texas; there were in the previous year 5,877 male students in the academic departments of the Southern state universities and 1,653 more in endowed institutions of similar grade: a population of over 23,000 bordering on high school graduation and widely distributed over the entire area. Our question is thus already answered. The best material for the making of a few hundred Southern doctors annually does not have to be torn from the plow.

But these figures convey by no means the whole truth. The South is in the midst of a genuine educational renaissance. Within the last few years every Southern state under the leadership of the state university, the state Department of Education, and certain endowed institutions like Vanderbilt University has set enthusiastically to work to develop its common and secondary school systems after the admirable model furnished by the robust communities of the Middle West.

The professors of secondary education in the state universities are the evangelists of this auspicious movement. Young, intelligent, well-trained, these sturdy leaders ceaselessly traverse the length and breadth of their respective states, stimulating, suggesting, guiding, organizing. It is an inspiring spectacle. Three years ago the high school had no legal standing in Virginia; today the state is dotted with two-year, three-year, and four-year high schools, created by local taxation, with a considerable subvention from the state treasury. There are already 2,511 boys in fairly well-equipped

four-year high schools, and as many more in private institutions of equal value; and the two-year and three-year schools are growing rapidly into fuller high school stature. It needs no argument to prove that Virginia can at once procure its doctors from among the bona fide graduates of such high schools and better. . . .

The situation is even clearer, insofar as it touches the rest of the country. We estimate that outside the South 1,500 doctors annually graduated will provide for all the real and many imaginary needs. There are at this date something like 8,000 public and over 1,000 private high schools, so widely dispersed over the area under consideration that on the average few boys need go over five miles to school. In the public high schools alone there are enrolled 300,000 boys. What excuse exists for cutting under the high school? We can indeed do better than accept as the basis of a medical education the high school "flat." In the colleges, universities, and technical schools of the North and West, exclusive of preparatory and professional departments, there were, in 1908, 120,000 male students. The number swells with unprecedented rapidity; long before the country has digested the number of doctors now struggling for a livelihood, it will have doubled.

Already, in 1907, 903 of the doctors graduated in that year held academic degrees; that is to say, fully one-half of the number the country actually needed could conform to the standard that has been urged, or better. There is at this moment absolutely nothing in the educational situation outside the South that countenances the least departure from the scientific basis necessary to the successful pursuit of modern medicine.

For whose sake is it permitted? Not really for the remote mountain districts of the South, for example, whence the "yarb doctor," unschooled and unlicensed, can in no event be dislodged; nor yet for that twilight zone, on the hither edge of which so many low-grade doctors huddle that there is no decent living for those already there and no tempting prospect for anybody better: ostensibly, "for the poor boy." For his sake, the terms of entrance upon a medical career must be kept low and easy. We have no right, it is urged, to set up standards which will close the profession to "poor boys."

What are the merits of this contention? The medical profession is a social organ, created not for the purpose of gratifying the inclinations or preferences of certain individuals but as a means of promoting health, physical vigor, happiness — and the economic independence and efficiency immediately connected with these factors. Whether most men support themselves or become charges on the community depends on their keeping well, or if ill, promptly getting well. Now, can anyone seriously contend that in the midst of abundant educational resources, a congenial or profitable career in medicine is to be made for an individual regardless of his capacity to satisfy the purpose for which the profession exists?

It is right to sympathize with those who lack only opportunity; still better to assist them in surmounting obstacles; but not at the price of certain injury to the common weal. Commiseration for the hand-spinner was not suffered for one moment to defeat the general economic advantage procurable through machine-made cloth. Yet the hand-spinner had a sort of vested right: society had tacitly induced him to enter the trade; he had grown up in it on that assurance; and he was now good for nothing else. Your "poor boy" has no right, natural, indefeasible, or acquired, to enter upon the practice of medicine unless it is best for society that he should. . . .

So much from the standpoint of the individual. The proper method of calculating cost is, however, social. Society defrays the expense of training and maintaining the medical corps. In the long run which imposes the greater burden on the community

— the training of a needlessly vast body of inferior men, a large proportion of whom break down, or that of a smaller body of competent men who actually achieve their purpose? When to the direct waste here in question there is added the indirect loss due to incompetency, it is clear that the more expensive type is decidedly cheaper. Aside from interest on investment, from loss by withdrawal of the student body from productive occupations, the cost of our present system of medical education is annually about $3 million as paid in tuition fees alone. The number of high-grade physicians really required could be educated for much less; the others would be profitably employed elsewhere; and society would be still further enriched by efficient medical service.

The argument is apt to shift at this point. If we refuse to be moved by the "poor boy," pity the small towns; for it is speciously argued that the well-trained, college-bred student will scorn them. Not sympathy for the poor boy requires us now to sacrifice the small town to him, but sympathy for the small town requires us to sacrifice the poor boy to it. Two vital considerations are overlooked in this plea. In the first place, the small town needs the best and not the worst doctor procurable. For the country doctor has only himself to rely on: he cannot in every pinch hail specialist, expert, and nurse. On his own skill, knowledge, resourcefulness, the welfare of his patient altogether depends. The rural district is therefore entitled to the best-trained physician that can be induced to go there.

But, we are told, the well-trained man will not go; he will not pay for a high-grade medical education and then content himself with a modest return on his investment. Now the six-year medical education (that based on two college years) and the four-year medical education (that based on the high school or equivalent) may, as we saw above, be made to cost the same sum. As far as cost is concerned, then, the better sort of four-year medical education must have precisely the same effect on distribution of doctors as the six-year training furnished by the state universities. . . .

The truth is that existing conditions are defended only by way of keeping unnecessary medical schools alive. The change to a higher standard could be fatal to many of them without in the least threatening social needs. Momentarily there would be a sharp shrinkage. But forethought would be thus effectively stimulated; trained men would be attracted into the field; readjustment would be complete long before any community felt the pinch. Despite prevailing confusion — legal, popular, and educational — as to what good training in medicine demands, the enrollment in the five schools which have during the last four years required two or more years of college work is already 1,186 students, and is increasing rapidly. . . .

It does not follow, however, that if schools generally rose to the college requirement, their losses would be only one-half and the recovery therefrom ultimately assured. For the schools that came off thus lightly were previously attended by a large proportion of high-grade men. A much greater loss would undoubtedly take place in the lower-grade schools; many of them would be practically annihilated. For the tendency of elevated standards and ideals is to reduce the number of students to something like parity with the demand, and to concentrate this reduced student body in fewer institutions, adequately supported. . . .

The reconstruction of our medical education on the basis of two years of required college work is not, however, going to end matters once and for all. It leaves untouched certain outlying problems that will all the more surely come into focus when the professional training of the physician is once securely established on a scientific basis. At that moment the social role of the physician will generally expand, and to support such expansion he will crave a more liberal and disinterested educational experience.

The question of age — not thus far important because hitherto our demands have been well within the limits of adolescence — will then require to be reckoned with. The college freshman averages nineteen years of age; two years of college work permit him to begin the study of medicine at twenty-one, to be graduated at twenty-five, to get a hospital year and begin practice at twenty-six or twenty-seven. No one familiar with the American college can lightly ask that this age be raised two years for everybody for the sake of the additional results to be secured from nonprofessional college work. There is, however, little question that compression in the elementary school, closer articulation between and more effective instruction within secondary school and college, can effect economies that will give the youth of twenty-one the advantage of a complete college education. The basis of medical education will thus have been broadened without deferring the actual start.

Meanwhile we are so far from endeavoring to force a single iron-clad standard on the entire country that our proposition explicitly recognizes at least three concurrent levels for the time being: (1) the state university entrance standard in the South; (2) the two-year college basis as legal minimum in the rest of the country; (3) the degree standard in a small number of institutions. . . .

No general legislation is at the moment feasible. The South, for instance, may well rest for a time if every state will at once restrict examinations for license to candidates actually possessing the M.D. degree, and require after, say, January 1, 1911, that every such degree shall emanate from a medical school whose entrance standards are at least those of the state university. Such legislation would suppress the schools that now demoralize the situation; it would concentrate the better students in a few solvent institutions to which the next moves may safely be left. Elsewhere, every available agency should be employed to bring examining boards to reinterpret the work "equivalent" and to adopt efficient machinery for the enforcement of the intended standard.

Equivalent means "equal in force, quality, and effect." The only authorities competent to pass on such values are trained experts. The entire matter would be in their hands if the state boards should in every state delegate the function of evaluating entrance credentials to a competently organized institution of learning. In many states, the state university could very properly perform this duty; elsewhere, an equally satisfactory arrangement could be made with an endowed institution. Whatever the standard fixed, it would thus be intelligently enforced.

The school catalogs would then announce that no student can be matriculated whose credentials are not filed within ten days of the opening of the session, and that no M.D. degree can be conferred until at least four years subsequent to complete satisfaction of the preliminary requirement. These credentials, sent at once to the secretary of the state board, would be by him turned over to the registrar of the state or other university, whose verdict would be final. A state that desired to enforce a four-year high school requirement could specify as satisfying its requirements:

1. Certificate of admission to a state university requiring a four-year high school education.

2. Certificate of admission to any institution that is a member of the Association of American Universities.

3. Medical student certificate of the regents of the University of the State of New York.

4. Certificates issued by the College Entrance Examination Board for fourteen units.

In exchange for such credentials, or for high school diplomas acceptable to the academic authorities acting for the state board, a medical student certificate would be issued; in default thereof, the student must by examination earn one of the aforesaid credentials, in its turn to be made the basis of his medical student certificate. In the Southern states, the legal minimum would be necessarily below the four-year high school; in Minnesota, above it. But the same sort of machinery would work. The schools would have nothing to do with it except to keep systematically registered the name of the student and the number of his certificate; the state board or the university acting for it would keep everything else, open to inspection.

This is substantially what takes place in New York, where the State Education Department superintends the process. What is wanted in other states is an agency similarly qualified. For the present nothing can so well perform the office within a given state as its state university, or, in default thereof, the best of its endowed institutions. This suggestion is perfectly fair to all medical schools, for the credentials would pass through the hands of the state board to the reviewing authority without information as to the purpose of the applicant. The directions required would take up less space in the medical school catalogs than the complicated details they now contain.

It should be further provided that the original credentials of every student be kept on file in the office of the state board or the reviewing university, and that they shall be open to inspection, without notice, by properly accredited representatives of medical and educational organizations. These simple measures would introduce intelligence and sincerity where subterfuge and disorder now prevail. The beneficial results to the high school and the medical school would be incalculable. Nor would the poor boy be subjected to the least hardship; for by exercising forethought, he could accumulate genuine scholastic credits by examination or otherwise, *pari passu*, during the time he is accumulating the money for his medical education.

So much actually accomplished, the rest will be easier. The reduced number of schools will not resist the forces making for a higher legal minimum. The state universities of the West will doubtless lead this movement; for once established on the two-year college basis, they will induce the states to protect their own sons and the public health against the lower-grade doctors made elsewhere. The University of Minnesota, having by statesmanlike action got rid of all other medical schools in the state, is thus backed up by the legislature and the state board. North Dakota and Indiana have taken the same stand. Michigan and Iowa will probably soon follow. "The adjustment is perhaps difficult, but not too difficult for American strength."

50.

WILLIAM ALLEN WHITE: The Growth of Democracy in America

During the first decade of this century, a number of states passed reform laws that reflected the demand for popular control of government. Some examples of the new trend were the initiative, referendum, and recall, the secret ballot, and the direct primary. In 1909 William Allen White, the editor of the Emporia (Kansas) Gazette, *who became famous after his editorial "What's the Matter with Kansas?" was published in 1896, wrote a series of articles based upon detailed research into state reform programs. The following year, the articles were collected in a book,* The Old Order Changeth. *The selection, taken from the chapter "The Beginnings of the Change," summarizes White's faith in Progressive reform.*

Source: *The Old Order Changeth*, New York, 1910, pp. 50-57.

IT WAS TWENTY YEARS AGO that Senator Ingalls of Kansas, one of the cleanest men in public life in that day, looking ahead to the limit of his vision, said: "The purification of politics is an iridescent dream."

But the secret ballot, the direct primary, and the purged party — which are now fairly well assured in American politics — do not set the metes and bounds of progress toward self-government in this country. They are fundamental reforms, it is true, and they are the steps that are necessary before there may be any real forward movement. For it will be seen that each one of these movements is a leveling process, a tendency to make money, capital, property, wealth, or financial distinction count for nothing save as an indirect influence in the ballot box. Each of these innovations, the secret ballot, the primary, and the reformed party, is a step toward democracy — a step toward the Declaration of Independence and away from the Constitution, which so feared majority rule that the majority was hedged about with checks and balances at every possible point.

In the early days of the republic, the people annulled the Constitution by getting a direct vote on the President, and thus obtained the executive branch of the government. Now they are capturing the legislative branch through the primary, which today puts over half the United States senators under the direct vote of the people. When one stops to think that in Oregon, Washington, Nevada, Idaho, California, North Dakota, South Dakota, Nebraska, Kansas, Oklahoma, Texas, Louisiana, Arkansas, Missouri, Iowa, Wisconsin, Ohio, Alabama, Mississippi, Florida, Georgia, Tennessee, South Carolina, Virginia, New Jersey, and Kentucky, United States senators at the next election will go directly to the people for nominations, and not to the railroads and the public service corporations of their respective states; in short, not to capital as they did ten years ago, one realizes how revolutionary are the changes that are coming into our system. The democracy that was gathering strength in the days of Hanna is beginning to move in the nation.

Indeed, the growth of fundamental democracy in this country is astonishing. Thirty years ago the secret ballot was regarded as a passing craze by professional politicians. Twenty years ago it was a vital issue in nearly every American state. Today the secret ballot is universal in American politics. Ten years ago the direct primary was the subject of an academic discussion in the University of Michigan by a young man named La Follette of Wisconsin. Now it is in active operation in over two-thirds of our American states, and over half of the American people use the direct primary as a weapon of self-government.

Five years ago the recall was a piece of freak legislation in Oregon. Today more American citizens are living under laws giving them the power of recall than were living under the secret ballot when Garfield came to the White House, and many times more people have the power to recall certain public officers today than had the advantages of the direct primary form of party nominations when Theodore Roosevelt came to Washington. The referendum is only five years behind the primary. Prophecy with these facts before one becomes something more than a rash guess.

The democracy has the executive and the legislative branches of the state and federal government under its direct control; for in the nomination of a majority of the members of the House and of the Senate the personification of property is unimportant. By making the party a legalized state institution, by paying for the party primaries with state taxes, by requiring candidates at primaries to file their expense accounts and a list of their contributors (as is done in some states), by limiting the amount to be spent (as is done in certain states), and by guaranteeing a secret vote and a fair count, the state has broken the power of money in politics. Capital is not eliminated from politics, but it is hampered and circumscribed and is not the dominant force that it was ten years ago. Then the political machine was financed by capital invested in public service corporations and was continually trying to avoid the responsibility of its public partnership. Then the political machine quietly sold special privileges to public service corporations. Now the political machine is in a fair way to be reduced to mere political scrap iron by the rise of the people.

Today, in states having the primary under the state control, the corporation candidate for any public office is handicapped. The men elected to the United States Senate from states having the Northern type of primary generally have been free men, free from machine and corporation taint. Under the primary system any clean, quick-witted man in these states can defeat the corporation senatorial candidate at the primary if the people desire to defeat him. This advance alone is worth the cost of the primary — something like $100,000 for each state biennially. Moreover, the fact that governors and state officers, legislators and county officers, also are free men makes the primary invaluable in terms of money.

Taft and Bryan, the two men who had less money behind them than any of their opponents, the two men whom the "interests" did not wish to see nominated, headed the tickets of the two great parties in 1908. And when those United States senators who win their nominations and elections without the aid of the railroads and the public service corporations, and win in the face of the opposition of these organizations of capital — when these senators begin to name federal judges, the Supreme Court will begin to reverse itself and the people will capture the lower federal courts — the last citadel of capital. But that is almost an "iridescent dream."

However, just now the people are finding a way around the legislative veto of the state courts. And this they are doing more generally than may be realized by many people. The voters are taking two methods of circumventing the legislative veto of the courts: first, by amending their state constitutions, or making new constitutions; and, second, by direct legislation, or the modification of it known as the initiative and referendum. State courts are elective and therefore are afraid of majorities. They cannot declare constitutional amendments unconstitutional, and they handle laws adopted by a direct vote of the people with great care. Hence the prevalence of the constitutional amendment in American states, and the growth of the initiative and referendum from Maine to California. The tendency to amend a state constitution is not a local phenomenon. In 1908 California voted on eighteen amendments and Missouri voted on eight.

If a state may be said to have a tendency to amend its constitution when it has voted upon one or more amendments at nearly every biennial election for half a dozen years, then the tendency is fairly marked in California, Alabama, Utah, Massachusetts, Oregon, Rhode Island, Texas, Minnesota, New Jersey, Montana, Florida, Maryland, and Mississippi; in New York, where the amendment is a slow and difficult process; in Vermont, where there is agitation for a constitutional convention; in Michigan, where a new constitution has just been adopted; in Illinois; in Maine, where the initiative and referendum has just been instituted by constitutional amendment; and in New Hampshire, Louisiana, Missouri, and Kansas. Where the habit of amending the state constitution becomes settled, as it is in California and Missouri, the habit amounts to a public referendum of many laws, and from the standpoint of direct legislation and government by the majority this habit is praiseworthy. If, however, the guarantee of absolutely unrestricted capital is considered more important than the majority rule, the habit of amending the constitution is dangerous and revolutionary.

The value of the initiative and referendum depends also upon the point from which it is viewed. In certain quarters politics is considered the science of government of the many by the few. Also a government is considered excellent when it protects investment, when it makes the right of contract more important than the welfare of citizens, when it protects vested rights even after they become vested wrongs. In those quarters the initiative and referendum, which is coming into American government as surely as the secret ballot came, will be deemed a dangerous menace to our institutions. Certainly it is a departure from the idea of a government by the few which inspired the fathers of the federal Constitution when Chief Justice John Marshall gave the federal judiciary the final veto on all laws passed by state or national legislatures.

And the issue should be met candidly. The friends of the movement for direct legislation should admit frankly that the purpose of their cause is twofold; first, to compel legislatures to act quickly and without evasion; and, second, to circumvent the veto of such courts as are elective and hence dependent upon popular majorities, and to put whatever righteousness there is in a definitely registered expression of popular will before such courts as are not elective to stay them in their vetoes. For the veto power of the American courts over legislation — under the assumed right to declare legislation "unconstitutional" — is one of the most ruthless checks upon democracy permitted by any civilized people. European kings and courts do not have such reactionary power; yet in the end it seems to make for righteousness. Because under that power in America people have developed a patience and a conscience and a patriotic self-abnegation which fits them to progress in the light of the vision within them. So the initiative and referendum — a most outlandish phrase — which is coming into state governments and city governments all over the country will be the instrument of a self-restrained people. It will not be the weapon of a mob.

51.

Theodore Roosevelt: The New Nationalism

In the summer of 1910, former President Theodore Roosevelt returned to active political life. His speech on August 31, 1910, at the dedication of the John Brown Battlefield at Osawatomie, Kansas, was heralded by many as the beginning of his bid for the 1912 presidential nomination. Adopting Herbert Croly's phrase "new nationalism," Roosevelt outlined a program for widespread reform. Roosevelt's Progressive sympathies are revealed in his stand for a "square deal" for the common man, a demand that, when it was made for labor in 1906, had enhanced his popularity. The speech, reprinted here in part, reflected his belief in a strong executive and contained his mature thinking on the responsibility of government to deal with social problems. It is one of the most influential speeches in American political history.

Source: *The New Nationalism*, New York, 1910, pp. 3-33.

I STAND FOR THE SQUARE DEAL. But when I say that I am for the square deal, I mean not merely that I stand for fair play under the present rules of the game but that I stand for having those rules changed so as to work for a more substantial equality of opportunity and of reward for equally good service. One word of warning, which, I think, is hardly necessary in Kansas. When I say I want a square deal for the poor man, I do not mean that I want a square deal for the man who remains poor because he has not got the energy to work for himself. If a man who has had a chance will not make good, then he has got to quit. And you men of the Grand Army, you want justice for the brave man who fought and punishment for the coward who shirked his work. Is not that so?

Now, this means that our government, national and state, must be freed from the sinister influence or control of special interests. . . . We must drive the special interests out of politics. That is one of our tasks today. Every special interest is entitled to justice — full, fair, and complete — and, now, mind you, if there were any attempt by mob violence to plunder and work harm to the special interest, whatever it may be, that I most dislike, and the wealthy man, whomsoever he may be, for whom I have the greatest contempt, I would fight for him, and you would if you were worth your salt. He should have justice. For every special interest is entitled to justice, but not one is entitled to a vote in Congress, to a voice on the bench, or to representation in any public office. The Constitution guarantees protection to property, and we must make that promise good. But it does not give the right of suffrage to any corporation.

The true friend of property, the true conservative, is he who insists that property shall be the servant and not the master of the commonwealth; who insists that the creature of man's making shall be the servant and not the master of the man who made it. The citizens of the United States must effectively control the mighty commercial forces which they have themselves called into being. There can be no effective control of corporations while their political activity remains. To put an end to it will be neither a short nor an easy task, but it can be done.

We must have complete and effective publicity of corporate affairs so that the people may know beyond peradventure whether the corporations obey the law and whether their management entitles them to the confidence of the public. It is necessary that laws should be passed to prohibit the use of corporate funds directly or indirectly for political purposes; it is still more necessary that such laws should be thoroughly enforced. Corporate expenditures for political purposes, and especially such expenditures by public service corporations, have supplied one of the principal sources of corruption in our political affairs.

It has become entirely clear that we must have government supervision of the capitalization, not only of public service corporations, including, particularly, railways, but of all corporations doing an interstate business. I do not wish to see the nation forced into the ownership of the railways if it can possibly be avoided, and the only alternative is thoroughgoing and effective regulation, which shall be based on a full knowledge of all the facts, including a physical valuation of property. This physical valuation is not needed, or, at least, is very rarely needed, for fixing rates; but it is needed as the basis of honest capitalization.

We have come to recognize that franchises should never be granted, except for a limited time, and never without proper provision for compensation to the public. It is my personal belief that the same kind and degree of control and supervision which should be exercised over public service corporations should be extended also to combinations which control necessaries of life, such as meat, oil, and coal, or which deal in them on an important scale. I have no doubt that the ordinary man who has control of them is much like ourselves. I have no doubt he would like to do well, but I want to have enough supervision to help him realize that desire to do well.

I believe that the officers, and, especially, the directors, of corporations should be held personally responsible when any corporation breaks the law.

Combinations in industry are the result of an imperative economic law which cannot be repealed by political legislation. The effort at prohibiting all combination has substantially failed. The way out lies, not in attempting to prevent such combinations but in completely controlling them in the interest of the public welfare. For that purpose the Federal Bureau of Corporations is an agency of first importance. Its powers, and, therefore, its efficiency, as well as that of the Interstate Commerce Commission, should be largely increased. We have a right to expect from the Bureau of Corporations and from the Interstate Commerce Commission a very high grade of public service. We should be as sure of the proper conduct of the interstate railways and the proper management of interstate business as we are now sure of the conduct and management of the national banks, and we should have as effective supervision in one case as in the other. The Hepburn Act, and the amendment to the act in the shape in which it finally passed Congress at the last session, represent a long step in advance, and we must go yet further.

There is a widespread belief among our people that, under the methods of making tariffs which have hitherto obtained, the special interests are too influential. Probably this is true of both the big special interests and the little special interests. These methods have put a premium on selfishness, and, naturally, the selfish big interests have gotten more than their smaller, though equally selfish, brothers. The duty of Congress is to provide a method by which the interest of the whole people shall be all that receives consideration. To this end there must be an expert tariff commission, wholly removed from the possibility of political pressure or of improper business influence. Such a commission can find the real difference between cost of production, which is mainly the difference of labor cost here and abroad. As fast as its recommendations are made, I believe in revising one schedule at a time. A general revision of the tariff almost inevitably leads to logrolling and the subordination of the general public interest to local and special interests.

The absence of effective state and, especially, national restraint upon unfair money getting has tended to create a small class of enormously wealthy and economically powerful men whose chief object is to hold and increase their power. The prime need is to change the conditions which enable these men to accumulate power which it is not for the general welfare that they should hold or exercise. We grudge no man a fortune which represents his own power and sagacity when exercised with entire regard to the welfare of his fellows. . . . We should permit it to be gained only so long as the gaining represents benefit to the community. This, I know, implies a policy of a far more active governmental interference with social and economic conditions in this country than we have yet had, but I think we have got to face the fact that such an increase in governmental control is now necessary.

No man should receive a dollar unless that dollar has been fairly earned. Every dollar received should represent a dollar's worth of service rendered — not gambling in stocks but service rendered. The really big fortune, the swollen fortune, by the mere fact of its size, acquires qualities which differentiate it in kind as well as in degree from what is possessed by men of relatively small means. Therefore, I believe in a graduated income tax on big fortunes, and in another tax which is far more easily collected and far more effective — a graduated inheritance tax on big fortunes, properly safeguarded against evasion and increasing rapidly in amount with the size of the estate.

The people of the United States suffer from periodical financial panics to a degree substantially unknown among the other nations which approach us in financial strength. There is no reason why we should suffer what they escape. It is of profound importance that our financial system should be promptly investigated and so thoroughly and effectively revised as to make it certain that hereafter our currency will no longer fail at critical times to meet our needs. . . .

Nothing is more true than that excess of every kind is followed by reaction; a fact which should be pondered by reformer and reactionary alike. We are face to face with new conceptions of the relations of property to human welfare, chiefly because certain advocates of the rights of property as against the rights of men have been pushing their claims too far. The man who wrongly holds that every human right is secondary to his profit must now give way to the advocate of human welfare, who rightly maintains that every man holds his property subject to the general right of the community o regulate its use to whatever degree the public welfare may require it.

But I think we may go still further. The right to regulate the use of wealth in the public interest is universally admitted. Let us admit also the right to regulate the terms and conditions of labor, which is the chief element of wealth, directly in the interest of the common good. The fundamental thing to do for every man is to give him a chance to reach a place in which he will make the greatest possible contribution to the public welfare. Understand what I say there. Give him a chance, not push him up if he will not be pushed. Help any man who stumbles; if he lies down, it is a poor job to try to carry him; but if he is a worthy man, try your best to see that he gets a chance to show the worth that is in him.

No man can be a good citizen unless he has a wage more than sufficient to cover the bare cost of living and hours of labor short enough so that after his day's work is done he will have time and energy to bear his share in the management of the community, to help in carrying the general load. We keep countless men from being good citizens by the conditions of life with which we surround them. We need comprehensive workmen's compensation acts, both state and national laws to regulate child labor and work for women, and, especially, we need in our common schools not merely education in book learning but also practical training for daily life and work. We need to enforce better sanitary conditions for our workers and to extend the use of safety appliances for our workers in industry and commerce, both within and between the states. Also, friends, in the interest of the workingman himself we need to set our faces like flint against mob violence just as against corporate greed; against violence and injustice and lawlessness by wage workers just as much as against lawless cunning and greed and selfish arrogance of employers.

If I could ask but one thing of my fellow countrymen, my request would be that, whenever they go in for reform, they remember the two sides, and that they always exact justice from one side as much as from the other. I have small use for the public servant who can always see and denounce the corruption of the capitalist, but who cannot persuade himself, especially before election, to say a word about lawless mob violence. And I have equally small use for the man, be he a judge on the bench, or editor of a great paper, or wealthy and influential private citizen, who can see clearly enough and denounce the lawlessness of mob violence, but whose eyes are closed so that he is blind when the question is one of corruption in business on a gigantic scale. . . .

I do not ask for overcentralization; but I do ask that we work in a spirit of broad and far-reaching nationalism when we work for what concerns our people as a whole. We are all Americans. Our common interests are as broad as the continent. I speak to you here in Kansas exactly as I would speak in New York or Georgia, for the most vital problems are those which affect us all alike. The national government belongs to the whole American people, and where the whole American people are interested, that interest can be guarded effectively only by the national government. The betterment which we seek must be accomplished, I believe, mainly through the national government.

The American people are right in demanding that New Nationalism, without which we cannot hope to deal with new problems. The New Nationalism puts the national need before sectional or personal advantage. It is impatient of the utter confusion that results from local legislatures attempting to treat national issues as local issues. It is still more impatient of the impotence which springs from overdivision of governmental powers, the impotence which makes it possible for local selfishness or for legal cunning, hired by wealthy special interests, to bring national activities to a deadlock. This New Nationalism regards the executive power as the steward of the public welfare. It demands of the judiciary that it shall be interested primarily in human welfare rather than in property, just as it demands that the representative body shall represent all the people rather than any one class or section of the people. . . .

One of the fundamental necessities in a representative government such as ours is to make certain that the men to whom the people delegate their power shall serve the people by whom they are elected and not the special interests. I believe that every national officer, elected or appointed, should be forbidden to perform any service or receive any compensation, directly or indirectly, from interstate corporations; and a similar provision could not fail to be useful within the states.

The object of government is the welfare of the people. The material progress and prosperity of a nation are desirable chiefly so far as they lead to the moral and material welfare of all good citizens. Just in proportion as the average man and woman are honest, capable of sound judgment and high ideals, active in public affairs — but, first of all, sound in their homelife, and the father and mother of healthy children whom they bring up well — just so far, and no farther, we may count our civilization a success. We must have — I believe we have already — a genuine and permanent moral awakening, without which no wisdom of legislation or administration really means anything; and, on the other hand, we must try to secure the social and economic legislation without which any improvement due to purely moral agitation is necessarily evanescent.

52.

William James: The Moral Equivalent of War

"It is instructive to find," wrote William James apropos of American intervention in Venezuela, "how near the surface in all of us the old fighting spirit lies and how slight an appeal will wake it up. Once really waked, there is no retreat." The observation was prophetic, for it was not long before the jingoism of the 1890s swept America into war with Spain. James was an anti-imperialist who watched with regret as "the country puked up its ancient principles" first in Cuba and then in the Philippines. But he was enough of a realist to recognize that war could not be abandoned as an instrument of national policy without finding a substitute for the passions that it satisfied. His famous essay on this subject is reprinted below in part.

Source: *McClure's*, August 1910.

The war against war is going to be no holiday excursion or camping party. The military feelings are too deeply grounded to abdicate their place among our ideals until better substitutes are offered than the glory and shame that come to nations as well as to individuals from the ups and downs of politics and the vicissitudes of trade. There is something highly paradoxical in the modern man's relation to war. Ask all our mil lions, North and South, whether they would vote now (were such a thing possible) to have our war for the Union expunged from history and the record of a peaceful transition to the present time substituted for that of its marches and battles, and probably hardly a handful of eccentrics would say yes.

Those ancestors, those efforts, those memories and legends, are the most ideal part of what we now own together, a sacred spiritual possession worth more than all the blood poured out. Yet ask those same people whether they would be willing in cold blood to start another Civil War now to gain another similar possession, and not one man or woman would vote for the proposition. In modern eyes, precious though wars may be, they must not be waged solely for the sake of the ideal harvest. Only when forced upon one, only when an enemy's injustice leaves us no alternative, is a war now thought permissible.

It was not thus in ancient times. The earlier men were hunting men, and to hunt a neighboring tribe, kill the males, loot the village, and possess the females was the most profitable, as well as the most exciting, way of living. Thus were the more martial tribes selected, and in chiefs and peoples a pure pugnacity and love of glory came to mingle with the more fundamental appetite for plunder.

Modern war is so expensive that we feel trade to be a better avenue to plunder; but modern man inherits all the innate pugnacity and all the love of glory of his ancestors. Showing war's irrationality and horror is of no effect upon him. The horrors make the fascination. War is the *strong* life; it is life *in extremis;* war taxes are the only ones men never hesitate to pay, as the budgets of all nations show us. . . .

The popular imagination fairly fattens on the thought of wars. Let public opinion once reach a certain fighting pitch and no ruler can withstand it. In the Boer War both governments began with bluff but couldn't stay there; the military tension was too much for them. In 1898 our people had read the word "war" in letters three inches high for three months in every newspaper. The pliant politician McKinley was swept away by their eagerness, and our squalid war with Spain became a necessity.

At the present day, civilized opinion is a curious mental mixture. The military instincts and ideals are as strong as ever, but are confronted by reflective criticisms which sorely curb their ancient freedom. Innumerable writers are showing up the bestial side of military service. Pure loot and mastery seem no longer morally avowable motives, and pretexts must be found for attributing them solely to the enemy. England and we, our Army and Navy authorities repeat without ceasing, arm solely for "peace"; Germany and Japan it is who are bent on loot and glory. "Peace" in military mouths today is a synonym for "war expected." The word has become a pure provocative, and no government wishing peace sincerely should allow it ever to be printed in a newspaper. Every up-to-date dictionary should say that "peace" and "war" mean the same thing, now *in posse,* now *in actu.* It may even reasonably be said that the intensely sharp competitive *preparation* for war by the nations *is the real war,* permanent, unceasing; and that the battles are only a sort of public verification of the mastery gained during the "peace" interval.

It is plain that on this subject civilized man has developed a sort of double personality. If we take European nations, no legitimate interest of any one of them would seem to justify the tremendous destructions which a war to compass it would necessarily entail. It would seem as though common sense and reason ought to find a way to reach agreement in every conflict of honest interests. I myself think it our bounden duty to believe in such international rationality as possible. But, as things stand, I see how desperately hard it is to bring the peace party and the war party together, and I believe that the difficulty is due to certain deficiencies in the program of pacificism which set the militarist imagination strongly, and to a certain extent justifiably, against it. In the whole discussion both sides are on imaginative and sentimental ground. It is but one utopia against another, and everything one says must be abstract and hypothetical. Subject to this criticism and caution, I will try to characterize in abstract strokes the opposite imaginative forces and point out what to my own very fallible mind seems the best utopian hypothesis, the most promising line of conciliation.

In my remarks, pacifist though I am, I will refuse to speak of the bestial side of the war regime (already done justice to by many writers) and consider only the higher aspects of militaristic sentiment. Patriotism no one thinks discreditable; nor does anyone deny that war is the romance of history. But inordinate ambitions are the soul of every patriotism and the possibility of violent death the soul of all romance. The militarily patriotic- and romantic-minded everywhere, and especially the professional military class, refuse to admit for a moment that war may be a transitory phenomenon in social evolution. The notion of a sheep's paradise like that revolts, they say, our higher imagination. Where then would be the steeps of life? If war had ever stopped, we should have to re-invent it, on this view, to redeem life from flat degeneration.

Reflective apologists for war at the present day all take it religiously. It is a sort of sacrament. Its profits are to the vanquished as well as to the victor; and quite apart from any question of profit, it is an absolute good, we are told, for it is human nature at its highest dynamic. Its "horrors" are a cheap price to pay for rescue from the only alternative supposed, of a world of clerks and teachers, of coeducation and zoophily, of "consumer's leagues" and "associated charities," of industrialism unlimited, and feminism unabashed. No scorn, no hardness, no valor anymore! Fie upon such a cattleyard of a planet!

So far as the central essence of this feeling goes, no healthy-minded person, it seems to me, can help to some degree partaking of it. Militarism is the great preserver of our ideals of hardihood, and human life with no use for hardihood would be contemptible. Without risks or prizes for the darer, history would be insipid indeed; and there is a type of military character which everyone feels that the race should never cease to breed, for everyone is sensitive to its superiority. The duty is incumbent on mankind, of keeping military characters in stock — of keeping them, if not for use, then as ends in themselves and as pure pieces of perfection — so that Roosevelt's weaklings and mollycoddles may not end by making everything else disappear from the face of nature.

This natural sort of feeling forms, I think, the innermost soul of army writings. Without any exception known to me, militarist authors take a highly mystical view of their subject, and regard war as a biological or sociological necessity, uncontrolled by ordinary psychological checks and motives. When the time of development is ripe, the war must come, reason or no reason, for the justifications pleaded are invariably fictitious. War is, in short, a permanent human *obligation*. Gen. Homer Lea, in his recent book, *The Valor of Ignorance*, plants himself squarely on this ground. Readiness for war is for him the essence of nationality, and ability in it the supreme measure of the health of nations.

Nations, General Lea says, are never stationary, they must necessarily expand or shrink according to their vitality or decrepitude. Japan now is culminating; and by the fatal law in question it is impossible that her statesmen should not long since have entered, with extraordinary foresight, upon a vast policy of conquest — the game in which the first moves were her wars with China and Russia and her treaty with England, and of which the final objective is the capture of the Philippines, the Hawaiian Islands, Alaska, and the whole of our coast west of the Sierra passes. This will give Japan what her ineluctable vocation as a state absolutely forces her to claim, the possession of the entire Pacific Ocean; and to oppose these deep designs we Americans have, according to our author, nothing but our conceit, our ignorance, our commercialism, our corruption, and our feminism.

General Lea makes a minute technical comparison of the military strength which we at present could oppose to the strength of Japan, and concludes that the Islands, Alaska, Oregon, and Southern California would fall almost without resistance, that San Francisco must surrender in a fortnight to a Japanese investment, that in three or four months the war would be over, and our republic, unable to regain what it had heedlessly neglected to protect sufficiently, would then "disintegrate," until perhaps some Caesar should arise to weld us again into a nation.

A dismal forecast indeed! Yet not unplausible, if the mentality of Japan's statesmen be of the Caesarian type of which history shows so many examples, and which is all that General Lea seems able to imagine. But there is no reason to think that women can no longer be the mothers of Napoleonic or Alexandrian characters; and if these come in Japan and find their opportunity, just such surprises as *The Valor of Ignorance* paints may lurk in ambush for us. Ignorant as we still are of the innermost recesses of Japanese mentality, we may be foolhardy to disregard such possibilities.

Other militarists are more complex and more moral in their considerations. The *Philosophie des Krieges* by S. R. Steinmetz, is a good example. War, according to this author, is an ordeal instituted by God, who

The Granger Collection

William James

weighs the nations in its balance. It is the essential form of the state, and the only function in which peoples can employ all their powers at once and convergently. No victory is possible save as the resultant of a totality of virtues, no defeat for which some vice or weakness is not responsible. Fidelity, cohesiveness, tenacity, heroism, conscience, education, inventiveness, economy, wealth, physical health, and vigor — there isn't a moral or intellectual point of superiority that doesn't tell, when God holds His assizes and hurls the peoples upon one another. *Die Weltgeschichte ist das Weltgericht* [The world's history is the world's judgment], and Dr. Steinmetz does not believe that in the long run chance and luck play any part in apportioning the issues.

The virtues that prevail, it must be noted, are virtues anyhow, superiorities that count in peaceful as well as in military competition; but the strain on them, being infinitely intenser in the latter case, makes war infinitely more searching as a trial. No ordeal is comparable to its winnowings. Its dread hammer is the welder of men into cohesive states, and nowhere but in such states can human nature adequately develop its capacity. The only alternative is "degeneration."

Dr. Steinmetz is a conscientious thinker, and his book, short as it is, takes much into account. Its upshot can, it seems to me, be summed up in Simon Patten's word, that mankind was nursed in pain and fear, and that the transition to a "pleasure economy" may be fatal to a being wielding no powers of defense against its disintegrative influences. If we speak of the *fear of emancipation from the fear regime*, we put the whole situation into a single phrase; fear regarding ourselves now taking the place of the ancient fear of the enemy.

Turn the fear over as I will in my mind, it all seems to lead back to two unwillingnesses of the imagination, one aesthetic and the other moral; unwillingness, first to envisage a future in which army life, with its many elements of charm, shall be forever impossible, and in which the destinies of peoples shall nevermore be decided quickly, thrillingly, and tragically, by force, but only gradually and insipidly by "evolution"; and, second, unwillingness to see the supreme theater of human strenuousness closed and the splendid military aptitudes of men doomed to keep always in a state of latency and never show themselves in action. These insistent unwillingnesses, no less than other aesthetic and ethical insistencies, have, it seems to me, to be listened to and respected. One cannot meet them effectively by mere counter-insistency on war's expensiveness and horror. The horror makes the thrill; and when the question is of getting the extremest and supremest out of human nature, talk of expense sounds ignominious.

The weakness of so much merely negative criticism is evident — pacifism makes no converts from the military party. The military party denies neither the bestiality nor the horror, nor the expense; it only says that these things tell but half the story. It only says that war is *worth* them; that, taking human nature as a whole, its wars are its best protection against its weaker and more cowardly self, and that mankind cannot *afford* to adopt a peace economy.

Pacificists ought to enter more deeply into the aesthetical and ethical point of view of their opponents. Do that first in any controversy, says J. J. Chapman, *then move the point*, and your opponent will follow. So long as antimilitarists propose no substitute for war's disciplinary function, no *moral equivalent* of war, analogous, as one might say, to the mechanical equivalent of heat, so long they fail to realize the full inwardness of the situation. And as a rule they do fail. The duties, penalties, and sanctions pictured in the utopias they paint are all too weak and tame to touch the military-minded. Tolstoi's pacificism is the only exception to this rule, for it is profoundly pessimistic as regards all this world's values, and makes the fear of the Lord furnish the moral spur provided elsewhere by the fear of the enemy.

But our socialistic peace advocates all believe absolutely in this world's values; and instead of the fear of the Lord and the fear of the enemy, the only fear they reckon with is the fear of poverty if one be lazy. This weakness pervades all the socialistic literature with which I am acquainted. Even in Lowes Dickinson's exquisite dialogue high wages and short hours are the only forces invoked for overcoming man's distaste for repulsive kinds of labor. Meanwhile, men at large still live as they always have lived, under a plain-and-fear economy — for those of us who live in an ease economy are but an island in the stormy ocean — and the whole atmosphere of present-day utopian literature tastes mawkish and dishwatery to people who still keep a sense for life's more bitter flavors. It suggests, in truth, ubiquitous inferiority.

Inferiority is always with us, and merciless scorn of it is the keynote of the military temper. "Dogs, would you live forever?" shouted Frederick the Great. "Yes," say our utopians, "let us live forever and raise our level gradually." The best thing about our "inferiors" today is that they are as tough as nails, and physically and morally almost as insensitive. Utopianism would see them soft and squeamish, while militarism would keep their callousness, but transfigure it into a meritorious characteristic, needed by "the service," and redeemed by that from the suspicion of inferiority. All the qualities of a man acquire dignity when he knows that the service of the collectivity that owns him needs them. If proud of the collectivity, his own pride rises in proportion. No collectivity is like an army for nourishing such pride; but it has to be confessed that the only sentiment which the image of pacific cosmopolitan industrialism is capable of arousing in countless worthy breasts is shame at the idea of belonging to *such* a collectivity. It is obvious that the United States of America as they exist today impress a mind like General Lea's as so much human blubber. Where is the sharpness and precipitousness, the contempt for life, whether one's own or another's? Where is the savage "yes" and "no," the unconditional duty? Where is the conscription? Where is the blood tax? Where is anything that one feels honored by belonging to?

Having said thus much in preparation, I will now confess my own utopia. I devoutly believe in the reign of peace and in the gradual advent of some sort of a socialistic equilibrium. The fatalistic view of the war function is to me nonsense, for I know that war-making is due to definite motives and subject to prudential checks and reasonable criticisms, just like any other form of enterprise. And when whole nations are the armies and the science of destruction vies in intellectual refinement with the sciences of production, I see that war becomes absurd and impossible from its own monstrosity. Extravagant ambitions will have to be replaced by reasonable claims, and nations must make common cause against them. I see no reason why all this should not apply to yellow as well as to white countries, and I look forward to a future when acts of war shall be formally outlawed as between civilized peoples.

All these beliefs of mine put me squarely into the antimilitarist party. But I do not believe that peace either ought to be or will be permanent on this globe, unless the states pacifically organized preserve some of the old elements of army discipline. A permanently successful peace economy cannot be a simple pleasure economy. In the more or less socialistic future, toward which mankind seems drifting, we must still subject ourselves collectively to those severities which answer to our real position upon this only partly hospitable globe. We must make new energies and hardihood continue the manliness to which the military mind so faithfully clings. Martial virtues must be the enduring cement; intrepidity, contempt of softness, surrender of private interest, obedience to command must still remain the rock upon which states are built — unless, indeed, we wish for dangerous reactions against commonwealths fit only for contempt and liable to invite attack whenever a center of crystallization for military-minded enterprise gets formed anywhere in their neighborhood.

The war party is assuredly right in affirming and reaffirming that the martial virtues, although originally gained by the race through war, are absolute and permanent human goods. Patriotic pride and ambition in their military form are, after all, only specifications of a more general competitive passion. They are its first form, but that is no reason for supposing them to be its last form. Men now are proud of belonging to a conquering nation, and without a murmur they lay down their persons and their wealth if by so doing they may fend off subjection. But who can be sure that *other aspects of one's country* may not, with time and education and suggestion enough, come to be regarded with similarly effective feelings of pride and shame? Why should men not someday feel that it is worth a blood tax to belong to a collectivity superior in *any* ideal respect? Why should they not blush with indignant shame if the community that owns them is vile in any way whatsoever?

Individuals, daily more numerous, now feel this civic passion. It is only a question of blowing on the spark till the whole population gets incandescent, and on the ruin of the old morals of military honor, a stable system of morals of civic honor builds itself up. What the whole community comes to believe in grasps the individual as in a vise. The war function has grasped us so far; but constructive interests may someday seem no less imperative and impose on the individual a hardly lighter burden.

53.

ROBERT HENRI: The New York Exhibition of Independent Artists

"What is necessary for art in America," Robert Henri wrote, "is first an appreciation of the great ideas native to the country and then the achievement of masterly freedom in expressing them." Greatly influenced by the French Impressionists, Henri and many of his colleagues, who became known as the "Ashcan School," painted canvases depicting the bleaker realities. In 1908 and again in 1910, Henri and his friends organized an independent exhibit in revolt against the National Academy, which had not been receptive to their work. In an article, reprinted here in part, Henri described the philosophy behind the exhibitions.

Source: *The Craftsman,* May 1910.

THE EXHIBITION OF INDEPENDENT ARTISTS is not a movement headed by any one man or small group of men. I think that one of the most damaging things that could happen to the progress of art in America would be to personalize this movement in any way. Neither is it an exhibition of the rejected nor an exhibition of people who have had their pictures accepted or refused by the Academy. It is not a gathering together of kickers

of any description but is an expression of the present tendency in America toward developing individuality. This tendency is a great underwave flowing all through America. From the North to the South, from the East to the West, there is an awakening in art matters.

This exhibition is practically an opportunity for individuality, an opportunity for experimenters. The people who got up the ex ibition did so with a view to bringing to-gether all workers, old or young, who have some definite direction in their work; not necessarily directions that the originators of the exhibition might care to follow or might like or even might be sure of under-standing, but a direction that the artist him-self really understands. For instance, if any-one in the exhibition should come to me and say, "Is this the kind of work you stand for?" I should reply, "That is not the question. This work is here because it is the kind of work its author stands for, and I am convinced that he means a definite thing in what he is doing. Therefore I consider that he is furnishing important evidence — that he is a valuable experimenter in this means of human expression."

Freedom to think and to show what you are thinking about, that is what the exhibi-tion stands for. Freedom to study and ex-periment and to present the results of such essay, not in any way being retarded by the standards which are the fashion of the time and not to be exempted from public view because of such individuality or strangeness in the manner of expression. What such an exhibition desires is all the new evidence, all the new opinions that the artists have, and then their work must either succeed by its integrity or fail from the lack of it.

We want to know the ideas of young men. We do not want to coerce them into accepting ours. Every art exhibit should hear from the young as well as the old, and in this one we want to present the indepen-dent personal evidence which each artist has to make and which must become a record of their time and a proof of the advance-ment of human understanding.

This is called an independent exhibition because it is a manifestation of indepen-dence in art and of the absolute necessity of such independence. It does not mean that it is an independent organization, but that it is made up of the independent points of view

of men who are investigating. What such an exhibition should show is the work of those who are pushing forward, who need and deserve recognition, who must have encour-agement, who should receive praise for ev-ery step of their advance. They deserve it because they are thinking. The world should stand and watch their progress, not to criticize, but to be criticized by these es-says.

When we walk into such an exhibition, we may expect to see things which we will not understand, but we should not express instantly the first idea which comes into our minds, because that idea is more apt than not to be an exclamation at the shock we receive at seeing something different from what we had expected. All important steps forward in the world have been received by critics and by the public generally as some-thing ridiculous, impossible — until they were accepted and lauded.

As I see it, there is only one reason for the development of art in America, and that is that the people of America learn the means of expressing themselves in their own time and in their own land. In this country, we have no need of art as a culture; no need of art as a refined and elegant perfor-mance; no need of art for poetry's sake, or any of these things for their own sake. What we do need is art that expresses the *spirit* of the people of today. What we want is to meet young people who are expressing this spirit and listen to what they have to tell us.

Those of us who are old should be anx-ious to be told the things by those who are to advance beyond us, and we should not hate to see them in their progress. We should rejoice that a building is rising on the foundation that we have helped and are still helping to erect. I personally want to see things advance; I want to see work done better by others than I have found possible in my life. I want to see progress.

It should be impossible to have any feeling of jealousy toward those who are young and who are to accomplish the future.

It is necessary for the people in this country to understand *what* art is, to understand *why* it is, to understand that it is the expression of the temperament of our people, that it is the development of the imagination which in the end must affect not only the production of painting, of sculpture, of poems, music, architecture, but every phase of our daily existence. If art is real it must come to affect every action in our lives, every product, every necessary thing. It is, in fact, the understanding of what is needed in life, and then the pursuit of the best means to produce it. It is not learning how to do something which people will call art, but rather inventing something that is absolutely necessary for the progress of our existence.

Our artists must be philosophers; they must be creators; they must be experimenters; they must acquire a knowledge of fundamental law in order that those who seek them and listen to them may learn that there are great laws controlling all existence, that through the understanding of these laws they may live in greater simplicity, greater happiness, and greater beauty. Art cannot be separated from life. It is the expression of the greatest need of which life is capable, and we value art, not because of the skilled product but because of its revelation of a life's experience. The artists who produce the most satisfactory art are in my mind those who are absorbed in the civilization in which they are living.

Take, for instance, Rockwell Kent. He is interested in everything — in political economy, in farming, in every phase of industrial prosperity. He cannot do without this interest in his art. The very things that he portrays on his canvas are the things that he sees written in the great organization of life, and his painting is a proclamation of the rights of man, of the dignity of man, of the dignity of creation. It is his belief in God. It is what art should mean.

Another is John Sloan, with his demand for the rights of man, and his love of the people; his keen observation of the people's folly, his knowledge of their virtues, and his surpassing interest in all things. I have never met Sloan but what he had something new to tell me of some vital thing in life that interested him, and which probably was eventually typified in his work.

William Glackens is in this exhibition, as usual, unique in mind, unique in his appreciation of human character, with an element of humor, an element of criticism, always without fear. He shows a wonderful painting of a nude that has many of the qualities that you notice in the Neo-Impressionist movement. But Glackens seems to me to have attained a greater beauty and a more fundamental truth. There is something rare, something new in the thing that he has to say. At first it may shock you a little, perhaps a great deal. You question, but you keep looking; you grow friendly toward his art; you come back and you get to feel toward the things that you have criticized as you do toward the defects in the face of a person whom you have grown to like very much. They become essential to you in the whole; and the whole with Glackens is always so much alive, so much the manifestation of a temperament intensely sincere and intensely brave.

A man whose work is beautiful because he is close to life is Jerome Myers. He is also a dreamer; he works close to the little people in this world of New York. He is a lover of people, and in his pictures he tells you what he knows of humanity's ways. You don't stop to question his technique, although that is good enough, too; but in studying his paintings you study the soul of the man and his knowledge of the world and the breadth of his kindness.

Not one of these men will talk to you of their technique or of any organization they are interested in or any effort to form a society. They will tell you that they want independence for their ideas, independence for every man's idea. Why, this country was founded with the idea of independence, with the idea of man's right for freedom. We do not think much about this, and yet it was the first idea that caused people to fight under the leadership of such a man as Patrick Henry. . . .

I do not wish to convey the idea that this exhibition was planned for the work of young people; at least, for those who are young in their abilities as artists, because most of the exhibitors are not young people. A few of them are older than some very old artists that I know. Take the picture, for instance, of Julius Golz, the painter of Blackwell's Island and the East River. What force and power is in this man's work. He seems to be the only man who has ever painted the East River, that wonderful snowswept fence against that absolutely deep and tragic water and then beyond, Blackwell's Island, and all done without a particle of sentimentality. As a canvas it stands as a striking piece of realism, and, yet, in the hanging, it is associated with and is a most natural accompaniment to the painting of Arthur Davies, the great imaginator. Side by side with the work of these two men is the painting showing the tenderness and bravery and the imagination of Homer Boss, and down the line is John Sloan's "clown," a wonderful piece of work.

I want to speak again of John Sloan, of his painting of the backs of houses, old Twenty-second Street houses, with the boys on the roof startling the pigeons into flight. It is a human document of the lives of the people living in those houses. You feel the incidents in the windows, the incidents in the construction of the houses, the incidents in the wear and tear on them; in fact, the life of that neighborhood is all shown in the little line of houses, yellow and red houses, warm in the sunlight. And the quality of the sunlight is that of a caress; the houses, the atmosphere are steeped in its warmth.

These are some of the things that it seems to me a person will see at the Independent Exhibition of pictures. Those who are looking for exhibitions of culture in some set form or fashion in art will probably not see these things, because of the prejudice of their point of view, because they are really looking in different directions. They are looking for the signs of the acquirement of the fashion in art of the day; they are not looking for the thoughts, the feelings, the life of a man; they are not searching for a personal record in a man's work. They seek an accomplishment in a trade. . . .   .

I have been asked if this Independent Exhibition will become a permanent organization. I have not the slightest doubt but what the *idea* will go on, but I personally have no interest whatever in forming it into a society; and if an institution were formed and I were to become a member of it, I would probably be the first man to secede from it, because I can see no advantage to art in the existence of art societies. The thing that interests me in this is the idea of it, the idea of independence, the idea of encouragement of independence and individuality in study, and the giving of an opportunity for greater freedom in exhibitions.

I have been thinking for a long time what possible substitute could be furnished for the Academy idea, in what way pictures could be exhibited entirely without the jury and the hanging committee, and suggest the following scheme, which seems practical to me. A gallery that might be of great educational value and of great honor to the city of New York could be established along the following lines: It would be perhaps some three or four times larger than the present Fine Arts Building on Fifty-seventh Street, New York. It would contain many rooms of equal value for exhibition purposes, these rooms to be at the service of artists who would form themselves into groups of twenty, gaining by the formation of their body the right to use one of the rooms for a period of one month. A waiting list might occur, because there might be many groups of twenty men who would care to associate themselves in one exhibition.

Such a gallery should be under the freest of direction. It should be a city institution, actually for the advancement and encouragement of the arts, a place for trying out the artists' ideas, a place where they could exhibit and where there was no judge except the public, and the nineteen other men of the same group. This proposition seems to me to do away with any permanent organization of artists, with any board of officers, with any presidents, with any body of men who sit in judgment on other men. All that is necessary is for a man to be acceptable to nineteen other artists who are sufficiently in accord to wish to ally themselves in an exhibition. Should a man go alone to this gallery and say, "I have absolutely the greatest thing in the world so far as art is concerned, but I cannot get a chance to exhibit. I want you to give me a place in your galleries," the reply would be, "Find nine-

teen other artists who believe in your sincerity or worth sufficiently to form themselves into a group and exhibit with you, and the room is yours. But you must ring true to nineteen other men thinking along your own lines and judging your work from the point of view of a fellow worker."

I have been asked what answer would be made if a group of students banded themselves together and asked for an opportunity of exhibiting. My immediate answer is, "Why not? We want to see what they are doing." Of course, there would be mistakes, but we could not make any more than we are successful in doing today in our institutions. We should at least have groups of men who believe in each other, who are trying to understand each other, and who if they criticize, do it from the point of view of intelligent understanding and sincerity. Such a gallery as this would furnish New York what it should wish to have — an open field for the searcher, the opportunity to show what he is searching for, the chance to be laughed at, if necessary, but at least the chance to prove that he knows what he is aiming at. It would be a battleground for the testing of new ideas and new intentions, and such a battleground should be free from all dictatorship. Every man should find it an open door to an open road, and it should stand for the truth about art in America.

Knowin' all about baseball is just about as profitable as bein' a good whittler.
                                                            KIN HUBBARD

1911

54.

ALBERT G. SPALDING: Our National Game

Baseball was a popular game even before the Civil War, but it was not until after the war that it became a professional sport. The National League was organized in 1876 as the controlling body of the newly established professional teams, and the American League was organized in 1901 as a competing association. From then on, baseball was big business as well as mass entertainment. Albert G. Spalding, who had helped organize the National League, gave some reasons why the game had taken such a strong hold on the American popular imagination.

Source: *America's National Game*, New York, 1911, pp. 3-14.

HAVE WE, OF AMERICA, a national game? Is there in our country a form of athletic pastime which is distinctively American? Do our people recognize, among their diversified field sports, one standing apart from every other, outclassing all in its hold upon the interest and affection of the masses? If a negative reply may truthfully be given to all or any of these queries, then this book should never have been published — or written.

But, if we have a national game; if we know a form of athletics which is peculiarly American and have adopted it as our own; if it is American in its spirit, its character, and its achievements; if it conforms in every way to the American temperament; if we have a field sport outranking all others in popularity, then it is indeed time that the writing, in personal reminiscence, of its story in book form should begin, "lest we forget" the salient points in the inception, evolution, and development of so important a factor in the widespread entertainment of the American people and the physical upbuilding of our youth.

To enter upon a deliberate argument to prove that baseball is our national game; that it has all the attributes of American origin, American character, and unbounded public favor in America, seems a work of supererogation. It is to undertake the elucidation of a patent fact, the sober demonstration of an axiom; it is like a solemn declaration that two plus two equal four.

Every citizen of this country who is blessed with organs of vision knows that whenever the elements are favorable and wherever grounds are available the great American game is in progress, whether in city, village, or hamlet, east, west, north, or south, and that countless thousands of interested spectators gather daily throughout the season to witness contests which are to determine the comparative excellence of competing local organizations or professional league teams.

The statement will not be successfully challenged that the American game of baseball attracts more numerous and larger gatherings of spectators than any other form of field sport in any land. It must also be admitted that it is the only game known for which the general public is willing day after day to pay the price of admission. In exciting political campaigns, presidential candidates and brilliant orators will attract thousands; but let there be a charge of half a dollar imposed, and only baseball can stand the test.

I claim that baseball owes its prestige as our national game to the fact that as no other form of sport it is the exponent of American courage, confidence, combativeness; American dash, discipline, determination; American energy, eagerness, enthusiasm; American pluck, persistency, performance; American spirit, sagacity, success; American vim, vigor, virility.

Baseball is the American game *par excellence*, because its playing demands brain and brawn, and American manhood supplies these ingredients in quantity sufficient to spread over the entire continent.

No man or boy can win distinction on the ball field who is not, as man or boy, an athlete, possessing all the qualifications which an intelligent, effective playing of the game demands. Having these, he has within him the elements of pronounced success in other walks of life. In demonstration of this broad statement of fact, one needs only to note the brilliant array of statesmen, judges, lawyers, preachers, teachers, engineers, physicians, surgeons, merchants, manufacturers, men of eminence in all the professions and in every avenue of commercial and industrial activity who have graduated from the ball field to enter upon honorable careers as American citizens of the highest type, each with a sane mind in a sound body.

It seems impossible to write on this branch of the subject — to treat of baseball as our national game — without referring to cricket, the national field sport of Great Britain and most of her colonies. Every writer on this theme does so. But, in instituting a comparison between these games of the two foremost nations of earth, I must not be misunderstood. Cricket is a splendid game, for Britons. It is a genteel game, a conventional game — and our cousins across the Atlantic are nothing if not conventional. They play cricket because it accords with the traditions of their country so to do; because it is easy and does not overtax their energy or their thought. They play it because they like it and it is the proper thing to do. Their sires, and grandsires, and great-grandsires played cricket — why not they? They play cricket because it is their national game, and every Briton is a patriot. They play it persistently — and they play it well. I have played cricket and like it. There are some features about that game which I admire more than I do some things about baseball.

But cricket would never do for Americans; it is too slow. It takes two and sometimes three days to complete a first-class cricket match; but two hours of baseball is quite sufficient to exhaust both players and spectators. An Englishman is so constituted by nature that he can wait three days for the result of a cricket match; while two hours is about as long as an American can wait for the close of a baseball game — or anything else, for that matter. The best cricket team ever organized in America had its home in Philadelphia — and remained there. Cricket does not satisfy the red-hot blood of young or old America.

The genius of our institutions is democratic; baseball is a democratic game. The spirit of our national life is combative; baseball is a combative game. We are a cosmopolitan people, knowing no arbitrary class distinctions, acknowledging none. The son of a President of the United States would as soon play ball with Patsy Flannigan as with Lawrence Lionel Livingstone, provided only that Patsy could put up the right article. Whether Patsy's dad was a banker or boilermaker would never enter the mind of the White House lad. It would be quite enough for him to know that Patsy was up in the game.

I have declared that cricket is a genteel game. It is. Our British cricketer, having finished his day's labor at noon, may don his negligee shirt, his white trousers, his gorgeous hosiery, and his canvas shoes, and sally forth to the field of sport, with his sweetheart on one arm and his cricket bat under the other, knowing that he may engage in his national pastime without soiling his linen or neglecting his lady. He may play cricket, drink afternoon tea, flirt, gossip, smoke, take a whiskey-and-soda at the customary hour, and have a jolly, conventional good time, don't you know?

Not so the American ball player. He may be a veritable Beau Brummell in social life. He may be the swellest swell of the smart set in Swelldom; but when he dons his baseball suit, he says good-bye to society, doffs his gentility, and becomes — just a ball player! He knows that his business now is to play ball, and that first of all he is expected to attend to business. It may happen to be his business to slide; hence, forgetting his beautiful new flannel uniform, he cares not if the mud is four inches deep at the base he intends to reach. His sweetheart may be in the grandstand — she probably is — but she is not for him while the game lasts.

Cricket is a gentle pastime. Baseball is war! Cricket is an athletic sociable, played and applauded in a conventional, decorous, and English manner. Baseball is an athletic turmoil, played and applauded in an unconventional, enthusiastic, and American manner.

The founder of our national game became a major general in the United States Army! The sport had its baptism when our country was in the preliminary agonies of a fratricidal conflict. Its early evolution was among the men, both North and South, who, during the war of the 1860s, played the game to relieve the monotony of camp life in those years of melancholy struggle. It was the medium by which, in the days following the "late unpleasantness," a million warriors and their sons, from both belligerent sections, passed naturally, easily, gracefully from a state of bitter battling to one of perfect peace.

Baseball, I repeat, is war! And the playing of the game is a battle in which every contestant is a commanding general, who, having a field of occupation, must defend it; who, having gained an advantage, must hold it by the employment of every faculty of his brain and body, by every resource of his mind and muscle.

But it is a bloodless battle; and when the struggle ends, the foes of the minute past are friends of the minute present, victims congratulating victors, conquerors pointing out the brilliant individual plays of the conquered.

It would be as impossible for a Briton, who had not breathed the air of this free land as a naturalized American citizen; for one who had no part or heritage in the hopes and achievements of our country, to play baseball, as it would for an American, free from the trammels of the English traditions, customs, conventionalities, to play the national game of Great Britain.

Let such an Englishman stand at the batter's slab on an American ball field, facing the son of an American President in the pitcher's box, and while he was ruminating upon the propriety of hitting, in his "best form," a ball delivered by the hands of so august a personage, the President's boy would probably shoot three hot ones over the plate, and the umpire's "Three strikes; you're out," would arouse our British cousin to a realization that we have a game too lively for any but Americans to play.

On the other hand, if one of our cosmopolitan ball artists should visit England and attempt a game of cricket, whether it were Cobb, Lajoie, Wagner, or any American batsman of Scandinavian, Irish, French, or German antecedents, simply because he was an American, and even though the cricket ball were to be bowled at his feet by King George himself, he would probably hit the sphere in regular baseball style, and smash all conventionalities at the same time, in his eager effort to clear the bases with a three bagger.

The game of baseball is American as to another peculiar feature. It is the only form of field sport known where spectators have an important part and actually participate in the game. Time was, and not long ago, when comparatively few understood the playing rules; but the day has come when nearly every man and boy in the land is versed in all the intricacies of the pastime; thousands of young women have learned it well enough to keep score, and the number of matrons who know the difference between the shortstop and the backstop is daily increasing.

But neither our wives, our sisters, our daughters, nor our sweethearts may play baseball on the field. They may play cricket, but seldom do; they may play lawn tennis, and win championships; they may play basketball, and achieve laurels; they may play golf, and receive trophies; but baseball is too strenuous for womankind, except as she may take part in grandstand, with applause for the brilliant play, with waving kerchief to the hero of the three bagger, and, since she is ever a loyal partisan to the home team, with smiles of derision for the umpire when he gives us the worst of it, and, for the same reason, with occasional perfectly decorous demonstrations when it becomes necessary to rattle the opposing pitcher.

But spectators of the sterner sex may play the game on field, in grandstand, or on bleachers, and the influence they exert upon the contest is hardly less than that of the competitors themselves.

In every town, village, and city is the local wag. He is a baseball fan from infancy. He knows every player in the league by sight and by name. He is a veritable encyclopaedia of information on the origin, evolution, and history of the game. He can tell you when the Knickerbockers were organized and knows who led the batting list in every team of the National and American Leagues last year. He never misses a game. His witticisms, ever seasoned with spice, hurled at the visitors and now and then at the umpire, are as thoroughly enjoyed by all who hear them as is any other feature of the sport. His words of encouragement to the home team, his shouts of derision to the opposing players find sympathetic responses in the hearts of all present.

But it is neither the applause of the women nor the jokes of the wag which make for victory or defeat in comparison with the work of the "rooter." He is ever present in large numbers. He is there to see the "boys" win. Nothing else will satisfy him. He is bound by no rules of the game and, too often, perhaps, by no laws of decorum. His sole object in life for two mortal hours is to gain victory for the home team, and that he is not overscrupulous as to the amount of racket emanating from his immediate vicinity need not be emphasized here.

And so it comes to pass that at every important game there is an exhibition in progress, in grandstand and on bleachers, that is quite as interesting in its features of excitement and entertainment as is the contest on the field of sport, and which, in its bearing upon the final result, is sometimes a factor nearly as potent as are the efforts of the contesting players.

It must be admitted that as the game of baseball has become more generally known; that is, as patrons of the sport are coming to be more familiar with its rules and its requirements, their enjoyment has immeasurably increased; because, just insofar as those in attendance understand the features presented in every play, so far are they able to become participators in the game itself. And beyond doubt it is to this growing knowledge on the part of the general public with the pastime that its remarkable popularity is due. For, despite the old adage, familiarity does *not* breed contempt, but fondness, and all America has come to regard baseball as its very own, to be known throughout the civilized world as the great American national game.

Finally, in one other particular, baseball has won its right to be denominated the American national game. Ever since its establishment in the hearts of the people as the foremost of field sports, baseball has "followed the flag." It followed the flag to the front in the 1860s, and received then an impetus which has carried it to half a century of wondrous growth and prosperity. It has followed the flag to Alaska, where, under the midnight sun, it is played on Arctic ice. It has followed the flag to the Hawaiian Islands, and at once supplanted every other form of athletics in popularity. It has followed the flag to the Philippines, to Puerto Rico, and to Cuba, and wherever a ship floating the stars and stripes finds anchorage today, somewhere on nearby shore the American national game is in progress.

55.

WOODROW WILSON: Commission City Government

Woodrow Wilson had earned a doctorate in political science, had been a professor of the subject and had written widely on it prior to his career as an active politician. His early writings are still considered astute analyses of our political institutions. In the following address, delivered at Seattle, Washington, May 20, 1911, shortly after he became governor of New Jersey, Wilson discussed a novel type of city government — the commission system — that was then gaining currency. It had many features that appealed to him: most particularly, its effective use of experts in municipal administration. Always interested in finding more efficient and honest ways of running a government, Wilson presented a cogent argument for the commission system.

Source: Library of Congress, Manuscript Division: Papers of Woodrow Wilson, Speech File.

NO SINGLE MOVEMENT of reform in our governmental methods has been more significant than the rapid adoption of the so-called commission form of government in the cities of the country. The rapid spread of this reform has been extraordinary. In almost every state, cities are now to be found which have adopted the new form of government, and everywhere, so far as I have been able to learn, the results have been admirable and the cities which have made the change have congratulated themselves upon it.

The most interesting thing about the reform is that it has a very much wider significance than a mere change in the form of city governments would have. There are principles involved in the change which it is very interesting to see coming rapidly into recognition, principles which only a few years ago would hardly have been willingly conceded in any quarter in America.

For one thing, the most conspicuous feature of the new form of city government negatives the greater part of our practice hitherto in trying to establish popular control. Until we began this new movement of reconstruction in city government, it was the commonly accepted doctrine in America that the way to make the people supreme was to make every office elective, to have as few appointive officers as possible, and to put every choice for office, whether the office were great or small, in the hands of the people. We now see that that was exactly the way in which not to make popular control effective.

I suppose that there is not a single voter who has ever voted a ticket with more than ten or fifteen names on it who will not admit that he knew absolutely nothing about most of the persons he was voting for and cared very little about them. Moreover, it has become obvious to anybody who knows anything of the practical operation of politics that the politicians who make up the long tickets with scores of names upon them feel that they have perfect control of all the nominations except those for a few conspicuous offices. They often feel that they have to be careful about a nomination for governor or for congressman or for mayor or for judge, but, beyond these few conspicuous offices, they can do what they please, depending upon the more or less excellent and well-known name to pull the rest of the ticket through. This means, of course, that they put up for genuine election one or two men and virtually appoint the rest to office.

Very few except those of the "inner circle" of the political machine can tell you anything about the nominees on a long ticket or what their nomination signifies and is meant to accomplish. The small talk of politics is full of stories, thought to be amusing, of how long tickets can be manipulated and all sorts of persons smuggled in at the pleasure of party managers.

It is evident upon the face of it that this is not a process of selection, or election either, on the part of the people. It is a process of appointment at the hands of the political managers. It has become an axiom among those who understand practical politics that if you give the people something to do which they cannot do, you virtually take it away from them. It is as impossible for the people to select a miscellany of officers to serve them in posts big and little as it would be for the head of a great business to select the whole body of his employees down to the boy who sweeps out the office. The only way in which he can make his business effective is to put these matters in the hands of responsible superintendents whom he must hold answerable for anything that goes wrong and for the inefficiency of their subordinates.

The very fact that they are almost everywhere adopting the commission form of government for their cities shows that the people have at last discovered this fundamental thing. The central feature of the commission form of government is the very short ballot used in municipal elections, a ballot containing not more than five or six names, the names of the commissioners who are to be held wholly responsible for the conduct of the government of the city, who are expected to choose their own subordinates, organize the various departments of the city government under their own immediate direction, and give the people what they demand — a businesslike, nonpartisan, economical, efficient government. Five or six men the people can watch and hold responsible; more than five or six would escape their notice and would constitute a crowd which they could not follow either with their applause or their censure.

The second thing manifest in the new form of government is that it abandons the idea with which we so long deceived our selves, that a city government is practically a state government in small, which must have its carefully separated executive and legislative branches. Of course there is an analogy between the power of a city council to pass ordinances and the power of a state legislature to pass statutes, but the ordinance-making power is rather regulative, not legislative, and the city is a great administrative organization, not a miniature copy of the government of a state.

Hitherto, moreover, we have not been content with drawing careful lines between executive and legislative action in our city governments. We have sought to multiply checks and balances as elaborately as possible. It has been a favorite device to set up independent boards of finance which should have control of the moneys of the city and determine how much the various departments of the city should be permitted to spend. We have had water boards and gas boards and boards of public works and boards of every kind, each with its independent set of powers, each with its independent derivation from the votes of the people, and have seemed almost of set purpose to multiply the clogs and jealousies and pullings hither and thither of a system which ought, in order to work effectively, to have worked in harmony as a unit and not as a system of rivalries and suspicious checks.

If we are, as now seems probable, to follow along the lines upon which we have started in the matter of our city governments, it is evident that we are going to benefit ourselves greatly by giving up our ancient ingenious art of creating ambushes and jungles in which our politicians can play hide-and-seek with us. The thing which the astute politician should most desire is that authority should be as much subdivided as possible; that each officer should have a function so obscure that nobody could have the time or the curiosity to watch him; that there should be no system of central control; that no one officer should be subordinated to any other officer; and that, above all, there should be independent elections to the several places to be filled. This delightful confusion constitutes the most admirable opportunity for management and contrivance and private combination imaginable. Anything that simplifies the system of necessity purifies it, because simplification means that there are no hiding places for schemes or "framed-up" combinations.

It cannot be an accident that the best governed cities in the world are those in which there is a short ballot, concentrated authority, and, by consequence, expert service; for expert service is bound to come in America, as elsewhere, by reason of this concentration of authority and simplification of political methods. There is no reason why our cities should not have a practical permanent corps of expert officials. In one or two instances the commission form of government has assumed this form. Instead of putting the actual administration of the government in the hands of a commission of five, each one of whom should have charge of a distinct department of the city government, it has been arranged in one or two American cities that the commissioners should be merely the guiding and consultative body. They have been authorized and directed to choose a business manager who should have charge of the administration of the city as their servant, subject to be removed by them at any time and obliged in all particulars to carry out their directions, but nevertheless employed as a professional, an expert, a genuine business manager.

Should this form of commission government be generally adopted, it would undoubtedly result in the growth of a professional class very much to be desired — the development of a body of men whose business it would be to understand the various departments of city government and to take charge of them. Our bureaus of municipal research are producing men who might easily be trained for such purposes, and it is not beyond hoping for that we may be within sight of the time when we shall be able to conduct our cities with real business efficiency at the hands of experts.

The indispensable conditions of success in city government, as in all government, are, first, publicity; and, second, alert public opinion guided in some definite way by those who really understand the business in hand. Nothing ought to be done by a city government, or by any other government, information regarding which is not accessible day by day to any citizen who desires to obtain it. Without publicity, public opinion has not sufficient matter to work upon. With publicity will come the necessity that those who conduct the government should explain the things which are not easily understood by the newspapers or by critics of any kind; and with the necessity of explaining will come as a natural consequence the necessity of leading.

It is the principal business of those who constitute the responsible governing authorities of a city or of a state to explain matters that need explanation and to guide opinion regarding them by something more than explanation, that is, by argument, by proposals of measures of various kinds, by all the legitimate means by which opinion is guided and developed. Government is of necessity in many of its parts a technical and complicated thing. We shall not be saved merely by having experts. We shall be safe only when we have experts who are also capable of being leaders.

56.

WILLIAM HOWARD TAFT: Veto of Arizona Enabling Act

In 1911 President Taft, objecting to the provision for judicial recall in Arizona's constitution, vetoed a joint resolution admitting New Mexico and Arizona to the Union. The veto upset many supporters of the bill, but Taft was a firm believer in the separation of powers of the branches of government and did not believe that the judiciary should be subject to the vagaries of the popular will. He described his reservations about the recall clause in his veto message of August 15, 1911, from which the following selection is taken. Arizona changed its constitution to conform to Taft's wishes but, after admission, restored the objectionable clause.

Source: *Record,* 62 Cong., 1 Sess., pp. 3964-3966.

To the House of Representatives:

I return herewith, without my approval, House Joint Resolution No. 14, "To admit the territories of New Mexico and Arizona as states into the Union on an equal footing with the original states." . . .

If I sign this joint resolution, I do not see how I can escape responsibility for the judicial recall of the Arizona constitution. The joint resolution admits Arizona with the judicial recall, but requires the submission of the question of its wisdom to the voters. In other words, the resolution approves the admission of Arizona with the judicial recall unless the voters themselves repudiate it.

Under the Arizona constitution all elective officers, and this includes county and state judges, six months after their election, are subject to the recall. It is initiated by a petition signed by electors equal to 25 percent of the total number of votes cast for all the candidates for the office at the previous general election. Within five days after the petition is filed the officer may resign. Whether he does or not, an election ensues in which his name, if he does not resign, is placed on the ballot with that of all other candidates.

The petitioners may print on the official ballot 200 words showing their reasons for recalling the officer, and he is permitted to make defense in the same place in 200 words. If the incumbent receives the highest number of the votes, he continues in his office; if not, he is removed from office and is succeeded by the candidate who does receive the highest number.

This provision of the Arizona constitution, in its application to county and state judges, seems to me so pernicious in its effect, so destructive of independence in the judiciary, so likely to subject the rights of the individual to the possible tyranny of a popular majority, and, therefore, to be so injurious to the cause of free government that I must disapprove a constitution containing it.

I am not now engaged in performing the office given me in the Enabling Act . . . approved June 20, 1910, which was that of approving the constitutions ratified by the peoples of the territories. It may be argued from the text of that act that in giving or withholding the approval under the act my only duty is to examine the proposed constitution, and if I find nothing in it inconsistent with the federal Constitution, the principles of the Declaration of Independence, or the Enabling Act, to register my approv-

al. But now I am discharging my constitutional function in respect to the enactment of laws, and my discretion is equal to that of the houses of Congress. I must therefore withhold my approval from this resolution if in fact I do not approve it as a matter of governmental policy.

Of course, a mere difference of opinion as to the wisdom of details in a state constitution ought not to lead me to set up my opinion against that of the people of the territory. It is to be their government, and while the power of Congress to withhold or grant statehood is absolute, the people about to constitute a state should generally know better the kind of government and constitution suited to their needs than Congress or the executive. But when such a constitution contains something so destructive of free government as the judicial recall, it should be disapproved.

A government is for the benefit of all the people. We believe that this benefit is best accomplished by popular government, because in the long run each class of individuals is apt to secure better provision for themselves through their own voice in government than through the altruistic interest of others, however intelligent or philanthropic. The wisdom of ages has taught that no government can exist except in accordance with laws and unless the people under it either obey the laws voluntarily or are made to obey them. In a popular government the laws are made by the people — not by all the people — but by those supposed and declared to be competent for the purpose, as males over twenty-one years of age, and not by all of these — but by a majority of them only.

Now, as the government is for all the people, and is not solely for a majority of them, the majority in exercising control either directly or through its agents is bound to exercise the power for the benefit of the minority as well as the majority. But all have recognized that the majority of a people, unrestrained by law, when aroused and without the sobering effect of deliberation and discussion, may do injustice to the minority or to the individual when the selfish interest of the majority prompts. Hence arises the necessity for a constitution by which the will of the majority shall be permitted to guide the course of the government only under controlling checks that experience has shown to be necessary to secure for the minority its share of the benefit to the whole people that a popular government is established to bestow.

A popular government is not a government of a majority, by a majority, for a majority of the people. It is a government of the whole people by a majority of the whole people under such rules and checks as will secure a wise, just, and beneficent government for all the people. It is said you can always trust the people to do justice. If that means all the people and they all agree, you can. But ordinarily they do not all agree, and the maxim is interpreted to mean that you can always trust a majority of the people. This is not invariably true; and every limitation imposed by the people upon the power of the majority in their constitutions is an admission that it is not always true. No honest, clearheaded man, however great a lover of popular government, can deny that the unbridled expression of the majority of a community converted hastily into law or action would sometimes make a government tyrannical and cruel.

Constitutions are checks upon the hasty action of the majority. They are the self-imposed restraints of a whole people upon a majority of them to secure sober action and a respect for the rights of the minority, and of the individual in his relation to other individuals, and in his relation to the whole people in their character as a state or government. . . .

What I have said has been to little purpose if it has not shown that judges to fulfill their functions properly in our popular government must be more independent than in any other form of government, and that need of independence is greatest where the individual is one litigant and the state, guided by the successful and governing majority, is the other. In order to maintain the rights of the minority and the individual and to preserve our constitutional balance, we must have judges with courage to decide against the majority when justice and law require.

By the recall in the Arizona constitution, it is proposed to give to the majority power to remove arbitrarily and without delay any judge who may have the courage to render an unpopular decision. . . . Other candidates are permitted to present themselves and have their names printed on the ballot, so that the recall is not based solely on the record or the acts of the judge but also on the question whether some other and more popular candidate has been found to unseat him. Could there be a system more ingeniously devised to subject judges to momentary gusts of popular passion than this?

We cannot be blind to the fact that often an intelligent and respectable electorate may be so roused upon an issue that it will visit with condemnation the decision of a just judge, though exactly in accord with the law governing the case, merely because it affects unfavorably their contest. Controversies over elections, labor troubles, racial or religious issues, issues as to the construction or constitutionality of liquor laws, criminal trials of popular or unpopular defendants, the removal of county seats, suits by individuals to maintain their constitutional rights in obstruction of some popular improvement — these and many other cases could be cited in which a majority of a district electorate would be tempted by hasty anger to recall a conscientious judge if the opportunity were open all the time.

No period of delay is interposed for the abatement of popular feeling. The recall is devised to encourage quick action and to ead the people to strike while the iron is hot. The judge is treated as the instrument and servant of a majority of the people and subject to their momentary will, not after a long term in which his qualities as a judge and his character as a man have been subjected to a test of all the varieties of judicial work and duty so as to furnish a proper means of measuring his fitness for continuance in another term. On the instant of an unpopular ruling, while the spirit of protest has not had time to cool, and even while an appeal may be pending from his ruling, in which he may be sustained, he is to be haled before the electorate as a tribunal, with no judicial hearing, evidence, or defense, and thrown out of office and disgraced for life because he has failed, in a single decision, it may be, to satisfy the popular demand.

Think of the opportunity such a system would give to unscrupulous political bosses in control, as they have been in control not only of conventions but elections! Think of the enormous power for evil given to the sensational, muckraking portion of the press in rousing prejudice against a just judge by false charges and insinuations, the effect of which in the short period of an election by recall it would be impossible for him to meet and offset! Supporters of such a system seem to think that it will work only in the interest of the poor, the humble, the weak, and the oppressed; that it will strike down only the judge who is supposed to favor corporations and be affected by the corrupting influence of the rich. Nothing could be further from the ultimate result. The motive it would offer to unscrupulous combinations to seek to control politics in order to control the judges is clear.

Those would profit by the recall who have the best opportunity of rousing the majority of the people to action on a sudden impulse. Are they likely to be the wisest or the best people in a community? Do they not include those who have money

enough to employ the firebrands and slanderers in a community and the stirrers-up of social hate? Would not self-respecting men well hesitate to accept judicial office with such a sword of Damocles hanging over them? What kind of judgments might those on the unpopular side expect from courts whose judges must make their decisions under such legalized terrorism? The character of the judges would deteriorate to that of trimmers and timeservers, and independent judicial action would be a thing of the past. As the possibilities of such a system pass in review, is it too much to characterize it as one which will destroy the judiciary, its standing, and its usefulness?

The argument has been made to justify the judicial recall that it is only carrying out the principle of the election of the judges by the people. The appointment by the executive is by the representative of the majority, and so far as future bias is concerned there is no great difference between the appointment and the election of judges. The independence of the judiciary is secured rather by a fixed term and fixed and irreducible salary. It is true that when the term of judges is for a limited number of years and reelection is necessary, it has been thought and charged sometimes that shortly before election, in cases in which popular interest is excited, judges have leaned in their decisions toward the popular side.

As already pointed out, however, in the election of judges for a long and fixed term of years, the fear of popular prejudice as a motive for unjust decisions is minimized by the tenure on the one hand, while the opportunity which the people have calmly to consider the work of a judge for a full term of years in deciding as to his reelection generally insures from them a fair and reasonable consideration of his qualities as a judge. While, therefore, there have been elected judges who have bowed before unjust popular prejudice or who have yielded to the power of political bosses in their decisions,

I am convinced that these are exceptional, and that, on the whole, elected judges have made a great American judiciary. But the success of an elective judiciary certainly furnishes no reason for so changing the system as to take away the very safeguards which have made it successful.

Attempt is made to defend the principle of judicial recall by reference to states in which judges are said to have shown themselves to be under corrupt corporate influence and in which it is claimed that nothing but a desperate remedy will suffice. If the political control in such states is sufficiently wrested from corrupting corporations to permit the enactment of a radical constitutional amendment like that of judicial recall, it would seem possible to make provision in its stead for an effective remedy by impeachment in which the cumbrous features of the present remedy might be avoided, but the opportunity for judicial hearing and defense before an impartial tribunal might be retained.

Real reforms are not to be effected by patent shortcuts or by abolishing those requirements which the experience of ages has shown to be essential in dealing justly with everyone. Such innovations are certain in the long run to plague the inventor or first user and will come readily to the hand of the enemies and corrupters of society after the passing of the just popular indignation that prompted their adoption.

Again, judicial recall is advocated on the ground that it will bring the judges more into sympathy with the popular will and the progress of ideas among the people. It is said that now judges are out of touch with the movement toward a wider democracy and a greater control of governmental agencies in the interest and for the benefit of the people. The righteous and just course for a judge to pursue is ordinarily fixed by statute or clear principles of law, and the cases in which his judgment may be affected by his political, economic, or social views

are infrequent. But even in such cases judges are not removed from the people's influence. Surround the judiciary with all the safeguards possible, create judges by appointment, make their tenure for life, forbid diminution of salary during their term, and still it is impossible to prevent the influence of popular opinion from coloring judgments in the long run.

Judges are men, intelligent, sympathetic men, patriotic men, and in those fields of the law in which the personal equation unavoidably plays a part, there will be found a response to sober popular opinion as it changes to meet the exigency of social, political, and economic changes. Indeed, this should be so. Individual instances of a hidebound and retrograde conservatism on the part of courts in decisions which turn on the individual economic or sociological views of the judges may be pointed out; but they are not many and do not call for radical action.

In treating of courts we are dealing with a human machine, liable, like all the inventions of man, to err, but we are dealing with a human institution that likens itself to a divine institution because it seeks and preserves justice. It has been the cornerstone of our gloriously free government, in which the rights of the individual and of the minority have been preserved, while governmental action of the majority has lost nothing of beneficent progress, efficacy, and directness. This balance was planned in the Constitution by its framers and has been maintained by our independent judiciary.

Precedents are cited from state constitutions said to be equivalent to a popular recall. In some, judges are removable by a vote of both houses of the legislature. This is a mere adoption of the English address of Parliament to the Crown for the removal of judges. It is similar to impeachment in that a form of hearing is always granted. Such a provision forms no precedent for a popular recall without adequate hearing and defense, and with new candidates to contest the election.

It is said the recall will be rarely used. If so, it will be rarely needed. Then why adopt a system so full of danger? But it is a mistake to suppose that such a powerful lever for influencing judicial decisions and such an opportunity for vengeance because of adverse ones will be allowed to remain unused.

But it is said that the people of Arizona are to become an independent state when created, and even if we strike out judicial recall now, they can reincorporate it in their constitution after statehood. To this I would answer that in dealing with the courts, which are the cornerstone of good government and in which not only the voters but the nonvoters and nonresidents have a deep interest as a security for their rights of life, liberty, and property, no matter what the future action of the state may be, it is necessary for the authority which is primarily responsible for its creation to assert in no doubtful tones the necessity for an independent and untrammeled judiciary.

57.

GEORGE SANTAYANA: The Genteel Tradition in American Philosophy

According to Santayana, the "genteel tradition" in American philosophy was an outmoded but still dominant way of thought that Americans had inherited from their colonial ancestors and had retained (albeit with modifications) long after it had been discarded in Europe. Santayana was particularly struck by the anachronistic character of American philosophical thought which seemed so at odds with the nation's marked superiority in invention and technological ingenuity. In a lecture originally delivered on August 25, 1911, to the Philosophical Union of the University of California, Santayana analyzed the American genteel tradition and pointed out how it was finally being decisively challenged by the pragmatism of William James — an observation that is now a commonplace. Part of the lecture appears here.

Source: *Winds of Doctrine*, New York, 1926.

THE PRIVILEGE OF ADDRESSING YOU today is very welcome to me, not merely for the honor of it, which is great, nor for the pleasures of travel, which are many, when it is California that one is visiting for the first time, but also because there is something I have long wanted to say which this occasion seems particularly favorable for saying.

America is still a young country, and this part of it is especially so; and it would have been nothing extraordinary if, in this young country, material preoccupations had altogether absorbed people's minds, and they had been too much engrossed in living to reflect upon life or to have any philosophy. The opposite, however, is the case. Not only have you already found time to philosophize in California, as your society proves, but the Eastern colonists from the very beginning were a sophisticated race. As much as in clearing the land and fighting the Indians they were occupied, as they expressed it, in wrestling with the Lord. The country was new, but the race was tried, chastened, and full of solemn memories. It was an old wine in new bottles; and America did not have to wait for its present universities, with their departments of academic philosophy, in order to possess a living philosophy — to have a distinct vision of the universe and definite convictions about human destiny.

Now this situation is a singular and remarkable one, and has many consequences, not all of which are equally fortunate. America is a young country with an old mentality: it has enjoyed the advantages of a child carefully brought up and thoroughly indoctrinated; it has been a wise child. But a wise child, an old head on young shoulders, always has a comic and an unpromising side. The wisdom is a little thin and verbal, not aware of its full meaning and grounds; and physical and emotional growth may be stunted by it, or even deranged. Or when the child is too vigorous for that, he will develop a fresh mentality of his own out of his observations and actual instincts; and this fresh mentality will interfere with the traditional mentality and tend to reduce it to something perfunctory, conventional, and perhaps secretly despised.

A philosophy is not genuine unless it inspires and expresses the life of those who cherish it. I do not think the hereditary philosophy of America has done much to atrophy the natural activities of the inhabitants; the wise child has not missed the joys of youth or of manhood; but what has happened is that the hereditary philosophy has grown stale, and that the academic philosophy afterwards developed has caught the stale odor from it.

America is not simply, as I said a mo-

ment ago, a young country with an old mentality: it is a country with two mentalities — one, a survival of the beliefs and standards of the fathers, the other, an expression of the instincts, practice, and discoveries of the younger generations. In all the higher things of the mind — in religion, in literature, in the moral emotions — it is the hereditary spirit that still prevails, so much so that Mr. Bernard Shaw finds that America is a hundred years behind the times. The truth is that one-half of the American mind, that not occupied intensely in practical affairs, has remained, I will not say high-and-dry, but slightly becalmed; it has floated gently in the backwater, while, alongside, in invention and industry and social organization, the other half of the mind was leaping down a sort of Niagara Rapids.

This division may be found symbolized in American architecture: a neat reproduction of the colonial mansion — with some modern comforts introduced surreptitiously — stands beside the skyscraper. The American will inhabits the skyscraper; the American intellect inhabits the colonial mansion. The one is the sphere of the American man; the other, at least predominantly, of the American woman. The one is all aggressive enterprise; the other is all genteel tradition.

Now, with your permission, I should like to analyze more fully how this interesting situation has arisen, how it is qualified, and whither it tends. And, in the first place, we should remember what, precisely, that philosophy was which the first settlers brought with them into the country. In strictness there was more than one; but we may confine our attention to what I will call Calvinism, since it is on this that the current academic philosophy has been grafted. I do not mean exactly the Calvinism of Calvin, or even of Jonathan Edwards; for in their systems there was much that was not pure philosophy, but rather faith in the externals and history of revelation. Jewish and Christian revelation was interpreted by these men, however, in the spirit of a particular philosophy, which might have arisen under any sky and been associated with any other religion as well as with Protestant Christianity. In fact, the philosophical principle of Calvinism appears also in the Koran, in Spinoza, and in Cardinal Newman; and persons with no very distinctive Christian belief, like Carlyle or like Professor Royce, may be, nevertheless, philosophically, perfect Calvinists.

Calvinism, taken in this sense, is an expression of the agonized conscience. It is a view of the world which an agonized conscience readily embraces if it takes itself seriously, as, being agonized, of course it must. Calvinism, essentially, asserts three things: that sin exists, that sin is punished, and that it is beautiful that sin should exist to be punished. The heart of the Calvinist is therefore divided between tragic concern at his own miserable condition and tragic exultation about the universe at large. He oscillates between a profound abasement and a paradoxical elation of the spirit. To be a Calvinist philosophically is to feel a fierce pleasure in the existence of misery, especially of one's own, in that this misery seems to manifest the fact that the Absolute is irresponsible or infinite or holy. Human nature, it feels, is totally depraved: to have the instincts and motives that we necessarily have is a great scandal, and we must suffer for it; but that scandal is requisite since, otherwise, the serious importance of being as we ought to be would not have been vindicated.

To those of us who have not an agonized conscience, this system may seem fantastic and even unintelligible; yet it is logically and intently thought out from its emotional premises. It can take permanent possession of a deep mind here and there, and under certain conditions it can become epidemic. Imagine, for instance, a small nation with an intense vitality, but on the verge of ruin, ecstatic and distressful, having a strict and minute code of laws that paints life in sharp and violent chiaroscuro, all pure righteousness and black abominations, and exaggerating the consequences of both perhaps to infinity. Such a people were the Jews after the exile, and again the early Protestants. If such a people is philosophical at all, it will not improbably be Calvinistic.

Even in the early American communities many of these conditions were fulfilled. The nation was small and isolated; it lived under pressure and constant trial; it was acquainted with but a small range of goods and evils. Vigilance over conduct and an absolute demand for personal integrity were not merely traditional things but things that practical sages, like Franklin and Washington, recommended to their countrymen, because they were virtues that justified themselves visibly by their fruits. But soon these happy results themselves helped to relax the pressure of external circumstances and indirectly the pressure of the agonized conscience within.

The nation became numerous; it ceased to be either ecstatic or distressful; the high social morality which on the whole it preserved took another color; people remained honest and helpful out of good sense and goodwill rather than out of scrupulous adherence to any fixed principles. They retained their instinct for order and often created order with surprising quickness; but the sanctity of law, to be obeyed for its own sake, began to escape them; it seemed too unpractical a notion, and not quite serious. In fact, the second and native-born American mentality began to take shape. The sense of sin totally evaporated. Nature, in the words of Emerson, was all beauty and commodity; and while operating on it laboriously and drawing quick returns, the American began to drink in inspiration from it aesthetically.

At the same time, in so broad a continent, he had elbowroom. His neighbors helped more than they hindered him; he wished their number to increase. Goodwill became the great American virtue; and a passion arose for counting heads, and square miles, and cubic feet, and minutes saved — as if there had been anything to save them for. How strange to the American now that saying of Jonathan Edwards, that men are naturally God's enemies! Yet that is an axiom to any intelligent Calvinist, though the words he uses may be different. If you told the modern American that he is totally depraved, he would think you were joking, as he himself usually is. He is convinced that he always has been, and always will be, victorious and blameless.

Calvinism thus lost its basis in American life. Some emotional natures, indeed, reverted in their religious revivals or private searchings of heart to the sources of the tradition; for any of the radical points of view in philosophy may cease to be prevalent, but none can cease to be possible. Other natures, more sensitive to the moral and literary influences of the world, preferred to abandon parts of their philosophy, hoping thus to reduce the distance which should separate the remainder from real life.

Meantime, if anybody arose with a special sensibility or a technical genius, he was in great straits; not being fed sufficiently by the world, he was driven in upon his own resources. The three American writers whose personal endowment was perhaps the finest — Poe, Hawthorne, and Emerson — had all a certain starved and abstract quality. They could not retail the genteel tradition; they were too keen, too perceptive, and too independent for that. But life offered them little digestible material, nor were they naturally voracious. They were fastidious, and under the circumstances they were starved. Emerson, to be sure, fed on books. There was a great catholicity in his reading; and he showed a fine tact in his comments and in his way of appropriating what he read. But he read transcendentally, not historically, to learn what he himself felt, not what others might have felt before him. And to feed on books, for a philosopher or a poet, is still to starve.

Books can help him to acquire form or to avoid pitfalls; they cannot supply him with substance, if he is to have any. Therefore the genius of Poe and Hawthorne, and even of Emerson, was employed on a sort of inner play, or digestion of vacancy. It was a refined labor, but it was in danger of being morbid, or tinkling, or self-indulgent. It was a play of intra-mental rhymes. Their mind was like an old music box, full of tender echoes and quaint fancies. These fancies expressed their personal genius sincerely, as dreams may; but they were arbitrary fancies in comparison with what a real observer would have said in the premises. Their manner, in a word, was subjective. In their own persons they escaped the mediocrity of the genteel tradition, but they supplied nothing to supplant it in other minds.

The churches, likewise, although they modified their spirit, had no philosophy to offer save a new emphasis on parts of what Calvinism contained. The theology of Calvin, we must remember, had much in it besides philosophical Calvinism. A Christian tenderness and a hope of grace for the individual came to mitigate its sardonic optimism; and it was these evangelical elements that the Calvinistic churches now emphasized, seldom and with blushes referring to hellfire or infant damnation. Yet philosophic Calvinism, with a theory of life that would perfectly justify hellfire and infant damnation, if they happened to exist, still dominates the traditional metaphysics. It is an ingredient, and the decisive ingredient, in what calls itself idealism. But in order to see just what part Calvinism plays in current idealism, it will be necessary to distinguish the other chief element in that complex system, namely, transcendentalism.

Transcendentalism is the philosophy which the romantic era produced in Germany, and independently, I believe, in America also. Transcendentalism proper, like romanticism, is not any particular set of dogmas about what things exist; it is not a system of the universe regarded as a fact or as a collection of facts. It is a method, a point of view, from which any world, no matter what it might contain, could be approached by a self-conscious observer. Transcendentalism is systematic subjectivism. It studies the perspectives of knowledge as they radiate from the self; it is a plan of those avenues of inference by which our ideas of things must be reached if they are to afford any systematic or distant vistas. In other words, transcendentalism is the critical logic of science. Knowledge, it says, has a station, as in a watchtower; it is always seated here and now, in the self of the moment. The past and the future, things inferred and things conceived, lie around it, painted as upon a panorama. They cannot be lighted up save by some centrifugal ray of attention and present interest, by some active operation of the mind. . . .

But the transcendental method, in its way, was also sympathetic to the American mind. It embodied, in a radical form, the spirit of Protestantism as distinguished from its inherited doctrines; it was autonomous, undismayed, calmly revolutionary; it felt that will was deeper than intellect; it focused everything here and now, and asked all things to show their credentials at the bar of the young self and to prove their value for this latest-born moment.

These things are truly American; they would be characteristic of any young society with a keen and discursive intelligence, and they are strikingly exemplified in the thought and in the person of Emerson. They constitute what he called self-trust.

Self-trust, like other transcendental attitudes, may be expressed in metaphysical fables. The romantic spirit may imagine itself to be an absolute force, evoking and molding the plastic world to express its varying moods. But for a pioneer who is actually a world builder, this metaphysical illusion has a partial warrant in historical fact; far more warrant than it could boast of in the fixed and articulated society of Europe, among the moonstruck rebels and sulking poets of the romantic era.

Emerson was a shrewd Yankee, by instinct on the winning side; he was a cheery, childlike soul, impervious to the evidence of evil, as of everything that it did not suit his transcendental individuality to appreciate or to notice. More, perhaps, than anybody that has ever lived, he practised the transcendental method in all its purity. He had no system. He opened his eyes on the world every morning with a fresh sincerity, marking how things seemed to him then, or what they suggested to his spontaneous fancy. This fancy, for being spontaneous, was not always novel; it was guided by the habits and training of his mind, which were those of a preacher. Yet he never insisted on his notions so as to turn them into settled dogmas; he felt in his bones that they were myths.

Sometimes, indeed, the bad example of other transcendentalists, less true than he to their method, or the pressing questions of unintelligent people, or the instinct we all have to think our ideas final, led him to the very verge of system making; but he stopped short. Had he made a system out of his notion of compensation, or the oversoul, or spiritual laws, the result would have been as thin and forced as it is in other transcendental systems. But he coveted truth; and he returned to experience, to history, to poetry, to the natural science of his day, for new starting points and hints toward fresh transcendental musings. . . .

Emerson had no system; and his coveting truth had another exceptional consequence: he was detached, unworldly, contemplative. When he came out of the conventicle or the reform meeting, or out of the rapturous close atmosphere of the lecture room, he heard nature whispering to him: "Why so hot, little sir?" No doubt the spirit or energy of the world is what is acting in us, as the sea is what rises in every little wave; but it passes through us, and cry out as we may, it will move on. Our privilege is to have perceived it as it moves. Our dignity is not in what we do but in what we understand. The whole world is doing things. We are turning in that vortex; yet within us is silent observation, the speculative eye before which all passes, which bridges the distances and compares the combatants. On this side of his genius, Emerson broke away from all conditions of age or country and represented nothing except intelligence itself.

There was another element in Emerson, curiously combined with transcendentalism, namely, his love and respect for nature. Nature, for the transcendentalist, is precious because it is his own work, a mirror in which he looks at himself and says (like a poet relishing his own verses), "What a genius I am! Who would have thought there was such stuff in me?" And the philosophical egotist finds in his doctrine a ready explanation of whatever beauty and commodity nature actually has. No wonder, he says to himself, that nature is sympathetic, since I made it. And such a view, one-sided and even fatuous as it may be, undoubtedly sharpens the vision of a poet and a moralist to all that is inspiriting and symbolic in the natural world. Emerson was particularly ingenious and clear-sighted in feeling the spiritual uses of fellowship with the elements. This is something in which all Teutonic poetry is rich and which forms, I think, the most genuine and spontaneous part of modern taste, and especially of American taste.

Just as some people are naturally enthralled and refreshed by music, so others are by landscape. Music and landscape make up the spiritual resources of those who cannot or dare not express their unfulfilled ideals in words. Serious poetry, profound religion (Calvinism, for instance), are the joys of an unhappiness that confesses itself; but when a genteel tradition forbids people to confess that they are unhappy, serious poetry and profound religion are closed to them by that; and since human life, in its depths, cannot then express itself openly, imagination is driven for comfort into abstract arts, where human circumstances are lost sight of and human problems dissolve in a purer medium. The pressure of care is thus relieved without its quietus being found in intelligence. To understand oneself is the classic form of consolation; to elude oneself is the romantic. In the presence of music or landscape, human experience eludes itself; and thus romanticism is the bond between transcendental and naturalistic sentiment. The winds and clouds come to minister to the solitary ego.

Have there been, we may ask, any successful efforts to escape from the genteel tradition, and to express something worth expressing behind its back? This might well not have occurred as yet; but America is so precocious, it has been trained by the genteel tradition to be so wise for its years, that some indications of a truly native philosophy and poetry are already to be found. I might mention the humorists, of whom you here in California have had your share. The humorists, however, only half escape the genteel tradition; their humor would lose its savor if they had wholly escaped it. They point to what contradicts it in the facts; but not in order to abandon the genteel tradition, for they have nothing solid to put in its place. When they point out how ill many facts fit into it, they do not clearly conceive that this militates against the stan-lard, but think it a funny perversity in the facts. Of course, did they earnestly respect the genteel tradition, such an incongruity would seem to them sad rather than ludicrous. Perhaps the prevalence of humor in America, in and out of season, may be taken as one more evidence that the genteel tradition is present pervasively, but everywhere weak. . . .

The one American writer who has left the genteel tradition entirely behind is perhaps Walt Whitman. For this reason educated Americans find him rather an unpalatable person, who they sincerely protest ought not to be taken for a representative of their culture; and he certainly should not, because their culture is so genteel and traditional. But the foreigner may sometimes think otherwise, since he is looking for what may have arisen in America to express, not the polite and conventional American mind but the spirit and the inarticulate principles that animate the community on which its own genteel mentality seems to sit rather lightly.

When the foreigner opens the pages of Walt Whitman, he thinks that he has come at last upon something representative and original. In Walt Whitman, democracy is carried into psychology and morals. The various sights, moods, and emotions are given each one vote; they are declared to be all free and equal, and the innumerable commonplace moments of life are suffered to speak like the others. Those moments formerly reputed great are not excluded, but they are made to march in the ranks with their companions — plain foot soldiers and servants of the hour. Nor does the refusal to discriminate stop there; we must carry our principle further down, to the animals, to inanimate nature, to the cosmos as a whole.

Whitman became a pantheist; but his pantheism, unlike that of the Stoics and of Spinoza, was unintellectual, lazy, and self-indulgent; for he simply felt jovially that everything real was good enough, and that he was good enough himself. In him, Bohemia rebelled against the genteel tradition; but the reconstruction that alone can justify revolution did not ensue. His attitude, in principle, was utterly disintegrating; his poetic genius fell back to the lowest level, perhaps, to which it is possible for poetic genius to fall. He reduced his imagination to a passive sensorium for the registering of impressions. No element of construction remained in it, and therefore no element of penetration. But his scope was wide; and his lazy, desultory apprehension was poetical. His work, for the very reason that it is so rudimentary, contains a beginning, or rather many beginnings, that might possibly grow into a noble moral imagination, a worthy filling for the human mind. An American in the 19th century who completely disregarded the genteel tradition could hardly have done more.

But there is another distinguished man, lately lost to this country, who has given some rude shocks to this tradition and who, as much as Whitman, may be regarded as representing the genuine, the long silent American mind — I mean William James. He and his brother Henry were as tightly swaddled in the genteel tradition as any infant geniuses could be, for they were born before 1850, and in a Swedenborgian household. Yet they burst those bands almost entirely. The ways in which the two brothers freed themselves, however, are interestingly different. Mr. Henry James has done it by adopting the point of view of the outer world, and by turning the genteel American tradition, as he turns everything else, into a subject matter for analysis. For him it is a curious habit of mind, intimately comprehended, to be compared with other habits of mind, also well known to him. Thus he has overcome the genteel tradition in the classic way, by understanding it.

With William James, too, this infusion of worldly insight and European sympathies was a potent influence, especially in his earlier days; but the chief source of his liberty was another. It was his personal spontaneity, similar to that of Emerson, and his personal vitality, similar to that of nobody else. Convictions and ideas came to him, so to speak, from the subsoil. He had a prophetic sympathy with the dawning sentiments of the age, with the moods of the dumb majority. His scattered words caught fire in many parts of the world. His way of thinking and feeling represented the true America, and represented in a measure the whole ultramodern, radical world. Thus he eluded the genteel tradition in the romantic way, by continuing it into its opposite.

The romantic mind, glorified in Hegel's dialectic (which is not dialectic at all, but a sort of tragi-comic history of experience), is always rendering its thoughts unrecognizable through the infusion of new insights and through the insensible transformation of the moral feeling that accompanies them, till at last it has completely reversed its old judgments under cover of expanding them. Thus the genteel tradition was led a merry dance when it fell again into the hands of a genuine and vigorous romanticist like William James. He restored their revolutionary force to its neutralized elements by picking them out afresh and emphasizing them separately, according to his personal predilections.

For one thing, William James kept his mind and heart wide open to all that might seem, to polite minds, odd, personal, or visionary in religion and philosophy. He gave a sincerely respectful hearing to sentimentalists, mystics, spiritualists, wizards, cranks, quacks, and impostors — for it is hard to draw the line, and James was not willing to draw it prematurely. He thought, with his usual modesty, that any of these might have something to teach him. The lame, the halt, the blind, and those speaking with tongues could come to him with the certainty of finding sympathy; and if they were not healed, at least they were comforted, that a famous professor should take them so seriously; and they began to feel that after all to have only one leg, or one hand, or one eye, or to have three, might be in itself no less beauteous than to have just two, like the stolid majority.

Thus William James became the friend and helper of those groping, nervous, half-educated, spiritually disinherited, passionately hungry individuals of which America is full. He became, at the same time, their spokesman and representative before the learned world; and he made it a chief part of his vocation to recast what the learned world has to offer, so that as far as possible it might serve the needs and interests of these people.

Yet the normal, practical, masculine American, too, had a friend in William James. There is a feeling abroad now, to which biology and Darwinism lend some color, that theory is simply an instrument for practice and intelligence merely a help toward material survival. Bears, it is said, have fur and claws, but poor, naked man is condemned to be intelligent, or he will perish. This feeling William James embodied in that theory of thought and of truth which he called pragmatism. Intelligence, he thought, is no miraculous, idle faculty by which we mirror passively any or everything that happens to be true, reduplicating the real world to no purpose. Intelligence has its roots and its issue in the context of events; it is one kind of practical adjustment, an experimental act, a form of vital tension. It does not essentially serve to picture other parts of reality but to connect them.

This view was not worked out by William James in its psychological and historical details; unfortunately he developed it chiefly in controversy against its opposite, which he called intellectualism, and which he hated with all the hatred of which his kind heart was capable. Intellectualism, as he conceived it, was pure pedantry; it impoverished and verbalized everything, and tied up nature in red tape. Ideas and rules that may have been occasionally useful it put in the place of the full-blooded irrational movement of life which had called them into being; and these abstractions, so soon obsolete, it strove to fix and to worship forever.

Thus all creeds and theories and all formal precepts sink in the estimation of the pragmatist to a local and temporary grammar of action; a grammar that must be changed slowly by time, and may be changed quickly by genius. To know things as a whole, or as they are eternally, if there is anything eternal in them, is not only beyond our powers but would prove worthless and perhaps even fatal to our lives. Ideas are not mirrors, they are weapons; their function is to prepare us to meet events, as future experience may unroll them. Those ideas that disappoint us are false ideas; those to which events are true are true themselves. . . .

Omniscience is impossible; time is real; what had been omniscience hitherto might discover something more today. "There shall be news," William James was fond of saying with rapture, quoting from the unpublished poem of an obscure friend, "there shall be news in Heaven!" There is almost certainly, he thought, a God now; there may be several gods, who might exist together, or one after the other. We might, by our conspiring sympathies, help to make a new one. Much in us is doubtless immortal; we survive death for some time in a recognizable form; but what our career and transformations may be in the sequel we cannot tell, although we may help to determine them by our daily choices. Observa-

tion must be continual if our ideas are to remain true. Eternal vigilance is the price of knowledge; perpetual hazard, perpetual experiment keep quick the edge of life.

This is, so far as I know, a new philosophical vista; it is a conception never before presented, although implied, perhaps, in various quarters, as in Norse and even Greek mythology. It is a vision radically empirical and radically romantic; and, as William James himself used to say, the visions and not the arguments of a philospher are the interesting and influential things about him. William James, rather too generously, attributed this vision to M. Bergson, and regarded him in consequence as a philosopher of the first rank, whose thought was to be one of the turning points in history. M. Bergson had killed intellectualism. It was his book on creative evolution, said James with humorous emphasis, that had come at last to *"écraser l'infâme."*

We may suspect, notwithstanding, that intellectualism, infamous and crushed, will survive the blow; and if the author of the Book of Ecclesiastes were now alive, and heard that there shall be news in heaven, he would doubtless say that there may possibly be news there, but that under the sun there is nothing new — not even radical empiricism or radical romanticism, which from the beginning of the world has been the philosophy of those who as yet had had little experience; for to the blinking little child it is not merely something in the world that is new daily but everything is new all day.

I am not concerned with the rights and wrongs of that controversy; my point is only that William James, in this genial, evolutionary view of the world, has given a rude shock to the genteel tradition. What! The world a gradual improvisation? Creation unpremeditated? God a sort of young poet or struggling artist? William James is an advocate of theism; pragmatism adds one to the evidences of religion; that is excellent. But is not the cool, abstract piety of the genteel getting more than it asks for? This empirical, naturalistic God is too crude and positive a force; He will work miracles, He will answer prayers, He may inhabit distinct places and have distinct conditions under which alone He can operate; He is a neighboring being whom we can act upon and rely upon for specific aids, as upon a personal friend, or a physician, or an insurance company. How disconcerting! Is not this new theology a little like superstition? And yet how interesting, how exciting, if it should happen to be true!

I am far from wishing to suggest that such a view seems to me more probable than conventional idealism or than Christian orthodoxy. All three are in the region of dramatic system-making and myth to which probabilities are irrelevant. If one man says the moon is sister to the sun and another that she is his daughter, the question is not which notion is more probable, but whether either of them is at all expressive. The so-called evidences are devised afterward, when faith and imagination have prejudged the issue.

The force of William James's new theology, or romantic cosmology, lies only in this: that it has broken the spell of the genteel tradition, and enticed faith in a new direction, which on second thoughts may prove no less alluring than the old. The important fact is not that the new fancy might possibly be true — who shall know that? — but that it has entered the heart of a leading American to conceive and to cherish it. The genteel tradition cannot be dislodged by these insurrections; there are circles to which it is still congenial and where it will be preserved. But it has been challenged and (what is perhaps more insidious) it has been discovered. No one need be browbeaten any longer into accepting it.

No one need be afraid, for instance, that his fate is sealed because some young prig may call him a dualist; the pint would call the quart a dualist if you tried to pour the quart into him. We need not be afraid of being less profound for being direct and sincere. The intellectual world may be traversed in many directions; the whole has not been surveyed; there is a great career in it open to talent. That is a sort of knell that tolls the passing of the genteel tradition. Something else is now in the field; something else can appeal to the imagination and be a thousand times more idealistic than academic idealism, which is often simply a way of whitewashing and adoring things as they are.

The illegitimate monopoly which the genteel tradition had established over what ought to be assumed and what ought to be hoped for has been broken down by the first-born of the family, by the genius of the race. Henceforth there can hardly be the same peace and the same pleasure in hugging the old proprieties. Hegel will be to the next generation what Sir William Hamilton was to the last. Nothing will have been disproved, but everything will have been abandoned. An honest man has spoken, and the cant of the genteel tradition has become harder for young lips to repeat.

With this I have finished such a sketch as I am here able to offer you of the genteel tradition in American philosophy. The subject is complex and calls for many an excursus and qualifying footnote; yet I think the main outlines are clear enough. The chief fountains of this tradition were Calvinism and transcendentalism. Both were living fountains; but to keep them alive they required, one an agonized conscience, and the other a radical subjective criticism of knowledge. When these rare metaphysical preoccupations disappeared — and the American atmosphere is not favorable to either of them — the two systems ceased to be inwardly understood; they subsisted as sacred mysteries only; and the combination of the two in some transcendental system of the universe (a contradiction in principle) was doubly artificial. Besides, it could hardly be held with a single mind.

Natural science, history, the beliefs implied in labor and invention, could not be disregarded altogether; so that the transcendental philosopher was condemned to a double allegiance and to not letting his left hand know the bluff that his right hand was making. Nevertheless, the difficulty in bringing practical, inarticulate convictions to expression is very great, and the genteel tradition has subsisted in the academic mind for want of anything equally academic to take its place.

The academic mind, however, has had its flanks turned. On the one side came the revolt of the Bohemian temperament, with its poetry of crude naturalism; on the other side came an impassioned empiricism, welcoming popular religious witnesses to the unseen, reducing science to an instrument of success in action, and declaring the universe to be wild and young and not to be harnessed by the logic of any school.

This revolution, I should think, might well find an echo among you, who live in a thriving society and in the presence of a virgin and prodigious world. When you transform nature to your uses, when you experiment with her forces and reduce them to industrial agents, you cannot feel that nature was made by you or for you, for then these adjustments would have been preestablished. Much less can you feel it when she destroys your labor of years in a momentary spasm. You must feel, rather, that you are an offshoot of her life; one brave little force among her immense forces.

When you escape, as you love to do, to your forests and your sierras, I am sure again that you do not feel you made them, or that they were made for you. They have grown, as you have grown, only more massively and more slowly. In their nonhuman beauty and peace they stir the subhuman depths and the superhuman possibilities of your own spirit. It is no transcendental logic that they teach; and they give no sign of any deliberate morality seated in the world. It is rather the vanity and superficiality of all logic, the needlessness of argument, the relativity of morals, the strength of time, the fertility of matter, the variety, the unspeakable variety, of possible life.

Everything is measurable and conditioned, indefinitely repeated, yet, in repetition, twisted somewhat from its old form. Everywhere is beauty and nowhere permanence, everywhere an incipient harmony, nowhere an intention, nor a responsibility, nor a plan. It is the irresistible suasion of this daily spectacle, it is the daily discipline of contact with things, so different from the verbal discipline of the schools, that will, I trust, inspire the philosophy of your children. A Californian whom I had recently the pleasure of meeting observed that, if the philosophers had lived among your mountains, their systems would have been different from what they are.

Certainly, I should say, very different from what those systems are which the European genteel tradition has handed down since Socrates; for these systems are egotistical; directly or indirectly they are anthropocentric and inspired by the conceited notion that man, or human reason, or the human distinction between good and evil, is the center and pivot of the universe. That is what the mountains and the woods should make you at last ashamed to assert. From what, indeed, does the society of nature liberate you, that you find it so sweet? It is hardly (is it?) that you wish to forget your past, or your friends, or that you have any secret contempt for your present ambitions. You respect these, you respect them perhaps too much; you are not suffered by the genteel tradition to criticize or to reform them at all radically.

No; it is the yoke of this genteel tradition itself that these primeval solitudes lift from your shoulders. They suspend your forced sense of your own importance not merely as individuals, but even as men. They allow you, in one happy moment, at once to play and to worship, to take yourselves simply, humbly, for what you are, and to salute the wild, indifferent, noncensorious infinity of nature. You are admonished that what you can do avails little materially, and in the end nothing. At the same time, through wonder and pleasure, you are taught speculation. You learn what you are really fitted to do, and where lie your natural dignity and joy, namely, in representing many things, without being them, and in letting your imagination, through sympathy, celebrate and echo their life.

Because the peculiarity of man is that his machinery for reaction of external things has involved an imaginative transcript of these things, which is preserved and suspended in his fancy; and the interest and beauty of this inward landscape, rather than any fortunes that may await his body in the outer world, constitute his proper happiness. By their mind, its scope, quality, and temper, we estimate men, for by the mind only do we exist as men, and are more than so many storage batteries for material energy. Let us therefore be frankly human. Let us be content to live in the mind.

58.

Franklin P. Adams: "The Rich Man"

Franklin Pierce Adams, or F.P.A. as he was known to his many readers, was the author of a famous newspaper column that ran for many years in several New York newspapers. The column, called "The Conning Tower," was the vehicle for Adams' searching and bittersweet observations on the follies and foibles of the men and women of his time. As often as not the column contained a short verse, of which "The Rich Man," originally published in 1911 and reprinted here, is a good example.

Source: *Toboganning on Parnassus*, Garden City, N.Y., 1911.

THE RICH MAN

The rich man has his motorcar,
　His country and his town estate.
He smokes a fifty-cent cigar
　And jeers at Fate.

He frivols through the livelong day,
　He knows not Poverty, her pinch.
His lot seems light, his heart seems gay;
　He has a cinch.

Yet though my lamp burns low and dim,
　Though I must slave for livelihood —
Think you that I would change with him?
　You bet I would!

The scene on Milk Street, Boston, about 1910

URBAN AMERICA

America's cities had by now taken on the structure and aspect characteristic of the present day; buildings would be replaced, neighborhoods would shift, and cities would spread wider and wider into the countryside, but the style of the 20th-century city was established. The urban population had grown to 46 percent of the total by 1910, and would overtake the rural portion before the next census. But as yet few could begin even to guess at the social and political changes that would be required or that would simply come unbidden as the nation became urban. Beyond the obvious fact that legal theories and practices dating from an agrarian or, at most, simple capitalist period were unsuitable — witness, for example, the legal obstacles to badly needed reforms — it was also true, though less clear, that whole philosophies and whole bodies of accustomed usage had to evolve with society. And just as with reform and the law, wherever structures or customs lagged behind the development of the environment, friction was assured.

Perhaps the real point is not that ideas lagged so far behind a changing reality, but that reality changed so quickly. Automobiles, the movies, airplanes, radio — all came into American life in an amazingly short time, and all were capable of exerting tremendous pressure on social organization and value. Space and time both faced a reappraisal in light of transportation advances; the mobility that followed began a second change that instant communication and common sources of information and entertainment completed: the final integration of regional populations into a fully common people.

OPPOSITE PAGE: (Top)
Looking down Broad Street
in Philadelphia to City
Hall, topped by a statue of
William Penn, 1905; Old
Plough Inn, Philadelphia, a
decaying remnant of an-
other era in the city

(Top) Horse-drawn wagons
bringing goods to Dock Street
in Philadelphia; (right)
a portion of the campus
of the University of Pennsylvania in 1904; (bot-
tom) residential street
in Germantown, Pa., 1908

Downtown Boston with Old South Church in the background, 1906

Looking down Park Street to the State House

Wagons loading and unloading at the Quincy Street Market in Boston, 1906

Boston at the turn of the century: (Right) Children playing in front of an Italian grocery occupying the building that was the home of Paul Revere; (center) looking down Commonwealth Avenue; (bottom) swan boats in Boston Gardens

(Top) View of Trinity Church and grounds in downtown Manhattan; (center) Macy's department store in 1908; (bottom) City College of New York in 1912

OPPOSITE PAGE: (Top) The construction of Pennsylvania Station in New York in 1908; (left) Bankers Trust Company Building, New York, 1911; (center right) tunnel work on the rapid transit system, 1901; (bottom right) Cross-section of the Pennsylvania Tube under the Hudson River during construction

(Top) View down Dexter Avenue to the State Capitol, Montgomery, Alabama, 1906; (left) Perry Avenue, Montgomery; (below) Marietta Street in Atlanta, Georgia, 1908

(Top) Bainbridge, Georgia; (above) Pulaski, Virginia, 1907 and (right) Main Street in Pulaski

Fifth Street in Quincy, Illinois, about 1910

Amherst Street in Milford, New Hampshire, about 1910

(Top) Pacific Avenue and 13th Street in Benson, Minn., 1908; crowds gathering for the county fair at Mankato, Minn.; (right) Atlantic Avenue in Benson

Crowds watching the fires set off by the earthquake in San Francisco in 1906, photo by Arnold Genthe; (below) general view of the destruction caused by the quake and fire

Owens River Aqueduct, carrying water from the Sierra to Los Angeles, was opened in 1913

(Above) Central Los Angeles, 1908; (below) water spurred Southern California's dramatic growth

(Top) Rosaka Lake, watering place for the herds on the Three Block Ranch near Richardson, New Mexico; photographed about 1910 by E. E. Smith; (right) cowboys celebrating at the railroad yards in Lubbock, Texas, 1907, after delivering a herd of cattle for shipment; (bottom) cowboys moving a herd of cattle at daybreak; photograph taken on the Three Block Ranch, 1908

59.

A Labor-Management Agreement

The labor-management agreement reprinted here is considered a landmark in the history of collective bargaining in the United States. Signed between the Chicago clothing firm of Hart, Schaffner & Marx and its employees, represented and led by Sidney Hillman, the contract established a form of industrial government in which the rights of employer, employee, and union are recognized and protected; and the forms in which the rights are guaranteed inhere in a structure comparable to the division of the federal government into executive, legislative, and judicial branches. The agreement ended the bitter strike of 1910-1911 against the company. Hillman organized the Amalgamated Clothing Workers in 1914 and later was a vice-president of the CIO. An important figure in the negotiations leading up to the contract was the eminent labor lawyer Clarence Darrow.

Source: Original in possession of Hart, Schaffner & Marx, Chicago, Illinois.

IT IS AGREED between Hart, Schaffner & Marx, and the employees of Hart, Schaffner & Marx, represented by Morris Feinberg, that a committee be and hereby is appointed, composed of E. D. Howard and Carl Meyer, representing Hart, Schaffner & Marx, Wm. O. Thompson and S. Hillman, representing the employees, and Charles H. Winslow (in his individual capacity and not in any way in his official capacity, and his services in no way to interfere with his official work or hours), said Winslow being selected by said other four members, for the following purposes:

(1) To create a board of such number as such committee shall determine upon for the purpose of adjusting and fixing prices when necessary, and adjusting any other matters that may be in dispute between Hart, Schaffner & Marx and its employees, and the neutral member of said board shall be appointed by said committee.

(2) To formulate and fix such rules and regulations for the guidance of said board as may be determined upon, such rules and regulations to be binding upon the parties hereto during the continuance of the agreement entered into between Hart, Schaffner & Marx and its employees, to wit: until April 1, 1913.

(3) It is expressly agreed that the agreement made on January 14 and the decision of Clarence Darrow and Carl Meyer, the arbitrators appointed under said agreement, which decision is dated March 13, 1911, shall remain in all respects in full force and effect, and neither said committee nor said board so appointed shall have any right to take up any question of increasing wages or of providing for any sort of what is commonly termed a closed shop, or to make any rules or regulations in violation of or inconsistent with any of the provisions of said agreement of January 14, 1911, or said decision of March 13, 1911.

Said board when appointed shall be solely for the purpose of acting as an original tribunal and an appeal shall always lie to the arbitration board created by the present agreements from the decisions of said board.

Said board shall be in existence during the life of the present agreement between said Hart, Schaffner & Marx and said employees, or until April 1, 1913.

60.

CLARENCE DARROW: The Closed Shop

Clarence Darrow won his first fame (and obloquy) as the defense attorney for Eugene Debs in the series of trials that followed the Pullman Strike of 1894, and for a number of years continued to defend labor leaders when they were accused of this heinous crime or that. In 1911 he conducted the defense of John J. McNamara and his brother James B., the union leaders who had been charged with organizing the bombing of the Los Angeles Times *Building. Los Angeles had been the center of a long struggle between labor and capital over the "closed shop," and in the article from which the following selection is taken Darrow presented what he termed "an authoritative statement of the labor unions' position" on the issue. The McNamara brothers made a public confession on December 1, 1911, and the AFL, claiming that it had been tricked, boycotted Darrow thereafter.*

Source: *American Magazine*, September 1911: "Why Men Fight for the Closed Shop."

WHY CAPITAL AND LABOR QUARREL

UNDER THE PRESENT SYSTEM of production, there are bound to be employers and employed. While the wage system lives there must be an employing class and a laboring class; the one who owns the lands, forests, railroads, factories, and mills — all the implements of production; and the other, the laborer, who must apply his labor to these raw materials for the production of wealth.

Gradually, the workmen of the world have been separated from the tools which were once owned by them and necessary to their trade. Neither the old-time artisan nor his simple tools have any place in the complex industry of today. The passing of machine production into larger hands means into fewer hands; means that the relative number of employers is growing less and that of the workmen constantly increasing. Even could any number of workmen by superior skill, frugality, or industry rise into the employing class, this phenomenon would not change the industrial processes or inherent relationship.

Capital goes on, ever busy inventing new methods for larger production, which means centralization and consolidation. The mileage of railroads under a single head is ever growing; factories growing larger; department stores driving out smaller business. Combinations take place in spite of human laws and in the teeth of public opinion. The steel trust, the tobacco trust, and the oil trust are doubtless illegal as they have been declared, because their present methods of business have outgrown the laws which were made for a primitive production.

But while these trusts are contrary to the laws of the country, the fact of their growth and persistency, even against law, shows that they are in harmony with the deeper laws of industrial life — laws which in the end control; and all legislative efforts to hamper this growth by civil and criminal laws are worse than futile — they are mischievous and meddlesome in the extreme. So long as there is economy in production under a larger scale, just so long will public opinion and public law be helpless to prevent it.

This process of centralization and consolidation is marked by the gradual crystallization of industrial classes; classes which in the very nature of things are mutually hostile. Surface thinkers are always condemning and classing as demagogues those who say there is a conflict between capital and labor. They stoutly contend that labor and capital are friends and co-workers, but both the employer and the workman understand that this is not true; that however friendly individual capitalists and laboring men may be, still, under present methods of industry, capital and labor are enemies.

The employer builds his factory and sells his goods. His profits are represented by the price he receives for his goods, less the cost of production. He needs wood and iron and coal. These he uses as the raw material to make up the finished product. He turns to the market of the world and he buys these at the lowest price. As a businessman he is not the friend of the coal dealer, the lumber dealer, or the ore dealer. He is trying to buy as cheaply as he can; the other is trying

to sell as high as he can. The capitalist then turns to the labor market, the same as to the coal market, and buys his labor as cheaply as it can be had.

In buying coal and iron and wood and labor, he can make a better bargain if the supply is unlimited and if the individual sellers of these commodities are forced into competition with one another. This effort of the capitalist to get labor as cheaply as possible makes him encourage the immigration of men and women with lower standards of living; makes him bid for the European in place of the American; for the Asiatic in place of the European; the woman instead of the man, and the child instead of the woman, while the constant invention of great machines has made the method of production simple and done away with the need of learning a trade. The capitalist is seeking to get his labor as cheaply as he can, and the workman, like the coal dealer, is using every effort to get as high a price as possible for the one thing which he has to sell — his toil.

The equities of the matter can have nothing to do with the case. Even though an employer might wish to pay higher wages, he is still bound by the laws of trade and cannot survive if he pays substantially more than others engaged in the same business with himself. The ethics of either side can have nothing to do with a business matter. Both are selfish. Both are bound to be selfish, and nothing but a change of the system of production and distribution can modify it. . . .

THE INDIVIDUAL LABORER MUST BE PROTECTED

NATURALLY THE CAPTAINS of industry stoutly oppose any force which would regulate their business. True it is that they have built up their combinations in defiance of law, yet just as strenuously they deny the right of the workingman to monopolize and control the one commodity he has to sell — his toil. It is only natural that employers should regard unions as hostile to their rights. The employer, of course, believes that the business is his and that no one has the right to interfere with his business. The labor unions have made it a business to organize workingmen for shorter hours, better conditions, safer tools, and a larger share of the common production than he could individually obtain. Naturally capital has resented this interference of organized labor with what they term their rights. They can never understand that labor should have a part in managing the industrial institutions of the land. The man who invests his labor in the mill or on a railroad is as much interested in its management, and should have as much to say as to hours, conditions, and terms of labor as the owner of the plant whose investment is money.

True it is that the employer has the title to the plant; can keep it idle or busy as he pleases. But it is just as true that the laborer, either singly or collectively, may refuse to take employment or enter upon a business agreement except upon such terms and conditions as he shall choose. Both employer and employed agree upon the one proposition, that labor is better protected and gets a larger share of the profits through trade unions than it would receive if trade unions were destroyed. The employer would destroy them for selfish purposes. The workmen would strengthen them for selfish purposes. And so long as selfishness is the rule and basis of business life, the conflict must go on with increasing bitterness, often with violence, and without ceasing.

The individual laborer today is helpless to make any terms with an employer. Imagine one of the 40,000 workmen of a great railroad system making a demand for shorter hours and better wages. He would be met by the answer: "If you don't like the terms, you can find another job." Individually, he is helpless. The employer has complete power over the isolated man. The man cannot make a real contract on an equal footing with the employer unless he goes to him clothed with the same power as the employer has, of putting him out of business unless he accepts his terms. A complete organization of workmen making a common demand would have the same power with the railroad company that the railroad company has with the workmen. And in this way only can a real contract be made.

Most things that are old gain a certain degree of respectability because of their age alone. Trade unionism is now so old that it is an established institution in the world, and most people concede theoretically its benefits and grant its necessity. Even many employers, who at heart are hostile to unions because at heart they are selfish, as they are bound to be under the industrial life of today, many of these profess their belief in trade unions provided trade unions "keep their place." They would not seriously object to a union which did nothing but hold meetings and pass resolutions. They object to the strikes, the boycotts, to the interference in politics, to the enforced demand for shorter hours, better conditions, easier life, and higher wages. In short, they do not object to the union itself, but only to those activities which make the union of any value to the workmen.

WHAT THE ISSUE NARROWS DOWN TO

TODAY, THE COMMON FEELING against trade unionism has narrowed down to the issue of the closed shop. The employer says he will employ union men, but he must have the right to employ nonunion men as well. He says, shall a man be deprived of the right to work because he does not belong to a union?

On the face of it, this position of the employer seems fair and right, and under an ideal system of society or method of business which did not control employers and workmen alike, no employer would be justified in asking whether a man was a member of a union anymore than he can ask today whether he is a member of a church. But this question, like all others, must be examined in the light of conditions, and whether the demand is reasonable on the part of the union depends entirely upon the industrial life under which workingmen live.

Theoretically there is nothing but words in the statement that a man has the right to work whether he belongs to a union or not. This statement is generally strengthened by adding the word "inalienable" — which sounds well when found in the Declaration of Independence but really means nothing there or anywhere else. An inalienable right is one which cannot be taken away, and it is plain that under the present conditions of work no such right exists; for a man's work can be taken away. This inalienable right to work is insisted upon by those who have appropriated all the coal, ore, and lumber, who control all the factories and railroads, and who have left the workman with nothing but his hands. And yet men cannot labor without an opportunity to apply their hands to these very bounties of nature; to these same materials from which things are made.

Neither can there be an inalienable right to work without a place to work. Neither the government nor those who declaim the loudest or insist the most have ever furnished the workmen an inalienable place to work. The inalienable right to work means simply the inalienable right of the employer, without let or hindrance, to go into the open market and bid for labor on the hardest terms. No government or great body of men ever made any demand or enforced any means that would give the workingman his inalienable right to work. And what about his inalienable right to work when the mines shut down, when the mills close,

when the seasons are dull or in times of industrial depression? All the rights a laborer has under the law, and without the protection of the union, is to go to an employer and *ask* him for work. His right to work depends upon his ability to find someone who has the means and inclination to hire him. He has no power to force himself upon an unwilling employer. Where or to whom is the workman to go to force his inalienable right? The phrase is a bit of birdlime used to catch the unthinking mass.

The inalienable right to work can be no greater than the inalienable right not to work, though it has been much more seriously urged. This is because those who most strongly defend his right to labor are more interested in his work than in his play.

No doubt the courts, if called upon, would declare that a man has an inalienable right to pursue happiness in ways not prohibited by law, provided that he amuse himself alone or found his pleasure in places of public amusement. But it is certain that no one would contend that the inalienable right to pursue happiness gave anyone the right to associate with another against his will; to enter his parlor or home or company without invitation and when his presence was not desired. The workman has the same right to choose the companions with whom he associates in labor as to choose the friends with whom he will spend his pastime; and the employer has no more right to force the society of another upon him during his hours of toil than during his hours of recreation.

WHY UNION MEN HATE "SCABS"

THE REASONS that appeal to a union man for not working with a nonunion man are manifest and obvious, but were it prejudice and nothing else he would have a right to indulge his prejudice, provided he was able to make terms with the employer, or should refuse to work for any employer who would not recognize his claim. . . . They have come to regard nonunion men not only as the enemies of their homes, the destroyers of their families, but as traitors to their class; as men who seek to undermine and destroy the organization which protects them, and, therefore, in the nature of things, there is a constant feud between them.

This is not a fact in trade unionism alone, but a deep, abiding fact in human life. In its last analysis it is the law of self-defense; and the employers have exactly the same feeling toward one of their members who gives his influence to the other side. Both feel that the offending man is disloyal to his class, and, though in both instances the offenders may be acting from the highest motives, they must pay the penalty of disloyalty. They must be regarded as traitors. And just so long as industry is carried on by two classes in hostile camps, this feeling must continue with both. . . .

One of the chief objects of the trade union is to permit their workmen to make a collective bargain, and to do this it is necessary to enroll in the union the largest proportion of organized men in each employment. Naturally the employer prefers to deal with individuals, as one man can be better dealt with than a combination of men. It has been only by the most bitter struggles, from the times when laws positively forbade unionism, that workmen have gained the right to collective bargaining, and without this right there could be no real bargaining whatever.

It is true that sometimes the unions have been narrow and exclusive, have fixed hard and unreasonable terms of membership, and have even unjustly limited apprentices so as to work a hardship to the laboring class. To this the workmen have the right to object. But in these methods they are like the rest of mankind. The constant increase of qualifications and time necessary to become a doctor or a lawyer are not made with an eye single to the benefit of the public, but with an eye almost single to the benefit of those already in those professions. These unjust terms are not, however, a part of the philosophy of trade unionism; are not a part of their principles or policies, or connected with the closed shop. The rule of the unions is simply to urge all members of the craft to unite on the easiest terms, without regard to any conditions except faithfulness to one another. . . .

THE EASIEST WAY TO DESTROY UNIONS

THE OPEN SHOP furnishes, and always has furnished, the best possible means of destroying the organization of the men. The closed shops are the only sure protection for the trade agreements and for the defense of the individual. When the master is left to hire or discharge either union or nonunion men as he sees fit, he naturally discharges the man that he thinks most hostile to his business and employs the one that will be subservient to his will. This does not come from the inherent or natural hardness of the master but from the hard facts of life. The master naturally discharges those who are most active in the unions, who interfere the most with his business, who are ever agitating for higher wages, who are insisting on better conditions and shorter hours. He does this for his own protection, and he naturally employs those who are most complaisant, those who have given the most hostages to fortune and who cannot afford to lose their jobs; those whom he can bring to be dependent upon his will.

The business officer, the agitator, the walking delegate is the last to be chosen. And when times are hard and someone must go, such men must walk the plank; while the complaisant man, the ready tool, the nonunion man is kept. In every employment there are always reasons for dismissal. In the management of complex affairs, accidents and mistakes occur. Under the open shop it is easy to find reasons for discharging the union man, to fix the blame for mistakes upon him, and it is likewise easy to find reasons for replacing him with a nonunion man.

In reality the open shop means only the open door through which the union man goes out and the nonunion man comes in to take his place. This is not theory alone. The open shop means uncertainties, anxiety, a shifting basis for the principles of trade unionism. The history of trade unionism has proven this fact from the beginning, and it is recognized by every union man. The open shop is a constant menace to his interests, ever present like the sword above the victim's head. He understands that his job is dependent upon the lack of interest in the union — the union which to him is all important. Then too, in every shop, in every grade of industry there are always easy jobs and hard ones, and under the open shop the easy one goes to the nonunion man, to the friend of the employer; the hard and dangerous task to the man whose devotion to his fellows incurs the enmity of the boss.

Trade unionism, like any ideal, calls for its sacrifices. To lay down your tools and to go out to look for bread for no injury to yourself, but on account of a wrong to your brother, calls for a loyalty and devotion of a noble order. Men who belong to the unions and accept these responsibilities cannot be persuaded to pay dues and make sacrifices for the benefit of the nonunion men who work by his side. And yet the nonunion man is always the first to claim and receive the benefit of every struggle made by the union. These benefits they receive without danger, without labor, and without cost. It cannot be expected that large numbers of workmen can be relied upon to support their union and to take the disadvantages that go with it, while the favors, the emoluments, and the victories all go to the men who make no sacrifices in return.

THE GREAT WORK UNIONS HAVE DONE

To prevent trade unionism from being conquered in detail; to keep its members from being thrown out through the open door; to maintain the best condition in shop and mill and factory and strive for others better still; to save the workman from long hours of toil and provide a shorter day still needs every effort of every union man; and without the right to protect themselves in a closed shop by refusing to work with those whose weakness or stupidity make them unfaithful to their class, trade unionism cannot hold that which it has won, still less look forward to greater victories to come.

I took the Isthmus, started the Canal, and then left Congress — not to debate the Canal but to debate me.
THEODORE ROOSEVELT, *New York Times*, March 24, 1911
The greatest liberty that man has taken with nature.
JAMES BRYCE, of the Panama Canal

61.

E. D. WHITE AND J. M. HARLAN: *Standard Oil Company of New Jersey et al.* v. *United States*

The Sherman Antitrust Act of 1890 had declared all combinations in restraint of trade to be unlawful, and the Supreme Court in a number of decisions had upheld the constitutionality of this provision of the Act. The Court's decision in the case of Standard Oil Company of New Jersey did not run explicitly counter to the earlier decisions, but it added an interpretation of this key provision of the Act that was to have great influence in the years to come. Standard Oil had been founded by John D. Rockefeller in 1882, and in 1907, when the government prosecution of the company began, it exercised a virtual monopoly of the entire petroleum industry of the country. The Court ordered the breakup of the Standard Oil "trust," with the result that numerous other Rockefeller-controlled oil companies were founded in other states besides New Jersey. But in so doing, the Court held that only unreasonable combinations in restraint of trade were illegal, and in effect that monopolies could not be legally attacked unless they clearly violated this canon. The "rule of reason" espoused by Chief Justice White in his opinion for the majority became a precedent that the Court looked to in all future antitrust suits. Portions of Justice Harlan's dissent (although he concurred in part) as well as of White's opinion of May 15, 1911, are reprinted here.

Source: 221 U.S. 1.

Mr. Chief Justice White: Both as to the law and as to the facts, the opposing contentions pressed in the argument are numerous and in all their aspects are so irreconcilable that it is difficult to reduce them to some fundamental generalization, which by being disposed of would decide them all. For instance, as to the law. While both sides agree that the determination of the controversy rests upon the correct construction and application of the 1st and 2nd sections of the Antitrust Act, yet the views as to the meaning of the Act are as wide apart as the poles, since there is no real point of agreement on any view of the Act. And this also is the case as to the scope and effect of authorities relied upon, even although in some instances one and the same authority is asserted to be controlling.

So also is it as to the facts. Thus, on the one hand, with relentless pertinacity and minuteness of analysis, it is insisted that the facts establish that the assailed combination took its birth in a purpose to unlawfully acquire wealth by oppressing the public and destroying the just rights of others, and that its entire career exemplifies an inexorable carrying out of such wrongful intents, since, it is asserted, the pathway of the combination from the beginning to the time of the filing of the bill is marked with constant proofs of wrong inflicted upon the public and is strewn with the wrecks resulting from crushing out, without regard to law, the individual rights of others.

Indeed, so conclusive, it is urged, is the proof on these subjects that it is asserted that the existence of the principal corporate defendant — the Standard Oil Company of New Jersey — with the vast accumulation of property which it owns or controls, because of its infinite potency for harm and the dangerous example which its continued existence affords, is an open and enduring menace to all freedom of trade and is a byword and reproach to modern economic methods.

On the other hand, in a powerful analysis of the facts, it is insisted that they demonstrate that the origin and development of the vast business which the defendants control was but the result of lawful competitive methods, guided by economic genius of the highest order, sustained by courage, by a keen insight into commercial situations, resulting in the acquisition of great wealth, but at the same time serving to stimulate and increase production, to widely extend the distribution of the products of petroleum at a cost largely below that which would have otherwise prevailed, thus proving to be at one and the same time a benefaction to the general public as well as of enormous advantage to individuals.

It is not denied that in the enormous volume of proof contained in the record in the period of almost a lifetime to which that proof is addressed, there may be found acts of wrongdoing, but the insistence is that they were rather the exception than the rule, and in most cases were either the result of too great individual zeal in the keen rivalries of business or of the methods and habits of dealing which, even if wrong, were commonly practised at the time. And to discover and state the truth concerning these contentions, both arguments call for the analysis and weighing, as we have said at the outset, of a jungle of conflicting testimony covering a period of forty years, a duty difficult to rightly perform and, even if satisfactorily accomplished, almost impossible to state with any reasonable regard to brevity.

Duly appreciating the situation just stated, it is certain that only one point of concord between the parties is discernible, which is, that the controversy in every aspect is controlled by a correct conception of the meaning of the first and second sections of the Antitrust Act. We shall therefore — departing from what otherwise would be the natural order of analysis — make this one point of harmony the initial basis of our examination of the contentions, relying upon the conception that by doing so some harmonious resonance may result adequate to dominate and control the discord with which the case abounds. That is to say, we shall first come to consider the meaning of the 1st and 2nd sections of the Antitrust Act by the text, and, after discerning what by that process appears to be its true meaning, we shall proceed to consider the respective contentions of the parties concerning the Act, the strength or weakness of those contentions, as well as the accuracy of the meaning of the Act as deduced from the text in the light of the prior decisions of this court concerning it. When we have done this we shall then approach the facts. . . .

We quote the text of the 1st and 2nd sections of the act, as follows:

Section 1. Every contract, combination in the form of trust or otherwise, or conspiracy, in restraint of trade or commerce among the several states, or with foreign nations, is hereby declared to be illegal. Every person who shall make any such contract or engage in any such combination or conspiracy shall be deemed guilty of a misdemeanor, and, on conviction thereof, shall be punished by fine not exceeding $5,000, or by imprisonment not exceeding one year, or by both said punishments, in the discretion of the court.

Section 2. Every person who shall monopolize, or attempt to monopolize, or combine or conspire with any other person or persons to monopolize any part of the trade or commerce among the several states, or with foreign nations, shall be deemed guilty of a misdemeanor, and, on conviction thereof, shall be punished by fine not exceeding $5,000, or by imprisonment not exceeding one year, or

"Next"; the Standard Oil octopus as cartooned in "Puck"

by both said punishments, in the discretion of the court.

The debates show that doubt as to whether there was a common law of the United States which governed the subject in the absence of legislation was among the influences leading to the passage of the Act. They conclusively show, however, that the main cause which led to the legislation was the thought that it was required by the economic condition of the times, that is, the vast accumulation of wealth in the hands of corporations and individuals, the enormous development of corporate organization, the facility for combination which such organizations afforded, the fact that the facility was being used, and that combinations known as trusts were being multiplied, and the widespread impression that their power had been and would be exerted to oppress individuals and injure the public generally. Although debates may not be used as a means for interpreting a statute (*United States* v. *Trans-Missouri Freight Association* . . .) that rule in the nature of things is not

violated by resorting to debates as a means of ascertaining the environment at the time of the enactment of a particular law, that is, the history of the period when it was adopted.

There can be no doubt that the sole subject with which the 1st section deals is restraint of trade as therein contemplated, and that the attempt to monopolize and monopolization is the subject with which the 2nd section is concerned. It is certain that those terms, at least in their rudimentary meaning, took their origin in the common law, and were also familiar in the law of this country prior to and at the time of the adoption of the act in question. . . .

Generalizing these considerations, the situation is this:

1. That by the common law, monopolies were unlawful because of their restriction upon individual freedom of contract and their injury to the public.

2. That as to necessaries of life, the freedom of the individual to deal was restricted where the nature and character of the deal-

ing was such as to engender the presumption of intent to bring about at least one of the injuries which it was deemed would result from monopoly, that is an undue enhancement of price.

3. That to protect the freedom of contract of the individual not only in his own interest but principally in the interest of the commonweal, a contract of an individual by which he put an unreasonable restraint upon himself as to carrying on his trade or business was void.

And that at common law the evils consequent upon engrossing, etc., caused those things to be treated as coming within monopoly and sometimes to be called monopoly and the same considerations caused monopoly because of its operation and effect, to be brought within and spoken of generally as impeding the due course of or being in restraint of trade. . . .

It is remarkable that nowhere at common law can there be found a prohibition against the creation of monopoly by an individual. This would seem to manifest, either consciously or intuitively, a profound conception as to the inevitable operation of economic forces and the equipoise or balance in favor of the protection of the rights of individuals which resulted. That is to say, as it was deemed that monopoly in the concrete could only arise from an act of sovereign power, and, such sovereign power being restrained, prohibitions as to individuals were directed, not against the creation of monopoly but were only applied to such acts in relation to particular subjects as to which it was deemed, if not restrained, some of the consequences of monopoly might result. After all, this was but an instinctive recognition of the truisms that the course of trade could not be made free by obstructing it, and that an individual's right to trade could not be protected by destroying such right. . . .

In this country . . . the acts from which it was deemed there resulted a part if not all of the injurious consequences ascribed to monopoly, came to be referred to as a monopoly itself. In other words, here as had been the case in England, practical common sense caused attention to be concentrated not upon the theoretically correct name to be given to the condition or acts which gave rise to a harmful result, but to the result itself and to the remedying of the evils which it produced. . . .

Without going into detail and but very briefly surveying the whole field, it may be with accuracy said that the dread of enhancement of prices and of other wrongs which it was thought would flow from the undue limitation on competitive conditions caused by contracts or other acts of individuals or corporations led, as a matter of public policy, to the prohibition or treating as illegal all contracts or acts which were unreasonably restrictive of competitive conditions, either from the nature or character of the contract or act or where the surrounding circumstances were such as to justify the conclusion that they had not been entered into or performed with the legitimate purpose of reasonably forwarding personal interest and developing trade; but on the contrary were of such a character as to give rise to the inference or presumption that they had been entered into or done with the intent to do wrong to the general public and to limit the right of individuals, thus restraining the free flow of commerce and tending to bring about the evils, such as enhancement of prices, which were considered to be against public policy.

It is equally true to say that the survey of the legislation in this country on this subject from the beginning will show, depending as it did upon the economic conceptions which obtained at the time when the legislation was adopted or judicial decision was rendered, that contracts or acts were at one time deemed to be of such a character as to justify the inference of wrongful intent which were at another period thought not to be of that character. But this again, as we have seen, simply followed the line of development of the law of England. . . .

In view of the common law and the law in this country as to restraint of trade . . . and the illuminating effect which that history must have under the rule to which we have referred, we think it results:

1. That the context manifests that the statute was drawn in the light of the existing practical conception of the law of restraint of trade, because it groups as within that class, not only contracts which were in restraint of trade in the subjective sense but all contracts or acts which theoretically were attempts to monopolize, yet which in practice had come to be considered as in restraint of trade in a broad sense.

2. That in view of the many new forms of contracts and combinations which were being evolved from existing economic conditions, it was deemed essential by an all-embracing enumeration to make sure that no form of contract or combination by which an undue restraint of interstate or foreign commerce was brought about could save such restraint from condemnation. The statute under this view evidenced the intent not to restrain the right to make and enforce contracts, whether resulting from combination or otherwise, which did not unduly restrain interstate or foreign commerce, but to protect that commerce from being restrained by methods, whether old or new, which would constitute an interference that is an undue restraint.

3. And as the contracts or acts embraced in the provision were not expressly defined, since the enumeration addressed itself simply to classes of acts, those classes being broad enough to embrace every conceivable contract or combination which could be made concerning trade or commerce or the subjects of such commerce, and thus caused any act done by any of the enumerated methods anywhere in the whole field of human activity to be illegal if in restraint of trade, it inevitably follows that the provision necessarily called for the exercise of judgment which required that some standard should be resorted to for the purpose of determining whether the prohibitions contained in the statute had or had not in any given case been violated. Thus not specifying but indubitably contemplating and requiring a standard, it follows that it was intended that the standard of reason which had been applied at the common law, and in this country in dealing with subjects of the character embraced by the statute, was intended to be the measure used for the purpose of determining whether in a given case a particular act had or had not brought about the wrong against which the statute provided. . . .

We see no cause to doubt the correctness of these conclusions, considering the subject from every aspect; that is, both in view of the facts established by the record and the necessary operation and effect of the law as we have construed it upon the inferences deducible from the facts, for the following reasons:

1. Because the unification of power and control over petroleum and its products which was the inevitable result of the combining in the New Jersey corporation by the increase of its stock and the transfer to it of the stocks of so many other corporations, aggregating so vast a capital, gives rise, in and of itself, in the absence of countervailing circumstances, to say the least, to the *prima facie* presumption of intent and purpose to maintain the dominancy over the oil industry, not as a result of normal methods of industrial development but by new means of combination which were resorted to in order that greater power might be added than would otherwise have arisen had normal methods been followed, the whole with the purpose of excluding others from the trade and thus centralizing in the combination a perpetual control of the movements of petroleum and its products in

the channels of interstate commerce.

2. Because the *prima facie* presumption of intent to restrain trade, to monopolize and to bring about monopolization resulting from the act of expanding the stock of the New Jersey corporation and vesting it with such vast control of the oil industry, is made conclusive by considering: (1) the conduct of the persons or corporations who were mainly instrumental in bringing about the extension of power in the New Jersey corporation before the consummation of that result and prior to the formation of the trust agreements of 1879 and 1882; (2) by considering the proof as to what was done under those agreements and the acts which immediately preceded the vesting of power in the New Jersey corporation as well as by weighing the modes in which the power vested in that corporation has been exerted and the results which have arisen from it.

Recurring to the acts done by the individuals or corporations who were mainly instrumental in bringing about the expansion of the New Jersey corporation during the period prior to the formation of the trust agreements of 1879 and 1882, including those agreements, not for the purpose of weighing the substantial merit of the numerous charges of wrongdoing made during such period but solely as an aid for discovering intent and purpose, we think no disinterested mind can survey the period in question without being irresistibly driven to the conclusion that the very genius for commercial development and organization which it would seem was manifested from the beginning soon begot an intent and purpose to exclude others which was frequently manifested by acts and dealings wholly inconsistent with the theory that they were made with the single conception of advancing the development of business power by usual methods; but which, on the contrary, necessarily involved the intent to drive others from the field and to exclude them from their right to trade and thus ac-

complish the mastery which was the end in view.

And, considering the period from the date of the trust agreements of 1879 and 1882 up to the time of the expansion of the New Jersey corporation, the gradual extension of the power over the commerce in oil which ensued, the decision of the Supreme Court of Ohio, the tardiness or reluctance in conforming to the commands of that decision, the method first adopted and that which finally culminated in the plan of the New Jersey corporation, all additionally serve to make manifest the continued existence of the intent which we have previously indicated and which among other things impelled the expansion of the New Jersey corporation.

The exercise of the power which resulted from that organization fortifies the foregoing conclusions, since the development which came, the acquisition here and there which ensued for every efficient means by which competition could have been asserted, the slow but resistless methods which followed by which means of transportation were absorbed and brought under control, the system of marketing which was adopted by which the country was divided into districts and the trade in each district in oil was turned over to a designated corporation within the combination and all others were excluded, all lead the mind up to a conviction of a purpose and intent which we think is so certain as practically to cause the subject not to be within the domain of reasonable contention.

The inference that no attempt to monopolize could have been intended and that no monopolization resulted from the acts complained of, since it is established that a very small percentage of the crude oil produced was controlled by the combination, is unwarranted. As substantial power over the crude product was the inevitable result of the absolute control which existed over the refined product, the monopolization of the one carried with it the power to control the other, and if the inferences which this situation suggests were developed, which we deem it unnecessary to do, they might well serve to add additional cogency to the presumption of intent to monopolize which we have found arises from the unquestioned proof on other subjects.

Mr. Justice Harlan: A sense of duty constrains me to express the objections which I have to certain declarations in the opinion just delivered on behalf of the Court.

I concur in holding that the Standard Oil Company of New Jersey and its subsidiary companies constitute a combination in restraint of interstate commerce, and that they have attempted to monopolize and have monopolized parts of such commerce — all in violation of what is known as the Antitrust Act of 1890. . . . The evidence in this case overwhelmingly sustained that view and led the Circuit Court, by its final decree, to order the dissolution of the New Jersey corporation and the discontinuance of the illegal combination between that corporation and its subsidiary companies.

In my judgment, the decree below should have been affirmed without qualification. But the Court, while affirming the decree, directs some modifications in respect of what it characterizes as "minor matters." It is to be apprehended that those modifications may prove to be mischievous. In saying this, I have particularly in view the statement in the opinion that

> it does not necessarily follow that because an illegal restraint of trade or an attempt to monopolize or a monopolization resulted from the combination and the transfer of the stocks of the subsidiary corporations to the New Jersey corporation, that a like restraint of trade or attempt to monopolize or monopolization would necessarily arise from agreements between one or more of the subsidiary corporations after the transfer of the stock by the New Jersey corporation.

Taking this language, in connection with other parts of the opinion, the subsidiary companies are thus, in effect, informed — unwisely, I think — that although the New Jersey corporation, being an illegal combination, must go out of existence, *they* may join in an agreement *to restrain commerce* among the states if such restraint be not "undue."

In order that my objections to certain parts of the Court's opinion may distinctly appear, I must state the circumstances under which Congress passed the Antitrust Act, and trace the course of judicial decisions as to its meaning and scope. This is the more necessary because the Court, by its decision, when interpreted by the language of its opinion, has not only upset the long-settled interpretation of the Act but has usurped the constitutional functions of the legislative branch of the government. With all due respect for the opinions of others, I feel bound to say that what the Court has said may well cause some alarm for the integrity of our institutions. Let us see how the matter stands.

All who recall the condition of the country in 1890 will remember that there was everywhere, among the people generally, a deep feeling of unrest. The nation had been rid of human slavery — fortunately, as all now feel — but the conviction was universal that the country was in real danger from another kind of slavery sought to be fastened on the American people, namely, the slavery that would result from aggregations of capital in the hands of a few individuals and corporations controlling, for their own profit and advantage exclusively, the entire business of the country, including the production and sale of the necessaries of life. Such a danger was thought to be then imminent, and all felt that it must be met firmly and by such statutory regulations as would adequately protect the people against oppression and wrong.

Congress, therefore, took up the matter and gave the whole subject the fullest consideration. All agreed that the national government could not, by legislation, regulate the domestic trade carried on wholly within the several states; for, power to regulate such trade remained with, because never surrendered by, the states. But, under authority expressly granted to it by the Constitution, Congress could regulate commerce among the several states and with foreign states. Its authority to regulate such commerce was and is paramount, due force being given to other provisions of the fundamental law devised by the fathers for the safety of the government and for the protection and security of the essential rights inhering in life, liberty, and property.

Guided by these considerations, and to the end that the people, *so far as interstate commerce* was concerned, might not be dominated by vast combinations and monopolies, having power to advance their own selfish ends, regardless of the general interests and welfare, Congress passed the Antitrust Act of 1890. . . .

After what has been adjudged, upon full consideration, as to the meaning and scope of the Antitrust Act, and in view of the usages of this Court when attorneys for litigants have attempted to reopen questions that have been deliberately decided, I confess to no little surprise as to what has occurred in the present case. The Court says that the previous cases . . . "cannot by any possible conception be treated as authoritative without the certitude that *reason* was resorted to for the purpose of deciding them." And its opinion is full of intimations that this Court proceeded in those cases, so far as the present question is concerned, without being guided by the "rule of reason," or "the light of reason."

It is more than once intimated, if not suggested, that if the Antitrust Act is to be construed as prohibiting *every* contract or combination, of whatever nature, which is in fact in restraint of commerce, regardless of the reasonableness or unreasonableness of such restraint, that fact would show that the Court had not proceeded, in its decision, according to "the light of reason," but had

disregarded the "rule of reason." If the Court, in those cases, was wrong in its construction of the Act, it is certain that it fully apprehended the views advanced by learned counsel in previous cases and pronounced them to be untenable. The published reports place this beyond all question. . . .

Is it to be supposed that any point escaped notice in those cases when we think of the sagacity of the justice who expressed the views of the Court, or of the ability of the profound, astute lawyers who sought such an interpretation of the Act as would compel the Court to insert words in the statute which Congress had not put there, and the insertion of which words would amount to "judicial legislation"? Now, this Court is asked to do that which it has distinctly declared it could not and would not do, and has now done what it then said it could not constitutionally do. It has, by mere interpretation, modified the Act of Congress and deprived it of practical value as a defensive measure against the evils to be remedied.

On reading the opinion just delivered, the first inquiry will be that, as the Court is unanimous in holding that the particular things done by the Standard Oil Company and its subsidiary companies, in this case, were illegal under the Antitrust Act, whether those things were in reasonable or unreasonable restraint of interstate commerce, why was it necessary to make an elaborate argument, as is done in the opinion, to show that according to the "rule of reason" the Act as passed by Congress should be interpreted as if it contained the word "unreasonable" or the word "undue"?

The only answer which, in frankness, can be given to this question is that the Court intends to decide that its deliberate judgment, fifteen years ago, to the effect that the Act permitted no restraint whatever of interstate commerce, whether reasonable or unreasonable, was not in accordance with the "rule of reason." In effect, the Court says that it will now, for the first time, bring the discussion under the "light of reason" and apply the "rule of reason" to the questions to be decided. I have the authority of this Court for saying that such a course of proceeding on its part would be "judicial legislation." . . .

I said at the outset that the action of the Court in this case might well alarm thoughtful men who revered the Constitution. I meant by this that many things are intimated and said in the Court's opinion which will not be regarded otherwise than as sanctioning an invasion by the judiciary of the constitutional domain of Congress — an attempt by interpretation to soften or modify what some regard as a harsh public policy. This Court, let me repeat, solemnly adjudged many years ago that it could not, except by *"judicial legislation,"* read words into the Antitrust Act not put there by Congress, and which, being inserted, give it a meaning which the words of the Act, as passed, if properly interpreted, would not justify. The Court has decided that it could not thus change a public policy formulated and declared by Congress; that Congress has paramount authority to regulate interstate commerce, and that it alone can change a policy once inaugurated by legislation.

The courts have nothing to do with the wisdom or policy of an act of Congress. Their duty is to ascertain the will of Congress, and if the statute embodying the expression of that will is constitutional, the courts must respect it. They have no function to declare a public policy nor to *amend* legislative enactments. "What is termed the policy of the government with reference to any particular legislation," as this Court has said, "is generally a very uncertain thing, upon which all sorts of opinions, each variant from the other, may be formed by different persons. It is a ground much too un-stable upon which to rest the judgment of the Court in the interpretation of statutes." . . .

After many years of public service at the national Capitol, and after a somewhat close observation of the conduct of public affairs, I am impelled to say that there is abroad, in our land, a most harmful tendency to bring about the amending of constitutions and legislative enactments by means alone of judicial construction. As a public policy has been declared by the Legislative Department in respect of interstate commerce, over which Congress has entire control under the Constitution, all concerned must patiently submit to what has been lawfully done, until the people of the United States — the source of all national power — shall, in their own time, upon reflection and through the Legislative Department of the government, require a change of that policy.

There are some who say that it is a part of one's liberty to conduct commerce among the states without being subject to governmental authority. But that would not be liberty, regulated by law; and liberty, which cannot be regulated by law, is not to be desired. The supreme law of the land — which is binding alike upon all — upon presidents, congresses, the courts and the people — gives to Congress, and to Congress alone, authority to regulate interstate commerce, and when Congress forbids *any* restraint of such commerce, in any form, all must obey its mandate. To overreach the action of Congress merely by judicial construction, that is, by indirection, is a blow at the integrity of our governmental system, and in the end will prove most dangerous to all. Mr. Justice Bradley wisely said, when on this bench, that illegitimate and unconstitutional practices get their first footing by silent approaches and slight deviations from legal modes of legal procedure.

62.

THEODORE ROOSEVELT: A Square Deal for the Trusts

Although Theodore Roosevelt was hailed — and attacked — as the leading "trustbuster" of his time, the succeeding Taft administration actually prosecuted more antitrust suits in four years than Roosevelt's administration had in eight. One case that attracted much attention was the prosecution of the United States Steel Corporation. Roosevelt, who had been severely criticized for failing to move against the giant steel company while he was President, explained why he thought the government was wrong in bringing suit against the U.S. Steel Corporation in an article published in 1911. The article is reprinted here in part.

Source: *Outlook,* November 18, 1911: "The Trusts, the People, and the Square Deal."

IT IS A VITALLY necessary thing to have the persons in control of big trusts of the character of the Standard Oil Trust and tobacco trust taught that they are under the law, just as it was a necessary thing to have the sugar trust taught the same lesson in drastic fashion by Mr. Henry L. Stimson when he was United States district attorney in the city of New York. But to attempt to meet the whole problem, not by administrative governmental action but by a succession of lawsuits, is hopeless from the standpoint of working out a permanently satisfactory solution. Moreover, the results sought to be achieved are achieved only in extremely insufficient and fragmentary measure by breaking up all big corporations, whether they have behaved well or ill, into a number of little corporations, which it is perfectly certain will be largely, and perhaps altogether, under the same control. Such action is harsh and mischievous if the corporation is guilty of nothing except its size; and where, as in the case of the Standard Oil, and especially the tobacco, trusts, the corporation has been guilty of immoral and antisocial practices, there is need for far more drastic and thoroughgoing action than any

that has been taken under the recent decree of the Supreme Court.

In the case of the tobacco trust, for instance, the settlement in the Circuit Court, in which the representatives of the government seem inclined to concur, practically leaves all of the companies still substantially under the control of the twenty-nine original defendants. Such a result is lamentable from the standpoint of justice. The decision of the Circuit Court, if allowed to stand, means that the tobacco trust has merely been obliged to change its clothes, that none of the real offenders have received any real punishment, while, as the *New York Times,* a pro-trust paper, says, the tobacco concerns, in their new clothes, are in positions of "ease and luxury" and "immune from prosecution under the law."

Surely, miscarriage of justice is not too strong a term to apply to such a result when considered in connection with what the Supreme Court said of this trust. That great Court, in its decision, used language which, in spite of its habitual and severe self-restraint in stigmatizing wrongdoing, yet unhesitatingly condemns the tobacco trust for moral turpitude, saying that the case shows an "ever present manifestation . . . of conscious wrongdoing" by the trust, whose history is

> replete with the doing of acts which it was the obvious purpose of the statute to forbid . . . demonstrative of the existence from the beginning of a purpose to acquire dominion and control of the tobacco trade, not by the mere exertion of the ordinary right to contract and to trade but by methods devised in order to monopolize the trade by driving competitors out of business, which were ruthlessly carried out upon the assumption that to work upon the fears or play upon the cupidity of competitors would make success possible.

The letters from and to various officials of the trust, which were put in evidence, show a literally astounding and horrifying indulgence by the trust in wicked and depraved business methods — such as the "endeavor to cause a strike in their [a rival business firm's] factory," or the "shutting off the market" of an independent tobacco firm by "taking the necessary steps to give them a warm reception," or forcing importers into a price agreement by causing and continuing "a demoralization of the business for such length of time as may be deemed desirable" (I quote from the letters). A trust guilty of such conduct should be absolutely disbanded, and the only way to prevent the repetition of such conduct is by strict government supervision and not merely by lawsuits.

The Antitrust Law cannot meet the whole situation, nor can any modification of the principle of the Antitrust Law avail to meet the whole situation. The fact is that many of the men who have called themselves Progressives, and who certainly believe that they are Progressives, represent in reality in this matter not progress at all but a kind of sincere rural Toryism. These men believe that it is possible by strengthening the Antitrust Law to restore business to the competitive conditions of the middle of the last century. Any such effort is foredoomed to end in failure and, if successful, would be

mischievous to the last degree. Business cannot be successfully conducted in accordance with the practices and theories of sixty years ago unless we abolish steam, electricity, big cities, and, in short, not only all modern business and modern industrial conditions but all the modern conditions of our civilization. The effort to restore competition as it was sixty years ago, and to trust for justice solely to this proposed restoration of competition, is just as foolish as if we should go back to the flintlocks of Washington's Continentals as a substitute for modern weapons of precision.

The effort to prohibit all combinations, good or bad, is bound to fail, and ought to fail; when made, it merely means that some of the worst combinations are not checked and that honest business is checked. Our purpose should be, not to strangle business as an incident of strangling combinations but to regulate big corporations in thoroughgoing and effective fashion so as to help legitimate business as an incident to thoroughly and completely safeguarding the interests of the people as a whole.

Against all such increase of government regulation the argument is raised that it would amount to a form of socialism. This argument is familiar; it is precisely the same as that which was raised against the creation of the Interstate Commerce Commission and of all the different utilities commissions in the different states, as I myself saw, thirty years ago, when I was a legislator at Albany, and these questions came up in connection with our state government. Nor can action be effectively taken by any one state. Congress alone has power under the Constitution effectively and thoroughly and at all points to deal with interstate commerce; and where Congress, as it should do, provides laws that will give the nation full jurisdiction over the whole field, then that jurisdiction becomes, of necessity, exclusive — although until Congress does act affirmatively and thoroughly it is idle to expect that the states will or ought to rest content with nonaction on the part of both federal and state authorities.

This statement, by the way, applies also to the question of "usurpation" by any one branch of our government of the rights of another branch. It is contended that in these recent decisions the Supreme Court legislated; so it did; and it had to, because Congress had signally failed to do *its* duty by legislating. For the Supreme Court to nullify an act of the legislature as unconstitutional except on the clearest grounds is usurpation; to interpret such an act in an obviously wrong sense is usurpation; but where the legislative body persistently leaves open a field which it is absolutely imperative, from the public standpoint, to fill, then no possible blame attaches to the official or officials who step in because they have to and who then do the needed work in the interest of the people. The blame in such cases lies with the body which has been derelict, and not with the body which reluctantly makes good the dereliction. . . .

Few will dispute the fact that the present situation is not satisfactory and cannot be put on a permanently satisfactory basis unless we put an end to the period of groping and declare for a fixed policy, a policy which shall clearly define and punish wrongdoing, which shall put a stop to the iniquities done in the name of business, but which shall do strict equity to business. . . .

Not only should any huge corporation which has gained its position by unfair methods and by interference with the rights of others, by demoralizing and corrupt practices, in short, by sheer baseness and wrongdoing, be broken up but it should be made the business of some administrative governmental body, by constant supervision, to see that it does not come together again, save under such strict control as shall insure the community against all repetition of the bad conduct. And it should never be permitted thus to assemble its parts as long as these parts are under the control of the original offenders, for actual experience has shown

that these men are, from the standpoint of the people at large, unfit to be trusted with the power implied in the management of a large corporation. But nothing of importance is gained by breaking up a huge interstate and international industrial organization *which has not offended otherwise than by its size*, into a number of small concerns without any attempt to regulate the way in which those concerns as a whole shall do business. Nothing is gained by depriving the American nation of good weapons wherewith to fight in the great field of international industrial competition. . . .

Either the Bureau of Corporations should be authorized, or some other governmental body similar to the Interstate Commerce Commission should be created, to exercise this supervision, this authoritative control. When once immoral business practices have been eliminated by such control, competition will thereby be again revived as a healthy factor, although not as formerly an all-sufficient factor, in keeping the general business situation sound. Wherever immoral business practices still obtain — as they obtained in the cases of the Standard Oil Trust and tobacco trust — the Antitrust Law can be invoked; and wherever such a prosecution is successful and the courts declare a corporation to possess a monopolistic character, then that corporation should be completely dissolved, and the parts ought never to be again assembled save on whatever terms and under whatever conditions may be imposed by the governmental body in which is vested the regulatory power.

Methods can readily be devised by which corporations sincerely desiring to act fairly and honestly can on their own initiative come under this thoroughgoing administrative control by the government and thereby be free from the working of the Antitrust Law. But the law will remain to be invoked against wrongdoers; and under such condition it could be invoked far more vigorously and successfully than at present.

1911 - 1912

63.

Senate Hearings on Interstate Commerce

The Interstate Commerce Commission, established in 1887, had no real power until the Hepburn Act of 1906 provided it with the authority to regulate railroad rates. From then on Progressive reformers agitated for further strengthening of the commission's authority, and during 1911 and 1912 the Senate conducted hearings to determine whether a need existed for additional legislation. The following three-part selection comprises portions of the testimony of J. R. Moorehead, C. U. Carpenter, and T. J. Brooks. Moorehead was secretary of the National Federation of Retail Merchants; Carpenter, a New York businessman, was also chairman of the Sherman Antitrust Committee of the New York Board of Trade; and Brooks was a farmer from Atwood, Tennessee.

Source: *Report of the Committee on Interstate Commerce, U.S. Senate,* 62 Congress, Washington, 1913, Vol. I, pp. 914-920, 1027-1032, Vol. II, pp. 2336-2338.

I.

J. R. MOOREHEAD:
The Plight of Small Business

YOU WILL ALL AGREE that there are grave problems confronting big business of this country, and there are grave problems confronting Congress and the people of the country in dealing with big business. I want to say that although it may not have been intentional on the part of those who are responsible for the present situation — and I have no reason to believe that it is — there are also grave problems confronting the small businessmen of the country.

I want to say in the beginning that many of the stones that are being cast at the big fellows are missing the mark and crossing the street and breaking the windows of the little fellows. In other words, the efforts that are being made to curb the powerful, the rich, and the grasping are recoiling upon that class of men in this country for whom we believe it was not intended, those who are the least able and the least organized to secure their rights and combat the opposition. In other words, we know that the antitrust law of the nation and the states as well is being perverted and is being used for ends that were never intended and, should present conditions continue, would bring about a situation that cannot be later on remedied.

There are no longer any uncertain theories confronting the little man in business. We have a condition, and had we come here oftener and made our wants known and our influence in politics felt long since, perhaps, the status of these I have the honor to represent could be better determined.

First, there is a great outcry in this country just now for the elimination of the "middleman," better known as the retail merchant, although the wholesaler and jobber may be classed as such. Our answer to this demand is that we do not propose to be eliminated if concerted action on our part should be able to show the Congress and the legislatures of the several states that we have a place in the economy of the country and that our preservation is for the best interest of the greatest number; best for their economical, political, and social welfare.

This outcry emanates from four principal sources: first, the great aggregations of capital known as mail-order houses; second, almost all of what are known as farm journals; third, a great part of the metropolitan press; fourth, many politicians seeking to curry favor with the farming and laboring classes. These elements in our national make up, along with others of lesser influence, have brought about a condition in the minds of the public adverse to the retail merchants, especially among the farmers and laboring men, that is no less than criminal.

To my mind, this is the most serious side of the whole question. Just to think that it has been possible in this country of ours to so organize and conduct a campaign of advertising to so poison the minds of hundreds of thousands of people scattered all over the country against their neighbors, the home merchant, that they will not even give us a chance to meet outside competition. Under these false representations, carried on for so long, the public seems not able to distinguish between our efforts to obtain a fair living and the practice of extortion. They set us down as extortionists, without argument or chance to be heard.

I am not here to criticize the President of the United States or the attorney general or any of his assistants. I have had occasion to more particularly call the President's attention to some of these facts and conditions, and the reply to my communication comes through the office of the attorney general to the effect that, "It is not the duty of those upon whom the responsibility of the enforcement of a law is imposed to consider general economic questions in determining whether a prosecution should be had for its violation." This being the case, which I am perfectly willing to admit without any question whatever, then it is the duty of Congress to settle economic questions if it is in their power so to do.

I have mentioned four of the principal elements that are just now, intentionally or not, working to the undoing of the little man in business. Gentlemen, the attempt at combination or concentration of business into the hands of a few is no more manifest or real than is now being brought about in the distribution of merchandise of every kind, known as the retail business. This country has been wonderfully prosperous in the last ten years. I venture to assert that there never was a time in the history of this country, taking into account the last five years or more, when there were so many people in every walk of life who were doing so well, making such a good living, getting such prices for farm products and livestock, making better wages, better housed, better fed, better clothed, and, taking all things into consideration, no greater general prosperity ever existed in the country. We can and do rejoice in this fact.

Not one of us would reduce the price of a single item raised upon our farms or produced by our labor; but I am confident that I am within the truth when I say that the million or more retail merchants of this country have received less of the benefits growing out of this great era of prosperity than any one other class of our people. I feel safe in saying that the little merchants of the country have not reaped their share of the reward. Their business nor their profits have grown in proportion to the general prosperity that surrounds us. Certainly there has been a greater consumption of merchandise in the shape of clothing, food, and every other class of goods used by humanity; but the increase has not fallen into the lap of the small retailer.

When you have the opportunity to go among your constituents, who are the retailers of merchandise, you will surely find that the great majority of them have done little more than hold their own. Many of them do not do that well. Farmlands have increased beyond all expectations, and I am not saying they are too high. Wages have increased, but I do not say that labor is too well-paid. No one knows better than those for whom I speak that upon these two elements rest our security and prosperity, and they have no better friends or defenders in the country than their home merchants; but we do assert, with emphasis, that the business, the storehouses, the homes, the stocks of goods, and the profits of the retailers have not grown in proportion to that obtained by either of the above-mentioned class or any others.

Where has it gone? Who has gathered the harvest? I have said that "mail-order houses" are one of the factors that has brought about this condition of affairs. What are some of the facts? It has gone the rounds of the press, and is no doubt a fact, that one of these houses alone sold more than $63 million of merchandise by mail last year. The business of one increased, it is said, 1,000 percent in three years — so much business that they were scarcely able to take care of it.

And while the "control of trusts" and the influence of Wall Street are pertinent questions for debate at this time, I venture to remind you that it is not disputed that the chairman of the Board of Directors of the largest mail-order house in this country is the president of one of the largest banks in New York. It might not be out of place to suggest that this would be a fruitful field for investigation. If the business of this class is to go on increasing, how long will it be before there will be dictation to the jobber, wholesaler, and manufacturer as to whom they shall sell, and we can imagine what would happen to the little fellows in business.

I have referred to the feeling of public sentiment which has obtained in the public mind against the retail merchant. Ever since this method of merchandising by mail began to take root in this country, a great part of their advertising has not been in praise of their wares but has been a tirade of insinuation, misrepresentation, and abuse for the home merchants, as being nothing more than robbers and thieves; and when we attempt to get together to protect our business, our homes, and our families, we find out how they are able to invoke in their own behalf the antitrust laws of the country. Almost without exception the greater part of the advertising revenue of the farm journals comes from the mail-order house, just as the daily press is largely supported by revenues from the large department stores. I think you can readily see why there is rarely ever a good word spoken for the little man in business from these sources. There are undoubtedly exceptions, but they are exceedingly rare. . . . .

I do not blame the farm journals for standing up for those who support them, for they could not exist without this kind of upport. I do not blame the daily press for alking for the great department stores vhich furnish them with such profitable usiness; they would be ingrates if they did ot. But I do complain, and we believe we ave a just complaint, when we find ourelves involved in this already unequal truggle and the government steps in and ays, "Stop; you are restraining the trade of he mail-order house, the manufacturers and he big fellows. You are operating a new ind of trust, a trust of power." What greater trust of power could there be than hat of a great aggregation of capital to pread it broadcast through the daily and arm press and catalogues that they can sell heir wares at half the price charged by the ome merchants?

To be more specific, a United States grand jury in Chicago recently indicted ourteen secretaries of as many retail lumber associations, and I am informed upon good authority, by the parties themselves, that he Retail Implement Dealers' Association and the Retail Coal Dealers' Association are undergoing the same kind of an investigaion. It is only fair to presume that these atter two organizations, and perhaps others, will meet the same fate as the lumber secrearies have; for, during the recent trip of the President across the country, he certainly made it plain that all, at least, would have o submit to the same methods of investigaion, and the legal department of the govrnment seems to be entirely in accord with his plan of procedure.

Civil action has also been brought against a number of the lumber associations, and I am quite sure, had the legal department of he government been willing to stop here, hat they would have welcomed the opporunity of finding out whether or not they vere violating a law which no one seems to e able to correctly interpret. I call your atention to the fact that in bringing indictments above referred to, the government had to admit, or at least could not charge, hat these organizations, which their secre-

taries represented, "had no incorporation, no capital stock, and did not even try to control prices among themselves"; and we are safe in saying that other organizations which will have to submit to like treatment will be able to show likewise.

But what is the charge? In short, it is that these retail merchants have been guilty of "restraining the trade of certain companies and corporations by furnishing information to its membership." As to their double dealing and duplicity, which I wish to remind you, it is in no wise charged as being false in any particular. If I steal a horse, and my neighbor or a newspaper charges me with the crime and the charge is proven in court, I have no recourse; but if I can show that I did not steal the horse, have I not recourse to the law against my neighbor or the newspaper for libel or damage to character? Nowhere, at no time, has any person, company, or corporation sought redress because of any false statements being made or published.

If it is unlawful to furnish information of this character to each other as to the action or practices of a manufacturer, wholesaler, or mail-order house, why is it not also unlawful for Dun's or Bradstreet's to furnish the manufacturers or wholesalers with the information that will enable them to avoid great loss in the sale of merchandise to the retailer? What is the difference? If a manufacturer or wholesaler sells me a stock of goods to be sold at retail and then turns around and sells to my customers, wherein is the difference between my telling or reporting this fact to my fellow merchants and a commercial agency reporting me as not being worthy of credit, or that I had mortgaged my property and was not therefore considered responsible for my obligations? But, gentlemen, that was not the milk in the coconut in the actions referred to.

A number of manufacturers, along with certain mail-order houses, were named in these indictments as being nominal plaintiffs in the case, but these manufacturers have almost without exception repudiated in writing any suggestion that their business had in any way been restrained. Therefore, this situation resolves itself into the only solution possible, that this is a fight for the retail business of the country between the little fellows and the mail-order house and, unfortunately for the little fellows, the government is furnishing the stronger with the ammunition and the attorneys to fight their battles.

When these indictments were brought, the headlines of the daily papers reporting them were reproduced in groups and sent broadcast over this country, both signed and anonymously, by the mail-order house. I had the great pleasure of having three of them handed to me, two of them from my bankers. It would appear that they would even attempt to injure our credit at home. Just consider, gentlemen, for one moment, what methods are being used to get business other than meeting competition with an article of merchandise which speaks for itself in quality and price.

You ask what has this to do with suggesting amendments to the Sherman Antitrust Law? Just this. The retail merchants, for whom I speak, do not ask you to pass any law or make any amendments to the present law that will in any way curtail the rights of those who are surely working to the reduction of the little merchants to nothing more than makeshifts; to serve as an accommodation when the people have no money to send away from home for what they want, when crops fail and when the strike is on. All that we ask is a chance for a fair fight and no favors; but we do insist that this law shall in some way be made so plain along these lines that the threat of being sent to jail will not be hanging over us when we join hands to fight for our business existence, upon which so much depends, our happiness and the welfare of our families and everyone in the communi-

ties in which we are perchance doing business.

It is out of all reason to think that the businessman has to submit or work under a law the uncertainties of which are such that he has no idea or conception of his standing before such a law until he has been brought into court and tried. Therefore, it would seem that it should be the aim of Congress to make it so plain insofar as it affects voluntary associations of businessmen not formed for making prices or profits that "he who runs may read." Does this seem to be an unreasonable demand, although the exact terms in which it is to be expressed may not at this time be clear? We are restless under suspicion and surveillance when government and state officials are upon our heels and delving into our business.

When we met in Chicago in October last to organize the federation, which I have the honor to represent, a government agent was there to watch us as if we were a lot of criminals; and I had not been secretary of the organization longer than thirty minutes until this government representative asked me for a copy of the minutes of our Board of Directors. I should like to ask, gentlemen, how much of an appropriation for the Secret Service would you vote for if a part of it was to be used to pay a man to stand at the door of this committee room and watch your every movement? Is the blood of the men I represent any less red than the members of Congress; or, in other words, of your constituency?

The retail merchant is not going to be put out of business, but he will be reduced to a mere means of accommodation to those who have not the cash to send away from home to supply their wants. We believe we have a right to more than this. We believe that we are of as much a necessity to the community as the farmer, laborer, the doctor, lawyer, or postmaster. We believe that a good live town, with live merchants making something more than a living, are as much of a necessity in our economy as is the farmer. For you cannot deny that every acre of land is increased in value in proportion to its proximity to a good town or city, and depreciates in value just in proportion to its distance from a good town or city. A good town or city is as much of a necessity to the farmer as the farmer to a good town. It appears to us that such a condition would be ideal in this country and should not be in anywise disturbed or discounted, even though it might be admitted that the farmer or any other citizen might save in a small way upon his purchases when sent to a city.

In this connection I want to say, although it might not be germane to the question to be decided by you, that the new shibboleth is the demand for a parcels post, a new link to be forged into the chain. I might not be competent to give advice, but, gentlemen, look well and you will find that the demand for this law emanates from the sources about which I have been speaking and is desired for the purpose of further crippling the small communities of this country to the advantage of the mail-order house and the city department store. Have we not already enough problems growing out of the drift of the population to the great centers? Do we want to increase our social, economical, and political problems along this line? . . .

In conclusion, let me say that it is my commission to tell you that if we do not, as little merchants, obtain our rights as we see them, it will not be because we have not asked for them and because we will not continue to ask for them henceforth. Surely you will, in considering this great question, not forget that this great body of our citizenship, which I have the honor to represent, must have due consideration in determining a future plan of action in dealing with this law.

Here is a class of our citizenship who pay more taxes and insurance, extend a greater line of credit, take the lead in every public enterprise, in schools, churches, charity, good roads, libraries, and work longer hours; and, yet, as a class, we are looked upon by a large part of our population as being no better than crooks and criminals and only fit for the gibes of the press and politicians. And it is my commission to say to you, with all due respect for the high position which you occupy, that against such persecutions more than a million of retail merchants in this country enter their protests and ask at your hands that we be given relief to the extent that we may fight for our rights untrammeled and under a law that we in no wise desire to violate when it can be ascertained just what constitutes a violation.

II.

C. U. Carpenter:
A Justification of Big Business

That the business of this country is in a greatly disturbed condition cannot be denied. This applies not only to the great corporations known as the monopolies but also to the smaller businesses operated by the average American businessman. Anyone who has traveled throughout the country and observed conditions carefully cannot but note that this general business distress is becoming alarming.

I have just come from the central west, let me say, and I find factories in the central western part of Ohio laying off men. They expect a great deal of business distress this winter. It will not be long before the manufacturing interests of the country begin laying off their workmen in large quantities. Indeed, it is a fact that this process of reducing working forces has been operating now for some months, and this business situation which has been so disturbing to our businessmen will soon affect a large portion of the American men seriously.

The fact is they are doing that now. I feel that this situation is really becoming serious enough to say that it will soon affect a large proportion of our American workingmen.

Businessmen generally place the largest share of blame for this condition upon the feeling of uncertainty over the Sherman Antitrust Law, its interpretation, and method of enforcement of the Sherman Act.

In my conversation with businessmen throughout the country, I find that they have now come to believe that there is a stern necessity for a regulating act which will control the greed of these monopolies. There is no question about it, but in my opinion much of the business distress occurs through the lawsuits which have been instituted by the government against corporations, or threatened lawsuits against corporations, which appear to be willing to adjust their businesses to whatever Congress shall decide.

The businessmen of this country are as patriotic as any other class of men, and their widespread opposition to the prosecutions under the Sherman Act is not based upon selfishness and greed, as seems to be so generally supposed. They feel that the situation demands "more statesmanship and fewer lawsuits." They feel that this business disturbance and industrial depression will soon become a serious matter for this country, and that Congress should take some wise steps to improve the situation that is becoming very serious, both to the businessman and his employees.

Now, gentlemen, of course it is not my province to criticize Congress or any of the messages, but it must be admitted that there still exists the greatest uncertainty as to where legality ends and illegality begins in our industrial corporations of today. Now, that is the feeling of businessmen generally. Whether it is warranted or not is another question, but they certainly feel it. Mere bigness of plant, no matter what the size, may not be illegal, but when this "bigness" incidentally results in elimination of competition, the result, apparently, would be an illegal corporation, no matter what the intent. . . .

There is a point that I wish to emphasize, that it is not a question of the changing of the Sherman Act; it is not a question of the Sherman Act being unjust. We need the Sherman Act, or need something like the Sherman Act. In my opinion, though, I think it bears the aspect of unfairness to prosecute these large corporations which were formed under the Sherman Act, which corporations are perfectly willing to disintegrate and reorganize according to any legal method that might be defined, and there, in my opinion, is the great reason for the disturbance today, the fact that the businessmen do not know what to do.

Many feel that inasmuch as the government has never really interpreted this law for over twenty years, that the government should give due consideration to the fact that they have allowed these corporate practices to exist and these corporations to grow up without protest; therefore, that in these widespread prosecutions there is a certain element of unfairness. Hence these suggestions that Congress enact a statute which will give the fair businessmen of this country a chance to comply with the law and at the same time protect their business interests.

If one believes in the rigorous enforcement of the present law and the suing under it, then naturally one must believe that unrestricted competition is a good thing for the country at large. Fair-minded businessmen do not approve of unrestricted competition as an economically correct condition. We cannot convince ourselves that the bitter costly fights, the cutting of prices too close to cost, business worries and failures, and the low wages resulting from such conditions represent conditions which are good for the country at large.

The average businessman of this country is as much opposed to unrestricted competition as he is to unrestricted monopoly. We cannot but recognize the enormous advantages and economies to be gained through combinations. The possibility of savings in both the selling and manufacturing ends of the business are too great to be neglected. This question has been so elucidated by men of great prominence, such as Mr. Gary and others, that this point needs no further elaboration.

The question of the enormous savings to be gained through combinations is undisputed. It is my belief that one of the greatest mistakes has been made by our large corporate interests in failing to give to the public the benefit of at least a portion of the savings resulting from these large combinations. The public hears much about the economies and savings that can be and have been made, but they see little or no evidence of it in the prices which they have to pay for the articles themselves, and naturally they are dissatisfied. They resent bitterly the fact that most large corporations have not given them at least some slight share in these savings and economies. In my opinion this condition explains much of the bitter attitude of the public against these large corporations.

It seems to me that the managers of the large corporations today have expended their energies largely in "capitalizing their possibilities" and have failed to recognize the rights as well as the demands of the public. Managers of corporations of all sizes recognize now that the insistent demand of the public for a proper and thorough degree of control over their corporations is a fair demand, a just demand, and one that must be complied with.

We have had the suggested remedy, first, of federal incorporation for all corporations doing an interstate business. In case it is desired to avoid conflict with the states, these corporations might be formed under state laws, with the provision for a federal license, a government fee, and government supervision. The regular state taxes should be paid to the state.

Second, in my opinion, a commission similar to the Interstate Commerce Commission should be appointed. This commission should have control over the question of the issuance of the stocks and bonds of such corporations, basing their calculations upon actual net assets, plus an allowance of, say, 20 percent for goodwill. Their work should include, not only the control of the primary issues of all stocks, bonds, etc., but also of any such issues that might be proposed after the company was incorporated.

It is useless for me to say to this committee that I think that we all feel that much of the mischief has been caused by our watering the stock — the issuing of stocks and bonds upon values that do not exist, except future values, and the possibility of making dividends.

To this commission should be submitted reports from such companies, based upon standardized methods of accounting and standardized methods of making reports. In my opinion, these reports should be published in full, in such a manner that the public may ascertain the exact facts in regard to the earnings of such corporations. I believe that it is safe to say that public sentiment and public opinion would soon force the managers of large corporations to lower their prices so that a fair return on the investment might be earned.

With stock and bond issues based upon actual assets, no other course but the lowering of prices would be possible, unless the managers cared to face an enraged public opinion and also to invite competition to enter the field.

Personally, I think it would be wise to take these steps first and then stop all further legislation until the government officials could note the effect of these steps.

Now, when such eminent men as Mr.

Wickersham and Mr. Gary speak of government control of prices, no American can fail to recognize that we are moving very rapidly and going very far. It seems to me that this is a most serious plunge. But government control of prices means that we would take some steps that we could never retrace, and it is a plunge, in my belief, that would prove most serious. . . .

In my opinion, the question of the government setting prices, notwithstanding the fact that the theory has been advanced by very eminent men, would be impracticable. It might do in some of the necessities of life, but you will have to go beyond that if you pass a law that will be general in its application — you get into fields where you are wandering in a jungle. By reason of that fact, as I say, you have the selling proposition to consider as well as the production.

Now, then, I beg to suggest here a somewhat different plan, and that is, if there has to be control, instead of the government trying to control prices, that the government shall control profits. If there has to be a measure of government control, I would prefer to have it a measure of control of the percentage of profit rather than try to have it set the prices. You gentlemen can readily see that if it were a question of control of profits it would be general in its application and very much simpler in its application than the application of the government setting prices.

Now, therefore, my suggestion would be, first, the federal incorporation law; second, a controlling commission; third, stocks and bonds issued to be based upon net assets, plus the 20 percent allowance for goodwill. I mention that allowance for goodwill because I think it very essential. In some businesses goodwill is not of so much value, but if you take a business where a magnificent selling organization has been built up, where you have salesmen all through the world, and where you have gone to the expense of many hundreds of thousands of dollars to build up that selling organization, that money spent represents your goodwill and represents dollars spent just as much as dollars for machinery. That is one reason why I say an allowance should be made for goodwill.

Fourth, allow a company to calculate their depreciation upon a basis to be determined by accepted methods of accounting. Of course, such items as taxes, insurance, etc., are fixed and require no ruling.

Fifth, allow that company to make a profit of only a certain percent, that percentage to be determined upon, say, 15 percent — that is merely a suggestion — 15 percent upon their capitalization. That means 10 percent for machinery, 5 percent for buildings — whatever the general account determines is a fair standard of depreciation. The reason I suggest 15 percent is because in a general manufacturing business there are lean years and good years, and good years must make up for lean years. Just now we are experiencing lean years and we need a good year to make up for what we are suffering now. Allow a further percent of earnings (say 10 percent) for surplus; this surplus to be built up until it equals the capital stock, and then it must stop.

Sixth, it might be necessary to restrict salary allowances to a fixed percentage on the capital stock, because otherwise their officials might vote themselves such huge salaries as would eat up the profits, with the result of higher prices.

Seventh, any earnings over and above these amounts should be turned back to the federal government, or, better still, to the state treasury in which the company is organized. The effect of this would be that the managers of the corporation would strive to keep the prices down so that practically no funds need be returned to the state; thus lower prices would result immediately.

III.

T. J. Brooks:
The Antitrust Laws as Applied
to Farmers

Mr. Chairman and gentlemen of the committee, the particular phase of this question which it is our purpose to discuss relates to that portion of the antitrust law which might be construed to apply to organizations of farmers.

I represent the Farmers' Educational Cooperative Union, the largest organization of farmers in the world. It extends from Virginia to California and from the state of Washington to Florida, including about thirty states.

The efforts upon the part of the farmer to adjust his business to the commercial demands of the age necessarily compel him to organize. When he is organized, for commercial purposes, the object of his organization should be proclaimed without reserve and understood thoroughly by the public.

The advantages of combination are the advantages of better organization and more effective operation, cheaper production and distribution. The disadvantages of combination have arisen chiefly from the misuse of the power of combination which develops into monopoly.

There is a great deal of difference between a monopoly whose purpose is to coerce and oppress, and cooperative organization whose purpose is to eliminate useless expense without in any degree practising extortion by withholding from the consumer, regardless of the law of supply and demand, in order to create fictitious values.

A great deal has been said about an elastic system of currency that would meet those periodic demands for enormous amounts of capital to move the great staple crops of the country from the producer to the consumer. In other words, when wheat is thrown on the market at harvest time, a great deal of money is required to purchase this wheat from the farmer, hold it till it is needed by the mills, and finally sold to the consumer — and the same way with cotton. In the fall of the year something over $800 million are required to purchase from the farmer his cotton crop. He usually markets it so fast that this volume of money is taken from other channels of trade to the inconvenience of our financial institutions in order to hold this cotton until the mills can use it.

Now, an organization of farmers who grow wheat or who grow cotton, which has for its purpose the establishing of a system whereby the farmers can assume the carrying function, and gradually market his wheat and his cotton throughout the year, should be exempt from any law that would hinder its operation. The purpose of the organization which I represent is to facilitate marketing according to the normal operation of the law of supply and demand, and is in no sense of the word an attempt to corner the market and create artificial prices. It takes a great deal less money to finance the holding of a crop than it does to purchase it outright; and by gradual marketing the periodic disturbance in our commercial world would be lessened and the evils of the exchanges mitigated.

None of the evils of overcapitalization, oppression of employees, or extortion of the public are inherent in the class of organizations to which we refer. A law whose purpose is to prevent injustice to the public should be so worded as to exempt all legitimate enterprises where there is no attempt to misuse the public confidence or destroy or pervert the natural operation of the law of supply and demand in the markets of the world. We believe that all corporations doing interstate business should be required to come to the strictest standard of account as to their tangible assets and methods of operation.

We wish it to be clearly provided for in

any antitrust law that no penalty shall attach to those promoting any organization or combination upon the part of producers having as its purpose the gradual marketing of farm products. We think it would be performing a great public service to so arrange the delivery of our staple crops each year as consumption called for them, instead of dumping them on the market regardless of the demands of trade. This is the basis of our contention, and upon this contention we rest our plea for exemption from antitrust legislation.

I do not claim that the present law makes the farmers' organizations now in existence subject to its penal provisions. I do not say that any amendments proposed would interfere with any business organization of the farmer. But what I do suggest is that if such provisions could by technical construction be construed to interfere, that they should be eliminated, and when amendments are passed, that they should be so worded as to exempt the organizations to which I refer from any liabilities to its prohibitory features.

I suppose there never would have been an antitrust law passed had it not been that there were combinations being formed which were calculated to do an injustice to the public. If any such organization has ever been formed by the agricultural classes, I have not seen any notice of it; I have not heard of any organization of farmers being accused of plotting for such a purpose. The condition of the farmer financially, as compared with that of other vocations, would indicate that he has not heretofore made use of any unfair means by which he could extort from his patrons. He is in a sense a manufacturer. He manufactures the soil, the sunshine, and the showers into the raw materials that feed and clothe the people of the world. He has never arrogated to himself the prerogatives that his power might indicate that he could if he so chose.

Beginning with 90 percent of the wealth, when this government was first launched among the sovereignties of the world, he has now only about one-fifth of the aggregate wealth of the nation; and only a part of the farmers own this percentage. A great percent of them are propertyless. In fact, one-half of the plowmen of this nation have no home. We have, approximately, 93 million people who are supported by about 12.5 million actual field hands, who produce the food and raiment that feeds and clothes the 93 million people at home and millions beyond the seas. Is it not an alarming state of affairs that one-half of these producers have no place on this planet that they can call their own? So a combination of the farmers when organized for mutual benefit should not run against some national statute intended for public protection.

According to the census of 1910 the manufacturers of the United States are worth approximately $20 billion, and their yearly output is valued at the same figures, employing 6.5 million hands and paying them $3,427,000,000. How is it that the farmer, who has something like $28 billion invested, twice as many hands, and the annual value of his crop, at farm prices, is only $9 billion?

We may see here some indication of the cause of the exits from the country to the towns and cities. The cry of "back to the farm," of which we have seen so much in the press of late, is invariably a command to "go" and not an entreaty to "come." In other words, the farmer is not begging the people to come from the city to help him farm, but the city man is urging people to go back to the country, but seldom does he take his own advice. I mention these things merely to show that the farmer is not holding his own in the race of life. We have about 1 million corporations in the United States which control 82 percent of the wealth of the nation.

1912

64.

William Dean Howells: The Cinematographic Show

As editor of Harper's Monthly *magazine, William Dean Howells wrote a regular column, the "Editor's Easy Chair," in which he discoursed on current literary fashions and popular taste. Howells was an influential critic who maintained that art should in general serve morality, that it should be educational rather than, or at least as well as, amusing. The "cinematographic show," as he called it, was still a novelty in 1912; but complaints were already beginning to be heard that movies debased the popular intelligence. Taking this as his starting point, Howells, in his column for the September 1912 issue of the magazine, made some suggestions — partly constructive, partly tongue-in-cheek — about how to make more worthwhile movies.*

Source: *Harper's Monthly*, September 1912.

IT IS PERHAPS the main characteristic, the ruling principle of this judgment seat to regard nothing human as alien to it. In the unbounded range of its interests, its amenities, all that concerns mankind is included, but from time to time it is able to afford its votaries a refreshing and invigorating surprise by something especially recondite in its inquiries.

With the Easy Chair there is no high, no low; or if not quite that, there is nothing too high or too low. It is not long, as years count in the age of nations, since it looked carefully into the nature of something so far beneath the regard of most philosophers as vaudeville and found much to praise in that variegated form of dramatic performance. Now it is moved by the course of events to invite its familiar circle of two or three million associate casuists to the consideration of that younger sister of vaudeville, the cinematographic show, its essence, its potentiality for good and evil, and its actual influence on the manners and morals of the community as one of the most novel of the social forces. We are the more eager to enter upon the question because it seems to us that the feeling against this sort of show, though most respectable in its origin, has been too exaggerated in its expression.

What to our experience (founded on a tolerant taste in such matters which we could not commend too highly to other observers) has appeared far more innocently tedious as well as innocently entertaining than the ordinary musical comedy or the problem play of commerce has been found by some experts in ethics deleterious in high degree. The pictures thrown upon the luminous curtain of the stage have been declared extremely corrupting to the idle young people lurking in the darkness before it. The darkness itself has been held a condition of inexpressible depravity and a means of allurement to evil by birds of prey hovering in the standing room and the foyers of the theaters.

Just how these predacious fowl operate, the censors of the moving-picture show have not felt it necessary to say; the lurid imagination of the public has been invoked without the specifications, and the moving-picture show has dropped to zero in the esteem of most self-respecting persons. It is possibly the showmen themselves who have therefore seen that something must be done, and who have sought for government approval of their films, quite unaware that this was a renunciation of individuality verging hard upon socialism. At any rate, the pictures shown are now proclaimed as bearing the warrant of censorship; and still another and more surprising step has been taken toward safeguarding the public morals. The pictures are sometimes shown in a theater lighted as broad as day, where not the silliest young girl or the wickedest young fellow can plot fully unseen, or even the most doting and purblind grandams and grandsires, who seem always to form a large part of the audience.

This ought, one would think, to be enough. But apparently it is not, if we may take in proof the case of a Massachusetts village where the moving-picture show prevails. The moving-picture show prevails everywhere, in Europe as well as America, and doubtless Asia, Africa, South America,

and Oceanica. It has become the most universally accepted of modern amusements; the circus compared with it is partial and provincial. But in this particular New England village it is of an evolution which peculiarly threatens the spiritual peace and the intellectual growth of the place unless its forces can be turned to the promise of ultimate good.

It began there in a simple town hall, which 300 people of every age and sex filled afternoon and evening at 10 cents each, and so prospered the proprietor that now, after two years, he has built a much roomier theater, which the villagers continue to throng. He gives them, it seems, a very acceptable amusement, and they in turn give him some $15,000 a year, or about twice the sum they pay in school taxes.

One would say this was very well, supposing the money of the villagers and their neighbors was not tainted money, and if they liked to spend it in that way. But it has been discovered in Massachusetts, if not in Europe, Asia, Africa, Oceanica, and the rest of North and South America, that the moving picture habit tends in both old and young to lethargy of mind and inertness of body, and that especially the schoolchildren, when they have become accustomed to looking at the scenes and incidents thrown upon the white curtain, acquire a fixed indifference to the claims of orthography, mathematics, history, and geography. This is said to be undeniably the case, and we could readily imagine it, just as we could imagine that a very fatuous type of fiction such as most of our people read might disgust them with every sort of edifying literature.

The question in Massachusetts, as elsewhere, is what shall be done about it. The moving-picture show, like some other things, "has come to stay"; it cannot be mocked or scolded away; but, as it has already shown itself capable of uplift, we may fitly ask ourselves not only what it esthetically is, but what it ethically may be.

> Oh, to what uses shall we put
>   The wild-weed flower that simply
>   blows,
> And is there any moral shut
>   Within the bosom of the rose?

But we need not decide at once that the moving-picture show is either a wild-weed flower or a rose, and poetically despair of its capacity to do nothing more than impart a "giddy pleasure of the eye." If the authorities wish to share in delighting as well as instructing youth, why should not they make this enemy their ally?

The moving-picture show is in a mechanical way not only the latest of "the fairy dreams of science," but it is the most novel of all the forms of dramatic entertainment. Yet if pantomime is one of the oldest forms of drama, the moving-picture show is of an almost Saturnian antiquity, for pantomime is what the moving picture is, whether representing a veritable incident or a fanciful invention. As even the frequenter of it may not realize, its scenes have been photographically studied from the action of performers more rather than less skilled than the average, who have given the camera a dress rehearsal of the story thrown upon the white curtain for his pleasure or improvement. The stage direction flashed on the same space between the acts or scenes offers the spectator the needed clue, and in the vivid action of the dumb show he scarcely misses the text which would be spoken in the theater. In fact, as most plays in most theaters are done, he is the gainer by the silent demonstration, which in the dress rehearsal may well have included spoken dialogue.

Of course, the stuff itself is crude enough, oftenest; yet sometimes it is not crude, and

the pantomime has its fine moments, when one quite loses oneself in the artistic pleasure of the drama. Where a veritable incident is portrayed, one has the delight of perceiving how dramatic life is, and how full of tragedy and comedy.

It is a convention of the moving picture that life is mostly full of farce, but that is an error which it shares with the whole modern stage, and it is probable that when the moving-picture show is asked to be serious, as we propose it shall be, it will purge itself of this error. Meanwhile our proposition is that the school committee of that dismayed Massachusetts town, who find their pupils and their pupils' money going to the moving-picture theater, shall make friends with its manager. They will possibly not find him a Mammon of unrighteousness, but a fellowman willing to cooperate with them to a good end if they can show him that it will pay. To this end they can contribute by actually paying him out of the school fund on condition that he will make his theater a part of the school system during certain hours of the day.

The educators now find that the children would rather give 10 cents of their parents' money to go and look idly on at a succession of fictitious and largely impossible events as portrayed on the white curtain of the theater than come to school for nothing, or for nothing more than their fathers and mothers must now pay in taxes, and pass the day in studying and reciting from textbooks which do not offer the allure of the picture show. But there is no reason why their studies, many of them, should not offer that allure.

It is difficult, of course, and very likely it is impossible, say, for English spelling to be made pictorially charming, but it might very easily be made amusing by throwing on the white curtain an illustrated series of the more preposterous instances in which our orthography insults the reason and sins against common sense. Arithmetic would not lend itself much more readily to the processes of the moving pictures, and yet the mathematical ambition of the children might be stimulated by the vision, say, of a lightning calculator working his miracles at a quivering blackboard. Every other branch of learning might be turned from the dry stock which now revolts the youthful mind, though it no longer threatens the youthful body so much as formerly, and set it before the charmed sense in all the bloom and sweetness of a living plant.

We do not know just what sciences are studied in our public schools, but we will suppose geology may be one of them, and we believe that nothing more attractive to the young is now set forth on the theater curtain than some scene of Eocene life would be. No imaginative boy could fail of high joy in the presentation of

> dragons of the prime
> That tare each other in the slime,

or even a peaceful moment when the ichthyosaurus and the plesiosaur amphibiously sported together on the shores of time and the pterodactyl floated in the warm air above them. A flower-loving little maid might usefully lose herself in the vision of a forest of tree ferns and in thinking of the specimens she could gather for her herbarium from them she might feel through the association of geology with botany the unity of all science.

We are trying, perhaps too playfully, to commend to the reader the possibility which we have seriously in mind. We would really like to convince our educators of the immense helpfulness which they might find in the managers of the moving-picture shows if it came to their joint instruction in geography, history, and the various branches of biology. Fancy the appeal which ethnology alone, presented in pictured studies of the different races and civilizations, would have! Realize the immense advantage of presenting human events in

pictures, which the most careless eye could not refuse to seize, over the actual method of teaching history by names and dates meaningless to most of the young minds which now reject them! Consider the charm which visual knowledge of the discoverers and explorers, conquerors, heroes of all sorts, reformers of every type, martyrs, inventors, authors — even authors — would have if the student could know them in their persons as well as their experiences and performances!

We would not trifle with the case as the authorities of that Massachusetts town conceive it. They have reason to be anxious if the moving pictures beguile once studious youth from the desire of learning; and wherever the moving-picture show prevails the custodians of childhood have the same reason to be anxious. But we would by no means have them vex the managers of such shows by vain opposition. Failing their cooperation, we would have the authorities take counsel with themselves whether moving pictures may not be introduced into the school curriculum. We are too little acquainted with the machinery and its working to suggest what steps should be taken to this end, but doubtless there are those who know. What we confidently look to is the excellent result.

The children will no longer waste their money on the private picture show when they can have the public one for nothing, and the school will not be so hateful when learning is to be acquired with no more labor than lolling in the seats of the cinematographic theater now costs them. The lessons will be largely object lessons. The wretched little boy or hapless little girl will not be obliged to try and guess what the different races of men are like; he or she will be shown the fact in photographs snapshotted from the originals in the streets of their cities or the depths of their jungles. At the mention of Columbus, the great admiral's best portrait will be reproduced on the white curtain, and Napoleon, Washington,

Lincoln, and George the Third will be likewise visualized as they looked in life.

The children can be shown a volcano in full blast, and its liquid rival, the waterspout, moving rapidly over the sea in pursuit of the nearest liner. A group of icebergs and a chain of mountains can be contrasted with equal advantage. An earthquake will not perhaps exceed the powers of the all-comprehending camera, and a modern battle with smokeless powder may be taught to rage before their eyes, and every detail of heads and legs blown off, that they may realize how glorious war is at close range; towns burning in the background and women and children flying for their lives will fill the perspective. A sea fight, with armored battleships sinking one another, could be as easily rendered if the films were recovered from the body of some witness representing an enterprising metropolitan journal in the engagement.

No economic or social fact need transcend the scope of the public-school picture show. The operations of some giant industry, such as coal mining or iron smelting, or some vast cotton mill, with children younger than themselves tending the machinery, and the directors in their Oriental-rugged and mahogany arm-chaired parlors could be illustrated for the entertainment and instruction of the school boys and girls. Strikers and strikebreakers in a street fight, or the spectacle of policemen clubbing mothers from a train in which they are trying to send their little ones out of town beyond the struggling and starving, would impart an idea of our civilization which no amount of study could without it.

Of course, the more pleasing branches of study can be taught as easily as those we have glanced at. Agriculture, for instance, which is becoming more and more a science with every year; forestry, which vitally concerns our deforested continent; dynamitic culture, by which the fertility of the earth, sick of having its mere surface scratched, is restored a hundredfold; fruit growing, cattle grazing can all be taught best with the help of illustration. It is only a summer or two ago since the Central Park authorities thought it advisable to show the poor, ignorant East Side children where milk came from, and by having a cow milked in their presence convince all that would come to see the process. But the ignorance of such a simple primary fact could be universally dispersed by a moving picture far less cumbrously and at incalculably less cost to the community.

We have said enough, we hope, to persuade the public-school committees everywhere to try first what may be done with the moving-picture managers. They may be assured that in any conflict with these managers they will be beaten; for the managers will have all the children on their side; clandestinely, we fear, they will have the parents, too. But by inviting the managers to cooperate with them, they will have a fair chance of winning them over and at the same time sugarcoating the pill of learning so that the youth of this fair land of ours will eagerly swallow it.

But if the managers hold out against the committees, and selfishly refuse to help them in their present strait, then we hope the committees will set up moving-picture shows of their own and make them an integral part of the public-school system. This, however, should be their final resort. It would savor of socialism, and socialism is the last thing we would advise, though as our whole public-school system is a phase of socialism, it might not be immediately anarchistic to try it.

Motion pictures are just a passing fancy and aren't worth comment in this newspaper.

ARTHUR BRISBANE, *Chicago Record-Herald*, 1913

65.

"The Titanic"

The Titanic, *which had been widely publicized as the first "unsinkable" ship in the history of the world, went to the bottom of the North Atlantic after colliding with an iceberg on its maiden voyage. The fateful day was April 15, 1912, and more than fifteen hundred people lost their lives, partly because there were not enough lifeboats to rescue everyone and partly because of the pusillanimity of some members of the crew. A number of prominent persons died in the tragedy, which was talked, written, and sung about by everyone for two years — until World War I forced it into the shadow. The events of that dreadful day were well known, among them that the passengers who could not find space in lifeboats gathered on the boat deck and sang "Nearer My God to Thee" as the waves splashed over the side. The song reprinted below was written by an unknown author shortly after the event. Its ironic tone was in keeping with the fundamental irony of the unsinkable ship that sank only a few days after leaving port for the first time.*

🎵 THE TITANIC

Oh, they built the ship *Titanic* to sail the ocean blue;
They thought they had a ship that the water wouldn't go through.
But the Lord's almighty hand knew this ship would never stand —
It was sad when that great ship went down.

Chorus:
Oh, it was sad; it was sad;
It was sad when that great ship went down (to the bottom of the) —
Husbands and wives and little children lost their lives —
It was sad when that great ship went down.

Oh, they sailed from England, they were almost to the shore,
When the rich refused to associate with the poor;
So they put them down below, where they were the first to go —
It was sad when that great ship went down.

The boat was full of sin, and the sides about to burst,
When the captain shouted: "Women and children first!"
Oh, the captain tried to wire, but the lines were all on fire —
It was sad when that great ship went down.

Oh, they swung the lifeboats out o'er the deep and raging sea,
And the band struck up with, "Nearer My God to Thee."
Little children wept and cried, as the waves swept o'er the side —
It was sad when that great ship went down.

66.

MARY ANTIN: The Promise of Free Education

America meant opportunity to all immigrants from Europe, but the opportunities were of various kinds. For some, America was a place where the streets were paved with gold and where the new arrival could become rich simply by stooping to pick up the wealth that lay everywhere for the taking. For others, it meant freedom from religious and political persecution. But for men and women like the parents of Mary Antin, America was a place where all could be educated and thereby attain the intellectual freedom that was reserved, in Europe, for the fortunate few. In the following excerpt from her autobiography, Miss Antin describes in moving terms what free education for all meant to at least some newcomers to "the promised land."

Source: *The Promised Land*, Boston, 1912, Ch. 9.

OUR INITIATION INTO AMERICAN ways began with the first step on the new soil. My father found occasion to instruct or correct us even on the way from the pier to Wall Street, which journey we made crowded together in a rickety cab. He told us not to lean out of the windows, not to point, and explained the word "greenhorn." We did not want to be "greenhorns," and gave the strictest attention to my father's instructions. . . .

The first meal was an object lesson of much variety. My father produced several kinds of food, ready to eat, without any cooking, from little tin cans that had printing all over them. He attempted to introduce us to a queer, slippery kind of fruit, which he called "banana," but had to give it up for the time being. After the meal, he had better luck with a curious piece of furniture on runners, which he called "rocking chair." There were five of us newcomers, and we found five different ways of getting into the American machine of perpetual motion, and as many ways of getting out of it. One born and bred to the use of a rocking chair cannot imagine how ludicrous

people can make themselves when attempting to use it for the first time. We laughed immoderately over our various experiments with the novelty, which was a wholesome way of letting off steam after the unusual excitement of the day.

In our flat we did not think of such a thing as storing the coal in the bathtub. There was no bathtub. So in the evening of the first day my father conducted us to the public baths. As we moved along in a little procession, I was delighted with the illumination of the streets. So many lamps, and they burned until morning, my father said, and so people did not need to carry lanterns. In America, then, everything was free, as we had heard in Russia. Light was free; the streets were as bright as a synagogue on a holy day. Music was free; we had been serenaded, to our gaping delight, by a brass band of many pieces, soon after our installation on Union Place.

Education was free. That subject my father had written about repeatedly, as comprising his chief hope for us children, the essence of American opportunity, the treasure that no thief could touch, not even misfortune or poverty. It was the one thing that he was able to promise us when he sent for us; surer, safer than bread or shelter. On our second day I was thrilled with the realization of what this freedom of education meant. A little girl from across the alley came and offered to conduct us to school. My father was out, but we five between us had a few words of English by this time.

We knew the word "school." We understood. This child, who had never seen us till yesterday, who could not pronounce our names, who was not much better dressed than we, was able to offer us the freedom of the schools of Boston! No application made, no questions asked, no examinations, rulings, exclusions; no machinations, no fees. The doors stood open for every one of us. The smallest child could show us the way.

This incident impressed me more than anything I had heard in advance of the freedom of education in America. It was a concrete proof — almost the thing itself. One had to experience it to understand it.

It was a great disappointment to be told by my father that we were not to enter upon our school career at once. It was too near the end of the term, he said, and we were going to move to Crescent Beach in a week or so. We had to wait until the opening of the schools in September. What a loss of precious time — from May till September! . . .

The apex of my civic pride and personal contentment was reached on the bright September morning when I entered the public school. That day I must always remember, even if I live to be so old that I cannot tell my name. To most people their first day at school is a memorable occasion. In my case the importance of the day was a hundred times magnified, on account of the years I had waited, the road I had come, and the conscious ambitions I entertained.

I am wearily aware that I am speaking in extreme figures, in superlatives. I wish I knew some other way to render the mental life of the immigrant child of reasoning age. I may have been ever so much an exception in acuteness of observation, powers of comparison, and abnormal self-consciousness; nonetheless were my thoughts and conduct typical of the attitude of the intelligent immigrant child toward American institutions. And what the child thinks and feels is a reflection of the hopes, desires, and purposes of the parents who brought him overseas, no matter how precocious and independent the child may be. Your immigrant inspectors will tell you what poverty the foreigner brings in his baggage, what want in his pockets. Let the overgrown boy of twelve, reverently drawing his letters in the baby class, testify to the noble dreams and high ideals that may be hidden beneath the greasy caftan of the immigrant. Speaking for the Jews, at least, I know I am safe in inviting such an investigation. . . .

And when the momentous day arrived, and the little sister and I stood up to be arrayed, it was Frieda herself who patted and smoothed my stiff new calico; who made me turn round and round to see that I was perfect; who stooped to pull out a disfiguring basting thread. If there was anything in her heart besides sisterly love and pride and goodwill, as we parted that morning, it was a sense of loss and a woman's acquiescence in her fate; for we had been close friends, and now our ways would lie apart. Longing she felt, but no envy. She did not grudge me what she was denied. . . .

The two of us stood a moment in the doorway of the tenement house on Arlington Street, that wonderful September morning when I first went to school. It was I that ran away, on winged feet of joy and expectation; it was she whose feet were bound in the treadmill of daily toil. And I was so blind that I did not see that the glory lay on her, and not on me.

Father himself conducted us to school. He would not have delegated that mission to the President of the United States. He had awaited the day with impatience equal to mine, and the visions he saw as he hurried us over the sun-flecked pavements transcended all my dreams. Almost his first act on landing on American soil, three years before, had been his application for naturalization. He had taken the remaining steps in the process with eager promptness, and at the earliest moment allowed by the law, he became a citizen of the United States. It is true that he had left home in search of bread for his hungry family, but he went blessing the necessity that drove him to America. The boasted freedom of the New World meant to him far more than the right to reside, travel, and work wherever he pleased; it meant the freedom to speak his thoughts, to throw off the shackles of superstition, to test his own fate, unhindered by political or religious tyranny. He was only a young man when he landed — thirty-two; and most of his life he had been held in leading-strings. He was hungry for his untasted manhood.

Three years passed in sordid struggle and disappointment. He was not prepared to make a living even in America, where the day laborer eats wheat instead of rye. Apparently the American flag could not protect him against the pursuing Nemesis of his limitations; he must expiate the sins of his fathers who slept across the seas. He had been endowed at birth with a poor constitution, a nervous, restless temperament, and an abundance of hindering prejudices. In his boyhood his body was starved, that his mind might be stuffed with useless learning. In his youth this dearly gotten learning was sold, and the price was the bread and salt which he had not been trained to earn for himself. Under the wedding canopy he was bound for life to a girl whose features were still strange to him; and he was bidden to multiply himself, that sacred learning might be perpetuated in his sons, to the glory of the God of his fathers. All this while he had been led about as a creature without a will, a chattel, an instrument.

In his maturity he awoke, and found himself poor in health, poor in purse, poor in useful knowledge, and hampered on all sides. At the first nod of opportunity he broke away from his prison and strove to atone for his wasted youth by a life of useful labor; while at the same time he sought to lighten the gloom of his narrow scholarship by freely partaking of modern ideas. But his utmost endeavor still left him far from his goal. In business, nothing prospered with him. Some fault of hand or mind or temperament led him to failure where other men found success. Wherever the blame for his disabilities be placed, he reaped their bitter fruit. "Give me bread!" he cried to America. "What will you do to earn it?" the challenge came back. And he found that he was master of no art, of no trade; that even his precious learning was of no avail, because he had only the most antiquated methods of communicating it.

So in his primary quest he had failed. There was left him the compensation of intellectual freedom. That he sought to realize in every possible way. He had very little opportunity to prosecute his education, which, in truth, had never been begun. His struggle for a bare living left him no time to take advantage of the public evening school; but he lost nothing of what was to be learned through reading, through attendance at public meetings, through exercising the rights of citizenship. Even here he was hindered by a natural inability to acquire the English language. In time, indeed, he learned to read, to follow a conversation or lecture; but he never learned to write correctly, and his pronunciation remains extremely foreign to this day.

If education, culture, the higher life were shining things to be worshiped from afar, he had still a means left whereby he could draw one step nearer to them. He could send his children to school, to learn all those things that he knew by fame to be desirable. The common school, at least, perhaps high school; for one or two, perhaps even college! His children should be students, should fill his house with books and intellectual company, and thus he would walk by proxy in the Elysian Fields of lib-

eral learning. As for the children themselves, he knew no surer way to their advancement and happiness.

So it was with a heart full of longing and hope that my father led us to school on that first day. He took long strides in his eagerness, the rest of us running and hopping to keep up.

At last the four of us stood around the teacher's desk; and my father, in his impossible English, gave us over in her charge, with some broken word of his hopes for us that his swelling heart could no longer contain.

67.

Louis D. Brandeis: Business as a Profession

Louis Dembitz Brandeis, a graduate of Harvard Law School, a highly successful Boston lawyer, and an adviser in the 1912 presidential campaign to the winning candidate, Woodrow Wilson, had a face of "melancholy nobility and brooding wisdom," according to Arthur Schlesinger, Jr., and "something of the aspect of a Jewish Lincoln." Not risen, like Lincoln, from the ranks of the common man, Brandeis was nonetheless their champion. In a commencement address delivered at Brown University in 1912, he revealed his sympathy for and understanding of the workingman, even as he outlined the criteria for success in business. The speech, reprinted here in part, was also notable for its statement of a conception of business that was advanced for its time.

Source: *Business — A Profession*, Boston, 1914, pp. 1-12.

EACH COMMENCEMENT SEASON we are told by the college reports the number of graduates who have selected the professions as their occupations and the number of those who will enter business. The time has come for abandoning such a classification. Business should be, and to some extent already is, one of the professions. The once meager list of the learned professions is being constantly enlarged. Engineering in its many branches already takes rank beside law, medicine, and theology. Forestry and scien-

tific agriculture are securing places of honor. The new professions of manufacturing, of merchandising, of transportation, and of finance must soon gain recognition. The establishment of business schools in our universities is a manifestation of the modern conception of business.

The peculiar characteristics of a profession as distinguished from other occupations I take to be these:

First, a profession is an occupation for which the necessary preliminary training is intellectual in character, involving knowledge and to some extent learning, as distinguished from mere skill.

Second, it is an occupation which is pursued largely for others and not merely for oneself.

Third, it is an occupation in which the amount of financial return is not the accepted measure of success.

Is not each of these characteristics found today in business worthily pursued?

The field of knowledge requisite to the more successful conduct of business has been greatly widened by the application to industry not only of chemical, mechanical and electrical science but also the new science of management; by the increasing difficulties involved in adjusting the relations of labor to capital; by the necessary intertwining of social with industrial problems; by the ever extending scope of state and federal regulation of business. Indeed, mere size and territorial expansion have compelled the businessman to enter upon new and broader fields of knowledge in order to match his achievements with his opportunities.

This new development is tending to make business an applied science. Through this development the relative value in business of the trading instinct and of mere shrewdness have, as compared with other faculties, largely diminished. The conception of trade itself has changed. The old idea of a good bargain was a transaction in which one man got the better of another. The new idea of a good contract is a transaction which is good for both parties to it.

Under these new conditions, success in business must mean something very different from mere moneymaking. In business the able man ordinarily earns a larger income than one less able. So does the able man in the recognized professions — in law, medicine, or engineering; and even in those professions more remote from moneymaking, like the ministry, teaching, or social work. The world's demand for efficiency is

so great and the supply so small that the price of efficiency is high in every field of human activity.

The recognized professions, however, definitely reject the size of the financial return as the measure of success. They select as their test excellence of performance in the broadest sense, and include, among other things, advance in the particular occupation and service to the community. These are the bases of all worthy reputations in the recognized professions. In them a large income is the ordinary incident of success; but he who exaggerates the value of the incident is apt to fail of real success.

To the business of today a similar test must be applied. True, in business the earning of profit is something more than an incident of success. It is an essential condition of success; because the continued absence of profit itself spells failure. But while loss spells failure, large profits do not connote success. Success must be sought in business also in excellence of performance; and in business, excellence of performance manifests itself, among other things, in the advancing of methods and processes; in the improvement of products; in more perfect organization, eliminating friction as well as waste; in bettering the condition of the workingmen, developing their faculties and promoting their happiness; and in the establishment of right relations with customers and with the community. . . .

The career of the Filenes of Boston affords [an] example of success in professionalized business. . . . The Filenes recognized that the function of retail distribution should be undertaken as a social service, equal in dignity and responsibility to the function of production; and that it should be studied with equal intensity in order that the service may be performed with high efficiency, with great economy, and with nothing more than a fair profit to the retailer. They recognized that to serve their own customers properly the relations of the retailer to the producer must be fairly and scientifically adjusted; and, among other things, that it was the concern of the retailer to know whether the goods which he sold were manufactured under conditions which were fair to the workers — fair as to wages, hours of work, and sanitary conditions.

But the Filenes recognized particularly their obligations to their own employees. They found, as the common and accepted conditions in large retail stores, that the employees had no voice as to the conditions or rules under which they were to work; that the employees had no appeal from policies prescribed by the management; and that in the main they were paid the lowest rate of wages possible under competitive conditions.

In order to insure a more just arrangement for those working in their establishment, the Filenes provided three devices:

First, a system of self-government for employees administered by the store cooperative association. Working through this association, the employees have the right to appeal from and to veto policies laid down by the management. They may adjust the conditions under which employees are to work, and, in effect, prescribe conditions for themselves.

Second, a system of arbitration through the operation of which individual employees can call for an adjustment of differences that may exist between themselves and the management as to the permanence of employment, wages, promotion, or conditions of work.

Third, a minimum wage scale, which provides that no woman or girl shall work in their store at a wage less than $8 a week, no matter what her age may be or what grade of position she may fill.

The Filenes have thus accepted and applied the principles of industrial democracy and of social justice. But they have done more; they have demonstrated that the introduction of industrial democracy and of social justice is at least consistent with marked financial success. They assert that the greater efficiency of their employees shows industrial democracy and social justice to be money-makers. The so-called practical businessman, the narrow moneymaker without either vision or ideals, who hurled against the Filenes . . . the silly charge of being "theorists," has been answered even on his own low plane of material success. . . .

The Filenes are of course exceptional men; but there are in America today many with like perception and like spirit. The paths broken by such pioneers will become the peopled highways. Their exceptional methods will become accepted methods. Then the term "big business" will lose its sinister meaning, and will take on a new significance. "Big business" will then mean business big not in bulk or power but great in service and grand in manner. "Big business" will mean professionalized business, as distinguished from the occupation of petty trafficking or mere moneymaking. And as the profession of business develops, the great industrial and social problems expressed in the present social unrest will one by one find solution.

My hat is in the ring. The fight is on and I am stripped to the buff.
        THEODORE ROOSEVELT, announcing informally to reporters that he would attempt to be Republican candidate for the presidency, February 1912

We stand at Armageddon, and we battle for the Lord.
        THEODORE ROOSEVELT, speech on eve of Republican Convention, June 1912

68.

Walter E. Weyl: The New Spirit of Socialism

Walter Weyl, along with Herbert Croly and the young Walter Lippmann, was one of the leading spokesmen of Progressivism. An economist by training, Weyl attempted to frame a social and political philosophy that would be relevant to the new industrial and urban America. Putting his faith in evolutionary socialism, Weyl nevertheless hoped to retain the traditional democratic virtues, especially emphasizing the element of enlightened self-interest. The following selection is reprinted from his book The New Democracy, *which first appeared in 1912.*

Source: *The New Democracy,* Revised edition, New York, 1914: "The Industrial Program of the Democracy."

THE INDUSTRIAL GOAL of the democracy is the socialization of industry. It is the attainment by the people of the largest possible industrial control and of the largest possible industrial dividend. The democracy seeks to attain these ends through government ownership of industry; through government regulation; through tax reform; through a moralization and reorganization of business in the interest of the industrially weak. . . .

The most characteristic feature of the industrial program of the democracy, as revealed in party platforms and in books, newspapers, and speeches, as well as in actual legislation, is the emphasis which is laid upon the state in industry. Government ownership and regulation — national, state, and local — are urged for more and more industries. The dividend from industry which people are demanding is more largely a joint than an individual dividend. It is a dividend which the individual citizen can obtain only through the intermediation of the state or nation; in other words, through an extension of state control over industry.

What the democracy desires, however, is not government ownership for itself but merely as much government ownership, regulation, or control as may be necessary to a true socialization of industry. The democracy's goal — the socialization of industry — is a viewing of our manifold business life from the standpoint of society and not solely from that of the present beneficiaries or directors of industry. It is such a coordination of business as will permanently give the greatest happiness and the highest development to the largest number of individuals and to society as a whole.

Socialization is thus a point of view. It is less a definite industrial program than the animating ideal of a whole industrial policy. It is a standard by which industrial conditions and industrial developments must be adjudged. . . .

Socialization considers industry as a whole. The national business is "one and indivisible"; an indissoluble union of autonomous, but linked, industries.

In emphasizing this oneness of business, socialization is doing on a large scale and from the point of view of society what the trust did on a smaller scale from the point of view of the profit taker. Like the trust, socialization subjects rival or dissimilar businesses to the sway of a single aim. Like the trust, socialization attains unity without sacrificing variety. The trust does not always end the separate existence of constituent companies. So, under a complete socialization of our national industry, we would have thousands of separate kinds of business under different forms of ownership, management, and control, but each continuing its existence and mode of life because adapted, in the opinion of society, to contribute its share to the best progress of industry as a whole.

Like the trust, also, socialization does not end competition. The trust encourages *internal* competition. The right hand is stimulated to do better than the left, and the left to excel the right. . . .

In actual fact, socialization, insofar as it involves the actual intervention of the state, is used largely to supplement or correct competition. It is where competition is atrophied, as in the case of monopolies, or where it appears in a pathological form, as in child labor, industrial parasitism, etc., that the intervention of the state is most needed. . . .

It is probable, however, that a considerable extension of the federal government's ownership and direction of business will take place in the future. Three factors are leading in this direction. One is the increasingly evident monopoly character of many large businesses; a second is the improvement in our civil service; a third is the progressive democratization of the government. As monopoly invades business, the choice lies between government and private monopoly, instead of between government monopoly and competition. The monopoly element in the business aligns "the many" against a few insiders. As the civil service improves, moreover, the government is enabled to conduct business both honestly and efficiently. As the state becomes increasingly democratized, the people accept it as their natural representative, as opposed to an entrenched industrial oligarchy in a monopolized business. . . .

What will ultimately decide in each case the question between government operation and government regulation (when one of the two is desirable) will be the relative efficiency of the two methods. There are certain definite limits set to an extension of government ownership by the necessity of preserving the highest possible industrial efficiency. While the federal government is becoming yearly more efficient, and while the vast private monopolies often show the same industrial weaknesses as government does, nevertheless there remains a certain advantage with the trust owing to the greater play of the desire for profits, the greater elasticity of its arrangements, and the wider latitude given to its directors.

Industrial autonomy, however clear its drawbacks, does at least produce a hard, alert, wide-awake industrial agent. The disadvantage of the trust is that it is too likely to sacrifice the public interest and even the interest of the investors to a series of private interests, which are excessively stimulated. The disadvantage of public ownership, on the other hand, is that it tends to develop too little that sharp private interest which leads to unobserved extra exertions and to a keener and more intelligent application.

A compromise between this public interest and the private interest is sought to be effected by government regulation. The object of government regulation is to combine the advantages of individual initiative and of public control.

I feel as fit as a bull moose.

THEODORE ROOSEVELT, reply to reporter on the eve of the Progressive Party Convention, Aug. 7, 1912

69.

The Progressive Party Platform

Theodore Roosevelt's break with President Taft led him to "throw his hat in the ring" in the election year of 1912. Taft's hold on the Republican Convention proved too strong for Roosevelt to gain the nomination, and he and his followers withdrew to form their own Progressive, or "Bull Moose," Party, as it soon came to be called. The party platform, reproduced below, was widely acclaimed by reformers and reflected Roosevelt's belief in regulating but not destroying big business. "The Progressive Platform," according to Jane Addams, "contains all I have been fighting for for a decade." The two Republican candidates together received a majority of the popular vote, but Woodrow Wilson won the election.

Source: *World Almanac for 1913*, pp. 693-697.

Declaration of Principles — The conscience of the people, in a time of grave national problems, has called into being a new party, born of the nation's awakened sense of injustice.

We of the Progressive Party here dedicate ourselves to the fulfillment of the duty laid upon us by our fathers to maintain that government of the people, by the people, and for the people whose foundations they laid.

We hold, with Thomas Jefferson and Abraham Lincoln, that the people are the masters of their Constitution to fulfill its purposes and to safeguard it from those who, by perversion of its intent, would convert it into an instrument of injustice. In accordance with the needs of each generation, the people must use their sovereign powers to establish and maintain equal opportunity and industrial justice, to secure which this government was founded and without which no republic can endure.

This country belongs to the people who inhabit it. Its resources, its business, its institutions, and its laws should be utilized, maintained, or altered in whatever manner will best promote the general interest. It is time to set the public welfare in the first place.

The Old Parties — Political parties exist to secure responsible government and to execute the will of the people. From these great tasks both the old parties have turned aside. Instead of instruments to promote the general welfare, they have become the tools of corrupt interests, which use them impartially to serve their selfish purposes. Behind the ostensible government sits enthroned an invisible government, owing no allegiance and acknowledging no responsibility to the people. To destroy this invisible government, to dissolve the unholy alliance between corrupt business and corrupt politics, is the first task of the statesmanship of the day.

The deliberate betrayal of its trust by the Republican Party, the fatal incapacity of the Democratic Party to deal with the new issues of the new time, have compelled the people to forge a new instrument of government through which to give effect to their will in laws and institutions.

Unhampered by tradition, uncorrupted by power, undismayed by the magnitude of the task, the new party offers itself as the instrument of the people to sweep away old abuses, to build a new and nobler commonwealth.

Covenant With the People — This declaration is our covenant with the people, and we hereby bind the party and its candidates in state and nation to the pledges made herein.

Rule of the People — The Progressive Party, committed to the principle of government by a self-controlled democracy expressing its will through representatives of the people, pledges itself to secure such alterations in the fundamental law of the several states and of the United States as shall insure the representative character of the government. In particular the party declares for direct primaries for the nomination of state and national officers, for nationwide preferential primaries for candidates for the presidency; for the direct election of United States senators by the people; and we urge on the states the policy of the short ballot, with responsibility to the people secured by the initiative, referendum, and recall.

Constitution Should Be Easily Amended — The Progressive Party, believing that a free people should have the power from time to time to amend their fundamental law so as to adapt it progressively to the changing needs of the people, pledges itself to provide a more easy and expeditious method of amending the federal Constitution.

Nation and State — Up to the limit of the Constitution, and later by amendment of the Constitution, if found necessary, we advocate bringing under effective national jurisdiction those problems which have expanded beyond reach of the individual states.

It is as grotesque as it is intolerable that the several states should by unequal laws in matter of common concern become competing commercial agencies, barter the lives of their children, the health of their women, and the safety and well-being of their working people for the benefit of their financial interests.

The extreme insistence on states' rights by the Democratic Party in the Baltimore platform demonstrates anew its inability to understand the world into which it has survived or to administer the affairs of a union of states which have in all essential respects become one people.

Social and Industrial Reform — The supreme duty of the nation is the conservation of human resources through an enlightened measure of social and industrial justice. We pledge ourselves to work unceasingly in state and nation for:

Effective legislation looking to the prevention of industrial accidents, occupational diseases, overwork, involuntary unemployment, and other injurious effects incident to modern industry.

The fixing of minimum safety and health standards for the various occupations, and the exercise of the public authority of state and nation, including the federal control over interstate commerce and the taxing power to maintain such standards.

The prohibition of child labor.

Minimum wage standards for working women, to provide a "living scale" in all industrial occupations.

The prohibition of night work for women and the establishment of an eight-hour day for women and young persons.

One day's rest in seven for all wage workers.

The eight-hour day in continuous twenty-four-hour industries.

The abolition of the convict contract labor system; substituting a system of prison production for governmental consumption only and the application of prisoners' earnings to the support of their dependent families.

Publicity as to wages, hours, and conditions of labor; full reports upon industrial accidents and diseases; and the opening to public inspection of all tallies, weights, measures, and check systems on labor products.

Standards of compensation for death by industrial accident and injury and trade diseases which will transfer the burden of lost earnings from the families of working people to the industry, and thus to the community.

The protection of homelife against the hazards of sickness, irregular employment, and old age through the adoption of a system of social insurance adapted to American use.

The development of the creative labor power of America by lifting the last load of illiteracy from American youth and establishing continuation schools for industrial education under public control and encouraging agricultural education and demonstration in rural schools.

The establishment of industrial research laboratories to put the methods and discoveries of science at the service of American producers.

We favor the organization of the workers, men and women, as a means of protecting their interests and of promoting their progress.

Regulation of Interstate Corporations — We believe that true popular government, justice, and prosperity go hand in hand; and, so believing, it is our purpose to secure that large measure of general prosperity which is the fruit of legitimate and honest business, fostered by equal justice and by sound progressive laws.

We demand that the test of true prosperity shall be the benefits conferred thereby on all the citizens, not confined to individuals or classes, and that the test of corporate efficiency shall be the ability better to serve the public; that those who profit by control of business affairs shall justify that profit and that control by sharing with the public the fruits thereof.

We therefore demand a strong national regulation of interstate corporations. The corporation is an essential part of modern business. The concentration of modern business, in some degree, is both inevitable and necessary for national and international business efficiency. But the existing concentration of vast wealth under a corporate system, unguarded and uncontrolled by the nation, has placed in the hands of a few men enormous, secret, irresponsible power over the daily life of the citizen — a power unsufferable in a free government and certain of abuse.

This power has been abused in monopoly of national resources, in stock watering, in unfair competition and unfair privileges, and, finally, in sinister influences on the public agencies of state and nation. We do not fear commercial power, but we insist that it shall be exercised openly, under publicity, supervision, and regulation of the most efficient sort, which will preserve its good while eradicating and preventing its evils.

To that end we urge the establishment of a strong federal administrative commission of high standing, which shall maintain permanent active supervision over industrial corporations engaged in interstate commerce, or such of them as are of public importance, doing for them what the government now does for the national banks, and what is now done for the railroads by the Interstate Commerce Commission.

Such a commission must enforce the complete publicity of those corporate transactions which are of public interest; must attack unfair competition, false capitalization, and special privilege, and by continuous trained watchfulness guard and keep open equally to all the highways of American commerce. Thus the businessman will have certain knowledge of the law and will be able to conduct his business easily in conformity therewith, the investor will find security for his capital, dividends will be rendered more certain, and the savings of the people will be drawn naturally and safely into the channels of trade.

Under such a system of constructive regulation, legitimate business, freed from confusion, uncertainty, and fruitless litigation, will develop normally in response to the energy and enterprise of the American businessman.

Commercial Development — The time has come when the federal government should cooperate with manufacturers and producers in extending our foreign commerce. To this end we demand adequate appropriations by Congress and the appointment of diplomatic and consular officers solely with a view to their special fitness and worth, and not in consideration of political expediency.

It is imperative to the welfare of our people that we enlarge and extend our foreign commerce. We are preeminently fitted to do this because, as a people, we have developed high skill in the art of manufacturing; our businessmen are strong executives, strong organizers. In every way possible our federal government should cooperate in this important matter.

Anyone who has had opportunity to study and observe first hand Germany's course in this respect must realize that their policy of cooperation between government and business has in comparatively few years made them a leading competitor for the commerce of the world. It should be remembered that they are doing this on a national scale and with large units of business, while the Democrats would have us believe that we should do it with small units of business, which would be controlled, not by the national government but by forty-nine conflicting sovereignties. Such a policy is utterly out of keeping with the progress of the times and gives our great commercial rivals in Europe — hungry for international markets — golden opportunities of which they are rapidly taking advantage.

The Tariff — We believe in a protective tariff which shall equalize conditions of competition between the United States and foreign countries, both for the farmer and the manufacturer, and which shall maintain for labor an adequate standard of living. Primarily the benefit of any tariff should be disclosed in the pay envelope of the laborer. We declare that no industry deserves protection which is unfair to labor or which is operating in violation of federal law. We believe that the presumption is always in favor of the consuming public.

We demand tariff revision because the present tariff is unjust to the people of the United States. Fair dealing toward the people requires an immediate downward revision of those schedules wherein duties are shown to be unjust and excessive.

We pledge ourselves to the establishment of a nonpartisan scientific tariff commission, reporting both to the President and to either branch of Congress, which shall report, first, as to the costs of production, efficiency of labor, capitalization, industrial organization, and efficiency, and the general competitive position in this country and abroad of industries seeking protection from Congress; second, as to the revenue-producing power of the tariff and its relation to the resources of government; and, third, as to the effect of the tariff on prices, operations of middlemen, and on the purchasing power of the consumer.

We believe that this commission should have plenary power to elicit information, and for this purpose to prescribe a uniform system of accounting for the great protected industries. The work of the commission should not prevent the immediate adoption of acts reducing these schedules generally recognized as excessive.

We condemn the Payne-Aldrich Bill as unjust to the people. The Republican organization is in the hands of those who have broken, and cannot again be trusted to keep, the promise of necessary downward revision. The Democratic Party is committed to the destruction of the protective system through a tariff for revenue only — a policy which would inevitably produce widespread industrial and commercial disaster.

Reciprocity With Canada — We demand the immediate repeal of the Canadian Reciprocity Act.

High Cost of Living — The high cost of living is due partly to worldwide and partly to local causes; partly to natural and partly to artificial causes. The measures proposed in this platform on various subjects, such as the tariff, the trusts, and conservation, will of themselves remove the artificial causes. There will remain other elements, such as the tendency to leave the country for the city, waste, extravagance, bad system of taxation, poor methods of raising crops, and bad business methods in marketing crops. To remedy these conditions requires the fullest information and, based on this information, effective government supervision and control to remove all the artificial causes. We pledge ourselves to such full and immediate inquiry and to immediate action to deal with every need such inquiry discloses.

Improvement of the Currency — We believe there exists imperative need for prompt legislation for the improvement of our national currency system. We believe the present method of issuing notes through private agencies is harmful and unscientific. The issue of currency is fundamentally a government function and the system should have as basic principles soundness and elasticity. The control should be lodged with the government and should be protected from domination or manipulation by Wall Street or any special interests.

We are opposed to the so-called Aldrich Currency Bill because its provisions would place our currency and credit system in private hands, not subject to effective public control.

Conservation of Natural Resources — The natural resources of the nation must be promptly developed and generously used to supply the people's needs, but we cannot safely allow them to be wasted, exploited, monopolized, or controlled against the general good. We heartily favor the policy of conservation and we pledge our party to protect the national forests without hindering their legitimate use for the benefit of all the people. Agricultural lands in the national forests are, and should remain, open to the genuine settler. Conservation will not retard legitimate development. The honest settler must receive his patent promptly without hindrance, rules, or delays.

We believe that the remaining forests, coal and oil lands, water powers, and other natural resources still in state or national control (except agricultural lands) are more likely to be wisely conserved and utilized for the general welfare if held in the public hands.

In order that consumers and producers, managers and workmen, now and hereafter, need not pay toll to private monopolies of power and raw material, we demand that such resources shall be retained by the state or nation and opened to immediate use under laws which will encourage development and make to the people a moderate return for benefits conferred.

In particular we pledge our party to require reasonable compensation to the public for waterpower rights hereafter granted by the public. We pledge legislation to lease the public grazing lands under equitable provisions now pending which will increase the production of food for the people and thoroughly safeguard the rights of the actual homemakers. Natural resources whose conservation is necessary for the national welfare should be owned and controlled by the nation.

Waterways — The rivers of the United States are the natural arteries of this continent. We demand that they shall be opened to traffic as indispensable parts of a great nationwide system of transportation in which the Panama Canal will be the central link, thus enabling the whole interior of the United States to share with the Atlantic and Pacific seaboards in the benefit derived from the Canal.

It is a national obligation to develop our rivers, and especially the Mississippi and its tributaries, without delay, under a comprehensive general plan covering each river system, from its source to its mouth, designed to secure its highest usefulness for navigation, irrigation, domestic supply, waterpower, and the prevention of floods. We pledge our party to the immediate preparation of such a plan, which should be made and carried out in close and friendly cooperation between the nation, the state, and the cities affected.

Under such a plan the destructive floods of the Mississippi and other streams, which represent a vast and needless loss to the nation, would be controlled by forest conservation and water storage at the headwaters, and by levees below; land sufficient to support millions of people would be reclaimed from the deserts and swamps, waterpower enough to transform the industrial standing of whole states would be developed, adequate water terminals would be provided, transportation would revive, and the railroads would be compelled to cooperate as freely with the boat lines as with each other.

The equipment, organization, and experience acquired in constructing the Panama Canal soon will be available for the Lakes-to-the-Gulf deep waterway and other portions of this great work, and should be utilized by the nation in cooperation with the various states at the lowest net cost to the people.

Panama Canal — The Panama Canal, built and paid for by the American people, must be used primarily for their benefit. We demand that the Canal shall be so operated as to break the transportation monopoly now held and misused by the transcontinental railroads by maintaining sea competition with them; that ships directly or indirectly owned or controlled by American railroad corporations shall not be permitted to use the Canal, and that American ships engaged in coastwise trade shall pay no tolls.

The Progressive Party will favor legislation having for its aim the development of friendship and commerce between the United States and Latin-American nations.

Alaska — The coal and other natural resources of Alaska should be opened to development at once. They are owned by the people of the United States and are safe from monopoly, waste or destruction only while so owned. We demand that they shall neither be sold nor given away except under the Homestead Law, but while held in government ownership shall be opened to use promptly upon liberal terms requiring immediate development.

Thus the benefit of cheap fuel will accrue to the government of the United States and to the people of Alaska and the Pacific Coast; the settlement of extensive agricultural lands will be hastened; the extermination of the salmon will be prevented, and the just and wise development of Alaskan resources will take the place of private extortion or monopoly.

We demand also that extortion or monopoly in transportation shall be prevented by the prompt acquisition, construction, or improvement by the government of such railroads, harbor, and other facilities for transportation as the welfare of the people may demand.

We promise the people of the Territory of Alaska the same measure of local self-government that was given to other American territories, and that federal officials appointed there shall be qualified by previous bona fide residence in the territory.

Woman Suffrage — The Progressive Party, believing that no people can justly claim to be a true democracy which denies political rights on account of sex, pledges itself to the task of securing equal suffrage to men and women alike.

Corrupt Election Practices — We pledge our party to legislation that will compel strict limitation of all campaign contributions and expenditures, and detailed publicity of both before as well as after primaries and elections.

Publicity and Public Service — We pledge our party to legislation compelling the registration of lobbyists; publicity of committee hearings, except on foreign affairs, and recording of all votes in committee; and forbidding federal appointees from holding office in state or national political organizations or taking part as officers or delegates in political conventions for the nomination of elective state or national officials.

Popular Review of Judicial Decisions — The Progressive Party demands such restriction of the power of the courts as shall leave to the people the ultimate authority to determine fundamental questions of social welfare and public policy. To secure this end, it pledges itself to provide:

First, that when an act, passed under the police power of the state, is held unconstitutional under the state constitution by the courts, the people, after an ample interval for deliberation, shall have an opportunity to vote on the question whether they desire the act to become law, notwithstanding such decision.

Second, that every decision of the highest Appellate Court of a state declaring an act of the Legislature unconstitutional on the ground of its violation of the federal Constitution shall be subject to the same review by the Supreme Court of the United States as is now accorded to decisions sustaining such legislation.

Administration of Justice — The Progressive Party, in order to secure to the people a better administration of justice, and by that means to bring about a more general respect for the law and the courts, pledges itself to work unceasingly for the reform of legal procedure and judicial methods.

We believe that the issuance of injunctions in cases arising out of labor disputes should be prohibited when such injunctions would not apply when no labor disputes existed.

We also believe that a person cited for contempt in labor disputes, except when such contempt was committed in the actual presence of the court or so near thereto as to interfere with the proper administration of justice, should have a right to trial by jury.

A Department of Labor — We pledge our party to establish a Department of Labor, with a seat in the cabinet, and with wide jurisdiction over matters affecting the conditions of labor and living.

Country Life — The development and prosperity of country life are as important to the people who live in the cities as they are to the farmers. Increase of prosperity on the farm will favorably affect the cost of living and promote the interests of all who dwell in the country and all who depend upon its products for clothing, shelter, and food.

We pledge our party to foster the development of agricultural credit and cooperation, the teaching of agriculture in schools, agricultural college extension, the use of mechanical power on the farm and to reestablish the Country Life Commission, thus directly promoting the welfare of the farmers and bringing the benefits of better farming, better business, and better living within their reach.

National Health Service — We favor the union of all the existing agencies of the federal government dealing with the public health into a single National Health Service, without discrimination against or for any one set of therapeutic methods, school of medicine, or school of healing, with such additional powers as may be necessary to enable it to perform efficiently such duties in the protection of the public from preventable disease as may be properly undertaken by the federal authorities, including the executing of existing laws regarding pure food; quarantine and cognate subjects; the promotion of appropriate action for the improvement of vital statistics and the extension of the registration area of such statistics, and cooperation with the health activities of the various states and cities of the nation.

Patents — We pledge ourselves to the enactment of a patent law which will make it impossible for patents to be suppressed or used against the public welfare in the interest of injurious monopolies.

Interstate Commerce Commission — We pledge our party to secure to the Interstate Commerce Commission the power to value the physical property of railroads. In order that the power of the commission to protect the people may not be impaired or destroyed, we demand the abolition of the Commerce Court.

Good Roads — We recognize the vital importance of good roads, and we pledge our party to foster their extension in every proper way, and we favor the early construction of national highways. We also favor the extension of the rural free delivery service.

Inheritance and Income Tax — We believe in a graduated inheritance tax as a national means of equalizing the obligations of holders of property to government; and we hereby pledge our party to enact such a federal law as will tax large inheritances, returning to the states an equitable percentage of all amounts collected. We favor the ratification of the pending amendment to the Constitution giving the government power to levy an income tax.

Peace and National Defense — The Progressive Party deplores the survival in our civilization of the barbaric system of warfare among nations, with its enormous waste of resources, even in time of peace, and the consequent impoverishment of the life of the toiling masses. We pledge the party to use its best endeavors to substitute judicial and other peaceful means of settling international differences.

We favor an international agreement for the limitation of naval forces. Pending such an agreement, and as the best means of preserving peace, we pledge ourselves to maintain for the present the policy of building two battleships a year.

Protection of American Citizens Abroad — We pledge our party to protect the rights of American citizenship at home and abroad. No treaty should receive the sanction of our government which discriminates between American citizens because of birthplace, race, or religion, or that does not recognize the absolute right of expatriation.

Immigration — Through the establishment of industrial standards we propose to secure to the able-bodied immigrant and to his native fellow workers a larger share of American opportunity.

We denounce the fatal policy of indifference and neglect which has left our enormous immigrant population to become the prey of chance and cupidity. We favor governmental action to encourage the distribution of immigrants away from the congested cities, to rigidly supervise all private agencies dealing with them, and to promote their assimilation, education, and advancement.

Pensions — We pledge ourselves to a wise and just policy of pensioning American soldiers and sailors and their widows and children by the federal government.

And we approve the policy of the Southern states in granting pensions to the ex-Confederate soldiers and sailors and their widows and children.

Parcels Post — We pledge our party to the immediate creation of a parcels post, with rates proportionate to distance and service.

The Civil Service Law — We condemn the violations of the Civil Service Law under the present administration, including the coercion and assessment of subordinate employees, and the President's refusal to punish such violation after a finding of guilty by his own commission; his distribution of patronage among subservient congressmen, while withholding it from those who refuse support of administration measures; his withdrawal of nominations from the Senate until political support for himself was secured, and his open use of the offices to reward those who voted for his renomination.

To eradicate these abuses we demand not only the enforcement of the Civil Service Act in letter and spirit but also legislation which will bring under the competitive system postmasters, collectors, marshals, and all other nonpolitical officers, as well as the enactment of an equitable retirement law; and we also insist on continuous service during good behavior and efficiency.

Government Business Organization — We pledge our party to readjustment of the business methods of the national government and a proper coordination of the federal bureaus which will increase the economy and efficiency of the government service, prevent duplications, and secure better results to the taxpayers for every dollar expended.

Supervision Over Investments — The people of the United States are swindled out of many millions of dollars every year through worthless investments. The plain people, the wage earners, and the men and women with small savings have no way of knowing the merit of concerns sending out highly colored prospectuses offering stock for sale, prospectuses that make big returns seem certain and fortunes easily within grasp.

We hold it to be the duty of the government to protect its people from this kind of piracy. We therefore demand wise, carefully thought-out legislation that will give us such governmental supervision over this matter as will furnish to the people of the United States this much-needed protection, and we pledge ourselves thereto.

Conclusion — On these principles and on the recognized desirability of uniting the progressive forces of the nation into an organization which shall unequivocally represent the progressive spirit and policy, we appeal for the support of all American citizens, without regard to previous political affiliations.

A presidential campaign may easily degenerate into a mere personal contest and so lose its real dignity. There is no indispensable man.

WOODROW WILSON, speech

70.

Woodrow Wilson: The Fear of Monopoly

The campaign of 1912 pitted four remarkable men against each other for the presidency, all of them with significant reform backgrounds. William Howard Taft, the incumbent, had the support of the regular Republicans and of some of the old-guard Progressives. Theodore Roosevelt was backed by most of the Progressives, who had banded together to organize the rump Republican "Bull Moose" Party. Eugene Debs was the Socialist candidate. And Woodrow Wilson, the enlightened governor of New Jersey, ex-professor of political science and ex-president of Princeton University, was the choice of the Democrats. Failing at first to find an issue with which to stir the voters, Wilson was persuaded by Louis D. Brandeis to stress the problem of the trusts, and with his oratorical gifts he was able to turn it into what was almost a one-man crusade. A portion of Wilson's campaign speech at Lincoln, Nebraska, delivered on October 5, 1912, is reprinted here.

Source: Library of Congress, Manuscript Division: Ray Stannard Baker Papers; Transcription, Swem Notes.

WE ARE NOT GOING TO DISCUSS tonight the sympathies, the susceptibilities, the enthusiasms of the several men who are seeking your suffrages for President of the United States. I am perfectly ready to believe and will admit for the sake of argument that Mr. Roosevelt's heart and soul are committed to that part of the third-term program which contains those hopeful plans of human betterment in which so many noble men and women in this country have enlisted their sympathies and their energies.

I am not here to criticize anybody who has been drawn to that party because of that part of the program. But I want to call their attention to the fact that you can't have a program that you can carry out through a resisting and unsuitable medium, and that the thing that it is absolutely necessary for every candid voter to remember with regard to the third party is that the means of government, the means of getting the things that this country needs, are exactly the same on that side that they are on

the side where Mr. Taft seeks the suffrages of the country.

Because, while the party of Mr. Taft says in its platform that monopoly ought not to exist, the section of the Republican Party that is following Mr. Roosevelt subscribes to the statement that monopoly ought to be adopted by the law, and by regulation should be the governing force in the development of American industry. So that all that the third party asks of the monopolists is that they should cooperate, and the only hope of a program of human uplift from that party is that the monopolists will cooperate.

Have you got any hopes in that direction? Don't you know what the Republican Party has provided you with up to this time? I have taken special pains to clear from my own mind, at any rate, the Republican conception of government. That conception is that the people cannot organize their opinion in such fashion as to control their own government. And that, therefore, it is necessary constantly to consult those whose material interests in the development of the country are larger than anybody else's, and then, through the hands of these trustees, administer the government, not through the people but for the people.

I am perfectly ready to believe — knowing some of the men concerned as I do, I must believe — that a great many men now engaged in the promotion of monopoly in this country really wish to see the United States prosperous, and really desire to adopt the means that will make it prosperous. But they are not willing to let anybody else yield the means of prosperity except themselves. I wonder at the frame of mind which makes them believe that they are the trustees of political discretion in this country, but I am willing to admit for the sake of argument that that is their candid and deliberate judgment.

What we have to fight, therefore, is not a body of deliberate enemies, it may be, but a body of mistaken men. And what I want to point out to you is that Mr. Roosevelt subscribes to the judgment of these mistaken men as to the influences which should govern America. That is the serious part of it. Mr. Roosevelt's judgment has been captured. Mr. Roosevelt's idea of the way in which the industries of this country ought to be controlled has been captured. He does not propose to set us free. He proposes to use monopoly in order to make us happy. And the project is one of those projects which all history cries out against as impossible.

The Democratic platform is the only platform which says that private monopoly is indefensible and intolerable, and any man who does not subscribe to that opinion does not know the way to set the people of the United States free, and to serve humanity. All that Mr. Roosevelt is asking you to do is to elect him president of the board of trustees. I do not care how wise, how patriotic the trustees may be; I have never heard of any group of men in whose hands I am

willing to put the liberties of America in trust. And, therefore, I am not in this campaign engaged in doubting any man's motives. I merely want to point out that these gentlemen are not proposing the methods of liberty but are proposing the methods of control. A control among a free people is intolerable.

I have been very much interested the last day or two in having described to me the industries of some of these smaller Western cities. I know in Indiana, for example, town after town was pointed out to me that still has the American characteristic, in which there are factories upon factories owned by men who live in the place — independent enterprises still unabsorbed by the great economic combinations which have become so threateningly inhuman in our economic organization — and it seems to me that these are outposts and symbols of the older and freer America. And after I had traveled through that series of towns and met the sturdy people that live in them, I entered in the city of Gary, which is a little way outside of Chicago, and realized that I had come from the older America into the newer America. But this was a town owned and built by a single monopolistic corporation. And I wondered which kind of America the people of America, if they could see this picture as I saw it, would choose?

Which do you want? Do you want to live in a town patronized by some great combination of capitalists who pick it out as a suitable place to plant their industry and draw you into their employment? Or do you want to see your sons and your brothers and your husbands build up business for themselves under the protection of laws which make it impossible for any giant, however big, to crush them and put them out of business, so that they can match their wits here in the midst of a free country with any captain of industry or merchant of finance to be found anywhere in the world, and put every man who now assumes to control and promote monopoly upon his mettle to beat them at initiative, at economy, at the organization of business, and the cheap production of salable goods? Which do you want?

Why, gentlemen, America is never going to submit to monopoly. America is never going to choose thralldom instead of freedom. Look what there is to decide! There is the tariff question. Can the tariff question be decided in favor of the people of the United States so long as the monopolies are the chief counselors at Washington? There is the great currency question. You know how difficult it is to move your crops every year. And I tremble, I must frankly tell you, to think of the bumper crops that are now coming from our fields, because they are going to need enormous bodies of cash to move them.

You have got to get that cash by calling in your loans and embarrassing people in every center of commercial activity, because there isn't cash enough under our inelastic currency to lend itself to this instrumentality. And are we going to settle the currency question so long as the government of the United States listens only to the counsel of those who command the banking situation in the United States? You can't solve the tariff, you can't solve the currency question under the domination which is proposed by one branch of the Republican Party and tolerated by the other.

Then there is the great question of conservation. What is our fear about conservation? The hands that will be stretched out to monopolize our forests, to preempt the use of our great power-producing streams, the hands that will be stretched into the bowels of the earth to take possession of the great riches that lie hidden in Alaska and elsewhere in the incomparable domain of the United States are the hands of monopoly. And is this thing merely to be regulated? Is this thing to be legalized? Are these men to continue to stand at the elbow of government and tell us how we are to save ourselves from the very things that we fear? You can't settle the question of conservation while monopoly exists if monopoly is close to the ears of those who govern. And the question of conservation is a great deal bigger than the question of saving our forests and our mineral resources and our waters. It is as big as the life and happiness and strength and elasticity and hope of our people.

The government of the United States has now to look out upon her people and see what they need, what should be done for them. Why, gentlemen, there are tasks waiting the government of the United States which it cannot perform until every pulse of that government beats in unison with the needs and the desires of the whole body of the American people. Shall we not give the people access of sympathy, access of counsel, access of authority to the instrumentalities which are to be indispensable to their lives?

When I think of the great things to be accomplished and then think of the danger that there is that the people of the United States will not choose free instruments to accomplish them, then I tremble to think of the verdict that may be rendered on the 5th of November. But when you look around when going through America, as I have recently been going through it, your heart rises again. Why, two years ago when I was running for governor in New Jersey, I used to come away from public meetings with a certain burden on my heart, because I knew I was not mistaken in feeling that I had seen in the faces and felt in the atmosphere of the great meetings that I addressed a certain sense of foreboding and anxiety as a people who were anxious about their future.

But I haven't seen anything of that kind in the year 1912. The people of the United States now know what they intend to do. They intend to take charge of their own affairs again and they see the way to do it. Great outpourings like this are not in compliment to an individual; they are in demonstration of a purpose. And all I have to say for the Democratic candidate for the presidency is that I pray God he may be shown the way not to disappoint the expectations of such people.

Only you can show him the way. You can't do it by proxy. You must determine the interests of your own life and then find spokesmen for those interests who will speak them as fairly as men have learned how to speak in Nebraska. The great emancipation which has been wrought for you by the fight for progressive democracy which has gone on from splendid stage to splendid stage in this state is that it has raised up for you men who fearlessly speak the truth. And that is not true of all parts of the country.

Why, there are parts of the country where I am considered brave if I speak in words what every man and woman in the audience knows to be true. Now, I have never known what it was to exercise courage when I knew that the stars in all their courses were fighting my way. Do you suppose a man needs be courageous to speak the truth, to attach his puny force to the great voice of the country which is truth itself? A man would be a coward that wouldn't speak the truth. A man would be a fool who didn't see that the only puissance in human affairs was the irresistible force of truth itself, and men are weak in proportion as they are mistaken; they are weak in proportion as their judgments are misled; they are weak in proportion as they do not see the practical terms into which the truth can be translated. But they are not courageous when they merely tell the truth, because, if they lie because they were afraid, do you suppose they would have very comfortable moments when they withdraw into the privacy of their own family?

I wonder how some men sleep of nights because they deceive themselves and deceive others all day long, and then actually go home and go to sleep. I don't know what their dreams can be. And they speak the things that they know are not true because they are afraid of something.

Fear is abroad in free America. There are men who dare not undertake certain business enterprises because they know that they would be crushed. There are men who dare not speak certain opinions because they know that they would be boycotted in influential circles upon which their credit and their advancement in their business depends.

Do you suppose that it is singular that men should rise up and fight through half a generation as your own champions have fought in order to dispel that fear? The only way to dispel fear is to bring the things that you are afraid of out in the open and challenge them there to meet the great moral force of the people of the United States. So that if these gentlemen will come out and avow their purposes, they will destroy all possibility of realizing those purposes.

One of the fine things of our time is that the whole game is disclosed. We now know the processes of monopoly, and we therefore know the processes of law by which monopoly can be destroyed. They have shown their hands and we know how to stay their use of illegitimate power.

Will we do them any damage? I tell you frankly that if I thought that any considerable portion of the enterprising men of America would be injured by the policies that I am interested in, I would hesitate. But I am clear in the conviction that to set the people of the United States free is to set the big enterprises free along with the little ones, because I have never heard of any business conditions which were dependent upon the subservience of great business, of enterprising businessmen. If you have to be subservient, you aren't even making the rich fellows as rich as they might be, because you are not adding your originative force to the extraordinary production of wealth in America.

America is as rich, not as Wall Street, not

as the financial centers in Chicago and St. Louis and San Francisco; it is as rich as the people that make its centers rich. And if those people hesitate in their enterprise, cowering in the face of power, hesitate to originate designs of their own, then the very fountains which make these places abound in wealth are dried up at the source; so that by setting the little men of America free you are not damaging the giants. You are merely making them behave like human beings.

Now, a giant ought to have more human nature in him than a Pygmy, and we want to reread the Decalogue to these big men who may not have heard it in some time. And by moralizing, we are going to set them free and their business free.

It may be that certain things will happen, for monopoly in this country is carrying a body of water such as no body of men ought to be asked to carry. And when by regulated competition — that is to say, fair competition, competition that fights fair — they are put upon their mettle, they will have to economize in their processes of business, and they can't economize unless they drop that water. I do not know how to squeeze the water out but they will get rid of it, if you will put them on their mettle. They will have to get rid of it, or those of us who don't carry tanks will outrun them in the race. Put all the business of America upon the footing of economy and efficiency, and then let the race be to the strongest and the efficient.

So that our program is a program of prosperity, only it is a program of prosperity that is a little more pervasive to the present program, and pervasive prosperity is more fruitful than that which is narrow and restrictive.

I congratulate the monopolists of the United States that they are not going to have their way, because, quite contrary to the old theory, the people of the United States are wiser than they are. The people of the United States understand the United States as these gentlemen do not, and if they will only give us leave, we will not only make them rich but we will make them happy, because then our consciences will have less to carry. They are waking up to this fact, ladies and gentlemen. The businessmen of this country are not deluded, and not all of the big business of this country are deluded.

Some men who have been led into wrong practice, who have been led into the practice of monopoly because that seemed to be the drift and inevitable method of supremacy of their times, are just as ready as we are to turn about and adopt the processes of freedom, because American hearts beat in a lot of those men just as they beat under our jackets. They will be as glad to be free as we have been to set them free. And then the splendid force which has led to the things that hurt us will lead to the things that benefit us.

We are coming to a common understanding, and only a common understanding is the tolerable basis of a free government. I congratulate you, therefore, ladies and gentlemen, that you are now coming to that point of fruition of which you have dreamed and for which you have planned in Nebraska for more than half a generation. . . .

What we propose, therefore, in this program of freedom, is a program of general advantage. Almost every monopoly that has resisted extinction has resisted the real interests of its own stockholders. And it has been very, very slow business convincing those who were responsible for the business of the country that that was the fact. After the 4th of March next, therefore, we are going to get together; we are going to stop serving special interests, and we are going to stop setting one interest up against another interest. We are not going to champion one set of people against another set of people, but we are going to see what common counsel can accomplish for the happiness and redemption of America.

71.

Victor L. Berger: Socialism and Economic Evolution

Victor Berger was the first Socialist to serve in the U.S. Congress, occupying a seat in the House from 1911 to 1913 and from 1923 to 1929. Calling himself a constructionist, he rejected the Marxist dogmas of violence and revolution, and instead hoped for Socialist triumphs in municipal and state elections as the basis of a national victory for his party. "While nominally Socialistic," the Saturday Evening Post *told its readers, Berger's political philosophy was "really civic and social reform . . . mild and gentle uplifting and thoroughly housebroken." In the article reprinted here, which was published in November 1912, Berger analyzed the relationship between progressivism and socialism.*

Source: *American Magazine,* November 1912: "Socialism, the Logical Outcome of Progressivism."

WHY AM I going to vote for Debs? As good a man as Eugene V. Debs is, I am not going to vote for him in the sense one is voting for Wilson, Taft, or Roosevelt — I simply vote the ticket of the Socialist Party. I have no hope that the Socialist Party will elect its candidate for President in this election. With us, the Socialist movement and its principles are paramount — not the candidate.

The Socialist Party stands for the collective ownership of all the social means of production and distribution in the interest of the whole people. Socialists say that this step is the necessary and natural outcome of the concentration of wealth and of the development of capitalism.

Antagonists of Socialism in the past claimed that collective ownership of an industry was impossible because the personal supervision and control of the owner was absolutely necessary to the success of any enterprise. Today we see that the greatest undertakings are those in which the stockholders and owners have nothing to do with the management of affairs and are only drawing dividends.

In all of our large industrial concerns — stock companies, railroads, and trusts — business is managed and carried on by a few paid officials. These men might just as well be paid by the state, or the nation (as the case may be), to carry on the enterprise in the interest of the people, as paid by a few wealthy men to carry it on for their individual profit.

Moreover, we find that whenever the nation, state, or community has undertaken to own and manage any large industry, railroad, mine, factory, telegraph, telephone, mill, or canal, etc., this invariably redounded to the benefit of the commonwealth — the inherent weakness of our political spoils system notwithstanding. This idea, carried out gradually and logically, involves a complete change of our economic and political system.

Political equality under the present system is a snare and delusion. The wage worker who depends upon a master or upon the master class for an opportunity to make a living is not on terms of equality with his master. Political liberty and economic despotism are incompatible. The Socialist Party proposed to supplement our political democracy by industrial democracy.

No one dreams of abolishing private property. On the contrary, we propose to secure private property to every citizen, to the many million men and women who under the present system have no chance of ever having any. Productive capital only is to be owned in common, by the nation, the state, or the municipality as the exigencies of the case may require. Business will be carried on for use and not for profit. This is the case now in the post office, waterworks, public school, etc., wherever owned and managed by the people.

Such is the aim of the Socialist Party.

The usual argument in defense of the present vicious system is not that it is right or good but that it is here and must stay. We Socialists think this a foolish assertion. We believe the American people great and strong enough to get rid of anything that is not good or harmful.

The Capitalist system did not always exist. It followed the Feudal system, which replaced a system based upon ancient chattel slavery. The Capitalist system has undoubtedly done some good in this world. The Capitalist system was useful. It has concentrated economic forces and has made possible the production of wealth on a very large scale. The Capitalist system was a step in the evolution to freedom, but only a step. It has now outlived its usefulness. It has become oppressive to the great majority of the people. Therefore it must pass away.

The growing restiveness of the people generally — the willingness of the trusts and other great industrial undertakings to accept governmental control — the crumbling of the two great Capitalist parties — the fact that the most intelligent of their politicians are trying to steal Socialistic planks and adopt them for their own platforms are so many signs of the change that is upon us.

The Socialist Party has not a majority as yet. But Socialistic ideas have permeated the great majority. The trusts and economic evolution, on one hand, and the natural discontent of the people with the lowering of their standard of living, on the other hand, are working for Socialism. Therefore, we laugh at the contention that the Socialist Party is still comparatively small. Every great party has had a small beginning — and the Socialist Party is growing exceedingly fast.

The phrase of "getting on the bandwagon" is a stupid phrase. Who is on the "band-wagon"? Not the common citizen, not the average voter. The scheming financiers, and the sleek office seekers are on the "band-wagon."

To the common citizen, the workingman, the underpaid clerk, the disappointed professional man — to the disinherited of every description — we Socialists say: "Better vote for what you want, even if you do not get it, than vote for what you do not want and get it!"

Why should we wait with our work until the majority of the votes is with us? The majority is always indolent and often ignorant. We cannot expect them to be anything else with their present social surroundings. The majority have never brought about consciously and deliberately any great social change. They have always permitted an energetic minority to prepare the way. But the majority was always there when the fact itself was to be accomplished.

Therefore, our sole object in state and nation for the next few years is to elect a respectable minority of Socialists.

We want a Socialist minority respected on account of its numbers — respected because it represents the most advanced economic and political intelligence of the day — respected because it contains the most sincere representatives of the proletariat, the class that has the most to gain and nothing to lose.

Given such a respectable minority in Congress and in the legislature of every state of the Union within the next few years, the future of our people, the future of this country will be safe.

72.

JAMES OPPENHEIM: "Bread and Roses"

The Lawrence, Massachusetts, textile workers' strike of 1912 began spontaneously when 20,000 workers walked out of the mills to protest a cut in wages. Numerous parades and marches followed the walkout, and on one occasion some young girls were seen carrying a banner with the slogan "We want bread and roses too." The banner gave James Oppenheim the idea for a poem that was then set to music by Caroline Kohlsaat. The song, a stirring statement of the textile workers' demands, became widely popular.

Source: *Songs of Work and Freedom*, Edith Fowke and Joe Glazer, eds., New York, 1960.

BREAD AND ROSES

As we come marching, marching, in the beauty of the day,
A million darkened kitchens, a thousand mill lofts gray,
Are touched with all the radiance that a sudden sun discloses,
For the people hear us singing: "Bread and roses! Bread and roses!"

As we come marching, marching, we battle too for men,
For they are women's children, and we mother them again.
Our lives shall not be sweated from birth until life closes;
Hearts starve as well as bodies; give us bread, but give us roses!

As we come marching, marching, unnumbered women dead
Go crying through our singing their ancient cry for bread.
Small art and love and beauty their drudging spirits knew.
Yes, it is bread we fight for — but we fight for roses, too!

As we come marching, marching, we bring the greater days.
The rising of the women means the rising of the race.
No more the drudge and idler — ten that toil where one reposes,
But a sharing of life's glories: Bread and roses! Bread and roses!

73.

Recommendations of the Aldrich Commission

After the Panic of 1907, many people began to agitate for a reform in banking practices. Congress created the National Monetary Commission in 1908 under the chairmanship of Senator Nelson W. Aldrich to study the problem. The Aldrich Commission, as it was called, produced a number of volumes that dealt mainly with the financial history of the United States. The following list of defects in the banking system, presented to Congress in 1912, reflected the Commission's judgment about the areas requiring reform. Woodrow Wilson's first Congress used this list as the basis for the Federal Reserve Act of 1913.

Source: 62 Congress, 2 Session, Senate Document No. 243, pp. 6-9.

THE ACT OF MAY 30, 1908, providing for the appointment of the National Monetary Commission was a direct consequence of the panic of 1907. We shall not attempt to recount the severe losses and misfortunes suffered by the American people of all classes as the result of this and similar crises. To seek for means to prevent the recurrence or to mitigate the severity of grave disasters of this character was, however, one of the primary purposes of its creation.

We have made a thorough study of the defects of our banking system, which were largely responsible for these disasters and have sought to provide effective remedies for these and other defects in the legislation we propose.

The principal defects in our banking system we believe may be summarized as follows:

1. We have no provision for the concentration of the cash reserves of the banks and for their mobilization and use wherever needed in times of trouble. Experience has shown that the scattered cash reserves of our banks are inadequate for purposes of assistance or defense at such times.

2. Antiquated federal and state laws restrict the use of bank reserves and prohibit the lending power of banks at times when, in the presence of unusual demands, reserves should be freely used and credit liberally extended to all deserving customers.

3. Our banks also lack adequate means available for use at any time to replenish their reserves or increase their loaning powers when necessary to meet normal or unusual demands.

4. Of our various forms of currency, the bank note issue is the only one which we might expect to respond to the changing needs of business by automatic expansion and contraction, but this issue is deprived of all such qualities by the fact that its volume is largely dependent upon the amount and price of United States bonds.

5. We lack means to insure such effective cooperation on the part of banks as is necessary to protect their own and the public interests in times of stress or crisis. There is

no cooperation of any kind among banks outside the clearinghouse cities. While clearinghouse organizations of banks have been able to render valuable services within a limited sphere for local communities, the lack of means to secure their cooperation or affiliation in broader fields makes it impossible to use these or similar local agencies to prevent panics or avert calamitous disturbances affecting the country at large. These organizations have, in fact, never been able to prevent the suspension of cash payments by financial institutions in their own localities in cases of emergency.

6. We have no effective agency covering the entire country which affords necessary facilities for making domestic exchanges between different localities and sections, or which can prevent disastrous disruption of all such exchanges in times of serious trouble.

7. We have no instrumentality that can deal effectively with the broad questions which, from an international standpoint, affect the credit and status of the United States as one of the great financial powers of the world. In times of threatened trouble or of actual panic, these questions, which involve the course of foreign exchange and the international movements of gold, are even more important to us from a national than from an international standpoint.

8. The lack of commercial paper of an established standard, issued for agricultural, industrial, and commercial purposes, available for investments by banks, leads to an unhealthy congestion of loanable funds in great centers and hinders the development of the productive forces of the country.

9. The narrow character of our discount market, with its limited range of safe and profitable investments for banks, results in sending the surplus money of all sections, in excess of reserves and local demands, to New York, where it is usually loaned out on call on Stock Exchange securities, tending to promote dangerous speculation and inevitably leading to injurious disturbances in reserves. This concentration of surplus money and available funds in New York imposes upon the managers of the banks of that city the vast responsibilities which are inherent in the control of a large proportion of the banking resources of the country.

10. The absence of a broad discount market in our system, taken together with the restrictive treatment of reserves, creates, at times when serious financial disturbances are anticipated, a condition of dependence on the part of individual banks throughout the country, and at the same time places the farmers and others engaged in productive industries at a great disadvantage in securing the credit they require for the growth, retention, and distribution of their products.

11. There is a marked lack of equality in credit facilities between different sections of the country, reflected in less-favored communities, in retarded development, and great disparity in rates of discount.

12. Our system lacks an agency whose influence can be made effective in securing greater uniformity, steadiness, and reasonableness of rates of discount in all parts of the country.

13. We have no effective agency that can surely provide adequate banking facilities for different regions promptly and on reasonable terms to meet the ordinary or unusual demands for credit or currency necessary for moving crops or for other legitimate purposes.

14. We have no power to enforce the adoption of uniform standards with regard to capital, reserves, examinations, and the character and publicity of reports of all banks in the different sections of the country.

15. We have no American banking institutions in foreign countries. The organization of such banks is necessary for the development of our foreign trade.

16. The provision that national banks shall not make loans upon real estate restricts their power to serve farmers and other borrowers in rural communities.

17. The provision of law under which the government acts as custodian of its own funds results in irregular withdrawals of money from circulation and bank reserves in periods of excessive government revenues,

and in the return of these funds into circulation only in periods of deficient revenues. Recent efforts to modify the independent treasury system by a partial distribution of the public moneys among national banks have resulted, it is charged, in discrimination and favoritism in the treatment of different banks.

74.

William Howard Taft: The Cabinet and the Congress

President Taft came to believe during the course of his administration that a number of reforms were needed to make the executive and legislative branches of the government more responsive to one another. In a message to Congress in 1912, he suggested a plan to allow a member of the Cabinet to be questioned by Congress when legislation affecting his department was being considered. Taft's suggestions were eventually implemented. The opening portion of his message to Congress on December 19, 1912, appears below.

Source: *Record*, 62 Cong., 3 Sess., pp. 895-898.

THIS IS THE THIRD OF A SERIES of messages in which I have brought to the attention of the Congress the important transactions of the government in each of its departments during the last year and have discussed needed reforms.

I recommended the adoption of legislation which shall make it the duty of heads of departments — the members of the President's Cabinet — at convenient times to attend the session of the House and the Senate, which shall provide seats for them in each house, and give them the opportunity to take part in all discussions and to answer questions of which they have had due notice.

The rigid holding apart of the executive

and the legislative branches of this government has not worked for the great advantage of either. There has been much lost motion in the machinery due to the lack of cooperation and interchange of views face to face between the representatives of the executive and the members of the two legislative branches of the government. It was never intended that they should be separated in the sense of not being in constant effective touch and relationship to each other. The legislative and the executive each performs its own appropriate function, but these functions must be coordinated.

Time and time again debates have arisen in each house upon issues which the information of a particular department head would have enabled him, if present, to end at once by a simple explanation or statement. Time and time again a forceful and earnest presentation of facts and arguments by the representative of the executive, whose duty it is to enforce the law, would have brought about a useful reform by amendment, which in the absence of such a statement has failed of passage. I do not think I am mistaken in saying that the presence of the members of the Cabinet on the floor of each house would greatly contribute to the enactment of beneficial legislation. Nor would this in any degree deprive either the legislative or the executive of the independence which separation of the two branches has been intended to promote. It would only facilitate their cooperation in the public interest.

On the other hand, I am sure that the necessity and duty imposed upon department heads of appearing in each house and in answer to searching questions, of rendering upon their feet an account of what they have done or what has been done by the administration, will spur each member of the Cabinet to closer attention to the details of his department, to greater familiarity with its needs, and to greater care to avoid the just criticism which the answers brought out in questions put and discussions arising between the members of either house and the members of the Cabinet may properly evoke.

Objection is made that the members of the administration having no vote could ex-ercise no power on the floor of the House and could not assume that attitude of authority and control which the English parliamentary government have and which enables them to meet the responsibilities the English system thrusts upon them. I agree that in certain respects it would be more satisfactory if members of the Cabinet could at the same time be members of both houses, with voting power, but this is impossible under our system; and while a lack of this feature may detract from the influence of the department chiefs, it will not prevent the good results which I have described above, both in the matter of legislation and in the matter of administration. The enactment of such a law would be quite within the power of Congress without constitutional amendment, and it has such possibilities of usefulness that we might well make the experiment; and if we are disappointed the misstep can be easily retraced by a repeal of the enabling legislation.

This is not a new proposition. In the House of Representatives, in the Thirty-eighth Congress, the proposition was referred to a select committee of seven members. The committee made an extensive report and urged the adoption of the reform. The report showed that our history had not been without illustration of the necessity and the examples of the practice by pointing out that in early days secretaries were repeatedly called to the presence of either house for consultation, advice, and information.

75.

Henry Cabot Lodge: Corollary to the Monroe Doctrine

Rumors that an American syndicate was intending to sell a portion of Lower California to Japanese fishing interests reached Congress in 1912. The area, which included Magdalena Bay, had strategic value, for a naval force based there could easily dominate the new Panama Canal. With this fact in mind, Senator Henry Cabot Lodge offered to the Senate on July 31, 1912, the resolution printed below. Approved by the Senate on August 2, it has become known as the Lodge Corollary to the Monroe Doctrine and marks the first time that the doctrine was applied to an Oriental power.

Source: *Record*, 62 Cong., 2 Sess., p. 10045.

Resolved, that when any harbor or other place in the American continents is so situated that the occupation thereof for naval or military purposes might threaten the communications or the safety of the United States, the government of the United States could not see without grave concern the possession of such harbor or other place by any corporation or association which has such a relation to another government, not American, as to give that government practical power of control for national purposes. . . .

This resolution rests on a generally accepted principle of the law of nations, older than the Monroe Doctrine. It rests on the principle that every nation has a right to protect its own safety, and that if it feels that the possession by a foreign power, for military or naval purposes, of any given harbor or place is prejudicial to its safety, it is its duty as well as its right to interfere.

I will instance as an example of what I mean the protest that was made successfully against the occupation of the port of Agadir, in Morocco, by Germany. England objected on the ground that it threatened her communication through the Mediterranean. That view was shared largely by the European powers, and the occupation of that port was prevented in that way. That is the principle upon which the resolution rests.

It has been made necessary by a change of modern conditions, under which, while a government takes no action itself, the possession of an important place of the character I have described may be taken by a corporation or association which would be under the control of the foreign government.

The Monroe Doctrine was, of course, an extension in our own interests of this underlying principle — the right of every nation to provide for its own safety. The Monroe Doctrine, as we all know, was applied, so far as the taking possession of territory was concerned, to its being open to further colonization and naturally did not touch upon the precise point involved here. But without any Monroe Doctrine, the possession of a harbor such as that of Magdalena Bay, which has led to this resolution, would render it necessary, I think, to make some declaration covering a case where a corporation or association was involved.

In this particular case it became apparent from the inquiries made by the committee and by the administration that no government was concerned in taking possession of Magdalena Bay; but it also became apparent that those persons who held control of the Mexican concession, which included the land about Magdalena Bay, were engaged in negotiations, which have not yet been completed certainly but which have only been tentative, looking to the sale of that bay and the land about it to a corporation either created or authorized by a foreign government or in which the stock was largely held or controlled by foreigners.

The passage of this resolution has seemed to the committee, without division, I think, to be in the interest of peace. It is always desirable to make the position of a country in regard to a question of this kind known beforehand and not to allow a situation to arise in which it might be necessary to urge a friendly power to withdraw when that withdrawal could not be made, perhaps, without some humiliation.

The resolution is merely a statement of policy, allied to the Monroe Doctrine, of course, but not necessarily dependent upon it or growing out of it. When the message came in, I made a statement as to the conditions at Magdalena Bay which had led to the resolution of inquiry and which has now led to the subsequent action of the committee. It seemed to the committee that it was very wise to make this statement of policy at this time, when it can give offense to no one and makes the position of the United States clear.

Of course I need not say to the Senate that the opening of the Panama Canal gives to the question of Magdalena Bay and to that of the Galapagos Islands, which have been once or twice before considered, an importance such as they have never possessed, and I think it eminently desirable in every interest that this resolution should receive the assent of the Senate.

76.

WILLIAM HOWARD TAFT: Dollar Diplomacy

In his message to Congress of December 3, 1912, in the course of a review of his foreign policy actions of the preceding year, President Taft characterized his program as "substituting dollars for bullets." The phrase was picked up by his critics and converted into "dollar diplomacy," a highly uncomplimentary term to describe Taft's dealings with other countries. Taft's encouragement of American business, especially in the Caribbean, where he felt that investors would have a stabilizing effect on the shaky governments of the region, came in for the sharpest criticism. The paragraphs from his last annual message reprinted here are a defense of Taft's policies.

Source: PRFA, 1912, pp. vii-xxvii.

THE FOREIGN RELATIONS of the United States actually and potentially affect the state of the Union to a degree not widely realized and hardly surpassed by any other factor in the welfare of the whole nation. The position of the United States in the moral, intellectual, and material relations of the family of nations should be a matter of vital interest to every patriotic citizen. The national prosperity and power impose upon us duties which we cannot shirk if we are to be true to our ideals. The tremendous growth of the export trade of the United States has already made that trade a very real factor in the industrial and commercial prosperity of the country. With the development of our industries, the foreign commerce of the United States must rapidly become a still more essential factor in its economic welfare.

Whether we have a farseeing and wise diplomacy and are not recklessly plunged into unnecessary wars, and whether our foreign policies are based upon an intelligent grasp of present-day world conditions and a clear view of the potentialities of the future, or are governed by a temporary and timid expediency or by narrow views befitting an infant nation, are questions in the alternative consideration of which must convince any thoughtful citizen that no department of national polity offers greater opportunity for promoting the interests of the whole people on the one hand, or greater chance on the other of permanent national injury, than that which deals with the foreign relations of the United States.

The fundamental foreign policies of the United States should be raised high above the conflict of partisanship and wholly dissociated from differences as to domestic policy. In its foreign affairs the United States should present to the world a united front. The intellectual, financial, and industrial interests of the country and the publicist, the wage earner, the farmer, and citizen of whatever occupation must cooperate in a spirit of high patriotism to promote that national solidarity which is indispensable to national efficiency and to the attainment of national ideals. . . .

The diplomacy of the present administration has sought to respond to modern ideas of commercial intercourse. This policy has been characterized as substituting dollars for bullets. It is one that appeals alike to idealistic humanitarian sentiments, to the dictates of sound policy and strategy, and to legitimate commercial aims. It is an effort frankly directed to the increase of American trade upon the axiomatic principle that the government of the United States shall extend all proper support to every legitimate and beneficial American enterprise abroad.

How great have been the results of this diplomacy, coupled with the maximum and minimum provision of the Tariff Law, will be seen by some consideration of the wonderful increase in the export trade of the United States. Because modern diplomacy is commercial, there has been a disposition in some quarters to attribute to it none but materialistic aims. How strikingly erroneous is such an impression may be seen from a study of the results by which the diplomacy of the United States can be judged.

In the field of work toward the ideals of peace, this government negotiated, but to my regret was unable to consummate, two arbitration treaties which set the highest mark of the aspiration of nations toward the substitution of arbitration and reason for war in the settlement of international disputes. Through the efforts of American diplomacy, several wars have been prevented or ended. I refer to the successful tripartite mediation of the Argentine Republic, Brazil, and the United States between Peru and Ecuador; the bringing of the boundary dispute between Panama and Costa Rica to peaceful arbitration; the staying of warlike preparations when Haiti and the Dominican Republic were on the verge of hostilities; the stopping of a war in Nicaragua; the halting of internecine strife in Honduras.

The government of the United States was thanked for its influence toward the restoration of amicable relations between the Argentine Republic and Bolivia. The diplomacy of the United States is active in seeking to assuage the remaining ill feeling between this country and the Republic of Colombia. In the recent civil war in China, the United States successfully joined with the other interested powers in urging an early cessation of hostilities. An agreement has been reached between the governments of Chile and Peru whereby the celebrated

Tacna-Arica dispute, which has so long embittered international relations on the west coast of South America, has at last been adjusted. Simultaneously came the news that the boundary dispute between Peru and Ecuador had entered upon a stage of amicable settlement.

The position of the United States in reference to the Tacna-Arica dispute between Chile and Peru has been one of nonintervention, but one of friendly influence and pacific counsel throughout the period during which the dispute in question has been the subject of interchange of views between this government and the two governments immediately concerned. In the general easing of international tension on the west coast of South America, the tripartite mediation, to which I have referred, has been a most potent and beneficent factor.

In China the policy of encouraging financial investment to enable that country to help itself has had the result of giving new life and practical application to the open door policy. The consistent purpose of the present administration has been to encourage the use of American capital in the development of China by the promotion of those essential reforms to which China is pledged by treaties with the United States and other powers. The hypothecation to foreign bankers in connection with certain industrial enterprises, such as the Hukuang railways, of the national revenues upon which these reforms depended, led the Department of State, early in the administration, to demand for American citizens participation in such enterprises, in order that the United States might have equal rights and an equal voice in all questions pertaining to the disposition of the public revenues concerned.

The same policy of promoting international accord among the powers having similar treaty rights as ourselves in the matters of reform, which could not be put into practical effect without the common consent of all, was likewise adopted in the case of the loan desired by China for the reform of its currency. The principle of international cooperation in matters of common interest upon which our policy had already been based in all of the above instances has admittedly been a great factor in that concert of the powers which has been so happily conspicuous during the perilous period of transition through which the great Chinese nation has been passing.

In Central America the aim has been to help such countries as Nicaragua and Honduras to help themselves. They are the immediate beneficiaries. The national benefit to the United States is twofold. First, it is obvious that the Monroe Doctrine is more vital in the neighborhood of the Panama Canal and the zone of the Caribbean than anywhere else. There, too, the maintenance of that doctrine falls most heavily upon the United States. It is therefore essential that the countries within that sphere shall be removed from the jeopardy involved by heavy foreign debt and chaotic national finances and from the ever present danger of international complications due to disorder at home. Hence, the United States has been glad to encourage and support American bankers who were willing to lend a helping hand to the financial rehabilitation of such countries because this financial rehabilitation and the protection of their customhouses from being the prey of would-be dictators would remove at one stroke the menace of foreign creditors and the menace of revolutionary disorder.

The second advantage to the United States is one affecting chiefly all the Southern and Gulf ports and the business and industry of the South. The republics of Central America and the Caribbean possess great natural wealth. They need only a measure of stability and the means of financial regeneration to enter upon an era of peace and prosperity, bringing profit and happiness to themselves and at the same time creating conditions sure to lead to a flourishing interchange of trade with this country.

I wish to call your especial attention to the recent occurrences in Nicaragua, for I believe the terrible events recorded there during the revolution of the past summer — the useless loss of life, the devastation of property, the bombardment of defenseless cities, the killing and wounding of women and children, the torturing of noncombatants to exact contributions, and the suffering of thousands of human beings — might have been averted had the Department of State, through approval of the loan convention by the Senate, been permitted to carry out its now well-developed policy of encouraging the extending of financial aid to weak Central American states, with the primary objects of avoiding just such revolutions by assisting those republics to rehabilitate their finances, to establish their currency on a stable basis, to remove the customhouses from the danger of revolutions by arranging for their secure administration, and to establish reliable banks.

During this last revolution in Nicaragua, the government of that republic having admitted its inability to protect American life and property against acts of sheer lawlessness on the part of the malcontents, and having requested this government to assume that office, it became necessary to land over 2,000 Marines and Bluejackets in Nicaragua. Owing to their presence the constituted government of Nicaragua was free to devote its attention wholly to its internal troubles, and was thus enabled to stamp out the rebellion in a short space of time. When the Red Cross supplies sent to Granada had been exhausted, 8,000 persons having been given food in one day upon the arrival of the American forces, our men supplied other unfortunate, needy Nicaraguans from their own haversacks.

I wish to congratulate the officers and men of the United States Navy and Marine Corps who took part in reestablishing order in Nicaragua upon their splendid conduct, and to record with sorrow the death of seven American Marines and Bluejackets. Since the reestablishment of peace and order, elections have been held amid conditions of quiet and tranquillity. Nearly all the American Marines have now been withdrawn. The country should soon be on the road to recovery. The only apparent danger now threatening Nicaragua arises from the shortage of funds. Although American bankers have already rendered assistance, they may naturally be loath to advance a loan adequate to set the country upon its feet without the support of some such convention as that of June 1911, upon which the Senate has not yet acted. . . .

It is not possible to make to the Congress a communication upon the present foreign relations of the United States so detailed as to convey an adequate impression of the enormous increase in the importance and activities of those relations. If this government is really to preserve to the American people that free opportunity in foreign markets which will soon be indispensable to our prosperity, even greater efforts must be made. Otherwise the American merchant, manufacturer, and exporter will find many a field in which American trade should logically predominate preempted through the more energetic efforts of other governments and other commercial nations.

There are many ways in which, through hearty cooperation, the legislative and executive branches of this government can do much. The absolute essential is the spirit of united effort and singleness of purpose. I will allude only to a very few specific examples of action which ought then to result.

America cannot take its proper place in the most important fields for its commercial activity and enterprise unless we have a Merchant Marine. American commerce and enterprise cannot be effectively fostered in those fields unless we have good American banks in the countries referred to. We need American newspapers in those countries and proper means for public information about them.

We need to assume the permanency of a trained foreign service. We need legislation enabling the members of the foreign service to be systematically brought in direct contact with the industrial, manufacturing, and exporting interests of this country in order that American businessmen may enter the foreign field with a clear perception of the exact conditions to be dealt with and the officers themselves may prosecute their work with a clear idea of what American industrial and manufacturing interests require.

Congress should fully realize the conditions which obtain in the world as we find ourselves at the threshold of our middle age as a nation. We have emerged full grown as a peer in the great concourse of nations. We have passed through various formative periods. We have been self-centered in the struggle to develop our domestic resources and deal with our domestic questions. The nation is now too mature to continue in its foreign relations those temporary expedients natural to a people to whom domestic affairs are the sole concern.

In the past, our diplomacy has often consisted, in normal times, in a mere assertion of the right to international existence. We are now in a larger relation with broader rights of our own and obligations to others than ourselves. A number of great guiding principles were laid down early in the history of this government. The recent task of our diplomacy has been to adjust those principles to the conditions of today, to develop their corollaries, to find practical applications of the old principles expanded to meet new situations. Thus are being evolved bases upon which can rest the superstructure of policies which must grow with the destined progress of this nation.

The successful conduct of our foreign relations demands a broad and a modern view. We cannot meet new questions nor build for the future if we confine ourselves to outworn dogmas of the past and to the perspective appropriate at our emergence from colonial times and conditions. The opening of the Panama Canal will mark a new era in our international life and create new and worldwide conditions which, with their vast correlations and consequences, will obtain for hundreds of years to come. We must not wait for events to overtake us unawares. With continuity of purpose we must deal with the problems of our external relations by a diplomacy modern, resourceful, magnanimous, and fittingly expressive of the high ideals of a great nation.

There can be no fifty-fifty Americanism in this country. There is room here for only 100 percent Americanism, only for those who are American and nothing else.

THEODORE ROOSEVELT

The 100 per cent American is 99 per cent an idiot.

GEORGE BERNARD SHAW

1912 - 1913

77.

The Armory Show

The International Exhibition of Modern Art of 1913 brought French Postimpressionist and Cubist painting to America for the first time. Held at the 69th Regiment Armory in New York City, the show was promoted by an avant-garde group known as The Eight. The exhibition was a shock to traditional American painters as well as to the public at large. According to muralist Kenyon Cox, Cézanne (whose work had not been known in America before) was "absolutely without talent," and Van Gogh was "too unskilled to give quality to an evenly laid coat of pigment." The reaction of Theodore Roosevelt, who preferred the Navaho rug in his bathroom to most of the paintings in the exhibit, was typical of that of most laymen. The following selection includes, besides Roosevelt's review, part of a letter of December 12, 1912, from Walt Kuhn, one of the sponsors, to publicist Walter Pach, and the preface to the catalogue of the exhibition written by Frederick James Gregg.

Source: *American Art 1700-1960*, John W. McCoubrey, ed., pp. 188-191, © 1965 by permission of Prentice-Hall, Inc., Englewood Cliffs, N.J. *Outlook*, March 29, 1913: "A Layman's View of an Art Exhibition."

I.

WALT KUHN: Letter to Walter Pach

I SHOULD HAVE WRITTEN you before this, but Davies and myself have been on the jump every minute since we landed. Today I gave the papers the list of European stuff which we know of definitely. It will be like a bombshell, the first news since our arrival.

You have no idea how eager everybody is about this thing and what a tremendous success it's going to be. Everybody is electrified when we quote the names, etc. The outlook is great, and, after having figured up the likely income, we stand to come out ahead of the game as far as money goes. The articles appearing from now on will increase the desire to help by the moneyed "classes." We owe you a tremendous lot for your indispensable help and advice, but you know that we are all in the same boat for this great chance to make the American think. I feel as though I had crowded an entire art education into these few weeks. Chicago has officially asked for the show, and of course we accepted.

I am very anxious to get a "thumbnail" biography of *all* the important men. Will you see what you can get for me, every little bit helps, anything of interest? The papers are also interested in portrait photos of the men themselves. Everything you can send me in this line will be of enormous help in securing good press notices. I have planned a press campaign to run from now right through the show, and then some — a snapshot of the Duchamp-Villon brothers in their garden, for instance, will help me get a special article on them. I await your story on them, also Redon. We are going to feature Redon big (BIG!). You see the fact that he is so little known will mean a still bigger success in publicity.

John Quinn, our lawyer and biggest booster, is strong for plenty of publicity. He says the New Yorkers are worse than rubes, and must be told. All this is not to my personal taste; I'd rather stay home and work hard at my pictures, shoving in some of the things I have learned; but we are all in deep water now and have got to paddle — don't disappoint me on this — our show must be talked about all over the U.S. before the doors open. . . .

We have a great opportunity in this show, and must try to make it truly wonderful and get all the people there, which owing to the extremely short duration of the show is very hard and can only be done through the press. So don't ignore my plea for minor information. It may be undignified but it brings the desired result. We want this old show of ours to mark the starting point of the new spirit in art, at least as far as America is concerned.

I feel that it will show its effect even further and make the big wheel turn over both hemispheres.

II.

Frederick Gregg: Preface to the Catalogue for the International Exhibition of Modern Art

Mr. Arthur B. Davies, president of the Association of American Painters and Sculptors, gave out the following statement on the last day of December 1912:

On behalf of the Executive Committee, I desire to explain the general attitude of the Association and especially in regard to the International Exhibition to be held in this city in February and March.

This is not an institution but an association. It is composed of persons of varying tastes and predilections, who are agreed on one thing, that the time has arrived for giving the public here the opportunity to see for themselves the results of new influences at work in other countries in an art way.

In getting together the works of the European Moderns, the society has embarked on no propaganda. It proposes to enter on no controversy with any institution. Its sole object is to put the paintings, sculptures, and so on on exhibition so that the intelligent may judge for themselves, by themselves.

Of course, controversies will arise, just as they have arisen under similar circumstances in France, Italy, Germany, and England. But they will not be the result of any stand taken by this Association as such; on the other hand, we are perfectly willing to assume full responsibility for providing the opportunity to those who may take one side or the other.

Any individual expression of opinion contrary to the above is at variance with the official resolutions of this Association.

The wide publicity given to the above in the public press all over the country showed to what an extent it was accepted as a definite and precise expression of the policy and the aims of the Association in its relation to the art of Europe and to the American public. That policy and those aims remain unchanged.

Anything that can be said further must be but an amplification of the statement. The foreign paintings and sculptures here shown are regarded by the committee of the Association as expressive of the forces which have been at work abroad of late, forces which cannot be ignored because they have had results.

The American artists exhibiting here consider the exhibition as of equal importance for themselves as for the lay public. The less they find their work showing signs of the developments indicated in the Europeans, the more reason they will have to consider whether or not painters and sculptors here have fallen behind through escaping the incidence through distance and for other reasons of the forces that have manifested themselves on the other side of the Atlantic.

Art is a sign of life. There can be no life without change, as there can be no development without change. To be afraid of what is different or unfamiliar is to be afraid of life. And to be afraid of life is to be afraid of truth, and to be a champion of superstition. This exhibition is an indication that the Association of American Painters and Sculptors is against cowardice even when it takes the form of amiable self-satisfaction.

III.

THEODORE ROOSEVELT: Modern Art

THE RECENT International Exhibition of Modern Art in New York was really noteworthy. Messrs. Davies, Kuhn, Gregg, and their fellow members of the Association of American Painters and Sculptors have done a work of very real value in securing such an exhibition of the works of both foreign and native painters and sculptors. Primarily their purpose was to give the public a chance to see what has recently been going on abroad. No similar collection of the works of European "Moderns" has ever been exhibited in this country. The exhibitors are quite right as to the need of showing to our people in this manner the art forces which of late have been at work in Europe, forces which cannot be ignored.

This does not mean that I in the least accept the view that these men take of the European extremists whose pictures are here exhibited. It is true, as the champions of these extremists say, that there can be no life without change, no development without change, and that to be afraid of what is different or unfamiliar is to be afraid of life. It is no less true, however, that change may mean death and not life, and retrogression instead of development.

Probably we err in treating most of these pictures seriously. It is likely that many of them represent in the painters the astute appreciation of the power to make folly lucrative which the late P. T. Barnum showed with his faked mermaid. There are thousands of people who will pay small sums to look at a faked mermaid; and now and then one of this kind with enough money will buy a Cubist picture, or a picture of a misshapen nude woman, repellent from every standpoint.

In some ways it is the work of the American painters and sculptors which is of most interest in this collection, and a glance at this work must convince anyone of the real good that is coming out of the new movements, fantastic though many of the developments of these new movements are. There was one note entirely absent from the exhibition and that was the note of the commonplace. There was not a touch of simpering, self-satisfied conventionality anywhere in the exhibition. Any sculptor or painter who had in him something to express and the power of expressing it found the field open to him. He did not have to be afraid because his work was not along ordinary lines. There was no stunting or dwarfing, no requirement that a man whose gift lay in new directions should measure upon or down to stereotyped and fossilized standards.

For all this there can be only hearty praise. But this does not in the least mean that the extremists whose paintings and pictures were represented are entitled to any praise, save, perhaps, that they have helped to break fetters. Probably in any reform movement, any progressive movement, in any field of life, the penalty for avoiding the commonplace is a liability to extravagance. It is vitally necessary to move forward and to shake off the dead hand, often the fossilized dead hand of the reactionaries; and yet we have to face the fact that there is apt to be a lunatic fringe among the votaries of any forward movement.

In this recent art exhibition the lunatic fringe was fully in evidence, especially in the rooms devoted to the Cubists and the Futurists, or Near-Impressionists. I am not entirely certain which of the two latter terms should be used in connection with some of the various pictures and representations of plastic art — and, frankly, it is not of the least consequence. The Cubists are entitled to the serious attention of all who find enjoyment in the colored puzzle pictures of the Sunday newspapers.

Of course there is no reason for choosing the cube as a symbol, except that it is probably less fitted than any other mathematical expression for any but the most formal decorative art. There is no reason why people should not call themselves Cubists, or Octagonists, Parallelopipedonists, or Knights of the Isosceles Triangle, or Brothers of the Cosine, if they so desire; as expressing anything serious and permanent, one term is as fatuous as another.

Take the picture which for some reason is called "A Naked Man Going Downstairs." There is in my bathroom a really good Navaho rug which, on any proper interpretation of the Cubist theory, is a far more satisfactory and decorative picture. Now if, for some inscrutable reason, it suited somebody to call this rug a picture of, say, "A Well-dressed Man Going Up a Ladder," the name would fit the facts just about as well as in the case of the Cubist picture of the "Naked Man Going Downstairs." From the standpoint of terminology each name would have whatever merit inheres in a rather cheap straining aftereffect; and from the standpoint of decorative value, of sincerity, and of artistic merit, the Navaho rug is infinitely ahead of the picture. . . .

Very little of the work of the extremists among the European "Moderns" seems to be good in and for itself; nevertheless it has certainly helped any number of American artists to do work that is original and serious; and this not only in painting but in sculpture. I wish the exhibition had contained some of the work of the late Marcius Symonds; very few people knew or cared for it while he lived; but not since Turner has there been another man on whose canvas glowed so much of that unearthly "light that never was on land or sea." But the exhibition contained so much of extraordinary merit that it is ungrateful even to mention an omission. To name the pictures one would like to possess — and the bronzes and tanagras and plasters — would mean to make a catalogue of indefinite length.

One of the most striking pictures was the "Terminal Yards" — the seeing eye was there, and the cunning hand. I should like to mention all the pictures of the president of the Association, Arthur B. Davies. As first-class decorative work of an entirely new type, the very unexpected pictures of Sheriff Bob Chandler have a merit all their own. The "Arizona Desert," the "Canadian Night," the group of girls on the roof of a New York tenement house, the studies in the Bronx Zoo, the "Heracles," the studies for the Utah monument, the little group called "Gossip," which has something of the quality of the famous Fifteenth Idyl of Theocritus, the "Pelf," with its grim suggestiveness — these, and a hundred others, are worthy of study, each of them; I am naming at random those which at the moment I happen to recall.

I am not speaking of the acknowledged masters, of Whistler, Puvis de Chavannes, Monet; nor of John's children; nor of Cézanne's old woman with a rosary; nor of Redon's marvelous color pieces — a worthy critic should speak of these. All I am trying to do is to point out why a layman is grateful to those who arranged this exhibition.

1913

78.

Lewis Einstein: America and Anglo-German Rivalry

American foreign policy under Roosevelt and Taft had been largely geared to promoting American interests in the Caribbean, in Latin America, and in Asia. Little attention had been paid to Europe. Diplomat Lewis Einstein, in an article published in 1913, pointed out the threat to America presented by Anglo-German rivalry, a struggle that he felt would lead to war. He challenged the prevalent belief that the United States was invulnerable to attack because of its geographical situation and that it could not be harmed by any European power. Portions of his article, which carefully analyzed the Anglo-German disagreement, appear below.

Source: *National Review* (London), January 1913.

PARADOXICAL AS IT MAY SEEM, the grave danger of the present relations between Great Britain and Germany lies in the fact that there is no real difficulty between the two powers. Where a concrete obstacle stands in the way, by compromise and mutual goodwill it may be removed. In recent years, the Anglo-French and Anglo-Russian negotiations, by a judicious policy of give-and-take, smoothed out through diplomatic means the colonial rivalry of a century. But between Germany and England similar adjustment is impossible. Their antagonism presents nothing concrete save rival ambition. . . .

Future war or peace is today in the hands of the English and German people far more than in that of their governments. The decision rests with them not to goad the latter into assuming positions or advancing pretensions from which honorable retreat will have become impossible.

Whatever be the future of this situation a farsighted statesmanship compels the United States, as it does every other nation, to take cognizance of the possibility of a conflict breaking out in the near future between Great Britain and Germany, and to consider in what manner its interests would be affected. It is an easy remedy to repeat the old adage about American proverbial noninterference in European affairs. With all respect toward a policy which in the past has been thoroughly sound, it cannot be said in this instance to offer a complete panacea. A struggle between the two nations, even though it did not set ablaze the rest of Europe, cannot leave America indifferent. In too many regions of the world would its interests be affected by such reality.

It would withal be absurd to deduce from this that the United States would be dragged into a war against all inclination. The alternative of arms is no necessary consequence of diplomatic interest, and in such a conflict direct participation would, with proper precautions, be most unlikely. This should not, however, excuse any neglect on the part of Americans to consider the various political, strategic, and economic points of view in different regions of the world, where such struggle would react upon them, or how the balance of power, which it should be the policy of the United States to preserve in Europe, would be affected by the contest.

An indication of its wide-reaching nature, independent of the actual field of hostilities, would, for instance, be presented in the Far East, where the even temporary withdrawal of European influence would leave America face to face with a commensurately more powerful Japan. To say nothing of the Philippines the situation thus created depends on the degree of stability and strength attained by China. It is not difficult, however, to conceive of circumstances where to ensure respect for the often-pledged integrity of that state would lead the United States toward a course of action which it would be obliged to adopt single-handed, and without the benefit of such diplomatic support as in the past it has received from friendly powers.

Omitting from consideration the extent to which the almost inevitable conflagration would affect the world in a conflict between Great Britain and Germany, three general possibilities are open: (1) the victory of the former; (2) the reverse; (3) a war of indefinite result.

So far as America is concerned, the first alternative would be the least likely to materially alter the existing status. England might conceivably recover a pecuniary indemnity and deal a deathblow to German overseas commerce. But the German colonies are not such as to sensibly attract a conqueror, nor would a change in their title affect other nations in any way. While the predominant position of Germany upon the European continent would be shattered, the balance of power would hardly be affected, even though the disposition of its weight were altered. The insular position of Great Britain debars her from continental ambitions, and any attempt to assert herself in such manner would both run counter to all her traditions and be stoutly resisted by former allied states.

It is fortunate that in modern times no nation has succeeded in being paramount on both land and sea. Great Britain has hitherto refrained from unduly developing her military strength and there is no reason to anticipate that flushed by victory she would adopt a different course. Her naval superiority, which is a matter of life and death, menaces no one, though it bars the way to Germany, already supreme on land. But for America it represents an essential element in the maintenance and stability of the European balance of power.

If the terms of peace after such a war were to be dictated in London, the situation as it affected the United States would be radically reversed. While defeat for Germany might prove disastrous to the dynasty, for Great Britain it would be fatal to the Empire, whose disintegration would almost inevitably ensue. It is apparent that the fate of Canada and the British possessions in America immediately concern the republic. Of Canadian loyalty to the Empire there is here no question. It is certain that like the other self-governing British colonies, she would, to the best of her ability, support the mother country. But if the fortune of war prove adverse, there is no reason to suppose that Canada would long continue under the control, however nominal, of a parent state deprived of prestige and authority and ruined by an unsuccessful war. . . .

Without going to the length of such extreme conclusions, a third and more likely possibility would be that of a contest being drawn out between the two countries wherein neither could obtain decisive advantage. In spite of the paper proof that a lengthy war presents today an economic impossibility, there is no practical evidence to substantiate this theory, and there are distinguished economists who believe that the modern system of credit is peculiarly adopted to facilitate the prolongation of war. When poor countries, like Japan and Russia, have been able to maintain in the field for a considerable duration armies of almost unprecedented size, there is no reason to suppose that the pinch of poverty alone would materially hasten the conclusion of a contest between England and Germany.

The financial aspect of this is also likely to concern America. If the struggle should be protracted, extensive borrowing will have to be undertaken, and New York is more and more becoming one of the money markets of the world. It is probable that it will be called upon, possibly by both sides, to furnish pecuniary assistance, even though the obligations of strict neutrality are somewhat questionable on this point.

The extended duration of the war may be expected from the policy Germany would presumably adopt in attempting to tire out the vigilance of a British blockading fleet by long continued inaction, while perhaps striking isolated blows in distant waters. The recent construction in Germany of large battle cruisers capable of holding the seas points to the inference that, in the event of war, hostilities would not remain confined to the vicinity of home ports. It would not be impossible if, as in the eighteenth century, sea fights might again take place in American waters. The capture of one of the Lesser Antilles from the English or French might offer to the Germans both a convenient haven and a pledge for subsequent negotiations.

The attitude of the United States in this event would be one of no little difficulty. Logically, a policy of strict neutrality should cause it to remain, if not indifferent, at least passive, but it is questionable if any American government could long tolerate the embarrassment caused by the extended continuance of hostilities in near waters, even though it led to no more regrettable nor permanent result.

If this remains a remote though possible contingency, it is otherwise with the effect of a great struggle upon economic interests. As all industry in the belligerent nations would be brought to a virtual standstill, it is likely that while American manufactured exports in Europe suffered, there would be a greatly increased demand for foodstuffs as well as for whatever might be of utility in the conduct of war. Such commercial losses as would be experienced in Europe could be more than counterbalanced by the opportunity presented elsewhere to acquire new markets and supplant former rivals. This would give an unwonted impetus to trade. American commerce should find before it in Latin America, South Africa, Australia, and the Far East new outlets and new opportunities as the consequence of such a struggle.

Without a Merchant Marine under the American flag, no adequate benefit would be derived from this situation. The export of American products would be rendered increasingly difficult by the few remaining neutral bottoms with the consequent increase in freight rates. The creation of an American Merchant Navy thus becomes a primary necessity whether affected by postal subventions, direct subsidies, or the admission of foreign-built ships. The sad anomaly of the present position in this respect can hardly be overstated, and until steps are taken to remedy the deficiency of existing navigation laws, all efforts to win new markets will be severely handicapped.

Pride is often the forerunner of real interest, and while it is only the former that suffers today by the absence of the American flag on the high seas, a European war, with its wide ramifications and consequences, would soon awaken the United States to realizing the shortcomings of its present policy. Unless remedy be found for existing conditions, it is not difficult to picture American factories and workmen reduced to idleness because a foreign war had brought about a virtual cessation of ocean transport.

Even more important than the creation of an American Merchant Marine is that, at a time of uncertainty like the present, with the future still befogged, no efforts be spared to maintain its relative naval strength. Already the United States has fallen from the second place which, for a decade, it had occupied, and without greater exertion is likely to sink still further in the scale. The decision of Congress to curtail the program of naval construction could not have been less auspiciously chosen in its moment. To desist from a normal development, which hardly aims to do more than replace timeworn unities when all the nations of the world, great and small, are arming, is to court a disaster and to lay the country open to the consequences of such imprudence. The apostles of any one-sided disarmament at a time like the present are blindly working to expose their land to a disgraceful war or a yet more disgraceful humiliation.

In the event of a European conflagration the American fleet, even if maintained at its present relative strength, might find difficulty in accomplishing its double task of preserving the status quo in the Far East and enforcing the neutrality of the Caribbean, where the presence of hostilities would certainly embarrass and possibly endanger American interests. The preservation of the *Pax Americana* as a corollary to the Monroe Doctrine should be its goal at all times. The United States has everything to gain by the peaceful and orderly evolution of existing conditions on the Western Hemisphere and nothing by sudden or violent changes, even where its interests do not appear to be immediately affected. Hence any attempt to make of American waters the scene of war would be extremely distasteful to its policy.

The question of neutrality of the Caribbean might even be broached by diplomatic channels in time of peace. To Great Britain and France it would in all likelihood be welcome, as ridding them of solicitude in respect to islands difficult of defense and where their sole ambition is to maintain but not to extend. Nor could Germany, possessing no territorial interests in such waters, avow pretensions which would place her in opposition to this view. An international agreement having this in sight would thus contribute toward guaranteeing a stability of present possession by keeping the peace in the event of a European conflict and removing the likelihood of possible future changes of title embarrassing to the strategic and political position the United States occupy there. The alternative of a German victory, with the acquisition of a base of operations or even of territorial advantages, close to Central America, where Germans already possess great interests, and commanding the approaches to Panama, could not leave the republic indifferent to the future of such prospect.

An Anglo-German conflict would thus affect the United States at various points and in various ways. There is hardly a branch of American national activity, governmental or economic, which would not feel its consequences in varying degree or be concerned by its outcome. While the American attitude in such contest would in the beginning be one of strict neutrality, which would be maintained as long as possible, this does not mean that a farsighted policy might not under certain contingencies impose a different course of action. However considerable the responsibility incurred, however great the bait offered, it would hardly be wise statesmanship to remain passive if England should by any series of disasters be crushed.

Even though the immediate consequence would be to throw Canada and the British Antilles into the lap of the United States, it would leave the latter confronted by an empire supreme on land and sea, and would force it to pursue a preparation of armaments which for its own preservation could not be inferior to what it might be called upon to face.

Unperceived by many Americans, the European balance of power is a political necessity which can alone sanction on the Western Hemisphere the continuance of an economic development unhandicapped by the burden of excessive armaments. At no time, even unknown to the United States, were European politics a matter of indifference to its actual interests. But if hitherto it was impotent to alter their march, a fortunate destiny preserved the existing balance.

Seeking, as little as in the past, any selfish benefit in the Old World, even though it were possible, America has today a distinct and legitimate duty in the family of great nations in contributing to preserve those elements which compose the balance of power, and to which it can only be blind at a later cost. The disappearance or diminution of any one state in Europe would be a calamity, varying with its degree. But while the importance of such extinction might not in most instances be sufficiently close to warrant or provoke active intervention, this would not be true with Great Britain. The disintegration of the British Empire would be a defeat for America by the erection of a power supreme on land and sea. . . .

To consider the possible contingency of such intervention by the United States as tantamount to an alliance with Great Britain would be untrue. Where there is no treaty there is no alliance. America does not keep England from war nor push her toward a conflict. In the event of hostilities the assertion of its neutrality would at once be made and strictly lived up to. If Germa-ny and England choose to indulge in the luxury of war, such is their right. However much one may lament the loss of life, it is no affair of the United States, even though England were defeated, so long as the general balance is preserved. But if ever decisive results are about to be registered of a nature calculated to upset what has for centuries been the recognized political fabric of Europe, America can remain indifferent thereto only at her own eventual cost. If it then neglects to observe that the interests of the nations crushed are likewise its own, America will be guilty of political blindness which it will later rue.

To guard against this danger the diplomatic role of the United States in Europe should be far more active than in the past. Properly understood and carried out by skillful agents, it would be one which instead of being resented should entitle it to the gratitude of all lovers of peace, since it would be apparent that without selfish designs of its own it aimed to preserve the rights of all.

It is mistaking the nature of diplomacy to think that this would involve America in entanglements wherein it had no concern. But it is likewise mistaking its scope for national utility to accord by an attitude of indifferent passivity a free field to the forceful ambition of any single state. Great Britain, by upholding the European balance of power, has contributed toward American development. If misfortune in arms await her, it would be as politically unwise as it would be ungenerous to allow her to suffer unduly. A disastrous defeat inflicted by an opponent unwilling to use moderation in his victory should invite on the part of America a friendly mediation which in the last extremity might have to be converted into more effective measures. Hence the advisability for the United States of preserving its strength in such a way as ever to make its counsel welcome and its action unnecessary.

The Board of Directors of the Hagerstown, Maryland, Bank in 1908

SCENES OF DIVERSITY

America before World War I was more than the mass of unrest and confusion that produced Progressivism. There was at the same time a new sort of optimism, stemming as did Progressivism from a basic faith in American progress and finding its affirmation in America's new political and economic power. In less than half a century the country had grown from a war-torn agricultural nation to a leading manufacturer and new, if somewhat overzealous, world power. The imperialism of the period was motivated by forces rather similar to those behind Progressivism, and the rhetoric of the two movements reflected similar senti-ments — orderly progress, reform, justice through law rather than through violence. Roosevelt illustrated the closeness of Progressivism and the new feeling of world power in his role as arbitrator, both at home, between labor and capital, and abroad, particularly between European and American nations. It is often forgotten that, like any other time, there was behind the large movements of the day a relatively quiet pattern of life. Novelty was adopted rapidly into routine; one day's toy was the next day's tool. While the period is remembered primarily for its differences, it consisted in itself largely of the ordinary.

(Above) Coaching in New York in the early 1900s

(Right) Members of the Ladies Four-in-Hand and Coaching Society, New York, 1906; (below) Greek pageant staged at the Maxine Elliott Theatre for the benefit of the New York Trade School for Girls, 1909

(Above) Little girls attending an outing at the Georgian Court Polo Grounds in Lakewood, N.J.; (below) view of the audience at an opera

(Above) Shops in a Jewish section of New York; photograph by the Tenement Housing Commission taken 1905-1910; (below) New York tenement of this period

(Above) Policeman on the beat in an Italian neighborhood in New York, 1911; (below left) Santa Claus collecting for charity at Christmas in the early 1900s; (below right) celebrating the Feast of St. Rocco in an Italian neighborhood; photo by Jacob Riis

Photos by Lewis Hine of working conditions in parts of the country: (Top) Union shop in the Tierra del Lago Cigar Co. of Tampa, Fla., 1909; (right) family tailoring business in New York. The children attend school afternoons and Saturdays. (Bottom) Workers in the mills of Amoskeag Manufacturing Co., 1909

OPPOSITE PAGE: (Top) Unloading bananas in Mobile, Ala., 1906; (center) type of farming done by early settlers on the plains in western Texas, 1900-15; (bottom) potato digging on a truck farm in Long Island, 1910

(Above) Priest in charge of the Mission of San Juan Capistrano, photographed in the Inner Court in 1900; (below) baptism of United Brethren in Left Hand Creek, Ni Wot, Colo., 1907

(Top) A nester family on the Three Block Ranch near Richardson, New Mexico, 1905-1910; (center) family in Fries, Virginia, 1911. Father works some and the two boys on the right have been in the cotton mill for four years. Photo by Hine. (Left) Chinese grocery in San Francisco's Chinatown in 1906

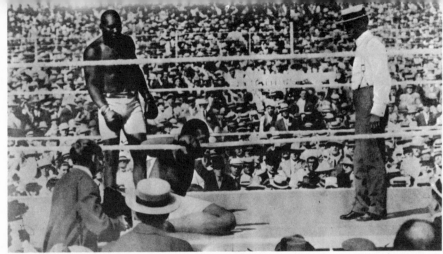

Jack Johnson, soon to be heavyweight champion, knocks out Jim Flynn in a 1907 bout

(Above left) Dorando and Hayes at the starting line for a race in 1908; (above right) Jack Johnson in 1915; (below) International Bowling Tournament in Madison Square Garden in 1909

(Above) Matthewson pitching in the 1913 World Series; (left) Cy Young; (below) Grover Cleveland Alexander; (bottom) Ty Cobb (right) and Hans Wagner (middle)

(Top) Manual training class in 1908; (left) saluting the flag in school in 1908; (bottom) children lined up at the swing during recess

OPPOSITE PAGE: (Top) Cast in a production of "Hamlet" at Washington and Lee, about 1900; (center) crowning the May Queen in May Day festivities in Forest Glen, Md., 1907; (bottom) Maypoles in Central Park, New York, in 1912

(Top) Amateur football game on the Boston Common, 1909, photo by Hine; (left) boy playing Diablo during a May Day festival in the early 1900s; (right) boy dressed as "Little Lord Fauntleroy" in 1908; (bottom) hitching a ride on a trolley car in Boston, 1909; Hine photo

79.

Charles Nagel: Against a Literacy Test for Immigrants

From the 1880s on, there was a persistent effort to reduce the number of immigrants entering the United States. Supported by the American Federation of Labor as well as by Progressives such as Theodore Roosevelt, legislators tried to pass restrictive measures to prevent the entry of foreigners, especially from southern and eastern Europe. In 1896 Congress passed a literacy test for immigrants that was vetoed by outgoing President Cleveland. On February 14, 1913, outgoing President Taft vetoed a similar bill. His veto was based largely upon the views of his secretary of commerce, Charles Nagel, part of whose letter to Taft of February 12 appears below. A literacy test was eventually passed in 1917 over the veto of President Wilson.

Source: Richardson, Supplement, pp. 8228-8230.

On the 4th instant, Mr. Hilles, by your direction, sent me Senate Bill 3175, "An act to regulate the immigration of aliens to and the residence of aliens in the United States," with the request that I inform you at my earliest convenience if I know of any objection to its approval. I now return the bill with my comments. . . .

With respect to the literacy test I feel compelled to state . . . in my opinion, this is a provision of controlling importance, not only because of the immediate effect which it may have upon immigration, and the embarrassment and cost it may impose upon the service, but because it involves a principle of far-reaching consequence with respect to which your attitude will be regarded with profound interest.

The provision as it now appears will require careful reading. In some measure the group system is adopted — that is, one qualified immigrant may bring in certain members of his family — but the effect seems to be that a qualified alien may bring in members of his family who may themselves be disqualified; whereas a disqualified member would exclude all dependent members of his family no matter how well qualified they might otherwise be. In other words, a father who can read a dialect might bring in an entire family of absolutely illiterate people, barring his sons over sixteen years of age, whereas a father who can not read a dialect would bring about the exclusion of his entire family, although every one of them can read and write.

Furthermore, the distinction in favor of the female members of the family as against the male members does not seem to me to rest upon sound reason. Sentimentally, of course, it appeals, but industrially considered it does not appear to me that the distinction is sound. Furthermore, there is no provision for the admission of aliens who have been domiciled here and who have simply gone abroad for a visit. The test would absolutely exclude them upon return.

In the administration of this law, very considerable embarrassment will be experienced. This at least is the judgment of members of the immigration force upon whose recommendations I rely. Delay will necessarily ensue at all ports, but on the borders of Canada and Mexico that delay will almost necessarily result in great friction and constant complaint. Furthermore, the force will have to be very considerably increased, and the appropriation will probably be in excess of present sums expended by as much as a million dollars.

The force of interpreters will have to be largely increased and, practically speaking, the bureau will have to be in a position to have an interpreter for any kind of language or dialect of the world at any port at any time. Finally, the interpreters will necessarily be foreigners, and with respect to only a very few of the languages or dialects will it be possible for the officials in charge to exercise anything like supervision.

I am of the opinion that this provision cannot be defended upon its merits. It was originally urged as a selective test. For some time, recommendations in its support upon that ground have been brought to our attention. The matter has been considered from that point of view, and I became completely satisfied that upon that ground the test could not be sustained. The older argument is now abandoned, and in the later conferences, at least, the ground is taken that the provision is to be defended as a practical measure to exclude a large proportion of undesirable immigrants from certain countries. The measure proposes to reach its results by indirection and is defended purely upon the ground of practical policy, the final purpose being to reduce the quantity of cheap labor in this country.

I cannot accept this argument. No doubt the law would exclude a considerable percentage of immigration from southern Italy, among the Poles, the Mexicans, and the Greeks. This exclusion would embrace probably in large part undesirable but also a great many desirable people, and the embarrassment, expense, and distress to those who seek to enter would be out of all proportion to any good that can possibly be promised for this measure.

My observation leads me to the conclusion that so far as the merits of the individual immigrant are concerned the test is altogether overestimated. The people who come from the countries named are frequently illiterate because opportunities have been denied them. The oppression with which these people have to contend in modern times is not religious, but it consists of a denial of the opportunity to acquire reading and writing. Frequently the attempt to learn to read and write the language of the particular people is discouraged by the government, and these immigrants in coming to our shores are really striving to free themselves from the conditions under which they have been compelled to live.

So far as the industrial conditions are concerned, I think the question has been superficially considered. We need labor in this country, and the natives are unwilling to do the work which the aliens come over to do. It is perfectly true that in a few cities and localities there are congested conditions. It is equally true that in very much larger areas we are practically without help. In my judgment, no sufficiently earnest and intelligent effort has been made to bring our wants and our supply together, and so far the same forces that give the chief support to this provision of the new bill have stubbornly resisted any effort looking to an intelligent distribution of new immigration to meet the needs of our vast country. In my judgment, no such drastic measure based upon a ground which is untrue and urged for a reason which we are unwilling to assert should be adopted until we have at least exhausted the possibilities of a rational distribution of these new forces.

Furthermore, there is a misapprehension as to the character of the people who come over here to remain. It is true that in certain localities newly arrived aliens live under deplorable conditions. Just as much may be said of certain localities that have been in-habited for a hundred years by natives of this country. These are not the general con-ditions, but they are the exceptions.

It is true that a very considerable portion of immigrants do not come to remain, but return after they have acquired some means, or because they find themselves unable to cope with the conditions of a new and ag-gressive country. Those who return for the latter reason relieve us of their own volition of a burden. Those who return after they have acquired some means certainly must be admitted to have left with us a consider-ation for the advantage which they have en-joyed. A careful examination of the charac-ter of the people who come to stay and of the employment in which a large part of the new immigration is engaged will, in my judgment, dispel the apprehension which many of our people entertain.

The census will disclose that with rapid strides the foreign-born citizen is acquiring the farmlands of this country. Even if the foreign-born alone is considered, the per-centage of his ownership is assuming a pro-portion that ought to attract the attention of the native citizens. If the second genera-tion is included, it is safe to say that in the Middle West and West a majority of the farms are today owned by foreign-born people or they are descendants of the first generation. This does not embrace only the Germans and the Scandinavians but is true, in large measure, for illustration, of the Bohemians and the Poles. It is true in sur-prising measure of the Italians; not only of the northern Italians but of the southern.

Again, an examination of the aliens who come to stay is of great significance. During the last fiscal year, 838,172 aliens came to our shores, although the net immigration of

the year was only a trifle above 400,000. But, while we received of skilled labor 127,016, and only 35,898 returned; we re-ceived servants, 116,529, and only 13,449 returned; we received farm laborers, 184,154, and only 3,978 returned, it ap-pears that laborers came in the number of 135,726, while 209,279 returned. These fig-ures ought to demonstrate that we get sub-stantially what we most need and what we cannot ourselves supply, and that we get rid of what we least need and what seems to furnish, in the minds of many, the chief jus-tification for the bill now under discussion.

The census returns show conclusively that the importance of illiteracy among aliens is overestimated and that these people are prompt after their arrival to avail of the op-portunities which this country affords. While, according to the reports of the Bu-reau of Immigration, about 25 percent of the incoming aliens are illiterate, the census shows that among the foreign-born people of such states as New York and Massachu-setts, where most of the congestion com-plained of has taken place, the proportion of illiteracy represents only about 13 per-cent.

I am persuaded that this provision of the bill is in principle of very great conse-quence, and that it is based upon a fallacy in undertaking to apply a test which is not calculated to reach the truth and to find re-lief from a danger which really does not ex-ist. This provision of the bill is new, and it is radical. It goes to the heart of the mea-sure. It does not permit of compromise, and, much as I regret it, because the other provisions of the measure are in most re-spects excellent and in no respect really ob-jectionable, I am forced to advise that you do not approve this bill.

To hell with Jews, Jesuits, and steamships.
    PRESCOTT HALL, when President Taft vetoed a bill requiring
    literacy for immigrants, 1911

80.

The Concentration of Economic Power

"The great monopoly in this country," Woodrow Wilson commented in 1911, "is the money monopoly." Congress shared Wilson's concern and in February 1912 appointed a subcommittee of the Banking and Currency Committee, chaired by Democrat Arsène P. Pujo, to investigate the "money trusts." The Pujo Committee's report shocked the public when it revealed the enormous concentration of wealth in the hands of a few — most notably J. P. Morgan (who testified before the Committee) and John D. Rockefeller. Passages from the report, which was made public on February 28, 1913, are reprinted below. The findings were among those that prompted the new Wilson administration to establish the Federal Reserve System and to reinforce the existing antitrust laws by means of the Clayton Act.

Source: 62 Congress, 3 Session, House Report No. 1593, pp. 55-103.

SECTION 1.

Two Kinds of Concentration

It is important at the outset to distinguish between concentration of the *volume of money* in the three central reserve cities of the national banking system — New York, Chicago, and St. Louis — and concentration of *control* of this volume of money and consequently of credit into fewer and fewer hands. They are very different things. An increasing proportion of the banking resources of the country might be concentrating at a given point at the same time that *control* of such resources at that point was spreading out in a wider circle.

Concentration of *control* of money, and consequently of credit, more particularly in the city of New York, is the subject of this inquiry. With concentration of the *volume* of money at certain points, sometimes attributed, so far as it is unnatural, to the provision of the national banking act permitting banks in the forty-seven other reserve cities to deposit with those in the three central reserve cities half of their reserves, we are not here directly concerned.

Whether under a different currency system the resources in our banks would be greater or less is comparatively immaterial if they continued to be controlled by a small group. We therefore regard the argument presented to us to show that the growth of concentration of the volume of resources in the banks of New York City has been at a rate slightly less than in the rest of the country, if that be the fact, as not involved in our inquiry. It should be observed in this connection, however, that the concentration of control of credit is by no means confined to New York City, so that the argument is inapplicable also in this respect.

SECTION 2.

Fact of Increasing Concentration Admitted

The resources of the banks and trust companies of the city of New York in 1911 were $5,121,245,175, which is 21.73 percent of the total banking resources of the country as reported to the comptroller of the currency. This takes no account of the unknown resources of the great private banking houses whose affiliations to the New York financial institutions we are about to discuss.

That in recent years concentration of control of the banking resources and consequently of credit by the group to which we will refer has grown apace in the city of New York is defended by some witnesses and regretted by others, but acknowledged by all to be a fact.

As appears from statistics compiled by accountants for the committee, in 1911, of the total resources of the banks and trust companies in New York City, the twenty largest held 42.97 percent; in 1906, the twenty largest held 38.24 percent of the total; in 1901, 34.97 percent.

SECTION 3.

Processes of Concentration

THIS INCREASED CONCENTRATION of control of money and credit has been effected principally as follows:

First, through consolidations of competitive or potentially competitive banks and trust companies, which consolidations in turn have recently been brought under sympathetic management.

Second, through the same powerful interests becoming large stockholders in potentially competitive banks and trust companies. This is the simplest way of acquiring control, but since it requires the largest investment of capital, it is the least used, although the recent investments in that direction for that apparent purpose amount to tens of millions of dollars in present market values.

Third, through the confederation of potentially competitive banks and trust companies by means of the system of interlocking directorates.

Fourth, through the influence which the more powerful banking houses, banks, and trust companies have secured in the management of insurance companies, railroads, producing and trading corporations, and

public utility corporations, by means of stockholdings, voting trusts, fiscal agency contracts, or representation upon their boards of directors, or through supplying the money requirements of railway, industrial, and public utilities corporations and thereby being enabled to participate in the determination of their financial and business policies.

Fifth, through partnership or joint account arrangements between a few of the leading banking houses, banks, and trust companies in the purchase of security issues of the great interstate corporations, accompanied by understandings of recent growth — sometimes called "banking ethics" — which have had the effect of effectually destroying competition between such banking houses, banks, and trust companies in the struggle for business or in the purchase and sale of large issues of such securities.

SECTION 4.

Agents of Concentration

IT IS A FAIR DEDUCTION from the testimony that the most active agents in forwarding and bringing about the concentration of control of money and credit through one or another of the processes above described have been and are: J. P. Morgan & Co.; First National Bank of New York; National City Bank of New York; Lee, Higginson & Co., of Boston and New York; Kidder, Peabody & Co., of Boston and New York; Kuhn, Loeb & Co. . . .

SECTION 11.

Interrelations of Members of the Group

Morgan & Co. and First National Bank.

Mr. Morgan, head of the firm of Morgan & Co. of New York and Drexel & Co. of Philadelphia, and Mr. Baker, head officer and dominant power in the First National Bank since shortly after its organization, have been close friends and business associates from almost the time they began business. . . .

Before becoming partners in Morgan & Co., Mr. Davison and Mr. Lamont, two of the most active members of the firm, were vice-presidents of the First National Bank, and still remain directors.

Next to Mr. Baker, Morgan & Co. is the largest stockholder of the First National, owning 14,500 shares, making the combined holdings of Mr. Baker and his son and Morgan & Co. about 40,000 shares out of 100,000 outstanding — a joint investment, based on the market value, of $41 million in this one institution.

Three of the Morgan partners — Mr. Morgan himself, Mr. Davison, and Mr. Lamont — are directors of the First National, and Mr. Morgan is a member of the Executive Committee of four. . . .

The First National has been associated with Morgan & Co. in the control of the Bankers Trust Co. . . . When the company was organized, its entire capital stock was vested in George W. Perkins, H. P. Davison, and Daniel G. Reid as voting trustees. Mr. Perkins was then a Morgan partner and Mr. Davison and Mr. Reid were, respectively, vice-president and a large stockholder of the First National. Mr. Davison, who has since become a Morgan partner, and Mr. Reid have continued as such trustees. Mr. Perkins has been succeeded by the attorney of the company, who is also Mr. Davison's personal counsel. Mr. Davison and Mr. Lamont, of the Morgan firm, and Mr. Hine, president; Mr. Norton, vice-president; and Mr. Hepburn, member of the Executive Committee of the First National, are codirectors of the Bankers Trust Co., Mr. Hine being also a member of its Executive Committee.

The First National likewise has been associated with Morgan & Co. in the control of the Guaranty Trust Co., Mr. Baker of the former being joined with Mr. Davison and Mr. Porter of the latter as voting trustees.

In the Astor Trust Co., controlled by Morgan & Co. through the Bankers Trust Co., Mr. Baker and Mr. Hine, chief officer of the First National, are directors. In the Liberty National Bank, controlled by Morgan & Co. through the Bankers Trust Co. Mr. Hine is also a director.

Since its organization in 1894, Mr. Morgan and Mr. Baker have been associated a voting trustees in the control of the Southern Railway, of which, also, Morgan & Co. and the First Security Co. are stockholders and Mr. Steele of the former and George F. Baker, Jr., and H. C. Fahenstock of the First National are directors. Mr. Morgan and Mr. Baker are also associated as voting trustees in the control of the Chicago Great Western Railway.

Mr. Morgan and Mr. Baker are further associated as directors and members of the Executive Committee of the New York Central Lines and as directors of the New York, New Haven & Hartford Railroad and the Pullman Co.

At Mr. Morgan's request, Mr. Baker became and has remained a director and member of the Finance Committee of the United States Steel Corporation which . . . was organized and always has been dominated by the former. At the request of Mr. Perkins, who, as a partner in Morgan & Co., was active in organizing the International Harvester Co., Mr. Baker became a director of that company, resigning only recently.

Mr. Stotesbury of Morgan & Co. and Mr. Baker are associated as voting trustees in the control of the William Cramp Ship & Engine Building Co.

In 1901 Mr. Baker and associates, cooperating with Mr. Morgan, transferred to Reading Co. a majority of the stock of the Central Railroad of New Jersey, thereby bringing under one control railroad systems transporting 33⅓ percent of the anthracite coal moving from the mines and coal companies owning or controlling 63 percent of the entire anthracite deposits. . . . In the same year Mr. Baker cooperated with Mr. Morgan in transferring to the Northern Securities Co. controlling stock interests in the Northern Pacific and Great Northern Railways, competitive transcontinental systems.

One or more members of Morgan & Co. and one or more officers or directors of the First National are associated as codirectors in the following additional corporations, among others: the Mutual Life Insurance Co. of New York; the anthracite railroads, including the Reading, the Central of New Jersey, the Lehigh Valley, the Erie, the New York, Susquehanna & Western, and the New York, Ontario & Western; the Northern Pacific Railway, in which also Mr. Steele of Morgan & Co., and Mr. Baker of the First National, are members of the Executive Committee; Adams Express Co.; American Telegraph & Telephone Co.; and The Baldwin Locomotive Works.

But nothing demonstrates quite so clearly the close and continuing cooperation between Morgan & Co. and the First National Bank as their joint purchases and underwritings of corporate securities. Since 1903 they have purchased for their joint account, generally with other associates, seventy-odd security issues of thirty different corporations, aggregating approximately $1,080 million. . . .

It is thus seen that through stockholdings, interlocking directors, partnership transactions, and other relations, Morgan & Co. and the First National Bank are locked together in a complete and enduring community of interest. Their relations in this regard are, indeed, a commonplace in the financial world. . . .

The resources of Morgan & Co. are unknown; its deposits are $163 million. The resources of the First National Bank are $150 million and those of its appendage, the First Security Co., at a very low estimate, $35 million. The resources of the National City Bank are $274 million; those of its appendage, the National City Co., are unknown, though the capital of the latter is

alone $10 million. Thus, leaving out of account the very considerable part which is unknown, the institutions composing this group have resources of upward of $632 million, aside from the vast individual resources of Messrs. Morgan, Baker, and Stillman.

Further, as heretofore shown, the members of this group, through stock holdings, voting trusts, interlocking directorates, and other relations, have become in some cases the absolutely dominant factor; in others, the most important single factor, in the control of the following banks and trust companies in the city of New York. . . .

Summary of directorships held by these members of the group. Exhibit 134-B shows the combined directorships in the more important enterprises held by Morgan & Co., the First National Bank, the National City Bank, and the Bankers and Guaranty Trust Cos., which latter two . . . are absolutely controlled by Morgan & Co. through voting trusts. It appears there that firm members or directors of these institutions together hold:

One hundred and eighteen directorships in 34 banks and trust companies having total resources of $2,679,000,000 and total deposits of $1,983,000,000; 30 directorships in 10 insurance companies having total assets of $2,293,000,000; 105 directorships in 32 transportation systems having a total capitalization of $11,784,000,000 and a total mileage (excluding express companies and steamship lines) of 150,200; 63 directorships in 24 producing and trading corporations having a total capitalization of $3,339,000,000; 25 directorships in 12 public utility corporations having total capitalization of $2,150,000,000 — in all, 341 directorships in 112 corporations having aggregate resources or capitalization of $22,245,000,000.

The members of the firm of J. P. Morgan & Co. hold 72 directorships in 47 of the greater corporations; George F. Baker, chairman of the Board, F. L. Hine, president, and George F. Baker, Jr., and C. D. Norton, vice-presidents, of the First National Bank of New York, hold 46 directorships in 37 of the greater corporations; and James Stillman, chairman of the Board, Frank A. Vanderlip, president, and Samuel McRoberts, J. T. Talbert, W. A. Simonson, vice-presidents, of the National City Bank of New York, hold 32 directorships in 26 of the greater corporations; making in all for these members of the group 150 directorships in 110 of the greater corporations. . . .

Relations between Morgan & Co., First National Bank, National City Bank, Lee Higginson & Co., Kidder, Peabody & Co., and Kuhn, Loeb & Co. Besides the group composed of Morgan & Co. and the First National Bank and the National City Bank, the principal banking agencies through which the greater corporate enterprises of the United States obtain capital for their operations are the international banking firms of Kuhn, Loeb & Co. of New York, and Kidder, Peabody & Co. and Lee Higginson & Co. of Boston and New York.

While it does not appear that these three last-named houses are affiliated with the group consisting of the first three in so definite and permanent a form of alliance as that existing between the latter, it is established that as issuing houses they do not as a rule act independently in purchasing security issues but rather in unison and cooperation with one or more members of that group, with the result that in the vastly important service of arranging credits for the great commercial enterprises of the country there is no competition or rivalry between those dominating that field, but virtually a monopoly the terms of which the borrowing corporations must accept.

The full extent to which they participate in one another's issues does not appear, owing to the absence of data as to the names of underwriters, other than in strictly joint-account transactions of the issues of securities made by Messrs. Morgan & Co. Kuhn, Loeb & Co., the First National Bank, and the National City Bank. The distinction between the cases in which one of the banks or banking houses assumes the relation of an underwriter of an issue of securities made by one of the others and that in which they act in joint account is that in the former case underwriters do not share in the primary bankers' profit, but insure the former against loss, while in the case of a joint account they are partners and as such share in the original risks and profits.

The course of business is for the house acquiring from a corporation the right of purchasing or underwriting an issue of its securities to offer participations in the purchase or underwriting to one or more of the associates named. . . .

Moreover, the banking houses which have joined in the plan of cooperation comprise the principal mediums through which the greater corporations of the country obtain their supplies of capital.

The charge for capital, which, of course enters universally into the prices of commodities and of service, is thus in effect determined by agreement among those supplying it, and not under the check of competition. If there be any virtue in the principle of competition, certainly any plan or arrangement which prevents its operation in the performance of so fundamental a commercial function as the supplying of capital is peculiarly injurious.

The possibility of competition between these banking houses in the purchase of securities is further removed by the understanding among them and others that one will not seek by offering better terms to take away from another a customer which it has theretofore served, and by the corollary of this, namely, that where given bankers have once satisfactorily united in bringing out an issue of a corporation they shall also join in bringing out any subsequent issue of the same corporation.

81.

Louis D. Brandeis: The Money Trust

Using the statistical evidence presented by the Pujo Committee Report on business consolidation, Louis D. Brandeis, the noted Progressive attorney and friend of President Wilson, wrote a series of articles for Harper's Weekly *in 1913. In his first article, on the "money trust," Brandeis described the operations of the investment banker, showing how firms such as J. P. Morgan & Co. were able to control a vast network of companies by pyramiding their financial holdings.*

Source: *Harper's Weekly*, November 22, 1913: "Breaking the Money Trust."

THE DOMINANT ELEMENT in our financial oligarchy is the investment banker. Associated banks, trust companies, and life insurance companies are his tools. Controlled railroads, public-service and industrial corporations are his subjects. Though properly but middlemen, these bankers bestride as masters America's business world, so that practically no large enterprise can be undertaken successfully without their participation or approval. These bankers are, of course, able men possessed of large fortunes; but the most potent factor in their control of business is not the possession of extraordinary ability or huge wealth. The key to their power is combination — concentration, intensive and comprehensive — advancing on three distinct lines:

First, there is the obvious consolidation of banks and trust companies; the less obvious affiliations — through stockholdings, voting trusts, and interlocking directorates — of banking institutions which are not legally connected; and the joint transactions, gentlemen's agreements, and "banking ethics" which eliminate competition among the investment bankers.

Second, there is the consolidation of railroads into huge systems, the large combinations of public-service corporations and the formation of industrial trusts, which, by making business so "big" that local, independent banking concerns cannot alone supply the necessary funds, has created dependence upon the associated New York bankers.

But combination, however intensive, along these lines only, could not have produced the money trust — another and more potent factor of combination was added.

Third, investment bankers, like J. P. Morgan & Co., dealers in bonds, stocks, and notes, encroached upon the functions of the three other classes of corporations with which their business brought them into contact. They became the directing power in railroads, public-service and industrial companies through which our great business operations are conducted — the makers of bonds and stocks. They became the directing power in the life insurance companies and other corporate reservoirs of the people's savings — the buyers of bonds and stocks. They became the directing power also in banks and trust companies — the depositaries of the quick capital of the country — the lifeblood of business, with which they and others carried on their operations. Thus, four distinct functions, each essential to business, and each exercised, originally, by a distinct set of men, became united in the investment banker. It is to this union of business functions that the existence of the money trust is mainly due.

The development of our financial oligarchy followed, in this respect, lines with which the history of political despotism has familiarized us — usurpation, proceeding by gradual encroachment rather than by violent acts; subtle and often long-concealed concentration of distinct functions, which are beneficent when separately administered and dangerous only when combined in the same persons. It was by processes such as these that Caesar Augustus became master of Rome. The makers of our own Constitution had in mind like dangers to our political liberty when they provided so carefully for the separation of governmental powers.

The original function of the investment banker was that of dealer in bonds, stocks, and notes; buying mainly at wholesale from corporations, municipalities, states, and governments which need money, and selling to those seeking investments. The banker performs, in this respect, the function of a merchant; and the function is a very useful one. Large business enterprises are conducted generally by corporations. The permanent capital of corporations is represented by bonds and stocks. The bonds and stocks of the more important corporations are owned, in large part, by small investors, who do not participate in the management of the company. Corporations require the aid of a banker-middleman, for they lack generally the reputation and clientele essential to selling their own bonds and stocks direct to the investor. Investors in corporate securities also require the services of a banker-middleman.

The number of securities upon the market is very large. Only a part of these securities is listed on the New York Stock Exchange; but its listings alone comprise about 1,600 different issues aggregating about $26.5 billion, and each year new listings are made averaging about 233, to an amount of $1.5 billion. For a small investor to make an intelligent selection from these many corporate securities — indeed, to pass an intelligent judgment upon a single one — is ordinarily impossible. He lacks the ability, the facilities, the training, and the time essential to a proper investigation. Unless his purchase is to be little better than a gamble, he needs the advice of an expert, who, combining special knowledge with judgment, has the facilities and incentive to make a thorough investigation.

This dependence, both of corporations and investors, upon the banker has grown in recent years, since women and others who do not participate in the management, have become the owners of so large a part of the stocks and bonds of our great corporations. Over half of the stockholders of the American Sugar Refining Company and nearly half of the stockholders of the Pennsylvania Railroad and of the New York, New Haven & Hartford Railroad are women.

Goodwill — the possession by a dealer of numerous and valuable regular customers — is always an important element in merchandising. But in the business of selling bonds and stocks, it is of exceptional value, for the very reason that the small investor relies so largely upon the banker's judgment. This confidential relation of the banker to customers — and the knowledge of the customers' private affairs acquired incidentally, is often a determining factor in the marketing of securities. With the advent of big business, such goodwill possessed by the older banking houses, preeminently J. P. Morgan & Co. and their Philadelphia house called Drexel & Co., by Lee, Higginson & Co. and Kidder, Peabody, & Co. of Boston, and by Kuhn, Loeb & Co. of New York, became of enhanced importance. The volume of new security issues was greatly increased by huge railroad consolidations, the development of the holding companies, and particularly by the formation of industrial trusts. The rapidly accumulating savings of our people sought investment. The field of operations for the dealer in securities was thus much enlarged. And, as the securities were new and untried, the services of the investment banker were in great demand, and his powers and profits increased accordingly.

But this enlargement of their legitimate field of operations did not satisfy investment bankers. They were not content merely to deal in securities. They desired to manufacture them also, and became promoters or allied themselves with promoters. Thus it was that J. P. Morgan & Company formed the steel trust, the Harvester trust, and the shipping trust. And, adding the duties of undertaker to those of midwife, the investment bankers became in times of corporate disaster, members of the security-holders' "Protective Committees"; then they participated as "Reorganization Managers" in the reincarnation of the unsuccessful corporations and ultimately became directors.

It was in this way that the Morgan associates acquired their hold upon the Southern Railway, the Northern Pacific, the Reading, the Erie, the Père Marquette, the Chicago and Great Western, and the Cincinnati, Hamilton & Dayton. Often they insured the continuance of that control by the device of the voting trust; but even where no voting trust was created, a secure hold was acquired upon reorganization. It was in this way also that Kuhn, Loeb & Co. became potent in the Union Pacific and the Baltimore & Ohio.

But the banker's participation in the management of the corporations was not limited to cases of promotion or reorganization. An urgent or extensive need of new money was considered a sufficient reason for the banker's entering a board of directors. And often without even such excuse the investment banker has secured a place upon the Board of Directors, through his powerful influence or the control of his customers' proxies. Such seems to have been the fatal entrance of Mr. Morgan into the management of the then prosperous New York, New Haven & Hartford Railroad in 1892. And when once a banker has entered the Board — whatever may have been the occasion — his grip proves tenacious and his influence usually supreme, for he controls the supply of new money.

The investment banker is naturally on the lookout for good bargains in bonds and stocks. Like other merchants, he wants to buy his merchandise cheap. But, when he becomes director of a corporation, he occupies a position which prevents the transaction by which he acquires its corporate securities from being properly called a bargain. Can there be real bargaining where the same man is on both sides of a trade? The investment banker, through his controlling influence on the Board of Directors, decides that the corporation shall issue and sell the securities, decides the price at which it shall sell them, and decides that it shall sell the securities to himself. The fact that there are other directors besides the banker on the Board does not, in practice, prevent this being the result. The banker, who holds the purse strings, becomes usually the dominant spirit.

Through voting trusteeships, exclusive financial agencies, membership on executive or finance committees, or by mere directorships, J. P. Morgan & Co. and their associates, hold such financial power in at least thirty-two transportation systems, public-utility corporations, and industrial companies — companies with an aggregate capitalization of $17,273,000,000. Mainly for corporations so controlled, J. P. Morgan & Co. procured the public marketing in ten years of security issues aggregating $1,950,000,000. This huge sum does not include any issues marketed privately nor any issues, however marketed, of intrastate corporations. Kuhn, Loeb & Co. and a few other investment bankers exercise similar control over many other corporations.

Such control of railroads, public-service and industrial corporations assures to the investment bankers an ample supply of securities at attractive prices; and merchandise well bought is half-sold. But these bond and stock merchants are not disposed to take even a slight risk as to their ability to market their goods. They saw that if they could control the security buyers, as well as the security makers, investment banking would, indeed, be "a happy hunting ground"; and they have made it so.

The numerous small investors cannot, in the strict sense, be controlled; but their dependence upon the banker insures their being duly influenced. A large part, however, of all bonds issued and of many stocks are bought by the prominent corporate investors; and most prominent among these are the life insurance companies, the trust companies, and the banks. The purchase of a security by these institutions not only relieves the banker of the merchandise but recommends it strongly to the small investor, who believes that these institutions are wisely managed. These controlled corporate investors are not only large customers, but may be particularly accommodating ones. Individual investors are moody. They buy only when they want to do so. They are sometimes inconveniently reluctant. Corporate investors, if controlled, may be made to buy when the bankers need a market. It was natural that the investment bankers proceeded to get control of the great life insurance companies, as well as of the trust companies and the banks.

The field thus occupied is uncommonly rich. The life insurance companies are our leading institutions for savings. Their huge surplus and reserves, augmented daily, are always clamoring for investment. No panic or money shortage stops the inflow of new money from the perennial stream of premiums on existing policies and interest on existing investments. The three great companies — the New York Life, the Mutual of New York, and the Equitable — would have over $55 million of *new* money to invest annually even if they did not issue a single new policy.

In 1904 — just before the Armstrong investigation — these three companies had together $1,247,331,738.18 of assets. They had issued in that year $1,025,671,126 of new policies. The New York legislature placed in 1906 certain restrictions upon their growth; so that their new business since has averaged $547,384,212, or only 53 percent of what it was in 1904. But the aggregate assets of these companies increased in the last eight years to $1,817,052,260.36. At the time of the Armstrong investigation the average age of these three companies was fifty-six years. *The growth of assets in the last eight years was about half as large as the total growth in the preceding fifty-six years.* These three companies must invest annually about $70 million of new money; and, besides, many old investments expire or are changed and the proceeds must be reinvested. A large part of all life insurance surplus and reserves are invested in bonds. The aggregate bond investments of these three companies on January 1, 1913, was $1,019,153,268.93.

It was natural that the investment bankers should seek to control these never failing reservoirs of capital. George W. Perkins was vice-president of the New York Life, the largest of the companies. While remaining such he was made a partner in J. P. Morgan & Co., and in the four years preceding the Armstrong investigation, his firm sold the New York Life $38,804,918.51 in securities. The New York is a mutual company, supposed to be controlled by its policyholders. But "the so-called control of life insurance companies by policyholders through mutualization is a farce" and "its only result is to keep in office a self-constituted, self-perpetuating management."

The Equitable Life Assurance Society is a stock company and is controlled by $100,000 of stock. The dividend on this stock is limited by law to 7 percent; but in 1910 Mr. Morgan paid about $3 million for $51,000, par value of this stock, or $5,882.35 a share. The dividend return on the stock investment is less than one-eighth of one percent; but the assets controlled amount now to over $500 million. And certain of these assets had an especial value for investment bankers; namely, the large holdings of stock in banks and trust companies.

The Armstrong investigation disclosed the extent of financial power exerted through the insurance company holdings of bank and trust company stock. The committee recommended legislation compelling the insurance companies to dispose of the stock within five years. A law to that effect was enacted, but the time was later extended. The companies then disposed of a part of their bank and trust company stocks; but, being controlled by the investment bankers, these gentlemen sold the bank and trust company stocks to themselves.

The banks and trust companies are depositaries, in the main, not of the people's savings but of the businessman's quick capital. Yet, since the investment banker acquired control of banks and trust companies, these institutions also have become, like the life companies, large purchasers of bonds and stocks. Many of our national banks have invested in this manner a large part of all their resources, including capital, surplus, and deposits. The bond investments of some banks exceed by far the aggregate of their capital and surplus and nearly equal their loanable deposits.

The goose that lays golden eggs has been considered a most valuable possession. But even more profitable is the privilege of taking the golden eggs laid by somebody else's goose. The investment bankers and their associates now enjoy that privilege. They control the people through the people's own money. If the bankers' power were commensurate only with their wealth, they would have relatively little influence on American business. Vast fortunes like those of the Astors are no doubt regrettable. They are inconsistent with democracy.

They are unsocial. And they seem peculiarly unjust when they represent largely unearned increment. But the wealth of the Astors does not endanger political or industrial liberty. It is insignificant in amount as compared with the aggregate wealth of America, or even of New York City. It lacks significance largely because its owners have only the income from their own wealth. The Astor wealth is static.

The wealth of the Morgan associates is dynamic. The power and the growth of power of our financial oligarchs comes from wielding the savings and quick capital of others. In two of the three great life insurance companies the influence of J. P. Morgan & Co. and their associates is exerted without any individual investment by them whatsoever. Even in the Equitable, where Mr. Morgan bought an actual majority of all the outstanding stock, his investment amounts to little more than one-half of one percent of the assets of the company. The fetters which bind the people are forged from the people's own gold.

But the reservoir of other people's money, from which the investment bankers now draw their greatest power, is not the life insurance companies but the banks and the trust companies. Bank deposits represent the really quick capital of the nation. They are the lifeblood of businesses. Their effective force is much greater than that of an equal amount of wealth permanently invested. The thirty-four banks and trust companies, which the Pujo Committee declared to be directly controlled by the Morgan associates, held $1,983,000,000 in deposits. Control of these institutions means the ability to lend a large part of these funds, directly and indirectly, to themselves; and what is often even more important, the power to prevent the funds being lent to any rival interests. These huge deposits can, in the discretion of those in control, be used to meet the temporary needs of their subject corporations. When bonds and stocks are issued to finance permanently these corporations, the bank deposits, can in large part be loaned by the investment bankers in control to themselves and their associates, so that the securities may be carried by them until sold to investors. Or these bank deposits may be loaned to allied bankers or jobbers in securities or to speculators, to enable them to carry the bonds or stocks.

Easy money tends to make securities rise in the market. Tight money nearly always makes them fall. The control by the leading investment bankers over the banks and trust companies is so great, that they can often determine for a time the market for money by lending or refusing to lend on the Stock Exchange. In this way, among others, they have power to affect the general trend of prices in bonds and stocks. Their power over a particular security is even greater. Its sale on the market may depend upon whether the security is favored or discriminated against when offered to the banks and trust companies, as collateral for loans.

Furthermore, it is the investment banker's access to other people's money in controlled banks and trust companies which alone enables any individual banking concern to take so large [a] part of the annual output of bonds and stocks. The banker's own capital, however large, would soon be exhausted. And even the loanable funds of the banks would often be exhausted but for the large deposits made in those banks by the life insurance, railroad, public-service, and industrial corporations which the bankers also control. On December 31, 1912, the three leading life insurance companies had deposits in banks and trust companies aggregating $13,839,189.08. As the Pujo Committee finds:

> The men, who through their control over the funds of our railroads and industrial companies are able to direct where such funds shall be kept and thus to create these great reservoirs of the people's money, are the ones who are in position to tap those reservoirs for the ventures in which they are interested and to prevent their being tapped for purposes of which they do not approve. The latter is quite as important a factor as the former. It is the controlling consideration in its effect on competition in the railroad and industrial world.

But the power of the investment banker over other people's money is often more direct and effective than that exerted through controlled banks and trust companies. J. P. Morgan & Co. achieve the supposedly impossible feat of having their cake and eating it too. They buy the bonds and stocks of controlled railroads and industrial concerns and pay the purchase price; and still do not part with their money. This is accomplished by the simple device of becoming the bank of deposit of the controlled corporations, instead of having the company deposit in some merely controlled bank in whose operation others have at least some share. When J. P. Morgan & Co. buy an issue of securities, the purchase money, instead of being paid over to the corporation, is retained by the banker for the corporation, to be drawn upon only as the funds are needed by the corporation. And as the securities are issued in large blocks, and the money raised is often not all spent until long thereafter, the aggregate of the balances remaining in the banker's hands are huge. Thus J. P. Morgan & Co. (including their Philadelphia house, called Drexel & Co.) held on November 1, 1912, deposits aggregating $162,491,819.65.

The operations of so comprehensive a system of concentration necessarily developed in the bankers overweening power. And the bankers' power grows by what it feeds on. Power begets wealth; and added wealth opens ever new opportunities for the acquisition of wealth and power. The operations of these bankers are so vast and numerous that even a very reasonable compensation for the service performed by the bankers, would, in the aggregate, produce for them incomes so large as to result in huge accumulations of capital. But the compensation taken by the bankers as commissions or profits is far from reasonable. Occupying, as they so frequently do, the inconsistent position of being at the same time seller and buyer, the standard for so-called compensation actually applied is not the "rule of reason" but "all the traffic will bear." And this is true even where there is no sinister motive. The weakness of human nature prevents men from being good judges of their own deservings.

The syndicate formed by J. P. Morgan & Co. to underwrite the United States Steel Corporation took for their services securities which netted $62.5 million in cash. Of this huge sum J. P. Morgan & Co. received, as syndicate managers, $12.5 million in addition to the share which they were entitled to receive as syndicate members. This sum of $62.5 million was only a part of the fees paid for the service of monopolizing the steel industry. In addition to the commissions taken specifically for organizing the United States Steel Corporation, large sums were paid for organizing the several companies of which it is composed. For instance, the National Tube Company was capitalized at $80 million of stock, $40 million of which was common stock. Half of this $40 million was taken by J. P. Morgan & Co. and associates for promotion services; and the $20 million stock so taken became later exchangeable into $25 million of Steel Common. Commissioner of Corporations Herbert Knox Smith found that:

> More than $150 million of the stock of the Steel Corporation was issued directly or indirectly (through exchange) for mere promotion or underwriting services. In other words, nearly one-seventh of the total capital stock of the Steel Corporation appears to have been issued directly or indirectly to promoters' services.

The so-called fees and commissions taken by the bankers and associates upon the organization of the trusts have been exceptionally large. But even after the trusts are successfully launched the exactions of the bankers are often extortionate. The syndicate which underwrote, in 1901, the Steel Corporation's preferred stock conversion plan, advanced only $20 million in cash and received an underwriting commission of $6.8 million.

The exaction of huge commissions is not confined to trust and other industrial concerns. The Interborough Railway is a most prosperous corporation. It earned last year nearly 21 percent on its capital stock, and secured from New York City, in connection with the subway extension, a very favorable contract. But when it financed its $170 million bond issue, it was agreed that J. P. Morgan & Co. should receive 3 percent, that is, $5.1 million, for forming this syndicate.

More recently, the New York, New Haven & Hartford Railroad agreed to pay J. P. Morgan & Co. a commission of $1,680,000, that is, 2½ percent, to form a syndicate to underwrite an issue at par of $67 million twenty-year 6 percent convertible debentures. That means: the bankers bound themselves to take at 97½ any of these 6 percent convertible bonds which stockholders might be unwilling to buy at 100. When the contract was made the New Haven's then outstanding 6 percent convertible bonds were selling at 114. And the new issue, as soon as announced, was in such demand that the public offered and has ever since been willing to buy at 106 — bonds which the company were to pay J. P. Morgan & Co. $1,680,000 to be willing to take at par.

These large profits from promotions, underwritings and security purchases led to a revolutionary change in the conduct of our leading banking institutions. It was obvious that control by the investment bankers of the deposits in banks and trust companies was an essential element in their securing these huge profits. And the bank officers naturally asked, "Why then should not the banks and trust companies share in so profitable a field? Why should not they themselves become investment bankers, too, with all the new functions incident to 'big business'?" To do so would involve a departure from the legitimate sphere of the banking business — which is the making of temporary loans to other business concerns.

But the temptation was irresistible. The invasion of the investment banker into the banks' field of operation was followed by a counterinvasion by the banks into the realm of the investment banker. And most prominent among the banks were the National City and the First National of New York. But theirs was not a hostile invasion. The contending forces met as allies, joined forces to control the business of the country and to "divide the spoils." The alliance was cemented by voting trusts, by interlocking directorates, and by joint ownerships. There resulted the fullest "cooperation"; and more railroads, public-service corporations, and great industrial concerns were brought into complete subjection.

82.

Woodrow Wilson: First Inaugural Address

Woodrow Wilson was sworn in as the twenty-eighth President of the United States on March 4, 1913. His first inaugural address, sometimes compared to Jefferson's first and to Lincoln's second, outlined the broad changes that he proposed for the country during the next four years. Interpreting his victory (despite his popular minority) as a mandate to clean house in Washington and especially to rid the government of the influence of privileged groups, Wilson pledged himself to reform the banking system and to lower tariffs. However, the address did not end the split among Progressives caused by the formation of Theodore Roosevelt's "Bull Moose" Party the previous year. In November 1914 Wilson pointed to the passage during the previous thirteen months of the Underwood Tariff Act, the Federal Reserve Act, the Clayton Antitrust Act, and the Federal Trade Commission Act as evidence that the main goals of Progressivism had been accomplished. But Herbert Croly complained in the New Republic *that the President had "utterly misconceived the meaning and the task of American progressivism" and had surrounded his misconception "with a halo of shimmering rhetoric."*

Source: *Record*, 63 Cong., 1 Sess., pp. 2-3.

There has been a change of government. It began two years ago, when the House of Representatives became Democratic by a decisive majority. It has now been completed. The Senate about to assemble will also be Democratic. The offices of President and Vice-President have been put into the hands of Democrats. What does the change mean? That is the question that is uppermost in our minds today. That is the question I am going to try to answer in order, if I may, to interpret the occasion.

It means much more than the mere success of a party. The success of a party means little except when the nation is using that party for a large and definite purpose. No one can mistake the purpose for which the nation now seeks to use the Democratic Party. It seeks to use it to interpret a change in its own plans and point of view.

Some old things with which we had grown familiar, and which had begun to creep into the very habit of our thought and of our lives, have altered their aspect as we have latterly looked critically upon them with fresh, awakened eyes; have dropped their disguises and shown themselves alien and sinister. Some new things, as we look frankly upon them, willing to comprehend their real character, have come to assume the aspect of things long believed in and familiar, stuff of our own convictions. We have been refreshed by a new insight into our own life.

We see that in many things that life is very great. It is incomparably great in its material aspects, in its body of wealth, in the diversity and sweep of its energy, in the industries which have been conceived and built up by the genius of individual men and the limitless enterprise of groups of men. It is great, also, very great, in its moral force. Nowhere else in the world have noble men and women exhibited in more striking forms the beauty and the energy of sympathy and helpfulness and counsel in their efforts to rectify wrong, alleviate suffering, and set the weak in the way of strength and hope. We have built up, moreover, a great system of government, which has stood through a long age as in many respects a model for those who seek to set liberty upon foundations that will endure against fortuitous change, against storm and accident. Our life contains every great thing, and contains it in rich abundance.

But the evil has come with the good, and much fine gold has been corroded. With riches has come inexcusable waste. We have squandered a great part of what we might have used and have not stopped to conserve the exceeding bounty of nature, without which our genius for enterprise would have been worthless and impotent, scorning to be careful, shamefully prodigal as well as admirably efficient. We have been proud of our industrial achievements, but we have not hitherto stopped thoughtfully enough to count the human cost, the cost of lives snuffed out, of energies overtaxed and broken, the fearful physical and spiritual cost to the men and women and children upon whom the dead weight and burden of it all has fallen pitilessly the years through. The groans and agony of it all had not yet reached our ears, the solemn, moving undertone of our life, coming up out of the mines and factories and out of every home where the struggle had its intimate and familiar seat. With the great government went many deep secret things which we too long delayed to look into and scrutinize with candid, fearless eyes. The great government we loved has too often been made use of for private and selfish purposes, and those who used it had forgotten the people.

At last a vision has been vouchsafed us of our life as a whole. We see the bad with the good, the debased and decadent with the sound and vital. With this vision we approach new affairs. Our duty is to cleanse, to reconsider, to restore, to correct the evil without impairing the good, to purify and humanize every process of our common life without weakening or sentimentalizing it.

There has been something crude and heartless and unfeeling in our haste to succeed and be great. Our thought has been "Let every man look out for himself, let every generation look out for itself," while we reared giant machinery which made it impossible that any but those who stood at the levers of control should have a chance to look out for themselves. We had not forgotten our morals. We remembered well enough that we had set up a policy which was meant to serve the humblest as well as the most powerful, with an eye single to the standards of justice and fair play, and remembered it with pride. But we were very heedless and in a hurry to be great.

We have come now to the sober second thought. The scales of heedlessness have fallen from our eyes. We have made up our minds to square every process of our national life again with the standards we so

Woodrow Wilson; photographed in 1912

proudly set up at the beginning and have always carried at our hearts. Our work is a work of restoration.

We have itemized with some degree of particularity the things that ought to be altered and here are some of the chief items: a tariff which cuts us off from our proper part in the commerce of the world, violates the just principles of taxation, and makes the government a facile instrument in the hands of private interests; a banking and currency system based upon the necessity of the government to sell its bonds fifty years ago and perfectly adapted to concentrating cash and restricting credits; an industrial system which, take it on all its sides, financial as well as administrative, holds capital in leading strings, restricts the liberties and limits the opportunities of labor, and exploits without renewing or conserving the natural resources of the country; a body of agricultural activities never yet given the efficiency of great business undertakings or served as it should be through the instrumentality of science taken directly to the farm, or afforded the facilities of credit best

suited to its practical needs; watercourses undeveloped, waste places unreclaimed, forests untended, fast disappearing without plan or prospect of renewal, unregarded waste heaps at every mine.

We have studied, as perhaps no other nation has, the most effective means of production, but we have not studied cost or economy as we should either as organizers of industry, as statesmen, or as individuals. Nor have we studied and perfected the means by which government may be put at the service of humanity, in safeguarding the health of the nation, the health of its men and its women and its children, as well as their rights in the struggle for existence.

This is no sentimental duty. The firm basis of government is justice, not pity. These are matters of justice. There can be no equality of opportunity, the first essential of justice in the body politic, if men and women and children be not shielded in their lives, their very vitality, from the consequences of great industrial and social processes which they cannot alter, control, or singly cope with. Society must see to it that it does not itself crush or weaken or damage its own constituent parts. The first duty of law is to keep sound the society it serves. Sanitary laws, pure-food laws, and laws determining conditions of labor which individuals are powerless to determine for themselves are intimate parts of the very business of justice and legal efficiency.

These are some of the things we ought to do, and not leave the others undone, the old-fashioned, never-to-be-neglected, fundamental safeguarding of property and of individual right. This is the high enterprise of the new day: to lift everything that concerns our life as a nation to the light that shines from the hearthfire of every man's conscience and vision of the right. It is inconceivable that we should do this as partisans; it is inconceivable we should do it in ignorance of the facts as they are or in blind haste.

We shall restore, not destroy. We shall

deal with our economic system as it is and as it may be modified, not as it might be if we had a clean sheet of paper to write upon; and step by step we shall make it what it should be, in the spirit of those who question their own wisdom and seek counsel and knowledge, not shallow self-satisfaction or the excitement of excursions whither they cannot tell. Justice, and only justice, shall always be our motto.

And yet it will be no cool process of mere science. The nation has been deeply stirred, stirred by a solemn passion, stirred by the knowledge of wrong, of ideals lost, of government too often debauched and made an instrument of evil. The feelings with which we face this new age of right and opportunity sweep across our heartstrings like some air out of God's own presence, where justice and mercy are reconciled and the judge and the brother are one. We know our task to be no mere task of politics but a task which shall search us through and through, whether we be able to understand our time and the need of our people, whether we be indeed their spokesmen and interpreters, whether we have the pure heart to comprehend and the rectified will to choose our high course of action.

This is not a day of triumph; it is a day of dedication. Here muster, not the forces of party but the forces of humanity. Men's hearts wait upon us; men's lives hang in the balance; men's hopes call upon us to say what we will do. Who shall live up to the great trust? Who dares fail to try? I summon all honest men, all patriotic, all forward-looking men, to my side. God helping me, I will not fail them, if they will but counsel and sustain me!

83.

WOODROW WILSON: Repudiation of "Dollar Diplomacy"

Through the initiative of President Taft in 1909, the United States was admitted to a four nation bank pool, known as the Four Power Consortium, whose aim was to aid railway construction in China. After China became a republic in 1911, it requested a $125 million loan, for which final arrangements were still being made when Woodrow Wilson became President in 1913. The American bankers in the Consortium, wishing government approval, told Wilson they would contribute their share of the loan only if he strongly desired it, as they were not enthusiastic about the financial (as opposed to the diplomatic) attractiveness of the venture. Wilson's reply to the bankers in March 1913 was seen as a repudiation of Taft's "dollar diplomacy." His opposition to the loan brought American participation in the Consortium to an end.

Source: *American Journal of International Law*, Vol. VII, pp. 338-339.

WE ARE INFORMED THAT, at the request of the last administration, a certain group of American bankers undertook to participate in the loan now desired by the government of China (approximately $125 million). Our government wished American bankers to participate along with the bankers of other nations, because it desired that the goodwill of the United States toward China should be exhibited in this practical way, that American capital should have access to that great country, and that the United States should be in a position to share with the other powers any political responsibilities that might be associated with the development of the foreign relations of China in connection with her industrial and commercial enterprises.

The present administration has been asked by this group of bankers whether it would also request them to participate in the loan. The representatives of the bankers through whom the administration was approached declared that they would continue to seek their share of the loan under the proposed agreements only if expressly requested to do so by the government. The administration has declined to make such request because it did not approve the conditions of the loan or the implications of responsibility on its own part which it was plainly told would be involved in the request.

The conditions of the loan seem to us to touch very nearly the administrative independence of China itself; and this administration does not feel that it ought, even by implication, to be a party to those conditions. The responsibility on its part which would be implied in requesting the bankers to undertake the loan might conceivably go to the length, in some unhappy contingency, of forcible interference in the financial, and even the political, affairs of that great Oriental state, just now awakening to a consciousness of its power and of its obligations to its people.

The conditions include not only the pledging of particular taxes, some of them antiquated and burdensome, to secure the loan but also the administration of those taxes by foreign agents. The responsibility on the part of our government implied in the encouragement of a loan thus secured and administered is plain enough and is obnoxious to the principles upon which the government of our people rests.

The government of the United States is not only willing but earnestly desirous of aiding the great Chinese people in every way that is consistent with their untrammeled development and its own immemorial principles. The awakening of the people of China to a consciousness of their possibilities under free government is the most significant, if not the most momentous, event of our generation. With this movement and aspiration the American people are in profound sympathy. They certainly wish to participate, and participate very generously, in opening to the Chinese and to the use of the world the almost untouched and perhaps unrivaled resources of China.

The government of the United States is earnestly desirous of promoting the most extended and intimate trade relationships between this country and the Chinese Republic. The present administration will urge and support the legislative measures necessary to give American merchants, manufacturers, contractors, and engineers the banking and other financial facilities which they now lack, and without which they are at a serious disadvantage as compared with their industrial and commercial rivals. This is its duty. This is the main material interest of its citizens in the development of China. Our interests are those of the open door — a door of friendship and mutual advantage. This is the only door we care to enter.

84.

Woodrow Wilson: Rebuke to the Tariff Lobby

Wilson had pledged in his campaign to lower the tariff, and shortly after becoming President he asked Congress to draft an appropriate bill. The effort was stymied by the tariff lobby and Wilson, exasperated and indignant, issued the following message to the press on May 26, 1913, denouncing the pressure tactics of the lobby. The public reaction was favorable to the President. His public statement is usually credited with having persuaded the legislators to carry out the Democratic pledge.

Source: *New York Times*, May 27, 1913.

I THINK THAT THE PUBLIC ought to know the extraordinary exertions being made by the lobby in Washington to gain recognition for certain alterations of the tariff bill. Washington has seldom seen so numerous, so industrious, or so insidious a lobby. The newspapers are being filled with paid advertisements calculated to mislead the judgment of public men not only, but also the public opinion of the country itself. There is every evidence that money without limit is being spent to sustain this lobby and to create an appearance of a pressure of public opinion antagonistic to some of the chief items of the tariff bill.

It is of serious interest to the country that the people at large should have no lobby and be voiceless in these matters, while great bodies of astute men seek to create an artificial opinion and to overcome the interests of the public for their private profit. It is thoroughly worth the while of the people of this country to take knowledge of this matter. Only public opinion can check and destroy it.

The government in all its branches ought to be relieved from this intolerable burden and this constant interruption to the calm progress of debate. I know that I am speaking for the members of the two houses, who would rejoice as much as I would to be released from this unbearable situation.

America is not a mere body of traders; it is a body of free men. Our greatness is built upon our freedom — is moral, not material. We have a great ardor for gain; but we have a deep passion for the rights of man.
Woodrow Wilson, speech, New York, Dec. 6, 1911

85.

P. Harvey Middleton: Movies Speed Up Labor

During the first years of their development in this country, motion pictures were used almost entirely for entertainment. But by 1913 other uses were becoming evident. In the article reprinted here, which first appeared in a technical journal in April 1913, P. Harvey Middleton described an attempt in a Rhode Island factory to use movies in a time and motion study of employees. The study reflected the growing interest of businessmen in scientific methods for increasing the efficiency of factory operations.

Source: *Technical World*, April 1913.

In the factory of a manufacturing company at Providence, Rhode Island, it was decided recently to call into service the moving-picture cameraman to speed up labor. This was at the suggestion of a modern business expert.

As a preliminary, the first task was to make an organization chart showing the exact locations of the various departments of the factory and of every machine on every floor. Then a "route engineer" examined minutely every product in the factory, from raw material to finished machine, and made a survey of the administrative offices.

Next, a model was built of the plant, and, with tapes of different colors, the manner in which the various parts under construction passed from department to department was shown. By following the course of a string of a certain color, one could see instantly the progress of that material in its different forms. "Waste motions," caused through the inconvenient situation of the various departments through which a given piece of machinery must pass, were thus clearly outlined. Then began the work of shortening the strings, or, in other words, arranging the departments in the natural order of the material's progress.

Finally, the moving-picture machine was called into play. It made its debut in the assembling of a braiding machine. The various parts of this machine came from the different departments of the factory, and the assembler was confronted with the complicated task of putting them together. The method previously in vogue was for the assembler to take the base of the machine, hunt around for the first support, put it in position, then hunt around for the second piece, put that in place, and so on, until the completed machine stood ready for the testers. Apparently the assembler was an efficient workman and did not waste a minute of his time.

The experts spent a day or so watching this operation. Then they set up the moving-picture camera and photographed the entire process. They developed the film, and then studied it carefully. As a result, they invented a frame, standing at a convenient height from the floor. This frame they provided with hooks placed at regular intervals and numbered. Then they numbered the various parts of the machine to correspond.

A boy was employed to receive all the parts as they came from the factory and place them on this frame in a certain order, which made each piece to be used next the most convenient one for the assembler to reach. By using a stand of convenient height, the assembler was saved the exertion of reaching too high or stooping too low. In a few days the assembler was building that machine in less than a quarter of the time he had formerly consumed on exactly the same job, and he was enthusiastic about the new system, for it enabled him to materially increase his earning power.

Then the moving-picture machine was used to make a record of the process of handling incoming coal and outgoing ashes, and a saving in the route traveled of 75 percent was made possible, with a resulting heavy saving in labor. Another device, invented after a study of the films recording an intricate operation, reduced the time consumed from 37½ minutes to 8½ minutes, and this without in any way "speeding up" the workman.

"The system does not drive the operative, as many people suppose," said the general manager, in discussing the subject. "The old-fashioned foreman grew angry if he saw an operative stop for an instant. To see one sitting around idle would bring on a brainstorm. But under this system, if an operative is doing nothing, nobody pays any attention to it, because it is known that there must be constant resting spells. In one form of work, loading pig iron, a business expert's investigations convinced him that the worker was most efficient if he rested 57 percent of the time. Every task has a proportion of active work and complete rest under which it is best performed. It is the aim of everybody connected with this system to determine what that proportion is."

To make the study more exact, a clock was placed beside the operative during the operation of the moving-picture camera, and the timepiece was photographed in each picture. The hand of this clock revolves once in six seconds, so that the divisions represent thousandths of a minute, and are easily read to half thousandths. The continuous motion-picture film thus furnishes a record of times and motions. The film is studied with a magnifying glass. . . .

A new workman at this Providence plant is taken into the factory's "movie" show and given a pictorial demonstration of the manner in which a skilled workman performs the work he has to do. When the "green" hand has been at work a few days, he attends a second demonstration, in which he sees himself at work, and his faults are shown by comparison with the record of the skilled workman.

"This micro-motion study furnishes a means for the transference of skill from man to machine," the general manager further stated. "It also furnishes a means for the transference of skill from the man who has it to the man who has never had it. We have used micro-motion study for determining the correct times of the best motions in many different kinds of work, and have found that it is the least expensive as well as the only accurate method of recording indisputable motion and time study data. It can be applied to operations that are done so rapidly that the eye cannot follow the motions. It has stood every test and exactly fills the bill. The apparatus can be set in position in less than an hour in any part of the shop, and the records taken. After that the records can be studied at leisure any number of times. Someday I believe we will have a library full of records of the correct times and motions, which will be classified and arranged so that they can be used as the basis of all time study.

"From the very first, we have had hardly any opposition from our men, and a pleasing feature of the installation of the system has been a series of weekly conferences of managers, foremen, and operatives, at which every phase of the system has been threshed out. The most painstaking efficiency engineer could not have studied the operations more earnestly than have the operatives in our plant. They have devoted both their spare time and their working hours to increasing their efficiency and earning power by the new method."

In the experts' planning room, every phase of every process was worked out so that the departments would feed each other without waste of time, in order to ensure that the moment an operative is ready for material, that material will be ready for him. And the arrangement of that material was the subject of earnest thought. If the subject under investigation was bench work, a portable bench was arranged on one side, an exact place for the product on the other, with tools arranged in front of the operative.

In this planning room, the route clerk lays out the route which the work must travel through the shop, determining the entire transportation career of the material from the time it is unloaded from the siding until it leaves the factory as a finished product. The instruction-card clerk prepares the order cards and gives directions to the tool-room to furnish at the proper time the tools required, and to the stockroom to furnish the materials. The time-and-cost clerk keeps the record of the job, recording the time it occupied, and the bonuses earned by the expert workman. Another functionary, called the "disciplinarian," is charged with the duty of engaging hands and settling all differences of opinion between foremen and their subordinates.

There is also a "speed boss," but he simply exists for the purpose of adjusting all the machines to the speed at which it has been found by moving-picture study that the workman can operate most efficiently. His work is aided by the "repair boss," whose duty it is to adjust and overhaul the machinery and thus prevent costly breakdowns. Then there are inspectors who watch the various processes of manufacture, devoting special attention to the first part made in any process to see that it conforms absolutely to the specifications. When this is done, the subsequent duplicates need little inspection.

86.

GEORGE K. TURNER: The Puzzle of the Underworld

The description of the urban delinquent that is reprinted here was published in July 1913 by George Turner, an astute New York crime reporter who clearly recognized in the criminal world of half a century ago the "culture within a culture" that is a commonplace of contemporary sociological writings. Turner also revealed his acute understanding of the intimate relationship that sometimes exists between organized crime and the police — a relationship that put an end to Commissioner Bingham's efforts at reform in New York before World War I, and that has frustrated the efforts of many reformers since.

Source: *McClure's*, July 1913.

MONTH AFTER MONTH the United States Army officer and the New England schoolteacher, who were directing the New York police five years ago, looked into their card catalogues and maps of crime and saw a significant thing. From one small spot on the East Side of New York crime arose and spread all over the city, like pestilence from a swamp.

Around Chatham Square and the lower

Bowery were the ancient dens of thieves, older than the memory of living men. There was the saloon of the old pickpockets, the yeggs's dingy meeting place and post office, kept by the "dope fiend" and banker of criminals, from which the tramp burglars started out to break country safes all over the United States. There were the nightly "hangouts" of the misshapen lumps of beggars, the noisy rendezvous of the paid ruffians and professional murderers. A few blocks to the west were the resorts of the Italian bombmen and counterfeiters and "white slavers"; a few blocks to the east, the coffee rooms, from which the young pickpockets and "cadets" and prostitutes sallied forth to invade the regions of the prosperous upper West Side. It was the center of the underworld of the city, never yet disturbed.

From time to time an impulse came to Commissioner Bingham and his deputy, Woods: Why not smash the nests of this thing? Why not destroy the holes from which, year after year, crime had crawled out and spread over the city? The moment this was proposed, the detective force — and the best and most conscientious men on it — protested.

"Don't do it," they said anxiously. "Don't! You'll make the greatest mistake of your life. You've got your thieves there now all together under your hand. If you scatter them, where will you find them?"

It was a cry of alarm from the deepest convictions of the old police. They were destroying the old hunting grounds of the detectives, tearing the heart out of the old traditions of the New York Police Force for handling crime. But underneath that honest protest, always distinct, was the sullen resistance of the "police system."

"Hands off our man-hunting grounds," said the police; "for the sake of the work of the department first — if not, hands off anyway."

This immemorial police system stood around them, listening, threatening, thwart-

ing, and defeating them. What was the thing? they asked themselves, as thousands of other men have done. The average policeman is a good fellow, certainly as honest as the average man in his circumstances. And yet, there they were, surrounded at their headquarters and at their chief agencies by men of evil purpose. Why should the body of police continually put at their head the men who made the system? It was not long before they found the main clue. The average patrolman, as a matter of fact, had small chance to become an officer in the department. There was an inherited aristocracy of crookedness which rose, generation after generation, to take the higher offices of the force.

The significant fact they saw was this: three-quarters of the police officers at the head of the department had started their careers on the force as plainclothesmen, operating at the centers of the underworld. They were sometimes members of the old Detective Bureau, but more often the plainclothes agents of the notorious old-time officers of the police — the graduates of the man who gave the Tenderloin its name, of the chief who opened the town and threw away the key. These men had been chosen plainclothes agents for obvious reasons: they were quick-witted, safe, and crooked; they alone had the political influence and the money needed to buy promotion in dishonest police administration; they alone had had that close observation and training in the work of the higher grades, which placed them at the head of examinations for promotion in the administrations that were honest. The average patrolman had no chance for advancement in competition with these men of the system.

Over a long period of years this police system has established its traditions, which it hands down from one generation to another. These traditions form a strange code of ethics. Thieves, according to this code, should be caught — if it is not too hard work — and not licensed to operate for money. Money may be taken from citizens who want their stolen goods recovered, but it is only the more crooked detectives who take the money of thieves. Yet "stool pigeons" must be employed as spies upon other criminals, and for this privilege they must have the right to operate in their minor specialties and get a living for themselves. Saloonkeepers and gamblers may be taxed for the privilege of breaking the law. They are a part of the "necessary evil" in a great city, as is prostitution.

Concerning the tax upon prostitution, the tradition of the system is a little different. This is "blood money" — "dirty money." It is always taken, but some officers let the plainclothes agents keep it. They give it up, not on moral grounds but because there is a widespread superstition that this graft is unlucky. A number of men in the system (their names are familiar in the force) who took it have had a great deal of trouble in their families. But someone takes this money, always.

Gradually the management of the New York police began to sense the situation. And, as they watched, crime and vice and criminals kept boiling up from the same old stews on the East Side.

General Bingham was an obstinate and headstrong man. "By ged," said Bingham, slamming his fist down on his desk — and his lower lip quivered and his pointed mustache stood out straight — "we're going after 'em, and we're going after 'em all."

He started first to smash the district with the ordinary police force. Nothing happened, except explanations. "No explanations!" said Bingham. "What I want is results. You're off that job."

Finally, instead of leaving vice to be handled by patrolmen, its suppression was delegated to specialists. This was not, indeed, a part of the theory of the Bingham administration, but it gradually became, in fact, its practice. The suppression of vicious resorts was first made the responsibility of the inspector in a particular district; but inspectors were moved along until one man was found who could be trusted to pound them. And afterward this man was moved from one district to another for the same purpose. He had become a specialist.

In addition, the ex-schoolmaster, Deputy Woods, with the aid of special squads, moved against the ancient dens around Chatham Square. Evidence was secured, new methods were devised for outwitting the sharp corps of lawyers under constant retainer by the various departments of the underworld, and the dives of Chatham Square, whose doors had never closed, day or night, for generations, were shut — and shut to stay.

There was no doubt of the success of this method. The handling of vice is exactly like the handling of crime. It is not a patrolman's business; it is the work of a specialist — of a detective. Evidence must be secured by detective methods — for obvious reasons. Vice is a business carried on by a body of persistent violators of the law, exactly as the great bulk of crime is carried on by professional criminals. And it requires a specially trained body of men who know its operations and its personnel to watch it.

That the methods of the Bingham administration were successful was shown by the growing chorus of threats which rose from the whole underworld. Word came from every direction: "We'll get you yet."

The slum politicians were busy howling day and night for the police commissioner's head. And finally, through the minor incident of photographing a juvenile offender for the detectives' gallery, the crisis came, and the first modern administration of the New York police was forced to a sudden end. At bottom, the fact was that the great forces of the underworld, with their endless ramifications, were too strong to be resisted. They "got" the Bingham administration of the New York police in exactly the same way and for the same reasons that the underworld and their politicians in Paris are credited with having "got" Lepine, the world-famous chief of the Paris police, this last winter.

Now, the Bingham administration, composed of educated and intelligent men, had taken control of the police of the greatest city on the continent in blank ignorance of police work. Their ignorance, plus their intelligence, was exact reason why they reformed it. They examined from the foundation up an organization built upon the traditions and customs of the great body of uneducated men who form police departments and made it over into an entirely different thing. And they demonstrated thoroughly the fact that American police should be commanded, not by a man who has risen within its ranks but by a man of an entirely different mental training who will introduce into the structure the methods of administration common to all really modern institutions.

These pioneers in police work had followed out, in their development of new methods, the simple, logical processes of an orderly, trained mind. They had brought modern organization and system to the suppression of crime in the Detective Bureau, and, passing beyond this, they had applied exactly similar methods to dealing with vice.

But, meanwhile, they had reached the ultimate limits of police work under the old idea of it and had touched a problem far deeper than the police could go. They had reached the system of the schools of the underworld, the source from which came up the constant stream of criminals which was discharged upon the city through the dens they were breaking up in Chatham Square and Second Avenue and Mott Street. To carry the campaign further, there must be recruited still another mental and moral force from outside the ranks of the police.

The theorist and reformer knows very little of the unfailing sources of criminals; he lives in another and less populous world than the one from which they come. But every common patrolman understands it —

for he has seen it all his life. And for this very reason — strange as it may seem — the handling of the thing must be taken from the province of the patrolman and given to the reformer, who is now just beginning to see this huge social problem, the recruiting of the criminal classes — that old evil whose roots grow far down into the awful idle nights and Sundays in the three-room tenements.

When any intelligent person stops to think of this thing, it is clear enough. The young human animal shut up idly in three or four crowded rooms causes a situation intolerable both to himself and to the adults with him. He drifts naturally, often he is driven bodily by his parents, out to the city streets. And there he learns the old unwritten lessons of the night schools of the pavements of New York.

The ingenuity of the young boy pitted against the problem of making a city street a playground is one of the most extraordinary things in a great city. Founded upon the elements of familiar outdoor games, he has invented or adapted half a dozen ways of amusing himself. A tin can is a football, a flight of stone steps and the sidewalk a baseball field, a pointed chip and a broken broomstick a ball and bat. And most elaborate systems count the score. Nothing could be more clever or more pathetic than the efforts of the boy to overcome the limitations of the city street. But, in the end, the street defeats him. The limitations of space turn him unwillingly but certainly from active athletic sports to gambling.

Within the last fifteen or twenty years a new game, by its perfect adaptation to city conditions, has become the most popular pastime of the young boys of big cities. It is the dice game of craps — as old, probably, as the world, but here always the Negro game — very possibly brought from Africa. At any rate, the Negro gambler, coming up from the South with his "bones," has taught it to the whole country. It has become, in the last decade or two, a prepossession of the boys of the tenement districts in New York. Marbles and tops and baseball have their seasons — they demand more space than is accessible. But a pair of "bones" in a boy's pocket, a group on the corner of the sidewalk, and a gang of boys is embarked for hours of excitement in one of the oldest fascinations of the race. It is the game of all seasons and of anyplace. Surpassing all others, this African Negroes' gambling game is now the almost universal pastime of the boy of great cities.

The extent and vitality of public gambling in the great city is a constant surprise to most men who were bred elsewhere. Generations of gamblers are educated, almost inevitably, on the sidewalks of New York and Chicago under existing conditions. And every generation of boys passes on the traditions to its juniors. Children of four or five are taught to "roll the bones" for their older brothers; by the time they are six or seven they know the somewhat complicated count; and in a year or two more they have made their own investment of a couple of cents, asked for the dice in the little newspaper shop around the corner, and are embarked in playing for their own pennies.

Now, the thief, as any city policeman will inform you, is almost invariably a gambler. This may seem odd, at first. But, if you know the city, you know that gambling and thieving almost necessarily go together. There is nothing more natural; for, from the dim edge of babyhood, the thief has stolen to gamble. There is a continual course in the education of crime in New York City, nicely adjusted upward from the first kindergarten lesson in craps to the electric chair.

This desperate juvenile game of craps is a fight to the finish; it usually ends only when all parties except one in the contest are cleaned out financially. And the natural result is a general foray of a good-sized group of boys for the purpose of replenishing their resources. The petty pilfering in a great city is constantly evident even to the most casual observer. Every now and then the passerby sees children scurrying back into a side street with bundles of wood or coal; and everywhere throughout the boundaries of New York there is the scratching of the fingers of juvenile thieves. A great share of their thieving is stimulated by the driving necessities of the popular pastime of the juvenile world which requires financial stakes.

Cement bags are very desirable — they bring 2 cents apiece; bags of kindling wood, taken from demolished buildings, have a market value in the tenement districts of 10 cents; small bags of coal grabbed from wharves are quoted at about the same price. This fuel, the ice from the docks in summer, and vegetables from hucksters' carts always find a ready and constant market among the poorer foreign tenement population — and no questions asked.

So sure is this source of income that boys sometimes conduct a regular little business delivering stolen coal and ice. On the extreme West Side of New York, gangs have made a practice of delivering groceries on Saturday on a regular route. They visit tenements, taking orders at a scale of prices about half the retail grocer's rates; go out in a group to grocery stores and steal enough to fill these orders; take the cash from their customers; and spend the entire afternoon devoting the proceeds to a crap game, from which one boy emerges with the entire sum. So, as naturally as they breathe, generations of gamblers are bred in the great city; and, just as naturally, the child who is destined to be a thief is always sure to be a gambler.

A great proportion of the boys of a city could not, if they would, make their living as professional gamblers or thieves. At fourteen or fifteen they must go to work. And thus they leave the social and political organization of their localities to the Idle Boy — that great social force which dominates to such an extent the recreations and politics of the great city. The Idle Boy —

whether he becomes a professional politician or a professional thief — continues his education through a common and well-defined course of training.

The professional thief — and most thieves, like most prostitutes, are nearer twenty than thirty — continues his education in gambling and thieving simultaneously. His favorite "hangout" is not the liquor saloon — according to the old-time popular belief — it is the cheap pool and billiard parlor or, in rarer cases, a small cigar store with its rear gambling room. The pool parlor, as every detective in the city knows, is the great grammar school of thieves and gamblers.

Pool itself is a promising field for gambling; the surface of the pool table makes an excellent place for the game of craps, and soon the pool parlor has added special crap tables and equipment for other gambling games. It is a little gambling center; and the older boys find that gambling in its higher courses is exactly as stimulating to thievery as is the kindergarten on the sidewalks.

The Idle Boy, who loafs about these places while other boys of his age are working, must have money. Gambling demands it; he needs it to maintain the sartorial effects that are required by the traditions of his set. The pool parlor and little gambling place become the centers at which young thieves originate and pass on methods of crime. And in an exceedingly short time that curious product of new environment, the modern city thief, is sent out into practical life.

He is a soft-handed youth who carefully maintains a code of dressing of his own — a particular haircut, fine-striped suits, deep-cuffed trousers. In his way, he is as vain and scrupulous of his appearance as an eighteenth-century fop. As a matter of fact, he is a most important social figure, with widespread social and political responsibilities.

Very few people realize how far the destinies of a great city are taken charge of by the Idle Boy. The one place where votes form naturally in bunches, ready to the hand of the professional politician, is in the gangs of youths just coming into manhood, into which a large part of New York and Chicago and other cities naturally divide themselves. And the apprentice politician who takes charge of them is, naturally, the Idle Boy, who is developing the physical and social traits of a leader. The more crooked the gang, the more votes it will cast; and, by natural sequence, the "wise boys" graduate successively to take charge of city governments.

It is the Idle Boy, also, who takes over the social life of the city. Dances and "rackets" are his by right of leadership. In the teens the instinct of sex-hunting develops in the gang and is directed by the Idle Boy. Everywhere today there is universal skepticism over the possible continence of the male population before marriage. In the crowded city tenement districts there is small question that nearly all boys begin their sexual experience in their teens.

The little girls are forced into the streets exactly as the boys are; and, in the boys' minds, they come to be divided roughly into "good girls" and "bad girls." The "good girls," it is stated, are those that "their folks make come in by 10 o'clock at night." They are the girls, in other words, whose parents take some care of them.

With the girls, as with the boys, the main trouble is the awful nights and Sundays in the tenements — the restlessness of youth against the bars of circumstance. It is on Sundays that the police must put out their "strong-arm" squad to beat down the wild boys, with half-savage manners, who "roughhouse" the city transportation lines. Special policemen must go here and there to break up the crap games run by the larger boys for bigger stakes, which are the regular Sunday morning institutions of the tenement districts. And all day in summer and all the afternoons in winter, the boys and girls give up Sundays to their own "rackets" or their Sunday matinee dances.

The promoter of these dances and country excursions is still the Idle Boy, backed, generally, by a syndicate of intimates. In summertime they run their trips and dances in the suburbs — their dollar "beer rackets," with dancing and unlimited free beer in some sordid "summer garden" or park, where a few dejected shrubs or a couple of papier-mâché palm trees work Sundays as a forest. In some cases, in Philadelphia and New York, suburban farms rent their grounds and buildings complete on Sundays to these picnic dancing parties. The Idle Boy is in charge of a great share of these entertainments, and he tends always to drag the institution down to his own level. The dance, to him, is a sex hunt.

The girls of the tenements dance early. The sidewalk dance around the street piano is one of the commonest games of their childhood, and they wait anxiously for the time, in their middle teens, when the etiquette of juvenile society first considers them of age to go to public dances. After nightfall, from September to June, all young New York is dancing. There are now nearly 600 licensed public dance halls, and their attendance runs nightly into tens of thousands and on Saturday nights and Sunday afternoons into hundreds of thousands of boys and girls in their teens and early twenties.

Every year in the past decade there has been a growth in the popularity of the public dance. In the last three or four years, since the arrival of the "nigger" dances and the "rags" and the "turkey trots," dancing has become a public obsession. Like the gambling game of craps — which has supplanted or changed the habits of boyhood from the traditions of sport of northern Europe to the games of the Negro — this new dancing is a curious recrudescence, apparently originating from the same source as the gambling game. The "nigger" dance seems to find its main origin in the crude and heathen sexual customs of middle Africa, afterward passing through the centers of prostitutes in large cities, where the contributions of city savages, from Paris to San Francisco, have been added to it.

This "nigger" dancing craze, moving from the South and West to the East, has swept the city populations of America like an epidemic. In most of its many variations, it is not taught by dancing academies with any concern for their reputations or their licenses. But its steps are passed from one person to another, from the youths to the children, until it has gone through the country with the thoroughness of a great popular song. In its simpler and grosser forms, it is the easiest kind of dancing ever introduced — being merely a modified form of walking. Thousands of people who never learned the older dances have picked this up, and the popularity of dancing has been widened tremendously by the fact. Even little children dance the grotesque steps upon the sidewalk.

The promoter of cheap dances has never before had such a public for his enterprises, and never before has dancing been such a provocation to immorality. The recent trend has been entirely toward the ideals of the Idle Boy. Around him centers the organization for sex-hunting of the boys who are seeking the "bad girls"; for strangers in the hall, he and his assistants are constant sources of information on the same subject. The natural instinct of the man to test and tempt the woman is solidified in the dance hall into what is, for all practical purposes, a perfect system.

The Idle Boy is the hero as well as the leader of these affairs. The swashbuckler type, who develops into the ruffian and gunman, has all the charms of masculine audacity suited to impress the immature and romantic female mind. And this and the amiable juvenile worship of reckless courage all feeds his ambition to "go the limit" in any crime he undertakes. The dressy pickpockets, who are naturally clothed in a manner suitable to their public walk in life, are also most attractive to feminine taste; and in a very short time the personal alliance is formed between the flashy or weak "bad girl" and the Idle Boy, in the inevitable semi-marital relation of the criminal and the prostitute.

And so, by gradual and natural steps, the solidarity of the criminal world is built up. The gambler is a thief, the thief is a "cadet"; the prostitute, part wife, part business partner, part slave of her man. And the vice promoters and the slum politicians and the crooked policemen are all a part of the same class.

It was the last focus of this criminal world — the place in the city where all the graduates of the schools found their gathering places — that Bingham, as New York police commissioner, had attacked. And for doing this the underworld, in turn, had broken him.

And then, with the fall and disorganization of the Bingham Police Force and the advent of a new city administration, all the underworld and its women ran wild, until it worked its own destruction and brought down with it its old ally, the police system, through the killing of the famous professional gambler Rosenthal by professional murderers in the hire of a New York police officer.

The attention of the city of New York, and of the nation, was centered by this event upon the police and their alliance with the criminal classes. What is a policeman, and what is his capability and proper sphere? the entire country asked itself.

In the course of the investigations in New York, the Municipal Research Bureau, acting with the Aldermanic Committee, took the statistics concerning the men who entered the New York Police Force in 1912. Of 421 appointed, 4 out of every 5 were born in New York City. The average age on entering the force was 24 years, and about 2 out of every 3 were unmarried. Only 2 of the 421 had an education reaching through a high school; the remainder had gone no further than the grammar grades.

They were drawn from a great variety of occupations — more than a quarter of them from positions like those of drivers and motormen, concerned with the traffic of the public streets; and nearly all of the remainder were drawn from work of a grade somewhat above that of the common laborer. Only about 10 percent had been in clerical positions. About one-third of these men had been arrested, nearly all for the minor offenses in which active, city-bred youths of their class are most apt to be concerned — the commonest charge being that of disorderly conduct.

The police, in short, are drawn from the boys brought up on the streets of New York. They know the poorer population as no reformer can ever know it; for they are a part of it.

In the older Police Force, the patrolman was assigned, whenever possible, to the district he grew up in. And, to some extent, he is still. To the patrolman observing an offense, someone has said, the practical question far too often is: "Shall I take my friend's money or send him to jail?" In the home district he is, naturally, everybody's friend. And, wherever he may be, the people in shady occupations are using every means, direct and indirect, to get upon a friendly footing with him.

Now, a class with the viewpoint and the associations of the patrolman could scarcely be expected, in any case, to originate methods of handling the great and delicate policies required for dealing with vice and crime in a great city. As a matter of fact, the Police Force has never originated any movement toward improvement in administering the law — especially in that greatest of all questions, the suppression of criminal immorality — of its own accord. This has always been the province of the outsider — of the reformer with the up-country ideals of human conduct.

Out of this source has arisen, in the last few years, another movement toward both a more rational and a more human treatment of crime and vice in great cities. From this, it may be hoped, will soon come the complete idea of a new police.

The present old-time idea of a police force is built upon the ideals and traditions of generations of constables and watchmen. At its best, it follows, through the rule-of-thumb processes of a class untrained in modern organization, the business of taking finished offenders, largely for committing crimes against property, and letting pass, as venial offenses, the "necessary evils" (according to its code of reasoning) of vice and gambling and the breaking of the liquor law.

An outline of the new police that American cities must have can be gathered from a consideration of the Bingham experiment in New York and the still broader reforms now being formulated and worked out in other large cities. The new police will put the patrolman into the place for which he is eminently fitted — the position of general neighborhood watchman and guardian. He will be trained for this not-too-easy work in police schools.

Modern commercialized crime, with its specialists, criminal and legal, will be met by the specialization of the Detective Force, helped by the most modern systems of following crimes and identifying criminals.

Vice and excise offenses and gambling will be handled in much the same way. They are carried on by perfectly well-known operators; they should be followed by specialists. It is definitely determined, in every mind that has any knowledge on the subject, that the underworld is a unit which cannot, by its nature, be dissected into artificial parts. The only way to arrest the thief without arresting the gambler or the "cadet" would be to split the individual offender in half, arbitrarily arrest the south side of him as a thief and let the north side go as a gambler.

Then, still beyond the matter of mere administration of law, must come the more important function now generally proposed for the new police — the focusing of the best and soundest sentiment of the community upon the great question of public morals.

For a number of years past, private organizations like the Parkhurst Society and the Committee of Fourteen in New York have been working on the general problem of vice. In the past half-dozen years this interest has quickened and extended. Local agencies in a great many of the cities of the country have been studying the question, and especially the relation of the unfortunate girl to it. One society, the American Vigilance Association, has become a general agency for conducting this work in widely separated cities.

From these movements, quite naturally, has developed a general interest in the personal life and diversions of the population from which criminal and vicious classes are drawn. One notable and most healthy expression of this has been seen in the movement, which has extended across the country, to offset the present wave of indecent dancing by offering opportunities, within the means of the poorest, for dancing under decent and attractive conditions.

And now the latest proposal is to consolidate all the movements of this type in different cities into general morals or public welfare commissions, which would, on the one side, bring the best sentiment of the community to bear upon the enforcement of the law by the police and, on the other, consolidate the movements for breaking up the schools for criminals and prostitutes, which have developed in all our cities, through establishing means for satisfying the normal tendencies and activities of childhood and youth, which are now let loose to run wild toward destruction.

The exact method of relating this new representation of public sentiment to the police is a somewhat debatable matter. The plan is being worked out somewhat differently in different cities — in New York and Pittsburgh and Chicago and San Francisco. But there seems no doubt now that public conscience in different cities will find a means, in these commissions, to express itself effectively upon this whole great subject of public morals in cities; and that this will go far toward effecting a radical change long needed in urban police.

That a new police with new ideals must come in our cities, and must come soon, no one can doubt. This is not merely a question of new methods of organization; it requires a great social reformation. And the outbreaks of strange and barbaric crime in all the great cities of the world — in London and Paris as well as in New York — show that it is one of the greatest and most pressing questions of modern city life which cannot much longer be ignored.

87.

Charles A. Beard: The Constitution as a Product of Economic Interests

Charles Beard's controversial study, An Economic Interpretation of the Constitution of the United States, *appeared in 1913 and influenced two generations of American historians. Beard's thesis was that the moneyed and propertied classes had created the U.S. Constitution to protect their vested interests, and it produced widespread opposition from those who venerated the Founding Fathers. One Marion, Ohio, newspaper called Beard "a chief Hyena" for his "libelous, vicious, and damnable catalogue of filthy lies and rotten perversions." Despite such criticism, Beard contended that his purpose was not to debunk, but rather to interpret history within the economic context in which it occurred; he did not believe, he said, that the American past was the unfolding of some higher destiny. The first chapter of his famous book appears below.*

Source: *An Economic Interpretation of the Constitution of the United States,*
New York, 1913: "Historical Interpretation in the United States."

Broadly speaking, three schools of interpretation have dominated American historical research and generalization. The first of these, which may be justly associated with the name of Bancroft, explains the larger achievements in our national life by reference to the peculiar moral endowments of a people acting under divine guidance; or perhaps it would be more correct to say, it sees in the course of our development the working out of a higher will than that of man. There is to be observed in the history of the struggle for the Constitution, to use Bancroft's words, "the movement of the divine power which gives unity to the universe, and order and connection to events."

Notwithstanding such statements, scattered through Bancroft's pages, it is impossible to describe in a single phrase the ideal that controlled his principles of historical construction, because he was so often swayed by his deference to the susceptibilities of the social class from which he sprang and by the exigencies of the public life in which he played a by no means inconspicuous part. Even telling the whole truth did not lie upon his conscience, for, speaking on the question of the number of Americans who were descendants from transported felons and indented servants, he said that "Having a hand full, he opened his little finger."

Nevertheless, Bancroft constantly recurs in his writings to that "higher power" which is operating in human affairs, although he avoids citing specific events which may be attributed to it. It appears to him to be the whole course of history, rather than any event or set of events, which justifies his theory. "However great," he says, "may be the number of those who persuade themselves that there is in man nothing superior to himself, history interposes with evidence that tyranny and wrong lead inevitably to decay; that freedom and right, however hard may be the struggle, always prove restless. Through this assurance ancient nations learn to renew their youth; the rising generation is incited to take a generous part in the grand drama of time; and old age, staying itself upon sweet Hope as its companion and cherisher, not bating a jot of courage, nor seeing cause to argue against the hand or the will of a higher power, stands waiting in the tranquil conviction that the path of humanity is still fresh with the dews of morning, that the Redeemer of the nations liveth."

The second school of historical interpretation, which in the order of time followed that of Bancroft, may be called the Teutonic, because it ascribes the wonderful achievements of the English-speaking peoples to the peculiar political genius of the Germanic race. Without distinctly repudiating the doctrine of the "higher power" in history, it finds the secret to the "free" institutional development of the Anglo-Saxon world in innate racial qualities.

The thesis of this school is, in brief, as follows. The Teutonic peoples were originally endowed with singular political talents and aptitudes; Teutonic tribes invaded England and destroyed the last vestiges of the older Roman and British culture; they then set an example to the world in the development of "free" government. Descendants of this specially gifted race settled America and fashioned their institutions after old English models. The full fruition of their political genius was reached in the creation of the federal Constitution.

For more than a generation the Teutonic theory of our institutions deeply influenced historical research in the United States; but it was exhausted in the study of local government rather than of great epochs; and it produced no monument of erudition comparable to Stubbs' *Constitutional History of England*. Whatever may be said of this school, which has its historical explanation and justification, it served one exceedingly useful purpose: it was scrupulously careful in the documentation of its preconceptions and thus cultivated a more critical spirit than that which characterized the older historians.

The third school of historical research is not to be characterized by any phrase. It is marked rather by an absence of hypotheses. Its representatives, seeing the many pitfalls which beset the way of earlier writers, have resolutely turned aside from "interpretation" in the larger sense, and concerned themselves with critical editions of the documents and with the "impartial" presentation of related facts. This tendency in American scholarship has been fruitful in its results, for it has produced more care in the use of historical sources and has given us many excellent and accurate surveys of outward events which are indispensable to the student who would inquire more deeply into underlying causes.

Such historical writing, however, bears somewhat the same relation to scientific history which systematic botany bears to ecology; that is, it classifies and orders phenomena, but does not explain their proximate or remote causes and relations. The predominance of such a historical ideal in the United States and elsewhere is not altogether inexplicable; for interpretative schools seem always to originate in social antagonisms. The monarchy, in its rise and development, was never correctly understood as long as it was regarded by all as a mystery which must not be waded into, as James I put it, by ordinary mortals. Without the old regime there would have been no Turgot and Voltaire; Metternich and Joseph de Maistre came after the Revolution.

But the origin of different schools of interpretation in controversies and the prevalence of many mere preconceptions bolstered with a show of learning should not lead us to reject without examination any new hypothesis, such as the theory of economic determinism, on the general assumption of Pascal "that the will, the imagination, the disorders of the body, the thousand concealed infirmities of the intelligence conspire to reduce our discovery of justice and truth to a process of haphazard, in which we more often miss than hit the mark." Such a doctrine of pessimism would make of equal value for the student who would understand, for instance, such an important matter as the origin of the state, Mr. Edward Jenk's severely scientific *History of Politics* and Dr. Nathaniel Johnston's *The Excellency of Monarchical Government, especially the English Monarchy, wherein is largely treated of the Several Benefits of Kingly Government and the Inconvenience of Commonwealths. . . . Likewise the Duty of Subjects and the Mischief of Faction, Sedition, and Rebellion*, published in 1686.

It is not without significance, however, that almost the only work in economic interpretation which has been done in the United States seems to have been inspired at the University of Wisconsin by Professor Turner, now of Harvard. Under the direction of this original scholar and thinker, the influence of the material circumstances of the frontier on American politics was first clearly pointed out. Under his direction also

the most important single contribution to the interpretation of the movement for the federal Constitution was made: O. G. Libby's *Geographical Distribution of the Vote of the Thirteen States on the Federal Constitution.*

In a preface to this work, Professor Turner remarks that the study was designed to contribute

> to an understanding of the relations between the political history of the United States, and the physiographic, social, and economic conditions underlying this history. . . . It is believed that many phases of our political history have been obscured by the attention paid to state boundaries and to the sectional lines of North and South. At the same time the economic interpretation of our history has been neglected. In the study of the persistence of the struggle for state particularism in American constitutional history, it was inevitable that writers should make prominent the state as a political factor. But, from the point of view of the rise and growth of sectionalism and nationalism, it is much more important to note the existence of great social and economic areas, independent of state lines, which have acted as units in political history, and which have changed their political attitude as they changed their economic organization and divided into new groups.

Although the hypothesis that economic elements are the chief factors in the development of political institutions has thus been used in one or two serious works, and has been more or less discussed as a philosophic theory, it has not been applied to the study of American history at large — certainly not with that infinite detailed analysis which it requires. Nor has it received at the hands of professed historians that attention which its significance warrants. On the contrary, there has been a tendency to treat it with scant courtesy and to dismiss it with a sharpness bordering on contempt. Such summary judgment is, of course, wholly unwarranted and premature; for as Dr. William Cunningham remarks, the validity of no hypothesis can be determined until it has been worked to its utmost limits. It is easier to write a bulky volume from statutes, congressional debates, memoirs, and diplomatic notes than it is to ascertain the geographical distribution and political significance of any important group of economic factors. The theory of economic determinism has not been tried out in American history, and until it is tried out, it cannot be found wanting.

Sadly as the economic factors have been ignored in historical studies, the neglect has been all the more pronounced in the field of private and public law. The reason for this is apparent. The aim of instruction in these subjects is intensely practical; there are few research professorships in law; and the "case" system of teaching discourages attempts at generalization and surveys. Not even the elementary work has been done. There has been no generous effort to describe the merely superficial aspects of the development of private law in the United States. There has been no concerted attempt to bring together and make available to students the raw materials of such a history. Most of the current views on the history of our law are derived from occasional disquisitions of judges which are all too frequently shot through with curious errors of fact and conception.

Nor has England advanced far beyond us in the critical interpretation of legal evolution its explanation in terms of, or in relation to, the shifting economic processes and methods in which the law is tangled. It is true that English scholars have produced admirable histories of the law in its outward aspects, such as the monumental work of Pollock and Maitland; and they have made marvelous collections of raw materials, like the publications of the Selden Society. But apart from scattered and brilliant suggestions thrown off occasionally by Maitland in passing, no interpretation has been ventured, and no effort has been made to connect legal phases with economic changes.

In the absence of a critical analysis of legal evolution, all sorts of vague abstractions dominate most of the thinking that is done in the field of law. The characteristic view of the subject taken by American commentators and lawyers immersed in practical affairs is perhaps summed up as finely by Carter as by any writer. "In free, popular states," he says, "the law springs from and is made by the people; and as the process of building it up consists in applying, from time to time, to human actions the popular ideal or standard of justice, justice is the only interest consulted in the work. . . . The law of England and America has been a pure development proceeding from a constant endeavor to apply to the civil conduct of men the ever advancing standard of justice." In other words, law is made out of some abstract stuff known as "justice." What set the standard in the beginning and why does it advance?

The devotion to deductions from "principles" exemplified in particular cases, which is such a distinguishing sign of American legal thinking, has the same effect upon correct analysis which the adherence to abstract terms had upon the advancement of learning — as pointed out by Bacon. The absence of any consideration of the social and economic elements determining the thought of the thinkers themselves is all the more marked when contrasted with the penetration shown by European savants like Jhering, Menger, and Stammler. Indeed, almost the only indication of a possible economic interpretation to be found in current American jurisprudence is implicit in the writings of a few scholars, like Professor Roscoe Pound and Professor Goodnow, and in occasional opinions rendered by Mr. Justice Holmes of the Supreme Court of the United States.

What has here been said about our private law may be more than repeated about our constitutional history and law. This subject, though it has long held an honorable position in the American scheme of learning, has not yet received the analytical study which its intrinsic importance merits. In the past, it has often been taught in the law schools by retired judges who treated it as a branch of natural and moral philosophy or by practical lawyers who took care for the instant need of things. Our great commentaries, Kent, Story, Miller, are never penetrating; they are generally confined to statements of fact; and designed to inculcate the spirit of reverence rather than of understanding. And of constitutional histories, strictly speaking, we have none, except the surveys of superficial aspects by Curtis and Bancroft.

In fact, the juristic theory of the origin and nature of the Constitution is marked by the same lack of analysis of determining forces which characterized older historical writing in general. It may be stated in the following manner: The Constitution proceeds from the whole people; the people are the original source of all political authority exercised under it; it is founded on broad general principles of liberty and government entertained, for some reason, by the whole people and having no reference to the interest or advantage of any particular group or class. "By calm meditation and friendly councils," says Bancroft, they [the people] had prepared a Constitution which, in the union of freedom with strength and order, excelled every one known before. . . . In the happy morning of their existence as one of the powers of the world, they had chosen justice for their guide; and while they proceeded on their way with a well-founded confidence and joy, all the friends of mankind invoked success on their endeavor as the only hope for renovating the life of the civilized world.

With less exaltation, Chief Justice Marshall states the theory, in his opinion in the case of *M'Culloch* v. *Maryland:*

The government proceeds directly from the people; is "ordained and established" in the name of the people; and is declared to be ordained "in order to form a more perfect union, to establish justice, insure domestic tranquillity, and secure the blessings of liberty" to themselves and to their posterity. The assent of the states, in their sovereign capacity, is implied in calling a convention, and thus submitting that instrument to the people. But the people were at perfect liberty to accept or reject it; and their act was final. . . . The government of the Union, then (whatever may be the influence of this fact on the case) is emphatically and truly a government of the people. In form and in substance it emanates from them. Its powers are granted by them, and are to be exercised directly on them, and for their benefit. . . . It is the government of all; its powers are delegated by all; it represents all, and acts for all.

In the juristic view, the Constitution is not only the work of the whole people, but it also bears in it no traces of the party conflict from which it emerged. Take, for example, any of the traditional legal definitions of the Constitution; Miller's will suffice:

A constitution, in the American sense of the word, is any instrument by which the fundamental powers of the government are established, limited, and defined, and by which these powers are distributed among the several departments for their more safe and useful exercise, for the benefit of the body politic. . . . It is not, however, the origin of private rights, nor the foundation of laws. It is not the cause, but the consequence of personal and political freedom. It declares those natural and fundamental rights of individuals, for the security and common enjoyment of which governments are established.

Nowhere in the commentaries is there any evidence of the fact that the rules of our fundamental law are designed to protect any class in its rights, or secure the property of one group against the assaults of another.

"The Constitution," declares Bancroft,

establishes nothing that interferes with equality and individuality. It knows nothing of differences by descent, or opinions, of favored classes, or legalized religion, or the political power of property. It leaves the individual alongside of the individual. . . . As the sea is made up of drops, American society is composed of separate, free, and constantly moving atoms, ever in reciprocal action . . . so that the institutions and laws of the country rise out of the masses of individual thought, which, like the waters of the ocean, are rolling evermore.

In turning from the vague phraseology of Bancroft to an economic interpretation of constitutional history, it is necessary to realize at the outset that law is not an abstract thing, a printed page, a volume of statutes, a statement by a judge. So far as it becomes of any consequence to the observer it must take on a real form; it must govern actions; it must determine positive relations between men; it must prescribe processes and juxtapositions. A statute may be on the books for an age, but unless, under its provisions, a determinate arrangement of human relations is brought about or maintained, it exists only in the imagination. Separated from the social and economic fabric by which it is, in part, conditioned and which, in turn, it helps to condition, it has no reality.

Now, most of the law (except the elemental law of community defense) is concerned with the property relations of men, which reduced to their simple terms mean the processes by which the ownership of concrete forms of property is determined or passes from one person to another. As society becomes more settled and industrial in character, mere defense against violence (a very considerable portion of which originates in forcible attempts to change the ownership of property) becomes of relatively less importance; and property relations increase in complexity and subtlety.

But it may be said that constitutional law is a peculiar branch of the law; that it is not concerned primarily with property or with property relations, but with organs of government, the suffrage, administration. The superficiality of this view becomes apparent at a second glance. Inasmuch as the primary object of a government, beyond the mere repression of physical violence, is the making of the rules which determine the property relations of members of society, the dominant classes whose rights are thus to be determined must perforce obtain from the government such rules as are consonant with the larger interests necessary to the continuance of their economic processes, or they must themselves control the organs of government. In a stable despotism the former takes place; under any other system of government, where political power is shared by any portion of the population, the methods and nature of this control become the problem of prime importance; in fact, the fundamental problem in constitutional law. The social structure by which one type of legislation is secured and another prevented — that is, the constitution — is a secondary or derivative feature arising from the nature of the economic groups seeking positive action and negative restraint.

In what has just been said there is nothing new to scholars who have given any attention to European writings on jurisprudence. It is based in the first instance on the doctrine advanced by Jhering that law does not "grow," but is, in fact, "made" — adapted to precise interests which may be objectively determined. It was not original with Jhering. Long before he worked out the concept in his epoch-making book, *Der Zweck im Recht,* Lassalle had set it forth in his elaborate *Das System der erworbenen Rechte,* and long before Lassalle had thought it through, our own Madison had formulated it, after the most wide-reaching researches in history and politics.

In fact, the inquiry which follows is based upon the political science of James Madison, the father of the Constitution and later President of the Union he had done so much to create. This political science runs through all of his really serious writings and is formulated in its most precise fashion in *The Federalist* as follows:

> The diversity in the faculties of men, from which the rights of property originate, is not less an insuperable obstacle to a uniformity of interests. The protection of these faculties is the first object of government. From the protection of different and unequal faculties of acquiring property, the possession of different degrees and kinds of property immediately results; and from the influence of these on the sentiments and views of the respective proprietors, ensues a division of society into different interests and parties. . . . The most common and durable source of factions has been the various and unequal distribution of property. Those who hold and those who are without property have ever formed distinct interests in society. Those who are creditors, and those who are debtors, fall under a like discrimination. A landed interest, a manufacturing interest, a mercantile interest, a moneyed interest, with many lesser interests, grow up of necessity in civilized nations and divide them into different classes, actuated by different sentiments and views. The regulation of these various and interfering interests forms the principal task of modern legislation, and involves the spirit of party and faction in the necessary and ordinary operations of the government.

Here we have a masterly statement of the theory of economic determinism in politics. Different degrees and kinds of property inevitably exist in modern society; party doctrines and "principles" originate in the sentiments and views which the possession of various kinds of property creates in the minds of the possessors; class and group divisions based on property lie at the basis of modern government; and politics and constitutional law are inevitably a reflex of these contending interests. Those who are inclined to repudiate the hypothesis of economic determinism as a European importation must, therefore, revise their views, on learning that one of the earliest, and certainly one of the clearest, statements of it

came from a profound student of politics who sat in the convention that framed our fundamental law.

The requirements for an economic interpretation of the formation and adoption of the Constitution may be stated in a hypothetical proposition which, although it cannot be verified absolutely from ascertainable data, will at once illustrate the problem and furnish a guide to research and generalization.

It will be admitted without controversy that the Constitution was the creation of a certain number of men, and it was opposed by a certain number of men. Now, if it were possible to have an economic biography of all those connected with its framing and adoption — perhaps about 160,000 men altogether — the materials for scientific analysis and classification would be available. Such an economic biography would include a list of the real and personal property owned by all of these men and their families: lands and houses, with incumbrances, money at interest, slaves, capital invested in shipping and manufacturing, and in state and continental securities.

Suppose it could be shown from the classification of the men who supported and opposed the Constitution that there was no line of property division at all; that is, that men owning substantially the same amounts of the same kinds of property were equally divided on the matter of adoption or rejection — it would then become apparent that the Constitution had no ascertainable relation to economic groups or classes, but was the product of some abstract causes remote from the chief business of life — gaining a livelihood.

Suppose, on the other hand, that substantially all of the merchants, money lenders, security holders, manufacturers, shippers, capitalists, and financiers and their professional associates are to be found on one side in support of the Constitution and that substantially all or the major portion of the opposition came from the nonslaveholding farmers and the debtors. Would it not be pretty conclusively demonstrated that our fundamental law was not the product of an abstraction known as "the whole people," but of a group of economic interests which must have expected beneficial results from its adoption? Obviously all the facts here desired cannot be discovered, but the data presented in the following chapters bear out the latter hypothesis, and thus a reasonable presumption in favor of the theory is created.

Of course, it may be shown (and perhaps can be shown) that the farmers and debtors who opposed the Constitution were, in fact, benefited by the general improvement which resulted from its adoption. It may likewise be shown, to take an extreme case, that the English nation derived immense advantages from the Norman Conquest and the orderly administrative processes which were introduced, as it undoubtedly did; nevertheless, it does not follow that the vague thing known as "the advancement of general welfare" or some abstraction known as "justice" was the immediate, guiding purpose of the leaders in either of these great historic changes. The point is, that the direct, impelling motive in both cases was the economic advantages which the beneficiaries expected would accrue to themselves first, from their action. Further than this, economic interpretation cannot go. It may be that some larger world process is working through each series of historical events; but ultimate causes lie beyond our horizon.

88.

Elihu Root: The Proper Pace of Political Change

In April 1913, while he was a senator from New York, Elihu Root was invited to deliver a series of lectures at Princeton University. Former secretary of state and winner of the Nobel Peace Prize in 1912, Root was one of the most respected and influential American politicians of the first quarter of the twentieth century. A conservative, he was nevertheless well aware of the pressures for change and reform, and on the whole he had been in agreement with Theodore Roosevelt's New Nationalism. But he was concerned that the pace of change be "reasonable." A passage from his first lecture, "Experiments in Government," is reprinted here.

Source: *Addresses on Government and Citizenship*, Robert Bacon and James B. Scott, eds., Cambridge, 1916, pp. 79-97.

In this country we have set forth in the Declaration of Independence the principles which we consider to lie at the basis of civil society: "that all men are created equal, that they are endowed by their Creator with certain unalienable rights, that among these are life, liberty, and the pursuit of happiness. That to secure these rights, governments are instituted among men, deriving their just powers from the consent of the governed."

In our federal and state constitutions we have established the institutions through which these rights are to be secured. We have declared what officers shall make the laws, what officers shall execute them, what officers shall sit in judgment upon claims of right under them. We have prescribed how these officers shall be selected and the tenure by which they shall hold their offices. We have limited them in the powers which they are to exercise, and, where it has been deemed necessary, we have imposed specific duties upon them. The body of rules thus prescribed constitute the governmental institutions of the United States.

When proposals are made to change these institutions there are certain general considerations which should be observed.

The first consideration is that free government is impossible except through prescribed and established governmental institutions which work out the ends of government through many separate human agents, each doing his part in obedience to law. Popular will cannot execute itself directly except through a mob. Popular will cannot get itself executed through an irresponsible executive, for that is simple autocracy. An executive limited only by the direct expression of popular will cannot be held to responsibility against his will, because, having possession of all the powers of government, he can prevent any true, free, and general expression adverse to himself, and unless he yields voluntarily he can be overturned only by a revolution.

The familiar Spanish-American dictatorships are illustrations of this. A dictator once established by what is, or is alleged to be, public choice never permits an expression of public will which will displace him, and he goes out only through a new revolution because he alone controls the machinery through which he could be displaced peaceably. . . .

We should, therefore, reject every proposal which involves the idea that the people can rule merely by voting, or merely by voting and having one man or group of men to execute their will.

A second consideration is that, in estimat-

ing the value of any system of governmental institutions, due regard must be had to the true functions of government and to the limitations imposed by nature upon what it is possible for government to accomplish. We all know of course that we cannot abolish all the evils in this world by statute or by the enforcement of statutes, nor can we prevent the inexorable law of nature which decrees that suffering shall follow vice and all the evil passions and folly of mankind. Law cannot give to depravity the rewards of virtue, to indolence the rewards of industry, to indifference the rewards of ambition, or to ignorance the rewards of learning. The utmost that government can do is measurably to protect men, not against the wrong they do themselves but against wrong done by others, and to promote the long, slow process of educating mind and character to a better knowledge and nobler standards of life and conduct.

We know all this, but when we see how much misery there is in the world and instinctively cry out against it, and when we see some things that government may do to mitigate it, we are apt to forget how little after all it is possible for any government to do, and to hold the particular government of the time and place to a standard of responsibility which no government can possibly meet.

The chief motive power which has moved mankind along the course of development which we call the progress of civilization has been the sum total of intelligent selfishness in a vast number of individuals, each working for his own support, his own gain, his own betterment. It is that which has cleared the forests and cultivated the fields and built the ships and railroads, made the discoveries and inventions, covered the earth with commerce, softened by intercourse the enmities of nations and races, and made possible the wonders of literature and of art. Gradually, during the long process, selfishness has grown more intelligent, with a broader view of individual benefit from the common good, and gradually the influences of nobler standards of altruism, of justice, and human sympathy have impressed themselves upon the conception of right conduct among civilized men.

But the complete control of such motives will be the millennium. Any attempt to enforce a millennial standard now by law must necessarily fail, and any judgment which assumes government's responsibility to enforce such a standard must be an unjust judgment. Indeed, no such standard can ever be forced. It must come, not by superior force but from the changed nature of man, from his willingness to be altogether just and merciful.

A third consideration is that it is not merely useless but injurious for government to attempt too much. It is manifest that to enable it to deal with the new conditions I have described we must invest government with authority to interfere with the individual conduct of the citizen to a degree hitherto unknown in this country. When government undertakes to give the individual citizen protection by regulating the conduct of others toward him in the field where formerly he protected himself by his freedom of contract, it is limiting the liberty of the citizen whose conduct is regulated and taking a step in the direction of paternal government. While the new conditions of industrial life make it plainly necessary that many such steps shall be taken, they should be taken only so far as they are necessary and are effective. Interference with individual liberty by government should be jealously watched and restrained, because the habit of undue interference destroys that independence of character without which in its citizens no free government can endure.

We should not forget that while institutions receive their form from national character they have a powerful reflex influence upon that character. Just so far as a nation allows its institutions to be molded by its weaknesses of character rather than by its strength it creates an influence to increase weakness at the expense of strength.

The habit of undue interference by government in private affairs breeds the habit of undue reliance upon government in private affairs at the expense of individual initiative, energy, enterprise, courage, independent manhood.

The strength of self-government and the motive power of progress must be found in the characters of the individual citizens who make up a nation. Weaken individual character among a people by comfortable reliance upon paternal government and a nation soon becomes incapable of free self-government and fit only to be governed: the higher and nobler qualities of national life that make for ideals and effort and achievement become atrophied and the nation is decadent.

A fourth consideration is that in the nature of things all government must be imperfect because men are imperfect. Every system has its shortcomings and inconveniences; and these are seen and felt as they exist in the system under which we live, while the shortcomings and inconveniences of other systems are forgotten or ignored.

It is not unusual to see governmental methods reformed and, after a time, long enough to forget the evils that caused the change, to have a new movement for a reform which consists in changing back to substantially the same old methods that were cast out by the first reform.

The recognition of shortcomings or inconveniences in government is not by itself sufficient to warrant a change of system. There should be also an effort to estimate and compare the shortcomings and inconveniences of the system to be substituted, for although they may be different they will certainly exist.

A fifth consideration is that whatever changes in government ought to be made, we should follow the method which undertakes as one of its cardinal points to hold fast that which is good.

Visitors to New York's Metropolitan Museum view Leutze's "Washington Crossing the Delaware"

ART AND THE FUTURE

The decade after 1900 brought intimations of radically new perceptions in the arts. In architecture, the prevailing styles ranged from Eclectic Cluttered to Tenement Squalid, but the largely ignored "prairie house" designs of Frank Lloyd Wright hinted at future developments. The art world was peaceful in its assimilation of conservative European traditions. There was some toying with the impressionists' insights into color, a certain grudging respect for the nativists, Homer and Eakins, but it was largely a time of secure values and perceptions. The calm was disturbed from two directions early in the 20th century: the "realists" like John Sloan, Robert Henri, and George Luks pointedly rejected idealization or academic exercise in painting, and were dubbed the "apostles of ugliness" by the established art world; and in Europe truly radical departures in technique and perception were developing which would descend on an unprepared American audience in 1913 in a swirl of definitions — cubist, fauvist, futurist, expressionist. During the same period the filmmakers were experimenting with their new medium, mastering its technical possibilities and developing viable forms. The inherent ambivalance of the medium as an art form was exposed from the beginning: the commercial potential was quickly recognized and exploited, while for those who saw its suitability for pure expression it was an exciting new field for discovery.

(Above) View of the Singer Building under construction in New York City in 1910; (below) interior of the House of Representatives in Harrisburg, Pa., 1906, as seen from the balcony

Biltmore Estate, Asheville, N.C.

United Press International

Richard Nickel

(Above) "Biltmore," designed for the Vanderbilts by Richard M. Hunt in the style of a chateau

The popular architect of 1910 was a skillful eclectic, capable of combining elements of older, proven styles into new and yet comfortably familiar structures. On the other hand, there was Frank Lloyd Wright, an architect of boundless daring, and one considered not quite safe. By 1915 Wright had already developed the basic theory of the "prairie house" style — the adaptation of a building to its function and its site, with an emphasis on the utilization of space, of the natural colors and textures of materials, and on the incorporation of human values and scales.

(Left) Frank Lloyd Wright; (below) the "Robie House" in Chicago, an early example of Wright's prairie house style, emphasizing horizontals

(Above) "The Bowery at Night," 1895; original drawing by Louis Sonntag, Jr.

American painters were producing imitations of 19th-century models to please the conservative art-buying public. Representational art, with themes based on nature and the common man, was the standard of aesthetics until February 17, 1913, when the Association of American Painters and Sculptors opened its now famous Armory Show in New York City. This singular event forced the experimental forms and ferment of European artists on an unprepared and generally unreceptive — even hostile — American art public.

(Left) "South Boston Pier," watercolor by Maurice B. Prendergast, 1896; (below) "Golden Afternoon, Oregon" by Childe Hassam, 1908

(Above) A gallery at the New York Armory Show, 1913; (bottom right) lampoon of Duchamp's controversial "Nude Descending a Staircase," which became a symbol of the general hostility aroused by abstract painting; (below) "Brooklyn Bridge" by Joseph Stella

The Armory Show was conceived as a comprehensive exhibit of the work of the most advanced American artists plus "a few radical things from abroad." Under the guidance of Arthur B. Davies, however, it grew into the most complete exhibition of contemporary art to be held anywhere in 25 years. Virtually every modern "master" was represented: Cezanne, Van Gogh, Gauguin, Matisse, Picasso, Dufy, Kandinsky, Leger, Rouault, and Marcel Duchamp, whose "Nude Descending a Staircase" was considered most radical by the curious throngs.

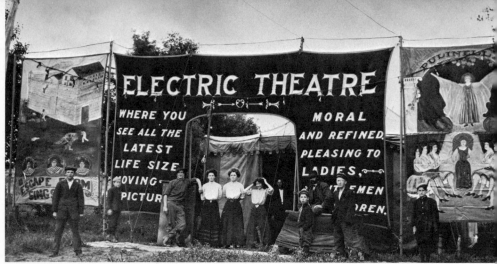

Charles Phelps Cushing

Traveling picture show set up in a Kansas town, 1910

George Eastman House

The movies progressed from a minor attraction in the arcades to a vaudeville time-filler to a major entertainment medium in a relatively short time. In 1903 Edwin S. Porter produced "The Great Train Robbery," firmly establishing the narrative capacity of the motion picture; in 1905 the first fully-equipped movie theater opened in Pittsburgh and was dubbed a nickelodeon. Within four years there were 8,000 such theaters, supplied by several competing production companies and already regulated by an industry monopoly.

(Left) Scene from Edison's film, "The Great Train Robbery," 1903; (bottom) the kinetographic theater at Edison's laboratory

Edison National Historic Site

(Above) Mack Swain, Gloria Swanson and the Sennett Bathing Beauties, 1916

(Left) Scene from the 1915 production, "Birth of a Nation" directed by D. W. Griffith; (below) Pearl White in the "Perils of Pauline"

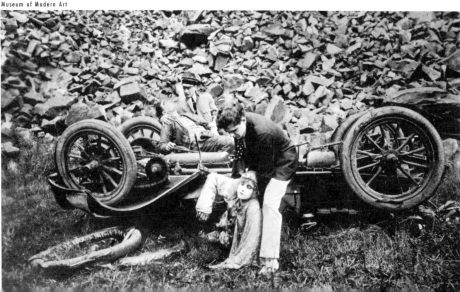

William Dean Howells, widely considered during his life the "dean of American letters," was important primarily in the encouragement and assistance he offered others. Howells' breadth of appreciation encompassed both Henry James and Mark Twain, often taken to represent opposite poles in American literature. Howells' own critical position, a half-hearted, melioristic realism, was fortunately subordinate to his recognition of ability; thus his proteges included Stephen Crane, Hamlin Garland, and Frank Norris, all hard realists and critics of American life.

(Above) **William Dean Howells**; (right) **Henry and William James**; (below) **Paul Lawrence Dunbar,** one of Howells' proteges; (right) **Mark Twain**

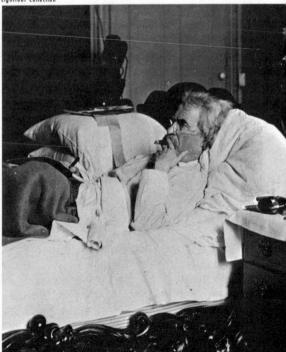

As the generation of James and Twain passed, new elements were appearing in American literature. The simple realism of Howells became progressively harsher and less "smiling"; from "Silas Lapham" to Crane's "Maggie" to Dreiser's naturalistic novels and finally to the explicit social and political doctrines of Upton Sinclair and Jack London, there was a direct and rapid progress from compromise to conscience.

(Above left) Emily Dickinson, whose poetry, published posthumously, achieved wide popularity; (above) Stephen Crane; (below left) Jack London; (below) O. Henry (William Sydney Porter)

In the literature of the period, there was, of course, the usual distance between the best and the popular; while pessimism and even despair fill the former, the latter was still a field of adventure and optimism. America's two original heroic characters, the frontiersman and the business success, exemplified these qualities, and dominated the vastly popular Dime Novel market. Declining after 1910, the Dime Novel, with its Buffalo Bill and Horatio Alger, lingered on in a generation raised on its myths, the reflections of an earlier age's fond dreams.

(Top) Horatio Alger (right) in an early magnesium flash light photograph by Edgar S. Hayes, 1889; (right) early Dime Novel by William F. Cody, published in 1884; (bottom) painting by C. M. Russell in the late 19th century for the state capitol in Helena, Mont., depicting the meeting between Lewis and Clark and the Flatheads

1914

89.

The Profit-Sharing Plan of the Ford Motor Company

To the surprise of labor leaders and the consternation of manufacturers, Henry Ford announced on January 5, 1914, that a minimum wage of $5 a day would be instituted immediately in the Ford Motor Company plants, along with a profit-sharing plan for all male employees. The average wage in 1914 in most industries was less than half that rate for a nine-hour day, and profit-sharing plans were extremely rare. Ford was attacked, but his decision was based on three important assumptions, all of which proved correct. First, he believed that there was a large market for the automobile if it could be produced and sold for a relatively small cost; second, that with an efficient assembly-line approach to production he could make cars for much less than other manufacturers; and, third (and perhaps most important), that if he paid his workers well, they would become his best customers. A newspaper account of Ford's announcement appears here.

Source: *Detroit Journal*, January 5, 1914.

THE FORD MOTOR COMPANY will give to its employees during the year of 1914 the sum of $10 million in addition to their wages.

This will not be a wage increase but a distribution of profits. It will be added, however, semimonthly to the pay envelopes of the men. In 1915, the distribution might be more or less than $10 million dependent on business conditions.

A minimum wage of $5 a day will be established by the addition of the profit distribution to wages. The present minimum wage in the great motorcar factory is $2.34. From next Monday to the end of the year, even the lowliest laborer and the man who merely sweeps the floors will get at least $5 a day.

Further, the eight-hour day is instituted. At present the Ford factory has two nine-hour shifts. It now will install three eight-hour shifts. . . .

Between 25,000 and 30,000 men will benefit greatly by the profit distribution. Fifteen thousand of them now work in the huge factory out Woodward Avenue. Four thousand more men are to be hired there during the present month and will come under the profit-sharing plan. The others who will share in the rich division number 7,000 to 8,000 and are scattered all over the world, working in Ford branches in Canada, Mexico, South America, Europe, Asia, Africa, and the Antipodes, even the Fiji Islands being included.

Every male Ford employee twenty-two years old will share at once in the distribution. About 10 percent of the employees in the factory here are women, engaged in the electrical department or in office work, and boys between eighteen and twenty-two. The women will not share in the distribution, not being considered the economic factors that men workers are, but they will get substantial wage boosts instead. Of the boys between eighteen and twenty-two, those who support their families or have others dependent on their earnings, will be included with their older fellow workers in the profit sharing.

No man will be discharged from the Ford employ except for unfaithfulness or proved inefficiency. Foremen will not be able to discharge employees. The employee will be given chances to make good in one department after another until the proper niche for him is found or his complete inefficiency is established.

If the factory is compelled to shut down for a time, things will be arranged to have the lay-off period come in the summertime, when farmers are calling for harvest hands and the man laid off will have a chance to step out of the factory and work the time in the fields.

The plan of profit distribution is one of social justice, the Ford Company declares. The extra money to the employees will not come out of the public, as price of cars will not be raised but will be lowered when possible. The money will be diverted from the stockholders to the workingmen.

The Ford Company financial statement as of September 30, 1912, showed assets of [about $21 million] and surplus of [about $14 million]. One year later, September 30, 1913, it showed assets of [about $35 million] and surplus of [about $28 million].

The profit-sharing plan of the Ford Motor Company, whereby its employees will divide $10 million in the present year, was announced to the newspapers of the city by Henry Ford, president, and James Couzens, vice-president and treasurer, Monday morning.

Seated in Mr. Couzens' office at the plant out Woodward Avenue, the two motorcar men discussed quietly the greatest step ever taken in industrial history. That the details of their plan would startle the whole world did not excite them. Mr. Ford announced simply that they had determined upon a plan to share their prosperity with their employees, and that first of all he wanted the newspapermen to know the details of the plan they had prepared.

Mr. Couzens then read from a statement covering the details, inviting questions on any points that needed elucidation.

Mr. Ford was looking out of the side window of the office when the discussion ended. From the window was a view down Woodward Avenue and along part of Manchester Avenue to the side of the factory buildings. Three or four hundred men were in the streets and on the sidewalks, some heading for the factory entrance to ask for work, others going back.

"There's the principal reason for the eight-hour day," said Mr. Ford, waving in the direction of the crowd. "With the eight-hour day and three shifts working we can put on 4,000 more of those men who are anxious to be at work."

"Yes," said Mr. Couzens, "we even considered a four-hour day so that still more men could be employed, but we could not work out such a day and retain our organization. So we adopted the eight-hour day."

The statement read by Mr. Couzens said:

The Ford Motor Company, the greatest and most successful automobile manufacturing company in the world, will, on January 12, inaugurate the greatest revolution in the matter of rewards for its workers ever known to the industrial world.

At one stroke it will reduce the hours of labor from nine to eight, and add to every man's pay a share of the profits of the house. The smallest amount to be received by any man twenty-two years old and upward will be $5 per day. The minimum wage is now $2.34 per day of nine hours.

All but 10 percent of the employees will at once share in the profits. Only 10 percent of the men now employed are under twenty-two and even every one of those under twenty-two will have a chance of showing himself entitled to $5 per day.

Instead of waiting until the end of the year to make a distribution of profits among their employees in one lump bonus sum, Mr. Ford and Mr. Couzens have estimated the year's prospective business and have decided upon what they feel will be a safe amount to award the workers. This will be spread over the whole year and paid on the regular semimonthly days.

The factory is now working two shifts of nine hours each. This will be changed to three shifts of eight hours each. The number employed is now about 15,000 and this will be increased by 4,000 or 5,000. The men who now earn $2.34 per day of nine hours will get at least $5 per day of eight hours.

This will apply to every man of twenty-two years of age or upward without regard to the nature of his employment. In order that the young men from eighteen to twenty-two years of age may be entitled to a share in the profits, he must show himself sober, saving, steady, industrious, and must satisfy the superintendent and staff that his money will not be wasted in riotous living.

Young men who are supporting families, widowed mothers, younger brothers and sisters will be treated like those over twenty-two.

It is estimated that over $10 million will be thus distributed over and above the regular wages of the men.

"The commonest laborer who sweeps the floor shall receive his $5 per day," said Henry Ford.

"It is our belief," said Mr. Couzens, "that social justice begins at home. We want those who have helped us to produce this great institution and are helping to maintain it to share our prosperity. We want them to have present profits and future prospects. Thrift and good service and sobriety all will be encouraged and recognized."

"If we are obliged," said Mr. Ford, "to lay men off for want of sufficient work at any season, we propose to so plan our year's work that the layoff shall be in the harvest time, July, August, and September, not in the winter. We hope in such case to induce our men to respond to the calls of the farmers for harvest hands and not to lie idle and dissipate their savings. We shall make it our business to get in touch with the farmers and to induce our employees to answer calls for harvest help.

"No man will be discharged if we can help it, except for unfaithfulness or inefficiency. No foreman in the Ford Company has the power to discharge a man. He may send him out of his department if he does not make good. The man is then sent to our 'clearinghouse' covering all the departments and is repeatedly tried in other work until we find the job he is suited for, provided he is honestly trying to render good service."

"We are quite sure," said Mr. Couzens, "that we shall still pay handsome dividends to our stockholders and will set aside reasonable amounts for additions and improvements and assembling plants in other parts of the country. And after that it is our hope to be able to do still better by our employees. We want them to be in reality partners in our enterprise."

Thus the Ford Motor Company sets the pace for prosperous employers everywhere. It shows the world a plan for dividing profits with its workers. In the discussion of the plan Mr. Couzens remarked:

"Believing as we do that a division of our earnings between capital and labor is unequal, we have sought a plan of relief suitable for our business. We do not feel sure that it is the best, but we have felt impelled to make a start and make it now. We do not agree with those employers who declare, as did a recent writer in a magazine in excusing himself for not practising what he preached, that 'the movement toward the bettering of society must be universal.' We think that one concern can make a start and create an example for other employers. And that is our chief object.

"The public need have no fear that this action of ours will result in any increase in prices of our products. On the contrary we hope to keep up our past record of reducing prices each year.

"We may have to make changes in our plan. If hard times should befall us we may have to reduce or modify our distribution of profits. But the outlook now is such as to justify this distribution for the present year."

"We believe," said Mr. Ford, "in making 20,000 men prosperous and contented rather than follow the plan of making a few slave drivers in our establishment multimillionaires."

"The girl and women employees will not share in the profit distribution?" Mr. Couzens was asked.

"No," he replied. "They are not the same economic factors as the men are. They do not control the standard of living. There are 200 or 300 women employed in the electrical department. The rest that are here do office work. The average woman employee cannot be regarded as a fixture in a business as a man can be. A woman will leave at almost any time, for almost any reason, and when she stays long enough to be a dependable worker, she is apt to get married and have someone else support her. It is the man we aim to benefit. However, in connection with the profit sharing, the women employees will not lose, for there will be substantial raises of wages for them."

"Will the profits be shared with employees of the company outside the city?"

"Yes, our employees all over the world will benefit. We have 15,000 men at work here now and about 50 percent of that number scattered in our branches in every corner of the world. They all will share in the profits.

"The sociological side of profit sharing is one of great importance and one to which we have given some consideration already, but will give a great deal more from now on," added Mr. Couzens. "We have a sociological department to look after our employees' welfare, and this will be greatly extended. Young men who have plenty of money may spend it wastefully or in riotous living. There are many now who make more than $5 a day, and they will get $7 to $10 a day under the new plan.

"We want to see that our employees do not lose their efficiency because of prosperity and will have our sociological department work along that line. Employees who cannot remain sober and industrious will be dismissed, but no one will be let out without being given every possible chance to make good. No one will be discharged until we find that he is of no use to us in any way whatever."

"When will the profit-sharing plan be announced to the employees?" Mr. Couzens was asked.

"It will have no announcement beyond the increase in their wages next payday and what they read in the newspapers," he replied.

Both Mr. Ford and Mr. Couzens said that it would be impossible to estimate what profits might be shared next year by the employees.

"Business conditions may change by that time," said Mr. Couzens. "Hard times might affect the business if they came. We might have competition that would reduce our profits. But if there is nothing changed over present conditions, it is possible that the profits to be shared would be greater next year than this. We are making a beginning now and will make any improvements to our plan that we can later."

90.

Vachel Lindsay: "Abraham Lincoln Walks at Midnight"

Vachel Lindsay began writing poems in 1897, but for years he published only pamphlets that attracted little attention. In January 1913, however, his "General William Booth Enters into Heaven," a not altogether complimentary study of a Salvation Army leader, was published in Harriet Monroe's Poetry: A Magazine of Verse, *and immediately established him as a poet of importance. Born in Springfield, Illinois, Lindsay was a lifelong admirer of Abraham Lincoln, and in 1914, when World War I broke out in Europe, he tried to imagine how the great Civil War President and martyr would have reacted to the event. "Abraham Lincoln Walks at Midnight," which reflected Lindsay's hatred of war as well as his almost religious belief in Lincoln's powers, was the result.*

Source: *Independent*, September 21, 1914.

ABRAHAM LINCOLN WALKS AT MIDNIGHT

(*In Springfield, Illinois*)

It is portentous, and a thing of state
That here at midnight, in our little town
A mourning figure walks, and will not rest,
Near the old courthouse pacing up and down.

Or by his homestead, or in shadowed yards
He lingers where his children used to play,
Or through the market, on the well-worn stones
He stalks until the dawn-stars burn away.

A bronzed, lank man! His suit of ancient black,
A famous high top-hat and plain worn shawl
Make him the quaint great figure that men love,
The prairie-lawyer, master of us all.

He cannot sleep upon his hillside now.
He is among us — as in times before!
And we who toss and lie awake for long
Breathe deep, and start, to see him pass the door.

His head is bowed. He thinks on men and kings.
Yea, when the sick world cries, how can he sleep?
Too many peasants fight, they know not why,
Too many homesteads in black terror weep.

The sins of all the warlords burn his heart.
He sees the dreadnaughts scouring every main.
He carries on his shawl-wrapped shoulders now
The bitterness, the folly and the pain.

He cannot rest until a spirit-dawn
Shall come — the shining hope of Europe free:
The league of sober folk, the Workers' Earth,
Bringing long peace to Cornland, Alp and Sea.

It breaks his heart that kings must murder still,
That all his hours of travail here for men
Seem yet in vain. And who will bring white peace
That he may sleep upon his hill again?

91.

Mary Antin: In Defense of the Immigrant

Mary Antin, a Russian immigrant child who came to America in 1894, grew up to become a writer who spoke with eloquence and understanding of the insecurity and fear of the many newcomers to our land. While some legislators were agitating for restrictive immigration laws, Miss Antin defended the immigrants, comparing their position to that of the early settlers who had come seeking religious freedom and economic opportunity. The following selection, "Judges in the Gate," is taken from a book by Miss Antin that was subtitled A Complete Gospel of Immigration.

Source: *They Who Knock at Our Gates*, Boston, 1914, Ch. 2.

Two classes of citizens are especially prone to fall under the tyranny of phrases: those whose horizon, through no fault of their own, is limited by the rim of an empty dinner pail; and those whose view of the universe is obstructed by the kitchen middens of too many dinners. There is no clear thinking on an empty stomach, and equally muddled are the thoughts of the overfull. When I hear of a public measure that is largely supported by these two classes of citizens, I know at once that the measure appeals to human prejudices rather than to divine reason.

Thus I became suspicious of the restrictionist movement when I realized that it was in greatest favor among the thoughtless poor and the thoughtless rich. I am well aware that the high priests of the cult include some of the most conscientious thinkers that ever helped to make history, and their earnestness is attested by a considerable body of doctrine, in support of which they quote statistics and special studies and scientific investigations. But I notice that the rank and file of restrictionists do not know as much as the titles of these documents. They have not followed the argument at all; they have only caught the catchwords of restrictionism. And these catchwords are the sort that appeal to the mean spots in human nature — the distrust of the stranger, the jealousy of possession, the cowardice of the stomach. Nothing else is expressed by such phrases as "the scum of Europe," "the exploitation of America's wealth," or "taking the bread from the mouth of the American workingman."

Even the least venomous formula of restrictionism, "Immigration isn't what it used to be," raises such a familiar echo of foolish human nature that I am bound to challenge its veracity. Does not every generation cry that the weather is not what it used to be, children are not what they used to be, society is not what it used to be? "The good old times" and "the old immigration" may be twin illusions of limited human vision.

If it is true that immigration is not what it used to be, the fact will appear from a detailed comparison of the "old" and the "new" immigration. But which of the immigrant stocks of the good old times shall be taken as a standard? . . .

If it was a merit in 1620 to flee from religious persecution, and in 1776 to fight against political oppression, then many of the Russian refugees of today are a little ahead of the *Mayflower* troop, because they have in their own lifetime sustained the double ordeal of fight and flight, with all their attendant risks and shocks.

To obtain a nice balance between the relative merits of these two groups of rebels, we remind ourselves that, for sheer adventurousness, migration to America today is not to be mentioned on the same page with the magnificent exploit of 1620, and we reflect that the moral glory of the Revolution of 1776 is infinitely greater than that of any subsequent revolt; because that, too, was a pathfinding adventure, with no compass but faith, no chart but philosophical invention.

On the other hand, it is plain that the Russian revolutionists moved against greater odds than the American colonists had to face. The Russians had to plot in secret, assemble in the dark, and strike with bare fists; all this under the very nose of the czar, with the benighted condition of the Russian masses hanging like a cloud over their enterprise. The colonists were able to lay the train of revolution in the most public manner — they had the local government in their hands, a considerable militia obedient to their own captains, and the advantage of distance from the enemy's resources, with a populace advanced in civic experience promising support to the leaders.

And what a test of heroism was that which the harsh nature of the Russian government afforded! The American rebels risked their charters and their property; for some of them, dungeons waited, and, for the leaders, dangled a rope, no doubt. But confiscation is not so bitter as Siberian exile, and a halter is less painful than the barbed whip of the Cossacks. The Minutemen at Concord Bridge defied a bully; the rioters in St. Petersburg challenged a tiger. And first of all to be thrust into the cage would be the rebels of Jewish faith, and nobody knew that better than the Jews themselves. . . .

If the Jewish spirit of freedom leaps from the grave of Barkochla to the hovels of the Russian ghetto, half across the world and half across the civilized era, shall we not look for similar prodigies from the more recent graves of Kosciuszko and Garibaldi? If the hook-nosed tailor can turn hero on occasion, why not the grinning organ-grinder, and the surly miner, and the husky lumberjack? We experienced a shock of surprise, a little while ago, when troops of our Greek immigrants deserted the bootblacking parlors and fruit stands and tumbled aboard anything that happened to sail for the Mediterranean, in their eagerness — it's hard to bring it out, in connection with a "Dago" bootblack! — in their eagerness to strike a blow for their country in her need. . . .

From these unexpected exploits of the craven Jew and the degenerate Greek, it would seem as if the different elements of the despised "new" immigration only await a spectacular opportunity to prove themselves equal to the "old" in civic valor. But if contemporary history fails to provide a war or revolution for each of our foreign nationalities, we are still not without the means of gauging the idealistic capacity of the aliens. Next after liberty, the Puritans loved education; and today, if you examine the registers of the schools and colleges they founded, you will find the names of recent immigrants thickly sprinkled from *A* to *Z*, and topping the honor ranks nine times out of ten. . . .

Go from the public school to the public library, from the library to the social settlement, and you will carry away the same story in a hundred different forms. The good people behind the desks in these public places are fond of repeating that they can hardly keep up with the intellectual demands of their immigrant neighbors. In the experience of the librarians it is the veriest commonplace that the classics have the greatest circulation in the immigrant quarters of the city; and the most touching proof of reverence for learning often comes from the illiterate among the aliens. On the East Side of New York, "Teacher" is a being adored. Said a bedraggled Jewish mother to her little boy who had affronted his teacher, "Don't you know that teachers is holy?" Perhaps these are the things the teachers have in mind when they speak with a tremor of the immense reward of work in the public schools. . . .

The great New England invention of compulsory education is more eagerly appropriated by the majority of our immigrants than by native Americans of the corresponding level. That is what the school-teachers say, and I suppose they know. They also say — they and all public educators in chorus — that while one foreign nationality excels in the love of letters, another excels in the love of music, and a third in the love of science; and all of them together constitute an army whose feet keep time with the noble rhythms of culture. . . . If it is the scum of Europe that we are getting in our present immigration, it seems to be a scum rich in pearls. . . .

What do the aliens show of the specific traits of manhood that go to the making of good citizens? Immersed in the tide of American life, do their spiritual secretions give off that fine luster of manhood that distinguished the noble Pilgrims of the first immigration? The genius of the few is obvious; the group virtue of the mass on exalted occasions, such as popular uprisings, has been sufficiently demonstrated. What we want to know now is whether the ordinary immigrant under ordinary circumstances comes anywhere near the type we have taken as a model.

There can be no effective comparison between the makers of history of a most romantic epoch and the vendors of bananas on our own thrice-commonplace streets. But the Pilgrims were not always engaged in signing momentous compacts or in effecting a historic landing. In a secondary capacity they were immigrants — strangers come to establish themselves in a strange land — and as such they may profitably be used as a model by which to measure other immigrants. . . .

The average immigrant of today, like the immigrant of 1620, comes to build — to build a civilized home under a civilized government, which diminishes the amount of barbarity in the world. He, too, like that earlier newcomer, has rebelled against the conditions of his life, and adventured halfway across the world in search of more acceptable conditions, facing exile and uncertainty and the terrors of the untried. He also pays as he goes along, and in very much the same coin as did the Pilgrims; awaiting God's miracle of human happiness in the grisly darkness of the mine, in the fierce glare of the prairie ranch, in the shriveling heat of coke ovens, beside roaring cotton gins, beside blinding silk looms, in stifling tailor shops, in nerve-racking engine rooms — in all those places where the assurance and pride of the state come to rest upon the courage and patience of the individual citizen. . . .

Measured by the exertions necessary to overcome them, the difficulties that beset the modern immigrant are no less formidable than those which the Pilgrims had to face. There has never been a time when it was more difficult to get something for nothing than it is today, but the unromantic setting of modern enterprises leads us to underestimate the moral qualities that make success possible today. Undoubtedly the pioneer with an axe over his shoulder is a more picturesque figure than the clerk with a pencil behind his ear, but we who have stood up against the shocks of modern life should know better than to confuse the picturesque with the heroic. Do we not know that it takes a *man* to beat circumstances today as in the days of the pioneers? And manliness is always the same mixture of courage, self-reliance, perseverance, and faith.

Inventions have multiplied since the days of the Pilgrims, but which of our mechanical devices takes the place of the old-fashioned quality of determination where obstacles are to be overcome? The New England wilderness retreated, not before the axe but before the diligence of the men who wielded the axe; and diligence it is which today transmutes the city's refuse into a loaf for the ragpicker's children. Resourcefulness — the ability to adjust the means to the end — enters equally in the subtle enterprises of the businessman and in the hardy exploits of the settler; and it takes as much patience to wait for returns on a petty investment of capital as it does to watch the sprouting of an acre of corn.

Hardiness and muscle and physical courage were the seventeenth-century manifestations of the same moral qualities which today are expressed as intensity and nerve and commercial daring. Our country being in part cultivated, in part savage, we need citizens with the endowment of the twentieth century and citizens with the pioneer endowment. The "new" immigration, however-er interpreted, consists in the main of these

two types. Whether we get these elements in the proportion best suited to our needs is another question, to be answered in its place. At this point it is only necessary to admit that the immigrant possesses an abundance of the homely virtues of the useful citizen in times of peace.

We arrived at this conclusion by a theoretical analysis of the qualities that carry a man through life today; and that was fair reasoning, since the great majority of aliens are known to make good, if not in the first generation, then in the second or the third. Any sociologist, any settlement worker, any census clerk will tell you that the history of the average immigrant family of the "new" period is represented by an ascending curve. The descending curves are furnished by degenerate families of what was once prime American stock. I want no better proof of these facts than I find in the respective vocabularies of the missionary in the slums of New York and the missionary in the New England hills. At the settlement on Eldridge Street they talk about hastening the process of Americanization of the immigrant; the country minister in the Berkshires talks about the rehabilitation of the Yankee farmer. That is, the one assists at an upward process, the other seeks to reverse a downward process.

Right here, in these opposite tendencies of the poor of the foreign quarters and the poor of the Yankee fastnesses, I read the most convincing proof that what we get in the steerage is not the refuse but the sinew and bone of all the nations. If rural New England today shows signs of degeneracy, it is because much of her sinew and bone departed from her long ago. Some of the best blood of New England answered to the call of "Westward ho!" when the empty lands beyond the Alleghenies gaped for population, while on the spent farms of the Puritan settlements too many sons awaited the division of the father's property. Of those who were left behind, many, of course, were detained by habit and sentiment, love of the old home being stronger in them than the lure of adventure. Of the aristocracy of New England, that portion stayed at home which was fortified by wealth and so did not feel the economic pressure of increased population; of the proletariat remained, on the whole, the less robust, the less venturesome, the men and women of conservative imagination.

It was bound to be so, because, wherever the population is set in motion by internal pressure, the emigrant train is composed of the stoutest, the most resourceful of those who are not held back by the roots of wealth or sentiment. Voluntary emigration always calls for the highest combination of the physical and moral virtues. The law of analogy, therefore, might suffice to teach us that with every shipload of immigrants we get a fresh infusion of pioneer blood. But theory is a tightrope on which every monkey of a logician can balance himself. We practical Americans of the twentieth century like to feel the broad platform of tested facts beneath our feet.

The fact about the modern immigrant is that he is everywhere continuing the work begun by our pioneer ancestors. So much we may learn from a bare recital of the occupations of aliens. They supply most of the animal strength and primitive patience that are at the bottom of our civilization. In California they gather the harvest, in Arizona they dig irrigation ditches, in Oregon they fell forests, in West Virginia they tunnel coal, in Massachusetts they plant the tedious crops suitable to an exhausted soil. In the cities they build subways and skyscrapers and railroad terminals that are the wonder of the world. Wherever rough work and low wages go together, we have a job for the immigrant.

The prouder we grow, the more we lean on the immigrant. The Wall Street magnate would be about as effective as a puppet were it not for the army of foreigners. who execute his schemes. The magic of stocks and bonds lies in railroad ties and in quarried stone and in axle grease applied at the right time. A Harriman might sit till doomsday gibbering at the telephone, and the Stock Exchange would take no notice of him if a band of nameless "Dagos" a thousand miles away failed to repair a telegraph pole. New York City is building an aqueduct that will surpass the works of the Romans, and the average New Yorker will know nothing about it until he reads in the newspapers the mayor's speech at the inauguration of the new water supply.

Our brains, our wealth, our ambitions flow in channels dug by the hands of immigrants. Alien hands erect our offices, rivet our bridges, and pile up the proud masonry of our monuments. Ignoring in this connection the fact that the engineer as well as the laborer is often of alien race, we owe to mere muscle a measure of recognition proportionate to our need of muscle in our boasted material progress. An imaginative schoolboy left to himself must presently catch the resemblance between the pick-and-shovel men toiling at our aqueducts and the heroes of the axe and rifle extolled in his textbooks as the "sturdy pioneers." Considered without prejudice, the chief difference between these two types is the difference between jean overalls and fringed buckskins.

Contemporaneousness takes the romance out of everything; otherwise we might be rubbing elbows with heroes. Whatever merit there was in hewing and digging and hauling in the days of the first settlers still inheres in the same operations today. Yes, and a little extra; for a stick of dynamite is more dangerous to handle than a crowbar, and the steam engine makes more widows in a year than ever the Indian did with bloody tomahawk and stealthy arrow.

There is no contention here that every fellow who successfully passes the entrance ordeals at Ellis Island is necessarily a hero. That there are weaklings in the train of the sturdy throng of foreigners nobody knows better than I. I have witnessed the pitiful struggles of the unfit and have seen the failures drop all around me. But no bold army ever marched to the field of action without a fringe of camp followers on its flanks. . . .

I am never so clear as to the basis of my faith in America as when I have been talking with the ungroomed mothers of the East Side. A widow down on Division Street was complaining bitterly of the hardships of her lot, alone in an alien world with four children to bring up. In the midst of her complaints the children came in from school. "Well," said the hard-pressed widow, "bread isn't easy to get in America, but the children can go to school, and that's more than bread. Rich man, poor man, it's all the same: the children can go to school."

The poor widow had never heard of a document called the Declaration of Independence, but evidently she had discovered in American practice something corresponding to one of the great American principles — the principle of equality of opportunity — and she valued it more than the necessaries of animal life. Even so was it valued by the fathers of the republic when they deliberately incurred the dangers of a war with mighty England in defense of that and similar principles.

The widow's sentiment was finely echoed by another Russian immigrant, a man who drives an ice wagon for a living. His case is the more impressive from the fact that he left a position of comparative opulence in the Old Country, under the protection of a wealthy uncle who employed him as steward of his estates. He had had servants to wait on him and money enough to buy some of the privileges of citizenship which the Russian government doles out to the favored few.

"But what good was it to me?" he asked. "My property was not my own if the police wanted to take it away. I could spend thousands to push my boy through the gymnasium, and he might get a little education as a favor, and still nothing out of it, if

he isn't allowed to be anything. Here I work like a slave, and my wife she works like a slave, too, — in the Old Country she had servants in the house — but what do I care, as long as I know what I earn I got it for my own? I got to furnish my house one chair at a time, in America, but nobody can take it away from me, the little that I got. And it costs me nothing to educate my family. Maybe they can, maybe they can't go to college, but all can go through grammar school, and high school, too, the smart ones. And all go together! Rich and poor, all are equal, and I don't get it as a favor."

Better a hard bed in the shelter of justice than a stuffed couch under the black canopy of despotism. Better a crust of the bread of the intellect freely given him as his right than the whole loaf grudgingly handed him as a favor. What nobler insistence on the rights of manhood do we find in the writings of the Puritans? . . .

There is a phrase in the American vocabulary of approval that sums up our national ideal of manhood. That phrase is "a self-made man." To such we pay the tribute of our highest admiration, justly regarding our self-made men as the noblest product of our democratic institutions. Now let anyone compile a biographical dictionary of our self-made men, from the romantic age of our history down to the prosaic year 1914, and see how the smell of the steerage pervades the volume! *There* is a sign that the practical man finds it easy to interpret. Like fruits grow from like seeds. Those who can produce under American conditions the indigenous type of manhood must be working with the same elements as the native American who starts out a yokel and ends up a senator. . . .

In the whole catalogue of sins with which the modern immigrant is charged, it is not easy to find one in which we Americans are not partners — we who can make and unmake our world by means of the ballot. The immigrant is blamed for the unsanitary conditions of the slums, when sanitary experts cry shame on our methods of municipal housecleaning. You might dump the whole of the East Side into the German capital and there would be no slums there, because the municipal authorities of Berlin know how to enforce building regulations, how to plant trees, and how to clean the streets. The very existence of the slum is laid at the door of the immigrant, but the truth is that the slums were here before the immigrants. Most of the foreigners hate the slums, and all but the few who have no backbone get out of them as fast as they rise in the economic scale. To "move uptown" is the dearest ambition of the average immigrant family.

If the slums were due to the influx of foreigners, why should London have slums, and more hideous slums than New York? No, the slum is not a by-product of the steerage. It is a sore on the social body in many civilized countries, due to internal disorders of the economic system. A generous dose of social reformation would do more to effect a cure than repeated doses of restriction of immigration.

A whole group of phenomena due to social and economic causes have been falsely traced, in this country, to the quantity and quality of immigration. Among these are the labor troubles, such as nonemployment, strikes, riots, etc. England has no such immigration as the United States, and yet Englishmen suffer from nonemployment, from riots and bitter strikes. Whom does the English workingman blame for his misery? Let the American workingman quarrel with the same enemy. If wage cutting is a sin more justly laid at the door of the immigrant, a minimum wage law might put a stop to that.

The immigrant undoubtedly contributes to the congestion of population in the cities, but not as a chief cause. Congestion is characteristic of city life the world over, and the remedy will be found in improved conditions of country life. Moreover, the immigrant has shown himself responsive to direction away from the city when a systematic attempt is made to help him find his place in the country. . . .

A good deal of anti-immigration feeling has been based on the vile conditions observed in labor camps, by another turn of that logic which puts the blame on the victims. A labor camp at its worst is not an argument against immigration, but an indictment of the brutality of the contractor who cares only to force a maximum of work out of the workmen and cares nothing for their lives; an indictment also of the government that allows such shameful exploitation of the laborers to go on. . . .

Immigrants are accused of civil indifference if they do not become naturalized, but when we look into the conditions affecting naturalization, we wonder at the numbers who do become citizens. Facilities for civic education of the adult are very scant and dependent mostly on the fluctuating enthusiasm of private philanthropies. The administration of the naturalization laws differs from state to state and is accompanied by serious material hindrances; while the community is so indifferent to the civic progress of its alien members that it is possible for a foreigner to live in this country for *sixteen years,* coming in contact with all classes of Americans, without getting the bare information that he may become a citizen of the United States if he wants to. Such a case, as reported by a charity worker of New Britain, Connecticut, makes a sensitive American choke with mortification. If we were ourselves as patriotic as we expect the immigrant to be, we would employ Salvation Army methods to draw the foreigner into the civic fold. Instead of that, we leave his citizenship to chance — or to the most corrupt political agencies.

I would rather not review the blackest of all charges against the immigrant, that he has a baleful effect on municipal politics: I am so ashamed of the implications. But sensible citizens will talk and talk about the immigrant selling his vote and not know whom they are accusing. Votes cannot be sold unless there is a market for them. Who creates the market for votes? The ward politician, behind whom stands the party boss, alert and powerful; and behind him — the indifferent electorate who allow him to flourish.

Among immigrants of the "new" order, the wholesale prostitution of the ballot is confined to those groups which are largely subjected to the industrial slavery of mining and manufacturing communities and construction camps. These helpless creatures, in their very act of sinning, bear twofold witness against us who accuse them. The foreman who disposes of their solid vote acquires his power under an economic system which delivers them up, body and soul, to the man who pays them wages, and turns it to account under a political system which makes the legislature subservient to the Stock Exchange. But let it be definitely noted that to admit that groups of immigrants under economic control fall an easy prey to political corruptionists is very far from proving any inherent viciousness in the immigrants themselves.

Neither does the immigrant's civic reputation depend entirely on negative evidence. New York City has the largest foreign population in the United States, and precisely in that city the politicians have learned that they cannot count on the foreign vote because it is not for sale. A student of New York politics speaks of the "uncontrollable and unapproachable vote of the ghetto." Repeated analyses of the election returns of the eighth district, which has the largest foreign population of all, show that "politically it is one of the most uncertain sections" in the city. Many generations of campaign managers have discovered to their sorrow that the usual party blandishments are wasted on the East Side masses.

Hester Street follows leaders and causes rather than party emblems. Nowhere is the art of splitting a ticket better understood. The only time you can predict the East Side vote is when there is a sharp alignment of the better citizens against the boss-ridden. Then you will find the naturalized citizens in the same camp with men like Jacob Riis and women like Lillian Wald. And the experience of New York is duplicated in Chicago and in Philadelphia and in every center of immigration. Ask the reformers.

How often we demand more civic virtue of the stranger than we ourselves possess! A little more time spent in weeding our own garden will relieve us of the necessity of counting the tin cans in the immigrant's backyard. . . .

Some of the things we say against the immigrants sound very strange from American lips. We speak of the corruption of our children's manners through contact with immigrant children in the public schools, when all the world is scolding us for our children's rude deportment. Finer manners are grown on a tiny farm in Italy than in the roaring subways of New York; and contrast our lunch-counter manners with the table manners of the Polish ghetto, where bread must not be touched with unwashed hands, where a pause for prayer begins and ends each meal, and on festival occasions parents and children join in folk songs between courses!

If there is a corruption of manners, it may be that it works in the opposite direction from what we suppose. At any rate, we ourselves admit that the children of foreigners, before they are Americanized, have a greater respect than our children for the Fifth Commandment.

We say that immigrants nowadays come only to exploit our country, because some of them go back after a few years, taking their savings with them. The real exploiters of our country's wealth are not the foreign laborers but the capitalists who pay them wages. The laborer who returns home with his savings leaves us an equivalent in the products of labor — a day's service rendered for every day's wages. The capitalists take away our forests and watercourses and mineral treasures and give us watered stock in return.

Of the class of aliens who do not come to make their homes here, but only to earn a few hundred dollars to invest in a farm or a cottage in their native village, a greater number than we imagine are brought over by industrial agents in violation of the Contract Labor Law. Put an end to the stimulation of immigration and we shall see very few of the class who do not come to stay. And even as it is, not all of those who return to Europe do so in order to spend their American fortune. Some go back to recover from ruin encountered at the hands of American land swindlers. Some go back to be buried beside their fathers, having lost their health in unsanitary American factories. And some are helped aboard on crutches, having lost a limb in a mine explosion that could have been prevented. When we watch the procession of cripples hobbling back to their native villages, it looks more as if America is exploiting Europe.

O that the American people would learn where their enemies lurk! Not the immigrant is ruining our country, but the venal politicians who try to make the immigrant the scapegoat for all the sins of untrammeled capitalism — these and their masters.

Find me the agent who obstructs the movement for the abolition of child labor and I will show you who it is that condemns able-bodied men to eat their hearts out in idleness; who brutalizes our mothers and tortures tender babies; who fills the morgues with the emaciated bodies of young girls and the infirmaries with little white cots; who fastens the shame of illiteracy on our enlightened land and causes American boys to grow up too ignorant to mark a ballot; who sucks the blood of the nation, fattens on its brains, and throws its heart to the wolves of the money market.

The stench of the slums is nothing to the stench of the child labor iniquity. If the foreigners are taking the bread out of the mouth of the American workingman, it is by the maimed fingers of their fainting little ones.

And if we want to know whether the immigrant parents are the promoters or the victims of the child labor system, we turn to the cotton mills, where forty thousand native American children between seven and sixteen years of age toil between ten and twelve hours a day, while the fathers rot in the degradation of idleness.

From all this, does it follow that we should let down the bars and dispense with the guard at Ellis Island? Only insofar as the policy of restriction is based on the theory that the present immigration is derived from the scum of humanity. But the immigrants may be desirable and immigration undesirable. We sometimes have to deny ourselves to the most congenial friends who knock at our door. At this point, however, we are not trying to answer the question whether immigration is good for us. We are concerned only with the reputation of the immigrant — and, incidentally, with the reputation of those who have sought to degrade him in our eyes. If statecraft bids us lock the gate, and our national code of ethics ratifies the order, lock it we must, but we need not call names through the keyhole.

Mount guard in the name of the republic if the health of the republic requires it, but let no such order be issued until her statesmen and philosophers and patriots have consulted together. Above all, let the voice of prejudice be stilled, let not self-interest chew the cud of envy in full sight of the nation, and let no syllable of willful defamation mar the oracles of state. For those who are excluded when our bars are down are exiles from Egypt, whose feet stumble in the desert of political and social slavery, whose hearts hunger for the bread of freedom. The ghost of the *Mayflower* pilots every immigrant ship, and Ellis Island is another name for Plymouth Rock.

92.

Robert Frost: "Mending Wall"

One of the ironies of Robert Frost, "the poet of New England" — he was the lineal descendant in the eighth generation of Nicholas Frost, who sailed from Plymouth to New England in 1634 — was that his poetry had first to be appreciated in England before anyone in America would pay attention to it. "Mending Wall" is one of his best-known poems, and appeared first in North of Boston, *a volume published in London in 1914 and then, to considerable acclaim (after it had received approbation from English critics), in his native land. The poem, besides being beautiful, is a dissertation on a perennial American subject, identified by Emerson in his book* Society and Solitude *(1870), but discussed by many others as well. Good fences may indeed, as the protagonist of Frost's lyric insists, "make good neighbors" — but there is also something, as the poet himself says, "that doesn't love a wall,/ That wants it down." Which in fact do we prefer: the solitude that means independence, or the fellowship of a society without walls?*

Source: *North of Boston*, New York, 2nd edition, 1915.

MENDING WALL

Something there is that doesn't love a wall,
That sends the frozen-ground-swell under it,
And spills the upper boulders in the sun;
And makes gaps even two can pass abreast.
The work of hunters is another thing:
I have come after them and made repair
Where they have left not one stone on a
    stone,
But they would have the rabbit out of
    hiding,
To please the yelping dogs. The gaps
    I mean,
No one has seen them made or heard them
    made,
But at spring mending-time we find them
    there.
I let my neighbor know beyond the hill;
And on a day we meet to walk the line
And set the wall between us once again.
We keep the wall between us as we go.
To each the boulders that have fallen
    to each.

And some are loaves and some so nearly
    balls
We have to use a spell to make them
    balance:
"Stay where you are until our backs are
    turned!"
We wear our fingers rough with handling
    them.
Oh, just another kind of outdoor game,
One on a side. It comes to little more:
There where it is we do not need the wall:
He is all pine and I am apple orchard.
My apple trees will never get across
And eat the cones under his pines, I tell him.
He only says, "Good fences make good
    neighbors."
Spring is the mischief in me, and I wonder
If I could put a notion in his head:
"*Why* do they make good neighbors?
    Isn't it
Where there are cows? But here there are
    no cows.
Before I built a wall I'd ask to know
What I was walling in or walling out,

And to whom I was like to give offense.
Something there is that doesn't love a wall,
That wants it down." I could say "Elves"
    to him,
But it's not elves exactly, and I'd rather
He said it for himself. I see him there
Bringing a stone grasped firmly by the top

In each hand, like an old-stone savage armed.
He moves in darkness as it seems to me,
Not of woods only and the shade of trees.
He will not go behind his father's saying,
And he likes having thought of it so well
He says again, "Good fences make good
    neighbors."

93.

George Harvey: Diplomats of Democracy

William Jennings Bryan, who had been titular leader of the Democratic Party since
1896, accepted the post of secretary of state during Woodrow Wilson's first term
as President. In this office Bryan was able to oversee the appointment of many who
served the State Department in foreign lands as ministers and ambassadors. His
main concern in filling appointments was to reward the party faithful, regardless of
qualifications, a policy that often meant dismissing able men from the Foreign Service
and replacing them with deserving Democrats who had waited nearly two decades to
gather the spoils of a presidential victory. Wilson, who had pledged not to follow such
a policy before the election, nevertheless supported Bryan up to a point. A number of
embarrassments resulted, most notably from the appointment of James M. Sullivan as
minister to the Dominican Republic. Bryan quickly became the object of scorn from
most of the American press. In February 1914, George Harvey, editor of the
North American Review, analyzed the Bryan appointments and their effect on
American diplomacy. His editorial is reprinted here in part.

Source: *North American Review*, February 1914.

SPEAKING to the National Civil Service Reform League at its annual convention on December 13, Dr. Charles W. Eliot, its president, said:

In general, the cabinet officers, with the exception of the secretary of state, have seemed to intend to conform to the declaration in their party platform and the well-known opinions of the President; but there have appeared some exceptions to this general policy.

Several of the appointments of obscure men to diplomatic posts have seemed to the public to be made in payment of political debts, but the public attributes these appointments, not to the President but to the secretary of state.

We shall deal presently with this singular division of responsibility as fashioned by the venerable president emeritus of Harvard University, to whom President Wilson proffered the position of ambassador to the Court of St. James.

Meanwhile, what are the facts?

Of the ministers plenipotentiary appointed to European courts by President Wilson, a majority, at least, rank easily as the peers, if not indeed the superiors, of their predecessors. . . . Can the like be said of the ambassadorships, the expensive "prizes" within the gift of the President?

Invariably, during the past twenty years, Democrats in convention and from the platform have denounced the Republican practice of bestowing these honors upon wealthy individuals in return for substantial campaign contributions. That Mr. Wilson was sincerely desirous of effecting a reform was evidenced immediately upon his inauguration by announcement from the White House of his determination to select "men without wealth, but possessing every other form of qualification." The difficulties attendant upon the putting of this policy into practice, however, became quickly apparent, and, after making a few abortive and in actual effect somewhat unfortunate attempts, the President abandoned the plan and reverted insensibly to the selective methods of his predecessors. The consequence is that, with the single exception of Mr. Walter H. Page, who contributed only William Bayard Hale and one hundred dollars in cash, all of those appointed are men who at one time or another supplied pecuniary aid to his canvass.

In this respect, therefore, there is little room for differentiation between the old enslavement and the new freedom. We advert to it, not by way of criticism but simply as a matter of fact and as a probably inevitable circumstance. At the very least, Mr. Wilson is entitled to credit, which could not be rightfully accorded to either Mr. Roosevelt or Mr. Taft, for making a commendable, though futile, endeavor to establish a higher and more truly American standard.

The relative merits of the ambassadors chosen may be summarized briefly. Of Mr. Thomas Nelson Page it may be said without hesitation, as of Dr. Van Dyke, that a more creditable appointment could not have been made. As a litterateur of high repute, a student of international affairs, and a cultivated linguist, he fully realizes the excellent traditions which in former years were generally observed. Despite the long and valuable experience of his predecessor, Mr. O'Brien, it must, we think, be conceded that Mr. Page is the better equipped for the services which devolve upon the American representative in the Eternal City.

So much, unhappily, cannot be said of his fellow Virginian, Mr. Willard, the new ambassador to Spain, whose sole qualification is his wealth and whose appointment can only be attributed to his generous donations to the cause. As the successor of Mr. Ide, former chief justice and governor general of the Philippines, who is fully acquainted with the language and customs of Spain, and a gentleman of modest fortune, Mr. Willard appears as a complete reversal of the President's aspiration. The appointments to Rome and Madrid link themselves naturally together, since, oddly enough, Mr. Page was nominated at the earnest solicitation of the senators from Virginia in return for their promise to secure confirmation of Mr. Willard, whose selection, being personal to the President, seemed likely to invite opposition. . . .

The appointment of Mr. Pindell, of Peoria, to be ambassador to Russia instead of internal revenue collector of the Third District of Illinois, still awaits confirmation by the Senate, whose hesitancy is said to be due less to considerations of fitness than to a curious lack of frankness concerning the reputed designation of postmasters to act as agents for Mr. Pindell's newspaper. We need not recall the peculiar circumstances which induced the making of this grotesque nomination. The most vivid imagining could add nothing to the limpid explanations adduced by the secretary of state and the ebullient senator from Illinois.

It is interesting to note, however, that the Russians themselves possess exclusive information to the effect that Mr. Pindell is a poet. They derived this impression from Senator Lewis's laudatory letter which was published in full in the *Novoe Vremya* and reprinted in part in the St. Petersburg *Press*. We quote from correspondence from the Russian capital:

If Mr. Pindell is really a poet, then his countrymen here owe him apologies, for none of them seem to be able to quote his verse. They were mildly surprised to read a telegram from Washington a few weeks ago saying that the appointment of the poet Pindell to be American ambassador in St. Petersburg had been confirmed. Even in Russia it is not usual to offer a high public appointment to a poet who seeks "plenty of enjoyment and the social advantages attached to the position (of Ambassador to the czar's court), especially for his daughter."

While freely admitting that, despite the seeming disrespect to their government implied in the appointment of an ambassador upon the terms outlined by Senator Lewis and Mr. Bryan, Mr. Pindell would be received without prejudice, the Russian ministers, nevertheless, "can scarcely believe that he will come here as ambassador from the United States."

That, of course, is a polite way of saying that, if Mr. Pindell should appear, his credentials would be accepted and he would be ignored. How could it be otherwise? Russia is a great and proud nation, wholly unaccustomed to playing enforced parts in opéra bouffe performances such as this has come to be. She is, moreover, the only one whose helpful friendship has never failed us, and is now frankly desirous of arranging the terms of a new treaty to our satisfaction and mutual advantage. To send Mr. Pindell to St. Petersburg under the conditions imposed by the administration, authorizing him to accept the hospitality of the Russian nation while withholding from him any real authority to represent our own, simply to do him honor and to please his little daughter, would be a gross impertinence.

We find it difficult to believe that President Wilson will permit the consummation of this absurd travesty. We do not presume to guess even at the reasons which induce his insistence upon the nomination; but we do declare plainly that the failure of Mr. Pindell to relieve the President of obvious embarrassment by demanding the withdrawal of his name betrays a deficiency in mental and moral perceptiveness, which leaves no doubt of his unfitness to serve as an ambassador of the United States to another power of equal rank, dignity, and national sensitiveness. . . .

We come now to the branch of the diplomatic service whose reformation upon a higher plane, initiated by Secretary Hay and scrupulously safeguarded by Secretary Root and Secretary Knox, with the full approval of Presidents McKinley, Roosevelt, and Taft, reflects the highest credit upon the Republican Party — and alas! the scene changes. We refer, of course, to the Latin American missions, obviously the most delicate and difficult of all in the present state of our relationship to the smaller republics of the Western Hemisphere. It was to the changes in these posts that President Eliot took exception in his report to the Civil Service Reform League. . . .

The average experience of the former ministers to these South and Central American republics was fifteen and one-third years, and their average age at the time of their expulsion was forty-seven. All spoke the language of the countries to which they were accredited. The average age of the new ministers is fifty-four and one-half, five being past sixty; no one of them, we believe, understands Spanish; and none, of course, has had diplomatic experience. In other words, twelve trained and capable representatives, several of whom entered the service under competitive examination and all of whom had long since forsaken partisanship, are superseded by mere party hacks whose ages clearly disqualify them for continuance in office for sufficient time to equip themselves for proper performance of their duties. A clearer case of partisan political debauchery cannot be imagined.

President Eliot affixes the blame to Secretary Bryan, whose henchmen, with the possible exception of two neighbors of Assistant President House in Austin, Texas, comprise the galaxy of incompetents. . . .

A President may authorize or request a secretary of state to submit recommendations, but it is the President himself who makes the appointments and signs the commissions, whose authority is "always in the last resort final and decisive." That Mr. Bryan, apparently abetted for personal reasons by Assistant President House, has availed himself of the opportunity to discharge peremptorily members of the diplomatic service who had won their places by merit and fidelity and had every moral right to expect that their faithfulness and honest endeavor no less than their developed capacity would be considered, and to put into their places his own personal followers, no one of whom can speak or write any language except his own, is sufficiently obvious. But who accorded him the privilege, if not the President?

Moreover, is Dr. Eliot quite fair in impugning the conduct of the secretary of state? To the best of our information, Mr. Bryan has never espoused the merit system.

While not going so far as to declare the right of the victors to the entire spoils, he did not hesitate in 1908 to pledge at least a half to his adherents in the event of success. And only last month his associate editor, Mr. Metcalfe, himself a beneficiary, pronounced it "ridiculous to suppose" that President Wilson would not "use the forthcoming canal organization as a means of reciprocating the efforts of those constituents who helped to place him where he is."

Surely no charge of false pretense or hypocrisy can lie against Mr. Bryan. He is a true-blue Jacksonian Democrat, avowedly amenable to "the unfortunate, the demoralizing influences which have been allowed to determine executive appointments since President Jackson's time," and has never pretended to be anything else. It was not the secretary of state who wrote:

> My warm advocacy and support both of the principle and of the bona fide practice of civil service reform is known to the whole country, and there is no danger that the spoils system will creep in with my approval or connivance.

It was Woodrow Wilson, President of the United States, who also said:

> The President may accept its [the Service Act's] directions or not, as he pleases. The only force that can hold him to the observance of its principle is the force of public opinion.

Truer words were never spoken; and we suspect that the force alluded to will be exercised and that its effect will be felt. But why does Woodrow Wilson do such things? How *can* he? Can anybody tell?

Can you let me know what positions you have at your disposal with which to reward deserving Democrats?

WILLIAM JENNINGS BRYAN, letter to W. W. Vick, receiver general of customs in Santo Domingo, August 1913

94.

Woodrow Wilson: The Tampico Affair

Mexico, in 1913, had been the scene of a military coup led by General Victoriano Huerta, whose regime President Wilson refused to recognize because it was, in his words, a "government of butchers." A crisis developed in April 1914 when some crew members of the U.S.S. Dolphin were arrested in Tampico, where the American ship had docked. Although the sailors were released immediately and an apology was extended, Admiral Mayo, commander of the American fleet off Veracruz, demanded a twenty-one gun salute to the American flag. When the salute was refused, the President went before Congress on April 20 to ask for permission to demand satisfaction from the Huerta administration. Wilson finally accepted an offer by Argentina, Brazil, and Chile (thereafter known as the ABC powers) to mediate, and war was averted. Wilson's message of April 20 appears below.

Source: PRFA, 1914, pp. 474-476.

It is my duty to call your attention to a situation which has arisen in our dealings with General Victoriano Huerta at Mexico City which calls for action, and to ask your advice and cooperation in acting upon it.

On the 9th of April a paymaster of the U.S.S. *Dolphin* landed at the Iturbide Bridge landing at Tampico with a whaleboat and boat's crew to take off certain supplies needed by his ship, and while engaged in loading the boat was arrested by an officer and squad of men of the army of General Huerta. Neither the paymaster nor anyone of the boat's crew was armed. Two of the men were in the boat when the arrest took place and were obliged to leave it and submit to be taken into custody, notwithstanding the fact that the boat carried, both at her bow and at her stern, the flag of the United States.

The officer who made the arrest was proceeding up one of the streets of the town with his prisoners when met by an officer of higher authority, who ordered him to return to the landing and await orders; and within an hour and a half from the time of the arrest, orders were received from the commander of the Huertista forces at Tampico for the release of the paymaster and his men. The release was followed by apologies from the commander and later by an expression of regret by General Huerta himself.

General Huerta urged that martial law obtained at the time at Tampico; that orders had been issued that no one should be allowed to land at the Iturbide Bridge; and that our sailors had no right to land there. Our naval commanders at the port had not been notified of any such prohibition; and, even if they had been, the only justifiable course open to the local authorities would have been to request the paymaster and his crew to withdraw and to lodge a protest with the commanding officer of the fleet. Admiral Mayo regarded the arrest as so serious an affront that he was not satisfied with the apologies offered, but demanded that the flag of the United States be saluted with special ceremony by the military commander of the port.

The incident cannot be regarded as a trivial one, especially as two of the men arrested were taken from the boat itself — that is to say, from the territory of the United States — but had it stood by itself it might have been attributed to the ignorance or arrogance of a single officer. Unfortunately, it was not an isolated case. A series of incidents have recently occurred which cannot but create the impression that the representatives of General Huerta were willing to go out of their way to show disregard for the dignity and rights of this government and felt perfectly safe in doing what they pleased, making free to show in many ways their irritation and contempt.

A few days after the incident at Tampico, an orderly from the U.S.S. *Minnesota* was arrested at Vera Cruz while ashore in uniform to obtain the ship's mail and was for a time thrown into jail. An official dispatch from this government to its embassy at Mexico City was withheld by the authorities of the telegraphic service until peremptorily demanded by our chargé d'affaires in person. So far as I can learn, such wrongs and annoyances have been suffered to occur only against representatives of the United States. I have heard of no complaints from other governments of similar treatment.

Subsequent explanations and formal apologies did not and could not alter the popular impression, which it is possible it had been the object of the Huertista authorities to create, that the government of the United States was being singled out, and might be singled out with impunity, for slights and affronts in retaliation for its refusal to recognize the pretensions of General Huerta to be regarded as the constitutional provisional president of the Republic of Mexico.

The manifest danger of such a situation was that such offenses might grow from bad to worse until something happened of so gross and intolerable a sort as to lead directly and inevitably to armed conflict. It was necessary that the apologies of General Huerta and his representatives should go

much further, that they should be such as to attract the attention of the whole population to their significance, and such as to impress upon General Huerta himself the necessity of seeing to it that no further occasion for explanations and professed regrets should arise.

I, therefore, felt it my duty to sustain Admiral Mayo in the whole of his demand and to insist that the flag of the United States should be saluted in such a way as to indicate a new spirit and attitude on the part of the Huertistas. Such a salute General Huerta has refused, and I have come to ask your approval and support in the course I now purpose to pursue.

This government can, I earnestly hope, in no circumstances be forced into war with the people of Mexico. Mexico is torn by civil strife. If we are to accept the tests of its own constitution, it has no government. General Huerta has set his power up in the City of Mexico, such as it is, without right and by methods for which there can be no justification. Only part of the country is under his control. If armed conflict should unhappily come as a result of his attitude of personal resentment toward this government, we should be fighting only General Huerta and those who adhere to him and give him their support, and our object would be only to restore to the people of the distracted republic the opportunity to set up again their own laws and their own government.

But I earnestly hope that war is not now in question. I believe that I speak for the American people when I say that we do not desire to control in any degree the affairs of our sister republic. Our feeling for the people of Mexico is one of deep and genuine friendship, and everything that we have so far done or refrained from doing has proceeded from our desire to help them, not to hinder or embarrass them. We would not wish even to exercise the good offices of friendship without their welcome and consent. The people of Mexico are entitled to settle their own domestic affairs in their own way, and we sincerely desire to respect their right. The present situation need have none of the grave implications of interference if we deal with it promptly, firmly, and wisely.

No doubt I could do what is necessary in the circumstances to enforce respect for our government without recourse to the Congress and yet not exceed my constitutional powers as President; but I do not wish to act in a matter possibly of so grave consequence except in close conference and cooperation with both the Senate and House. I, therefore, come to ask your approval that I

should use the armed forces of the United States in such ways and to such an extent as may be necessary to obtain from General Huerta and his adherents the fullest recognition of the rights and dignity of the United States, even amidst the distressing conditions now unhappily obtaining in Mexico.

There can in what we do be no thought of aggression or of selfish aggrandizement. We seek to maintain the dignity and authority of the United States only because we wish always to keep our great influence unimpaired for the uses of liberty, both in the United States and wherever else it may be employed for the benefit of mankind.

95.

WALTER LIPPMANN: The Trusts and Private Property

When Herbert Croly's The Promise of American Life *appeared in 1909, Walter Lippmann was president of the Harvard Socialist Club; and when Walter Weyl's* The New Democracy *was published three years later, Lippmann was secretary to the Socialist mayor of Schenectady, New York. In 1914, when Croly and Weyl began the Progressive journal the* New Republic, *Lippmann, aged twenty-five, joined them. He was no longer a Socialist, although his thinking remained "in direction socialist." His* Drift and Mastery *(1914), a portion of which is reprinted here, closely paralleled the earlier books by Croly and Weyl; and Theodore Roosevelt hailed him as "the most brilliant young man of his age in the United States."*

Source: *Drift and Mastery,* New York, 1914: "The Magic of Property."

THE ORDINARY EDITORIAL WRITER is a strong believer in what he calls the sanctity of private property. But as far as highly organized business is concerned, he is a pilgrim to an empty shrine. The trust movement is doing what no conspirator or revolutionist could ever do: it is sucking the life out of private property. For the purposes of modern industry the traditional notions have be-

come meaningless: the name continues, but the fact is disappearing. You cannot conduct the great industries and preserve intact the principles of private property. And so the trusts are organizing private property out of existence, are altering its nature so radically that very little remains but the title and the ancient theory.

When a man buys stock in some large

corporation he becomes in theory one of its owners. He is supposed to be exercising his instinct of private property. But how in fact does he exercise that instinct which we are told is the only real force in civilization? He may never see *his* property. He may not know where his property is situated. He is not consulted as to its management. He would be utterly incapable of advice if he were consulted. Contact with *his* property is limited to reading in the newspapers what it is worth each day, and hoping that dividends will be paid.

The processes which make him rich in the morning and poor in the evening, increase his income or decrease it — are inscrutable mysteries. Compare him with the farmer who owns his land, the homesteader or the prospector, compare him with anyone who has a real sense of possession, and you will find, I think, that the modern shareholder is a very feeble representative of the institution of private property.

No one has ever had a more abstract relation to the thing he owned. The absentee landlord is one of the sinister figures of history. But the modern shareholder is not only an absentee, he is a transient too. The week ending January 10, 1914, was generally regarded as a dull one in Wall Street. Yet on the New York Stock Exchange alone the total sales amounted to 1,777,038 shares. About 340,000 shares of private property in Reading changed hands.

With a few thousand dollars I can be an owner in Massachusetts textile mills on Monday, in Union Pacific on Tuesday. I can flit like a butterfly from industry to industry. I don't even have to use my judgment as to where I shall alight. All I have to do is to choose some well-known stockbroker and put myself into his hands.

And when I read in books on political economy that any profit I make is a reward for my foresight, my courage in the face of risk, I laugh. I know that I can't have any foresight. I don't understand the inner workings of the business world. I'm not allowed to know. That is reserved for specialists like stockbrokers and private bankers.

In the modern world, investing has become a highly skilled profession, altogether beyond the capacities of the ordinary shareholder. The great mass of people who have saved a little money can no more deal with their property on their own initiative than they can deal with disease or war on their own initiative. They have to act through representatives. Just as they need physicians and organized armies, so they have to have stockbrokers, financial experts, public service commissions, and the rest.

There has been in recent years a great outcry against the concentrated control of credit. It was found that the decision as to how money should be invested had passed away from the people who owned the money. The enormous power of Morgan consisted in his ability to direct the flow of capital. He was the head of a vast system which had taken out of the hands of investors the task of deciding how their money was to be used. It was no doubt a colossal autocracy.

There has been a great effort to break it up, to decentralize the power that concentrated about Morgan. But no one proposes to put back into the hands of the investor the decision as to the financing of industry. The investors are a scattered mob incapable of such decisions. The question of where money is to be applied is a matter for experts to answer. And so reform of the credit system does not consist in abolishing the financial expert. It consists in making him a public servant.

The Wilson Currency Bill seems to be an effort to make banking responsive to business needs all over the country. It gives businessmen a larger control over financial experts. How that control is to be extended to the citizens at large is one of the subtlest problems of democracy. I do not venture here to answer it. I wish rather to keep more closely to the fact that whatever system is devised, it will have to recognize that the investor no longer can decide in modern industry, that "foresight" has become an organized, technical profession, and is ceasing to be one of the duties of private property.

Not long ago the Interstate Commerce Commission gave a very neat recognition to this change. It issued a report on the bankruptcy of the Frisco Railway, which contained a condemnation of certain private bankers for offering bonds to the investing public when the bankers should have known that the road was insolvent. The Commission was saying that the investor couldn't know, that he was in the hands of experts, and that the experts have a trust to perform. You couldn't very well go to greater lengths in announcing the impotence of private property. For where in the name of sanity have all the courage, foresight, initiative gone to; what has happened to all the rugged virtues that are supposed to be inherent in the magic of property?

They have gone a-glimmering with the revolutionary change that the great industry has produced. Those personal virtues belong to an earlier age when men really had some personal contact with their property. But today the central condition of business is that capital shall be impersonal, "liquid," "mobile." The modern shareholder as a person is of no account whatever. It mattered very much what kind of people the old landlords were. But it matters not at all what kind of person the shareholder is. He may be ignorant or wise, he may be a child in arms or a greybeard in his dotage, he may live in Iceland or Patagonia: he has no genuine role in the conduct of industry. He cannot fulfill any responsibility to the property he owns. That is why it is so futile to attack clergymen and reformers who happen to own stock in some ruthless factory. They have no real power to alter the situation.

You often hear it said that the stockholders must be made to realize their duties. Not long ago, for example, when the wretched working conditions of the steel mills were exposed, a very well-meaning minority stockholder did protest and cause a slight flurry in the newspapers. But the notion that the 200,000 owners of the steel trust can ever be aroused to energetic, public-spirited control of "their" property — that is as fantastic as anything that ever issued from the brain of a lazy moralist. Scattered all over the globe, changing from day to day, the shareholders are the most incompetent constituency conceivable.

Think how difficult it is to make the voters in one town exhibit any capacity for their task. Well, the voters in the government of the steel trust do not meet each other every day, do not read the same newspapers: the suffrage qualifications for the steel trust have nothing to do with age, sex, nationality, residence, literacy; the one qualification is the possession of some money and the desire for more. Shareholders are a heterogeneous collection with a single motive, and from that material some people pretend to expect a high sense of social responsibility.

I do not mean to imply, of course, that because a man owns stock he is necessarily ignorant or tyrannical. He may be as benevolent as you please. But the fact that he owns stock will not enable him to practice his benevolence. He will have to find other ways of expressing it. For shareholding in the modern world is not adapted to the exercise of any civilizing passion. It is too abstract, too scattered, too fluctuating.

All this is a natural result of the large-scale corporation. In the partnership and firm, owners and managers are in general the same people, but the corporation has separated ownership from management. Ownership has been opened to a far larger number of people than it ever was before, and it means less than it used to. Each stockholder owns a smaller share in a far greater whole. The trusts have concentrated control and management, but ownership they have diffused and diluted till it means very little more than a claim to residual profits, after expenses are paid, after the bondholders are satisfied, and perhaps, after the insiders have decided which way they wish the stock market to fluctuate.

Let no stockholder come to the radical, then, and charge him with attacking the sanctity of private property. The evolution of business is doing that at a rate and with a dispatch which will make future historians gasp. If the reformers should, for example, arrive at the point of deciding to abolish private property in railroads, they would discover that most of the rights of property had already disappeared. Management has long ago passed out of the hands of the stockholders; the right to fix rates has been absorbed by the state; the right to fix wages is conditioned by very powerful unions. They would find stockholding in the last stages of decay, where not even the dividends were certain. And one of the most difficult problems reformers may have to face will be the eagerness of railroad owners to give up the few vestiges of private property which are left to them, if they can secure instead government bonds. They may feel far happier as creditors of the United States than as representatives of the institution of private property.

Government ownership will probably be a very good bargain for railroad stockholders. Today they are a little less than creditors; they loan their money, and they are not sure of a return. Government ownership may make them real creditors — that is the highest hope which remains from the shattered glamor that came from the magic of property.

What has happened to the railroads is merely a demonstration of what is likely to happen to the other great industries —

steel, oil, lumber, coal, and all the others which are adapted to large-scale production. Private property will melt away; its functions will be taken over by the salaried men who direct them, by government commissions, by developing labor unions. The stockholders deprived of their property rights are being transformed into money-lenders.

It is evident that the question of nationalizing industries is not a choice between the maintenance of private property and its abolition. In amateur socialist discussions this is always made the issue whenever someone proposes to substitute public operation for private. It betrays an unreal sense of the problem. There is no very essential difference between holding the securities of the steel trust and those of the U.S. government. The government bonds are, if anything, a more certain investment. But there is some difference between public and private enterprise: what is it?

Opponents of collectivism argue that government work is inefficient. They seem to imply that the alleged superiority of private management is due to the institution of private property. That, it seems to me, is a striking example of what logicians call false cause. If the steel trust is efficient, it is not due to the existence of its 200,000 stockholders. It is due to the fact that the management is autocratic, that administrators are highly paid and given power adequate to their responsibility. When governments are willing to pursue that course, they can be just as efficient as private management. The construction of the Panama Canal is a classic example of what government can do if it is ready to centralize power and let it work without democratic interruption.

The real problem of collectivism is the difficulty of combining popular control with administrative power. Private property is no part of the issue; for any industry which was ready for collectivism would have abolished private property before the question arose. What would remain for discussion would be the conflict between democracy and centralized authority. That is the line upon which the problems of collectivism will be fought out — how much power shall be given to the employees, how much to the ultimate consumer, how much to sectional interests, how much to national ones. Anyone who has watched the disillusionment of labor with the earlier socialism and has understood the meaning of the syndicalist trend will know how radically the real difficulties of public enterprise differ from those presented in theoretical debates.

I do not wish at this point to draw any conclusion as to the solution of the trust problem. I am trying to sketch very roughly the main elements in the actual situation. The incentive of the men who conduct modern industry was the first point of interest. It is obvious that the trusts have created a demand for a new type of businessman — for a man whose motives resemble those of the applied scientist and whose responsibility is that of a public servant. Nothing would be easier than to shout for joy and say that everything is about to be fine: the businessmen are undergoing a change of heart. That is just what an endless number of American reformers are shouting, and their prophet is Gerald Stanley Lee.

The notion seems to be that workers, politicians, consumers and the rest are to have no real part in the glorious revolution which is to be consummated for their benefit. It is not hard to understand the habit of mind which leads men to these conclusions. The modern world is brain-splitting in its complexity, and if you succeed in disentangling from it some hopeful trend there is nothing more restful than to call it the solution of the problem. Those who have seen the change in business motives have, I believe, good ground for rejoicing, but they might in decency refrain from erecting upon it a mystic and rhetorical commercialism.

For the same reason, it is well not to take too literally the revolution in private property. This revolution has not happened to all property. It is most advanced in the railroads and what we call public service corporations. It is imminent in the big staple industries which are adapted to large-scale production. But there remains a vast amount of genuine private property in agricultural land, in competitive business.

In the great industries themselves, however, it is important to notice that with the diminishing importance of ownership, the control has passed for the time being into the hands of investment experts, the banking interests. That control is challenged now, not by the decadent stockholders but by those most interested in the methods of industry — the consumer, the worker, and the citizen at large.

———————◆———————

They were upon their great theme: "When I get to be a man!" Being human, though boys, they considered their present state too commonplace to be dwelt upon. So, when the old men gather, they say: "When I was a boy!" It really is the land of nowadays that we never discover.

BOOTH TARKINGTON, *Penrod*, 1914

President Roosevelt posed on a steam shovel at Culebra Cut during his visit to Panama, 1906

PROGRESSIVE POLITICS

In March 1910 a coalition of Democrats and liberal Republicans succeeded in restricting the power of Speaker Joseph G. Cannon. In the fall the midterm election gave an overwhelming House majority to the Democrats. It was clear that the Republican Party, lacking the unity that Roosevelt's dynamism had provided, was on the verge of splitting. The break, when it came in 1912, was instrumental in electing Wilson. But in addition, the Democrats had succeeded finally in finding the pulse of the Progressive spirit. The repeated failure of Bryan to attract substantial Progressive support was indicative of the middle-class origin of the movement; with Wilson, Progressive voters had no fear of the radical tendencies of Populism. The popular sentiment for reform peaked during the early years of the Wilson administration and there was every hope that the country would move forward on a higher moral plane than ever before. Much was accomplished; but a tragic involvement in foreign affairs, never a hospitable field for idealism, brought Progressivism to a sudden and final end.

Brown Brothers

Library of Congress

The Granger Collection

Thomas Stauffer

(Top) The vigor of Roosevelt's speaking style has failed to arouse the reporters or the dignitaries on this occasion; (above) cartoons celebrating the apparent force and effect of Roosevelt's antitrust policies; the cartoon at right more accurately represents the relative positions of business and government in the antitrust battles. Odysseus Roosevelt is tied to the mast of the ship of state in order to resist the Siren's call of Rockefeller, Morgan, and Carnegie, representing the trusts

The Drago Doctrine of 1902 and Roosevelt's 1904 Corollary to the Monroe Doctrine insured unified hemisphere support for resisting the use of European arms in the Americas, whether for territorial gain or for the collection of debts. Latin America had, however, no comparable protection against the U.S., which had assumed the power of deciding unilaterally when military intervention was necessary. Predictably, the conditions of the Corollary were rapidly broadened until the U.S. was intervening for the protection of American investment or simply of the status quo.

(Top) The "Big Stick" in Latin America: T. R.'s version of the Monroe Doctrine, which included a lot of gunboat diplomacy, sought in effect to make the area safe for American investment; (left) Elihu Root, secretary of state, 1904-09; (below) Brazilian reaction to T. R.; T. R. reviewing the fleet

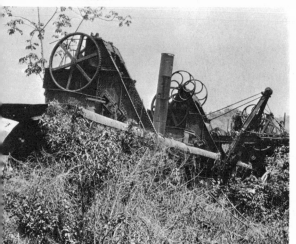

When, in 1903, the purchase by the U.S. of French canal rights in the Isthmus of Panama failed of ratification by the Colombian government, the United States promptly encouraged and supported with armed force a revolution in Panama. The Roosevelt administration appealed to an 1846 treaty under which the U.S. had intervened in Colombia, but always to help suppress revolution. With the canal at stake, Roosevelt allowed international law to go by the board.

(Top) Remains of unsuccessful American canal in Nicaragua, 1889; (left) debris left by French canal company in Panama, 1883; (below) U.S. blocks plans to take up the De Lesseps project and T. R. helps detach Panama from Colombia to insure American canal rights

Steam dredges at work in the Culebra Cut over-mountain portion of the Panama Canal

(Left) Col. William Gorgas, medical officer, who cleared the Canal Zone of yellow fever, making work possible; (right) George Goethals, head of the project; (below) locks in construction

T. R.'s active assertion of U.S. power and influence, particularly his offer to mediate the Russo-Japanese War, brought the charge that he wanted to "police the world"

At the request of Japan, which despite several victories was nearing the end of its resources, Roosevelt mediated an end to the Russo-Japanese War. Applying pressure through Great Britain and Germany, he forced the Treaty of Portsmouth in 1905. By balancing Russian and Japanese ambitions, Roosevelt hoped to keep the Orient open to America. To this end, even the Open Door was ignored in an informal agreement trading American acquiescence in Japan's annexation of Korea for a guarantee of Philippine security.

War Secretary Taft and Alice Roosevelt on a goodwill mission to Japan and the Philippines, 1905; float in parade welcoming them to the Philippines, showing planned capitol

Japanese warship in action off the coast of Manchuria, 1904; (below) native carries the belongings of Japanese officers ashore at Chemulpo; (above right) Russian officer

(Below) Japanese victory parade, complete with imitation Roman arch. The Japanese victory was the beginning of the end for Tsarist Russia and marked the entry of Japan into world politics

Based on the Miles Standish legend, this cartoon has T. R. taking up Taft's coy courtship of the nomination: "Why don't you speak for yourself, Theodore?"

Believing that his filling of McKinley's place from 1901 to 1904 constituted a first term, Roosevelt declared that he would not run in the 1908 election. Instead, he promoted his good friend, William H. Taft. Taft won easily, but lacked Roosevelt's leadership, and often found himself at odds with the Progressives. Displeased, Roosevelt opposed Taft in 1912, in the convention and then with the splinter Bull Moose Party. The Republican split virtually assured a Democratic victory.

(Left) Both Taft and Bryan court the favor of labor; (below) After the 1912 campaign Taft and T. R. lie exhausted, each saying: "Cheer up! I might have won."

(Above) Henry L. Stimson, war secretary (1911-13). He later served as secretary of state for Hoover and war secretary during World War II; (right) Taft opens a major Southwestern irrigation project, 1909. In the spirit of the Second Hague Peace Conference (1907), Secretary Root had negotiated 25 ''Reciprocity Treaties,'' agreeing to submit disputes to arbitration. In 1911 treaties were signed with Britain (below) and France, agreeing not to join attacks on each other or any other party to an arbitration treaty. The Senate inserted a restatement of U.S. primacy in Latin America before ratification.

(Above) President-elect Wilson and President Taft, Inauguration Day, 1913; (below) the lamp of Diogenes is passed to Wilson in recognition of his honesty and moral tone

"Uncle Joe" Cannon, conservative speaker of the house, 1903-1911

The first exercise of Wilsonian idealism in foreign affairs was in the fluid and violent Mexican situation. When the dictator Diaz was overthrown by the liberal Madero, the U.S. immediately recognized the new government. Recognition was, however, withheld when Madero fell to the counterrevolutionary Gen. Huerta; Wilson refused recognition even after most European countries had granted it. Basing his decision on the belief that the Huerta regime was illegitimate and immoral, Wilson thus obligated the U.S. to interfere should the government survive. The culmination was the occupation of Veracruz in 1914 to blockade a shipment of ammunition for Huerta.

U.S. troops at Veracruz, Mexico, 1914; one of many interventions in Latin America

(Above) Continued instability in Mexico and the marauding of Pancho Villa led to another intervention in 1916 of 15,000 troops under General Pershing; (below) "The Masses" comments

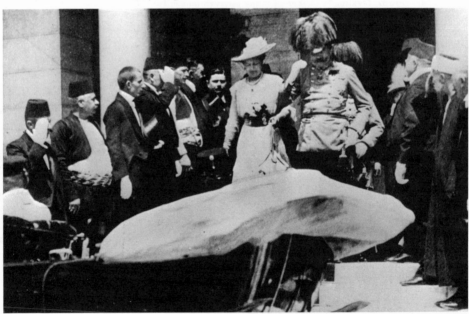

(Top) An unfinished sketch for a cartoon by Thomas Nast done about 1900. The "Peace Lord" (Christ) faces the "War Lord" (the Kaiser) in a prophetic foreshadowing of both the course of events and the moralistic anti-Hun frame of reference that eventually gripped the U.S.; (above) Archduke Ferdinand of Austria and his wife, Sophie, in Sarajevo (Bosnia), 5 minutes before they were killed; (right) capture of the assassin, Gavrilo Princip

96.

The Clayton Antitrust Act

The differences of economic policy between Wilson's New Freedom and Roosevelt's New Nationalism of 1912 did not seem so "fundamental and irreconcilable" two years later, when, as it seemed to many Progressives, the President had adopted much of the Roosevelt program. Wilson's policy on the trusts was embodied in two important pieces of legislation, both passed in 1914: the Federal Trade Commission Act, passed September 26, and the Clayton Antitrust Act, passed nineteen days later. The old Sherman Antitrust Act of 1890 had been made ineffective by several Supreme Court decisions, and the Clayton Act was intended to reinforce it. The purpose of the legislation, in Wilson's view, was "to make men in a small way of business as free to succeed as men in a big way, and to kill monopoly in the seed." A portion of the Clayton Act is reprinted below.

Source: *Statutes*, XXXVIII, Pt. 1, pp. 730-740.

An act to supplement existing laws against unlawful restraints and monopolies, and for other purposes.

Be it enacted by the Senate and House of Representatives of the United States of America in Congress assembled, that "antitrust laws," as used herein, includes the act entitled "An act to protect trade and commerce against unlawful restraints and monopolies," approved July 2, 1890; sections 73 to 75, inclusive, of an act entitled "An act to reduce taxation, to provide revenue for the government, and for other purposes," of August 27, 1894; an act entitled "An act to amend sections 73 and 76 of the act of August 27, 1894, entitled 'An act to reduce taxation, to provide revenue for the government, and for other purposes,'" approved February 12, 1913; and also this act.

"Commerce," as used herein, means trade or commerce among the several states and with foreign nations, or between the District of Columbia or any territory of the United States and any state, territory, or foreign nation, or between any insular pos-

sessions or other places under the jurisdiction of the United States, or between any such possession or place and any state or territory of the United States or the District of Columbia or any foreign nation, or within the District of Columbia or any territory or any insular possession or other place under the jurisdiction of the United States: *Provided,* that nothing in this act contained shall apply to the Philippine Islands.

The word "person" or "persons" wherever used in this act shall be deemed to include corporations and associations existing under or authorized by the laws of either the United States, the laws of any of the territories, the laws of any state, or the laws of any foreign country.

Section 2. That it shall be unlawful for any person engaged in commerce, in the course of such commerce, either directly or indirectly to discriminate in price between different purchasers of commodities, which commodities are sold for use, consumption, or resale within the United States or any territory thereof or the District of Columbia or any insular possession or other place under the jurisdiction of the United States, where the effect of such discrimination may be to substantially lessen competition or tend to create a monopoly in any line of commerce: *Provided,* that nothing herein contained shall prevent discrimination in price between purchasers of commodities on account of differences in the grade, quality, or quantity of the commodity sold, or that makes only due allowance for difference in the cost of selling or transportation, or discrimination in price in the same or different communities made in good faith to meet competition: *And provided further,* that nothing herein contained shall prevent persons engaged in selling goods, wares, or merchandise in commerce from selecting their own customers in bona fide transactions and not in restraint of trade.

Section 3. That it shall be unlawful for any person engaged in commerce, in the course of such commerce, to lease or make a sale or contract for sale of goods, wares, merchandise, machinery, supplies, or other commodities, whether patented or unpatented, for use, consumption, or resale within the United States or any territory thereof or the District of Columbia or any insular possession or other place under the jurisdiction of the United States, or fix a price charged therefor, or discount from, or rebate upon, such price, on the condition, agreement, or understanding that the lessee or purchaser thereof shall not use or deal in the goods, wares, merchandise, machinery, supplies, or other commodities of a competitor or competitors of the lessor or seller, where the effect of such lease, sale, or contract for sale or such condition, agreement, or understanding may be to substantially lessen competition or tend to create a monopoly in any line of commerce. . . .

Section 6. That the labor of a human being is not a commodity or article of commerce. Nothing contained in the antitrust laws shall be construed to forbid the existence and operation of labor, agricultural, or horticultural organizations, instituted for the purposes of mutual help, and not having capital stock or conducted for profit, or to forbid or restrain individual members of such organizations from lawfully carrying out the legitimate objects thereof; nor shall such organizations, or the members thereof, be held or construed to be illegal combinations or conspiracies in restraint of trade under the antitrust laws.

Section 7. That no corporation engaged in commerce shall acquire, directly or indirectly, the whole or any part of the stock or other share capital of another corporation engaged also in commerce, where the effect of such acquisition may be to substantially lessen competition between the corporation whose stock is so acquired and the corporation making the acquisition, or to restrain such commerce in any section or community, or tend to create a monopoly of any line of commerce.

No corporation shall acquire, directly or indirectly, the whole or any part of the stock or other share capital of two or more corporations engaged in commerce where the effect of such acquisition, or the use of such stock by the voting or granting of proxies or otherwise, may be to substantially lessen competition between such corporations, or any of them, whose stock or other share capital is so acquired, or to restrain such commerce in any section or community, or tend to create a monopoly of any line of commerce. . . .

Section 8. That from and after two years from the date of the approval of this act, no person shall at the same time be a director or other officer or employee of more than one bank, banking association, or trust company, organized or operating under the laws of the United States, either of which has deposits, capital, surplus, and undivided profits aggregating more than $5 million; and no private banker or person who is a director in any bank or trust company, organized and operating under the laws of a state, having deposits, capital, surplus, and undivided profits aggregating more than $5 million, shall be eligible to be a director in any bank or banking association organized or operating under the laws of the United States. The eligibility of a director, officer, or employee under the foregoing provisions shall be determined by the average amount of deposits, capital, surplus, and undivided profits as shown in the official statements of such bank, banking association, or trust company filed as provided by law during the fiscal year next preceding the date set for the annual election of directors; and when a director, officer, or employee has been elected or selected in accordance with the provisions of this act, it shall be lawful for him to continue as such for one year thereafter under said election or employment.

No bank, banking association, or trust company, organized or operating under the laws of the United States, in any city or incorporated town or village of more than 200,000 inhabitants, as shown by the last preceding decennial census of the United States, shall have as a director or other officer or employee any private banker or any director or other officer or employee of any other bank, banking association, or trust company located in the same place: *Provided*, that nothing in this section shall apply to mutual savings banks not having a capital stock represented by shares: *Provided further*, that a director or other officer or employee of such bank, banking association, or trust company may be a director or other officer or employee of not more than one other bank or trust company organized under the laws of the United States or any state where the entire capital stock of one is owned by stockholders in the other: *And provided further*, that nothing contained in this section shall forbid a director of Class A of a Federal Reserve bank, as defined in the Federal Reserve Act, from being an officer or director or both an officer and director in one member bank.

That from and after two years from the date of the approval of this act, no person at the same time shall be a director in any two or more corporations, any one of which has capital, surplus, and undivided profits aggregating more than $1 million, engaged in whole or in part in commerce, other than banks, banking associations, trust companies, and common carriers subject to the act to regulate commerce, approved February 4, 1887, if such corporations are or shall have been theretofore, by virtue of their business and location of operation, competitors, so that the elimination of competition by agreement between them would constitute a violation of any of the provisions of any of the antitrust laws. The eligibility of a director under the foregoing provision shall be determined by the aggregate amount of the capital, surplus, and undivided profits, exclusive of dividends declared but not paid to stockholders, at the end of the fiscal year of said corporation next preceding the election of directors; and when a director has been elected in accordance with the provisions of this act it shall be lawful for him to continue as such for one year thereafter.

When any person elected or chosen as a director or officer or selected as an employee of any bank or other corporation subject to the provisions of this act is eligible at the time of his election or selection to act for such bank or other corporation in such capacity, his eligibility to act in such capacity shall not be affected and he shall not become or be deemed amenable to any of the provisions hereof by reason of any change in the affairs of such bank or other corporation from whatsoever cause, whether specifically excepted by any of the provisions hereof or not, until the expiration of one year from the date of his election or employment. . . .

Section 10. That after two years from the approval of this act, no common carrier engaged in commerce shall have any dealings in securities, supplies, or other articles of commerce, or shall make or have any contracts for construction or maintenance of any kind, to the amount of more than $50,000, in the aggregate, in any one year, with another corporation, firm, partnership, or association when the said common carrier shall have upon its board of directors or as its president, manager, or as its purchasing or selling officer, or agent in the particular transaction, any person who is at the same time a director, manager, or purchasing or selling officer of, or who has any substantial interest in, such other corporation, firm, partnership, or association, unless and except such purchases shall be made from, or such dealings shall be with, the bidder whose bid is the most favorable to such common carrier, to be ascertained by competitive bidding under regulations to be prescribed by rule or otherwise by the Interstate Commerce Commission. No bid shall be received unless the name and address of the bidder or the names and addresses of the officers, directors, and general managers thereof if the bidder be a corporation, or of the members· if it be a partnership or firm, be given with the bid. . . .

Section 11. That authority to enforce compliance with sections 2, 3, 7, and 8 of this act by the persons respectively subject thereto is hereby vested: in the Interstate Commerce Commission where applicable to common carriers, in the Federal Reserve Board where applicable to banks, banking associations, and trust companies, and in the Federal Trade Commission where applicable to all other character of commerce. . . .

Section 19. That every order of injunction or restraining order shall set forth the reasons for the issuance of the same, shall be specific in terms, and shall describe in reasonable detail, and not by reference to the bill of complaint or other document, the act or acts sought to be restrained, and shall be binding only upon the parties to the suit, their officers, agents, servants, employees, and attorneys, or those in active concert or participating with them, and who shall, by

personal service or otherwise, have received actual notice of the same.

Section 20. That no restraining order or injunction shall be granted by any court of the United States, or a judge or the judges thereof, in any case between an employer and employees, or between employers and employees, or between employees, or between persons employed and persons seeking employment, involving, or growing out of, a dispute concerning terms or conditions of employment, unless necessary to prevent irreparable injury to property, or to a property right, of the party making the application, for which injury there is no adequate remedy at law; and such property or property right must be described with particularity in the application, which must be in writing and sworn to by the applicant or by his agent or attorney.

And no such restraining order or injunction shall prohibit any person or persons, whether singly or in concert, from terminating any relation of employment, or from ceasing to perform any work or labor, or from recommending, advising, or persuading others by peaceful means so to do; or from attending at any place where any such person or persons may lawfully be, for the purpose of peacefully obtaining or communicating information, or from peacefully persuading any person to work or to abstain from working; or from ceasing to patronize or to employ any party to such dispute, or from recommending, advising, or persuading others by peaceful and lawful means so to do; or from paying or giving to, or withholding from, any person engaged in such dispute, any strike benefits or other moneys or things of value; or from peaceably assembling in a lawful manner and for lawful purposes; or from doing any act or thing which might lawfully be done in the absence of such dispute by any party thereto; nor shall any of the acts specified in this paragraph be considered or held to be violations of any law of the United States.

97.

Woodrow Wilson: Appeal for Neutrality

"It would be the irony of fate," Woodrow Wilson remarked before his inauguration, "if my administration had to deal chiefly with foreign affairs." His worst fears were realized when the general European war began in August 1914 and soon became the most significant crisis he had to confront. Americans reacted to the outbreak of war with disbelief and with disgust, and with a strong determination not to become involved. Wilson's message to the Senate on August 19, which is reprinted here, echoed the sentiments of most of the nation. "We must be impartial," he declared, "in thought as well as in action." The remark became famous and was often quoted in the ensuing months of the war.

Source: 63 Congress, 2 Session, Senate Document No. 566.

I suppose that every thoughtful man in America has asked himself, during these last troubled weeks, what influence the European war may exert upon the United States; and I take the liberty of addressing a few words to you in order to point out that it is entirely within our own choice what its effects upon us will be, and to urge very earnestly upon you the sort of speech and conduct which will best safeguard the nation against distress and disaster.

The effect of the war upon the United States will depend upon what American citizens say and do. Every man who really loves America will act and speak in the true spirit of neutrality, which is the spirit of impartiality and fairness and friendliness to all concerned. The spirit of the nation in this critical matter will be determined largely by what individuals and society and those gathered in public meetings do and say, upon what newspapers and magazines contain, upon what ministers utter in their pulpits and men proclaim as their opinions on the street.

The people of the United States are drawn from many nations, and chiefly from the nations now at war. It is natural and inevitable that there should be the utmost variety of sympathy and desire among them with regard to the issues and circumstances of the conflict. Some will wish one nation, others another, to succeed in the momentous struggle. It will be easy to excite passion and difficult to allay it. Those responsible for exciting it will assume a heavy responsibility, responsibility for no less a thing than that the people of the United States, whose love of their country and whose loyalty to its government should unite them as Americans all, bound in honor and affection to think first of her and her interests, may be divided in camps of hostile opinion, hot against each other, involved in the war itself in impulse and opinion if not in action.

Such divisions among us would be fatal to our peace of mind and might seriously stand in the way of the proper performance of our duty as the one great nation at peace, the one people holding itself ready to play a part of impartial mediation and speak the counsels of peace and accommodation, not as a partisan but as a friend.

I venture, therefore, my fellow countrymen, to speak a solemn word of warning to you against that deepest, most subtle, most essential breach of neutrality which may spring out of partisanship, out of passionately taking sides. The United States must be neutral in fact as well as in name during these days that are to try men's souls. We must be impartial in thought as well as in action, must put a curb upon our sentiments as well as upon every transaction that might be construed as a preference of one party to the struggle before another.

My thought is of America. I am speaking, I feel sure, the earnest wish and purpose of every thoughtful American that this great country of ours, which is, of course, the first in our thoughts and in our hearts, should show herself in this time of peculiar trial a nation fit beyond others to exhibit the fine poise of undisturbed judgment, the dignity of self-control, the efficiency of dispassionate action; a nation that neither sits in judgment upon others nor is disturbed in her own counsels and which keeps herself fit and free to do what is honest and disinterested and truly serviceable for the peace of the world.

Shall we not resolve to put upon ourselves the restraints which will bring to our people the happiness and the great and lasting influence for peace we covet for them?

98.

Theodore Roosevelt: On Speaking Softly and Carrying a Big Stick

The nation as a whole quietly heeded President Wilson's admonition in 1914 "to put a curb upon our sentiments" concerning the war that raged ever more fiercely in Europe as the year wore on. Even a later ardent interventionist such as Theodore Roosevelt was unmoved, at least publicly, by the fate of innocent Belgium, quickly overrun by Germany after the outbreak of hostilities. But Roosevelt had no illusions about any nation's ability to protect its interests, even if they included remaining neutral, without backing its position by force. Emphasizing that he was not taking sides, he declared that the lesson of Belgium was clearly preparedness. The following selection comprises portions of an article published when the war was seven weeks old.

Source: *Outlook*, September 23, 1914: "The World War: Its Tragedies and Its Lessons."

OUR COUNTRY STANDS well-nigh alone among the great civilized powers in being unshaken by the present worldwide war. For this we should be humbly and profoundly grateful. All of us on this continent ought to appreciate how fortunate we are that we of the Western world have been free from the working of the causes which have produced the bitter and vindictive hatred among the great military powers of the Old World. We owe this immunity primarily to the policies grouped together under the title of the Monroe Doctrine. The Monroe Doctrine is as vital to the interests of this hemisphere today as it ever has been. Nations like Brazil, Argentina, and Chile are as deeply concerned in its maintenance as we are ourselves.

We of the United States have a twofold duty in this crisis. We must profit by reading aright the lesson writ in fire and steel before our eyes, and therefore we must safeguard our own future against the onfall of any similar disaster. Moreover, we must not only stand ready to act as an instrument for the achievement of a just peace if or when the opportunity arises, but also do whatever we can to formulate and secure adhesion to some kind of efficient international agreement whereby the chances of the recurrence of such worldwide disaster shall at least be minimized. To serve these various ends we, all of us, without regard to party differences, must stand ready loyally to support the administration, asking nothing except that the policy be one that in truth and in fact tells for the honor and interest of our nation, and in truth and in fact is helpful to the cause of a permanent and righteous world peace.

Of course, peace is worthless unless it serves the cause of righteousness. Peace which consecrates militarism is of small service. Peace obtained by crushing the liberty and life of just and unoffending people is as cruel as the most cruel war. It should ever be our honorable effort to serve one of the world's most vital needs by doing all in our power to bring about conditions which will give some effective protection to weak or small nations which themselves keep order and act with justice toward the rest of mankind. There can be no higher international duty than to safeguard the existence and independence of industrious, orderly states, with a high personal and national standard of conduct, but without the military force of the great powers; states, for instance, such as Belgium, Holland, Switzerland, the Scandinavian countries, Uruguay, and others. A peace which left Belgium's wrongs unredressed and which did not provide against the recurrence of such wrongs as those from which she has suffered would not be a real peace. . . .

The Belgians, when invaded, valiantly defended themselves. . . . They fought valiantly, and they were overcome. They were then stamped underfoot. Probably it is physically impossible for our people, living softly and at ease, to visualize to themselves the dreadful woe that has come upon the people of Belgium, and especially upon the poor people. . . .

The prime fact as regards Belgium is that Belgium was an entirely peaceful and genuinely neutral power which had been guilty of no offense whatever. What has befallen her is due to the further fact that a great, highly civilized military power deemed that its own vital interests rendered imperative the infliction of this suffering on an inoffensive although valiant and patriotic little nation.

I think, at any rate I hope, I have rendered it plain that I am not now criticizing, that I am not passing judgment one way or the other, upon Germany's action. I admire and respect the German people. I am proud of the German blood in my veins. When a nation feels that the issue of a contest in which, from whatever reason, it finds itself engaged will be national life or death, it is inevitable that it should act so as to save itself from death and to perpetuate its life. What has occurred to Belgium is precisely what would occur under similar conditions to us, unless we were able to show that the action would be dangerous.

If any Old World military power, European or Asiatic, were engaged in war, and deemed such action necessary *and safe*, it would at once seize the Panama Canal, or the Danish or Dutch West Indies, or Magdalena Bay, exactly as Belgium and Luxembourg have been overrun by Germany, as

Korea has been seized by Japan. They would certainly so act if they thought we would in any real crisis pay heed to the political theories resulting in the all-inclusive arbitration treaties that have just been negotiated in Washington. They would refrain from so acting only if they knew we would instantly and resolutely act ourselves in such manner as to forestall and defeat their action.

The rights and wrongs of these cases where nations violate the rules of abstract morality in order to meet their own vital needs can be precisely determined only when all the facts are known and when men's blood is cool. I am not at this time striving to lay down a general law, although I believe that it is imperative, in the interest of civilization, to create international conditions which shall neither require nor permit such action in the future. I am not at this time criticizing the particular actions of which I speak. But I do wish to point out just what these actions are, and just what lessons we of the United States should learn from them so far as our own future is concerned.

There are several such lessons. One is how complicated instead of how simple it is to decide what course we ought to follow as regards any given action supposed to be in the interest of peace. . . .

Our first duty is to hold ourselves ready to do whatever the changing circumstances demand in order to protect our own interests in the present and in the future; although, for my own part, I desire to add to this statement the proviso that under no circumstances must we do anything dishonorable, especially toward unoffending weaker nations. Neutrality may be of prime necessity in order to preserve our own interests, to maintain peace in so much of the world as is not affected by the war, and to conserve our influence for helping toward the reestablishment of general peace when the time

comes; for if any outside power is able at such time to be the medium for bringing peace, it is more likely to be the United States than any other. But we pay the penalty of this action on behalf of peace for ourselves, and possibly for others in the future, by forfeiting our right to do anything on behalf of peace for the Belgians in the present.

We can maintain our neutrality only by refusal to do anything to aid unoffending weak powers which are dragged into the gulf of bloodshed and misery through no fault of their own. Of course it would be folly to jump into the gulf ourselves to no good purpose; and very probably nothing that we could have done would have helped Belgium. We have not the smallest responsibility for what has befallen her, and I am sure that the sympathy of this country for the suffering of the men, women, and children of Belgium is very real.

Nevertheless, this sympathy is compatible with full acknowledgment of the unwisdom of our uttering a single word of official protest unless we are prepared to make that protest effective; and only the clearest and most urgent national duty would ever justify us in deviating from our rule of neutrality and noninterference. But it is a grim comment on the professional pacifist theories as hitherto developed that our duty to preserve peace for ourselves may necessarily mean the abandonment of all effective effort to secure peace for other unoffending nations which through no fault of their own are dragged into the war.

The next lesson we should learn is of far more immediate consequence to us than speculations about peace in the abstract. Our people should wake up to the fact that it is a poor thing to live in a fool's paradise. What has occurred in this war ought to bring home to everybody what has of course long been known to all really well-informed men who were willing to face the truth and not try to dodge it. Until some method is devised of putting effective force behind arbitration and neutrality treaties, neither these treaties nor the vague and elastic body of custom which is misleadingly termed international law will have any real effect in any serious crisis between us and any save perhaps one or two of the great powers. The average great military power looks at these matters purely from the standpoint of its own interests. . . .

Hysteria does not tend toward edification; and in this country hysteria is unfortunately too often the earmark of the ultrapacifist. Surely at this time there is more reason than ever to remember Professor Lounsbury's remark concerning the "infinite capacity of the human brain to withstand the introduction of knowledge." The comments of some doubtless well-meaning citizens of our own country upon the lessons taught by this terrible cataclysm of war are really inexplicable to any man who forgets the truth that Professor Lounsbury thus set forth. A writer of articles for a newspaper syndicate the other day stated that Germany was being opposed by the rest of the world because it had "inspired fear." This thesis can, of course, be sustained.

But Belgium has inspired no fear. Yet it has suffered infinitely more than Germany. Luxembourg inspired no fear. Yet it has been quietly taken possession of by Germany. The writer in question would find it puzzling to point out the particulars in which Belgium and Luxembourg — not to speak of China and Korea — are at this moment better off than Germany. Of course they are worse off; and this because Germany *has* "inspired fear," and they have not. Nevertheless, this writer drew the conclusion that "fear" was the only emotion which ought not to be inspired; and he advocated our abandonment of battleships and other means of defense, so that we might never inspire "fear" in anyone. He forgot

that, while it is a bad thing to inspire fear, it is a much worse thing to inspire contempt.

Another newspaper writer pointed out that on the frontier between us and Canada there were no forts, and yet peace obtained; and drew the conclusion that forts and armed forces were inimical to national safety. This worthy soul evidently did not know that Luxembourg had no forts or armed forces, and therefore succumbed without a protest of any kind. If he does not admire the heroism of the Belgians and prefers it to the tame submission of the Luxembourgers, then this writer is himself unfit to live as a freeman in a free country. The crown of ineptitude, however, was reached by an editor who announced, in praising the recent all-inclusive peace treaties, that "had their like been in existence between some of the European nations two weeks ago, the world might have been spared the Great War."

It is rather hard to deal seriously with such a supposition. At this very moment the utter worthlessness of even the rational treaties drawn to protect Belgium and Luxembourg has been shown. To suppose that under such conditions a bundle of bits of paper representing mere verbiage, with no guarantee, would count for anything whatever in a great crisis is to show ourselves unfit to control the destinies of a great, just, and self-respecting people.

These writers wish us to abandon all means of defending ourselves. Some of them advocate our abandoning the building of an efficient fleet. Yet at this moment Great Britain owes it that she is not in worse plight than Belgium solely to the fact that with farsighted wisdom her statesmen have maintained her Navy at the highest point of efficiency. . . .

It is our duty to be patient with every kind of folly, but it is hard for a good American, for a man to whom his country is dear, and who reveres the memories of Washington and Lincoln, to be entirely patient with the kind of folly that advocates reducing this country to the position of China and Luxembourg.

There is even a possible question whether we are not ourselves, like other neutral powers, violating obligations which we have explicitly or implicitly assumed in The Hague treaties. In Chapter I of the Convention defining the rights and duties of neutrals, the 10th Article reads: "The fact of a neutral power resisting even by force attempts to violate its neutrality cannot be regarded as a hostile act." The precise worth of this particular provision — and of all other provisions in all these treaties, save as they are backed by force — is beautifully illustrated by what has befallen Belgium at this time. All that she has suffered has been exactly and precisely because she did "resist by force attempts to violate her neutrality." In theory, so far as paper treaties go, she cannot be considered to have committed "hostile acts." In practice, Germany so treats her acts. Under actual conditions this Hague guarantee would excite laughter were not the tragedy such as to move us to tears instead.

One of the main lessons to learn from this war is embodied in the homely proverb, "Speak softly and carry a big stick." Persistently only half of this proverb has been quoted in deriding the men who wish to safeguard our national interest and honor. Persistently the effort has been made to insist that those who advocate keeping our country able to defend its rights are merely adopting "the policy of the big stick." In reality, we lay equal emphasis on the fact that it is necessary to speak softly; in other words, that it is necessary to be respectful toward all people and scrupulously to refrain from wronging them, while at the same time keeping ourselves in condition to prevent wrong being done to us. If a nation does not in this sense speak softly, then sooner or later the policy of the big stick is certain to result in war. But what befell Luxembourg six weeks ago, what has befallen China again and again during the past quarter of a century shows that no amount of speaking softly will save any people which does not carry a big stick.

I earnestly believe in peace. I respect every sincere and upright man who with wisdom and proper sense of perspective does all he can at peace conferences, or by the negotiation of reasonable arbitration treaties, or by the utilization of The Hague International Court in proper cases, to minimize the chances of war among civilized nations, and to give the opportunity to use other means than war for the settlement of international disputes. A little good can come from all these movements, but only on condition that there is no attempt made to erect shams and say they are truths or to pretend to be doing what we are not doing. A little good can come, but only on condition that nations remember that as yet arbitration treaties, neutrality treaties, treaties for the erection of independent tribunals, treaties of all kinds can do nothing to save a nation in great crises unless that nation is able to defend its own honor, its own vital interests.

America should have a coherent policy of action toward foreign powers, and this should primarily be based on the determination never to give offense when it can be avoided, always to treat other nations justly and courteously, and, as long as present conditions exist, to be prepared to defend our own rights ourselves. No other nation will defend them for us. No paper guarantee or treaty will be worth the paper on which it is written if it becomes to the interest of some other power to violate it, unless we have strength, and courage and ability to use that strength, back of the treaty. Every public man, every writer who speaks with wanton offensiveness of a foreign power or of a foreign people, whether he attacks England or France or Germany, whether he assails the Russians or the Japanese, is doing an injury to the whole American body politic. We have plenty of shortcomings at home to correct before we start out to criticize the shortcomings of others.

Now and then it becomes imperatively necessary in the interests of humanity, or in our own vital interest, to act in a manner which will cause offense to some other power. This is a lamentable necessity; but when the necessity arises we must meet it and act as we are honorably bound to act, no matter what offense is given. We must always weigh well our duties in such a case, and consider the rights of others as well as our own rights, in the interest of the world at large. If, after such consideration, it is evident that we are bound to act along a certain line of policy, then it is mere weakness to refrain from doing so because offense is thereby given. But we must never act wantonly or brutally, or without regard to the essentials of genuine morality — a morality considering our interests as well as the interests of others, and considering the interests of future generations as well as of the present generation.

We must so conduct ourselves that every big nation and every little nation that behaves itself shall never have to think of us with fear, and shall have confidence not only in our justice but in our courtesy. Submission to wrongdoing on our part would be mere weakness and would invite and insure disaster. We must not submit to wrong done to our honor or to our vital national interests. But we must be scrupulously careful always to speak with courtesy and self-restraint to others, always to act decently to others, and to give no nation any justification for believing that it has anything to fear from us as long as it behaves with decency and uprightness.

Above all, let us avoid the policy of peace with insult, the policy of unpreparedness to defend our rights, with inability to restrain our representatives from doing wrong to or publicly speaking ill of others. The worst policy for the United States is to combine the unbridled tongue with the unready hand.

We in this country have of course come lamentably short of our ideals, but our ideals have been high, and at times we have measurably realized them. Last spring some of our foes in Veracruz were guilty of the same misconduct as that because of the existence of which, as is alleged, Louvain was destroyed; but it never entered our heads to destroy Veracruz. When we found that our share of the Chinese indemnity paid us after the Boxer outrages was excessive, we returned it to China. When we gave our word to make Cuba independent, we kept our word — and none of the chancelleries of Europe thought we would do so.

From the beginning we have recognized what is taught in the words of Washington, and again in the great crisis of our national life in the words of Lincoln, that in the past free peoples have generally split and sunk on that great rock of difficulty caused by the fact that a government which recognizes the liberties of the people is not usually strong enough to preserve the liberties of the people against outside aggression. Washington and Lincoln believed that ours was a strong people, and therefore fit for a strong government. They believed that it was only weak peoples that had to fear strong governments, and that to us it was given to combine freedom and efficiency. They belonged among that line of statesmen and public servants whose existence has been the negation of the theory that goodness is always associated with weakness, and that strength always finds its expression in violent wrongdoing. . . .

There is, however, another lesson which this huge conflict may at least possibly teach. There is at least a chance that from this calamity a movement may come which will at once supplement and in the future perhaps altogether supplant the need of the kind of action so plainly indicated by the demands of the present. It is at least possible that the conflict will result in a growth of democracy in Europe, in at least a partial substitution of the rule of the people for the rule of those who esteem it their God-given right to govern the people. This, in its turn, would render it probably a little more unlikely that there would be a repetition of such disastrous warfare. I do not think that at present it would prevent the possibility of warfare. I think that in the great countries engaged, the peoples as a whole have been behind their sovereigns on both sides of this contest. Certainly the action of the Socialists in Germany, France, and Belgium, and, so far as we know, of the popular leaders in Russia would tend to bear out the truth of this statement. But the growth of the power of the people, while it would not prevent war, would at least render it more possible than at present to make appeals which might result in some cases in coming to an accommodation based upon justice; for justice is what popular rule must be permanently based upon and must permanently seek to obtain or it will not itself be permanent.

Moreover, the horror that right-thinking citizens feel over the awful tragedies of this war can hardly fail to make sensible men take an interest in genuine peace movements and try to shape them so that they shall be more practical than at present. I most earnestly believe in every rational movement for peace. My objection is only to movements that do not in very fact tell in favor of peace or else that sacrifice righteousness to peace. Of course this includes objection to all treaties that make believe to do what, as a matter of fact, they fail to do. Under existing conditions, universal and all-inclusive arbitration treaties have been utterly worthless, because where there is no power to compel nations to arbitrate, and where it is perfectly certain that some na-

tions will pay no respect to such agreements unless they can be forced to do so, it is mere folly for others to trust to promises impossible of performance; and it is an act of positive bad faith to make these promises when it is certain that the nation making them would violate them. But this does not in the least mean that we must abandon hope of taking action which will lessen the chance of war and make it more possible to circumscribe the limits of war's devastation. . . .

In view of what has occurred in this war, surely the time ought to be ripe for the nations to consider a great world agreement among all the civilized military powers *to back righteousness by force*. Such an agreement would establish an efficient World League for the Peace of Righteousness. Such an agreement could limit the amount to be spent on armaments and, after defining carefully the inalienable rights of each nation which were not to be transgressed by any other, could also provide that any cause of difference among them, or between one of them and one of a certain number of designated outside nonmilitary nations, should be submitted to an international court, including citizens of all these nations, chosen not as representatives of the nations *but as judges* — and perhaps in any given case the particular judges could be chosen by lot from the total number. To supplement and make this effectual it should be solemnly covenanted that if any nation refused to abide by the decision of such a court the others would draw the sword on behalf of peace and justice and would unitedly coerce the recalcitrant nation.

This plan would not automatically bring peace, and it may be too soon to hope for its adoption; but if some such scheme could be adopted, in good faith and with a genuine purpose behind it to make it effective, then we would have come nearer to the day of world peace. World peace will not come save in some such manner as that whereby we obtain peace within the borders of each nation; that is, by the creation of reasonably impartial judges and by putting an efficient police power — that is, by putting force in efficient fashion — behind the decrees of the judges.

At present each nation must in the last resort trust to its own strength if it is to preserve all that makes life worth having. At present this is imperative. This state of things can be abolished only when we put force, when we put the collective armed power of civilization, behind some body which shall with reasonable justice and equity represent the collective determination of civilization to do what is right.

99.

CARL SANDBURG: "Chicago"

The son of Swedish immigrants, Carl Sandburg had little formal education. After enlisting in the 6th Illinois Infantry during the Spanish-American War, he was sent to Puerto Rico for eight months. There he became close friends with a student at Lombard College, in Sandburg's hometown of Galesburg, Illinois, and returned after the war to attend the college. His interest in poetry grew, and he began to write verse. In 1914, Poetry: A Magazine of Verse *published several of his poems, including "Chicago," and he was on his way. The description of Chicago has seemed apt to many readers, and Chicagoans themselves are likely to say that their city is still "Stormy, husky, brawling," and that the Midwestern metropolis remains the "City of the Big Shoulders."*

Source: *Poetry,* March 1914.

CHICAGO

Hog Butcher for the World,
Tool Maker, Stacker of Wheat,
Player with Railroads and the Nation's
    Freight Handler;
Stormy, husky, brawling,
City of the Big Shoulders:

They tell me you are wicked and I believe them, for I
    have seen your painted women under the gas lamps
    luring the farm boys.
And they tell me you are crooked and I answer: Yes, it
    is true I have seen the gunman kill and go free to kill
    again.

And they tell me you are brutal and my reply is: On the
faces of women and children I have seen the marks of
wanton hunger.

And having answered so I turn once more to those who
sneer at this my city, and I give them back the sneer
and say to them:

Come and show me another city with lifted head singing
so proud to be alive and coarse and strong and cunning.

Flinging magnetic curses amid the toil of piling job on
job, here is a tall bold slugger set vivid against the
little soft cities;

Fierce as a dog with tongue lapping for action, cunning
as a savage pitted against the wilderness,

    Bareheaded,

    Shoveling,

    Wrecking,

    Planning,

    Building, breaking, rebuilding,

Under the smoke, dust all over his mouth, laughing with
white teeth,

Under the terrible burden of destiny laughing as a young
man laughs,

Laughing even as an ignorant fighter laughs who has never
lost a battle,

Bragging and laughing that under his wrist is the pulse,
and under his ribs the heart of the people,

        Laughing!

Laughing the stormy, husky, brawling laughter of
Youth, half-naked, sweating, proud to be Hog
Butcher, Tool Maker, Stacker of Wheat, Player with
Railroads and Freight Handler to the Nation.

1915

100.

Congressional Commission on Industrial Relations

The U.S. Commission on Industrial Relations, created by an act of Congress on August 23, 1912, conducted hearings for several years, interviewed over a thousand witnesses, and published eleven volumes of testimony. The investigation, touching on every contact between labor and all levels of management, included efforts to uncover the causes of the unrest and violence that marked labor-management relations at the turn of the century, as well as to define the relation between labor and the law. The testimony reprinted here is taken from that of Louis D. Brandeis (January 23, 1915), a prominent labor lawyer, and that of John Lawson (January 29, 1915), an organizer for the United Mine Workers. Lawson's testimony was given immediately after the end of the fifteen-month strike at Colorado Fuel and Iron in which the miners were decisively defeated. Brandeis addressed himself to the threat posed by absentee ownership to political liberty, a right hardly worth mentioning, he thought, without the industrial democracy that would give labor a share in the management of business.

Source: 64 Congress, 1 Session, Senate Document No. 415, Vol. VIII, pp. 7657-7681, 8003-8013.

I.

Louis D. Brandeis: Industrial Absolutism

Chairman Walsh. Have you observed the effect of the growth of large corporations on conditions of labor in American industry and the general industrial relations?

Mr. Brandeis. I have endeavored to study that among other things.

Chairman Walsh. Would you kindly state what your observation has been with respect to the question as to whether or not the high concentration and the growth of these corporations have improved the physical conditions under which workmen are employed, or otherwise.

Mr. Brandeis. I think, in many instances, they have improved their physical conditions; that is, large and successful organizations have been able to provide the best-planned and best-equipped factories, and they have, to a very considerable extent, built new factories. And there is, both among large corporations and the small —

or large factories and the small — a clear development of better factory conditions — more light, better ventilation, greater safety; and, insofar as the large corporations have been leaders in various branches of manufacturing and have constructed these new factories, they have undoubtedly improved in that way the physical condition of labor.

Chairman Walsh. Have the large corporations increased the wages as rapidly as the prices of commodities have increased, or shortened working hours as rapidly as the development of the industry would warrant?

Mr. Brandeis. It is difficult to answer that comprehensively. I should feel quite certain that in some respects they had not — certain corporations, and very prominent ones, have not increased wages as rapidly as the profits of the organization warranted, nor have they reduced hours. But I think that is true also of many corporations that are small.

Chairman Walsh. Does the corporate type of organization tend to produce a higher grade of workmen and citizens?

Mr. Brandeis. I should think not.

Chairman Walsh. Have the large corporations acted as a bulwark to prevent the growth of trade unions, from your observation, Mr. Brandeis?

Mr. Brandeis. Yes.

Chairman Walsh. I wish you would state what information you have, generally, of course, upon which you base that answer.

Mr. Brandeis. I think that the large industrial corporations have found this possible. That is true of the trusts and true also of large corporations which are not among those technically known as trusts, but which have powerful financial organizations; for instance, the steel trust, the tobacco trust, the sugar trust. It seems to me that they have possessed the power against which, in the main, the unions, union organizations, have struggled in vain.

There have been a very large number,

undoubtedly, of other employers who were not large, who had exactly the same desires and the same economic views as those who control these great corporations, but they had not the power of resistance, the power of endurance, and the influence and connections which enabled them to make their will law. It was a difference, not of motive in the main but of conditions.

Chairman Walsh. Have you observed the extent to which potential control over labor conditions is concentrated in the hands of financial directors of large corporations?

Mr. Brandeis. To a certain extent. I think that goes necessarily with the control of the corporations themselves. There has been undoubtedly great financial concentration — direct to a certain extent and indirect to a greater extent — and that influence which came from the concentration in comparatively few hands of a deciding voice in important financial and industrial questions almost necessarily affects the labor problems as it does other problems, although it may not have been the design primarily to deal with the labor problem.

Chairman Walsh. Have you observed the extent to which this potential control is exercised in connection with labor matters? Do you know of individual instances in which the control is directly used?

Mr. Brandeis. Well, the report of the Stanley Investigating Committee indicated that it had been used quite effectively in the steel trade.

Chairman Walsh. Do such financial directors, in your opinion, Mr. Brandeis, have sufficient knowledge of industrial conditions and social conditions to qualify them to direct labor policies involving hundreds of thousands of men?

Mr. Brandeis. I should think most of them did not; but what is perhaps more important or fully as important is the fact that neither these same men nor anybody else can properly deal with these problems without a far more intimate knowledge of the facts than it is possible for men to get who undertake to have a voice in so many different businesses. They are prevented from obtaining an understanding, not so much because of their point of view or motive but because of human limitations. These men have endeavored to cover far more ground than it is possible for men to cover properly, and without an intimate knowledge of the facts they cannot possibly deal with the problems involved.

Chairman Walsh. Does the fact that many large corporations with thousands of stockholders, among whom are large numbers of employees, in anyway whatever affect the policy of large corporations?

Mr. Brandeis. I do not believe that the holding of stock by employees — what is practically almost an insignificant participation, considering their percentage to the whole body of stockholders in large corporations — improves the condition of labor in those corporations. I think its effect is rather the opposite.

Chairman Walsh. I wish you would elucidate that a little, if you will, please, Mr. Brandeis; state the reasons for it.

Mr. Brandeis. Perhaps I would have to go a little further into my general feeling in this respect ——

Chairman Walsh. I wish you would do so, Mr. Brandeis.

Mr. Brandeis. As to the causes of the difficulty and of the unrest.

Chairman Walsh. I wish you would please do so.

Mr. Brandeis. My observation leads me to believe that while there are many contributing causes to unrest there is one cause which is fundamental. That is the necessary conflict — the contrast between our political liberty and our industrial absolutism. We are as free politically, perhaps, as free as it is possible for us to be. Every male has his voice and vote; and the law has endeavored to enable, and has succeeded practically, in enabling him to exercise his political

franchise without fear. He therefore has his part and certainly can secure an adequate part in the government of the country in all of its political relations; that is, in all relations which are determined directly by legislation or governmental administration.

On the other hand, in dealing with industrial problems, the position of the ordinary worker is exactly the reverse. The individual employee has no effective voice or vote. And the main objection, as I see it, to the very large corporation is that it makes possible — and in many cases makes inevitable — the exercise of industrial absolutism. It is not merely the case of the individual worker against employer which, even if he is a reasonably sized employer, presents a serious situation calling for the interposition of a union to protect the individual.

But we have the situation of an employer so potent, so well-organized, with such concentrated forces and with such extraordinary powers of reserve and the ability to endure against strikes and other efforts of a union, that the relatively loosely organized masses of even strong unions are unable to cope with the situation. We are dealing here with a question, not of motive but of condition.

Now, the large corporation and the managers of the powerful corporation are probably in large part actuated by motives just the same as an employer of a tenth of their size. Neither of them, as a rule, wishes to have his liberty abridged; but the smaller concern usually comes to the conclusion that it is necessary that it should be, where an important union must be dealt with. But when a great financial power has developed — when there exists these powerful organizations which can successfully summon forces from all parts of the country, which can afford to use tremendous amounts of money in any conflict to carry out what they deem to be their business principle, and can also afford to suffer large losses — you have necessarily a condition of inequality between the two contending forces.

Such contests, though undertaken with the best motives and with strong conviction on the part of the corporate managers that they are seeking what is for the best interests not only of the company but of the community lead to absolutism. The result, in the cases of these large corporations, may be to develop a benevolent absolutism, but it is an absolutism all the same; and it is that which makes the great corporation so dangerous. There develops within the state a state so powerful that the ordinary social and industrial forces existing are insufficient to cope with it.

I noted, Mr. Chairman, that the question you put to me concerning the employees of these large corporations related to their physical condition. Their mental condition is certainly equally important. Unrest, to my mind, never can be removed — and fortunately never can be removed — by mere improvement of the physical and material condition of the workingman. If it were possible, we should run great risk of improving their material condition and reducing their manhood. We must bear in mind all the time that however much we may desire material improvement and must desire it for the comfort of the individual that the United States is a democracy, and that we must have, above all things, men. It is the development of manhood to which any industrial and social system should be directed.

We Americans are committed not only to social justice in the sense of avoiding things which bring suffering and harm, like unjust distribution of wealth, but we are committed primarily to democracy. The social justice for which we are striving is an incident of our democracy, not the main end. It is rather the result of democracy — perhaps its finest expression — but it rests upon democracy, which implies the rule by the people. And therefore the end for which we must strive is the attainment of rule by the

people, and that involves industrial democracy as well as political democracy.

That means that the problems of a trade should be no longer the problems of the employer alone. The problems of his business, and it is not the employer's business alone, are the problems of all in it. The union cannot shift upon the employer the responsibility for conditions, nor can the employer insist upon determining, according to his will, the conditions which shall exist. The problems which exist are the problems of the trade; they are the problems of employer and employee. Profit sharing, however liberal, cannot meet the situation. That would mean merely dividing the profits of business. Such a division may do harm or it might do good, dependent on how it is applied.

There must be a division not only of profits but a division also of responsibilities. The employees must have the opportunity of participating in the decisions as to what shall be their condition and how the business shall be run. They must learn also in sharing that responsibility that they must bear to the suffering arising from grave mistakes, just as the employer must. But the right to assist in making the decisions, the right of making their own mistakes, if mistakes there must be, is a privilege which should not be denied to labor. We must insist upon labor sharing the responsibilities for the result of the business.

Now, to a certain extent we are gradually getting it — in smaller businesses. The grave objection to the large business is that, almost inevitably, the form of organization, the absentee stockholdings, and its remote directorship prevent participation, ordinarily, of the employees in such management. The executive officials become stewards in charge of the details of the operation of the business, they alone coming into direct relation with labor. Thus we lose that necessary cooperation which naturally flows from contact between employers and employees

— and which the American aspirations for democracy demand. It is in the resultant absolutism that you will find the fundamental cause of prevailing unrest; no matter what is done with the superstructure, no matter how it may be improved in one way or the other, unless we eradicate that fundamental difficulty, unrest will not only continue but, in my opinion, will grow worse.

Chairman Walsh. From your observation, Mr. Brandeis, what would you say is the responsibility of these so-called absentee owners of industries for conditions, wages, and other conditions existing in the corporations in which they are financially interested?

Mr. Brandeis. They must be held absolutely responsible. There is no such thing, to my mind, applying it in this connection, as an innocent stockholder. He may be innocent in fact, but socially he cannot be held innocent. He accepts the benefits of a system. It is his business and his obligation to see that those who represent him carry out a policy which is consistent with the public welfare. If he fails in that, so far as a stockholder fails in producing a result, that stockholder must be held absolutely responsible, except so far as it shall affirmatively appear that the stockholder endeavored to produce different results and was overridden by a majority.

Of course, stockholders may be innocent if they have been active and have been outvoted; but stockholders cannot be innocent merely by reason of the fact that they have not personally had anything to do with the decision of questions arising in the conduct of the business. That they have personally selected gentlemen or given their proxies to select gentlemen of high standing in the community is not sufficient to relieve them from responsibility. As a matter of course, most stockholders do have very little to do with the management and in these great corporations they have practically nothing to do.

It is largely the financial interests who determine policies and the practical results. But the stockholder is morally responsible although he actually has nothing to do with the management because he cannot justify himself in being a stockholder unless he assumes the obligations which go with stockholdership; and stockholdership is practically partnership in the establishment so far as concerns the questions now under consideration.

Chairman Walsh. You have probably noticed that practical — I was going to say practical unanimity, but that might be putting it a little too strong — the very general and broad statements that are made by directors in these corporations, especially those located in the city here, to the effect that they feel that they discharge their duties when labor policies are left to their local officials or to their exective officers here.

Mr. Brandeis. I have not read with any care the reports of what was testified to and that you have reference to.

Chairman Walsh. There are exceptions, but generally that has been the statement; that is, that they leave that to the executive officers.

Mr. Brandeis. That position, so far as it may have been taken, seems to me absolutely unsound. It is a position which, I think, must be deemed a relic of those earlier days when the labor problem was not regarded as the prime problem in the industrial world. The obligation of a director must be held to be absolute. Of course, I said a little while ago that one of the grave objections to this situation with large corporations was the directors did not know what was going on, and they could not therefore pass an intelligent judgment on these questions of the relations between employer and employee, because they did not have the facts.

Nobody can form a judgment that is worth having without a fairly detailed and intimate knowledge of the facts, and the circumstances of these gentlemen, largely bankers of importance, with a multitude of different associations and occupations — the fact that those men cannot know the facts is conclusive to my mind against a system by which the same men are directors in many different companies. I doubt whether anybody who is himself engaged in any important business has time to be a director in more than one large corporation. If he seeks to know about the affairs of that one corporation as much as he should know, not only in the interest of the stockholders but in the interest of the community, he will have a field for study that will certainly occupy all the time that he has.

Chairman Walsh. Have you observed, Mr. Brandeis, in the development of these large corporations, the percentage of stock which might give control, or in practical everyday life does give control — what I mean is this: There seems to be an impression in some quarters that the controllers had to have a majority of the stock — 51 percent, for instance.

Mr. Brandeis. I think it is true, not only of these very large corporations but of very much smaller corporations in which the stock is listed and widely distributed, that not only a small percentage of the stock may give control but that for a long series of years control is held sometimes without the ownership of any stock whatsoever, or of practically no more stock than is necessary to qualify directors.

I had a professional experience in connection with one corporation whose capitalization is very small as compared to those to which you refer, Mr. Chairman, but which runs into the millions, where I represented the outside stockholders who wanted to get control. The contest lasted a considerable time. We ultimately got control of the management, and when we examined the books we found that the management had practically sold itself out of all stock years before and held practically no stock at all;

that the president of the corporation had not only sold his stock holdings but had sold out even his qualifying shares, and had to go to the market the next day and buy five shares of stock in order to qualify as director.

I mean these corporations are not controlled through a majority of the stock; they are controlled very largely by position. And that is an almost inevitable result of the wide distribution of stock.

From the standpoint of the community, the welfare of the community and the welfare of the workers in the company, what is called a democratization in the ownership through the distribution of stock, is positively harmful. Such a wide distribution of the stock dissipates altogether the responsibility of stockholders, particularly of those with five shares, ten shares, fifteen shares, or fifty shares. They recognize that they have no influence in a corporation of hundreds of millions of dollars capital. Consequently they consider it immaterial whatever they do, or omit to do, the net result is that the men who are in control, it becomes almost impossible to dislodge, unless there should be such a scandal in the corporation as to make it clearly necessary for the people on the outside to combine for self-protection. Probably even that necessity would not be sufficient to ensure a new management. That comes rarely except when those in control withdraw because they have been found guilty of reprehensible practices resulting in financial failure. The wide distribution of stock, instead of being a blessing, constitutes, to my mind, one of the gravest dangers to the community. It is absentee landlordism of the worst kind. It is more dangerous, far more dangerous, than the absentee landlordism from which Ireland suffered. There, at all events, control was centered in a few individuals. By the distribution of nominal control among 10,000 or 100,000 stockholders, there is developed a sense of absolute irresponsibility on the part of the person who holds that stock. The few men that are in position continue absolute control without any responsibility except that to their stockholders of continuing and possibly increasing the dividends. Now, that responsibility, while proper enough in a way, may lead to action directly contrary to the public interest.

Chairman Walsh. For the purpose of illustration, take a corporation such as the Steel Corporation and explain what you mean by the democratization of industry, and to apply it to a concrete corporation, take that one.

Mr. Brandeis. I think the difficulty of applying it to that corporation, I mean a corporation as large as that and as powerful as that, is this: The unit is so large that it is almost inconceivable that the men in control can be made to realize the necessity of yielding a part of their power to the employee.

Now, when they resist a particular labor policy, for instance, the unionization of shops, and they do resist it violently, most of the officials do so in absolute good faith, convinced that they are doing what they ought to do. They have in mind the excesses of labor unions and their obligations to stockholders to protect the property; and having those things in mind and exaggerating, no doubt, the dangers of the situation, they conclude that they cannot properly submit to so-called union demands. They are apt to believe that it is "un-American" to do so — and declare it to be contrary to our conceptions of liberty and the rest. And they believe they are generally sincere in their statements.

The possession of almost absolute power makes them believe this. It is exactly the same condition that presents itself often in the political world. . . .

It is almost inconceivable to my mind that a corporation with powers so concentrated as the Steel Corporation could get to a point where it would be willing to treat with the employees on equal terms. And unless they treat on equal terms then there is no such thing as democratization. The treatment on equal terms with them involves not merely the making of a contract; it must develop into a continuing relation. The making of a contract with a union is a long step. It is collective bargaining — a great advance. But it is only the first step.

In order that collective bargaining should result in industrial democracy, it must go further and create practically an industrial government — a relation between employer and employee where the problems as they arise from day to day, or from month to month, or from year to year, may come up for consideration and solution as they come up in our political government. In that way conditions are created best adapted to securing proper consideration of any question arising. The representative of each party is heard — and strives to advance the interest he represents. It is the conflict of these opposing forces which produces the contract ultimately.

But to adequately solve the trade problems there must be some machinery which will deal with these problems as they arise from day to day. You must create something akin to a government of the trade before you reach a real approach to democratization. You must create a relation of employer to employee similar to that which exists in the trade under the protocol with the preferential union shop.

Chairman Walsh. Past experience indicates that large corporations can be trusted to bring about these reforms themselves?

Mr. Brandeis. I think all of our human experience shows that no one with absolute power can be trusted to give it up, even in part. That has been the experience with political absolutism; it must prove the same with industrial absolutism. Industrial democracy will not come by gift. It has got to be won by those who desire it. And if the situation is such that a voluntary organization like a labor union is powerless to bring about the democratization of a business, I think we have in this fact some proof that the employing organization is larger than is consistent with the public interest. I mean by larger, is more powerful, has a financial influence too great to be useful to the state; and the state must in some way come to the aid of the workingmen if democratization is to be secured.

Chairman Walsh. Are the workmen employed by large corporations in a position to work out their own salvation by trade-union organization today?

Mr. Brandeis. I think our experience, taking the steel trade as an example, has certainly shown that they are not. And this is true also of many other lines of business. Even in case of corporations very much smaller than the Steel Corporation, where the unions have found it impossible to maintain their position against the highly centralized, well-managed, highly financed company. Such corporations as a means of overcoming union influence and democratization frequently grant their employees more in wages and comforts than the union standard demands. But "man cannot live by bread alone." Men must have industrial liberty as well as good wages.

Chairman Walsh. Do you believe that the existing state and federal legislation is adequately and properly drawn to provide against abuses in industry so far as the employees are concerned?

Mr. Brandeis. I have grave doubt as to how much can be accomplished by legislation, unless it be to set a limit upon the size of corporate units. I believe in dealing with this labor problem as in dealing with the problem of credit. We must meet this question.

Chairman Walsh. Of what? Excuse me.

Mr. Brandeis. Size. And in dealing with the problem of industrial democracy there underlies all of the difficulties the question of the concentration of power. This factor

so important in connection with the subject of credit and in connection with the subject of trusts and monopolies is no less important in treating the labor problem. As long as there is such concentration of power no effort of the workingmen to secure democratization will be effective. The statement that size is not a crime is entirely correct when you speak of it from the point of motive. But size may become such a danger in its results to the community that the community may have to set limits.

A large part of our protective legislation consists of prohibiting things which we find are dangerous, according to common experience. Concentration of power has been shown to be dangerous in a democracy, even though that power may be used beneficently. For instance, on our public highways we put a limit on the size of an auto-truck, no matter how well it is run. It may have the most skillful and considerate driver, but its mere size may make it something which the community cannot tolerate in view of the other uses of the highway and the danger inherent in its occupation to so large an extent by a single vehicle.

II.

JOHN LAWSON:
Working Conditions at Colorado Fuel and Iron

Chairman Walsh. What is your present position or employment?

Mr. Lawson. I am a member of the International Executive Board of the United Mine Workers of America, representing District 15, which comprises Colorado, Utah, and New Mexico; and act as international organizer because of that fact.

Chairman Walsh. You addressed a communication to this commission asking to be heard at this time, I believe?

Mr. Lawson. Yes, sir.

Chairman Walsh. Please state why you wished to be heard at this hearing.

Mr. Lawson. When the miners of Colorado learned that the Rockefeller Foundation fund was going to be investigated here, they felt that it was within their duty to come to New York and request that they be permitted to put their side of the question before the commission, feeling that when every man lost 100 pounds of coal he contributed to the Foundation fund; that when he failed to receive payment for dead work he contributed to that same fund; that when he was not paid a sufficient amount of wages for his labor he contributed to that fund. So, Mr. Chairman, we decided to come here and to bring Mr. Edward P. Costigan, our legal representative, with us, and ask your permission to state these facts. . . .

Chairman Walsh. Is there anything in the testimony of Mr. Rockefeller that you would care to comment upon?

Mr. Lawson. Yes, Mr. Chairman, there are several things that I would like to comment on. I would like to comment on some testimony given before this commission and perhaps before the congressional hearing. I have with me a brief document that I have prepared, and I should like, with your permission, to read it into the record.

Chairman Walsh. Do you desire to read it at this time?

Mr. Lawson. Yes.

Chairman Walsh. You may proceed.

Mr. Lawson. I would like to state very much, Mr. Chairman, that in giving testimony before this commission at this time relating to the Foundation fund and the Colorado situation that I hope to do it without any malice and with the most kindly feeling. And I sincerely hope it will be taken in that way. I feel it my duty that this commission should get at the facts as far as we can give them.

The Commission on Industrial Relations was created to inquire into the underlying causes of industrial unrest. Speaking for the many thousands of men, women, and children who suffered through the recent coal strike in Colorado, I say to your honorable body that you can well afford to let the testimony of John D. Rockefeller, Jr., bring your investigation to an end. Out of this mouth came a reason for every discontent that agitates the laboring class in the United States today, and if remedies are provided for the injustices that he disclosed, a long step will be taken away from industrial disturbance.

For more than ten years he has been a director of the Colorado Fuel & Iron Co., vested with what is virtually the power of life and death over 12,000 men and their families, for the isolated nature of the coal-mining industry lends itself to an absolutism unknown in other activities. This power, let it be pointed out, came to him by no healthful process of struggle and achievement, but entirely through the fact that he was the son of his father. His huge control of men and money was, in effect, a gift that marked the attainment of his maturity.

In those first days, when he might have been expected to possess a certain enthusiasm in his vast responsibilities, Colorado was shaken by the coal strike of 1903-4. It is a matter of undisputed record that a mercenary militia, paid openly by the mine operators, crushed this strike by the bold violation of every known constitutional right that the citizen was thought to possess. Men were herded in bullpens like cattle, homes were shattered, the writ of habeas corpus suspended, hundreds were loaded on cars and dumped into the desert without food or water, others were driven over the snow of the mountain ranges, a governor elected by 15,000 majority was unseated, a man never voted on for that office was made governor, and when there came a thing called peace, the blacklist gave 6,000 miners the choice between starvation or exile.

The Colorado Fuel & Iron Co. organized and led that attack on the liberties of freemen, and yet you heard from Mr. Rockefeller's own lips that he never inquired into the causes of the strike, the conduct of his executives, or the fate of those who lost. So little interest did he take in the affair, so faint was the impression it made upon him, that he could not even answer your questions as to its larger facts.

To take the place of the banished workers, thousands were imported, and the extent of the company's dragnet for new material may be judged from the fact that over thirty languages and dialects have been spoken in the mines since 1904.

Ten years pass, and, in 1913, Colorado is once more pushed to the verge of bankruptcy by another strike. Many strikebreakers of 1903, reaching the limit of human endurance, followed the example of those whose places they had taken, choosing hunger and cold in tents on the mountainside and plains in preference to a continuance of unbearable conditions in the mines. By actual count, the union was supporting 21,508 men, women, and children in the various colonies in January 1914.

What course did Mr. Rockefeller pursue in connection with this upheaval of employees? His duty was clear, for he is on record with this admission, "I think it is the duty of every director to ascertain the conditions as far as he can, and if there are abuses, to right them." Putting their justice to one side, the fact remains that we claimed many abuses and cited them specifically.

The statute law of Colorado ordered a semimonthly payday, checkweighmen so that we might not be cheated, the right to form unions, the eight-hour day, and payment in cash — not scrip. We charged that the Colorado Fuel & Iron Co. had violated these and other laws, and in addition we told of evil housing conditions, high rents, company-store extortions, saloon environment, armed guards, and the denial of freedom in speech, education, religion, and politics. When 12,000 men back up such claims by taking their wives and children into windswept tents, surely they would seem to be deserving of consideration.

Yet upon the stand, throughout three whole days this week, John D. Rockefeller, Jr., insisted that he was absolutely ignorant of every detail of the strike. He stated that he had not received reports on labor conditions, he could not tell within several thousands how many men worked for him in Colorado, he did not know what wages they received or what rent they paid, he had never considered what the proper length of a working day should be, he did not know what constituted a living wage, and, most amazing of all, he had never even read the list of grievances that the strikers filed with the governor of Colorado and gave to the world through the press.

He did not know whether or not 50 percent of his employees worked twelve hours a day, and when asked whether or not he considered twelve hours a day in front of a blast furnace to be a hardship, he answered that he was not familiar enough with the work to judge. He did not know how many of his employees worked seven days a week the year around, but judged that it would be a hardship; yet when asked what part of a year could be worked under such conditions without hardship, refused to approximate an opinion.

He knew that there was a system by which injured men or their families were compensated, yet he did not know what the system was, and when a list was read showing the beggarly amounts paid to cripples, mangled miners, he would say nothing but that they were not matters that a board of directors would pass on. He did not know that his company's control of the courts had resulted in a condition where not one damage suit has been filed against it in years, and he did not know that men were treated like criminals for daring to mention unionism. He could not even define collective bargaining, nor had he ever made the slightest study of the great union or its principles against which the Colorado Fuel & Iron Co. threw its power and its millions. He expressed himself in favor of unions and then proceeded to negative this belief by refusing to answer affirmatively a number of questions that bore upon the manner in which unionization could be achieved.

Asked whether he would vote to discharge an executive officer if it should be proved that he had spent money to corrupt the electorate, he answered, "I should want to know the conditions." He did not know what the capitalization was of the subcompany that operates the mine stores or what it paid on the investment.

He did not know that the company built special buildings for saloons, charging high rental, or that church meetings were compelled to be held near saloons, and that in some cases saloons were in close contact with the schools. He knew that the company had maintained a sociological department, but he did not know what its activities were, nor was he aware that his officials dictated the appointment of our preachers and school teachers, and exercised the right of discharge if they offended by criticism.

As an excuse for this amazing lack of knowledge, he insisted that the Board of Directors had placed control of such matters in the hands of J. F. Welborn and L. M. Bowers and held them responsible for wise and just administration of labor affairs. He admitted that, aside from these two, he had knowledge of no others who would be responsible for labor conditions.

On the witness stand, L. M. Bowers, who gave his residence as Binghamton, N.Y., stated that he was concerned only with the finances of the Colorado Fuel & Iron Co., and knew nothing of labor conditions. J. F. Welborn admitted that, until his election to the presidency, he had been con-

nected with the sales department, always in Denver, and that it was not his habit to visit the mines. They pointed to E. H. Weitzel as the man in charge of labor conditions, and Weitzel stated that while he did not visit all the camps "frequently," he got to them as often as he could.

What has been Mr. Rockefeller's attitude to this development? Has he, in spite of his own lack of knowledge, instituted any investigation to discover whether Bowers and Welborn, his trusted executives, are equally ignorant and indifferent? I invite him to point to one single admission that would show the slightest activity in this direction or the least intent to summon these men before the Board of Directors to give an account of their stewardship. His answer was, "I have not had the opportunity." Fourteen months, thousands of men, women, and children suffered on the mountainsides and prairies, and two more months have gone since we called off the strike as a result of President Wilson's proposal, and yet he has not had the opportunity for a personal investigation.

His excuse for his lack of knowledge and his failures is that he is "too busy." What is his business? He explained it by stating that "I spend a large part of my time in directing, with others, the various foundations which my father has established and in giving time to questions of investment." I beg you to contrast this attitude with that of Henry Ford, a man who has built up his tremendous business with his own hands, and who follows every detail in its huge ramifications, and yet who finds the time to take a deep personal interest in every one of the 18,000 workers in his employ.

In reply to this, he spoke of the rich returns given by [the] Ford business as compared with the beggarly returns of the Colorado Fuel & Iron Co. He complained that his father had only received $371,000 in all of his stock, which was but a 3½ (⅔) percent interest on the cash investment. It was only under questioning that he confessed that his father had received $8,889,000 from his bonds; that the assets of the company were $23 million in excess of liabilities; and that this item did not take in an appreciation in property values of some $19 million. Nor did he mention the vast holdings that the Colorado Fuel & Iron Co. refuses to develop, keeping it idle while the population increase adds to its value.

Let me say to you in this connection — and I have spent a large part of my life in direct contact with the Colorado Fuel & Iron Co. — that whatever appearance of poverty clings to the company is not due to anything but its own stupid and corrupt policy. Had it taken the money it has spent in controlling officials and the electorate, in purchasing machine guns, the employment of gunmen, and in crushing the aspirations of human beings and spent it in wages and the improvement of working conditions, they would have had rich returns in increased productivity. Henry Ford's 15 percent wage increase, it will be noted, was followed by a 30 percent increase in efficiency.

These, Messrs. Commissioners — this record of indifference respecting human life and human happiness — are vital causes of industrial discontent. An employer who is never seen and whose power over us is handed down from man to man until there is a chain that no individual can climb; our lives and our liberties passed over as a birthday gift or by will; our energies and futures capitalized by financiers in distant cities; our conditions of labor held of less account than dividends; our masters too often men who have never seen us, who care nothing for us, and will not, or cannot, hear the cry of our despair.

There is another cause of industrial discontent, and this, too, flows from a Rockefeller source. This is the skillful attempt that is being made to substitute philanthropy for justice. There is not one of these founda-

tions now spreading their millions over the world in showy generosity that does not draw those millions from some form of industrial injustice. It is not their money that these lords of commercialized virtue are spending but the withheld wages of the American working class.

I sat in this room and heard Mr. Rockefeller read the list of activities that his Foundation felt calculated "to promote the well-being of mankind" — an international health commission to extend to foreign countries and peoples the work of eradicating the hookworm, $10 million for the Bureau of Municipal Research, a retreat for migratory birds in Louisiana, $100,000 for the American Academy in Rome, the promotion of medical education and health in China, $34 million for the University of Chicago, $1 million for the Belgians, $20,000 a year for widows' pensions in New York, the investigation of vice conditions in Europe, and $34 million for a general education board.

A wave of horror swept over me during that reading, and I say to you that that same wave is now rushing over the entire working class in the United States. Health for China, a refuge for birds, food for the Belgians, pensions for New York widows, university training for the elect, and never a thought or a dollar for the many thousand of men, women, and children who starved in Colorado, for the widows robbed of husbands, children of their fathers, by law-violating conditions in the mines, or for the glaring illiteracy of the coal camps. There are thousands of Mr. Rockefeller's ex-employees in Colorado today who wish to God that they were in Belgium to be fed or birds to be cared for tenderly.

As if this were not enough, labor is now informed that this Foundation has appropriated $1 million for the purpose of doing what this commission was appointed to do. An industrial-relations division has been formed to find out why we are discontented. Who, let it be asked, are the directors of this foundation out of which comes this investigation? The two Rockefellers; their professional advisers, Murphy, Gates, Green, and Heydt; their secretaries, Flexner and Rose, on the Rockefeller payroll; and three others, Eliot, Hepburn, and Judson, who furnish an outward appearance of independence. The same control that has directed the affairs of the Colorado Fuel & Iron Co., the same voice that declared through young Rockefeller that the defeat of the union in Colorado was a great American principle, for which he was willing to sacrifice his money and the lives of his workers; and they ask the laboring class to believe that what they feel as coal-company directors they will not feel as directors of the Foundation.

And who is the man chosen to conduct this million-dollar investigation into industrial unrest? One Mackenzie King, an alien, whose contribution to the industrial problem is a law that prescribes a jail sentence for the worker who dares to lay down his tools. If labor had any doubt as to his real intent, that doubt was removed by the letter read at this hearing. Under date of August 6, 1914, Mackenzie King wrote to John D. Rockefeller, Jr., as follows:

> It will not be long, however, before the inevitable effects of the European war on American labor conditions are certain to make themselves felt, and, once this becomes apparent, the unions will have to revise considerably some of their present policies. Looking at the ultimate rather than the immediate effect, there is, speaking generally, going to be a large amount of unemployment as a consequence of the war; in certain industries it is going to be easy for employers to find all the labor they desire, and unions will be confronted with a new problem. Here, it seems to me, lies a possible avenue of approach toward restoring normal conditions in Colorado.

The same thought was stated by President Welborn in a letter to Director McClement when he expressed pleasure over a two-foot fall of snow in Colorado, exclaiming, "This ought to make a good many of the strikers who are living in tents provided by the organization to seek the comfortable houses and employment at the mines."

Even were the source of the investigation less objectionable, what bearing can it possibly have on existing conditions? Mr. Rockefeller himself admitted that the Mackenzie King investigation will probably take many years. What is labor to do in the meantime? What is Colorado going to do? In response to this, Mr. Rockefeller says that "the problem now is for all concerned to develop increasing goodwill." Labor has been crushed by machine guns and hired soldiery; men, women, and children have died; homes have been ruined and futures blighted; new thousands have been imported for another decade of exploitation; and we are to "let bygones be bygones."

Mr. Rockefeller, Sr., is quoted as saying that God must be brought to New York. In Colorado there is a suffering multitude that asks only for a little of the spirit of the Christ, who died for human brotherhood.

The causes of industrial unrest, Mr. Commissioners, are not to be removed by promises of endless investigations or by a sudden willingness to hold conferences. They lie in the treatment of freemen, not as chattels, to be disposed of by deed and will, in absentee landlordism, in the theft of natural resources, or in indifferences to the necessities and aspirations of those who toil in the dark for the benefit of those in the light. Nor will Mr. Rockefeller's proposal for the election of men in coal camps meet the needs of collective bargaining. This is in truth the shadow and not the substance, for men so elected, unless backed by an organization wider even than state lines, will be utterly helpless in the hands of those who have sanctioned past grievances.

Nothing has been more clearly shown by

your investigation than that workers are unable to protect themselves as individuals, but can only gain this protection through organization in local, state, national, and international forms. It has been admitted by great operators that wage scales in nonunion mines, as well as the working conditions, are based upon the wages and conditions won by the efforts of organized labor.

In theory, at least, Mr. Rockefeller agrees to the principle of unionism. All that remains is to give his theory purpose and effect, something that cannot be done by simple expressions of goodwill or a suddenly expressed desire for meetings.

The United Mine Workers of America is the one organization that represents labor in this great industry. It has been in existence for twenty-five years. It has a present membership of more than 400,000 and enjoys contractual relations with employers in seventeen states. It has kept these contracts inviolate.

With these facts held clearly in mind, I insist that Mr. Rockefeller cannot give effect to his new point of view except with the cooperation of the United Mine Workers of America. By official conference with the executives of this organization, action should be taken to guarantee the enforcement of the mining and labor laws long violated in Colorado and the establishment of the principle in practice of collective bargaining.

Press reports give great publicity to meetings that are alleged to have been arranged between Mr. Rockefeller and the United Mine Workers' officials. Let me say on that subject that our one great desire is for lasting industrial peace. We rejoice that after all these years Mr. Rockefeller is at last disposed to consider and confer with the workers his company officials have despised, ignored, and endeavored to crush.

We welcome any and every conference, but these meetings should be official and purposeful, not mere social visits designed to give the utterly false impression that industrial war has had no more vital cause than a failure on Mr. Rockefeller's part to shake hands. So far as possible the remedies must equal and be as real as our great wrongs.

Chairman Walsh. In your opinion, Mr. Lawson, does the machinery for securing representation by the men in the management of the Colorado Fuel & Iron Co., as outlined by Mr. Rockefeller, and now being put into effect in Colorado, constitute an effective basis for collective bargaining?

Mr. Lawson. No, Mr. Chairman, it does not.

Chairman Walsh. Why not?

Mr. Lawson. In the first place, under the plan as outlined by Mr. Rockefeller and being put into effect by the operators in Colorado, the men are completely at the mercy of the operators, as much as they ever were, for this reason: Under this plan the miners have no organization behind them, they do not even have a local union organization, and the miners in this country today, without local unions, without state organizations, and without an international organization to stand behind them in enforcing their just demands, are without power, and I say again, entirely at the mercy of the employers.

Chairman Walsh. What are the essentials of collective bargaining?

Mr. Lawson. The essentials of collective bargaining are strong unions on each side, with a division of power in which each side may be represented properly and equally by those who are intelligent enough to bring about and negotiate agreements and have power enough to enforce just demands.

Chairman Walsh. Why do you say a national organization is required? Why would not a state or even a local organization do as well?

Mr. Lawson. Because, in this day and age of great combinations of capital — great corporations combined — labor must also put itself in a position that, when the workers are compelled to strike against injustice, they shall have some way — they must have some manner — of getting relief from some other source than among themselves, and they cannot do that, Mr. Chairman, for the reason that if a body of men have been compelled to go on strike — workingmen, the world over, are usually within a very few days of starvation, and it is necessary to have this relief so that they can maintain themselves and exist until the employers shall grant their demands.

101.

Ralph Chaplin: "Solidarity Forever"

"Solidarity Forever," by Ralph Chaplin, first appeared in the January 9, 1915, issue of Solidarity, *the labor newspaper published by the Industrial Workers of the World. "I wanted a song to be full of revolutionary fervor," Chaplin wrote later, "and to have a chorus that was singing and defiant." It became the best-known union song in America, virtually the anthem of the labor movement. Chaplin was a member of the IWW and one of its most able propagandists in verse.*

Source: *Songs of Work and Freedom*, Edith Fowke and Joe Glazer, eds., New York, 1960.

SOLIDARITY FOREVER

When the union's inspiration through the workers' blood shall run,
There can be no power greater anywhere beneath the sun.
Yet what force on earth is weaker than the feeble strength of one?
But the union makes us strong.

> *Chorus:*
> Solidarity forever!
> Solidarity forever!
> Solidarity forever!
> For the union makes us strong.

They have taken untold millions that they never toiled to earn,
But without our brain and muscle not a single wheel can turn.
We can break their haughty power, gain our freedom when we learn
That the union makes us strong.

In our hands is placed a power greater than their hoarded gold,
Greater than the might of armies magnified a thousandfold.
We can bring to birth the new world from the ashes of the old,
For the union makes us strong.

102.

W. A. Hamor: The Role of Chemistry in Industry

In the years after 1900 many manufacturing companies grew so quickly and haphazardly that their owners and executives had neither the time nor the inclination to reflect upon the reasons for their success. However, some forward-looking businessmen recognized that scientific research could be extremely valuable for industrial and financial growth. The Mellon Institute of Industrial Research at the University of Pittsburgh, for example, encouraged industrialists to utilize the staff of the university for work on specific research problems bearing on their manufacturing interests. In an article that was published in October 1915 and that is reprinted here in part, W. A. Hamor of the Mellon Institute discussed the value of industrial research.

Source: *Scientific Monthly*, October 1915.

THE AIM OF ALL INDUSTRIAL OPERATIONS is toward perfection, both in process and mechanical equipment, and every development in manufacturing creates new problems. It is only to be expected, therefore, that the industrial researcher is becoming less and less regarded as a burden unwarranted by returns. Industrialists have, in fact, learned to recognize chemistry as the intelligence department of industry, and manufacturing is accordingly becoming more and more a system of scientific processes. The accruement of technical improvements in particularly the great chemical industry is primarily dependent upon systematic industrial research, and this is being increasingly fostered by American manufacturers.

Ten thousand American chemists are at present engaged in pursuits which affect over 1 million wage earners and produce over $5 billion worth of manufactured products each year. These trained men have actively and effectively collaborated in bringing about stupendous results in American industry. There are, in fact, at least nineteen American industries in which the chemist has been of great assistance, either in founding the industry, in developing it, or in refining the methods of control or of manufacture, thus ensuring profits, lower costs, and uniform outputs.

At the recent symposium on the contributions of the chemist to American industries, at the 50th meeting of the American Chemical Society in New Orleans, the industrial achievements of that scientific scout, the chemist, were brought out clearly.

The chemist has made the wine industry reasonably independent of climatic conditions; he has enabled it to produce substantially the same wine, year in and year out, no matter what the weather; he has reduced the spoilage from 25 percent to 0.46 percent of the total; he has increased the shipping radius of the goods and has made preservatives unnecessary. In the copper industry he has learned and has taught how to make operations so constant and so continuous that in the manufacture of blister copper, valuations are less than $1 apart on every $10,000 worth of product, and in refined copper, the valuations of the product do not differ by more than $1 in every $50,000 worth of product. The quality of output is maintained constant within microscopic differences.

Without the chemist the corn-products industry would never have arisen, and in 1914 this industry consumed as much corn as was grown in that year by the nine states of Maine, New Hampshire, Vermont, Massachusetts, Rhode Island, Connecticut, New York, New Jersey, and Delaware combined. This amount is equal to the entire production of the state of North Carolina and about 80 percent of the production of each of the states of Georgia, Michigan, and Wisconsin. The chemist has produced over 100 useful commercial products from corn, which, without him, would never have been produced.

In the asphalt industry, the chemist has taught how to lay a road surface that will always be good, and he has learned and taught how to construct a suitable road surface for different conditions of service. In the cottonseed-oil industry, the chemist standardized methods of production, reduced losses, increased yields, made new use of wastes and by-products, and has added somewhere between $10 and $12 to the value of each bale of cotton grown. In the cement industry, the chemist has ascertained new ingredients, has utilized theretofore waste products for this purpose, has reduced the waste heaps of many industries and made them his starting material; he has standardized methods of manufacture, introduced methods of chemical control, and has insured constancy and permanency of quality and quantity of output.

In the sugar industry, the chemist has been active for so long a time that "the memory of man runneth not to the contrary." The sugar industry without the chemist is unthinkable. The Welsbach mantle is distinctly a chemist's invention and its successful and economical manufacture depends largely upon chemical methods. It would be difficult to give a just estimate of the economic effect of this device upon illumination, so great and valuable is it. In the textile industry, he has substituted uniform, rational, well-thought out, and simple methods of treatment of all the various textile fabrics and fibers where mystery, empiricism, "rule of thumb," and their accompanying uncertainties reigned.

In the fertilizer industry, it was the chemist who learned and who taught how to make our immense beds of phosphate rock useful and serviceable to man in the enrichment of the soil; he has taught how to make waste products of other industries useful and available for fertilization, and he has shown how to make the gasworks contribute to the fertility of the soil. In the soda industry, the chemist can successfully claim that he has founded it, developed it, and brought it to its present state of perfection and utility, but not without the help of other technical men; the fundamental ideas were and are chemical.

In the leather industry, the chemist has given us all of the modern methods of mineral tanning, and without them the modern leather industry is unthinkable. In the case of vegetable-tanned leather, he has also stepped in, standardized the quality of incoming material and of outgoing product. In the flour industry, the chemist has learned and taught how to select the proper grain for specific purposes, to standardize the product, and how to make flour available for certain specific culinary and food purposes.

In the brewing industry, the chemist has standardized the methods of determining the quality of incoming material and of outgoing products, and has assisted in the development of a product of a quality far beyond that obtaining prior to his entry into that industry. In the preservation of foods, the chemist made the fundamental discoveries; up to twenty years ago, however, he took little or no part in the commercial operations, but now is almost indispensable to commercial success. In the water supply of cities, the chemist has put certainty in the place of uncertainty; he has learned and has shown how, by chemical methods of treatment and control, raw water of varying quality can be made to yield potable water of substantially uniform composition and quality.

The celluloid industry and the nitrocellulose industry owe their very existence and much of their development to the chemist. In the glass industry, the chemist has learned and taught how to prepare glasses suitable for the widest ranges of uses and to control the quality and quantity of the output. In the pulp and paper industry, the chemist made the fundamental observations, inventions, and operations, and today he is in control of all the operations of the plant itself. To the chemist also is due the cheap production of many of the materials entering into this industry, as well as the increased and expanding market for the product itself.

Sufficient has been presented to show that certain industries of the United States have been elevated by an infusion of scientific spirit through the medium of the chemist, and that manufacturing, at one time entirely a matter of empirical judgment and individual skill, is more and more becoming a system of scientific processes. The result is that American manufacturers are growing increasingly appreciative of scientific research and are depending upon industrial researchers — "those who catalyze raw materials by brains" — as their pathfinders. It is now appropriate to consider just how industrialists are taking advantage of the universities and the products of these.

THE METHODS EMPLOYED IN THE ATTACK OF INDUSTRIAL PROBLEMS

WHEN AN INDUSTRY HAS PROBLEMS requiring solution, these problems can be attacked either inside or outside of the plant. If the policy of the industrialist is that all problems are to be investigated only within the establishment, a research laboratory must be provided for the plant or for the company. At present, in the United States, probably not more than 100 chemical manufacturing establishments have research laboratories or employ research chemists, although at least 5 companies are spending over $100,000 per year in research.

In Germany, and perhaps also in England, such research laboratories, in connection with chemical industries, have been much more common. The great laboratories of the Badische Anilin und Soda Fabrik and of the Elberfeld Company are striking examples of the importance attached to such research work in Germany, and it would be difficult to adduce any stronger argument in support of its value than the marvelous achievements of these great firms.

A frequent difficulty encountered in the employment of researchers or in the establishment of a research laboratory is that many manufacturers have been unable to grasp the importance of such work or know how to treat the men in charge so as to secure the best results. The industrialist may not even fully understand just what is the cause of his manufacturing losses or to whom to turn for aid. If he eventually engages a researcher, he is sometimes likely to regard him as a sort of master of mysteries who should be able to accomplish wonders; and, if he cannot see definite results in the course of a few months, is occasionally apt to consider the investment a bad one and to regard researchers, as a class, as a useless lot. It has not been unusual for the chemist to be told to remain in his laboratory and not to go in or about the works, and he must also face the natural opposition of workmen to any innovations and reckon with the jealousies of foremen and of various officials.

From the standpoint of the manufacturer, one decided advantage of the policy of having all problems worked out within the plant is that the results secured are not divulged, but are stored away in the laboratory archives and become part of the assets and working capital of the corporation which has paid for them; and it is usually not until patent applications are filed that this knowledge, generally only partially and imperfectly, becomes publicly known. When it is not deemed necessary to take out patents, such knowledge is often permanently buried.

In this matter of the dissemination of knowledge concerning industrial practice, it must be evident to all that there is but little cooperation between manufacturers and the universities. Manufacturers, and especially chemical manufacturers, have been quite naturally opposed to publishing any discoveries made in their plants since "knowledge is power" in manufacturing, as elsewhere, and new knowledge gained in the laboratories of a company may often very properly be regarded as among the most valuable assets of the concern. The universities and the scientific societies, on the other hand, exist for the diffusion of knowledge, and from their standpoint the great disadvantage of the above policy is this concealment of knowledge; for it results in a serious retardation of the general growth and development of science in its broader aspects, and renders it much more difficult for the universities to train men properly for such industries, since all the textbooks and general knowledge available would in all probability be far behind the actual manufacturing practice.

Fortunately, the policy of industrial secrecy is becoming more generally regarded in the light of reason, and there is a growing inclination among manufacturers to disclose the details of investigations, which, according to tradition, would be carefully guarded.

These manufacturers appreciate the facts that public interests in chemical achievements is stimulating to further fruitful research, that helpful suggestions and information may come from other investigators upon the publication of any results, and that the exchange of knowledge prevents many costly repetitions.

INDUSTRIAL FELLOWSHIPS

IF THE MANUFACTURER ELECTS to refer his problem to the university or technical school — and, because of the facilities for research to be had in certain institutions, industrialists are following this plan in constantly increasing numbers — such reference may take the form of an industrial fellowship and much has been said and may be said in favor of these fellowships. They allow the donor to keep secret for three years the results secured, after which they may be published with the donor's permission. They also secure to him patent rights. They give highly specialized training to properly qualified men, and often secure for them permanent positions and shares in the profits of their discoveries.

It should be obvious at the outset that a fellowship of this character can be successful only when there are close confidential relations obtaining between the manufacturer and the officer in charge of the research; for no such cooperation can be really effective unless based upon a thorough mutual familiarity with the conditions and an abiding faith in the integrity and sincerity of purpose of each other. It is likely to prove a poor investment for a manufacturer to seek the aid of an investigator if he is unwilling to take such expert into his confidence and to familiarize him with all the local and other factors which enter into the problem from a manufacturing standpoint.

103.

GRAHAM R. TAYLOR: Industrial Suburbs

Prompted by a desire for cheap land and lower taxes, many industrial firms fled the growing congestion of the cities at the turn of the century. The workers followed along, of course, and suburbs came into existence. The resulting metropolitan complexes drew the attention in 1915 of Graham R. Taylor, a Chicago minister and social worker who was concerned about living conditions in the new setting. His Satellite Cities *was a collection of articles about industrial suburbanization originally published in* The Survey *magazine.*

Source: *Satellite Cities: A Study of Industrial Suburbs,* New York, 1915: "The Outer Rings of Industry."

"BACK TO THE LAND" has come to mean more than the migration of a few tenement dwellers to farms. The big opportunity for the escape from crowded cities is through the wholesale removal of the work which city people do. Huge industrial plants are uprooting themselves bodily from the cities. With households, small stores, saloons, lodges, churches, schools clinging to them like living tendrils, they set themselves down ten miles away in the open.

While we spend years of effort in reconstructing our civic centers, only to have our schemes stalled by costly obstructions of brick and mortar and suspended by condemnation proceedings, city extension as a process is going on every week and every month on the edges of our cities.

Towns made to order entirely or with some little village as a core snatch bundles of papers from the morning trains, smudge new postmarks over sheet after sheet of red postage stamps, edge their way into the telephone tollbooks and the freight tariffs, scrawl their names on the tags of newcoming immigrants at Ellis Island and become part and parcel of up-and-doing municipal America before most of their slower-going sister cities have even heard of their existence.

From the middle of Philadelphia, several departments of the Baldwin Locomotive Works have been shunted out into a small suburb. Flint, Michigan, two hours from Detroit, has been seized as the place for huge automobile factories. While the population was trebling in the first three years, several hundred operatives had to be housed in tents throughout one summer. A big corn-products plant moved from the middle of Chicago to the nearby prairies and a "glucose city," Argo, started up. It occupies part of a tract of ten square miles, which one promoting company is developing as an "industrial district" and into which Chicago has already emptied more than two dozen establishments. Just outside Cincinnati a residential suburb, Norwood, is now the home of a score of manufacturing concerns.

Impelled partly by the arbitrary tolls charged on coal carried across the Mississippi River, industrial plants have moved over the bridges from St. Louis and founded a group of new towns in Illinois. The Standard Oil Company, a few years ago, poured out $3,500,000 on the bank of the Missouri a few miles from Kansas City, and the town of Sugar Creek sprang up. Yonkers long since lost its staid old character in a smother of hat and carpet factories. The metropolitan manufacturing district stretches out in belts and flanges from New York into Long Island, Staten Island, and New Jersey; while eastern Massachusetts is a mosaic of mill towns. In some sections of the South, scarcely a city of any size lacks one or more satellites thrumming with spindle and shuttle.

Gary, with its population nearing 50,000, where in 1906 there were only rolling sand dunes covered with scrub oak, is thus seen to be but the largest and most spectacular example of the far-reaching industrial exodus. Far-reaching and fast-moving, for Gary had scarcely attained four-year-old dignity when work started on a still newer member of the United States Steel Corporation's brood of steel towns — Fairfield, first known as Corey, on the edge of Birmingham, Alabama. On the heels of Fairfield came the news that more millions and another plant would found another steel town near Duluth.

This industrial exodus from city center to suburb was first seen conspicuously in the establishment of Pullman and Homestead in the early eighties. These two places were by no means the only forerunners. South Omaha, for example, in 1883, sprang up around the stockyards at a railway junction so rapidly as to win the name "Magic City." These exceptional towns, suddenly created at the dictate of pioneer master minds of the new industrialism, thrilled the popular imagination. . . .

Many reasons are readily apparent for the location of these new industrial communities. The impulse toward cheap land, low taxes, and elbowroom throws them out from the large centers of population. These are the centrifugal forces. The centripetal forces are equally powerful and bind them as satellites beyond the outer rings of the mother city. Even the towns which, like Gary, have attained a considerable measure of self-sufficiency and lie perhaps across state boundaries are bound by strong economic ties.

Through switchyards and belt lines, practically all the railroad facilities developed during years of growth which are at the disposal of a downtown establishment are at the service of the industry in the suburb. It means much to be within easy reach of at least one large market for finished product. Proximity to a big labor market is a more important factor.

The purpose of these pages, however, is not primarily to discuss the economic causes which lead to the sudden investment of large sums of capital in establishing suburban plants. It is rather to explore a little way into what the movement means for the great numbers of work people who are caught up and swept out with it. How do these new work places pan out as communities of people living together — families, neighbors, citizens? . . .

There is a public challenge in the very fact that in these localities civic and industrial conditions are being created brand-new, on a wholesale scale, without the handicaps and restrictions which high land values and prior improvements impose on every effort to reconstruct the congested centers. Are we turning these advantages to account? In our general municipal development we pay more and more heed to the counsel of city planner, housing expert, and sanitarian. We struggle to reshape our rigid, old-established conditions to fit newer and more workable molds, just as the manufacturer has to tear out, rebuild, and build higher if he stays in the midst of congestion while his business expands.

But have we set ourselves to inquire whether these made-to-order industrial cities, involving living conditions for thousands of people, are so shaped at the outset? In the planning of the great suburban industrial plant, marvelous skill and foresight are shown in adapting buildings and machinery to the processes through which stuff becomes finished product. Is a similar skill and foresight applied to the development of the things through which houses may become homes, a construction camp a community, and livelihood life? Apparently the answer is often the negative.

Whereas in the Gary plant, for example, the utmost ingenuity was shown in scheming out shortcuts, the street planning of the town was on the old checkerboard system. The placing of the blast furnaces was dictated by the speed of a laboring locomotive on a curving switch track. Instead of setting the stacks parallel or at right angles to the tracks, they were "placed at an angle of 22°, allowing a 200-foot radius for the entering switch." By such careful computations it was sought to avoid the moment wasted, to save the smallest fraction of a degree of heat which must otherwise be regained.

So much for transporting metal. But a workman who lives a mile away from the mill gate has needlessly to crisscross the checkerboard streets of the town, for a distance easily calculable by the old formula that the square of the hypotenuse of a right-angled triangle is equal to the sum of the squares of the other two sides.

Our general failure to bring city planning to bear where it will count for most — that is, in zones of new construction — was personified in this instance by those Middle Western officials of the Steel Corporation who, as members of the Commercial Club of Chicago, were at this time contributing from their own pockets toward the $100,000 fund raised to work out in map and design the present magnificent city plan for Chicago, in which the genius of Daniel H. Burnham had its final expression. Yet as company officials they had not thought to secure the services of an expert city planner to lay out a brand-new town which, including the plant, involved an investment of

over $75 million. The Chicago city plan calls for a cutting of diagonal streets through old territory at enormous expense; the Gary town plan is likely to create in a decade conditions which can only be remedied by a similar Caesarean operation.

The contention is raised, however, by some industrial leaders that they are in the business not of building cities but of establishing mills and factories, that the making of a town is a side matter into which they go only so far as necessity compels them. They want to avoid paternalism. It is significant to hear from their lips time and again a frank recognition of the mistakes of Pullman given as a justification for a "do-as-little-as-you-have-to" policy in shaping town conditions.

Yet it must be entirely evident that the early stage of choosing location and of laying the framework of plant and town is crucial. The citizens who are to people the town have not yet arrived. Their very absence imposes a greater obligation upon those with whose fiat goes such enormous power. Through such a serious miscarriage of judgment and stewardship by the company which built Lackawanna, in the outskirts of Buffalo, many of the workers were long housed on stilts in a swampy bottomland. The efforts of the present administration to overcome the situation insofar as is possible illustrate the slow recognition (by a corporation which has learned through experience) that efficiency hangs on health and human well-being and that a mill town in a swamp is as misplaced as a garden patch on a slag pile.

A manufacturing concern which makes highly finished cardboard products recently moved from the center of a large city to its outskirts, stating as one reason for the change that the smoky atmosphere prevalent in the city center caused great damage to the goods. Yet the effect of the same atmosphere on human lungs seemed to have been scarcely thought of. It was merely one of the fortunate coincidences of Providence that what was good for keeping stock clean happened also to be good for the health of the workers.

The scientific thoroughness which would follow the technique of efficiency and health down to the details of street planning is illustrated by the drawings for the construction of a large state prison by the Westinghouse, Church, Kerr Company. The firm went to the length of studying astronomical observations to determine the exact angle of the compass at which the building should stand in order to secure in each twelve months the maximum amount of sunlight. If it is worthwhile to take such care in housing the prisoners of a state, it seems reasonable to think that the same care might also be expended on street plans and the housing of free city dwellers.

How far we have yet to go in these directions in guiding development with reference to the community as a whole is illustrated by the fact that even at Flint —

where a few years ago public-spirited citizens secured a well-known city planner to lay out a scheme for parks, boulevards, and other civic features — one section after another of the industrial quarter was laid out adjacent to the automobile plants "without any special regulation except the understanding that no street was to be less than sixty feet in width." Fairfield is an example of a planned mill suburb.

It seems extraordinary that we do not require in the case of every new subdivision — just as we require of every new tenement house — a careful plan on lines broadly laid down by public authority and submitted to it for approval. The Washington (state) proposal that one-tenth of the area of every such subdivision must be set aside for parks and playgrounds is a step in the right direction. To safeguard the future in old towns as well as new, such broad legislation as is found in the English Town Planning Act is essential in this country.

104.

WALKER D. HINES: Our Irresponsible State Governments

By 1915, Progressivism in American politics had succeeded in bringing about the direct election of U.S. senators and in challenging graft and inefficient rule in many city governments. Walker D. Hines, who believed that the state governments also needed reforming, argued that their weaknesses were owing to inherent constitutional shortcomings. The typical Progressive belief that the removal of corrupt officials would correct all governmental problems was considered naïve by Hines. In an article reprinted here in part, he offered some suggestions about how the legislatures of state governments could be improved.

Source: *Atlantic Monthly*, May 1915.

THE AMERICAN PEOPLE disagree widely and variously upon innumerable subjects of public concern, but they are practically unanimous in the belief that our state legislatures pass a great mass of unnecessary laws, and

that many of the necessary laws are crudely drawn, inconsistent with one another, badly adapted to the ends in view, and largely ineffective. There is a correspondingly unanimous conviction that the affairs of the state governments are managed in a thoroughly unbusinesslike way, and that there is a widespread disregard of state laws and a general laxity in their enforcement. With a fatalistic resignation we expect the worst from our state legislatures and are prepared for the worst from our state administrative officers; and it is far too rare that we receive the agreeable surprise of beholding efficient work in either department.

The writer believes that to an important extent these unsatisfactory conditions are due to the fact that our scheme of state government carries the idea of divided responsibility to such an extreme that no public official is or can be held responsible in an effective sense for making the law or for enforcing the law; that this condition reacts upon the public and renders its supervision of those in public life less vigilant and intelligent; and that these things tend to produce public officers without training, talent, or sustained purpose for efficient public service.

Let us take first the Legislative Department. Its functions in the protection and promotion of the public interest are complex and difficult. There are needed an intelligent understanding of the various subjects upon which legislation is required or proposed; a knowledge of the history of former laws and their operation and of the effect of existing laws; sound judgment as to whether additional legislation is necessary; and originality in devising the best form of legislation. Vigilance is requisite in scrutinizing proposed legislative measures to see whether they are in the public interest, and initiative and persistence are needed to push through those measures which ought to be passed and to oppose those measures which are contrary to the general welfare. Thus the situation calls for wide information, hard study, originality, initiative, and persistence in order to carry on in an efficient way the business of governing the state. Always there is the general public in-

terest to be guarded, and this is far more important than any temporary or local interest of any particular community.

In considering the machinery which our state constitutions provide for dealing with this situation, let us look at the lower house of the state legislature, consisting, say, of 150 members. Not one of these members is primarily charged with studying or protecting the general public interests. Each member has the same measure of duty in this respect as every other member. It is a case where the protection of the public interest is "everybody's business"; and therefore it generally becomes in practice "nobody's business." It is ordinarily impossible to place the blame on any particular member for any important act which proves to be contrary to the public interest. Generally he is able to share that blame equally with every other member of the majority which acted or failed to act.

But in the rare cases where some member can be singled out as having a noticeable responsibility, that responsibility is exclusively to his local constituency and not to the state at large; his action may have been highly prejudicial to the state as a whole, but if he can satisfy his own constituency, perhaps through securing in another direction some local benefit, he suffers no embarrassment on account of his failure to discharge his duty to the general public. Such a condition tends to reduce to the minimum any motive to protect the general public interest, and to raise to the maximum the motive to secure local benefits for the restricted constituency upon which the member is dependent for support.

Every student of public or private affairs involving collective action appreciates that leadership is indispensable to the obtaining of results in any assemblage; but our system provides no leadership. Of course, as to any particular measure, some leadership arises, but ordinarily it is merely the leadership of some aggressive member who happens to be interested in the particular measure, and is not a comprehensive and continuous leadership in the public interest. In national affairs, party leadership upon party measures assumes a more tangible and responsible form; but in state legislatures the most important measures are frequently not party matters, and party leadership has very restricted operation. Therefore in state legislatures such leadership as exists is ordinarily fragmentary and accidental and is not the product of either the constitution or tradition. Public sentiment ordinarily fails to try to hold any such legislative leader responsible for results; and, in any event, his responsibility is not to the state whose interests he is shaping but to the locality which he represents.

Under such conditions, legislation affecting the public interest is shaped (or in a haphazard way shapes itself) in one house, and then goes to the other house, where it finds a similar division of responsibility, or lack of responsibility, and a similar raising of local interests above the interests of the state as a whole.

It cannot fairly be said that the evils referred to are substantially cured by the fact that measures have to pass two houses rather than one. On the contrary, these evils are frequently intensified thereby, because the mere splitting up of responsibility between the two houses makes each house even less attentive to the public interest than it would be if it had the sole responsibility. The house that passes a measure first has the feeling that its action is not final, and therefore need not be deliberate and thorough. The sanction thus given to the measure sometimes emboldens the second house to accept it without full and independent consideration.

At other times, the second house resents "being put in a hole" by being forced to take the responsibility of rejecting a measure already passed by the first house, and lets the measure go through. But whatever the outcome, a member of either house can share his responsibility (in the rare instances where it can be located at all) with members of the other house; and any shred of responsibility that finally sticks to him is confined entirely to his own constituency, who will probably disregard the matter altogether, being more interested in some other subject of purely local concern.

In addition to all the adverse factors already mentioned, still another division of responsibility confronts us. This arises from the fact that the governor has (in many states) the power of veto, and the legislature is not responsible for what the governor does. May not the carefree spirit with which a legislature passes doubtful measures be induced in many instances by the feeling that it is not taking final action, but is merely "putting things up to the governor"? And is it not a natural sequence to this spirit that the governor shall decline to veto measures which the representatives of the people have "put up to him" in this manner? . . .

Thus we have a system without constitutional leadership in either house; with responsibility split up until it reaches the vanishing point; with no member, even the most active, feeling any concern except for his own small body of constituents; with each house able to shift the responsibility to the other; with both houses able to shift the responsibility to the governor; and with the governor able to pass it back to the two houses. The legislature has no special concern as to whether its laws will be workable, and every member is anxious to pass a law because that is the only function which he has a chance to exercise. . . .

The usual constitutional provision that the governor "shall see that the laws shall be faithfully executed" is a mere passing counsel of perfection. Perhaps it is a survival of a time when the head of the Executive Department was the head in substance as well as in form. Ordinarily the governor has no power to enforce the laws and no substantial control over the officers who do have that power.

Frequently the state officers charged with the administration of the state's own business affairs, such as the heads of the various administrative departments, are wholly independent of the governor and of each other, and each is free to follow his own tendencies. These conditions, together with the aimlessness and irresponsibility of state legislatures, largely account for the impressive extravagance in public expenditures and for the rapid increase in the burdens of taxation.

When we come to the all-important function of making the individuals and business concerns in the state comply with the laws of the state, we find that, with a few exceptions, no state officer representing the state as a whole has any definite function or power because the enforcement of the laws ordinarily rests with the various county authorities. Law enforcement in a state is generally an exclusively local matter. A law of vital concern to the state as a whole is enforced or not in a particular community according to the degree of interest and efficiency manifested by the local authorities elected in that community.

Law enforcement is not an easy job. It requires vigilance, aggressiveness, and industry in detecting and locating the offenders and in preparing cases so that prosecutions will be prompt and successful. Yet we rarely find any well-considered scheme of county government whereby the responsibility for the conduct of these important functions is so centralized as to obtain effective results. The detection of offenses is largely accidental. The responsibility for instituting prosecutions is widely scattered. Frequently the local prosecuting attorney is in the comfortable position of being able to initiate such prosecutions as appeal to him, and to blame the grand jury, or some other functionaries, for not initiating prosecutions which do not appeal to him.

The preparation and conduct of a prosecution when initiated are generally under the control of a prosecuting attorney without effective supervision by any department of the state government. Such methods may be adequate with respect to crimes of violence, which are obvious and arouse the community's instinct of self-protection, but ordinarily they are inadequate with respect to much of the important legislation of the state. In these conditions we find some of the reasons why so little respect is commonly paid to state laws.

Another phenomenon which is widely observed is that frequently, when a law of special importance is passed, the legislature is likely to create some new board or commission to enforce that law. The result is that our state and local governments are plastered over with all sorts of expensive boards with anomalous and sometimes conflicting functions. Is not this condition largely due to the fact that the Executive Department is so poorly organized, and the responsibility therein is so divided and dissipated, that the public and the legislature assume, quite correctly, that the new law will not be vigorously enforced through existing channels? This anticipated inadequacy of the Executive Department (sometimes aided by the desire of people in public office to create more offices for their friends and supporters) seems to be the basic reason for the creation of so many boards and commissions. . . .

If to a substantial extent the foregoing criticisms of our present scheme of government are justified, the question remains, what improvement is practicable. It is a far too ambitious task for any individual to bring forward a scheme of government, and certainly the present writer does not propose to do so. But it does seem appropriate to suggest certain steps as worthy of consideration.

Any change in the direction of providing a constitutional leadership in the legislature, responsible to the state as a whole, will be worthy of serious consideration. The plan of giving the governor himself this leadership is probably best, because thereby the serious disadvantages of separating the law-making function from the law-enforcing function will be substantially overcome. It is open to serious question whether a legislature of a single house would not be an improvement over a legislature of two houses. It is reasonably clear that to make the governor the real instead of merely the nominal head of the Executive Department would be a wise step. Perhaps there will be little disagreement that county government ought to be centralized to the point where there will be a definite, single-headed responsibility for the enforcement of law in each county, such responsibility covering comprehensive and continuous work in the detection of offenders, in the preparation of cases against them, in the initiation of prosecutions, and in the prompt and effective conduct of such prosecutions.

Perhaps it is also worthy of consideration whether this central county responsibility ought not to be in some way put under the supervision of the executive head of the state, so that he can measure local results and aid in coordinating these activities throughout the state, to the end that the state laws, whose enforcement is of vital importance to the people of the state as a whole, shall be more adequately enforced in every part of the state.

Naturally the question arises whether the disadvantages of the present system, serious as they are, justify a departure from the theory of keeping separate the Legislative and Executive departments.

Today, there is much emphatic criticism of the executive's usurpation of the powers of the legislature. The claim is made that a strong and aggressive executive forces his will upon the legislature, which abdicates its constitutional functions and, without deliberation, registers the dictates of the executive. The suggestion may be made that the defects incident to such a practice would be intensified by a constitutional blending of the Executive and Legislative departments. The writer believes that the contrary would be true, because to a very great extent the present predominance of the executive is due to the weakness of the legislature, and this weakness in turn is due to the enfeebling effects of the scattering of responsibility. If the legislative and executive functions should be exercised by the same department of the government — the leaders of the legislative assembly being the executives — the legislature, through its increase of responsibility, would be strengthened in purpose and in personnel and would show a degree of originality and deliberation which at present is generally wanting.

As to the suggestion, not advocated but mentioned as worthy of consideration, that one legislative chamber be substituted for two, the answer will probably be made that a second chamber is necessary to correct the errors of the first. But is it not possible that a single chamber, realizing that its results will be final, will act with so much greater deliberation that its decisions will be more wise and sound than a decision arrived at by the present method? If the present method makes each house careless of the result, can it be said that we achieve better results by putting together two careless and irresponsible considerations than we would achieve by a single deliberation made in the light of the fact that the deliberation is final, and that responsibility therefore will rest exclusively upon those who participate in it, without the opportunity to divide it with another tribunal?

First, let it be pointed out that that theory would not be violated at all by providing a constitutional and responsible leadership in the Legislative Department answerable to the state as a whole; or by making the governor the real instead of merely the nominal executive head of the state, with control over all other state administrative officers; or by centralizing the executive power in each county in some way to secure responsibility and efficiency; or by making such centralized county power subject to the governor's supervision. All of these steps could be carried out without impairing the separation of the two departments, and the result would probably be to strengthen each of them as a separate department and make it really responsible to the state as a whole for the general public welfare.

It is conceded that the proposition to give to the head of the Executive Department the constitutional leadership in the legislature would involve a departure from the principle that the Executive and Legislative departments should be kept separate. But it is suggested that there is a serious question whether there is any adequate reason for keeping these two departments separate. It

is fair to inquire whether the blending of these two departments would not be in the direction of strengthening representative government, making it more responsive to the popular will and at the same time more efficient. And, along with all this, would not such a course accomplish a better training of the public, so as to give it the ability and the purpose to locate responsibility, to reward effectiveness, and to punish inefficiency? Popular government promises to be increasingly more complicated and difficult and to call for a higher order of training on the part of the public itself, and also on the part of the public's representatives. It is a fair question whether the accomplishment of these important results would not be promoted by blending the Executive and Legislative departments.

105.

ELIHU ROOT: The Invisible Government

Elihu Root, speaking before the New York Constitutional Convention on August 30, 1915, analyzed the evils of the "invisible government" that, he declared, had run New York state for many years. This government, he maintained, was not elected and was responsible only to the party boss in control of the state. Even worse, the party chief, through patronage, was able to control the legislative and executive branches of the state government. Root hoped that changes in the state's constitution would put an end to the system. Reprinted below is a portion of his speech in favor of the so-called Short Ballot Amendment, the intent of which was to facilitate the task of the voter in the voting booth, and hence to make government more responsive to the popular will.

Source: *Record of the Constitutional Convention of the State of New York, 1915,*
         Albany, 1915, Vol. III, pp. 3381-3389.

THE MOST IMPORTANT THING in constituting government is to unite responsibility with power, so that a certain known person may be definitely responsible for what ought to be done; to be rewarded if he does it, pun-

ished if he does not do it, and that the person held responsible shall have the power to do the thing. Under our system we have divided executive power among many separately elected heads of departments, and we have thus obscured responsibility, because in the complicated affairs of our government it is hard for the best informed to know who is to be blamed, or who is to be praised, who ought to be rewarded and who punished. . . .

Twenty years ago, when James Bryce wrote his *American Commonwealth,* the government of American cities was a by-word and a shame for Americans all over the world. Heaven be thanked, the government of our cities has now gone far toward redeeming itself and us from that disgrace, and the government of American cities today is in the main far superior to the government of American states. I challenge contradiction to that statement. How has it been reached? How have our cities been lifted up from the low grade of incompetency and corruption on which they stood when the *American Commonwealth* was written? It has been done by applying the principles of this bill to city government, by giving power to the men elected by the people to do the things for which they were elected. But I say it is quite plain that that is not all. It is not all.

I am going to discuss a subject now that goes back to the beginning of the political life of the oldest man in this Convention, and one to which we cannot close our eyes, if we keep the obligations of our oath. We talk about the government of the constitution. We have spent many days in discussing the powers of this and that and the other officer. What is the government of this state? What has it been during the forty years of my acquaintance with it? The government of the constitution? Oh, no; not half the time, or halfway. When I ask what do the people find wrong in our state government, my mind goes back to those periodic fits of public rage in which the people rouse up and tear down the political leader, first of one party and then of the other party. It goes on to the public feeling of resentment against the control of party organizations, of both parties and of all parties.

Library of Congress

Elihu Root

Now, I treat this subject in my own mind not as a personal question to any man. I am talking about the system. From the days of Fenton, and Conkling, and Arthur and Cornell, and Platt, from the days of David B. Hill down to the present time, the government of the state has presented two different lines of activity, one of the constitutional and statutory officers of the state and the other of the party leaders — they call them party bosses. They call the system — I don't coin the phrase, I adopt it because it carries its own meaning — the system they call "invisible government." For I don't remember how many years, Mr. Conkling was the supreme ruler in this state; the governor did not count, the legislatures did not count; comptrollers and secretaries of state and whatnot did not count. It was what Mr. Conkling said, and in a great outburst of public rage he was pulled down.

Then Mr. Platt ruled the state; for nigh

upon twenty years he ruled it. It was not the governor; it was not the legislature; it was not any elected officers; it was Mr. Platt. And the capitol was not here; it was at 49 Broadway — Mr. Platt and his lieutenants. It makes no difference what name you give, whether you call it Fenton or Conkling or Cornell or Arthur or Platt, or by the names of men now living. The ruler of the state during the greater part of the forty years of my acquaintance with the state government has not been any man authorized by the constitution or by the law; and, sir, there is throughout the length and breadth of this state a deep and sullen and long-continued resentment at being governed thus by men not of the people's choosing.

The party leader is elected by no one, accountable to no one, bound by no oath of office, removable by no one. Ah! My friends here have talked about this bill's creating an autocracy. The word points with admirable facility the very opposite reason for the bill. It is to destroy autocracy and restore power so far as may be to the men elected by the people, accountable to the people, removable by the people. I don't criticize the men of the invisible government. How can I? I have known them all, and among them have been some of my dearest friends. I can never forget the deep sense of indignation that I felt in the abuse that was heaped upon Chester A. Arthur, whom I honored and loved, when he was attacked because he held the position of political leader. But it is all wrong. It is all wrong that a government not authorized by the people should be continued superior to the government that is authorized by the people.

How is it accomplished? How is it done? Mr. Chairman, it is done by the use of patronage, and the patronage that my friends on the other side of this question have been arguing and pleading for in this Convention is the power to continue that invisible government against that authorized by the people. Everywhere, sir, that these two systems of government coexist, there is a conflict, day by day and year by year, between two principles of appointment to office, two radically opposed principles. The elected officer or the appointed officer, the lawful officer who is to be held responsible for the administration of his office desires to get men into the different positions of his office who will do their work in a way that is creditable to him and his administration. Whether it be a president appointing a judge, or a governor appointing a superintendent of public works, whatever it may be, the officer wants to make a success, and he wants to get the man selected upon the ground of his ability to do the work.

How is it about the boss? What does the boss have to do? He has to urge the appointment of a man whose appointment will consolidate his power and preserve the organization. The invisible government proceeds to build up and maintain its power by a reversal of the fundamental principle of good government, which is that men should be selected to perform the duties of the office; and to substitute the idea that men should be appointed to office for the preservation and enhancement of power of the political leader. The one, the true one, looks upon appointment to office with a view to the service that can be given to the public. The other, the false one, looks upon appointment to office with a view to what can be gotten out of it.

Gentlemen of the Convention, I appeal to your knowledge of facts. Every one of you knows that what I say about the use of patronage under the system of invisible government is true. Louis Marshall told us the other day about the appointment of wardens in the Adirondacks, hotelkeepers and people living there, to render no service whatever. They were appointed, not for the service that they were to render to the state, they were appointed for the service they were to render to promote the power of a political organization.

Mr. Chairman, we all know that the halls of this capitol swarm with men during the session of the legislature on payday. A great number, seldom here, rendering no service, are put on the payrolls as a matter of patronage, not of service, but of party patronage. Both parties are alike; all parties are alike. The system extends through all. Ah, Mr. Chairman, that system finds its opportunity in the division of powers, in a six-headed executive, in which, by the natural workings of human nature, there shall be opposition and discord and the playing of one force against the other; and so, when we refuse to make one governor elected by the people the real chief executive, we make inevitable the setting up of a chief executive not selected by the people, not acting for the people's interest, but for the selfish interest of the few who control the party, whichever party it may be.

Think for a moment of what this patronage system means. How many of you are there who would be willing to do to your private client, or customer, or any private trust, or to a friend or neighbor what you see being done to the state of New York every year of your lives in the taking of money out of her treasury without service? We can, when we are in a private station, pass on without much attention to inveterate abuses. We can say to ourselves, I know it is wrong, I wish it could be set right; it

cannot be set right, I will do nothing. But here, here, we face the duty, we cannot escape it, we are bound to do our work, face to face, in clear recognition of the truth, unpalatable, deplorable as it may be; and the truth is that what the unerring instinct of the democracy of our state has seen in this government is that a different standard of morality is applied to the conduct of affairs of states than that which is applied in private affairs.

I have been told forty times since this Convention met that you cannot change it. We can try, can't we? I deny that we cannot change it. I repel that cynical assumption which is born of the lethargy that comes from poisoned air during all these years. I assert that this perversion of democracy, this robbing democracy of its virility, can be changed as truly as the system under which Walpole governed the Commons of England, by bribery, as truly as the atmosphere which made the *crédit mobilier* scandal possible in the Congress of the United States has been blown away by the force of public opinion.

We cannot change it in a moment, but we can do our share. We can take this one step toward, not robbing the people of their part in government, but toward robbing an irresponsible autocracy of its indefensible and unjust and undemocratic control of government, and restoring it to the people to be exercised by the men of their choice and their control.

———◆———

There is such a thing as a man being too proud to fight.
WOODROW WILSON, speech at Philadelphia, May 10, 1915

Out of the Trenches and Back to Their Homes by Christmas.
HENRY FORD, slogan of peace delegation sent to Europe to stop the war, December 1915

106.

VAN WYCK BROOKS: Highbrow and Lowbrow

Van Wyck Brooks, whose long literary career was launched with The Wine of the
Puritans *(1909), continued his interpretation of cultured life in* America's
Coming-of-Age. *He had been greatly influenced by his professor, George Santayana,
who also believed that there was an unfortunate dichotomy in American culture. On
the one hand, there was Puritanism — an evil that Brooks and many in his generation
viewed with disgust; on the other hand, there was what Brooks called "catchpenny
opportunism." Both traditions were deemed undesirable; Brooks labeled the Puritan
strain "highbrow," and the opportunistic tendency "lowbrow" — words that, with a
somewhat altered meaning, have since become a part of ordinary American usage. In
the following selection, Brooks describes the background of this dual tradition and its
meaning in the twentieth century.*

Source: *America's Coming-of-Age,* New York, 1915, Ch. 1.

I

THE VERY ACCENT OF THE WORDS "highbrow" and "lowbrow" implies an instinctive perception that this is a very unsatisfactory state of affairs. For both are used in a
derogatory sense. The "highbrow" is the
superior person whose virtue is admitted
but felt to be an inept unpalatable virtue;
while the "lowbrow" is a good fellow one
readily takes to, but with a certain scorn for
him and all his works. And what is true of
them as personal types is true of what they
stand for. They are equally undesirable, and
they are incompatible; but they divide
American life between them.

II

THEY ALWAYS HAVE DIVIDED American life
between them; and to understand them one
has to go back to the beginning of things
— for without doubt the Puritan Theocra-
cy is the all-influential fact in the history of
the American mind. It was the Puritan con-

ception of the Deity as not alone all-
determining but precisely responsible for
the practical affairs of the race, as constituting, in fact, the state itself, which precluded
in advance any central bond, any responsibility, any common feeling in American affairs and which justified the unlimited centrifugal expediency which has always
marked American life. And the same instinct that made against centrality in government made against centrality in thought,
against common standards of any kind. The
imminent eternal issues the Puritans felt so
keenly, the equally imminent practical issues
they experienced so monotonously, threw
almost no light on one another; there was
no middle ground between to mitigate,
combine, or harmonize them.

So it is that from the beginning we find
two main currents in the American mind
running side by side but rarely mingling —
a current of overtones and a current of un-
dertones — and both equally unsocial; on
the one hand, the current of Transcendentalism, originating in the piety of the Puri-

tans, becoming a philosophy in Jonathan Edwards, passing through Emerson, producing the fastidious refinement and aloofness of the chief American writers, and, as the coherent ideals and beliefs of Transcendentalism gradually faded out, resulting in the final unreality of most contemporary American culture; and, on the other hand, the current of catchpenny opportunism, originating in the practical shifts of Puritan life, becoming a philosophy in Franklin, passing through the American humorists, and resulting in the atmosphere of contemporary business life. . . .

V

HUMAN NATURE itself in America exists on two irreconcilable planes, the plane of stark theory and the plane of stark business; and in the back of its mind is heaven knows what world of poetry, hidden away, too inaccessible, too intangible, too unreal in fact ever to be brought into the open, or to serve, as the poetry of life rightly should serve, in harnessing thought and action together, turning life into a disinterested adventure.

Argue which way you will, from the individual to society or from society to the individual, it is the same. Just as the American attitude toward the state has been the attitude of an oratorical and vague patriotism which has not based itself on a concrete interest in public affairs; just as, in consequence of this, the "invisible government" of business has swept in and taken possession of the field and become the actual government under which we live, overgrowing and supplanting the government we recognize; so also in the case of the individual; the cherishing of ideals that are simply unmapped regions to which nobody has the least intention of building roads, the baccalaureate sermons that are no just, organic comment on the educational system that precedes them — precisely these themselves strengthen the forces from below; the invisible government of self-interest, built up carefully from the beginning by maxim and example, fills the vacuum a disinterested purpose ought to have occupied.

Twenty, even ten, years ago, it would have been universally assumed that the only hope for American society lay in somehow lifting the "lowbrow" elements in it to the level of the "highbrow" elements. But that quickening realism which belongs to contemporary thought makes it plain, on the one hand, that the mere idealism of university ethics, the mere loftiness of what is called culture, the mere purity of so-called good government, left to themselves, not only produce a glassy inflexible priggishness on the upper levels which paralyzes life but that the lower levels have a certain humanity, flexibility, tangibility which are indispensable in any program; that Tammany has quite as much to teach good government as good government has to teach Tammany; that slang has quite as much in store for so-called culture as culture has for slang; that the universities, while emphatically not becoming more "practical," must base their disinterestedness on human, moral, social, artistic, and personal needs, impulses, and experience.

But society cannot become humane of itself; and it is for this reason that the movements of reform are so external and so superficial. The will to reform springs from a conviction *ex post facto* and is strictly analogous to the frame of mind of businessmen who retire at sixty and collect pictures. Nothing so exemplifies it as the spectacle of Mr. Carnegie spending three-quarters of his life in providing steel for battleships and the last quarter of it in trying to abolish war. He himself surely has not been conscious of any inward revolution; plainly with him as with others the will to create disorder and the will to reform it spring from the same inner condition of mind. The impetus of reform is evidently derived from the hope that a sufficient number of reformers can be trained and brought into the field to match the forces of business — the one group cancelling the other group. The ideal of reform, in short, is the attainment of zero.

Nothing is more absurd than to attack business as such. But the motives and circumstances of business vary from age to age, and there is a world of difference between industry conceived as a social process and trade conceived as a private end. A familiar distinction between the 19th century and the 20th is that the problem of civilization is no longer the problem of want but the problem of surplus. Roughly speaking, the hereditary American class — the prevailing class, I mean — is faced with the problem not of making money but of spending it; the prevailing American class is in a position of relative, but relatively great, economic freedom, and under these conditions it is plain that in them economic self-assertion ("enterprise") has become to a large extent a vicious anachronism. But force of habit, the sheer impetus and ground swell of an antiquated pioneering spirit finds them with no means of personal outlet except a continued economic self-assertion, on the one hand, and, on the other, a reckless and essentially impersonal overflow of surplus wealth which takes the form of doing what everybody else does, and doing it as much more so as possible.

Because it was for so long the law of the tribe, economic self-assertion still remains to most Americans a sort of moral obligation; while self-fulfillment still looks like a pretty word for selfishness. Yet self-fulfillment through science, or literature, or mechanics, or industry itself — the working out of one's own personality, one's own inventiveness through forms of activity that are directly social, as all these activities *are* directly social — gives a man, through his very sociality, through the feeling he has that as a good workman he is cooperating with all

other good workmen, a life interest apart from his rewards. And just as this principle becomes generally diffused and understood, the incentive is withdrawn from economic self-assertion, a relative competence being notoriously satisfying to the man whose prime end is the fulfilling of his own creative instincts; and the wealth of the world is already socialized.

You cannot have personality, you cannot have the expressions of personality so long as the end of society is an impersonal end, like the accumulation of money. For the individual whose personal end varies too greatly from the end of the mass of men about him not only suffers acutely and becomes abnormal, he actually cannot accomplish anything healthily fine at all. The best and most disinterested individual can only express the better intuitions and desires of his age and place; there must be some sympathetic touch between him and some visible or invisible host about him, since the mind is a flower that has an organic connection with the soil it springs from.

The only serious approach to society is the personal approach, and what I have called the quickening realism of contemporary social thought is at bottom simply a restatement for the mass of commercialized men, and in relation to issues which directly concern the mass of men as a whole, of those personal instincts that have been the essence of art, religion, literature — the essence of personality itself — since the beginning of things. It will remain of the least importance to patch up politics, to become infected with social consciousness, or to do any of the other easy popular contemporary things unless, in some way, personality can be made to release itself on a middle plane between vaporous idealism and self-interested practicality; unless, in short, self-fulfillment as an ideal can be substituted for self-assertion as an ideal. On the economic plane that implies socialism; on every other plane it implies something which a majority of Americans in our day certainly do not possess — an object in living.

VI

IT IS PERHAPS JUST AS WELL that Cervantes lived and died in Spain 300 years ago. Had he been born an American of the 20th century he might have found the task of satire an all too overwhelming one. Yet his fable, which has its personal bearing in all men always, has in America a social bearing that is perhaps unique. Don Quixote is the eternal "highbrow" under a polite name, just as Sancho Panza is the eternal "lowbrow"; and if the adorable Dulcinea is not a vision of the night and a daily goal in the mind of our professors, then there is no money in Wall Street. One admits the charm of both extremes, the one so fantastically above, the other so fantastically below the level of right reason; to have any kind of relish for muddled humanity is necessarily to feel the charm of both extremes. But where is all that is real, where is personality and all its works, if it is not essentially somewhere, somehow, in some not very vague way, between?

107.

WALTER PRICHARD EATON: Class-Consciousness and the Movies

By 1915 movies were the most popular entertainment in the country. Since they were an inexpensive amusement catering to a desire for adventure and violence that presumably characterized lower-class audiences, movies, it was argued, preserved class distinctions. The rich attended live dramas, presented in small, expensive theaters, while the poor went to movie houses. This, at least, was the argument of critics such as Walter Prichard Eaton.

Source: *Atlantic Monthly,* January 1915.

MOTION PICTURES, or the "movies" as they are popularly called, are a development of the 20th century. We can all remember when they were unknown; then a considerable period when they were exhibited in the vaudeville houses, always at the end of the program — the good-night act; then the time, scarcely more than a decade ago, when little theaters began to crop out devoted exclusively to motion pictures, and charging an admission fee of only 5 or 10 cents. At the present time it is almost safe to say that there is not a town of over 5,000 inhabitants in the country without its motion-picture theater, and in many sections the films are exhibited at least once a week in towns as small as 1,000.

Various calculations have been made to determine the number of people who daily attend the movies in the United States, the figures ranging from an inside estimate of 4 million to an outside figure of 10 million.

Even the smaller estimate is sufficiently impressive, but probably, in prosperous times at least, the higher is more nearly correct. Ten percent of our population, then, are patrons of the motion pictures.

These facts, I am aware, have been stated over and over, to the point of weariness, and various interpretations put upon them or deductions drawn from them. It has been pointed out, with truth, that the motion pictures, owing to their cheap price of admission and their extreme mobility, have added an entirely new source of amusement for small communities, where in the old days regular, or even, sometimes, occasional, dramatic entertainment was out of the question. It has also been pointed out that in the larger communities an individual, and more especially a family, can secure an evening of relaxation and entertainment much more frequently than before, because the head of a household, for example, can take his wife and three children to the movies for the price of one gallery seat at a regular playhouse.

It has been still further pointed out that not only is the outlay smaller but the return is more certain, and the sense of disappointment less, also, if the entertainment does not please. At the motion-picture theater more than one drama is presented — often four or five. At least one of them is bound to please. Paying five times as much admission even to the top gallery, the patron of the spoken drama, in any town except the few large centers, is generally taking chances with an unknown play and unknown players. The smallest town, however, sees the same motion-picture players as the largest — there are no second companies in the film world. John Bunny and Mary Pickford "star" in a hundred towns at once. . . .

Now, just what does all this mean? It means, the optimists will tell you, that the masses of the people are getting at last cheap amusement, on the whole of a good grade. Better and better productions are be-

ing made by the motion-picture firms, better actors are appearing on the screens, the Pathé Frères are presenting interesting and truly educational pictures of current events all over the world, a board of censors sees to it that objectionable film dramas are for the most part eliminated, and the spoken drama is learning to adapt itself successfully to the new conditions. There appear to be just as many regular theaters as ever and an even greater interest among educated people in the art of the playhouse. Moreover, as the motion pictures improve in quality, these same optimists say, they will "educate" many of their patrons to a desire for higher things. They will act as a school of appreciation for the spoken drama; they will breed new audiences for the legitimate playhouse.

This is a comforting — and a comfortable — view. It is a view we all wish we could hold. The present writer stuck to it as long as he could. But one does not need to be a Marxian Socialist, it seems to me, to detect, with a little thought and some observation of actual conditions, the economic basis of motion-picture popularity, and to feel that, so long as that economic basis exists, the breach between the film drama and the spoken drama will always exist also. You cannot, of course, draw any hard-and-fast line which will not be crossed at many points.

In Atlanta, Georgia, for example, you may often see automobiles parked two deep along the curb in front of a motion-picture theater, which hardly suggests an exclusively proletarian patronage. It does, however, suggest that Atlanta has a meager supply of the higher type of dramatic entertainment. On the other hand, when Sothern and Marlowe used to play Shakespeare at the old Academy of Music or the Manhattan Opera House in New York, the galleries were always packed with a proletarian audience. Nevertheless, it is perfectly safe to say that in the larger towns, where the higher-priced drama coexists with the motion-picture plays, the line of cleavage is sharply drawn in the character of the audience, and this line is the same line which marks the proletariat from the *bourgeoisie* and capitalist class.

In the smaller towns, of course, the line is much less sharply drawn, and in the villages, where "regular plays" never come, it is hardly drawn at all. But it is just in these villages, also, we must note, where modern industrialism has its least hold, that elder American institutions and social conditions most persist. In the average American village of a few thousand souls, even today, you will not find class-consciousness developed. The proletariat is not aware of itself. The larger the town, the greater the degree of class-consciousness — and the sharper the line of cleavage between the audiences at the spoken drama and at the movies. Indeed, in a certain New England city of 35,000 people, a concerted attempt was made two years ago by several wealthy men to provide good theatrical fare. They purchased the best theater in the town and installed an excellent stock company. The gallery seats sold for as low as 10 cents, thus competing with the movies. But the theater was on the "fashionable" side of town, it was looked upon by the 6,000 mill operatives and their families (constituting a proletariat which numbered more than 50 percent of the population) as something that belonged to the other class — and they would not go near it. Consequently, the well-meant attempt was a failure, while the movies continued to flourish as the green bay tree.

That is, perhaps, in the present state of things, an extreme example, showing rather how matters are going to be than how they generally are. At present, it is certainly not necessary to find any definite state of feeling to explain the cleavage between the two audiences. The economic explanation is quite sufficient. . . .

No, so long as the economic structure of our society remains as it is, and so long as our theaters are conducted as they are at present, the movies will not be to any appreciable extent a training school for audiences, fitting them for an appreciation of the spoken drama; nor will the movies grow any fewer in the land. Instead, the line of demarcation between theatrical audiences and movie audiences will grow ever sharper, the one representing entirely the *bourgeoisie* and upper classes, and the other the proletariat. The movies will become ever more powerfully a factor in the growth of class-consciousness. Already, as I have indicated, this result may be seen in the legitimate theaters as well as in the movie houses.

When theaters are built without galleries or balconies, when they are decorated like drawing rooms and no seat is sold for less than $2, or even $2.50, what chance is there of a democratic audience? More and more our playhouses are shrinking in size. There has not been a theater built to house dramas in New York in recent years which could not almost be placed on the stage of the old Boston Theatre. This is said to be a result of the changed conditions of the drama itself, modern realism having dictated an intimate type of playhouse.

In part that is true — but only in part. It is almost equally true that in recent years the managers (who would not care a snap about the proper presentation of intimate drama if they could fill the Metropolitan Opera House with it improperly presented, or with something else) found that they could not fill the larger houses. The upper galleries were just so much waste space. Their support came from what they call "the $2 crowd." Therefore they built for the $2 crowd — they built gilded drawing rooms. That development continues today. So does the development of the movies. Already the spoken drama and the silent drama are far apart. Each is the amusement, the pastime of a separate and antagonistic class.

I do not think that it would be at all difficult to show that this is bound to have a bad effect on the spoken drama, but I am rather less concerned with that phase of the question here than with the effect on the proletariat. It is surely a matter of record that the great periods of the drama have been coincident with periods of national awakening — true of all branches of the arts, perhaps. The Athenian drama and the Athenian state went hand in hand, for instance. The name of Shakespeare and the name of Drake can hardly be separated. Ibsen and modern Norway were a joint growth. The drama in France has always been close to the consciousness of the nation. We have no native opera in America; it is an imported pastime of the capitalist class — as we may call them in this paper — which set out with a title borrowed from the Socialists.

But you may hear any Italian laborer digging a ditch or laying a railroad burst into an air from Verdi, because opera is his national speech. To think of Vienna is to think of Johann Strauss. We have as yet no body of American drama worthy of the name. Bronson Howard, James A. Herne, and Clyde Fitch gave us the beginnings of such a drama, and other men still living and active have striven to carry on the work, men especially like Eugene Walter and Augustus Thomas. But of late there has been a disappointing lack of progress.

It is not that dramas are not written by Americans, or even that they are not well written by Americans. George Cohan's *Seven Keys to Baldpate* was extraordinarily well written — or shall we say well made? Rather it is that they never get down to national fundamentals, that they have no intellectual seriousness (which does not mean tragedy, or even necessarily any lack of comedy, as our present-day audiences seem to suppose). When Clyde Fitch's play, *The Truth*, was revived last winter after nine years, it was almost shocking to see how much more seriously he took his task as a dramatist than our entertainers of the hour. He was tracking down a woman's character; the hunt that thrilled was the hunt for her soul.

Today the plot is the thing, and just now the dramatist who can give a new and unexpected twist to a "situation" or tell his story backward is acclaimed as king. Is this not a symptom of sophistication? Is not sophistication bound to come in at the window when the proletariat goes out by the door, even if it is the back door? It is always true, I think, that a person who has never been obliged to earn his own living lacks a certain solidarity of view that neither sympathy nor good intentions nor moral character can supply. Just so the wage earners of a nation, who have lived perpetually close to the sterner realities, supply an element which the drama needs, which it must have, to achieve the universality and power demanded of any truly national expression in the arts. A theater without a gallery means a drama without a soul.

No doubt this point could be elaborated upon at considerable length, but after all it less concerns our present discussion than does the effect of the movies upon the proletariat. When we speak of class-consciousness, we do not mean the consciousness of "class." Certain people have always been quite conscious that they were superior beings, even in democracies like our own. There is nothing new about that. But what we mean by class-consciousness, as a revolutionist term, is the consciousness of the proletariat; not that it is socially inferior at present, but that it proposes to be economically equal in the future, and that this result is to be achieved by concerted class action, whether forcible or parliamentary. . . .

In practically shutting off the proletariat from the spoken drama, as we are doing (our New England city of 35,000 showed a proletariat of at least 20,000 who would not or did not attend the legitimate playhouse), and throwing them back on an exclusive amusement diet of motion pictures, what are we doing to them? Are we helping them or harming them? Should their own leaders rejoice at a gain in class-consciousness, or consider gravely the other side of the balance — the loss of romance, of poetry, of intellectual stimulation — all the varied aesthetic appeal of the most universal of the fine arts, the art of the theater?

I am perfectly well aware that many people will consider this question of but trivial importance. I am also well aware that many others will retort, and retort truly, that very often the movies are an excellent institution, supplying innocent amusement, often educational in value, to people who would otherwise be without resources for amusement. I do not for a moment deny it. In the smaller towns the movies are a boon. I myself would infinitely rather see *Cabiria* on the motion-picture screen, for that matter, than half the melodramas on Broadway. But the small town which never had an amusement center till the movies came is far from the heart of the problem, and *Cabiria* and its kind are far from the normal motion picture. The question is not between the movies and nothing but between the movies, the average 5- and 10-cent movies (*Cabiria* was exhibited on Broadway at $1 a seat) and the spoken drama — in other words, between a semimechanical pantomime and a fine art.

Let us put the matter a little differently. In our schools we attempt to teach the best literature, to inculcate ideals of good music and sound art. We open museums and establish free libraries. Why? For the simple reason that we believe, and rightly believe, that a knowledge and love of these better things is a bulwark of our civilization. We do not open museums of fine paintings for one class and museums of photographic re-productions of poor paintings for the proletariat. That would be inconceivable. We do not establish libraries of the world's choice literature for one class and, for the proletariat, provide endless editions of dime novels. That, too, would be inconceivable. In our socialistic institution, the school, we give alike to all; in our socialistic institution, the public library, we give alike to all; even in our semiphilanthropic institution, the museum, we give alike to all; and always for the same reason, that our civilization may be bulwarked to its foundation by what we call culture.

But what of the drama, the most universal, the most vividly appealing, the most direct and potent of the arts? Many people read but occasionally. Still more are but slightly reached, if at all, through the medium of pure vision — by painting and sculpture. Yet the drama goes home to everybody, old and young, rich and poor, educated and uneducated. It has ever been so, and will ever be so. It is inherent in our very natures. So instinctive is our response to it that it has almost never been regarded as "cultural" or "educational." It is regarded as amusement. We are all willing to pay for it, within our means. How can it fail, then, to reach us more surely than any other art? How can it fail, in a deeper, truer sense, to be potentially of the very highest cultural value? . . .

We have not yet realized the place of the theater in the life of a nation. Still Puritans at heart, we do not yet believe that anything we enjoy so much can be of value to our souls! The democratizing of the drama on the Continent has been accomplished under benevolent despotism — and think of the gains which have resulted to all the allied arts of the theater! Such a method would be impossible here, no doubt, without the sanction of the popular vote. With that sanction, we should achieve a socialized theater, and the superbly direct and vivid arts of the playhouse would be open to all, and in them all would feel proprietorship.

Every municipality large enough to support a theater comfortably should have a municipal playhouse, not of the tiny and "intimate" type but large enough to provide many seats competing in price with the movies; and in the trusteeship and management of this theater the proletariat should have equal share. In the larger centers there should be branch theaters, just as there are branch libraries, for the performance, under the simplest of conditions and at the minimum price, of fine plays close to the homes of the workers. When we think that the plays of Galsworthy were first performed in America at Hull House, we need not fear the lack of proletarian appreciation. That appreciation is essential, indeed, to the dramatist who would grapple with fundamental things, and without it no large body of serious national drama is likely ever to be written.

But here is neither the time nor the space to expand a scheme for a civic theater. My purpose was to show the need therefor, a need which has arisen in our nation just in proportion as a proletariat has arisen, and which is now emphasized and made more insistent by the growth of the movies with the consequent deflection of almost the entire wage-earning population away from the spoken drama to the infinitely inferior and spiritually stultifying mechanical film play. And with the steady increase of class-consciousness effected by this cleavage, the task of bridging the gulf again will be rendered constantly more difficult, if only because the proletariat will become constantly less susceptible to finer aesthetic appeals.

The problem, if it is ever tackled at all, will perhaps be given up as hopeless by the leaders of our present regime; it will be labeled a utopian dream. But utopian dreams are just what the Socialists thrive upon. The civil theater is hereby commended to them, as a needed propaganda. Thrilling songs may yet be sung and stirring dramas written to the steady tramp of revolution!

108.

Joseph H. Odell: Billy Sunday

Billy Sunday was the most popular revivalist of his day. His meetings attracted thousands, and everywhere he preached, eager audiences accepted his message of salvation. His down-to-earth language and his simple message — "Personal work is what counts" — appealed to many of his listeners. In an article, a portion of which appears here, Joseph Odell analyzed "The Mechanics of Revivalism," assessing the place of this kind of religion in American culture.

Source: *Atlantic Monthly*, May 1915.

There was something unmistakably spontaneous about the movements led by the great evangelists of former periods. They were devoid of devices for gathering results; there is no evidence of staging for effects; plotting, pre-arrangement, preliminary stimuli are absent. . . .

We do not come to the deliberately planned, prepared, and committed revival until we reach the middle of the last century. It started in America, and was probably the conscious outgrowth of the Methodist camp meeting. There was something weirdly compelling about those open-air meetings, held among the trees on warm summer evenings, with the flare of torches, the lilt of plaintive melodies, and the perfervid appeals of half-educated preachers to uneducated audiences. Their success indicated what could be done when such contributory elements were organized and established as permanent features.

Thus "gospel hymns" were brought into vogue. The part they play in modern revivalism is tremendous. Some of them have a hypnotic influence when used by a skilled director. "Just as I am, without one plea," and "I am coming home," sung with a diminishing cadence, have a lure that few emotional people can withstand. Such pieces are invariably used softly, appealingly, tenderly, at the time when the revivalist is seeking his results. Anyone who is at all familiar with modern evangelistic methods can recall many occasions when the appeal of the preacher has failed to bring a single penitent forward, and has noticed a change steal over the congregation as the wistful, pleading, melting melody has floated out softly from a choir trained to use the proper modulation.

If it be true that "the song that stirs a nation's heart is in itself a deed," we need not be hasty or harsh in our judgment. But unfortunately there is a mercenary side to this use of music. Hardly any of the great standard hymns of the Christian Church are copyrighted. But nearly all of the effective ones of the present-day revivalism are copyrighted and jealously guarded. Not because they are valuable as music or as poetry but for the simple reason that they are a lucrative sideline of profit for the evangelist or his musical director.

Sankey's success, as Moody's musical co-adjutor, pioneered the way for this financial by-product. Rodeheaver, Billy Sunday's aide, is interested in a publishing company that bears his name and that prints and sells the hymnbooks used exclusively in the Sunday campaigns. If one may judge from the well-known cost of producing such books side by side with the vast number that must be sold each year, it should be a very profitable flier. Indeed, one prominent evangelist has seriously warned his fellow evangelists that the commercial aspects and activities of their campaigns are bringing, not only their office but the whole cause of religion into disrepute. And it is not only hymnbooks. The writer has a very vivid impression of one mission conducted by the Rev. Reuben A. Torrey, D.D., in which the sale of his various publications seemed to bulk more largely than the conversion of souls.

Another feature of the commercialism is the compensation received by the revivalist himself. As Billy Sunday is undoubtedly the most successful evangelist, we may use him as an example. Just over a year ago he conducted a revival in Pittsburgh. He received as his honorarium or compensation about $45,000. True, it was a free-will offering, but the financial committee of the campaign took particular pains to see those who were able and likely to contribute the larger units.

Of course, it is nobody's business what he does with the money, anymore than it is anybody's concern what President Wilson does with his salary. It is also true that the amount is not net to Sunday. He pays one-third of the salaries of his personal helpers; for instance, he pays Rodeheaver $40 a week and the local committee makes up the balance. No one will raise the question whether Sunday earns such vast sums of money, but there are aspects to the situation that are fraught with pain to many ingenuous and earnest people.

For instance, Billy Sunday could not have a campaign unless he were invited by the local clergymen; it is they who do all

Billy Sunday in New York, 1917

impugning the purity of Billy Sunday's motives or even hinting that his spiritual or ethical value to any given community receives disproportionate compensation. Mr. Carnegie, who has no pretensions to evangelistic zeal and does not profess to be an expert in the saving of souls, once said that it was a scandal for any man to die rich. The financial peril of the revivalistic profession is very real, and the acute ethical sense of America is not to be toyed with.

To CONTINUE THE DISCUSSION of the nature and mechanics of modern revivalism, we can pursue no more scientific method than to make a "clinic" of a Billy Sunday campaign and a study of Billy Sunday's personality and method. A man who can command a reception in Washington, on a casual visit, second to none given to a President or a national hero, is worth consideration. Naturally he is now in such demand that his campaigns must be booked a year or even two years ahead. And his terms are explicit. Practically all the Evangelical Protestant churches must unite in inviting him and must agree to close their doors while he is in town. Months before the date of his debut, the community is carefully districted and prayer meetings are held in private homes.

A central committee takes over all the arrangements and underwrites the expenses. These are heavy, the largest item being the erection of a huge, turtleback, modern tabernacle planned to seat from 10,000 to 20,000 people. The purpose of underwriting the campaign is to protect the executive committee if anything should happen to Sunday and he failed to come. If he comes, the collections during the first two or three weeks are sufficient to meet all obligations. On February 1, 1915, when Sunday was less than halfway through his mission in Philadelphia, the collections amounted to $43,151.19.

the preliminary work; it is their faithful, sacrificial service that has made it possible for him to deliver an effective appeal; they must garner the results and conserve the converts after he has left. Yet, in the course of his meetings, he subjects them to the most outrageous indignities: he calls them "mutts," "deadheads," "stiffs," and many other opprobrious names; he degrades them and flaunts them in the eyes of the audience and the community.

And still it is well known that the average salary of a minister of the gospel in America is well under $1,000 a year. Supposing Billy Sunday paid out $10,000 as his share of the salaries of his helpers in Pittsburgh, his net gain would be as much for eight weeks of work as the average minister receives for a whole lifetime of plodding, drudging, conscientious, and self-forgetting service. This can all be said without

A few weeks before the meetings begin, an advance agent arrives, who takes the ushers in charge to train them in the handling of vast throngs and to impress upon them the need and nature of personal work. Personal work is chiefly speaking to individuals and leading them forward when the appeal for converts is made. A choir from 500 to 1,000 voices is gathered and drilled. On his staff of aides, Sunday has special workers for women, experts in Bible study, a physical trainer, a pianist and a chorister, a director of noon meetings in mills and factories, and a secretary. Each has his duty as clearly defined as that of a member of the military staff at a brigade headquarters. Not a detail of the campaign is left to chance, not an exigency but has been foreseen and discounted; not an opportunity for any form of religious work can arise that has not been provided for. All of the efficiency methods and forms of organization known to a typical modern business are utilized.

Billy Sunday himself is known formally as the Rev. William A. Sunday, D.D., a member of the Presbytery of Chicago, in good and regular standing. He presents no psychological problem. We may concede at once that he is absolutely sincere. Even in his postures and his gestures there is nothing artificial or studied. He preaches with the physical freedom of a natural athlete, and quite often, in the self-oblivion of delivering his message, he strikes the familiar attitudes of the diamond. His nature is very elemental and direct.

There is not the shadow of doubt that he believes all he teaches. He accepts the verbal inspiration and inerrancy of the entire Bible; he believes in a hell that is as materially real and consuming as the flames of a burning house; he cannot conceive of a Unitarian being saved unless the error is repented of and the Trinity of the historical creeds is accepted; he holds it to be very sinful to play cards, to see plays, to dance. There is no duplicity in him; he does not preach these things for their effect and yet cherish personal reservations. Heartily, unfeignedly, and with his whole nature he believes them.

Men who repudiate his creed and abhor his methods nevertheless admit his sincerity, his transparency, his convictions. And this is one of the chief reasons of his tremendous power over men. Everyone feels his reality; he may be crude and cruel, ignorant and narrow, dogmatic and archaic — or any one of a score of other things that are said about him — but he is real. His faith triumphs over the reluctance of many a man who rejects his belief. For example, he denounces the higher criticism in the most volcanic language, but many cultivated and learned clergymen who accept the findings of the higher critics smile and continue to work with him; he ridicules and misrepresents evolution and consigns it to hell, but scores of men who are thoroughly trained scientists and accept the hypothesis of evolution as they do that of gravitation nevertheless go on with the campaign and cooperate in the mission. And the reason is that they care absolutely nothing for Sunday's second-hand opinions on such questions of scholarship, but they are certain that he is a man who whole-heartedly, passionately stands for God and for righteousness, and does it with a measure of effectiveness that is beyond question.

For the same reason Sunday's use of slang is pardoned. And he is the supreme artist in American slang; Chimmie Fadden was a novice and a purist beside him. At first it seems irreverent, and there are many who never cease to shudder; but they tolerate it because it is the language Billy Sunday speaks naturally, and it is the language that the men of the shops and foundries hear every day and readily grasp. It is slang only to the educated, and if they are truly educated, they have learned the meaning of toleration in unessentials. There is no doubt that it is effective; by its use, Sunday gains the ear of thousands who would turn away from pure English. And it serves the purpose of showing to the mass of men that the evangelist is of them and understands them. There are refined people in the audience who know that the prologue to the Gospel of Luke is the only pure Greek of the New Testament, and that Jesus taught, even in his sublimest and loftiest parables, in the *patois* of the mean streets and the common people.

But it does not matter what defects of form or taste there may be in Sunday's sermons; the outstanding, unmistakable, undisguisable thing is that he is a genuine man devoting his strength without reserve to preaching the one gospel by which he believes men may be saved from hell. He is not a scholar, not a thinker, not a sophist, not an actor — but a healthy, frank, fearless, and irrepressible man, who offers no apology for doing the one thing he feels that his God has told him to do: preach a Puritan gospel to a godless generation. One cannot explain his success by stressing anything else. If every detail of his organization were perfected and anyone else were to take his place as the central figure, the movement would end as a farce.

He is easily the most compelling personality in America. There was a time when Colonel Roosevelt could have gone to Philadelphia and commanded an audience of 20,000 people for one night; but what other living man can command 20,000 hearers twice each day and three times on Sunday? And not for a week but for eight weeks. As a phenomenon in crowd gathering it is the most remarkable in history. The statistics, as gathered carefully by a responsible Philadelphia paper, the *Evening Ledger*, show on March 10: number of sermons preached to date, 122; total attendance, 2,330,000. And it may be added that scores, perhaps hundreds, of thousands have been turned away for lack of space.

JUDGED BY A PRAGMATICAL standard, the results are rather confused: bad and good. On the one side there are evils that will seem trivial or tremendous according to the standards of those who sit in judgment. The first thing noticeable is a tone of apparent irreverence in the churches. Perhaps the tendency of all religious organizations is toward a frigid conventionality; but that conventionality, from long familiarity, forms the only environment in which some people can worship. Anything flippant, humorous, or corybantic destroys at once the habit of the mind and the mood of the heart. There are some churches in a community which can continue the atmosphere of the tabernacle services and thrive, for there are always plenty of modern men and women who genuinely enjoy ragtime hymns, a parity and a camaraderie with God in prayer, and bizarre testimonies of personal salvation. But the writer has known of attempts to conduct this type of service in a church where people of refinement and thoughtfulness have been wont to worship; and though they have held their peace out of pure charity, they have suffered severely. In such a church the effects of the Billy Sunday campaign may continue for awhile, but they are bound to pass away.

Another difficulty lies in the artificial conscience that is created. In the stress of the campaign, many converts, particularly youths, pledge themselves against all worldly amusements as deadly forms of sin, "leading plumb to hell," in the revivalist's pungent words. But in numberless cases the vows are broken before many months pass, and dancing, card playing, and theatergoing are resumed. This tampering with conscience leads to a lower regard of all the sanctions and sanctities, and ministers have serious trouble in bringing their young people back to a healthy ethical tone.

That is not the only heritage of the churches following such a campaign. Unitarians, Universalists, Christian Scientists, and all who differ from the medieval theology of the evangelist have been so ridiculed, denounced, and consigned repeatedly to hell that it is extremely difficult for anyone to be tolerant or charitable. And with this teaching there has been so much premillenarianism and prophecy-mongering taught that the Bible has become a fetish which only those who have cryptic keys can understand or interpret aright. Even those who are eager to concede everything that is good in modern revivalism, as represented by Billy Sunday, have much to regret and condemn.

But that positive good does come from it hardly anyone close to the facts will deny. Wherever such a campaign is conducted, religion becomes the dominant topic of thought and speech. Men and women are recalled from indifference and contempt to reflection upon the most sacred subjects. One does not care to discuss the spiritual quality of conversion, but there are cases far too obvious in changed personal characteristics to be misunderstood, and far too obvious in ethical effects to be discounted.

Men cease to be profane; long-established habits of intemperance are suddenly broken; dishonesty gives place to honesty; vice becomes repugnant and virtue glorious. Thousands betake themselves to the study of the Bible, and many homes grow radiant that had been centers of gloom. Testimony of this nature can be collected, not only immediately after a Billy Sunday campaign but even when years have elapsed. The effect is so marked that employers of labor have asserted that they could afford to pay Sunday very liberally out of the funds of their corporations for the increased efficiency that comes to their plants in the reduction of accidents and enlarged productivity caused by the men's cutting out intoxicating liquor.

It is safe to say that, if testimony means anything at all, every community visited by Billy Sunday could send men into a Circuit or Supreme Court whose word would be accepted as relevant and material evidence. Psychologists may explain it one way and religionists another, but there are certain facts of changed character, altered habit, transformed temperament that lie thick in the wake of every Billy Sunday revival.

For the above reasons there are multitudes of men and women with aesthetic tastes and a high degree of personal spiritual culture who approve, defend, and even advocate this modern revivalism, although it makes no direct contribution to their own religious development. They take the ground that it is a form of human conservation, a renaissance of civic virtue, a dynamic of political morality. There are many level-headed and calculating businessmen who are willing to back it because the saloons and the dives and the gang leaders are so desperately antagonistic to it.

How far it will spread or how long it will persist, no one can tell. Already there are scores of little Billy Sundays setting up their tabernacles, duplicating his organization, borrowing his methods, and plagiarizing his speech; but it is impossible to estimate the sum of their influence. The historic revivals have rarely lasted more than a generation and have been associated invariably with one distinct personality. Billy Sunday appears to be the religious phenomenon of the opening of the twentieth century.

There will be no unanimity as to his value; such a verdict history has never known and will never reach. Many philosophers, most dramatists, and some saints have called this age spiritually dead and less responsive to religious appeal than any other through the centuries. To such, and to those who have accepted their characterization as true, Billy Sunday and his work are certainly worth studying.

109.

WASHINGTON GLADDEN: Religion and the Public Schools

Washington Gladden, long a leading spokesman for the Social Gospel, was disturbed by a trend among Roman Catholics and Lutherans toward educating their children in separate parochial schools. Gladden advocated a truly public school in which children of different races and religions would learn side by side. Religion should be taught, according to Gladden, in the church and the home. His essay "Religion and the Schools" was published in January 1915 and is reprinted here in part.

Source: *Atlantic Monthly*, January 1915.

I

THE PLACE OF RELIGION in popular education is not a new problem, but it bids fair to be one of considerable urgency in the near future. In all the more advanced nations, the government has assumed the responsibility for the education of the people; and, at the same time, in most of these nations, the government has been gradually withdrawing its hand from the direction of the religious life of the people. As a necessary consequence of both these tendencies, the religious element in popular education has been constantly diminishing. In our own country we may say that religious teaching has practically disappeared from the public schools. By many good citizens this fact is greatly deplored. All our Roman Catholic neighbors point to it as a radical defect in our system of popular education and assert that it is having grave consequences in the godlessness and immorality of the generations thus neglected; and many earnest Protestants substantially agree with them.

The non-Catholic elements in our population are, however, divided in sentiment upon this question, many of them maintaining that this exclusion of religious teaching from the public schools is the only possible policy; that, because of the conflicting views concerning religion, the state can by no means undertake to determine what shall be taught, and that such an attempt would violate the spirit of our Constitution, which forbids the government to impose upon its citizens any religious observances. Not only by secularists and agnostics but by many staunch churchmen is this denial of the right of the political power to prescribe religious instruction or practice of any kind strongly maintained.

II

THE ROMAN CATHOLICS, for their part, carry their objection to the nonreligious character of our public schools so far that they have withdrawn a large proportion of their children from the lower grades and are educating them at their own expense in parochial schools. According to late figures, there are now in such schools more than 1 million pupils under the care of 20,000 teachers, at an annual cost of more than $15 million — the property devoted to this purpose amounting to $100 million. It is a great price that our Roman Catholic brethren are willing to pay that their children may be religiously educated.

Most of these parochial schools are elementary schools; it is deemed especially important that the younger children be thoroughly instructed in the principles of religion; it is assumed that those thus grounded in the faith will be less likely to be drawn away from it in the later stages of their pupilage. Great efforts are being made, however, by the Catholics to develop their secondary schools. It is also true that the parochial schools are generally confined to the cities and large towns; in the rural districts the Catholic children attend the common schools. The church authorities strictly require the erection of separate schools wherever possible; but they recognize the difficulty of maintaining them among sparse populations, and in such cases permit their children to make use of the local schools. "It has been estimated," says one authority,

> that from one-fourth to one-third of the number of Catholic children of school age live in country districts. In towns and cities, therefore, where alone it is possible, generally speaking, to build and maintain Catholic schools, it may be said that all but about one-fourth to one-sixth of the Catholic population attending school is being educated in the parish schools. The number of children in the parish schools is also steadily increasing.

The parochial schools are sometimes "pay" schools, supported by fees collected from the parents; but more often they are a charge upon the parish and are made free to the pupils. Most of the teachers belong to religious orders; the average salary of females is from $200 to $300, and of males, $300 to $400. That is, the salaries are about half as large as those of public school teachers. "It has been estimated," says the *Catholic Encyclopedia*, "that the average annual per capita cost of parish school education in the United States is $8." This would mean that the 1,237,251 pupils in the parish schools during 1909-10 cost approximately for that year $9,898,008. The education of the same pupils in the public schools for the same year would, according to the estimate referred to, cost approximately $30,511,000; and if the annual in-

terest on the necessary property investment were added, the total would be upwards of $34 million.

The reasons given by the Roman Catholics for this withdrawal of their children are briefly these. Religion is the foundation of character and the first essential of education. It can no more be separated from education than light can be separated from color. It is the supreme interest in the training of the child. It requires to be made a constant element in all the processes of teaching. Morality cannot be adequately taught apart from religion. It is by no means sufficient to teach religion one day in seven; it must be made an integral part of the life of every day. All the relations of teacher and pupil, and of the pupils with one another, should be hallowed by it. Many of the subjects taught in the school cannot be correctly taught apart from their religious implications. Because the state cannot teach religion, the state cannot adequately conduct the work of educating its youth. For agnostics and for non-Catholics, to whom these interests of religion are not vital, the state may maintain secular schools; but Roman Catholics must not entrust the souls of their children to such defective care.

This puts a considerable burden on the Catholic citizens, who are taxed, of course, to maintain the public schools. They maintain that this is an injustice, and they are asking for relief. It does not seem to be practicable to remit that portion of the tax which is expended on the schools, and the alternative is a plea for the subsidizing of Catholic parish schools from the public treasury. Concerning this we are told that there is not entire unanimity among Catholics; that there are those who object to such subvention on the ground that the schools would thus be in danger of losing their independence, since state aid would necessarily mean some measure of inspection and regulation by the public authorities. Rather than risk this interference, they would continue to bear their present burden. Most of the Catholic leaders, however, appear to be willing to face that peril, and the demand for state aid to parochial schools is likely soon to be articulate and urgent.

III

THE LUTHERANS ARE ALSO to be reckoned with in this matter of public education. They agree substantially with the Roman Catholics with respect to the primacy of religion among the essentials of education. They hold that a training from which definite religious instruction is omitted is radically defective. This, at least, is true of the Central and Western synods, comprising more than half of the 2,123,245 communicant members. The Eastern synods are less strenuous in this demand. But among the Central and Western congregations of this church, there were last year no less than 6,085 parochial schools, with 295,581 pupils. Each of these schools is a purely congregational enterprise; it is supported, as the pastor is supported, by the voluntary contributions of the communicants. Fees are charged, however, in some cases.

In some places, as in my own city, the parochial school cooperates with the public school system. There are several Lutheran churches, but there is only one parochial school, and its course of instruction covers only the seventh and eighth grades. Up to and including the sixth grade, the children attend the public school; then they pass to the parochial school, where the course of study is the same as in the public schools, but there is added thereto "religious instruction embracing Bible history, catechism, hymns, and Bible reading"; at the end of the eighth grade the pupils are admitted to the examinations of the public schools and then pass into the high school. In such cases the Lutherans content themselves with keeping their children separate from the rest for only a portion of the elementary period; with two years of systematic religious instruction they are fain to be

satisfied. But in a large majority of the Western congregations the curriculum of the parochial schools cover the entire eight elementary grades.

In their attitude toward the state, however, the Lutherans differ widely from the Roman Catholics. With them there is no question as to the entire separation of state and church. They maintain that the state has no right to teach religion and that there must be no attempt at religious instruction in the public schools. Religion must be left wholly to the family and the church. For this purpose the parochial schools are provided. But the Lutherans refuse all state subventions. The burden of maintaining religious instruction for their children they will bear. They do not decry the public schools; they insist that the state must furnish them, and they gladly bear their share of that expense; but the education of their own children they prefer to keep, so far as possible, in their own hands. . . .

VII

IN NORTH DAKOTA and in Colorado attempts have been made to arrange for biblical studies to be conducted outside the schools, credit for such studies to be given by the school authorities on the completion of the course. A syllabus of Bible study has been prepared and published by the State School Board of North Dakota, covering the geographical and historical facts of both Testaments, the great narratives and the great characters, with a number of passages to be memorized; this can be studied in Sunday school or at home, and to every high-school student who passes an examination based on this syllabus and conducted by the school authorities, a half-credit is given on his high-school course. The course is elective, but with the active cooperation of ministers and Sunday-school superintendents a goodly number of students might be persuaded to take it. The cultural value of the Bible is not by this method, greatly emphasized; the intention is rather to make the pupil intelligent upon the main facts included in the biblical literature.

It is evident, however, that we have not yet in sight any plan by which the segregation of the Roman Catholic and the Lutheran children can be prevented so long as the people of those communions remain in their present state of mind. Such cultural study of the Bible as I have advocated would not answer their demands; and such a device as that resorted to in North Dakota would be regarded as wholly inadequate. The Lutheran authorities have, I understand, repudiated the North Dakota plan.

Several attempts have been made to provide a *modus vivendi* by which the church schools should be incorporated in the educational system. In Poughkeepsie and a few other cities and towns in New York the School Board leased, for a nominal rent, the Catholic school buildings, agreed to keep them in repair, prescribed the courses of study, retained the nuns in charge as teachers, and paid their salaries out of the public treasury. The instruction required by the public school board was given; whatever other instruction the teachers wished to give they were at liberty to impart. The arrangement continued for several years and appeared to be satisfactory; but the legality of it was doubtful, and the state superintendent of public instruction finally abrogated it, and his decision was confirmed by the Supreme Court.

A similar arrangement was made by Archbishop Ireland in the cities of Faribault and Stillwater, Minnesota; only in these cases it was stipulated that the religious instruction should be given outside the regular school hours. This was not satisfactory to the Catholics, and there was much controversy about it. Pope Leo XIII gave his approval to the plan, under certain limitations, and it is still in operation in various Western localities.

It does not, however, appear to be probable that these attempted adjustments will prove satisfactory on any large scale. The Lutherans, for their part — those of them who are supporting parochial schools — appear to be entirely satisfied with the existing situation. They are bearing the burden of elementary education for their children, and they are willing to bear it. They will not agree that the state shall meddle with religion in any way, and they want no aid from the state in maintaining their schools. So far as elementary education is concerned, they are outside the educational life of the community and they prefer to stay outside. Respecting the high schools, they are less rigid; many of their pupils pass from the parochial schools to the high schools; but up to the fourteenth year they endeavor to keep their children apart from the children of their neighbors during school hours.

The Roman Catholics also relax their inhibition somewhat at the end of the elementary period; many of the parochial pupils pass to the public high schools. But they complain of the injustice of being compelled to maintain the elementary schools at their own expense, and claim a share of the public money. The plan which they urge is substantially that adopted in England, where, in addition to the board schools, provided and wholly controlled by the public authorities, voluntary schools, under denominational control, are also aided by taxation. A considerable amount of supervision of these denominational schools is also exercised by government authorities; the state undertakes to see that the preparation of its young people for citizenship is effectively carried on; but the schools are left free to conduct religious education in their own way.

It should be said that in the English schools provided and managed wholly by the state, religion is taught, quite systematically; the curriculum of these schools includes a fair amount of instruction in the Bible and in the elementary principles of revealed religion. There has been a strong demand in England for a purely secular system of public education, but public opinion in that country has, thus far, successfully resisted that demand.

For some such arrangement as that which prevails in England, the Roman Catholics of the United States are disposed to contend. But the deep-rooted antagonism to any form of alliance between the church and the state has, hitherto, effectually negatived every such proposition. With such a miscellaneous swarm of faiths and cults and creeds as confronts us upon these shores, it does not seem practicable to recognize any as specially entitled to recognition by the state. There are a good many of them who would like to separate themselves from the community and have their tenets taught at the public expense. When once the principle was established, there would be no lack of sects which would make haste to avail themselves of its provision. Where should we draw the line? The logrolling would be quickly organized and the educational porkbarrel would soon assume dimensions. The practical difficulty of extending assistance to religious denominations for the maintenance of their religious belief seems well-nigh insuperable.

VIII

MUST WE THEN FACE the probability of a permanent division of our population upon this most vital interest of our communal life? Are our children, in their schooldays, to be separated into unsympathetic and unfriendly groups, suspicious of each other, never singing the national songs together, never feeling the thrill of a common emotion as the great days of old are recalled and the great deeds are recited? Nations whose traditions are feudal and whose social system rests on caste, may be content to have their youthful populations separated by such lines of division; but it is hard to understand how they can be tolerated in a democracy like ours. And it seems deplorable that so many children should grow up

among us who owe no debt of gratitude for their education to the land of their birth — to whom such a passionate devotion as that of Mary Antin must always be a thing unknown. Should not good citizens consider well whether or not they ought wholly to sever this tie between the lives of their children and their native land?

For my own part I have always been grateful that my children were permitted to grow up with Catholic and Jewish and Irish and Italian boys and girls, that a Catholic boy was my boy's seatmate in school and his most intimate friend; that little Catholic girls were playmates of my little girls. My children learned in this way sympathy and toleration; is it not a lesson that all children need to learn? And can we afford to establish and perpetuate an educational system which makes all this impossible? Is there not something here very sacred and precious which we ought to preserve?

I confess that I have no ready-made solution of this problem. I see the difficulties; I believe that I understand, to some extent, the scruples which make these Christian brethren insist on the policy which they have adopted. But I wonder whether it is not possible to find some line of accommodation by which we might, without sacrificing anything essential to faith, strengthen and preserve the spirit of community which these educational divisions threaten to destroy.

Is it not an infinite pity — nay, is it not a burning shame — that our religion, which ought to be the bond of peace, the principle of integration in our social life, should be the wedge that divides us, the force that prevents us from dwelling together in unity? Something is the matter with the religion of which this is true.

It must be remembered, however, that no arrangement respecting our public schools is possible by which the problem of religious education can be adequately solved. When we have done the best we can possibly do through the state, the largest part of that work will remain undone. My own belief is that the work of reviving and restoring the agencies of religious education has been seriously retarded by the discussion about replacing the Bible in the public schools. In pushing that agitation the real work to be done has been largely overlooked. For nothing is clearer than that our entire reliance for this work must be placed upon the church and the home.

It is with the home, of course, that the primary responsibility rests, and here we are confronted with the appalling fact that homelife has become almost an impossible thing to a large proportion of our population. The first thing to be sought is such a reordering of our social life as shall permit larger numbers of our people to live in homes wherein family religion can be cultivated.

No doubt the sense of responsibility for the religious education of their children greatly needs to be deepened in the minds of most parents. That burden has in large measure been shunted upon the day school and the Sunday school, and this is the fundamental cause of whatever religious decadence now exists.

The church is responsible for enforcing upon parents this obligation. If the church would but give to this business of developing family life half the time and money and energy which it devotes to sensational evangelisms, we should soon see very different conditions in this country. Much has been done, during the past decade by the Religious Education Association to enforce upon the churches their responsibility for the religious education of the children of the state, but it is still indifferently apprehended by the great majority of them. To say that this is the one thing which the church of this generation needs would not be true; the church is in crying need of a number of things; but this is one of them.

110.

Randolph Bourne: Who Owns the Universities?

Scott Nearing, a professor of economics at the Wharton School, was an ardent Socialist and pacifist whose articulate expression of his political views led to his dismissal in 1915. In the following selection, Randolph Bourne, a frequent writer on educational subjects, discussed the unhappy state of affairs in which university trustees, intimidated by state publications, determined educational policy. In an editorial of July 17, 1915, Bourne considered the difference between professors and corporate employees.

Source: *New Republic,* July 17, 1915.

The marked and immediate reaction of the thinking public to the Scott Nearing case shows a growing conviction that all is not well with the conventional forms of university control. It implies a sense that universities, whether supported by the state or privately, are becoming too vitally institutions of public service to be much longer directed on the plan of a private corporation.

University trustees are generally men of affairs, and as men of affairs they naturally tend to hold the same attitude toward the university that they do to the other institutions — the churches and railroads and corporations — they may direct. The university officers whom they appoint seem to have exactly the same duties of upholding the credit of the institution, of securing funds to meet its pressing needs, of organizing the administrative machinery, which their corporation officers would have.

Professors are engaged by contract as any highly skilled superintendent would be engaged in a factory. If a well-paid subordinate of a mining corporation could not get along with his colleagues and his men, or if he consorted with the IWW or made revolutionary speeches in the streets, his services would be dispensed with as readily as the Pennsylvania trustees rid themselves of the unpleasantness of Professor Nearing. Trustees may respect a professor more than they do intrinsically a fourth vice-president. They may tend to err, as Chancellor Day has suggested, on the side of "merciful consideration." But they cannot see that the amenities of the case materially alter the professor's status.

This would be the case of university trustees stated in its rawest terms. That they tend so often to act as if they were a mere board of directors of a private corporation gives rise to endless suspicion that they consult their own interests and the interests of the donors of the vested wealth they represent as trustees of the university, just as they would protect, as faithful corporation directors, the interests of the shareholders of the company.

It is just this attitude which the thinking public is no longer inclined to tolerate. We are acquiring a new view of the place of the university in the community. When the American college was no more than an advanced boys' academy, there may have been some excuse for this form of control by self-perpetuating and irresponsible boards of trustees. But many things have changed

since Harvard and Yale, Princeton, Pennsylvania, and Columbia were founded.

In the case of Harvard and Yale, there was, it is true, a semblance of public control. The self-perpetuating corporation of president and fellows of Harvard were responsible to overseers named by the legislature; the Yale Corporation included the governor, the lieutenant governor, and six state senators. But the other three colleges were organized under straight self-perpetuating boards, the charter of Columbia College (1810) giving the trustees full power and authority "forever" to prescribe courses of study, administer discipline, appoint the president and all officers and instructors, all of whom were to hold office at the pleasure of the trustees. Furthermore, it was explicitly provided that no officer or professor should ever be a trustee.

Now, this determined autocracy may not have worked so badly when most of the trustees and practically all of the instructors were ministers of the gospel, although even in those days faculties sometimes complained that their careful plans were overridden by men ignorant of collegiate business and little interested in educational policy. The demand that trustees' functions should be limited to the management of funds, leaving the faculties to regulate administration and control appointments, is a hoary one.

But with the passing of control from the ghostly to the moneyed element, the gulf between trustee and professor has become extreme. Professors have fallen into a more and more subordinate place, and the president, who used to be their representative, has now become almost entirely the executive agent of the trustees, far removed in power and purse and public distinction from the professor. The university president in this country has become a convenient symbol for autocratic power, but even when he has become a "mayor of the palace" and professors may not approach their governors except through him, the real autocracy still lies in the external board behind him.

This absentee and amateur form of university control is being constantly ratified by our American notions of democracy, and that folkway, which runs so omnipresently through our institutional life, of giving the plain ultimate citizen control, in order that we may be protected from the tyranny of the bureaucrat. The newer state universities are controlled in exactly the same spirit. Regents, elected by legislatures, have shown themselves quite as capable as the most private trustees of representing vested political interests.

Nor has democracy been achieved by the cautious admission, in recent years, of alumni trustees, as in the case of Columbia, or, as in the case of Harvard and Yale, by the substitution of alumni for the former state officials. Self-perpetuating boards will always propagate their own kind, and even if alumni trustees were inclined to be anything but docile, their minority representation would always be ineffective for democracy.

The issues of the modern university are not those of private property but of public welfare. Irresponsible control by a board of amateur notables is no longer adequate for the effective scientific and sociological laboratories for the community that the universities are becoming. The protests in the most recent case imply a growing realization that a professor who has a dynamic and not a purely academic interest in social movements is an asset for the whole community.

The latest controversy between trustee and professors seems to have been very definitely an issue between interested policy and accurate, technical fact. It seems to have been clearly a case of old tradition against new science, the prejudiced guesses of corporation officials against the data of a scientific student of economics. Any form of university control which gives the prejudiced guess the power over the scientific research is thus a direct blow at our own social knowledge and effectiveness.

The public simply cannot afford to run this risk of having the steady forging ahead of social and economic research curtailed and hampered. We cannot afford to depend on the tempering of trustees by the fear of the clamor of public opinion. It is wholly undesirable that trustees should be detained only by "merciful consideration" from discharging professors whom they find uncongenial or who they feel are spreading unsound doctrine. Make university trustees directors of a private corporation and you give them the traditional right of terminating contracts with their employees without giving reasons or any form of trial. But if the university is not to be a mere degree manufactory, or a prevocational school representing the narrow interests of a specialized economic class, but is to be that public intellectual and scientific service that we all want it to be, the governance must be different from that of a mining company, and the status of the professor different from that of a railroad employee. Professors should have some security of office.

An interested public which feels this way will demand that the faculties be represented strongly in the determination of all university policy and in the selection and dismissal of the instructors. It may even demand that the community itself be represented. Trustees who really envisage the modern university as a public service, as a body of scientific and sociological experts, will gladly share their power. If they do not, they will demonstrate how radically their own conception of a university differs from the general one, and it will be the duty of professors to assert their rights by all those forms of collective organization whereby controlled classes from the beginning of time have made their desires effective.

111.

Proposals for Academic Freedom

The American Association of University Professors was formed in 1915 to define and protect the rights of professors. One of its first and most significant acts was the appointment of a Committee on Academic Freedom and Academic Tenure. Headed by Edwin R. A. Seligman of Columbia University, the committee drafted a report that remains the outstanding summary of American educators' views on the subject of academic freedom. The report attacked the not uncommon conception of a university as an ordinary business venture, and of academic teaching as a purely private employment. Its main contention was not that individual teachers should be subject to no restraint, but that disciplinary action could with safety be imposed only by members of the academic profession. The practical proposals that concluded the report, which are reprinted here, were designed to institutionalize this position. The committee report was adopted by the Association on January 1, 1916.

Source: *American Economic Review,* March 1916, Supplement.

THE ENDS TO BE ACCOMPLISHED are chiefly three:

First, to safeguard freedom of inquiry and of teaching against both covert and overt attacks, by providing suitable judicial bodies, composed of members of the academic profession, which may be called into action before university teachers are dismissed or disciplined, and may determine in what cases the question of academic freedom is actually involved.

Second, by the same means, to protect college executives and governing boards against unjust charges of infringement of academic freedom, or of arbitrary and dictatorial conduct — charges which, when they gain wide currency and belief, are highly detrimental to the good repute and the influence of universities.

Third, to render the profession more attractive to men of high ability and strong personality by insuring the dignity, the independence, and the reasonable security of tenure of the professorial office.

The measures which it is believed to be necessary for our universities to adopt to realize these ends — measures which have already been adopted in part by some institutions — are four:

A. *Action by Faculty Committees on Reappointments.* Official action relating to reappointments and refusals of reappointment should be taken only with the advice and consent of some board or committee representative of the faculty. Your committee does not desire to make at this time any suggestion as to the manner of selection of such boards.

B. *Definition of Tenure of Office.* In every institution there should be an unequivocal understanding as to the term of each appointment; and the tenure of professorships and associate professorships, and of all positions above the grade of instructor after ten years of service, should be permanent (subject to the provisions hereinafter given for removal upon charges). In those state universities which are legally incapable of making contracts for more than a limited period, the governing boards should announce their policy with respect to the presumption of reappointment in the several classes of position, and such announcements, though not legally enforceable, should be regarded as morally binding. No university teacher of any rank should, except in cases of grave moral delinquency, receive notice of dismissal or of refusal of reappointment later than three months before the close of any academic year, and in the case of teachers above the grade of instructor, one year's notice should be given.

C. *Formulation of Grounds for Dismissal.* In every institution the grounds which will be regarded as justifying the dismissal of members of the faculty should be formulated with reasonable definiteness; and in the case of institutions which impose upon their faculties doctrinal standards of a sectarian or partisan character, these standards should be clearly defined and the body or individual having authority to interpret them, in case of controversy, should be designated. Your committee does not think it best at this time to attempt to enumerate the legitimate grounds for dismissal, believing it to be preferable that individual institutions should take the initiative in this.

D. *Judicial Hearings Before Dismissal.* Every university or college teacher should be entitled, before dismissal or demotion, to have the charges against him stated in writing in specific terms and to have a fair trial on those charges before a special or permanent judicial committee chosen by the faculty senate or council, or by the faculty at large. At such trial the teacher accused should have full opportunity to present evidence, and, if the charge is one of professional incompetency, a formal report upon his work should be first made in writing by the teachers of his own department and of cognate departments in the university, and, if the teacher concerned so desire, by a committee of his fellow specialists from other institutions, appointed by some competent authority.

112.

Rufus M. Jones: The Incompatibility of War and Christianity

From 1914 until 1917, while war raged in Europe, there was widespread debate over the desirability of America's entering the conflict. The majority of the population, especially in the Midwest and Far West, seemed opposed to any American involvement in Europe. But for those who held pacifist views, the question was the larger one of the categorical evil of war. Quaker Rufus M. Jones, in the following article published on April 3, 1915, outlined the "peace position" of the Society of Friends.

Source: *The Survey,* April 3, 1915: "The Quaker Peace Position."

THE WORLD AT LARGE has had for the most part a very vague conception of the central religious ideas of Quakerism, but everybody who knows the name "Quaker," knows and always has known that it is the popular name of a people who stand unconditionally for peace. Their peace testimony has in the mind of the great public always been their most characteristic mark and badge. This Quaker position has been treated sometimes with ridicule and sometimes with respect, but in either case their fundamental attitude has seldom been understood. It will perhaps not be out of place in the midst of this din and clash of arms to interpret briefly the Quaker idea.

We have grown familiar during the last score of years with the accumulation of economic reasons against war, and we have followed with interest the congresses and conferences that have piled up and driven home these impressive economic arguments. They, however, generally, if not always, end with a caveat or hedging clause to the effect that "peace at any price" is not part of the intention and is not implied in the argument.

The Quaker idea is fundamentally different from this economic idea. The Quaker is not primarily concerned with the question whether war pays or does not pay for the people engaged in it; whether it succeeds in its aim or does not succeed. The Quaker flatly insists that it is absolutely and eternally wrong morally; that Christianity and war are utterly incompatible. He does not blame or judge others — and they are vastly the majority — who think differently; but for himself the light of his truth is clear, and he cannot see otherwise.

This position goes back to and is grounded in the Quaker's idea of the nature of human personality, for this is the taproot of all Quaker idealisms. There is something divine, something of God, in every person. The eternal passion of God, the whole redemptive story of the gospels, gets its significance in the tremendous fact that man and God belong together, are meant for each other, and that beings like us are potential sons of God. To become a person, in the real sense of the word, is to awake to the consciousness of the divine relationship, to feel the inherent possibilities of sonship with God, to draw upon the inexhaustible supplies of grace, to enter into the actual inheritance of this divine-human privilege, and to live in it and practise it.

But this process of realizing the possibilities of life, this mighty business of becoming persons, can go on only in an atmosphere of human love and fellowship, and in an environment of cooperation. . . .

For one who has found his way through Christ to the full meaning of life, to the real worth of man, to the inestimable ministry of love and brotherhood, war is simply impossible. It is no longer a question of expediency; with the Quaker view of life one cannot engage in killing men, whatever may be involved in the refusal.

Through pain and struggle the world has slowly discovered the immense possibilities of democracy. We are just at the dawn of a real human emancipation. Vast processes of liberation are at work. Human rights, quite undreamed of when the Declaration of Independence was written, are gradually being won and enjoyed by common men and women. Social transformations are well under way which some day will bring new heavens and a new earth.

But war interferes with all these social undertakings; it postpones the realization of all ideals and human hopes. Pledged as he is to the advancement of human emancipation and to the achievement of a society which furnishes and guarantees richer and fuller and freer opportunities of life, the Quaker opposes all war and war methods because he believes they defeat this supreme business in which the best men and women are engaged.

Holding such views of man and of life, partaking of a kingdom in which war is flatly an impossible course, what is the Quaker's business and mission in a world organized as ours is today? One of the first things that is laid upon him is the business of making his idea of life, his grasp of Christianity clear and luminous to men. He should simplify it, strip it of outgrown phraseology, and make it march with quick, vital, human interpretation. He should, then, be ready to take unflinchingly whatever amount of suffering is involved in his truth, and he should verify it in its length and depth by going all the way through with his faith, even at the uttermost cost; for no prophet-visions of life can ever be wrought into the fabric of the everyday world except through the patient suffering of those who are privileged to see.

It becomes, further, a very essential part of his business, as George Fox, the Quaker founder, saw, to live in the virtue of that life and power which does away with the occasion of war. That is, if Quakerism is to be anything more than an empty abstraction and the name for an ideal in a vacuum, the Quaker is bound to practise a kind of life that abolishes the spirit that leads to war — the spirit of avarice and covetousness, tendencies of suspicion and hate, actions of injustice and selfishness. He must exhibit, hard as is the call, a life that puts his ideas of God and man, of divine and human interfellowship, of love and self-giving full into play. He must weave his idea into the visible stuff of daily life.

Then he must be gentle and tenderly respectful toward all Christians who feel the stern necessity of continuing the world-old way of settling differences and of working out national issues. It is never safe to assume the role of special favorite or sole guardian of truth, or remnant of the elect. Other Christians are also serious and honest, sincere and conscientious, and possessed of their profound convictions; and the Quaker, in holding on the way which seems sun-clear to him, must avoid all reflection upon the motives or the Christian loyalty of other faiths.

And whether in times of war or times of peace, the Quaker is under peculiar obligation to assist and to forward movements and forces which make for peace in the world and which bind men together in ties of unity and fellowship. In times of war, every avenue of loving service, of heroic devotion, or of self-forgetful ministry should be entered, that the Quaker may vie with the soldier in his blood-red loyalty and devotion to his cause.

The moment war is over, and in times of peace, those who hold this high and costly faith in God and man must not be content to conduct mild and lukewarm peace meetings and to issue commonplace resolutions — "helpless as spilled beans on a dresser," as Hosea Bigelow puts it. They must take a thoroughly virile and robust part in the work of creating higher national ideals and in forming a truer public sentiment and a healthier social atmosphere.

There must be no withdrawal from the complicated life of the world into any of the subtle forms of cloistered piety. Religious ideals must be interpreted and reinterpreted in terms of present-day thought; the ties of human sympathy must be linked up and woven in between all classes of men; every opportunity must be seized for directing and perfecting methods of public education and for raising the moral tone and quality of the press; and a full share of responsibility for the character of local and national government must be taken up and borne with the same fidelity that the Quaker has always shown to the inner voice in matters of intimate, personal duty.

A peace testimony is thus a heavy undertaking and calls for all the courage and all the sacrifice of a battlefield, though the "weapons" are of a vastly different sort from Krupp guns and Mauser rifles.

It is obviously far easier to work out and consistently to maintain such a peace position as this for the individual and for a small group of religious idealists than to put it into effective operation for a great nation living in complicated relations with the peoples of the world. The Quaker is forced to admit that so far in the history of the races no great nation has yet risked its honor and its very existence in an unconditional experiment of peace at all costs and hazards. It is a plain, clear fact that men everywhere are, even at this late stage of evolution, powerfully supplied with fighting instincts.

This present war proves conclusively that the fighting instinct is far from being smothered or eradicated. Never has the flower of a nation gone more willingly to danger and death than in this latest crowning year of man's civilization; and it is probably true that more persons during human history have gone to danger and death under the spur and thrust of this instinct than for any other single cause, perhaps, indeed, for all causes put together.

Then, again, we cannot miss the fact that nations have been and still are carried forward into wars almost unconsciously by the emotional force of deep-seated ideas, or theories or doctrines in reference to their supposed destiny — often enough doctrines essentially ungrounded or false. Certain economic theories or abstract ideas of peril to be feared from expanding and developing races frequently obsess nations, produce fears, suspicions, and hates and finally eventuate in war.

Nations are composed of many types of persons; they are striking instances of "multiple personality." There will for generations to come be higher and lower selves in the nations of the world, and we must not expect a millennium nation to come by express train or by aeroplane. Statesmen will still form entangling alliances when we are not watching, and they will get their nation into such a "fix" that citizens will be swept with the war spirit and will bring the ancient instincts into play.

What we must do, then, is to form in as large groups as possible higher convictions, more idealistic faiths, and greater compulsions, which in the long run — in these matters the run is often very long! — will penetrate and permeate ever wider groups, and so make new nations, or at least a new national spirit.

There can, of course, be no sure or permanent peace for the world nations until these higher convictions, these more idealistic faiths, these greater compulsions are formed in the moral fiber of the people themselves and are the controlling springs

of action. But it is quite possible that one great nation — our own beloved country — might already take the risk of depending for its defenses wholly on the fairness of its claims, the justice of its demands, the righteousness of its dealings.

President Wilson's noble words asking for a reversal of the provision of the Panama Canal Act of 1912 exempting from tolls United States vessels engaged in coastwise trade point the way toward a national spirit which would eventually do away with the occasion for war. He said:

> We are too big and too powerful a nation and too self-respecting a nation to interpret with too strained or refined a reading of words our own promises just because we have power enough to give us leave to read them as we please. The large thing to do is the only thing we can do — voluntary withdrawal from a position everywhere questioned and misunderstood.

The preparation, however, for putting the Quaker ideal full into play among the nations of the world is no doubt still a long future process. It calls for a far greater perfection of international courts, perhaps even the formation of an international parliament. It involves, further, a sounder education; the cultivation of clearer, truer insight; a keener and more searching analysis of facts; a greater elimination of prejudices in the formation of historic and economic theories, and a stronger control of will under the impact of such abstract theories. Just such moral, intellectual, and volitional advance, however, is the true glory of a nation and the promotion of it is the real business of the best patriots.

"Dreamers of dreams!" We take the
    taunt with gladness,
Knowing that God, beyond the years you
    see,
Hath wrought the dreams that count
    with you for madness,
Into the substance of the life to be.

113.

William Jennings Bryan: American Protest Over the Sinking of the *Lusitania*

On May 7, 1915, a German submarine sank the giant English liner Lusitania, *killing 1,198 of the passengers and crew, including 128 Americans. The American people were indignant and demanded strong action against Germany. Although President Wilson observed that "there is such a thing as a man being too proud to fight," he agreed with his advisers, including his secretary of state, William Jennings Bryan, that a protest note must be sent. Bryan, an avowed pacifist, was reluctant to issue too strong a rebuke for fear that it would draw the United States into the war. But he sent the following note on May 13, 1915, to the U.S. ambassador in Germany. This was the first of three so-called Lusitania Notes. In September Germany promised that no more surprise sinkings would take place, and in May 1916 declared that her submarine warfare would be conducted according to international law provided the United States would compel the Allies to do likewise. These promises were not long kept.*

Source: PRFA, 1915, Supplement: *The World War,* pp. 393-396.

PLEASE CALL ON THE MINISTER of foreign affairs and, after reading to him this communication, leave him with a copy.

In view of recent acts of the German authorities in violation of American rights on the high seas which culminated in the torpedoing and sinking of the British steamship *Lusitania* on May 7, 1915, by which over 100 American citizens lost their lives, it is clearly wise and desirable that the government of the United States and the Imperial German government should come to a clear and full understanding as to the grave situation which has resulted.

The sinking of the British passenger steamer *Falaba* by a German submarine on March 28, through which Leon C. Thrasher, an American citizen, was drowned; the attack on April 28 on the American vessel *Cushing* by a German aeroplane; the torpedoing on May 1 of the American vessel *Gulflight* by a German submarine, as a result of which two or more American citizens met their death; and, finally, the torpedoing and sinking of the steamship *Lusitania* constitute a series of events which the government of the United States has observed with growing concern, distress, and amazement.

Recalling the humane and enlightened attitude hitherto assumed by the Imperial German government in matters of international right, and particularly with regard to the freedom of the seas; having learned to recognize the German views and the German influence in the field of international obligation as always engaged upon the side of justice and humanity; and having understood the instructions of the Imperial German government to its naval commanders to be upon the same plane of humane action prescribed by the naval codes of other nations, the government of the United States was loath to believe — it cannot now bring itself to believe — that these acts, so absolutely contrary to the rules, the practices, and the spirit of modern warfare, could have the countenance or sanction of that great government. It feels it to be its duty, therefore, to address the Imperial German government concerning them with the utmost frankness and in the earnest hope that it is not mistaken in expecting action on the part of the Imperial German government which will correct the unfortunate impressions which have been created and vindicate once more the position of that government with regard to the sacred freedom of the seas.

The government of the United States has been apprised that the Imperial German government considered themselves to be obliged by the extraordinary circumstances of the present war and the measures adopted by their adversaries in seeking to cut Germany off from all commerce, to adopt methods of retaliation which go much beyond the ordinary methods of warfare at sea, in the proclamation of a war zone from which they have warned neutral ships to keep away. This government has already taken occasion to inform the Imperial German government that it cannot admit the adoption of such measures or such a warning of danger to operate as in any degree an abbreviation of the rights of American shipmasters or of American citizens bound on lawful errands as passengers on merchant ships of belligerent nationality; and that it must hold the Imperial German government to a strict accountability for any infringement of those rights, intentional or incidental.

It does not understand the Imperial German government to question those rights. It assumes, on the contrary, that the Imperial government accept, as of course, the rule that the lives of noncombatants, whether they be of neutral citizenship or citizens of one of the nations at war, cannot lawfully or rightfully be put in jeopardy by the capture or destruction of an unarmed merchantman, and recognize also, as all other nations do, the obligation to take the usual precaution of visit and search to ascertain whether a suspected merchantman is in fact of belligerent nationality or is in fact carrying contraband of war under a neutral flag.

The government of the United States, therefore, desires to call the attention of the Imperial German government, with the utmost earnestness, to the fact that the objection to their present method of attack against the trade of their enemies lies in the practical impossibility of employing submarines in the destruction of commerce without disregarding those rules of fairness, reason, justice, and humanity which all modern opinion regards as imperative. It is practically impossible for the officers of a submarine to visit a merchantman at sea and examine her papers and cargo. It is practically impossible for them to make a prize of her; and, if they cannot put a prize crew on board of her, they cannot sink her without leaving her crew and all on board of her to the mercy of the sea in her small boats.

These facts it is understood the Imperial German government frankly admit. We are informed that in the instances of which we have spoken time enough for even that poor measure of safety was not given, and, in at least two of the cases cited, not so much as a warning was received. Manifestly, submarines cannot be used against merchantmen, as the last few weeks have shown, without an inevitable violation of many sacred principles of justice and humanity.

American citizens act within their indisputable rights in taking their ships and in traveling wherever their legitimate business calls them upon the high seas, and exercise those rights in what should be the well-justified confidence that their lives will not be endangered by acts done in clear violation of universally acknowledged international obligations, and certainly in the confidence that their own government will sustain them in the exercise of their rights.

There was recently published in the newspapers of the United States, I regret to inform the Imperial German government, a formal warning, purporting to come from the Imperial German Embassy at Washington, addressed to the people of the United States, and stating, in effect, that any citizen of the United States who exercised his right of free travel upon the seas would do so at his peril if his journey should take him within the zone of waters within which the Imperial German Navy was using submarines against the commerce of Great Britain and France, notwithstanding the respectful but very earnest protests of his government, the government of the United States. I do not refer to this for the purpose of calling the attention of the Imperial German government at this time to the surprising irregularity of a communication from the Imperial German Embassy at Washington addressed to the people of the United States through the newspapers, but only for the purpose of pointing out that no warning that an unlawful and inhumane act will be committed can possibly be accepted as an excuse or palliation for that act or as an abatement of the responsibility for its commission.

Long acquainted as this government has been with the character of the Imperial German government and with the high principles of equity by which they have in the past been actuated and guided, the government of the United States cannot believe that the commanders of the vessels which committed these acts of lawlessness did so except under a misapprehension of the orders issued by the Imperial German naval authorities. It takes it for granted that, at least within the practical possibilities of every such case, the commanders even of submarines were expected to do nothing that would involve the lives of noncombatants or the safety of neutral ships, even at the cost of failing of their object of capture or destruction. It confidently expects, therefore, that the Imperial German government will disavow the acts of which the government of the United States complains, that they will make reparation so far as reparation is possible for injuries which are without measure, and that they will take immediate steps to prevent the recurrence of anything so obviously subversive of the principles of warfare for which the Imperial German government have in the past so wisely and so firmly contended.

The government and the people of the United States look to the Imperial German government for just, prompt, and enlightened action in this vital matter with the greater confidence because the United States and Germany are bound together, not only by special ties of friendship but also by the explicit stipulations of the treaty of 1828 between the United States and the Kingdom of Prussia.

Expressions of regret and offers of reparation in the case of the destruction of neutral ships sunk by mistake, while they may satisfy international obligations, if no loss of life results, cannot justify or excuse a practice, the natural and necessary effect of which is to subject neutral nations and neutral persons to new and immeasurable risks.

The Imperial German government will not expect the government of the United States to omit any word or any act necessary to the performance of its sacred duty of maintaining the rights of the United States and its citizens and of safeguarding their free exercise and enjoyment.

Why fear death? It is the most beautiful adventure of life.
        CHARLES FROHMAN, last words before going down with the *Lusitania*, May 7, 1915

114.

Thomas Hoier: "Don't Bite The Hand That's Feeding You"

Feeling against the immigrant was running high in 1915. For example, on January 28 President Wilson vetoed a congressional bill requiring a literacy test of all new immigrants, which would have greatly restricted their number. Thomas Hoier's "Don't Bite The Hand That's Feeding You," a song that expressed the view that all immigrants were ingrates, was popular among nativists at the time.

Source: *Legion Airs: Songs of the Armed Forces*, Lee O. Smith, ed., New York, 1960.

🎵 DON'T BITE THE HAND THAT'S FEEDING YOU

Last night, as I lay a-sleeping,
A wonderful dream came to me:
I saw Uncle Sammy weeping
For his children from over the sea.
They had come to him friendless and starving,
When from tyrant's oppression they fled,
But now they abuse and revile him,
Till at last in just anger he said:

> *Chorus:*
> "If you don't like your Uncle Sammy,
> Then go back to your home o'er the sea,
> To the land from where you came, whatever be it's name,
> But don't be ungrateful to me!
> If you don't like the stars in Old Glory,
> If you don't like the Red, White and Blue,
> Then don't act like the cur in the story,
> Don't bite the hand that's feeding you!"

You recall the day you landed,
How I welcomed you to my shore?
When you came here empty handed,
And allegiance forever you swore?
I gathered you close to my bosom,
Of food and of clothes you got both,
So, when in trouble I need you,
You will have to remember your oath.

115.

Robert Herrick: Recantation of a Pacifist

Most religious and educational leaders were opposed to American intervention in the
European war, but there were a few who viewed the conflict as a crusade for a better
world and who urged America to enter it. One such was Robert Herrick, a novelist
and a university professor, who came to see the war in this light after a tour of
the battlefields in 1915. Herrick had been a pacifist, and his "Recantation," which
appeared in the New Republic *in October, caused a stir among intellectuals.*

Source: *New Republic,* October 30, 1915.

After four months of living in Europe, I have returned to America with the deep conviction that war is not the worst of human evils, terrible as its waste and suffering are. I have become ashamed of that vague pacifism which I, like so many others, voiced under the first shock of the European war — the expression of an anemic idealism due to an imaginative dislike of the unpleasant and to an abstract sense of the folly of war. The timidities and unrealities preached by Bryan and other professional pacifists seem to me merely an evidence of sickliness in our national spirit, as well as of provincialism in our thinking.

Equally provincial is the often expressed fear that European civilization is in danger of extinction from the present terrific conflict. I see rather the coming of a better civilization through the settlement of fundamental principles. It is with this faith that the enormous sacrifices are being made freely in France, in England, in Italy. "It is of little importance what happens to us," a Frenchman said to me in Rheims, whose home had been shelled that morning, whose son had already been killed in battle. "There will be a better world for those who are to come because of what we have endured."

That is what the American mind cannot seem to understand — the necessity of a present sacrifice for a better future, the cost in blood and agony of ultimate principle.

We Americans use the word "peace" too loosely, as if it meant an absolute state of being which through our innate virtues and happy accidents we had realized. "Peace" is a purely relative term. To describe the social conditions of these United States since I have been old enough to be conscious of them as "peace" is a subterfuge; there has been an almost constant state of industrial warfare — a guerrilla and banditti warfare more evil in some ways than any military war. One need but mention the Chicago riots, the '93 strikes, Haverhill, Ludlow, Colorado. A vast deal more has gone on secretly under cover of political corruption, ignored as far as possible by the comfortable classes until it fermented in abortive protest in the progressive movement.

Bullets and shells are not the only means of taking life, nor invasion and rapine the only way of destroying civilization. What our talkative pacifists desire is not peace, but bloodlessness. American pacifism is rooted in the same sentimental humanitarianism which encourages the breeding of the unfit, which shrinks in horror from any practical method of restricting the increase of diseased, degenerate, and insane lives. It is proof less of a superior moral elevation than of a softness of fiber and vagueness of thinking. We do not like to look nature in the face; we prefer to add almshouses to hospitals and asylums, and feel comfortable "preserving lives."

This war is leading us all back to the basic commonplaces of thinking. Is life under any and all conditions sacred? Our reason says not. It tells us that the diseased and weak-minded should not be permitted to breed; also that an existence of struggle under degenerating influences, such as the industrially exploited must lead, is not worth calling life. We shudder at the term "cannon food." Why not shudder at the terms "factory food," "mine food," "sweat-shop food"? We sentimentalize as no European ever does over those brave young lives that have been spent by the hundreds of thousands in the trenches and on the battlefields of France and Poland, but we are placidly unconscious of the lives ground out in industrial competition.

Between the two methods of eating up, of maiming, of suppressing human lives, I feel that the battle method is more humane. I should prefer it for myself, for my child. We should be honest enough to recognize that for many human beings, perhaps a majority even in our prosperous, war-free society, a violent death is by no means the worst event in life. It may be the happiest if the individual feels that the sacrifice of his existence will help others to realize a better life. That is the hope, the faith of every Frenchman who falls in this struggle, of every French father and mother who pays with a son for the endurance of France.

If we rise from the depressing ranks of the exploited, the disinherited, whose lives even a pacifist might grant were as well spent in solving the issues of this great world struggle as in helping to create some new colossal fortune for others to enjoy and dispose of, then we come to the level of "us" — free beings with a modicum of self-determination, comfort, achievement, happiness. There are many of this favored class who have "fallen on the field of honor," whose lives if lived out under normal peace conditions might have meant much to themselves, possibly to humanity. They are the only ones whom the generalizing pacifists can have in mind, unconscious of the ironic fact that only a minority of our hundred millions will ever achieve sufficient liberty to enjoy the blessings of his peace.

I have seen many of these better-conditioned youths, the flower of the nations to come. I have seen them wounded, mutilated past all usefulness, dying; I have never heard a complaint from them of their fate. The doctors and nurses who serve in the hospitals will tell you the same thing. Much as I feel the awful price which they have been obliged to pay, I am sure that the finer spirits among them have lived more fully in the few crowded weeks of their struggle than if they had been permitted to live out their lives in all the gratifications of our comfortable democracies. The letters from the living and from the dead are an extraordinary revelation of those priceless things gained by these soldiers through sacrifice.

War is a great developer as well as a destroyer of life. Nothing else, it would seem in our present stage of development, presses the cup of human experience so full of realization and understanding as battle and death. These men who are paying for their beliefs with their lives are living more in moments and hours than we who have escaped the ordeal can ever live. For life cannot be measured by time or comfort or enjoyment. It is too subtle for that. A supreme effort, even a supreme agony, may have more real living worth than years of "normal" existence. The youths whose graves now dot the pleasant fields of France have drunk deeper than we can dream of the mystery of life.

For the nation, for that whole for whose endurance they have given their individual lives, there is no question of the great benefit of this war. We Americans are fond of measuring loss and gain in figures; we reckon up the huge war debts, the toll of killed and wounded, and against this heavy charge we set down nothing. It is all dead loss. Yet even today, in the crisis of struggle, there is not a Frenchman who will not tell you of the immense good that has already come to his people, that will come increasingly from the bloody sacrifice. It has united all classes, swept aside the trivial and the base, revealed the nation to itself.

The French have discovered within themselves and shown to the world qualities unsuspected or forgotten of chivalry, steadiness, seriousness; and they have renewed their familiar virtues of bravery and good humor. The French soldier, the French citizen, the French woman are today marvelously molded in the heroic type of their best tradition; in the full sense of the word they are gallant — chivalrous and self-forgetful. Is there any price too great to pay for this resurrection of nobility? I need not enumerate the many incidental benefits that are already showing themselves even through the ashes of devastation. A new, a larger, a more vital life has already begun for invaded and unconquered France.

I have cited France rather than any other of the warring countries because I have seen the French in their trials and because, outside of Belgium, I believe that France has the clearest record of all in this war. Hence has come to her the greatest reward. For in order to reap the blessings of war a nation must have an irreproachable cause.

I know that many Americans are still unable to determine for themselves that any fundamental issue is at stake in Europe today. Extraordinary as it seems to me, I hear intelligent people referring to the great war as if it were some local quarrel of no real concern to us. But even the humblest *poilu,* the simplest workman in France, is eternally assured that he is fighting not merely his own righteous battle of self-defense but the battle of the whole world in defense of its best ideals, its best traditions. His cause is big enough to consecrate him.

Having realized, then, something of the blessing as well as the curse of war, having witnessed the marvelous inspiration that has come to at least one great people through its bitterest agony, I have come to understand that war is far from being the most evil aspect of humanity. It may be lamentable that humanity is still so firmly in the grip of biologic law that it must kill in order to decide its disputes, but it is idle to shut one's eyes to the facts. And it is weak to assume that all wars can be prevented by any system of parliamenting or litigation, by any paper scheme of international arbitration.

No man — and no nation — is worthy of life who is not ready to lay it down at necessity. And some matters are of a primary necessity — unarguable, fundamental. It is proof not of European degeneracy that Europe has suffered from many wars, is today bleeding under the greatest of all wars, but of vigor and of vitality in beliefs. It is only the weakling who finds nothing worth fighting about. Whoever cares greatly will give all, even life.

It simply is not true that war never settles anything.
FELIX FRANKFURTER

116.

Leonard Wood: Military Unpreparedness

German submarine attacks on American and British ships in 1915 convinced many Americans that the only security for America lay in a formidable buildup of military power. The "preparedness" advocates, as they were called, argued that the ability to wage war was the first prerequisite of remaining neutral. The argument, of course, cut both ways, and the position was severely criticized by those who maintained that preparedness was in fact the first step toward active involvement in the conflict. Major General Wood, a staunch preparedness advocate, helped organize the "Plattsburgh" volunteers in the summer of 1915. He wrote the book from which the following selection is taken earlier in the year.

Source: *The Military Obligation of Citizenship,* Princeton, 1915, Ch. 1:
"The Policy of the United States in Raising and Maintaining Armies."

THE PEOPLE OF THE UNITED STATES are singularly lacking in information concerning both the military history of their country and its military policy. Students in school and college as a rule receive entirely erroneous ideas on both of these subjects. The average young man, unless he has really made a study of the country's history, is firmly convinced that the Revolutionary War was characterized throughout by the highest quality of patriotism and devotion to the best interests of the country on the part of the people as a whole.

He is not at all familiar with the desperate struggle which was made by Washington, various colonial assemblies, and the Confederation of Colonies to keep in the field even a small force of troops. He hears very little of the bickerings, mutinies, desertions, and frequent changes of personnel which made the war a difficult one to conduct and served to bring out into strong relief the remarkable qualities of Washington — those qualities of patience, good judgment, discretion, and again patience, and more patience, which made it possible for him to hold the illy-equipped, disjointed, and discordant elements together, and to have always available some kind of a fighting force, although seldom an effective one.

We have as a nation neglected the lessons of past wars and have learned little from the example of the great military nations, and, as Emory Upton truthfully says: "Our general policy has followed closely that of China." Perhaps this statement may be somewhat extreme in all which applies to conditions up to the end of the Civil War, but it is not in any way extreme when applied to conditions which exist today. The great nations with policies to uphold and interests to defend have made what they believe to be adequate military preparation.

The United States has been drifting for years. No real military preparations of an adequate character have been made. Military preparedness means the organization of all the resources of a nation — men, material, and money — so that the full power of the nation may be promptly applied and continued at maximum strength for a considerable period of time. War today, when initiated by a country prepared for war, comes with great suddenness, because all preparations have been made in advance; plans have been worked out to the last detail, organization completed, and reserve supplies purchased and assembled long in advance, and the whole force of the mighty machine can be applied in a very brief period of time at any designated point.

Back of the machine itself is the railroad service, so organized as to be turned over immediately to the military authorities. Back of this come the civil hospitals, the bakeries, and the supply departments of all sorts, each with its responsibility fixed in case of operations within its area or in case of a demand for supplies in other sections of the theater of war. The capacity of every ship is known and plans completed for her use as a troop ship; and when war threatens, the whereabouts of the shipping is closely watched, and ships are assembled quietly to meet any demand which may be required for oversea operations. These are but an outline of what is meant by military preparedness.

Mere numbers of men and undeveloped military resources are of little value. It has been well said that in the sudden onrush of modern war undeveloped military resources are of no more use than an undeveloped gold mine in Alaska would be in a panic on Wall Street. The comparison is not overdrawn. You must remember, all of you, that this country has never yet engaged in war with a first-class power prepared for war.

You must remember also that once sea power is lost or held in check an enormous force can be landed on these shores within a month — a force sufficient to go where it will and to hold whatever it desires to hold.

Why have we failed to make adequate preparation? Partly because of ignorance of the true facts concerning our utter unpreparedness and partly due to a conceit fostered by the average Fourth of July orator and politician, through statements to the effect that we possess peculiar and remarkable military characteristics which make our soldiers trained and efficient without preparation, and as good as equally brave and equally sound men of other countries who have spent years in training. Again there is the curious Anglo-Saxon prejudice against a large standing army and the feeling that it is always a menace to civil liberty.

In our past wars we were not confronted by great nations with highly organized military machines; steam navigation had not appeared; our possible enemies were without standing armies of any size and lacked entirely that complete military organization which characterizes them today. It took a long time to get troops together and prepare supplies for them and a considerable period of time to cross the ocean.

Our forefathers had more time to prepare. Then, again, they were more familiar with the use of arms; weapons were of a simple type; they could be made quickly and instruction in their use was a relatively simple matter.

Now, highly organized military establishments are the rule among our possible antagonists. Rapid steam transportation in vast amount is available. The arms of war are extremely complicated and costly; it takes a long time to make them and a long time to instruct soldiers in their use. In other words, today everything is in favor of the prepared aggressor and everything against the unready pacific nation. The blow comes more quickly and with greater force, and it is not possible to provide even a semblance of protection against it unless wise measures have been taken long in advance.

Since the foundation of the republic, war has existed as follows: Revolutionary War, 7 years; War of 1812-14, 2½ years; Mexican War, 2 years; Florida War, 7 years; Civil War, 4 years; War with Spain and Philippine Rebellion, 2 years — not to mention numerous Indian wars and internal disturbances requiring the use of troops.

We have struggled through these wars and have emerged generally successfully, but in none of them has there been any evidence of well-thought-out preparations or the application of a sound military policy. Our people remember only the success and forget entirely the great and unnecessary cost in blood and treasure in which our defective method of conducting these wars resulted. By faulty methods I mean that we have generally conducted war as a confederacy instead of as a nation. We have permitted altogether too much interference by states. Too many officers have been appointed by the governors of states. New regiments have been raised oftentimes in order that new officers might be appointed and political patronage increased, whereas the old regiments should have been filled up as they had acquired experience, some traditions and *esprit*, and were much more valuable than new regiments. This is seen in the Civil War in case of the Wisconsin organizations. Wisconsin had the good sense to veteranize her regiments, and the result is seen when one remembers the term "Iron Brigade" applied to a Wisconsin brigade.

Then again we have had frequently the intervention of civilians, either through the activities of the secretary of war or of the civil arms of the government. There has been a general lack of a sense of individual responsibility for military service. Reliance on volunteer enlistments has continued and has been one of the gravest sources of danger to the Republic. The experience of the Revolution should have taught us that it is not safe in a real war to depend upon volunteers. There is an enthusiastic response by a certain proportion of the best element in the early days of war, but this response cannot be counted upon to continue throughout a long war involving severe strains upon the population, nor is it right or just to throw the burden of military service upon a portion of the population. It is a universal obligation and the country will never be secure or safe until it is recognized as such and measures are taken to develop military preparation on a basis of universal military obligation. . . .

The voluntary system failed us in the past and will fail us in the future. It is uncertain in operation, prevents organized preparation, tends to destroy that individual sense of obligation for military service which should be found in every citizen, costs excessively in life and treasure, and does not permit that condition of preparedness which must exist if we are to wage war successfully with any great power prepared for war.

The question is: What shall we do to adequately prepare ourselves for war without establishing a huge standing army or bringing about a condition which might be described as one of militarism, which term, as I use it, means the condition under which the military forces of a nation demand and secure special recognition, both socially and officially, and exercise an undue influence in the conduct of the civil affairs of the government, both at home and abroad? In other words, a condition which may be described as one under which the military element dominates the nation's policy. Nothing could be more unfortunate than the establishment of such a condition in this country or elsewhere, so far as development on normal lines is concerned. However, a condition of thorough preparedness can be established without creating a condition of militarism. . . .

Do not place any dependence upon the statements of these charlatans who speak of a million men flocking to arms between sun and sun, but remember when you hear fallacies of this sort the words of old "Light-Horse Harry" Lee, which are as true today as they were when they were uttered. We must preserve our ideals, strive for world peace, and do what we can to build up the adjustment of international difficulties through arbitration, but we must not fail to give due heed to the conditions under which we live. Whatever we may hope for in the way of universal peace does not justify us in disregarding the conditions which surround us today.

If we want to hand down to our children the heritage which has come to us from our fathers, we must not place confidence in idle boasting but give serious heed to well-thought-out preparation and adopt a policy for the future with reference to our military establishment very different from that which has existed in the past. We can do this without violating our ideals. If I were to state such a military policy I would say, briefly, have an army sufficient for the peace needs of the nation, a good militia, an adequate navy, and behind them the largest possible number of men trained to be efficient soldiers if needed; but in time of peace following their ordinary civil occupations — ready to come when wanted. A country so prepared will have the largest possible measure of peace.

117.

HENRY L. STIMSON: American Military Needs

Henry L. Stimson, secretary of war from 1911 to 1913, was a staunch advocate of military "preparedness" in the years preceding America's entry into World War I. In the autumn of 1914, he joined with other preparedness spokesmen such as Theodore Roosevelt and Major General Leonard Wood to form the National Security League, whose avowed purpose was to propagandize for increased military expenditures. Through articles, books, and speeches, the League hoped to persuade the public and to pressure Congress into passing the desired legislation. In the following bulletin, published by the League in 1915, Stimson outlined what he considered to be the defense needs of the country.

Source: *America at War*, Albert B. Hart, ed., New York, 1918, pp. 185-189.

IN ANY DISCUSSION OF THE MILITARY NEEDS of this country, the first thing to be avoided is the formulation of any ill-matured suggestions by civilians who have no special knowledge on the subject. Constant change and lack of continuity have been characteristic faults from which our military policy has suffered since the beginning of our national history. . . .

NATIONAL DEFENSIVE NEEDS

THE ARMY AND NAVY are peculiar sufferers from our "pork-barrel" system, which is the result of our lack of any national executive budget. So long as the men who are responsible for the efficiency of these two services as a whole — the secretaries of war and of the Navy — have no hand in the preparation of a budget and no voice to defend such a budget on the floor of the houses of Congress, while the men who wish to spend the Army and Navy appropriations upon unnecessary Army posts or unfit Navy yards have such a voice as well as a vote, a great degree of waste and extravagance is sure to result. Our military system can never be made highly or permanently efficient until a budget system is adopted in this country similar to that which exists in substantially all other civilized countries. This general governmental need is the first need of our Army and Navy.

Roughly stated, our national defensive needs, as discussed in the above-enumerated report of the General Staff, and as agreed to by all competent military and naval authorities, are comprised under the following heads:

First, an adequate and efficient navy as the primary line of defense.

Second, an adequate system of coast defense to prevent the naval bombardment of our principal seaports and cities.

Third, a small but highly efficient regular army to serve in time of peace as a protection against civil disorder; in time of war, as a temporary protection against invasion; and in times of both peace and war, to be a pattern and nucleus for the organization of the larger citizens' army upon which, in any serious conflict, our protection must ultimately depend.

Fourth, a citizens' army composed of men who do not make arms their vocation, but who have been willing to spend a short portion of their lives in undergoing the training which modern methods of war make absolutely necessary as a condition of usefulness on the battlefield. . . .

THE NAVY

IN OUR NEED of an adequate and efficient navy, the United States comes second only to Great Britain. We have 21,000 miles of coastline and a rapidly increasing commerce to defend. The general purpose of a navy is purely defensive, although tactically it must always be able to act on the offensive for the purpose of making effective defense of the country. Standing by itself, a navy is not designed for military aggression, such as the invasion of another country. Its function, on the contrary, is to defend our own country and our commerce against such aggression. Yet, in order to do this, it must be able to seek the enemy's fleet and attack it wherever the conditions for American success are most certain. To scatter the fleet or to tie it down to operations near our own coast is to destroy its real defensive ability. In the Napoleonic Wars, England was saved from invasion by victories of her fleet which took place hundreds of miles away from her coasts; and a policy which would prevent our own fleet from adopting such a course of operation would be hazardous to our safety.

These considerations, in addition to the fact that we have distant foreign possessions, require that we should have a seagoing navy of adequate size and efficiency. The many vital questions which are still unsettled in naval tactics require that we should have a navy which is up-to-date in all of the various branches of the service.

As a matter of fact, naval authorities today agree that not only has our Navy been falling behind, in its general relative strength to that of other nations, but it is strikingly deficient in certain vital particulars. It is extremely short in personnel; it is deficient in the number of our capital ships; it has no battle cruisers and practically no scout cruisers; it is extremely lacking in effective submarines and destroyers.

In view of the fact that the Navy is practically our only existing defense today, its needs should meet with the promptest and most earnest attention.

COAST DEFENSE

OUR SYSTEM OF COAST DEFENSE is in the best relative condition of any of our land defenses. But its function is very limited. Its purpose is merely to protect our seacoast cities from a naval raid and damage such as recently befell Scarborough and Hartlepool. It offers no defense against an enemy who has control of the sea and can land an army at any unprotected point of our huge coastline.

Even in our coast defense there are great

deficiencies. Our military policy contemplates that its personnel should be supplied half from the regular army and half from the militia. Substantially 50 percent of each of these two quotas is lacking and, in the case of a sudden emergency, against which it is the purpose of the coast defense to be a protection, many of our forts would be hopelessly undermanned. The amount of ammunition is deficient. The plans of our military advisers contemplate only sufficient ammunition for an hour's firing. The actual supply at present is very considerably behind even the most modest standard and, in many cases of our most important seacoast guns, would be sufficient for only thirty or forty minutes' firing. . . .

THE CITIZENS' ARMY

IT HAS BEEN THE HISTORIC POLICY of this country to depend upon a voluntary army of citizens, called out at the outbreak of war, to defend it in case of any serious conflict. The development of the art of war during the last half century has been such as to make radical changes in this policy necessary if it is to be successful. Hitherto we have relied upon training and equipping our volunteers after the outbreak of war. In our previous wars we have escaped disaster under this method largely on account of conditions which will in all probability never occur again.

In the Civil War we were fighting against an enemy who was as unprepared as ourselves. Each side trained the other as the conflict proceeded. In the War of 1812 we were fighting a nation which was almost wholly absorbed in a great European war and which spent very little attention upon us. Yet in that war we called out, from first to last, 527,000 men to defend us against an enemy which never had a force of 16,000 men in the field at any one time and whose total forces throughout the war aggregated only about 54,000 altogether. We were defeated in most of our battles,

and we lost our Capitol at Washington after a force of 5,400 untrained Americans had run away from less than 1,500 British on suffering a loss of only 8 killed.

We can safely assume that any serious antagonist whom we shall have in the future will not be unprepared. Modern war is fought with weapons which require time to construct and training to use to an extent hitherto unknown. Our citizens today are wholly unaccustomed to the use of the military rifle, let alone the modern fieldpiece. The training, equipment, and discipline of the modern army is much more complicated than that of fifty years ago and requires very much greater time and expert knowledge. The conditions surrounding the raising and equipment of a force of citizen soldiery have therefore completely changed since the Civil War. To attempt to organize such a force of volunteers in the way in which we did it then would be to invite disaster against practically any army of modern Europe.

TRAINING OF MEN AND OFFICERS

UNDER THESE CIRCUMSTANCES it is inevitable that new and broader foundations must be laid for the creation of a body of citizen soldiery in time of war; provision must be made for the training of a force of reserve officers to constitute the junior officers of such a force. Steps have already been taken by the War Department in the institution of summer camps, where young school and college graduates can, in association with the regular army, get a brief, intensive training. We believe that this should be supplemented by a legislation permitting the graduates of such camps to obtain temporary commissions as junior officers in the regular army, on condition of becoming thereafter reserve officers, subject to call in time of war.

Provision should also be made for general training in rifle shooting among our young men, both in schools and in colleges. To this end we call attention to the steps which have already been taken in Switzerland and Australia — two of the most advanced and liberal governments in the world — where, from early boyhood, their young men are trained to use the rifle as a necessary part of their education. In these two countries, representing in their respective ways the most advanced types of modern democracy and going hand in hand with their freedom of thought and liberalism, we find the doctrine that every man owes to his country, not only to die for her if necessary but also to spend a little of his life in learning how to die for her effectively. We believe that the institution of a somewhat similar system in this country is not only highly important with a view to its defense in the time of war but we believe that the necessary self-control and discipline which is inherent to such training would be highly conducive to the moral, mental, and physical betterment of our youth in time of peace.

WAR MATERIAL

FINALLY, WE FIND that there is a great shortage in the material in this country necessary to equip a citizen's army for war: particu-larly in the vital element of field artillery and field-artillery ammunition. Such equipment cannot be extemporized nor can it always be purchased after war breaks out. It takes at least five months for the manufacture of a modern battery of field guns within the United States. At present we have in stock but little more than half the necessary number of field guns to equip a citizens' army of the minimum size believed by our military advisers to be necessary. And we have ammunition sufficient to serve those guns, at the rate ammunition is now used, rather less than one day and a half of fighting. We are very insufficient in aeroplanes, being outranked by at least thirteen other nations. Immediate steps should be taken to bring up these shortages.

Taken as a whole, we find that the condition of military unpreparedness of the United States is most serious and lamentable. We believe it is the duty of our citizens, without respect to party, to take the present occasion, when the interest of the country has been aroused by the European war, for insisting that Congress give to the subject its most earnest attention to the end that the foregoing deficiencies may be speedily remedied.

What this country needs is a good five-cent cigar.
> THOMAS RILEY MARSHALL, during a boring debate, when a senator began enumerating what the country needed. F. P. A. noted that "What this country needs is a good five-cent nickel," and Will Rogers added that "Our country has plenty of good five-cent cigars but the trouble is they charge fifteen cents for them."

118.

Francis G. Wickware: Suspicions of Sabotage

In order to carry on the war, the Allies were dependent on outside help, especially from America. From the point of view of the German high command, the policy of unrestricted submarine warfare against "neutral" ships carrying arms and other supplies to England was no more than a natural extension of the German war effort. A further extension of the same policy, the destruction by sabotage of the American munitions industry, seems to have been adopted by the German commanders in 1915, at a time when the submarine attacks were discontinued for diplomatic reasons. At any rate, attempts at sabotage were made, and as these became public they fortified the growing Allied sentiment in the country. The American reaction culminated in the passage of the Sabotage Act, the Espionage Act, and the Sedition Act by 1918. Francis Wickware, editor of the American Year Book, *discussed some early acts of sabotage in the 1915 edition of this work.*

Source: *The American Year Book . . . 1915,* New York, 1916: "Neutrality."

Domestic Problems of Neutrality. From transgressions on neutral American rights by the European belligerents, we turn finally to the domestic problems of neutrality, and especially to those involved in the tremendous and sustained campaign conducted in the United States on behalf of the Germanic alliance, the most remarkable example in history of mission work carried on in a neutral country in the interest of a belligerent.

Pro-German propaganda in its earliest phase of persuasion and apology appeared before hostilities were well begun, and in the early days of the war Dr. Bernhard Dernburg, sometime colonial minister in the Imperial German government, arrived as a special emissary of Berlin to instruct the American people on the aggressive responsibility of Great Britain and her allies, the righteousness of the German cause, and the superiority of German *Kultur.* This campaign of education, conducted by Dr. Dernburg and other German and German-American leaders with the utmost vigor on the platform, in the press, and through the mails, failed utterly to change American opinion on the origin and issues of the war or to lessen the antipathy inspired by the invasion of Belgium and its attendant horrors. Sometimes unscrupulous, often insulting, and always lacking in imagination, the propaganda alienated more sympathy than it attracted, and it was not long before the futile efforts to convert a sentiment generally strongly adverse to the German cause were overshadowed by a campaign of attack on American neutrality. . . .

Passport Frauds. Another annoying phase of German activity was the fraudulent use of American passports to facilitate the return of reservists to Germany. Early in the year the government discovered indications of a systematic plan to obtain passports for this purpose through fraud, but prompt convictions in two cases effactually discouraged the conspirators before the plot had any important success. The first case involved four German reservists bearing passports issued to American citizens who were taken from a Norwegian steamer leaving

New York on January 2. The passports were traced to Carl Ruroede, a steamship agent of Brooklyn, who pleaded guilty to a charge of conspiracy to defraud the government and was sentenced to three years' imprisonment on March 8.

In the second case, the confession of one of the principals charged Captain Boy-Ed with being the instigator of the fraud. Richard P. Stegler, a German reservist arrested on February 24 on a charge of conspiracy to obtain an American passport by impersonating an American citizen, declared that Captain Boy-Ed had persuaded him to go to England as a spy in the guise of a commercial agent for American firms, and had suggested the means and supplied the money by which he had obtained the birth certificate of an American citizen as a preliminary to securing a passport. Captain Boy-Ed issued an emphatic denial of Stegler's charges. Stegler was sentenced on March 19 to sixty days' imprisonment, and his two accomplices in the transfer of the birth certificate to ten months.

The Campaign for an Embargo on Arms. As an overt campaign of defense and persuasion, the pro-German propaganda ended with the sinking of the *Lusitania* early in May. The horror and disgust inspired by that barbarous act extinguished the tolerance with which the American people had hitherto endured German instruction and complaint; and it responded to Dr. Dernburg's attempted defense of the massacre with an outburst of exasperation which permanently silenced that protagonist of *Kultur* and resulted, with some official suggestion, in his departure for Germany on June 12. Thereafter, German effort pursued by different methods its supreme objective of the prevention of exports of munitions of war to the Allies. . . .

The Criminal Campaign. Failing to stop the export of munitions to the Allies by persuasion, legislation, or diplomacy, German effort turned as a last resort to direct action against the sources of supply and the means of transport to Europe. The last half of the year, in which this criminal campaign against American industries was chiefly operative, was ushered in by an attempt on the life of J. Pierpont Morgan by an insane instructor in German in Cornell University, known as Frank Holt, later identified as Erich Muenter, a former instructor in Harvard University who disappeared after indictment for the murder of his wife in 1906. As a preliminary to the attack on the head of the banking firm acting as chief fiscal and purchasing agents of the British and French governments, Holt placed a bomb in the Capitol in Washington on July 2 which wrecked the Senate reception room.

On the morning of the 3rd, he sought Mr. Morgan at his country home at Glen Cove, Long Island, for the purpose of forcing from him an agreement to use his influence to have an embargo put on shipments of ammunition. In attempting to disarm his assailant, Mr. Morgan was shot twice, neither bullet doing any permanent injury. Holt committed suicide in his cell in the Nassau County Jail at Mineola on the 6th.

The attack on Mr. Morgan, fortunately the sole attempt at direct assassination, exemplified the workings of propaganda on a disordered mind. In its effective manifestations the criminal campaign displayed a high order of prevision and resource. Beginning with an incendiary fire causing $1.5 million loss at the works of the John A. Roebling's Sons Co. at Trenton, N.J., on January 18, disasters to industrial plants engaged in the manufacture of munitions were reported with increasing frequency throughout the year. Within twenty-four hours, on November 10-11, for example, fire attacked the Roebling works a second time, with damage estimated at $1 million, destroyed a shop of the Bethlehem Steel Co. with equal loss, and caused smaller damages at the plants of the Midvale Steel & Ordnance Co. at Midvale, O., and the Baldwin Locomotive Works at Eddystone, Pa.

Among numerous disasters to ammunition factories, an explosion at one of the plants of the du Pont Powder Co. near Wilmington, Del., on November 30 caused the loss of thirty-one lives, and on December 9 the du Pont factory town of Hopewell, near Richmond, Va., was practically destroyed by fire. Equally numerous were cases of attempted destruction of ocean steamers. Bombs were discovered on several vessels, and, on many more, fires attributed to the same agency broke out in port or at sea. So visited were the *Touraine* of the French Line in March, the *Minnehaha* of the Atlantic Transport Line in July, the *Sant' Anna* of the Italian Line in September, and the *Rochambeau* of the French Line in November. . . .

So far as the destruction of munitions plants and the burning of ships and cargoes could be attributed with any shadow of probability to accident or natural causes, that allowance was made. But in the last quarter of the year the conviction has been forced home that disasters so numerous and widespread could be neither the result of coincidence nor the work of a few scattered fanatics, but must be the product of organized warfare on the munitions industry. Hitherto, however, the conspirators have operated with comparative impunity. The government has disclosed no evidence of a directing agency, and arrests have been made in very few cases, the most important being those of Charles C. Crowley, apprehended with several alleged accomplices at San Francisco in November on charges of criminal activities against shipping and munitions plants on the Pacific Coast; and of Robert Fay, who claims to be an officer in the German Army, arrested with another German near Weehawken, N.J., on October 24, on charges of conspiracy to blow up vessels sailing from American ports with cargoes of munitions for the Allies.

Three other alleged conspirators with Fay were taken into custody later. Fay was found to have large quantities of explosives in his possession, which he admitted were for the purpose of manufacturing time bombs to be attached as mines to munitions ships. In a voluntary statement made on October 25, Fay confessed that he had been taken from active service especially for this work, that he had been sent to the United States under instructions from the German Secret Service, and that he had reported his mission to Capt. Karl Boy-Ed and Capt. Franz von Papen, the German naval and military attachés at Washington.

On November 8 a federal grand jury in New York found indictments against Fay and the other defendants, charging conspiracy to destroy vessels to the detriment of the owners of the ships and cargoes and of the underwriters of insurance thereon. Five other indictments were found on December 6, intended to cover all possible phases of the offenses alleged, the additional charges including conspiracy to commit assault and murder.

The third and last of the principal manifestations of the criminal campaign has been an effort to foment strikes among seamen and workers in munitions plants. In June, Andrew Furuseth, president of the International Seamen's Union of America, declared that a plan was on foot, backed apparently with unlimited funds, to promote a world's strike of seamen and thus immobilize all ocean shipping. On August 17, Samuel Gompers issued a statement that his aid in foreign tampering with American labor had been solicited for months, and the Executive Committee of the American Federation of Labor reported officially in November that attempts had been made unsuccessfully to corrupt a number of labor leaders. Beginning with a strike on a new munitions factory at Bridgeport, Conn., in July, an epidemic of strikes swept over the East, especially among machinists in munitions plants. In four months, 102 distinct strikes and 6 lockouts of machinists were recorded, and Bridgeport alone reported 55 strikes in various trades in a space of ten weeks. . . . Even more certainly than in the case of incendiary and bomb conspiracies, the labor troubles of munitions makers exceeded the probability of coincidence and chance.

The labor conspiracy the government claims to have traced to a definite source. Early in December a federal grand jury in New York began an investigation of the activities of Labor's National Peace Council, an organization formed late in June by the promoters of a so-called peace meeting, of a very Teutonic cast, addressed by Mr. Bryan in New York on June 19.

On December 28 an indictment was found under the Sherman Act against Representative Frank Buchanan of Illinois, first president of Labor's National Peace Council; Jacob C. Taylor, his successor in that office; H. Robert Fowler, a former representative from Illinois, is general counsel; Frank S. Monnett, former attorney general of Ohio, a chairman of committee; Henry B. Martin, secretary; Henry Schulteis, a member; David Lamar, the so-called wolf of Wall Street; and Franz Rintelen, a captain in the German Navy, alleged to be a close friend of the Kaiser and now imprisoned in London as a spy. These men, the indictment charges, conspired to restrain the foreign commerce of the United States in war materials by fomenting, by propaganda and bribery, strikes among the workers in munitions plants. A fund of $500,000 for this purpose is alleged to have been disbursed through the other seven by Rintelen, who is said also to have promoted a revolution in Mexico under General Huerta.

119.

EDGAR LEE MASTERS: Spoon River Epitaphs

*"I feel that no poet in English or American history had a harder life than mine was,"
wrote Edgar Lee Masters, ". . . among a people whose flesh and whose vibrations were
better calculated to poison, to pervert, and even to kill a sensitive nature." This and
other remarks of the same kind reflect the deep-seated and ineradicable misanthropy
of Masters, whose* Spoon River Anthology *is nevertheless one of the finest and
most influential volumes of verse published in America in the twentieth century.
Inspired by a friend who introduced him to the* Greek Anthology, *Masters was seized
with the idea of composing a similar series of free-verse epitaphs in the form of
monologues spoken from the grave by former inhabitants of Spoon River, a fictitious
village modeled after two Illinois towns of the poet's childhood. The epitaphs,
however, were not fictitious enough, and the families of some of Masters' subjects
never forgave him.*

Source: *Spoon River Anthology,* New York, 1915.

ANNE RUTLEDGE

Out of me unworthy and unknown
The vibrations of deathless music;
"With malice toward none, with charity for all."
Out of me the forgiveness of millions toward millions,

And the beneficent face of a nation
Shining with justice and truth.
I am Anne Rutledge who sleep beneath these weeds,
Beloved in life of Abraham Lincoln,
Wedded to him, not through union,
But through separation.
Bloom forever, O Republic,
From the dust of my bosom!

KNOWLT HOHEIMER

I was the first fruits of the battle of Missionary Ridge.
When I felt the bullet enter my heart
I wished I had staid at home and gone to jail
For stealing the hogs of Curl Trenary,
Instead of running away and joining the army.
Rather a thousand times the county jail
Than to lie under this marble figure with wings
And this granite pedestal
Bearing the words, *"Pro Patria."*
What do they mean, anyway?

EDITOR WHEDON

To be able to see every side of every question;
To be on every side, to be everything, to be nothing long;
To pervert truth, to ride it for a purpose,
To use great feelings and passions of the human family
For base designs, for cunning ends,
To wear a mask like the Greek actors —
Your eight-page paper — behind which you huddle,
Bawling through the megaphone of big type:
"This is I, the giant."
Thereby also living the life of a sneak-thief,
Poisoned with the anonymous words
Of your clandestine soul.
To scratch dirt over scandal for money,
And exhume it to the winds for revenge,
Or to sell papers,
Crushing reputations, or bodies, if need be,
To win at any cost, save your own life,
To glory in demonaic power, ditching civilization,
As a paranoiac boy puts a log on the track
And derails the express train.
To be an editor, as I was.
Then to lie here close by the river over the place
Where the sewage flows from the village,
And the empty cans and garbage are dumped,
And abortions are hidden.

Index of Authors

The numbers in brackets
indicate selection numbers
in this volume

ADAMS, FRANKLIN P. (Nov. 15, 1881-March 23, 1960), journalist and humorist. Conducted and wrote a column, "The Conning Tower," (1922-31) in the *New York World*, (1931-37) in the *New York Herald Tribune*, and (1938-41) in the *New York Post;* wrote *In Other Words* (1912), *The Diary of Our Own Samuel Pepys* (1935). **[58]**

ANTIN, MARY (1881-May 15, 1949), author and authority on immigrants. Born Russia; studied (1901-04) at Columbia University; wrote *From Polotzk to Boston* (1899), *The Promised Land* (1912), *They Who Knock at Our Gates* (1914). **[66, 91]**

BEARD, CHARLES A. (Nov. 27, 1874-Sept. 1, 1948), historian and educator. Professor of politics (1907-17) at Columbia University; a founder of the New School for Social Research, N.Y.C.; wrote *American Government and Politics* (1910), *An Economic Interpretation of the Constitution* (1913), *The Rise of American Civilization* (1927), *A Basic History of the United States* (1944). **[87]** See also Author Index, Vols. 14, 15.

BENNETT, EDWARD H. (May 12, 1874-Oct. 14, 1954), architect and artist. Specialist in city planning (from 1904); author of city planning reports (1905) for San Francisco, (1909) for Chicago, (1915) for Ottawa and Hull, Canada, and (1917) for Minneapolis; exhibited oil and watercolor paintings. **[41]**

BERGER, VICTOR L. (Feb. 28, 1860-Aug. 7, 1929), editor and Socialist political leader. Edited (1892-98) the *Milwaukee Daily Vorwaerts*, (1900) the *Social Democratic Herald*, and (from 1911) the *Milwaukee Leader;* U.S. representative from Wisconsin (1911-13, 1918-19); excluded by Congress for disloyalty to U.S. (1919); reelected and seated (1923-29). **[71]**

BOURNE, RANDOLPH (May 30, 1886-Dec. 22, 1918), pacifist and essayist. Contributed to the periodicals *The Masses* and *Seven Arts;* wrote *Youth and Life* (1913), *Education and Living* (1917), *The History of a Literary Radical* (1920). **[110]** See also Author Index, Vol. 14.

BRANDEIS, LOUIS D. (Nov. 13, 1856-Oct. 5, 1941), jurist. Special counsel for the people in minimum wage and work hour law cases in Illinois, Ohio, California, and Oregon (1907-14); associate justice (1916-39) of the U.S. Supreme Court. **[6, 67, 81, 100]** See also Author Index, Vol. 15.

BROOKS, T. J. (fl. 1911-1912), Tennessee farmer. Representative of the Farmers' Educational Cooperative Union. [63]

BROOKS, VAN WYCK (Feb. 16, 1886-May 2, 1963), essayist, critic, and translator. Edited (1920-24) *The Freeman*; translated modern French authors; wrote *America's Coming-of-Age* (1915), *The Ordeal of Mark Twain* (1920), *The Flowering of New England, 1815-1865* (1936), *New England: Indian Summer, 1865-1915* (1940). [106]

BRYAN, VINCENT (fl. 1905), lyricist. [12]

BRYAN, WILLIAM JENNINGS (March 19, 1860-July 26, 1925), lawyer and political leader. U.S. representative from Nebraska (1891-95); free-silver advocate; thrice defeated (1896, 1900, 1908) candidate for President of the United States; edited (from 1901) the weekly *Commoner*; secretary of state (1913-15) under Wilson; a prosecuting attorney in the Scopes "monkey trial" at Dayton, Tenn. (1925). [113] See also Author Index, Vol. 12.

BURNHAM, DANIEL H. (Sept. 4, 1846-June 1, 1912), architect and city planner. Chief of construction for Chicago World's Fair (1893); designed the Montauk Building, Chicago (first to be called a "skyscraper"), Flatiron Building, N.Y.C., and Union Railroad Station, Washington, D.C.; consultant on city planning for Chicago, Cleveland, San Francisco, and Manila. [41]

CARPENTER, C. U. (fl. 1911-1912), businessman. Chairman of the Sherman Antitrust Committee of the New York Board of Trade; vice-president and general manager of American Stamp and Ticket Vending Machine Company. [63]

CHANUTE, OCTAVE (Feb. 18, 1832-Nov. 23, 1910), civil engineer and pioneer aviator. Born France; consulting engineer for U.S. railroad and bridge-building projects; president (1891-92) of the American Society of Civil Engineers; wrote *Progress in Flying Machines* (1894). [26]

CHAPLIN, RALPH (fl. 1915), songwriter and labor organizer. Member of the Industrial Workers of the World; wrote "Solidarity Forever," a popular union song. [101]

CLEMENS, SAMUEL L., "Mark Twain" (Nov. 30, 1835-April 21, 1910), author and humorist. Journeyman printer (1847-56); Mississippi river pilot (1857-61); prospector (1861) and newspaper reporter (1862) in Nevada; wrote, among others, *Innocents Abroad* (1869), *The Adventures of Tom Sawyer* (1876), *The Prince and the Pauper* (1880), *Life on the Mississippi* (1883), *The Adventures of Huckleberry Finn* (1884), *The Man That Corrupted Hadleyburg* (1900). [22] See also Author Index, Vol. 10.

COHAN, GEORGE M. (July 3, 1878-Nov. 5, 1942), actor, playwright, and producer. Wrote and acted in plays (*Little Johnny Jones*, 1904; *The Song and Dance Man*, 1923) and composed popular songs ("I'm a Yankee Doodle Dandy," "You're a Grand Old Flag," "Give My Regards to Broadway," "Over There"). [19] See also Author Index, Vols. 12, 14.

CROLY, HERBERT (Jan. 23, 1869-May 17, 1930), editor and author. Edited (1900-06) the *Architectural Record*; founded and edited (from 1914) the *New Republic*; wrote *The Promise of American Life* (1909), *Progressive Democracy* (1914). [45]

CUBBERLEY, ELLWOOD P. (June 6, 1868-Sept. 15, 1941), educator. Professor of education (1898-1933) at Stanford University; wrote *Changing Conceptions of Education* (1909), *Rural Life and Education* (1913), *Public Education in the U.S.* (1919), *A History of Education* (1921). [42]

DARROW, CLARENCE (April 18, 1857-March 13, 1938), lawyer. Counsel for Eugene V. Debs in American Railway Union conspiracy case (1894), for labor interests in Pennsylvania anthracite strike arbitrations (1902-03), for John Scopes charged with violating a Tennessee law forbidding teaching evolution theory (1925); president of the American League to Abolish Capital Punishment; wrote *Crime, its Cause and Treatment* (1925). [60]

DEBS, EUGENE V. (Nov. 5, 1855-Oct. 20, 1926), labor organizer and Socialist leader. National secretary and treasurer (1880-97) of the Brotherhood of Locomotive Firemen and leader in the Chicago Pullman Strike (1894); organizer (1898) of the Social Democratic Party and its candidate (1900, 1904, 1908,

1912, 1920) for President of the United States. [31]

DE LEON, DANIEL (Dec. 14, 1852-May 11, 1914), lawyer and labor leader. Lecturer in Latin-American diplomacy (1883-89) at Columbia University; founded (1895) the Socialist Trade and Labor Alliance; editor (from 1900) of the Socialist Labor Party organ, *The People.* [5] See also Author Index, Vol. 12.

DUNNE, FINLEY PETER (July 10, 1867-April 24, 1936), editor and humorist. An editor (1892-97) for the *Chicago Evening Post* and *Chicago Times Herald* and (1897-1900) for the *Chicago Journal;* wrote *Mr. Dooley in Peace and War* (1898), *Mr. Dooley's Philosophy* (1900), *Mr. Dooley Says* (1910). [14] See also Author Index, Vol. 12.

DWIGHT, FREDERICK (fl. 1908), author. [25]

EATON, WALTER PRICHARD (Aug. 24, 1878-Feb. 26, 1957), author and critic. Professor of playwriting (1933-47) at Yale; wrote *Green Trails and Upland Pastures* (1917), *Queen Victoria* (1923), *The Drama in English* (1930). [107]

EINSTEIN, LEWIS (March 15, 1877-1949), diplomat. Officer in U.S. Foreign Service (1903-30), serving in Paris, London, Constantinople, Peking, Costa Rica, Bulgaria, and Czechoslovakia; wrote books on history, diplomacy, and art. [78]

FLEXNER, ABRAHAM (Nov. 13, 1866-Sept. 21, 1959), educator. Staff member (1908-12) of the Carnegie Foundation for the Advancement of Teaching; secretary (1913-25) and director of the division of studies (1925-28) of the General Education Board; director (1930-39) of the Institute for Advanced Study, Princeton University. [49]

FROST, ROBERT (March 26, 1874-Jan. 29, 1963), poet. Professor of English (1916-20, 1924, 1926-38, 1949-63) at Amherst; professor of poetry (1939-43) at Harvard and (1943-49) at Dartmouth; among his books of poetry are *A Boy's Will* (1913), *North of Boston* (1914), *Mountain Interval* (1916), *New Hampshire* (1923), *West-running Brook* (1928), *A Further Range* (1936), *A Witness Tree* (1942), and *In the Clearing* (1962). [92] See also Author Index, Vols. 14, 15, 16.

GIACOSA, GIUSEPPE (1847-1906), Italian dramatist. Collaborated on librettos for Verdi's *La Bohème* and *Madame Butterfly.* [27]

GLADDEN, WASHINGTON (Feb. 11, 1836-July 2, 1918), Congregational clergyman. Pastor (1875-82) at Springfield, Mass., and (1882-1918) at Columbus, Ohio; wrote *Plain Thoughts on the Art of Living* (1868), *Working People and Their Employers* (1876), *Social Salvation* (1901). [109] See also Author Index, Vol. 11.

GREGG, FREDERICK JAMES (fl. 1913), art critic. Member of the Association of American Painters and Sculptors. [77]

HADLEY, ARTHUR TWINING (April 23, 1856-March 6, 1930), educator. Professor of political science (1886-91) and of political economy (1891-99) at Yale, and president (1899-1921) of the university; wrote *Economics* (1896), *Standards of Political Morality* (1907), *Some Influences in Modern Philosophic Thought* (1913). [30]

HAMOR, W. A. (March 27, 1887-Nov. 23, 1961), industrial chemist. Assistant director (1914-59) of the Mellon Institute of Industrial Research; co-inventor of cellulosic food products, certain processes for food preservation, and methods of distilling sulfur. [102]

HARLAN, JOHN M. (June 1, 1833-Oct. 14, 1911) jurist. Attorney general of Kentucky (1863-67); associate justice (1877-1911) of the U.S. Supreme Court. [3, 61] See also Author Index, Vols. 10, 12.

HARVEY, GEORGE (Feb. 16, 1864-Aug. 20, 1928), political journalist. Owner and editor (1899-1926) of the *North American Review;* president (1900-15) of Harper & Bros., publishers; editor (1901-13) of *Harper's Weekly* and (1918-21) of *Harvey's Weekly;* ambassador to Great Britain (1921-23). [93]

HENRI, ROBERT (June 25, 1865-July 12, 1929), painter. Taught at Philadelphia and Paris, and at the Veltin, Chase, and Ferrar schools and (1915-23) at the Art Students' League in New York; wrote *The Art Spirit* (1923). [53]

HEPBURN, WILLIAM P. (Nov. 4, 1833-Feb. 7, 1916), lawyer and public official. U.S. representative from Iowa (1881-87,

1893-1909); sponsored the Hepburn Railroad Act (1906) and the Pure Food and Drug Act (1906); solicitor of the treasury under Benjamin Harrison. [13]

HERRICK, ROBERT (April 26, 1868-Dec. 23, 1938), novelist and educator. Teacher of English (1893-1923) at the University of Chicago; wrote many novels, including *The Gospel of Freedom* (1898), *The World Decision* (1916), *Sometime* (1933). [115]

HILL, JAMES J. (Sept. 16, 1838-May 29, 1916), railroad promoter and financier. Merged several railroad properties into the Great Northern Railway (1890); president of the road (to 1907); with J. P. Morgan engaged in stock market battle against Harriman and Schiff for control of Northern Pacific Rd.; organized Northern Securities Co. to hold his properties; company dissolved by U.S. Supreme Court decree (1904). [36]

HILL, JOE (1882-1915), IWW songwriter. Born Sweden; member of the Industrial Workers of the World; wrote numerous popular union songs; convicted of murder in Salt Lake City, Utah, and executed (Nov. 19, 1915); one day before his execution, sent a telegram to IWW headquarters: "Don't waste time mourning. Organize." [7]

HILLQUIT, MORRIS (Aug. 1, 1869-Oct. 7, 1933), lawyer and Socialist leader. Born Latvia; member (from 1901) of the executive board of the Socialist Party and its unsuccessful candidate (1917) for mayor of New York City; wrote *History of Socialism in the United States* (1903), *Socialism Summed Up* (1912). [44]

HINES, WALKER D. (Feb. 2, 1870-Jan. 14, 1934), lawyer and railroad official. General counsel (1906-18) for the Atchison, Topeka and Santa Fe Railway Co.; assistant U.S. director-general (1918-19) and director-general (1919-20) of railroads. [104]

HOIER, THOMAS (fl. 1915), lyricist. [114]

HOLMES, OLIVER WENDELL, JR. (March 8, 1841-March 6, 1935), jurist. Son of physician and author Oliver Wendell Holmes; professor of law (1882) at Harvard Law School; associate justice (1883-99) and chief justice (1899-1902) of the

Massachusetts Supreme Court; associate justice (1902-32) of the U.S. Supreme Court. [3] See also Author Index, Vols. 12, 14.

HOWELLS, WILLIAM DEAN (March 1, 1837-May 10, 1920), novelist and editor. Wrote (1856-61) for the *Ohio State Journal*, (1866-91) for *Harper's Magazine*, and (1891-92) for *Cosmopolitan Magazine*; editor (1866-81) of the *Atlantic Monthly*; wrote *Venetian Life* (1866), *The Rise of Silas Lapham* (1885), *A Hazard of New Fortunes* (1890), *Criticism and Fiction* (1891). [64] See also Author Index, Vol. 11.

JAMES, WILLIAM (Jan. 11, 1842-Aug. 26, 1910), psychologist and philosopher. Son of Henry James, Sr., and brother of Henry James; professor (1872-1907) at Harvard; established (1875) the first psychological research laboratory in U.S.; leading advocate of pragmatism; wrote *The Principles of Psychology* (1890), *The Will to Believe and Other Essays* (1897), *The Varieties of Religious Experience* (1902), *Pragmatism* (1907), *The Meaning of Truth* (1909). [52] See also Author Index, Vol. 12.

JONES, RUFUS M. (Jan. 25, 1863-June 16, 1948), Quaker philosopher. Chairman (1917-27, 1934-44) of the American Friends Service Committee for European Relief; Professor of philosophy (1901-34) at Haverford College; wrote *Practical Christianity* (1899), *The Church's Debt to Heretics* (1925), *The Radiant Life* (1944). [112]

JORDAN, DAVID STARR (Jan. 19, 1851-Sept. 19, 1931), naturalist and educator. Member (1877-91) of U.S. Fish Commission; professor of zoology (1879-85) and president (1885-91) of Indiana University; president (1891-1913) and chancellor (1913-16) of Stanford University. [34]

KELLEY, FLORENCE (Sept. 12, 1859-Feb. 17, 1932), social worker. Illinois state inspector of factories (1893-97); secretary (1899) of National Consumers' League; social worker (1891-99) at Hull House, Chicago, and (1899-1924) at Henry Street Settlement, New York City. [20]

KLEIN, FÉLIX (1862-?), French Roman Catholic clergyman. Professor at the Institut Catholique, Paris; chaplain of the American War Hospital, Paris; toured America (1904) and recorded his impressions as *In the Country of "the Strenuous Life"* (1905). **[10]**

KUHN, WALT (Oct. 27, 1877-July 13, 1949), painter. An organizer and executive secretary of the International Exhibition of Modern Art (Armory Show) of 1913; Instructor (1908-09) at New York School of Art and (1926-27) at Art Students League; wrote, designed, and produced stage pantomimes and satirical ballets. **[77]**

LAWSON, JOHN (fl. 1915), labor union official. Member of the International Executive Board of the United Mine Workers of America and international organizer for that union. **[100]**

LINDSAY, VACHEL (Nov. 10, 1879-Dec. 5, 1931), poet. Wrote *General William Booth Enters into Heaven and Other Poems* (1913), *The Congo and Other Poems* (1914), *The Chinese Nightingale* (1917), *The Golden Whales of California* (1920), *Going-to-the-Sun* (1923). **[90]** See also Author Index, Vol. 14.

LINDSEY, BEN B. (Nov. 25, 1869-March 26, 1943), jurist. Authority on juvenile court law and juvenile delinquency; judge (1900-27) of the Juvenile Court of Denver, Colo.; judge (from 1934) of the Superior Court of California; wrote *Problems of the Children* (1903), *The Revolt of Modern Youth* (1925). **[46]**

LIPPMANN, WALTER (Sept. 23, 1889-　　), editor and author. Assisted in preparation of the Fourteen Points and the League of Nations plan for the Paris Peace Conference (1918-19); a co-founder (1914) and editor of the *New Republic;* syndicated political columnist (1931-67) for the *New York Herald Tribune;* wrote *Public Opinion* (1927), *A Preface to Morals* (1929), *The Good Society* (1937), *U.S. Foreign Policy: Shield of the Republic* (1943), *Essays in the Public Philosophy* (1955). **[95]** See also Author Index, Vols. 14, 15, 16, 17, 18.

LODGE, HENRY CABOT (May 12, 1850-Nov. 9, 1924), public official and author. U.S. representative from Massachusetts (1887-93); U.S. senator (from 1893); wrote *The Story of the American Revolution* (2

vols., 1898), *The Senate and the League of Nations* (1925), and several biographies. **[75]** See also Author Index, Vols. 12, 14.

LONDON, JACK (Jan. 12, 1876-Nov. 22, 1916), author. At various times a sailor, gold miner, salmon fisher, and longshoreman; arrested several times for making Socialist speeches; war correspondent in the Far East and Mexico; wrote *The Call of the Wild* (1903), *The Sea-Wolf* (1904), *South Sea Tales* (1911). **[11]**

McCLINTOCK, HARRY (fl. 1897-1926), songwriter. **[48]** See also Author Index, Vol. 12.

MASTERS, EDGAR LEE (Aug. 23, 1869-March 5, 1950), lawyer and author. Wrote novels, plays, biographies (*Lincoln — The Man*, 1931; *Vachel Lindsay, A Poet in America*, 1935; *Whitman*, 1937), poetry (*Songs and Satires*, 1916; *Poems of People*, 1936; *Illinois Poems*, 1941), and a volume of verse epitaphs, *Spoon River Anthology* (1915). **[119]**

MIDDLETON, P. HARVEY (fl. 1913), journalist. **[85]**

MOOREHEAD, J. R. (fl. 1911-1912), Missouri businessman. First secretary of the National Federation of Retail Merchants. **[63]**

NAGEL, CHARLES (Aug. 9, 1849-Jan. 5, 1940), lawyer and political leader. Lecturer (1885-1909) at St. Louis Law School; secretary of commerce and labor under Taft. **[79]**

ODELL, JOSEPH H. (May 20, 1871-Aug. 29, 1929), Presbyterian clergyman. Born England; pastor (1894-1902) in Fulton, N.Y., (1902-14) in Scranton, Pa., and (1915-18) in Troy, N.Y.; editor (1913-14) of *Scranton Tribune-Republican* and *Scranton Truth.* **[108]**

OPPENHEIM, JAMES (May 24, 1882-Aug. 4, 1932), poet and novelist. Edited (1916-17) the monthly *Seven Arts;* collections of poetry include *Monday Morning and Other Poems* (1909) and *Golden Bird* (1923); novels include *Wild Oats* (1910) and *The Olympian* (1912). **[72]**

PECKHAM, RUFUS W. (Nov. 8, 1838-Oct. 24, 1909), jurist. Justice (1883-86) of New York Supreme Court; judge (1886-95) of the New York Court of Appeals;

associate justice (from 1896) of U.S. Supreme Court. **[3]**

PHILLIPS, DAVID GRAHAM (Oct. 31, 1867-Jan. 24, 1911), author. Exposed political corruption in his magazine series "The Treason of the Senate" (*Cosmopolitan*, 1906-07) wrote "muckraking" novels such as *The Cost* (1904), *The Husband's Story* (1910), and *Susan Lenox: Her Fall and Rise* (1917). **[15]**

RAUSCHENBUSCH, WALTER (Oct. 4, 1861-July 25, 1918), Baptist clergyman and theologian. Professor of New Testament exegesis (from 1897) at Rochester Theological Seminary; wrote *Christianity and the Social Crisis* (1907), *The Social Principles of Jesus* (1916). **[21]**

ROCKEFELLER, JOHN D. (July 8, 1839-May 23, 1937), industrialist and financier. Founder (1870) and president of Standard Oil Trust, which was dissolved by court decree (1911); established and endowed four large charitable corporations (Rockefeller Foundation, General Education Board, Laura Spelman Rockefeller Memorial, and Rockefeller Institute for Medical Research). **[43]** See also Author Index, Vol. 12.

ROOSEVELT, THEODORE (Oct. 27, 1858-Jan. 6, 1919), soldier, historian, and statesman. Twenty-sixth President of the United States (1901-09); assistant secretary of the navy (1897-98) under McKinley; served in Cuba (1898) as colonel of "Roosevelt's Rough Riders" volunteer cavalry regiment; governor of New York (1899-1900); Vice-President of the United States (1901) under McKinley; succeeded to the Presidency upon McKinley's death (Sept. 14, 1901); received Nobel Peace Prize (1906); wrote *The Naval War of 1812* (1882), *The Winning of the West* (4 vols., 1889-96). **[1, 37, 39, 51, 62, 77, 98]** See also Author Index Vols. 11, 12, 14.

ROOT, ELIHU (Feb. 15, 1845-Feb. 7, 1937), lawyer and statesman. Secretary of war (1899-1903) under McKinley and Theodore Roosevelt, and secretary of state (1905-09) under Roosevelt; U.S. senator from New York (1909-15); member (1910-17) of The Hague Tribunal; president (1910-25) of the Carnegie Endowment for International Peace; received Nobel Peace Prize (1912); headed special

diplomatic mission to Russia (1917). **[88, 105]** See also Author Index, Vol. 14.

RYAN, JOHN A. (May 25, 1869-Sept. 16, 1945), Roman Catholic clergyman. Professor of moral theology and sociology (1915-39) at Catholic University of America; wrote *A Living Wage: Its Ethical and Economic Aspects* (1906), *The Church and Labor* (1920), *The State and the Church* (1922), *Catholic Principles of Politics* (1940). **[18]**

SANDBURG, CARL (Jan. 6, 1878-July 22, 1967), poet and author. Poetry collections include *Cornhuskers* (1918), *Smoke and Steel* (1920), *The People, Yes* (1936), and *Complete Poems* (1950); edited collections of folk songs (*The American Songbag*, 1927); wrote histories (*Abraham Lincoln — The Prairie Years*, 1926; *Abraham Lincoln — The War Years*, 1939). **[99]** See also Author Index, Vols. 14, 15.

SANTAYANA, GEORGE (Dec. 16, 1863-Sept. 26, 1952), philosopher, poet, novelist, and literary critic. Born Spain; teacher of philosophy (1889-1912) at Harvard; wrote *The Sense of Beauty* (1896), *The Life of Reason* (5 vols., 1905-06), *Skepticism and Animal Faith* (1923), *The Realms of Being* (4 vols., 1927-40), *The Last Puritan* (1935), and an autobiography, *Persons and Places* (3 vols., 1944-45, 1953). **[57]** See also Author Index, Vol. 14.

SINCLAIR, UPTON (Sept. 20, 1878-Nov. 25, 1968), novelist and politician. Socialist Party candidate for state and national offices (1906-30); founded American Civil Liberties Union in California; wrote *The Jungle* (1906), *Oil!* (1927), *Boston* (1928), and the Lanny Budd series of historical novels (1940-53). **[17]**

SMITH, CHARLES SPRAGUE (April 27, 1853-March 30, 1910), educator. Instructor and professor of German (1880-91) at Columbia University; founded (1897) the People's Institute at Cooper Union, N.Y.; wrote *Barbizon Days* (1902), *Working with the People* (1904). **[23]**

SPALDING, ALBERT G. (Sept. 2, 1850-Sept. 9, 1915), businessman and sportsman. Played professional baseball with teams in Boston (1871-75) and Chicago (1876); manager (1876-77) and president (1882-91) of the Chicago National League team; edited (1878-80) *Spalding's Official Baseball Guide.* [54]

STIMSON, HENRY L. (Sept. 21, 1867-Oct. 20, 1950), lawyer and public official. Secretary of war (1911-13) under Taft; special representative to Nicaragua (1927); governor of the Philippine Islands (1927-29); secretary of state under Hoover; chairman (1932) of U.S. delegation to the Disarmament Conference; secretary of war (1940-45) under F. D. Roosevelt [117] See also Author Index, Vol. 15.

TAFT, WILLIAM HOWARD (Sept. 15, 1857-March 8, 1930), jurist and statesman. Twenty-seventh President of the United States (1909-13); U.S. solicitor general (1890-92); judge (1892-1900) of U.S. Circuit Court; president (1900-04) of U.S. Philippines Commission and civil governor (1901-04) of Philippine Islands; secretary of war (1904-08) under Theodore Roosevelt; provisional governor (1906) of Cuba; professor of law (1913-21) at Yale; chief justice (from 1921) of the U.S. Supreme Court. [40, 56, 74, 76] See also Author Index, Vol. 14.

TAYLOR, GRAHAM R. (May 2, 1851-Sept. 26, 1938), Dutch Reformed clergyman and sociologist. Taught theology and sociology (1888-92) at Hartford Theological Seminary, (from 1892) at Chicago Theological Seminary, and (from 1903) at the University of Chicago; founder and resident warden (from 1894) of Chicago Commons Social Settlement; wrote *Religion in Social Action* (1913), *Pioneering on Social Frontiers* (1930). [103]

TEVIS, CHARLES V. (fl. 1908), journalist. [29]

TURNER, GEORGE K. (fl. 1913), journalist. [86]

VAUGHN, JOHN (fl. 1906), journalist. [16]

VAY DE VAYA UND ZU LUSKOD, Count (fl. 1908), Hungarian churchman. [28]

WALSH, GEORGE E. (March 12, 1865-Feb. 4, 1941), journalist and author. Free-lance contributor to many periodicals; author of many serials and short stories. [24]

WEYL, WALTER E. (March 11, 1873-Nov. 9, 1919), economist. Associate editor (1914-16) of the *New Republic;* wrote *The New Democracy* (1912), which influenced the Progressive Party program in the campaign of 1912, and *American World Politics* (1917). [68]

WHITE, EDWARD D. (Nov. 3, 1845-May 19, 1921), jurist. Associate justice (1878-91) of the Louisiana Supreme Court; U.S. senator (1891-94); associate justice (1894-1910) and chief justice (from 1910) of U.S. Supreme Court. [61]

WHITE, HERVEY (fl. 1908), journalist. [35]

WHITE, WILLIAM ALLEN (Feb. 10, 1868-Jan. 29, 1944), journalist and author. Known as "the Sage of Emporia" for his work as owner and editor (from 1895) of the *Emporia* (Kan.) *Gazette;* wrote *The Real Issue and Other Stories* (1896), *A Puritan in Babylon* (1938), *The Changing West* (1939), *Autobiography* (1946). [50] See also Author Index, Vols. 12, 14, 15.

WICKWARE, FRANCIS G. (Jan. 31, 1883-Oct. 12, 1940), journalist. Associate editor (1907-11) of *Engineering Magazine;* editor (1911-20) of *American Year Book.* [118]

WILCOX, DAVID (fl. 1905), businessman. President of the Delaware and Hudson Railroad Company. [2]

WILSON, WOODROW (Dec. 28, 1856-Feb. 3, 1924), lawyer, historian, educator, and statesman. Twenty-eighth President of the United States (1913-21); instructor in history (1885-88) at Bryn Mawr College and (1888-90) at Wesleyan University; professor of jurisprudence and political economy (1890-1902) at Princeton University; president (1902-10) of Princeton; governor of New Jersey (1911-13); received Nobel Peace Prize (1919); wrote *A History of the American People* (5 vols., 1902). [55, 70, 82, 83, 84, 94, 97] See also Author Index, Vols. 11, 14.

WOOD, LEONARD (Oct. 9, 1860-Aug. 7, 1927), soldier and physician. Commanded "Roosevelt's Rough Riders" in Cuba (1898); military governor of Santiago (1898) and of Cuba (1899-1902); commanded U.S. forces in the Philippines (1903-08); chief of staff of U.S. Army (1910-14); governor-general of the Philippines (from 1921). [116]

WRIGHT, RICHARD R., JR. (fl. 1900-1905), clergyman. Pastor of Trinity Mission, Chicago; active in the Negro labor movement in Chicago. [9]